Siddhartha Rao

Sams **Teach Yourself**

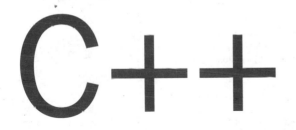

in **One Hour** a Day

Seventh Edition

SAMS | 800 East 96th Street, Indianapolis, Indiana 46240

Sams Teach Yourself C++ in One Hour a Day, Seventh Edition

ISBN-13: 978-0-672-33567-9
ISBN-10: 0-672-33567-0

The Library of Congress Cataloging-in-Publication Data is on file.

Printed in the United States of America

Fourth Printing: November 2013

Trademarks

All terms mentioned in this book that are known to be trademarks or service marks have been appropriately capitalized. Sams Publishing cannot attest to the accuracy of this information. Use of a term in this book should not be regarded as affecting the validity of any trademark or service mark.

Warning and Disclaimer

Every effort has been made to make this book as complete and as accurate as possible, but no warranty or fitness is implied. The information provided is on an "as is" basis. The author and the publisher shall have neither liability nor responsibility to any person or entity with respect to any loss or damages arising from the information contained in this book.

Bulk Sales

Sams Publishing offers excellent discounts on this book when ordered in quantity for bulk purchases or special sales. For more information, please contact

U.S. Corporate and Government Sales
1-800-382-3419
corpsales@pearsontechgroup.com

For sales outside of the U.S., please contact

International Sales
international@pearsoned.com

Acquisitions Editor
Mark Taber

Development Editor
Songlin Qiu

Managing Editor
Sandra Schroeder

Project Editor
Mandie Frank

Copy Editor
Charlotte Kughen

Indexer
Tim Wright

Proofreader
Megan Wade

Technical Editor
Jon Upchurch

Publishing Coordinator
Vanessa Evans

Designer
Gary Adair

Compositor
Studio Galou, LLC

Contents at a Glance

Table of Contents

About the Author

Siddhartha Rao is a technologist at SAP AG, the world's leading supplier of enterprise software. As the head of SAP Product Security India, his primary responsibilities include hiring expert talent in the area of product security as well as defining development best practices that keeps SAP software globally competitive. Awarded Most Valuable Professional by Microsoft for Visual Studio–Visual C++, he is convinced that C++11 will help you program faster, simpler, and more efficient C++ applications.

Siddhartha also loves traveling and discovering new cultures given an opportunity to. For instance, parts of this book have been composed facing the Atlantic Ocean at a quaint village called Plogoff in Brittany, France—one of the four countries this book was authored in. He looks forward to your feedback on this global effort!

Dedication

This book is dedicated to my lovely parents and my wonderful sister for being there when I have needed them the most.

Acknowledgments

I am deeply indebted to my friends who cooked and baked for me while I burned the midnight oil working on this project. I am grateful to the editorial staff for their very professional engagement and the wonderful job in getting this book to your shelf!

We Want to Hear from You!

As the reader of this book, *you* are our most important critic and commentator. We value your opinion and want to know what we're doing right, what we could do better, what areas you'd like to see us publish in, and any other words of wisdom you're willing to pass our way.

You can email or write directly to let us know what you did or didn't like about this book—as well as what we can do to make our books stronger.

Please note that we cannot help you with technical problems related to the topic of this book, and that due to the high volume of mail we receive, we might not be able to reply to every message.

When you write, please be sure to include this book's title and author as well as your name and phone number or email address.

E-mail: feedback@samspublishing.com

Mail: Reader Feedback
            Sams Publishing
            800 East 96th Street
            Indianapolis, IN 46240 USA

Reader Services

Visit our website and register this book at informit.com/register for convenient access to any updates, downloads, or errata that might be available for this book.

Introduction

2011 was a special year for C++. With the ratification of the new standard, C++11 empowers you to write better code using new keywords and constructs that increase your programming efficiency. This book helps you learn C++11 in tiny steps. It has been thoughtfully divided into lessons that teach you the fundamentals of this object-oriented programming language from a practical point of view. Depending on your proficiency level, you will be able to master C++11 one hour at a time.

Learning C++ by doing is the best way—so try the rich variety of code samples in this book hands-on and help yourself improve your programming proficiency. These code snippets have been tested using the latest versions of the available compilers at the time of writing, namely the Microsoft Visual C++ 2010 compiler for C++ and GNU's C++ compiler version 4.6, which both offer a rich coverage of C++11 features.

Who Should Read This Book?

The book starts with the very basics of C++. All that is needed is a desire to learn this language and curiosity to understand how stuff works. An existing knowledge of C++ programming can be an advantage but is not a prerequisite. This is also a book you might like to refer to if you already know C++ but want to learn additions that have been made to the language in C++11. If you are a professional programmer, Part III, "Learning the Standard Template Library (STL)," is bound to help you create better, more practical C++11 applications.

Organization of This Book

Depending on your current proficiency levels with C++, you can choose the section you would like to start with. This book has been organized into five parts:

- Part I, "The Basics," gets you started with writing simple C++ applications. In doing so, it introduces you to the keywords that you most frequently see in C++ code of a variable without compromising on type safety.

- Part II, "Fundamentals of Object-Oriented C++ Programming," teaches you the concept of classes. You learn how C++ supports the important object-oriented programming principles of encapsulation, abstraction, inheritance, and polymorphism.

Lesson 9, "Classes and Objects," teaches you the new C++11 concept of move constructor followed by the move assignment operator in Lesson 12, "Operator Types and Operator Overloading." These performance features help reduce unwanted and unnecessary copy steps, boosting the performance of your application. Lesson 14, "An Introduction to Macros and Templates," is your stepping stone into writing powerful generic C++ code.

- Part III, "Learning the Standard Template Library (STL)," helps you write efficient and practical C++ code using the STL `string` class and containers. You learn how `std::string` makes simple string concatenation operations safe and easy and how you don't need to use C-style `char*` strings anymore. You will be able to use STL dynamic arrays and linked lists instead of programming your own.

- Part IV, "More STL," focuses on algorithms. You learn to use `sort` on containers such as `vector` via iterators. In this part, you find out how C++11 keyword `auto` has made a significant reduction to the length of your iterator declarations. Lesson 22, "C++11 Lambda Expressions," presents a powerful new feature that results in significant code reduction when you use STL algorithms.

- Part V, "Advanced C++ Concepts," explains language capabilities such as smart pointers and exception-handling, which are not a must in a C++ application but help make a significant contribution toward increasing its stability and quality. This part ends with a note on best practices in writing good C++11 applications.

Conventions Used in This Book

Within the lessons, you find the following elements that provide additional information:

NOTE
| These boxes provide additional information related to material you read. |

C++11

These boxes highlight features new to C++11. You may need to use the newer versions of the available compilers to use these language capabilities.

CAUTION
> These boxes alert your attention to problems or side effects that can occur in special situations.

TIP
> These boxes give you best practices in writing your C++ programs.

DO	DON'T
DO use the "Do/Don't" boxes to find a quick summary of a fundamental principle in a lesson.	DON'T overlook the useful information offered in these boxes.

This book uses different typefaces to differentiate between code and plain English. Throughout the lessons, code, commands, and programming-related terms appear in a computer typeface.

Sample Code for this Book

The code samples in this book are available online for download from the publisher's website.

LESSON 1
Getting Started

Welcome to *Sams Teach Yourself C++ in One Hour a Day*! You're ready to get started on becoming a proficient C++ programmer.

In this lesson, you find out

- Why C++ is a standard in software development
- How to enter, compile, and link your first working C++ program
- What's new in C++11

A Brief History of C++

The purpose of a programming language is to make consumption of computational resources easier. C++ is not a new language, yet one that is popularly adopted and still being improved. The latest version of C++ being ratified by the ISO Standards Committee in 2011 is called C++11.

Connection to C

Initially developed by Bjarne Stroustroup at Bell Labs in 1979, C++ was designed to be a successor to C. C is a procedural language in which one defines functions that take certain actions. In contrast, C++ was designed to be an object-oriented language, and it implements concepts such as inheritance, abstraction, polymorphism, and encapsulation. C++ features classes that are used to contain member data and member methods that operate on that data. (Methods are akin to functions in C.) The effect is that the programmer thinks of data and what he wishes to do with it. C++ compilers have traditionally supported C programming, too. This has had its advantages as far as backward compliance of legacy code goes; however, it has come with its share of disadvantages as compilers have become incredibly complex in providing programmers with this backward compliance while still implementing all the new features that evolution of the language has required.

Advantages of C++

C++ is considered an intermediate-level programming language, which means that it allows for high-level programming of applications as well as low-level programming of libraries that work close to the hardware. For many programmers, C++ provides the optimal mix of being a high-level language that lets one develop complex applications while supplying flexibility in allowing the developer to extract the best performance via accurate control of resource consumption and availability.

In spite of the presence of newer programming languages such as Java and others based on .NET, C++ has remained relevant and has also evolved. Newer languages provide certain features like memory management via garbage collection implemented in a runtime component that endear them to some programmers. Yet, often these very programmers would still choose C++ for cases where they need accurate control over their application's performance. A tiered architecture where a web server is programmed in C++ while the front-end application is in HTML, Java, or .NET is commonplace now.

Evolution of the C++ Standard

Years of evolution resulted in C++ being widely accepted and adopted albeit in many different forms because of the many different compilers, which each having its own idiosyncrasies. This popularity and the resulting deviations in the versions available led to a lot of interoperability problems and porting issues. Hence, there emerged a need to standardize it all.

In 1998, the first standard version of C++ was ratified by the ISO Committee in ISO/IEC 14882:1998. This was followed by a revision in 2003 (ISO/IEC 14882:2003). The current version of the C++ Standard was ratified in August 2011. It is officially called C++11 (ISO/IEC 14882:2011) and contains some of the most ambitious and progressive changes the standard has ever seen.

NOTE

A lot of documentation on the Internet still refers to a version of C++ called C++0x. It was expected that the new standard would be ratified in 2008 or 2009, and x was used as a marker for the year. Finally in August 2011, the proposed new standard was approved and is appropriately called C++11.

In other words, C++11 is the new C++0x.

Who Uses Programs Written in C++?

Irrespective of who you are or what you do—a seasoned programmer or one who uses the computer for a specific purpose—chances are that you are constantly consuming C++ applications and libraries. Be it operating systems, device drivers, office applications, web servers, cloud-based applications, search engines, or even some of the newer programming languages, C++ is often the language of choice for creating them.

Programming a C++ Application

When you start Notepad or VI on your computer, you actually are telling the processor to run an executable of that program. The executable is the finished product that can be run and should do what the programmer intended to achieve.

Steps to Generating an Executable

Writing a C++ program is a first step towards creating an executable that can eventually run on your operating system. The basic steps in creating applications in C++ are the following:

1. Writing (or programming) C++ code using a text editor
2. Compiling code using a C++ compiler that converts it to a machine language version contained in "object files"
3. Linking the output of the compiler using a linker to get an executable (.exe in Windows, for example)

Note that the microprocessor cannot consume text files, which is essentially what you create when you program. Compilation is the step where code in C++ contained typically in .CPP text files is converted into byte code that the processor can eventually understand. The compiler converts one code file at a time, generating an object file with a .o or .obj extension and ignoring dependencies that this CPP file may have on code in another file. Joining the dots and resolving these dependencies is the job of the linker. In addition to bringing the various object files together, it establishes dependencies, and in the event of successful linkage, it creates an executable for the programmer to execute and eventually distribute.

Analyzing Errors and Firefighting

Most complex applications, especially those developed by many programmers working in a team, rarely compile and work perfectly at the first run. A huge or complex application programmed in any language—C++ included—often needs many runs and re-runs to analyze the problems and detect bugs. The bugs are then fixed, the program is rebuilt, and the process continues. Thus, in addition to the three steps of programming, compiling, and linking, development often involves a step called debugging in which the programmer analyzes anomalies and errors in the application using tools, such as watches, and debugging features, such as executing the application one line at a time.

Integrated Development Environments

Many programmers prefer using an Integrated Development Environment (IDE) in which the programming, compiling, and linking steps are integrated within a unified user interface that also supplies debugging features that make it easier to detect errors and solve problems.

1

TIP

There are many freely available C++ IDEs and compilers. The popular ones are Microsoft Visual C++ Express for Windows and the GNU C++ Compiler called g++ for Linux. If you're programming on Linux, you can install the free Eclipse IDE to develop C++ applications using the g++ compiler.

CAUTION

Although no compiler completely supports the C++11 Standard at the time of writing this book, many major features have already been supported by the aforementioned compilers.

DO	DON'T
DO either use a simple text editor such as Notepad or gedit to create your source code or use an IDE.	**DON'T** use rich text editors because they often add their own markup in addition to the code you program.
DO save your files with the .cpp extension.	**DON'T** use a .c extension because many compilers treat such files as C code instead of C++ code.

Programming Your First C++ Application

Now that you know the tools and the steps involved, it is time to program your first C++ application, which follows tradition and prints a "Hello World!" on your screen.

If you are on Windows and using Microsoft Visual C++ Express, you can follow these steps:

1. Create a new project via the menu option File, New, Project.

2. Choose type Win32 Console Application and uncheck the Use Precompiled Header option.

3. Name your project **Hello** and replace the automatically generated contents in Hello.cpp with the code snippet shown in Listing 1.1.

    If you are programming on Linux, use a simple text editor (I used gedit on Ubuntu) to create a CPP file with contents as seen in Listing 1.1.

LISTING 1.1   `Hello.cpp`, the Hello World Program

```
1:  #include <iostream>
2:
3:  int main()
4:  {
5:    std::cout << "Hello World!" << std::endl;
6:    return 0;
7:  }
```

This simple application does nothing more than print a line to the screen using `std::cout`. `std::endl` instructs `cout` to end that line, and the application exits by returning 0 to the operating system.

NOTE

To read a program to yourself, it might help if you know how to pronounce the special characters and keywords.

For instance, you can call `#include` hash-include. Other versions are sharp-include or pound-include, depending on where you come from.

Similarly, you can read `std::cout` as standard-c-out.

CAUTION

Remember, the devil is in the details, meaning that you need to be typing your code in exactly the same way as it is shown in the listing. Compilers are notorious for expecting compliance to their expectations. If you mistakenly put a `:` at the end of a statement where a `;` is expected, all hell will certainly break loose!

Building and Executing Your First C++ Application

If you're using Microsoft Visual C++ Express, press Ctrl + F5 to run your program directly via the IDE. This compiles, links, and executes your application. You could also do the individual steps:

1. Right-click the project and select Build to generate the executable.

2. Navigate to the path of the executable using the command-prompt (typically under the Debug directory of the project folder).

3. Run it by typing the name of the executable.

Your program composed in Microsoft Visual C++ will look quite similar to that illustrated in Figure 1.1.

FIGURE 1.1
A simple "Hello World" C++ program edited in Microsoft Visual C++ 2010 Express.

If you are on Linux, invoke the g++ compiler and linker using the command line:

```
g++ -o hello Hello.cpp
```

Entering this tells g++ to create an executable named "hello" by compiling your C++ file `Hello.cpp`. Executing `.\hello` on Linux or `Hello.exe` on Windows returns the following output:

```
Hello World!
```

Congratulations! You have started on your way to learning one of the most popular and powerful programming languages of all times!

Significance of the C++ ISO Standard

As you can see, standard compliance helps the code snippet in Listing 1.1 be compiled and executed on multiple platforms or operating systems—the prerequisite being the availability of a standard compliant C++ compiler. Thus, if you need to create a product that needs to be run by Windows as well as Linux users, for example, standard compliant programming practices (that don't use a compiler or platform-specific semantics) give you an inexpensive way to reach more users without needing to program specifically for every environment you need to be supporting. This, of course, works optimally for applications that don't need much interaction at an operating system level.

Understanding Compiler Errors

Compilers are painfully exact in their requirements, yet good ones make a decent effort at telling you where you have made mistakes. If you face a problem in compiling the application in Listing 1.1, you might get errors that look quite like the following (introduced deliberately by omitting the semicolon in Line 5):

```
hello.cpp(6): error C2143: syntax error : missing ';' before 'return'
```

This error message from the Visual C++ Compiler is quite descriptive: It tells the name of the file that contains the error, the line number (6, in this case) where you missed a semicolon, and a description of the error itself accompanied by the error number (C2143, in this case). Though the punctuation mark was deleted from the fifth line for this example, the error reported is in the line after because the error became apparent to the compiler only when it analyzed the return statement which indicated that the previous statement ought to have been terminated before the return. You can try to add the semicolon at the start of the sixth line and the program compiles just fine!

NOTE	Line-breaks don't automatically terminate statements as they do in some languages such as VBScript. In C++, it is possible to have a statement spanning multiple lines.

What's New in C++11

If you are an experienced C++ programmer, you might have noticed that the basic C++ program in Listing 1.1 hasn't changed one bit. Although it's true that C++11 remains backward compliant with previous versions of C++, a lot of work has been done in making the language simpler to use and to program in.

Features such as auto allow you to define a variable whose type is deduced automatically by the compiler, compacting wordy iterator declarations for instance without compromising on type-safety. "Lambda functions" are functions without a name. They allow you to write compact function objects without long class definitions, reducing lines of code significantly. C++11 promises programmers the ability to write portable, multi-threaded, and yet standard-compliant C++ applications. These applications, when correctly built, support concurrent execution paradigms and are well positioned to scale in performance when the user boosts the capability of his hardware configuration by increasing the number of CPU cores.

These are some of the many improvements featured in C++11 that are discussed throughout this book.

Summary

In this lesson you learned how to program, compile, link, and execute your first C++ program. This lesson also gave you a brief overview on the evolution of C++ and demonstrated the effectiveness of a standard in showing that the same program can be compiled using different compilers on different operating systems.

1

Q&A

Q Can I ignore warning messages from my compiler?

A In certain cases, compilers issue warning messages. Warnings are different from errors in that the line in question is syntactically correct and compile-worthy. However, there possibly is a better way to write it, and good compilers issue a warning with a recommendation for a fix.

The suggested correction can mean a more secure way of programming or one that lets your application work with characters and symbols from non-Latin languages. You should heed these warnings and improve your program accordingly. Don't mask the warning messages, unless you are sure that they're false positives.

Q How does an interpreted language differ from a compiled language?

A Languages such as Windows Script are interpreted. There is no compilation step. An interpreted language uses an interpreter that directly reads the script text file (code) and performs the desired actions. Consequently, you need to have the interpreter installed on a machine where the script needs to be executed; consequently, performance usually takes a hit as the interpreter works as a runtime translator between the microprocessor and the code written.

Q What are runtime errors, and how are they different from compile-time errors?

A Errors that happen when you execute your application are called *runtime errors*. You might have experienced the infamous "Access Violation" on older versions of Windows, which is a runtime error. Compile-time errors don't reach the end-user and are an indication of syntactical problems; they keep the programmer from generating an executable.

Workshop

The Workshop provides quiz questions to help you solidify your understanding of the material covered and exercises to provide you with experience in using what you've learned. Try to answer the quiz and exercise questions before checking the answers in Appendix D, and be certain you understand the answers before continuing to the next lesson.

Quiz

1. What is the difference between an interpreter and a compiler?

2. What does the linker do?

3. What are the steps in the normal development cycle?

4. How does the C++11 Standard better support multicore CPUs?

Exercises

1. Look at the following program and try to guess what it does without running it:

```
 1: #include <iostream>
 2: int main()
 3: {
 4:    int x = 8;
 5:    int y = 6;
 6:    std::cout << std::endl;
 7:    std::cout << x - y << " " << x * y << " " << x + y;
 8:    std::cout << std::endl;
 9:    return 0;
10:}
```

2. Type in the program from Exercise 1 and then compile and link it. What does it do? Does it do what you guessed?

3. What do you think is the error in this program:

```
1: include <iostream>
2: int main()
3: {
4:     std::cout << "Hello Buggy World \n";
5:     return 0;
6: }
```

4. Fix the error in the program in Exercise 3, compile, link, and run it. What does it do?

LESSON 2
The Anatomy of a C++ Program

C++ programs consist of classes, functions, variables, and other component parts. Most of this book is devoted to explaining these parts in depth, but to get a sense of how a program fits together, you must see a complete working program.

In this lesson, you learn

- The parts of a C++ program

- How the parts work together

- What a function is and what it does

- Basic input and output operations

Part of the Hello World Program

Your first C++ program in Lesson 1, "Getting Started," did nothing more than write a simple "Hello World" statement to the screen. Yet this program contains some of the most important and basic building blocks of a C++ program. You use Listing 2.1 as a starting point to analyze components all C++ programs contain.

LISTING 2.1   HelloWorldAnalysis.cpp: Analyze a C++ Program

```
1:  // Preprocessor directive that includes header iostream
2: #include <iostream>
3:
4: // Start of your program: function block main()
5: int main()
6: {
7:    /* Write to the screen */
8:    std::cout << "Hello World" << std::endl;
9:
10:   // Return a value to the OS
11:   return 0;
12: }
```

This C++ program can be broadly classified into two parts: the preprocessor directives that start with a # and the main body of the program that starts with int main().

NOTE

Lines 1, 4, 7, and 10, which start with a // or with a /*, are comments and are ignored by the compiler. These comments are for humans to read.

Comments are discussed in greater detail in the next section.

Preprocessor Directive #include

As the name suggests, a *preprocessor* is a tool that runs before the actual compilation starts. Preprocessor directives are commands to the preprocessor and always start with a pound sign #. In Line 2 of Listing 2.1, *#include <filename>* tells the preprocessor to take the contents of the file (iostream, in this case) and include them at the line where the directive is made. iostream is a standard header file that is included because it contains the definition of std::cout used in Line 8 that prints "Hello World" on the screen. In other words, the compiler was able to compile Line 8 that contains std::cout because we instructed the preprocessor to include the definition of std::cout in Line 2.

> **NOTE**
>
> In professionally programmed C++ applications, not all includes are only standard headers. Complex applications are typically programmed in multiple files wherein some need to include others. So, if an artifact declared in FileA needs to be used in FileB, you need to include the former in the latter. You usually do that by putting the following `include` statement in FileA:
>
> ```
> #include "...relative path to FileB\FileB"
> ```
>
> We use quotes in this case and not angle brackets in including a self-created header. <> brackets are typically used when including standard headers.

The Body of Your Program `main()`

Following the preprocessor directive(s) is the body of the program characterized by the function `main()`. The execution of a C++ program always starts here. It is a standardized convention that function `main()` is declared with an `int` preceding it. `int` is the return value type of the function `main()`.

> **NOTE**
>
> In many C++ applications, you find a variant of the `main()` function that looks like this:
>
> ```
> int main (int argc, char* argv[])
> ```
>
> This is also standard compliant and acceptable as main returns `int`. The contents of the parenthesis are "arguments" supplied to the program. This program possibly allows the user to start it with command-line arguments, such as
>
> ```
> program.exe /DoSomethingSpecific
> ```
>
> `/DoSomethingSpecific` is the argument for that program passed by the OS as a parameter to it, to be handled within `main`.

Let's discuss Line 8 that fulfills the actual purpose of this program!

```
std::cout << "Hello World" << std::endl;
```

cout ("console-out", also pronounced see-out) is the statement that writes "Hello World" to the screen. cout is a stream defined in the standard namespace (hence, std::cout), and what you are doing in this line is putting the text "Hello World" into this stream by using the stream insertion operator <<. std::endl is used to end a line, and inserting it into a stream is akin to inserting a carriage return. Note that the stream insertion operator is used every time a new entity needs to be inserted into the stream.

The good thing about streams in C++ is that similar stream semantics used with another stream type result in a different operation being performed with the same text—for example, insertion into a file instead of a console. Thus, working with streams gets intuitive, and when you are used to one stream (such as `cout` that writes text to the console), you find it easy to work with others (such as `fstream` that helps write text files to the disk).

Streams are discussed in greater detail in Lesson 27, "Using Streams for Input and Output."

> **NOTE**
>
> The actual text, including the quotes `"Hello World"`, is called a *string literal*.

Returning a Value

Functions in C++ need to return a value unless explicitly specified otherwise. `main()` is a function, too, and always returns an integer. This value is returned to the operating system (OS) and, depending on the nature of your application, can be very useful as most OSes provide for an ability to query on the return value of an application that has terminated naturally. In many cases, one application is launched by another and the parent application (that launches) wants to know if the child application (that was launched) has completed its task successfully. The programmer can use the return value of `main()` to convey a success or error state to the parent application.

> **NOTE**
>
> Conventionally programmers return 0 in the event of success or -1 in the event of error. However, the return value is an integer, and the programmer has the flexibility to convey many different states of success or failure using the available range of integer return values.

> **CAUTION**
>
> C++ is case-sensitive. So, expect compilation to fail if you write `Int` instead of `int`, `Void` instead of `void`, and `Std::Cout` instead of `std::cout`.

The Concept of Namespaces

The reason you used std::cout in the program and not only cout is that the artifact (cout) that you want to invoke is in the standard (std) namespace.

So, what exactly are namespaces?

Assume that you didn't use the namespace qualifier in invoking cout and assume that cout existed in two locations known to the compiler—which one should the compiler invoke? This causes a conflict and the compilation fails, of course. This is where namespaces get useful. Namespaces are names given to parts of code that help in reducing the potential for a naming conflict. By invoking std::cout, you are telling the compiler to use that one unique cout that is available in the std namespace.

2

> **NOTE**
>
> You use the std (pronounced "standard") namespace to invoke functions, streams, and utilities that have been ratified by the ISO Standards Committee and are hence declared within it.

Many programmers find it tedious to repeatedly add the std namespace specifier to their code when using cout and other such features contained in the same. The using namespace declaration as demonstrated in Listing 2.2 will help you avoid this repetition.

LISTING 2.2   The using namespace Declaration

```
1: // Pre-processor directive
2: #include <iostream>
3:
4: // Start of your program
5: int main()
6: {
7:     // Tell the compiler what namespace to search in
8:     using namespace std;
9:
10:    /* Write to the screen using std::cout */
11:    cout << "Hello World" << endl;
12:
13:    // Return a value to the OS
14:    return 0;
15: }
```

Analysis ▼

Note Line 8. By telling the compiler that you are using the namespace `std`, you don't need to explicitly mention the namespace on Line 11 when using `std::cout` or `std::endl`.

A more restrictive variant of Listing 2.2 is shown in Listing 2.3 where you do not include a namespace in its entirety. You only include those artifacts that you wish to use.

LISTING 2.3   Another Demonstration of the using Keyword

```
1: // Pre-processor directive
2: #include <iostream>
3:
4: // Start of your program
5: int main()
6: {
7:    using std::cout;
8:    using std::endl;
9:
10:    /* Write to the screen using cout */
11:    cout << "Hello World" << endl;
12:
13:    // Return a value to the OS
14:    return 0;
15: }
```

Analysis ▼

Line 8 in Listing 2.2 has now been replaced by Lines 7 and 8 in Listing 2.3. The difference between `using namespace std` and `using std::cout` is that the former allows all artifacts in the `std` namespace to be used without explicitly needing to specify the namespace qualifier `std::`. With the latter, the convenience of not needing to disambiguate the namespace explicitly is restricted to only `std::cout` and `std::endl`.

Comments in C++ Code

Lines 1, 4, 10 and 13 in Listing 2.3 contain text in a spoken language (English, in this case) yet do not interfere with the ability of the program to compile. They also do not alter the output of the program. Such lines are called *comments*. Comments are ignored by the compiler and are popularly used by programmers to explain their code—hence, they are written in human- (or geek-) readable language.

C++ supports comments in two styles:

- `//` indicates that the line is a comment. For example:

  ```
  // This is a comment
  ```

- `/*` followed by `*/` indicates the contained text is a comment, even if it spans multiple lines:

  ```
  /* This is a comment
  and it spans two lines */
  ```

NOTE

It might seem strange that a programmer needs to explain his own code, but the bigger a program gets or the larger the number of programmers working on a particular module gets, the more important it is to write code that can be easily understood. It is important to explain what is being done and why it is being done in that particular manner using well-written comments.

DO	DON'T
Do add comments explaining the working of complicated algorithms and complex parts of your program.	**Don't** use comments to explain or repeat the obvious.
Do compose comments in a style that fellow programmers can understand.	**Don't** forget that adding comments will not justify writing obscure code.
	Don't forget that when code is modified, comments might need to be updated, too.

Functions in C++

Functions in C++ are the same as functions in C. Functions are artifacts that enable you to divide the content of your application into functional units that can be invoked in a sequence of your choosing. A function, when called (that is, invoked), typically returns a value to the calling function. The most famous function is, of course, `main()`. It is recognized by the compiler as the starting point of your C++ application and has to return an `int` (i.e., an integer).

You as a programmer have the choice and usually the need to compose your own functions. Listing 2.4 is a simple application that uses a function to display statements on the screen using `std::cout` with various parameters.

LISTING 2.4   Declaring, Defining, and Calling a Function That Demonstrates Some Capabilities of std::cout

```cpp
 1: #include <iostream>
 2: using namespace std;
 3:
 4: // Function declaration
 5: int DemoConsoleOutput();
 6:
 7: int main()
 8: {
 9:    // Call i.e. invoke the function
10:    DemoConsoleOutput();
11:
12:    return 0;
13: }
14:
15: // Function definition
16: int DemoConsoleOutput()
17: {
18:    cout << "This is a simple string literal" << endl;
19:    cout << "Writing number five: " << 5 << endl;
20:    cout << "Performing division 10 / 5 = " << 10 / 5 << endl;
21:    cout << "Pi when approximated is 22 / 7 = " << 22 / 7 << endl;
22:    cout << "Pi more accurately is 22 / 7 = " << 22.0 / 7 << endl;
23:
24:    return 0;
25: }
```

Output ▶

```
This is a simple string literal
Writing number five: 5
Performing division 10 / 5 = 2
Pi when approximated is 22 / 7 = 3
Pi more accurately is 22 / 7 = 3.14286
```

Analysis ▶

Lines 5, 10, and 15 through 25 are those of interest. Line 5 is called a *function declaration*, which basically tells the compiler that you want to create a function called DemoConsoleOutput() that returns an int (integer). It is because of this *declaration* that the compiler agrees to compile Line 10, assuming that the *definition* (that is, the implementation of the function) comes up, which it does in Lines 15 through 25.

This function actually displays the various capabilities of cout. Note how it not only prints text the same way as it displayed "Hello World" in previous examples, but also the result of simple arithmetic computations. Lines 21 and 22 both attempt to display the result of pi (22 / 7), but the latter is more accurate simply because by diving 22.0 by 7, you tell the compiler to treat the result as a real number (a `float` in C++ terms) and not as an integer.

Note that your function is stipulated to return an integer and returns 0. As it did not perform any decision-making, there was no need to return any other value. Similarly, `main()` returns 0, too. Given that `main()` has delegated all its activity to the function `DemoConsoleOutput()`, you would be wiser to use the return value of the function in returning from `main()` as seen in Listing 2.5.

LISTING 2.5   Using the Return Value of a Function

```
1: #include <iostream>
2: using namespace std;
3:
4: // Function declaration and definition
5: int DemoConsoleOutput()
6: {
7:    cout << "This is a simple string literal" << endl;
8:    cout << "Writing number five: " << 5 << endl;
9:    cout << "Performing division 10 / 5 = " << 10 / 5 << endl;
10:    cout << "Pi when approximated is 22 / 7 = " << 22 / 7 << endl;
11:    cout << "Pi more accurately is 22 / 7 = " << 22.0 / 7 << endl;
12:
13:    return 0;
14: }
15:
16: int main()
17: {
18:    // Function call with return used to exit
19:    return DemoConsoleOutput();
20: }
```

Analysis ▶

The output of this application is the same as the output of the previous listing. Yet, there are slight changes in the way it is programmed. For one, as you have defined (i.e., implemented) the function before `main()` at Line 5, you don't need an extra declaration of the same. Modern C++ compilers take it as a function declaration and definition in one. `main()` is a bit shorter, too. Line 19 invokes the function `DemoConsoleOutput()` and simultaneously returns the return value of the function from the application.

NOTE

In cases such as this where a function is not required to make a decision or return success or failure status, you can declare a function of return type `void`:

`void DemoConsoleOutput()`

This function cannot return a value, and the execution of a function that returns `void` cannot be used to make a decision.

Functions can take parameters, can be recursive, can contain multiple return statements, can be overloaded, can be expanded in-line by the compiler, and lots more. These concepts are introduced in greater detail in Lesson 7, "Organizing Code with Functions."

Basic Input Using `std::cin` and Output Using `std::cout`

Your computer enables you to interact with applications running on it in various forms and allows these applications to interact with you in many forms, too. You can interact with applications using the keyboard or the mouse. You can have information displayed on the screen as text, displayed in the form of complex graphics, printed on paper using a printer, or simply saved to the file system for later usage. This section discusses the very simplest form of input and output in C++—using the console to write and read information.

You use `std::cout` (pronounced "standard see-out") to write simple text data to the console and use `std::cin` ("standard see-in") to read text and numbers (entered using the keyboard) from the console. In fact, in displaying "Hello World" on the screen, you have already encountered `cout`, as seen in Listing 2.1:

```
8:    std::cout << "Hello World" << std::endl;
```

The statement shows `cout` followed by the insertion operator `<<` (that helps insert data into the output stream), followed by the string literal "Hello World" to be inserted, followed by a newline in the form of `std::endl` (pronounced "standard end-line").

The usage of `cin` is simple, too, and as `cin` is used for input, it is accompanied by the variable you want to be storing the input data in:

```
std::cin >> Variable;
```

Thus, `cin` is followed by the extraction operator `>>` (extracts data from the input stream), which is followed by the variable where the data needs to be stored. If the user input needs to be stored in two variables, each containing data separated by a space, then you can do so using one statement:

```
std::cin >> Variable1 >> Variable2;
```

Note that cin can be used for text as well as numeric inputs from the user, as shown in Listing 2.6.

LISTING 2.6   Use cin and cout to Display Number and Text Input by User

```cpp
1: #include <iostream>
2: #include <string>
3: using namespace std;
4:
5: int main()
6: {
7:     // Declare a variable to store an integer
8:     int InputNumber;
9:
10:     cout << "Enter an integer: ";
11:
12:     // store integer given user input
13:     cin >> InputNumber;
14:
15:     // The same with text i.e. string data
16:     cout << "Enter your name: ";
17:     string InputName;
18:     cin >> InputName;
19:
20:     cout << InputName << " entered " << InputNumber << endl;
21:
22:     return 0;
23: }
```

Output ▶

```
Enter an integer: 2011
Enter your name: Siddhartha
Siddhartha entered 2011
```

Analysis ▶

Line 8 shows how a variable of name InputNumber is declared to store data of type int. The user is requested to enter a number using cout in Line 10, and the entered number is stored in the integer variable using cin in Line 13. The same exercise is repeated with storing the user's name, which of course cannot be held in an integer but in a different type called string as seen in Lines 17 and 18. The reason you included <string> in Line 2 was to use type string later inside main(). Finally in Line 20, a cout statement is used to display the entered name with the number and an intermediate text to produce the output Siddhartha entered 2011.

This is a very simple example of how basic input and output work in C++. Don't worry if the concept of variables is not clear to you as it is explained in good detail in the following Lesson 3, "Using Variables, Declaring Constants."

Summary

This lesson introduced the basic parts of a simple C++ program. You understood what main() is, got an introduction to namespaces, and learned the basics of console input and output. You are able to use a lot of these in every program you write.

Q&A

Q What does #include do?

A This is a directive to the preprocessor that runs when you call your compiler. This specific directive causes the contents of the file named in <> after #include to be inserted at that line as if it were typed at that location in your source code.

Q What is the difference between // comments and /* comments?

A The double-slash comments (//) expire at the end of the line. Slash-star (/*) comments are in effect until there is a closing comment mark (*/). The double-slash comments are also referred to as *single-line comments*, and the slash-star comments are often referred to as *multiline comments*. Remember, not even the end of the function terminates a slash-star comment; you must put in the closing comment mark or you will receive a compile-time error.

Q When do you need to program command-line arguments?

A To allow the user to alter the behavior of a program. For example, the command ls in Linux or dir in Windows enables you to see the contents within the current directory or folder. To view files in another directory, you would specify the path of the same using command-line arguments, as seen in ls / or dir \.

Workshop

The Workshop provides quiz questions to help you solidify your understanding of the material covered and exercises to provide you with experience in using what you've learned. Try to answer the quiz and exercise questions before checking the answers in Appendix D, and be certain you understand the answers before continuing to the next lesson.

Quiz

1. What is the problem in declaring Int main()?
2. Can comments be longer than one line?

Exercises

1. **BUG BUSTERS:** Enter this program and compile it. Why does it fail? How can you fix it?

```
1: #include <iostream>
2: void main()
3: {
4:      std::Cout << Is there a bug here?";
5: }
```

2. Fix the bug in Exercise 1 and recompile, link, and run it.
3. Modify Listing 2.4 to demonstrate subtraction (using –) and multiplication (using *).

LESSON 3
Using Variables, Declaring Constants

Variables are tools that help the programmer temporarily store data for a finite amount of time. *Constants* are tools that help the programmer define artifacts that are not allowed to change.

In this lesson, you find out

- How to use C++11 keywords auto and constexpr
- How to declare and define variables and constants
- How to assign values to variables and manipulate those values
- How to write the value of a variable to the screen

What Is a Variable?

Before you actually explore the need and use of variables in a programming language, take a step back and first see what a computer contains and how it works.

Memory and Addressing in Brief

All computers, smart phones, and other programmable devices contain a microprocessor and a certain amount of memory for temporary storage called Random Access Memory (RAM). In addition, many devices also allow for data to be persisted on a storage device such as the hard disk. The microprocessor executes your application, and in doing so it works with the RAM to fetch the application to be executed as well as the data associated with it, which includes that displayed on the screen and that entered by the user.

The RAM itself can be considered to be a storage area akin to a row of lockers in the dorms, each locker having a number—that is, an address. To access a location in memory, say location 578, the processor needs to be asked via an instruction to fetch a value from there or write a value to it.

Declaring Variables to Access and Use Memory

The following examples will help you understand what variables are. Assume you are writing a program to multiply two numbers supplied by the user. The user is asked to feed the multiplicand and the multiplier into your program, one after the other, and you need to store each of them so that you can use them later to multiply. Depending on what you want to be doing with the result of the multiplication, you might even want to store it for later use in your program. It would be slow and error-prone if you were to explicitly specify memory addresses (such as 578) to store the numbers, as you would need to worry about inadvertently overwriting existing data at the location or your data being overwritten at a later stage.

When programming in languages like C++, you define variables to store those values. Defining a variable is quite simple and follows this pattern:

```
variable_type variable_name;
```

or

```
variable_type variable_name = initial_value;
```

The variable type attribute tells the compiler the nature of data the variable can store, and the compiler reserves the necessary space for it. The name chosen by the programmer is a friendly replacement for the address in the memory where the variable's value is stored. Unless the initial value is assigned, you cannot be sure of the contents of that memory location, which can be bad for the program. Therefore, initialization is optional, but it's often a good programming practice. Listing 3.1 shows how variables are declared, initialized, and used in a program that multiplies two numbers supplied by the user.

LISTING 3.1 Using Variables to Store Numbers and the Result of Their Multiplication

```
1: #include <iostream>
2: using namespace std;
3:
4: int main ()
5: {
6:    cout << "This program will help you multiply two numbers" << endl;
7:
8:    cout << "Enter the first number: ";
9:    int FirstNumber = 0;
10:   cin >> FirstNumber;
11:
12.   cout << "Enter the second number: ";
13:   int SecondNumber - 0;
14:   cin >> SecondNumber;
15:
16:   // Multiply two numbers, store result in a variable
17:   int MultiplicationResult = FirstNumber * SecondNumber;
18:
19:   // Display result
20:   cout << FirstNumber << " x " << SecondNumber;
21:   cout << " = " << MultiplicationResult << endl;
22:
23:   return 0;
24: }
```

Output ▼

```
This program will help you multiply two numbers
Enter the first number: 51
Enter the second number: 24
51 x 24 = 1224
```

Analysis ▼

This application asks the user to enter two numbers, which the program multiplies and displays the result. For the application to be able to use numbers entered by the user, it needs to store them in the memory. Variables FirstNumber and SecondNumber declared in Lines 9 and 13 do the job of temporarily storing integer values entered by the user. You use std::cin in Lines 10 and 14 to accept input from the user and to store them in the two integer variables. The cout statement in Line 21 is used to display the result on the console.

3

Take a variable declaration and analyze it further:

```
9:    int FirstNumber = 0;
```

What this line declares is a variable of type `int`, which indicates an integer, and a name `FirstNumber`. Zero is assigned to the variable as an initial value.

Thus, in comparison to assembly programming, in which you need to explicitly ask the processor to store the multiplicand in a location—say 578—C++ enables you to access memory locations to store and retrieve data using friendlier concepts such as the `FirstNumber` variable. The compiler does the job of mapping this variable `FirstNumber` to a location in memory and takes care of the associated bookkeeping for you.

The programmer thus works with human-friendly names, leaving it to the compiler to convert the variable into an address and create instructions for the microprocessor and RAM to work with.

> **CAUTION**
>
> Naming variables appropriately is important for writing good, understandable, and maintainable code.
>
> Variable names can be alphanumeric, but they cannot start with a number. They cannot contain spaces and cannot contain arithmetic operators (such as +, –, and so on) within them. You can elongate variable names using an underscore.
>
> Variables names also cannot be reserved keywords. For example, a variable named `return` causes compilation failures.

Declaring and Initializing Multiple Variables of a Type

In Listing 3.1, `FirstNumber`, `SecondNumber`, and `MultiplicationResult` are all of the same type—integers—and are declared in three separate lines. If you wanted to, you could condense the declaration of these three variables to one line of code that would look like this:

```
int FirstNumber = 0, SecondNumber = 0, MultiplicationResult = 0;
```

> **NOTE**
>
> As you can see, C++ makes it possible to declare multiple variables of a type at once and even to declare variables at the beginning of a function. Yet, declaring a variable when it is first needed is often better as it makes the code readable—one notices the type of the variable when the declaration is close to its point of first use.

> **CAUTION**
>
> Data stored in variables is data stored in RAM. This data is lost when a computer is shut down or an application is terminated unless the programmer explicitly persists the data on a storage medium like a hard disk.
>
> Storing to a file on disk is discussed in Lesson 27, "Using Streams for Input and Output."

Understanding the Scope of a Variable

Ordinary variables have a well-defined scope within which they're valid and can be used. When used outside their scope, the variable names will not be recognized by the compiler and your program won't compile. Beyond its scope, the variable is an unidentified entity that the compiler knows nothing of.

To better understand the scope of a variable, reorganize the program in Listing 3.1 into a function MultiplyNumbers() that multiplies the two numbers and returns the result. See Listing 3.2.

3

LISTING 3.2 Demonstrating the Scope of the Variables

```
1: #include <iostream>
2: using namespace std;
3:
4: void MultiplyNumbers ()
5: {
6:    cout << "Enter the first number: ";
7:    int FirstNumber = 0;
8:    cin >> FirstNumber;
9:
10:    cout << "Enter the second number: ";
11:    int SecondNumber = 0;
12:    cin >> SecondNumber;
13:
14:    // Multiply two numbers, store result in a variable
15:    int MultiplicationResult = FirstNumber * SecondNumber;
16:
17:    // Display result
18:    cout << FirstNumber << " x " << SecondNumber;
19:    cout << " - " << MultiplicationResult << endl;
20: }
21: int main ()
22: {
23:    cout << "This program will help you multiply two numbers" << endl;
24:
25:    // Call the function that does all the work
```

LISTING 3.2   Continued

```
26:     MultiplyNumbers();
27:
28:     // cout << FirstNumber << " x " << SecondNumber;
29:     // cout << " = " << MultiplicationResult << endl;
30:
31:     return 0;
32: }
```

Output ▼

```
This program will help you multiply two numbers
Enter the first number: 51
Enter the second number: 24
51 x 24 = 1224
```

Analysis ▼

Listing 3.2 does exactly the same stuff as Listing 3.1 and produces the same output. The only difference is that the bulk of the work is delegated to a function called MultiplyNumbers() invoked by main(). Note that variables FirstNumber and SecondNumber cannot be used outside of MultiplyNumbers(). If you uncomment Line 28 or 29 in main(), you experience compile failure, most likely of type undeclared identifier.

This is because the scope of the variables FirstNumber and SecondNumber is local and limited to the function they're declared in, in this case MultiplyNumbers(). A local variable can be used in a function after its declaration till the end of the function. The curly brace (}) that indicates the end of a function also limits the scope of variables declared in the same. When a function ends, all local variables are destroyed and the memory they occupied returned.

When compiled, variables declared within MultiplyNumbers() perish when the function ends, and if they're used in main(), compilation fails as the variables have not been declared in there.

CAUTION

If you declare another set of variables with the same name in main(), then don't still expect them to carry a value that might have been assigned in MultiplyNumbers().

The compiler treats the variables in main() as independent entities even if they share their names with a variable declared in another function, as the two variables in question are limited by their scope.

Global Variables

If the variables used in function MultiplyNumbers() in Listing 3.2 were declared outside the scope of the function MultiplyNumber() instead of within it, then they would be usable in both main() and MultiplyNumbers(). Listing 3.3 demonstrates global variables, which are the variables with the widest scope in a program.

LISTING 3.3   Using Global Variables

```
 1: #include <iostream>
 2: using namespace std;
 3:
 4: // three global integers
 5: int FirstNumber = 0;
 6: int SecondNumber = 0;
 7: int MultiplicationResult = 0;
 8:
 0: void MultiplyNumbers ()
10: {
11:    cout << "Enter the first number: ";
12:    cin >> FirstNumber;
13:
14:    cout << "Enter the second number: ";
15:    cin >> SecondNumber;
16:
17:    // Multiply two numbers, store result in a variable
18:    MultiplicationResult = FirstNumber * SecondNumber;
19:
20:    // Display result
21:    cout << "Displaying from MultiplyNumbers(): ";
22:    cout << FirstNumber << " x " << SecondNumber;
23:    cout << " = " << MultiplicationResult << endl;
24: }
25: int main ()
26: {
27:    cout << "This program will help you multiply two numbers" << endl;
28:
29:    // Call the function that does all the work
30:    MultiplyNumbers();
31:
32:    cout << "Displaying from main(): ";
33:
34:    // This line will now compile and work!
35:    cout << FirstNumber << " x " << SecondNumber;
36:    cout << " = " << MultiplicationResult << endl;
37:
38:    return 0;
39: }
```

3

Output ▼

```
This program will help you multiply two numbers
Enter the first number: 51
Enter the second number: 19
Displaying from MultiplyNumbers(): 51 x 19 = 969
Displaying from main(): 51 x 19 = 969
```

Analysis ▼

Listing 3.3 displays the result of multiplication in two functions, neither of which have declared the variables FirstNumber, SecondNumber, and MultiplicationResult. These variables are global as they have been declared in Lines 5–7, outside the scope of any function. Note Lines 23 and 36 that use these variables and display their values. Pay special attention to how MultiplicationResult is assigned in MultiplyNumbers() yet is effectively reused in main().

CAUTION

> Using global variables indiscriminately is generally considered poor programming practice.
>
> Global variables can be assigned values in any function and can contain an unpredictable state, especially if different function modules are programmed by different programmers in a team.
>
> An elegant way of having the result of multiplication in main() as required in Listing 3.3 is to have MultiplyNumbers() return that result to main.

Common Compiler-Supported C++ Variable Types

In most of the examples this far, you have defined variables of type int—that is, integers. However, C++ programmers have a variety of fundamental variable types supported directly by the compiler to choose from. Choosing the right variable type is as important as choosing the right tools for the job! A Phillips screwdriver won't work well with a regular screw head just like an unsigned integer can't be used to store values that are negative! Table 3.1 enlists the various variable types and the nature of data they can contain. This information is very important in writing efficient and reliable C++ programs.

TABLE 3.1 Variable Types

Type	Values
bool	true or false
char	256 character values
unsigned short int	0 to 65,535
short int	–32,768 to 32,767
unsigned long int	0 to 4,294,967,295
long int	–2,147,483,648 to 2,147,483,647
unsigned long long	0 to 18,446,744,073,709,551,615
long long	–9,223,372,036,854,775,808 to 9,223,372,036,854,775,807
int (16 bit)nt data type	–32,768 to 32,767
int (32 bit)nt data type	–2,147,483,648 to 2,147,483,647
unsigned int (16 bit)	0 to 65,535
unsigned int (32 bit)	0 to 4,294,967,295
float	1.2e–38 to 3.4e38
double	2.2e–308 to 1.8e308

The following sections explain the important types in greater detail.

Using Type bool to Store Boolean Values

C++ provides a type that is specially created for containing boolean values true or false, both of which are reserved C++ keywords. This type is particularly useful in storing settings and flags that can be ON or OFF, present or absent, available or unavailable, and the like.

A sample declaration of an initialized Boolean variable is

```
bool AlwaysOnTop = false;
```

An expression that evaluates to a Boolean type is

```
bool DeleteFile = (UserSelection == "yes");
// evaluates to true only if UserSelection contains "yes", else to false
```

Using Type char to Store Character Values

Use type char to store a single character. A sample declaration is

```
char UserInput = 'Y'; // initialized char to 'Y'
```

3

Note that memory is comprised of bits and bytes. Bits can be either 0 or 1, and bytes can contain numeric representation using these bits. So, working or assigning character data as shown in the example, the compiler converts the character into a numeric representation that can be placed into memory. The numeric representation of Latin characters A–Z, a–z, numbers 0–9, some special keystrokes (for example, DEL), and special characters (such as backspace) has been standardized by the American Standard Code for Information Interchange, also called ASCII.

You can look up the table in Appendix E, "ASCII Codes," to see that the character 'Y' assigned to variable UserInput has the ASCII value 89 in decimal. Thus, what the compiler does is store 89 in the memory space allocated for UserInput.

The Concept of Signed and Unsigned Integers

Sign implies positive or negative. All numbers you work with using a computer are stored in the memory in the form of bits and bytes. A memory location that is 1 byte large contains 8 bits. Each bit can either be a 0 or 1 (that is, carry one of these two values at best). Thus, a memory location that is 1 byte large can contain a maximum of 2 to the power 8 values—that is, 256 unique values. Similarly, a memory location that is 16 bits large can contain 2 to the power 16 values—that is, 65,536 unique values.

If these values were to be unsigned—assumed to be only positive—then one byte could contain integer values ranging from 0 through 255 and two bytes would contain values ranging from 0 through 65,535, respectively. Look at Table 3.1 and note that the unsigned short is the type that supports this range, as it is contained in 16 bits of memory. Thus, it is quite easy to model positive values in bits and bytes (see Figure 3.1).

FIGURE 3.1
Organization of bits in a 16-bit unsigned short integer.

How to model negative numbers in this space? One way is to "sacrifice" a bit as the sign-bit that would indicate if the values contained in the other bits are positive or negative (see Figure 3.2). The sign-bit needs to be the most-significant-bit (MSB) as the least-significant-one would be required to model odd numbers. So, when the MSB contains sign-information, it is assumed that 0 would be positive and 1 would mean negative, and the other bytes contain the absolute value.

FIGURE 3.2
Organization of
bits in a 16-bit
signed short
integer.

15 . . . . Bit 0

15 bits contain absolute value

Sign Bit
0: Indicates positive integer
1: Indicates negative integer

Thus, a signed number that occupies 8 bits can contain values ranging from −128 through 127, and one that occupies 16 bits can contain values ranging from −32768 through 32767. If you look at Table 3.1 again, note that the (signed) short is the type that supports positive and negative integer values in a 16-bit space.

Signed Integer Types `short`, `int`, `long`, and `long long`

These types differ in their sizes and thereby differ in the range of values they can contain. int is possibly the most used type and is 32 bits wide on most compilers. Use the right type depending on your projection of the maximum value that particular variable would be expected to hold.

Declaring a variable of a signed type is quite simple:

```
short int SmallNumber = -100;
int LargerNumber = -70000;
long PossiblyLargerThanInt = -70000; //on some platforms, long is an int
long long LargerThanInt = -70000000000;
```

Unsigned Integer Types `unsigned short`, `unsigned int`, `unsigned long`, and `unsigned long long`

Unlike their signed counterparts, unsigned integer variable types cannot contain sign information, and hence they can actually support twice as many positive values.

Declaring a variable of an unsigned type is as simple as this:

```
unsigned short int SmallNumber = 255;
unsigned int LargerNumber = 70000;
// on some platforms, long is int
unsigned long PossiblyLargerThanInt = 70000;
unsigned long long LargerThanInt = 70000000000;
```

NOTE

You would use an unsigned variable type when you expect only positive values. So, if you're counting the number of apples, don't use int; use unsigned int. The latter can hold twice as many values in the positive range as the former can.

CAUTION

So, an unsigned type might not be suited for a variable in a banking application used to store the account balance.

Floating-Point Types `float` and `double`

Floating-point numbers are what you might have learned in school as real numbers. These are numbers that can be positive or negative. They can contain decimal values. So, if you want to store the value of pi (22 / 7 or 3.14) in a variable in C++, you would use a floating-point type.

Declaring variables of these types follows exactly the same pattern as the int in Listing 3.1. So, a `float` that allows you to store decimal values would be declared as the following:

```
float Pi = 3.14;
```

And a double precision `float` (called simply a `double`) is defined as

```
double MorePrecisePi = 22 / 7;
```

NOTE

The data types mentioned in the table are often referred to as POD (Plain Old Data). The category POD contains these as well as aggregations (structs, enums, unions, or classes) thereof.

Determining the Size of a Variable Using `sizeof`

Size is the amount of memory that the compiler reserves when the programmer declares a variable to hold the data assigned to it. The size of a variable depends on its type, and C++ has a very convenient operator called `sizeof` that tells you the size in bytes of a variable or a type.

The usage of `sizeof` is quite simple. To determine the size of an integer, you invoke `sizeof` with parameter `int` (the type) as demonstrated by Listing 3.4.

```
cout << "Size of an int: " << sizeof (int);
```

LISTING 3.4   Finding the Size of Standard C++ Variable Types

```
 1: #include <iostream>
 2:
 3: int main()
 4: {
 5:    using namespace std;
 6:    cout << "Computing the size of some C++ inbuilt variable types" << endl;
 7:
 8:    cout << "Size of bool: " << sizeof(bool) << endl;
 9:    cout << "Size of char: " << sizeof(char) << endl;
10:    cout << "Size of unsigned short int: " << sizeof(unsigned short) << endl;
11:    cout << "Size of short int: " << sizeof(short) << endl;
12:    cout << "Size of unsigned long int: " << sizeof(unsigned long) << endl;
13:    cout << "Size of long: " << sizeof(long) << endl;
14:    cout << "Size of int: " << sizeof(int) << endl;
15:    cout << "Size of unsigned long long: "<< sizeof(unsigned long long)<<
endl;
16:    cout << "Size of long long: " << sizeof(long long) << endl;
17:    cout << "Size of unsigned int: " << sizeof(unsigned int) << endl;
18:    cout << "Size of float: " << sizeof(float) << endl;
19:    cout << "Size of double: " << sizeof(double) << endl;
20:
21:    cout << "The output changes with compiler, hardware and OS" << endl;
22:
23:    return 0;
24: }
```

Output ▼

```
Computing the size of some C++ inbuilt variable types
Size of bool: 1
Size of char: 1
Size of unsigned short int: 2
Size of short int: 2
Size of unsigned long int: 4
Size of long: 4
Size of int: 4
Size of unsigned long long: 8
Size of long long: 8
Size of unsigned int: 4
Size of float: 4
Size of double: 8
The output changes with compiler, hardware and OS
```

Analysis ▼

The output of Listing 3.4 reveals sizes of various types in bytes and is specific to my platform: compiler, OS, and hardware. This output in particular is a result of running the program in 32-bit mode (compiled by a 32-bit compiler) on a 64-bit operating system. Note that a 64-bit compiler probably creates different results, and the reason I chose a 32-bit compiler was to be able to run the application on 32-bit as well as 64-bit systems. The output tells that the `sizeof` a variable doesn't change between an unsigned or signed type; the only difference in the two is the MSB that carries sign information in the former.

NOTE

> All sizes seen in the output are in bytes. The size of an object is an important parameter when allocating memory for it, particularly when this allocation is made by the programmer dynamically.

C++11

Using `auto`, the Compiler's Type Inference Capabilities

There are cases where the type of a variable is apparent given the initialization value it is being assigned. For example, if a variable is being initialized with the value `true`, the type of the variable can be best estimated as `bool`. In C++11, you have the option to not explicitly specify the type when you use keyword `auto` instead.

auto Flag = true;

We have left the task of defining an exact type for variable `Flag` to the compiler. What the compiler does is check the nature of the value the variable is being initialized to and then decide on the best possible type that suits this variable. In this particular case, it is clear that an initialization value of `true` best suits a variable that is of type `bool`. The compiler thus determines `bool` as the type that suits variable `Flag` best and internally treats `Flag` as a `bool`, as is also demonstrated by Listing 3.5.

LISTING 3.5   Using auto Keyword and Relying on the Compiler's Type-inference Capabilities

```
1: #include <iostream>
2: using namespace std;
3:
4: int main()
5: {
6:     auto Flag = true;
7:     auto Number = 2500000000000;
8:
9:     cout << "Flag = " << Flag;
10:    cout << " , sizeof(Flag) = " << sizeof(Flag) << endl;
11:    cout << "Number = " << Number;
12:    cout << " , sizeof(Number) = " << sizeof(Number) << endl;
13:
14:    return 0;
15: }
```

3

Output ▼

```
Flag = 1 , sizeof(Flag) = 1
Number = 2500000000000 , sizeof(Number) = 8
```

Analysis ▼

See how instead of deciding that Flag should be of type bool or that Number should be a long long, you have used the auto keyword in Lines 6 and 7 where the two variables have been declared. This delegates the decision on the type of variable to the compiler, which uses the initialization value as a ballpark. You have used sizeof to actually check if the compiler created the types you suspected it would, and you can check against the output of Listing 3.4 to verify that it really did.

> **NOTE**
>
> Using auto requires you to initialize the variable for the compiler, which needs this initialization value in deciding what the variable type can be.
>
> When you don't initialize a variable of type auto, you get a compile error.

Even if auto seems to be a trivial feature at first sight, it makes programming a lot easier in those cases where the type variable is a complex type. Take the case where you declare a dynamic array of integers in the form of a std::vector, called MyNumbers:

```
std::vector<int> MyNumbers;
```

You access or iterate elements in the array and display them using the following code:

```
for ( vector<int>::const_iterator Iterator = MyNumbers.begin();
     Iterator < MyNumbers.end();
     ++Iterator )
   cout << *Iterator << " ";
```

Neither the std::vector nor the for loop has been explained to you yet, so don't worry if the preceding code looks like Greek and Latin. What it does is that for every element in the vector, starting at begin() and ending before end(), it displays the value using cout. Look at the complexity of the first line that declares a variable Iterator and assigns it an initial value, as returned by begin(). This variable Iterator is of type vector<int>::const_iterator, which is quite a complicated thing for the programmer to learn and write. Instead of knowing this by heart, the programmer can rely on the return type of begin() and simplify this for loop to the following:

```
for( auto Iterator = MyNumbers.begin();
    Iterator < MyNumbers.end();
    ++Iterator )
   cout << *Iterator << " ";
```

Note how compact the first line has become. The compiler checks the initialization value of Iterator that is the return value of begin() and assigns it the same type as the return value. This simplifies C++ coding, especially when you use templates quite a bit.

Using typedef to Substitute a Variable's Type

C++ allows you to substitute variable types to something that you might find convenient. You use the keyword typedef for that. Here is an example where a programmer wants to call an unsigned int a descriptive STRICTLY_POSITIVE_INTEGER.

```
typedef unsigned int STRICTLY_POSITIVE_INTEGER;
STRICTLY_POSITIVE_INTEGER PosNumber = 4532;
```

When compiled, the first line tells the compiler that a STRICLY_POSITIVE_INTEGER is nothing but an unsigned int. At later stages when the compiler encounters the already defined type STRICLY_POSITIVE_INTEGER, it substitutes it for unsigned int and continues compilation.

NOTE _____ | typedef or type substitution is particularly convenient when dealing with complex types that can have a cumbersome syntax, for example those using templates.

What Is a Constant?

Imagine you are writing a program to calculate the area and the circumference of a circle. The formulas are

```
Area = Pi * Radius * Radius;

Circumference = 2 * Pi * Radius of circle
```

In this formula, Pi is the constant of value 22 / 7. You don't want the value of Pi to change anywhere in your program. You also don't want accidental assignments of possibly incorrect values to Pi, say via an inadvertent copy-paste or find-replace error. C++ enables you to define Pi as a constant that cannot be changed after declaration. In other words, after it's defined the value of a constant cannot be altered. Assignments to a constant in C++ cause compilation errors.

Thus, constants are like variables in C++ except that these cannot be changed. Similar to variables, constants also occupy space in the memory and have a name to identify the address where the space is reserved. However, the content of this space cannot be overwritten. Constants in C++ can be

- Literal constants
- Declared constants using the const keyword
- Constant expressions using the constexpr keyword (new to C++11)
- Enumerated constants using the enum keyword
- Defined constants that are not recommended and deprecated

Literal Constants

Look at Listing 3.1 again—the simple program that multiplies two numbers. We have declared an integer called FirstNumber, like this:

```
9:    int FirstNumber = 0;
```

3

The integer called `FirstNumber` is assigned an initial value of zero. Here zero is a part of the code, gets compiled into the application, is unchangeable, and is called a literal constant. Literal constants can be of many types—bool, integer, string, and so on. In your very first C++ program in Listing 1.1, you displayed "Hello World" using the following:

```
std::cout << "Hello World" << std::endl;
```

In here, "Hello World" is a string literal constant.

Declaring Variables as Constants Using `const`

The most important type of constants in C++ from a practical and programmatic point of view are declared by using keyword `const` before the variable type. The generic declaration looks like the following:

```
const type-name constant-name;
```

Let's see a simple application that displays the value of a constant called `Pi` (see Listing 3.6).

LISTING 3.6 Declaring a Constant Called `Pi`

```
 1: #include <iostream>
 2:
 3: int main()
 4: {
 5:    using namespace std;
 6:
 7:    const double Pi = 22.0 / 7;
 8:    cout << "The value of constant Pi is: " << Pi << endl;
 9:
10:    // Uncomment next line to fail compilation
11:    // Pi = 345;
12:
13:    return 0;
14: }
```

Output ▼

```
The value of constant Pi is: 3.14286
```

Analysis ▼

Note the declaration of constant `Pi` in Line 7. We use the `const` keyword to tell the compiler that `Pi` is a constant of type `double`. If you uncomment Line 11 where the programmer tries to assign a value to a variable you have defined as a constant, you see a compile failure that says something similar to, "You cannot assign to a variable that is const." Thus, constants are a powerful way to ensure that certain data cannot be modified.

> **NOTE**
>
> It is good programming practice to define variables that are not supposed to change their values as const. The usage of the const keyword ensures that the programmer has thought about ensuring the constant-ness of data and ensures his application against inadvertent changes to this constant.
>
> This is particularly useful in a multi-programmer environment.

Constants are useful when declaring the length of static arrays, which are fixed at compile time. Listing 4.2 in Lesson 4, "Managing Arrays and Strings," includes a sample that demonstrates the use of a const int to define the length of an array.

C++11

Declaring Constants Using constexpr

3

The concept of constexpr always existed in C++ even before C++11 but was not formalized to a keyword. Note the example in Listing 3.5 in which 22.0 / 7 is a constant expression supported by pre-2011 compilers, too. However, pre-2011 compilers did not allow for defining functions that could be evaluated at compile time. In C++11, you can now define this:

```
constexpr double GetPi() {return 22.0 / 7;}
```

GetPi() used in combination with another constant such as this still makes a valid statement:

```
constexpr double TwicePi() {return 2 * GetPi();}
```

The difference between const and constexpr is very little at first look; however, there are new optimization possibilities from the compiler's and application's point of view. The second statement (without the constexpr) would've been a runtime computation in pre-2011 compilers—evaluated when the application is running—but is an expression resolved at compile-time with C++11-compliant compilers, which makes the application run faster.

> **NOTE**
>
> At time of writing this book, constexpr was not supported by Microsoft Visual C++ Express Compiler. constexpr is supported by GNU's g++ compiler.

Enumerated Constants

There are situations where a particular variable can take only a certain set of values. These are situations where you don't want the colors in the rainbow to contain Turquoise or the directions on a compass to contain Left. In both these cases, what you want is a type of a variable whose values are restricted to a certain set defined by you. Enumerated constants are exactly the tool you need in this situation and are characterized by the keyword enum.

For example, the following is an enumerated constant that specifies colors in a rainbow:

```
enum RainbowColors
{
    Violet = 0,
    Indigo,
    Blue,
    Green,
    Yellow,
    Orange,
    Red
};
```

Here's another that contains the cardinal directions:

```
enum CardinalDirections
{
    North,
    South,
    East,
    West
};
```

Note that these enumerated constants can now be used as variable types that can accept values restricted to those that they have been declared to contain. So, if defining a variable that contains the colors of a Rainbow, you declare the variable like this:

```
RainbowColors MyWorldsColor = Blue; // Initial value
```

In the preceding line of code, you have declared an enumerated constant MyWorldsColor of type RainbowColors. This enumerated constant variable is restricted to contain any of the legal VIBGYOR colors, and no other value.

<table>
<tr>
<td>

NOTE

</td>
<td>

When declaring an enumerated constant, the compiler converts the enumerated values such as Violet and so on into integers. Each enumerated value specified is one more than the previous value. You have the choice of specifying a starting value and if this is not specified, the compiler takes it as 0. So, North is evaluated as value 0.

If you want to, you can also specify an explicit value against each of the enumerated constants by initializing them.

</td>
</tr>
</table>

Listing 3.7 demonstrates how enumerated constants are used to hold the four cardinal directions, with an initializing value supplied to the first one.

LISTING 3.7   Using Enumerated Values to Indicate Cardinal Wind Directions

```
1: #include <iostream>
2: using namespace std;
3:
4: enum CardinalDirections
5: {
6:    North = 25,
7:    South,
8:    East,
9:    West
10: };
11:
12: int main()
13: {
14:    cout << "Displaying directions and their symbolic values" << endl;
15:    cout << "North: " << North << endl;
16:    cout << "South: " << South << endl;
17:    cout << "East: " << East << endl;
18:    cout << "West: " << West << endl;
19:
20:    CardinalDirections WindDirection = South;
21:    cout << "Variable WindDirection = " << WindDirection << endl;
22:
23:    return 0;
24: }
```

3

Output ▼

```
Displaying directions and their symbolic values
North: 25
South: 26
East: 27
West: 28
Variable WindDirection = 26
```

Analysis ▼

Note how we have defined the four cardinal directions as enumerated constants but have given the first North an initial value of 25 (see Line 6). This automatically ensures that the following constants are assigned values 26, 27, and 28 as demonstrated in the output. In Line 20 you create a variable of type CardinalDirections that is assigned an initial value South. When displayed on the screen in Line 21, the compiler dispatches the integer value associated with South, which is 26.

TIP

> You may want to take a look at Listings 6.4 and 6.5 in Lesson 6,"Controlling Program Flow." They use enum to enumerate the days of the week and conditional processing to tell what the day of the user's choosing is named after.

Defining Constants Using #define

First and foremost, don't use this if you are writing a program anew. The only reason this book analyzes the definition of constants using #define is to help you understand certain legacy programs that do define Pi using this syntax:

```
#define Pi 3.14286
```

This is a preprocessor macro, and what is done here is that all mentions of Pi henceforth are replaced by 3.14286 for the compiler to process. Note that this is a text replacement (read: non-intelligent replacement) done by the preprocessor. The compiler neither knows nor cares about the actual type of the constant in question.

CAUTION

> Defining constants using the preprocessor via #define is deprecated and should not be used.

Naming Variables and Constants

There are many different ways to name variables and many different conventions. Some programmers prefer prefixing their variable names with a few characters that indicate type. For example:

```
bool bIsLampOn = false;
```

Here, b is the prefix that the programmer has added to indicate that the variable is of type bool. This kind of notation is called Hungarian Notation and was initially developed and promoted by Microsoft. However, C++ is a strongly type-safe language and the compiler knows what a variable is, not by the prefix on its name, but because of the type definition that is bool. So, these days programmers are strongly recommended to not follow the Hungarian Notation. It is necessary that the variable is understandable, even if that means the name gets a little long. Assuming that the Boolean variable in the example was used to program the electronics of a car, a slightly better variant would be the following:

```
bool IsHeadLampOn = false;
```

Note, both these variants are better and recommended over something like this:

```
bool b = false;
```

Such nondescriptive variable names should be avoided at all costs.

3

DO	DON'T
DO give variables descriptive names, even if that makes them long.	**DON'T** give names that are too short or contain just a character.
DO ensure that the name of the variable explains its purpose.	**DON'T** give names that use exotic acronyms known only to you.
DO put yourself into the shoes of one who hasn't seen your code yet and think if the name would make sense to him or her.	**DON'T** give names that are reserved C++ keywords as these won't compile.
DO check if your team is following certain naming conventions and follow them.	

Keywords You Cannot Use as Variable or Constant Names

Some words are reserved by C++, and you cannot use them as variable names. These keywords have special meaning to the C++ compiler. Keywords include if, while, for, and main. A list of keywords defined by C++ is presented in Table 3.2 as well as in Appendix B, "C++ Keywords." Your compiler might have additional reserved words, so you should check its manual for a complete list.

TABLE 3.2   The C++ Keywords

asm	else	new	this
auto	enum	operator	throw
bool	explicit	private	true
break	export	protected	try
case	extern	public	typedef
catch	false	register	typeid
char	float	reinterpret_cast	typename
class	for	return	union
const	friend	short	unsigned
const_cast	goto	signed	using
continue	if	sizeof	virtual
default	inline	static	void
delete	int	static_cast	volatile
do	long	struct	wchar_t
double	mutable	switch	while
dynamic_cast	namespace	template	

In addition, the following words are reserved:

And	bitor	not_eq	xor
and_eq	compl	or	xor_eq
bitand	not	or_eq	

Summary

In this lesson you learned about using memory to store values temporarily in variables and constants. You learned that variables have a size determined by their type and that the operator `sizeof` can be used to determine the size of one. You got to know of different types of variables such as `bool`, `int`, and so on and that they are to be used to contain different types of data. The right choice of a variable type is important in effective programming, and the choice of a variable that's too small for the purpose can result in a wrapping error or an overflow situation. You learned the new C++11 keyword `auto`, where you let the compiler decide the data-type for you on the basis of the initialization value of the variable.

You also learned about the different types of constants and usage of the most important ones among them using keywords `const` and `enum`.

Q&A

Q Why define constants at all if you can use regular variables instead of them?

A Constants, especially those declared using the keyword `const`, are your way of telling the compiler that the value of a particular variable be fixed and not allowed to change. Consequently, the compiler always ensures that the constant variable is never assigned another value, not even if another programmer was to take up your work and inadvertently try to overwrite the value. So, declaring constants where you know the value of a variable should not change is a good programming practice and increases the quality of your application.

Q Why should I initialize the value of a variable?

A If you don't initialize, you don't know what the variable contains for a starting value. The starting value is just the contents of the location in the memory that are reserved for the variable. Initialization such as that seen here:

```
int MyFavoriteNumber = 0;
```

writes the initial value of your choosing, in this case 0, to the memory location reserved for the variable `MyFavoriteNumber` as soon as it is created. There are situations where you do conditional processing depending on the value of a variable (often checked against nonzero). Such logic does not work reliably without initialization because an unassigned or initiated variable contains junk that is often nonzero and random.

Q **Why does C++ give me the option of using `short int` and `int` and `long int`? Why not just always use the integer that always allows for the highest number to be stored within?**

A C++ is a programming language that is used to program for a variety of applications, many running on devices with little computing capacity or memory resources. The simple old cell phone is one example where processing capacity and available memory are both limited. In this case, the programmer can often save memory or speed or both by choosing the right kind of variable if he doesn't need high values. If you are programming on a regular desktop or a high-end smartphone, chances are that the performance gained or memory saved in choosing one integer type over another is going to be insignificant and in some cases even absent.

Q **Why should I not use global variables frequently? Isn't it true that they're usable throughout my application and I can save some time otherwise lost to passing values around functions?**

A Global variables can be read and assigned globally. The latter is the problem as they can be changed globally. Assume you are working on a project with a few other programmers in a team. You have declared your integers and other variables to be global. If any programmer in your team changes the value of your integer inadvertently in his code—which even might be a different .CPP file than the one you are using—the reliability of your code is affected. So, sparing a few seconds or minutes should not be criteria, and you should not use global variables indiscriminately to ensure the stability of your code.

Q **C++ is giving me the option of declaring unsigned integers that are supposed to contain only positive integer values and zero. What happens if I decrement a zero value contained in an `unsigned int`?**

A You see a wrapping effect. Decrementing an unsigned integer that contains 0 by 1 means that it wraps to the highest value it can hold! Check Table 3.1—you see that an `unsigned short` can contain values from 0 to 65535. So, declare an `unsigned short` and decrement it to see the unexpected:

```
unsigned short MyShortInt = 0;  // Initial Value
MyShortInt = MyShortInt - 1; // Decrement by 1
std::cout << MyShortInt << std::endl; // Output: 65535!
```

Note that this is not a problem with the `unsigned short`, rather with your usage of the same. An unsigned integer (or short or long) is not to be used when negative values are within the specifications. If the contents of `MyShortInt` are to be used to dynamically allocate those many number of bytes, a little bug that allows a zero value to be decremented would result in 64KB being allocated! Worse, if

`MyShortInt` were to be used as an index in accessing a location of memory, chances are high that your application would access an external location and would crash!

Workshop

The Workshop provides quiz questions to help you solidify your understanding of the material covered and exercises to provide you with experience in using what you've learned. Try to answer the quiz and exercise questions before checking the answers in Appendix D, and be certain that you understand the answers before continuing to the next lesson.

Quiz

1. What is the difference between a signed and an unsigned integer?
2. Why should you not use #define to declare a constant?
3. Why would you initialize a variable?
4. Consider the enum below. What is the value of QUEEN?
   ```
   enum YOURCARDS {ACE, JACK, QUEEN, KING};
   ```
5. What is wrong with this variable name?
   ```
   int Integer = 0;
   ```

Exercises

1. Modify enum YOURCARDS in quiz question 4 to demonstrate that the value of QUEEN can be 45.
2. Write a program that demonstrates that the size of an unsigned integer and a normal integer are the same, and that both are smaller in size than a long integer.
3. Write a program to calculate the area and circumference of a circle where the radius is fed by the user.
4. In Exercise 3, if the area and circumference were to be stored in integers, how would the output be any different?
5. BUGBUSTERS: What is wrong in the following initialization:
   ```
   auto Integer;
   ```

3

LESSON 4

Managing Arrays and Strings

In previous lessons, you declared variables used to contain a single `int`, `char`, or `string` to mention a few instances. However, you may want to declare a collection of objects, such as 20 `ints` or a litter of `Cats`.

In this lesson, you find out

- What arrays are and how to declare and use them
- What strings are and how to use character arrays to make them
- A brief introduction to `std::string`

What Is an Array?

The dictionary definition of an *array* gets really close to what we want to be understanding. According to Merriam Webster, an *array* is "a group of elements forming a complete unit, for example an array of solar panels."

The following are characteristics of an array:

- An array is a collection of elements.
- All elements contained in an array are of the same kind.
- This collection forms a complete set.

In C++, arrays enable you to store data elements of a type in the memory, in a sequential and ordered fashion.

The Need for Arrays

Imagine that you are writing a program where the user can type in five integers and you display them back to him. One way would be to have your program declare five distinct and unique integer variables and use them to store and display values. The declarations would look like this:

```
int FirstNumber = 0;
int SecondNumber = 0;
int ThirdNumber = 0;
int FourthNumber = 0;
int FifthNumber = 0;
```

If your user wants this program to store and display 500 integers at a later stage, you need to declare 500 such integers using the preceding system. This still is doable given generous amounts of patience and time. However, imagine the user asks you to support 500,000 integers instead of 5—what would you do?

You would do it right and do it smart from the point go by declaring an array of five integers each initialized to zero, like this:

```
int MyNumbers [5] = {0};
```

Thus, if you were asked to support 500,000 integers, your array would scale up quite quickly, like this:

```
int ManyNumbers [500000] = {0};
```

An array of five characters would be defined as

```
char MyCharacters [5];
```

Such arrays are called *static arrays* because the number of elements they contain as well as the memory the array consumes is fixed at the time of compilation.

Declaring and Initializing Static Arrays

In the preceding lines of code, you have declared an array called `MyNumbers` that contains five elements of type `int`—that is, integer—all initialized to a value 0. Thus, array declaration in C++ follows a simple syntax:

```
element-type array-name [number of elements] = {optional initial values}
```

You can even declare an array and initialize its contents on a per-element basis, like this integer array where each of the five integers is initialized to five different integer values:

```
int MyNumbers [5] = {34, 56, -21, 5002, 365};
```

You can initialize all elements of an array to one value, like this:

```
int MyNumbers [5] = {100}; // initialize all integers to 100
```

You can also partially initialize elements in an array, like this:

```
int MyNumbers [5] = {34, 56}; // initialize first two elements
```

You can define the length of an array (that is, the number of elements in one) as a constant and use that constant in your array definition:

```
const int ARRAY_LENGTH = 5;
int MyNumbers [ARRAY_LENGTH] = {34, 56, -21, 5002, 365};
```

4

This is particularly useful when you need to access and use the length of the array at multiple places, such as when iterating elements in one, and then instead of having to change the length at each of those places, you just correct the initialization value at the `const int` declaration.

NOTE

When partially initializing arrays, it is possible that certain compilers initialize those elements ignored by you to an initial value 0.

You can opt to leave out the number of elements in an array if you know the initial values of the elements in the array:

```
int MyNumbers [] = {2011, 2052, -525};
```

The preceding code creates an array of three integers with the initial values 2011, 2052, and –525.

How Data Is Stored in an Array

Think of books placed on a shelf, one next to the other. This is an example of a one-dimensional array, as it expands in only one dimension, that is the number of books on it. Each book is an element in the array, and the rack is akin to the memory that has been reserved to store this collection of books as shown in Figure 4.1.

FIGURE 4.1
Books on a shelf: a one-dimensional array.

It is not an error that we started numbering the books with 0. As you later see, indexes in C++ start at 0 and not at 1. Similar to the five books on a shelf, the array MyNumbers containing five integers looks quite similar to Figure 4.2.

Note that the memory space occupied by the array is comprised of five blocks, each of equal size, that is defined by the type of data to be held in the array, in this case integer. If you remember, you studied the size of an integer in Lesson 3, "Using Variables, Declaring Constants." The amount of memory reserved by the compiler for the array MyNumbers is hence sizeof(int) * 5. In general, the amount of memory reserved by the compiler for an array in bytes is

```
Bytes consumed by an array = sizeof(element-type) * Number of Elements
```

FIGURE 4.2
Organization of an array of five integers, MyNumbers, in memory.

Accessing Data Stored in an Array

Elements in an array can be accessed using their zero-based index. These indexes are called zero-based because the first element in an array is at index 0. So, the first integer value stored in the array MyNumbers is MyNumbers[0], the second is MyNumbers[1], and so on. The fifth is MyNumbers[4]. In other words, the index of the last element in an array is always (Length of Array − 1).

When asked to access element at index N, the compiler uses the memory address of the first element (positioned at index zero) as the starting point and then skips N elements by adding the offset computed as N*sizeof(element) to reach the address containing the (N+1)th element. The C++ compiler does not check if the index is within the actual defined bounds of the array. You can try fetching the element at index 1001 in an array of only 10 elements, putting the security and stability of your program at risk. The onus of ensuring that the array is not accessed beyond its bounds lies solely on the programmer.

CAUTION

Accessing an array beyond its bounds results in unpredictable behavior. In many cases this causes your program to crash. Accessing arrays beyond their bounds should be avoided at all costs.

Listing 4.1 demonstrates how you declare an array of integers, initialize its elements to integer values, and access them to display them on the screen.

LISTING 4.1   Declaring an Array of Integers and Accessing Its Elements

```
0:  #include <iostream>
1:
2:  using namespace std;
3:
4:  int main ()
5:  {
6:     int MyNumbers [5] = {34, 56, -21, 5002, 365};
7:
8:     cout << "First element at index 0: " << MyNumbers [0] << endl;
9:     cout << "Second element at index 1: " << MyNumbers [1] << endl;
10:    cout << "Third element at index 2: " << MyNumbers [2] << endl;
11:    cout << "Fourth element at index 3: " << MyNumbers [3] << endl;
12:    cout << "Fifth element at index 4: " << MyNumbers [4] << endl;
13:
14:    return 0;
15: }
```

Output ▼

```
First element at index 0: 34
Second element at index 1: 56
Third element at index 2: -21
Fourth element at index 3: 5002
Fifth element at index 4: 365
```

Analysis ▼

Line 6 declares an array of five integers with initial values specified for each of them. The subsequent lines simply display the integers using cout and using the array variable MyNumbers with an appropriate index.

NOTE

> To familiarize you with the concept of zero-based indexes used to access elements in arrays, we started numbering lines of code in Listing 4.1 and beyond with the first line being numbered as Line 0.

Modifying Data Stored in an Array

In the previous code listing, you did not enter user-defined data into the array. The syntax for assigning an integer to an element in that array is quite similar to assigning an integer value to an integer variable.

For example, assigning a value 2011 to an integer is like the following:

```
int AnIntegerValue;
AnIntegerValue = 2011;
```

Assigning a value 2011 to the fourth element in your array is like this:

```
MyNumbers [3] = 2011; // Assign 2011 to the fourth element
```

Listing 4.2 demonstrates the use of constants in declaring the length of an array and shows how individual array elements can be assigned values during the execution of the program.

LISTING 4.2   Assigning Values to Elements in an Array

```
0: #include <iostream>
1: using namespace std;
2:
3: int main()
4: {
5:     const int ARRAY_LENGTH = 5;
6:
7:     // Array of 5 integers, initialized to zero
8:     int MyNumbers [ARRAY_LENGTH] = {0};
9:
10:    cout << "Enter index of the element to be changed: ";
11:    int nElementIndex = 0;
12:    cin >> nElementIndex;
13:
14:    cout << "Enter new value: ";
15:    cin >> MyNumbers [nElementIndex];
16:
17:    cout << "First element at index 0: " << MyNumbers [0] << endl;
18:    cout << "Second element at index 1: " << MyNumbers [1] << endl;
19:    cout << "Third element at index 2: " << MyNumbers [2] << endl;
20:    cout << "Fourth element at index 3: " << MyNumbers [3] << endl;
21:    cout << "Fifth element at index 4: " << MyNumbers [4] << endl;
22:
23:    return 0;
24: }
```

4

Output ▼

```
Enter index of the element to be changed: 2
Enter new value: 2011
First element at index 0: 0
Second element at index 1: 0
Third element at index 2: 2011
Fourth element at index 3: 0
Fifth element at index 4: 0
```

Output ▼

The array declaration syntax in Line 8 makes use of a const integer ARRAY_LENGTH initialized to five before that. As this is a static array, the length of the array is fixed at compile time. So, the compiler substitutes ARRAY_LENGTH by 5 and compiles considering MyArray to be an array of integers containing five elements. In Lines 10 through 12, the user is asked what element he wants to set in the array and that zero-based index is stored in an integer ElementIndex. This integer is used in Line 14 to modify the contents of the array. The output shows that modifying element at index 2 and actually modifies the third element in the array, as indexes are zero-based entities. You have to get used to this.

NOTE

Many novice C++ programmers assign the fifth value at index five in an array of five integers. Note that this exceeds the bound of the array as the compiled code tries accessing the sixth element in the array which is beyond its defined bounds.

This kind of error is called a fence-post error. It's named after the fact that the number of posts needed to build a fence is always one more than the number of sections in the fence.

CAUTION

Something very fundamental is missing in Listing 4.2: It does not check if the index entered by the user is within the bounds of the array. The previous program should actually verify if ElementIndex is within 0 and 4 and reject all other entries. This missing check allows the user to potentially assign a value beyond the bounds of the array. This can potentially cause the application—and the system, in a worst-case scenario—to crash.

Performing checks is explained in Lesson 6, "Controlling Program Flow."

Using Loops to Access Array Elements

When working with arrays and their elements in serial order, you should access them (in other words, iterate) using loops. See Lesson 6 and Listing 6.10 in particular to quickly learn how elements in an array can be efficiently inserted or accessed using a for loop.

DO	DON'T
Do always initialize arrays, or else they will contain junk values. **Do** always ensure that your arrays are used within their defined boundaries.	**Don't** ever access the Nth element using index N, in an array of N elements. **Don't** forget that the first element in an array is accessed using index 0.

Multidimensional Arrays

The arrays that we have seen this far have been akin to books on a shelf. There can be more books on a longer shelf and fewer books on a shorter one. That is, the length of the shelf is the only dimension defining the capacity of the shelf, hence it is one-dimensional. Now, what if we were to use arrays to model an array of solar panels as shown in Figure 4.3? Solar panels, unlike bookshelves, expand in two dimensions: in length and in breadth.

FIGURE 4.3
Array of solar panels on a roof.

4

As you see in Figure 4.3, six solar panels are placed in a two-dimensional arrangement comprised of two rows and three columns. From one perspective, you can see this arrangement as an array of two elements, each element itself being an array of three panels—in other words, an array of arrays. In C++, you can model two-dimensional arrays, but you are not restricted to just two dimensions. Depending on your need and the nature of the application, you can model multidimensional arrays in memory, too.

Declaring and Initializing Multidimensional Arrays

C++ enables you to declare multidimensional arrays by indicating the number of elements you want to reserve in each dimension. So, a two-dimensional array of integers representing the solar panels in Figure 4.3 is

```
int SolarPanelIDs [2][3];
```

Note that in Figure 4.3, you have also assigned each panel an ID ranging from 0 through 5 for the six panels in the solar array. If you were to initialize the integer array in the same order, it would look like the following:

```
int SolarPanelIDs [2][3] = {{0, 1, 2}, {3, 4, 5}};
```

As you see, the initialization syntax you have used is actually similar to one where we initialize two one-dimensional arrays. Note that it is not two because this is a two-dimensional array, rather we have two arrays because there are two rows. If this were to be an array comprised of three rows and three columns, it would look like this:

```
int ThreeRowsThreeColumns [3][3] = {{-501, 206, 2011}, {989, 101, 206}, {303, 456, 596}};
```

<table>
<tr><td>**NOTE**</td><td>Even though C++ enables us to model multidimensional arrays, the memory where the array is contained is one-dimensional. So, the compiler maps the multidimensional array into the memory space, which expands only in one direction.

If you wanted to, you could've also initialized the array called `SolarPanelIDs` like the following, and it would still be the same:

`int SolarPanelIDs [2][3] = {0, 1, 2, 3, 4, 5};`

However, the other method makes a better example because it's easier to imagine and understand a multidimensional array as an array of arrays.</td></tr>
</table>

Accessing Elements in a Multidimensional Array

Think of a multidimensional array as an array of arrays. So, when dealing with a two-dimensional array comprised of three rows and three columns containing integers, you can visualize it as handling an array comprised of three elements, where each element is an array comprised of three integers.

So, when you need to access an integer in this array, you would need to use a first subscript to address the array where the integer is and the second subscript to address that integer in this array. Consider this array:

```
int ThreeRowsThreeColumns [3][3] = {{-501, 206, 2011}, {989, 101, 206}, {303, 456, 596}};
```

It has been initialized in a way you can visualize three arrays, each containing three integers. Here, the integer element with value 206 is at position [0][1]. The element with value 456 is at position [2][2]. Listing 4.3 explains how integer elements in this array can be accessed.

LISTING 4.3 Accessing Elements in a Multidimensional Array

```
0: #include <iostream>
1: using namespace std;
2:
3: int main()
4: {
5:     int ThreeRowsThreeColumns [3][3] = \
6:     {{-501, 206, 2011}, {989, 101, 206}, {303, 456, 596}};
7:
8:     cout << "Row 0: " << ThreeRowsThreeColumns [0][0] << " " \
9:                       << ThreeRowsThreeColumns [0][1] << " " \
10:                      << ThreeRowsThreeColumns [0][2] << endl;
11:
12:
13:    cout << "Row 1: " << ThreeRowsThreeColumns [1][0] << " " \
14:                      << ThreeRowsThreeColumns [1][1] << " " \
15:                      << ThreeRowsThreeColumns [1][2] << endl;
16:
17:    cout << "Row 2: " << ThreeRowsThreeColumns [2][0] << " "\
18:                      << ThreeRowsThreeColumns [2][1] << " " \
19:                      << ThreeRowsThreeColumns [2][2] << endl;
20:
21:    return 0;
22: }
```

4

Output ▼

```
Row 0: -501 206 2011
Row 1: 989 101 206
Row 2: 303 456 596
```

Analysis ▼

Note how you have accessed elements in the array row-wise, starting with the array that is Row 0 (the first row, with index 0) and ending with the array that is Row 2 (third row, with index 2). As each of the rows is an array, the syntax for addressing the third element in the first row is seen in Line 10.

NOTE

In Listing 4.3 the length of the code increases dramatically with the increase in the number of elements in the array or dimensions thereof. This code is actually unsustainable in a professional development environment.

You can see a more efficient way to program accessing elements in a multidimensional array in Listing 6.14 in Lesson 6, in which you use a nested `for` loop to access all elements in such an array. Using `for` loops is actually shorter and less error prone, and the length of the program is not affected by changing the number of elements in the array.

Dynamic Arrays

Consider an application that stores medical records for hospitals. There is no good way for the programmer to know what the upper limits of the number of records his application might need to handle are. He can make an assumption that is way more than the reasonable limit for a small hospital to err on the safe side. In those cases, he is reserving huge amounts of memory without reason and reducing the performance of the system.

The key is to not use static arrays like the ones we have seen this far, rather to choose dynamic arrays that optimize memory consumption and scale up depending on the demand for resources and memory at execution-time. C++ provides you with very convenient and easy-to-use dynamic arrays in the form of `std::vector` as shown in Listing 4.4.

LISTING 4.4   Creating a Dynamic Array of Integers and Adding Values Dynamically

```
0: #include <iostream>
1: #include <vector>
2:
3: using namespace std;
4:
5: int main()
6: {
7:     vector<int> DynArrNums (3);
8:
9:     DynArrNums[0] = 365;
10:     DynArrNums[1] = -421;
11:     DynArrNums[2]= 789;
12:
13:     cout << "Number of integers in array: " << DynArrNums.size() << endl;
```

```
14:
15:     cout << "Enter another number for the array" << endl;
16:     int AnotherNum = 0;
17:     cin >> AnotherNum;
18:     DynArrNums.push_back(AnotherNum);
19:
20:     cout << "Number of integers in array: " << DynArrNums.size() << endl;
21:     cout << "Last element in array: ";
22:     cout << DynArrNums[DynArrNums.size() - 1] << endl;
23:
24:     return 0;
25: }
```

Output ▼

```
Number of integers in array: 3
Enter another number for the array
2011
Number of integers in array: 4
Last element in array: 2011
```

Analysis ▼

Don't worry about the syntax in Listing 4.4 as vector and templates have not been explained as yet. Try to observe the output and correlate it to the code. The initial size of the array according to the output is 3, consistent with the declaration of the vector at Line 7. Knowing this, you still ask the user to enter a fourth number at Line 15, and, interestingly enough, you are able to push this number into the vector using push_back() at Line 18. The vector dynamically resizes itself to accommodate more data. This can be then seen in the size of the array that increases to 4. Note the usage of the familiar static array syntax to access data in the vector. Line 22 accesses the last element (wherever that might be, given a position calculated at run-time) using the zero-based index, where the last element is at index "size − 1", and size() returns the total number of elements (integers) in the vector.

4

NOTE

To use the dynamic array class std::vector, you need to include header vector, which is also shown in Line 1 of Listing 4.4.

#include <vector>

Vectors are explained in greater detail in Lesson 17, "STL Dynamic Array Classes."

C-style Strings

C-style strings are a special case of an array of characters. You have already seen some examples of C-style strings in the form of string literals that you have been writing into your code:

```
std::cout << "Hello World";
```

This is equivalent to using the array declaration:

```
char SayHello[] = {'H', 'e', 'l', 'l', 'o', ' ', 'W', 'o', 'r', 'l', 'd', '\0'};
std::cout << SayHello << std::endl;
```

Note that the last character in the array is a null character '\0'. This is also called the string-terminating character because it tells the compiler that the string has ended. Such C-style strings are a special case of character arrays in that the last character always precedes the null-terminator '\0'. When you embed a string literal in your code, the compiler does the job of adding a '\0' after it.

If you inserted '\0' anywhere in the middle of the array, it would not change the size of the array; it would only mean that string-processing using the array as input would stop at that point. Listing 4.5 demonstrates this point.

NOTE

'\0' might look like two characters to you, and it indeed is two characters typed using the keyboard. Yet, the backslash is a special escape code that the compiler understands and \0 means null—that is, it asks the compiler to insert a null or zero in there.

You could not write '0' directly because that would be accepted as character zero, which has the non-zero ASCII code 48.

Check the table in Appendix E, "ASCII Codes," to see this and other ASCII values.

LISTING 4.5   Analyzing the Null Terminator in a C-style String

```
0: #include <iostream>
1: using namespace std;
2:
3: int main()
4: {
5:     char SayHello[] = {'H','e','l','l','o',' ','W','o','r','l','d','\0'};
6:     cout << SayHello << endl;
```

```
7:     cout << "Size of array: " << sizeof(SayHello) << endl;
8:
9:     cout << "Replacing space with null" << endl;
10:    SayHello[5] = '\0';
11:    cout << SayHello << endl;
12:    cout << "Size of array: " << sizeof(SayHello) << endl;
13:
14:    return 0;
15: }
```

Output ▼

```
Hello World
Size of array: 12
Replacing space with null
Hello
Size of array: 12
```

Analysis ▼

Line 10 is where we replace the space in "Hello World" by the null terminating character. Note that the array now has two null-terminators, but it's the first one that occurs that creates an effect. When the space character has been replaced by null, the result of displaying the string results in it being truncated to just "Hello". `sizeof()` at Lines 7 and 12 indicate that the size of the array has not changed, even if the displayed data changed a lot.

4

CAUTION

> If you forget to add the '\0' when declaring and initializing the character array in Listing 4.5 at Line 5, then expect the output to contain garbled characters after printing "Hello World"; this is because `std::cout` does not stop with printing the array until it reaches a null character, even if it means exceeding the bounds of the array.
>
> This mistake can cause your program to crash and, in some cases, compromise the stability of the system.

C-style strings are fraught with danger. Listing 4.6 demonstrates the risks involved in using one.

LISTING 4.6 A Risky Application Using C-style Strings and User Input

```
0: #include <iostream>
1: using namespace std;
2:
3: int main()
4: {
5:    cout << "Enter a word NOT longer than 20 characters:" << endl;
6:
7:    char UserInput [21] = {'\0'};
8:    cin >> UserInput;
9:
10:    cout << "Length of your input was: " << strlen (UserInput) << endl;
11:
12:    return 0;
13: }
```

Output ▼

```
Enter a word NOT longer than 20 characters:
Don'tUseThisProgram
Length of your input was: 19
```

Analysis ▼

The danger is visible in the output. The program is begging the user to not enter data longer than 20 characters. The reason it does so is that the character buffer declared in Line 7 meant to store user input has a fixed—static—length of 21 characters. As the last character in the string needs to be a null-terminator '\0', the maximum length of text stored by the buffer is limited to 20. Note the usage of strlen in Line 10 to compute the length of the string. strlen walks the character buffer and counts the number of characters crossed until it reaches the null terminator that indicates the end of the string. This null terminator has been inserted by cin at the end of the user's input. This behavior of strlen makes it dangerous as it can easily walk past the bounds of the character array if the user has supplied text longer than the mentioned limit. See Listing 6.2 in Lesson 6 to learn how to implement a check that ensures that an array is not written beyond its bounds.

C++ Strings: Using std::string

C++ standard string is the most efficient way to deal with text input—and in performing string manipulations like concatenations.

CAUTION

Applications programmed in C (or in C++ by programmers who have a strong C background) often use string copy functions such as strcpy, concatenation functions such as strcat, and strlen to determine the length of a string, in addition to others of this kind.

These functions take C-style strings as input and are dangerous as they seek the null-terminator and can exceed the boundaries of the character array they're using if the programmer has not ensured the presence of the terminating null.

C++ offers you genuinely powerful, yet safe, options in manipulating strings using std::string, as shown in Listing 4.7. std::string is not static in size like a regular char array implementation of a C-style string is and can scale up when more data needs to be stored in it.

LISTING 4.7 Using std::string to Initialize, Store User Input, Copy, Concatenate, and Determine the Length of a String

```
0: #include <iostream>
1: #include <string>
2:
3: using namespace std;
4:
5: int main()
6: {
7:     string Greetings ("Hello std::string!");
8:     cout << Greetings << endl;
9:
10:     cout << "Enter a line of text: " << endl;
11:     string FirstLine;
12:     gotline(cin, FirstLine);
13:
14:     cout << "Enter another: " << endl;
15:     string SecLine;
16:     getline(cin, SecLine);
17:
18:     cout << "Result of concatenation: " << endl;
19:     string Concat = FirstLine + " " + SecLine;
20:     cout << Concat << endl;
21:
22:     cout << "Copy of concatenated string: " << endl;
23:     string Copy;
24:     Copy = Concat;
25:     cout << Copy << endl;
```

```
26:
27:    cout << "Length of concat string: " << Concat.length() << endl;
28:
29:    return 0;
30: }
```

Output ▼

```
Hello std::string!
Enter a line of text:
I love
Enter another:
C++ strings
Result of concatenation:
I love C++ strings
Copy of concatenated string:
I love C++ strings
Length of concat string: 18
```

Analysis ▼

Try to understand the output and correlate it to the various elements in code. Don't let new syntax features bother you at this stage. The program starts with displaying a string that has been initialized in Line 7 to "Hello `std::string`". It then asks the user to enter two lines of text, which are stored in variables `FirstLine` and `SecLine`, in Lines 12 and 16. The actual concatenation is quite simple and looks like an arithmetic addition in Line 19, where even a space has been added to the first line. The act of copying is a simple act of assigning, in Line 24. Determining the length of the string is done by invoking `length()` on it, in Line 27.

NOTE	To use a C++ string, you need to include the header `string`:
	`#include <string>`
	This is also visible in Line 1 in Listing 4.7.

To learn the various functions of `std::string` in detail, take a quick look at Lesson 16, "The STL `string` Class." Because you have not learned about classes and templates, ignore sections that seem unfamiliar in that lesson and concentrate on understanding the gist of the samples.

Summary

This lesson taught you about the basics of arrays, what they are, and where they can be used. You learned how to declare them, initialize them, access elements in an array, and write values to elements in an array. You learned how important it is to not exceed the bounds of an array. That is called a *buffer overflow*, and ensuring that input is checked before using to index elements helps ensure that the limits of an array are not crossed.

Dynamic arrays are those where the programmer doesn't need to worry about fixing the max length of an array at compile time, and they allow for better memory management in the event of usage that is lesser than the expected maximum.

You also learned that C-style strings are a special case of `char` arrays where the end of the string is marked by a null-terminating character `'\0'`. More importantly, though, you learned that C++ offers a far better option in the `std::string`, which provides convenient utility functions that enable you to determine the length, concatenate, and perform similar actions.

Q&A

Q Why take the trouble to initialize a static array's elements?

A Unless initialized, the array, unlike a variable of any other type, contains junk and unpredictable values as the memory at that location was left untouched after the last operations. Initializing arrays ensures that the information therein has a distinct and predictable initial state.

Q Would you need to initialize the elements in a dynamic array for the same reasons as mentioned in the first question?

A Actually, no. A dynamic array is quite a smart array. Elements in the array don't need to be initialized to a default value unless there is a specific reason related to the application that needs you to have certain initial values in the array.

Q Given a choice, would you use C-style strings that need a null terminator?

A Yes, but only if someone places a gun to your head. C++ `std::string` is a lot safer and supplies features that should make any good programmer stay away from using C-style strings.

Q Does the length of the string include the null-terminator at the end of it?

A No, it doesn't. The length of string "Hello World" is 11, including the space and excluding the null character at the end of it.

4

Q **Well, I still want to use C-style strings in char arrays defined by myself. What should be the size of the array I am using?**

A Here you go with one of the complications of using C-style strings. The size of the array should be one greater than the size of the largest string it will ever contain. This is essential so that it can accommodate for the null character at the end of the largest string. If "Hello World" was to be the largest string your char array would ever hold, then the length of the array needs to be $11 + 1 = 12$ characters.

Workshop

The Workshop provides quiz questions to help you solidify your understanding of the material covered and exercises to provide you with experience in using what you've learned. Try to answer the quiz and exercise questions before checking the answers in Appendix D, and be certain you understand the answers before continuing to the next lesson.

Quiz

1. Check the array MyNumbers in Listing 4.1. What are the indexes of the first and last elements in that array?

2. If you need to allow the user to input strings, would you use C-style strings?

3. How many characters are in '\0' as seen by the compiler?

4. You forget to end your C-style string with a null terminator. What happens when you use it?

5. See the declaration of vector in Listing 4.4 and try composing a dynamic array that contains elements of the type char.

Exercises

1. Declare an array that represents the squares on the chessboard; the type of the array can be an enum that defines the nature of the pieces on the board.

2. **BUG BUSTERS:** What is wrong with this code fragment?
```
int MyNumbers[5] = {0};
MyNumbers[5] = 450; // Setting the 5th element to value 450
```

3. **BUG BUSTERS:** What is wrong with this code fragment?
```
int MyNumbers[5];
cout << MyNumbers[3];
```

LESSON 5
Working with Expressions, Statements, and Operators

At its heart, a program is a set of commands executed in sequence. These commands are programmed into expressions and statements and use operators to perform specific calculations or actions.

In this lesson, you learn

- What statements are

- What blocks or compound statements are

- What operators are

- How to perform simple arithmetic and logical operations

Statements

Languages—spoken or programmed—are composed of statements that are executed one after another. Let's analyze the first important statement you learned:

```
cout << "Hello World" << endl;
```

A statement using cout displays text using the console on the screen. All statements in C++ end with a semicolon (;), which defines the boundary of a statement. This is similar to the period (.) you add when ending a sentence in English. The next statement can start immediately after the semicolon, but for convenience and readability you often program successive statements on successive lines. In other words, this is actually a set of two statements in a line:

```
cout << "Hello World" << endl; cout << "Another hello" << endl; // One line, two
➥statements
```

> **NOTE**   Whitespaces typically are not visible to the compiler. This includes spaces, tabs, line feeds, carriage returns, and so on. Whitespaces within string literals, though, make a difference to the output.

The following would be invalid:

```
cout << "Hello
    World" << endl; // new line in string literal not allowed
```

Such code typically results in an error indicating that the compiler is missing a closing quote (") and a statement-terminating semicolon (;) in the first line. If you need to spread a statement over two lines for some reason, you can do it by inserting a backslash (\) at the end:

```
cout << "Hello \
    World" << endl; // split to two lines is OK
```

Another way of writing the preceding statement in two lines is to write two string literals instead of just one:

```
cout << "Hello "
   "World" << endl; // two string literals is also OK
```

In the preceding example, the compiler notices two adjacent string literals and concatenates them for you.

Splitting a statement into many lines can be quite useful when you have long text elements or complex expressions comprised of many variables that make a statement much longer than what most displays can allow.

Compound Statements or Blocks

When you group statements together within braces { . . . }, you create a compound statement or a block.

```
{
    int Number = 365;
    cout << "This block contains an integer and a cout statement" << endl;
}
```

A block typically groups many statements to indicate that they belong together. Blocks are particularly useful when programming conditional if statements or loops, which are explained in Lesson 6, "Controlling Program Flow."

Using Operators

Operators are tools that C++ provides for you to be able to work with data, transform it, process it, and possibly make decisions on the basis of it.

The Assignment Operator (=)

The assignment operator is one that you already have been using intuitively in this book:

```
int MyInteger = 101;
```

The preceding statement uses the assignment operator in initializing the integer to 101. The assignment operator replaces the value contained by the operand to the left (called l-value) by that on the right (called r-value).

Understanding l-values and r-values

l-values often refer to locations in memory. A variable such as MyInteger from the preceding example is actually a handle to a memory location and is an l-value. r-values, on the other hand, can be the very content of a memory location.

5

So, all l-values can be r-values, but not all r-values can be l-values. To understand it better, look at the following example, which doesn't make any sense and therefore won't compile:

```
101 = MyInteger;
```

Operators to Add (+), Subtract (-), Multiply (*), Divide (/), and Modulo Divide (%)

You can perform an arithmetic operation between two operands by using + for addition, - for subtraction, * for multiplication, / for division, and % for modulo operation:

```
int Num1 = 22;
int Num2 = 5;
int addition = Num1 + Num2; // 27
int subtraction = Num1 - Num2; // 17
int multiplication = Num1 * Num2; // 110
int division = Num1 / Num2; // 4
int modulo = Num1 % Num2; // 2
```

Note that the division operator (/) returns the result of division between two operands. In the case of integers, however, the result contains no decimals as integers by definition cannot hold decimal data. The modulo operator (%) returns the remainder of a division operator, and it is applicable only on integer values. Listing 5.1 is a simple program that demonstrates an application to perform arithmetic functions on two numbers input by the user.

LISTING 5.1   Demonstrate Arithmetic Operators on Integers Input by the User

```
0: #include <iostream>
1: using namespace std;
2:
3: int main()
4: {
5:    cout << "Enter two integers:" << endl;
6:    int Num1 = 0, Num2 = 0;
7:    cin >> Num1;
8:    cin >> Num2;
9:
10:    cout << Num1 << " + " << Num2 << " = " << Num1 + Num2 << endl;
11:    cout << Num1 << " - " << Num2 << " = " << Num1 - Num2 << endl;
12:    cout << Num1 << " * " << Num2 << " = " << Num1 * Num2 << endl;
13:    cout << Num1 << " / " << Num2 << " = " << Num1 / Num2 << endl;
14:    cout << Num1 << " % " << Num2 << " = " << Num1 % Num2 << endl;
15:
16:    return 0;
17: }
```

Output ▼

```
Enter two integers:
365
25
365 + 25 = 390
365 - 25 = 340
365 * 25 = 9125
365 / 25 = 14
365 % 25 = 15
```

Analysis ▼

Most of the program is quite self explanatory. The line of most interest is possibly the one that uses the % modulo operator. What this does is return the remainder that is the result of dividing Num1 (365) by Num2 (25).

Operators to Increment (++) and Decrement (--)

Sometimes you need to count in increments of one. This is particularly required in variables that control loops where the value of the variable needs to be incremented or decremented every time a loop has been executed.

C++ includes the ++ (increment) and -- (decrement) operators to help you with this task.

The syntax for using these is the following:

```
int Num1 = 101;
int Num2 = Num1++; // Postfix increment operator
int Num2 = ++Num1; // Prefix increment operator
int Num2 = Num1--; // Postfix decrement operator
int Num2 = --Num1; // Prefix decrement operator
```

As the code sample indicates, there are two different ways of using the incrementing and decrementing operators: before and after the operand. Operators that are placed before the operand are called prefix increment or decrement operators, and those that are placed after are called postfix increment or decrement operators.

To Postfix or to Prefix?

It's important to first understand the difference between prefix and postfix and then use the one that works for you. The result of execution of the postfix operators is that the l-value is first assigned the r-value and after that assignment the r-value is incremented (or decremented). This means that in all cases where a postfix operator has been used, the value of Num2 is the old value of Num1 (before the increment or decrement operation).

5

Prefix operators have exactly the opposite in behavior. The r-value is first incremented and then assigned to the l-value. In these cases, Num2 and Num1 carry the same value. Listing 5.2 demonstrates the effect of prefix and postfix increment and decrement operators on a sample integer.

LISTING 5.2 Demonstrate the Difference Between Postfix and Prefix Operators

```
0: #include <iostream>
1: using namespace std;
2:
3: int main()
4: {
5:     int MyInt = 101;
6:     cout << "Start value of integer being operated: " << MyInt << endl;
7:
8:     int PostFixInc = MyInt++;
9:     cout << "Result of Postfix Increment = " << PostFixInc << endl;
10:    cout << "After Postfix Increment, MyInt = " << MyInt << endl;
11:
12:    MyInt = 101; // Reset
13:    int PreFixInc = ++MyInt;
14:    cout << "Result of Prefix Increment = " << PreFixInc << endl;
15:    cout << "After Prefix Increment, MyInt = " << MyInt << endl;
16:
17:    MyInt = 101;
18:    int PostFixDec = MyInt--;
19:    cout << "Result of Postfix Decrement = " << PostFixDec << endl;
20:    cout << "After Postfix Decrement, MyInt = " << MyInt << endl;
21:
22:    MyInt = 101;
23:    int PreFixDec = --MyInt;
24:    cout << "Result of Prefix Decrement = " << PreFixDec << endl;
25:    cout << "After Prefix Decrement, MyInt = " << MyInt << endl;
26:
27:    return 0;
28: }
```

Output ▼

```
Start value of integer being operated: 101
Result of Postfix Increment = 101
After Postfix Increment, MyInt = 102
Result of Prefix Increment = 102
After Prefix Increment, MyInt = 102
Result of Postfix Decrement = 101
After Postfix Decrement, MyInt = 100
Result of Prefix Decrement = 100
After Prefix Decrement, MyInt = 100
```

Analysis ▼

The results show that the postfix operators were different from the prefix ones in that the l-values being assigned in Lines 8 and 18 contain the original values of the integer before the actual increment or decrement operations. The prefix operations in Lines 13 and 23, on the other hand, result in the l-value being assigned the incremented or decremented value. This is the most important difference that needs to be kept in perspective when choosing the right operator type.

Note that in the following statements, the prefix or postfix operators make no difference to the output of the program:

```
MyInt++; // Is the same as…
++MyInt;
```

This is because there is no assignment of an initial value, and the end result in both cases is just that the integer is incremented.

NOTE

You often hear of cases where prefix increment or decrement operators are preferred on grounds of better performance. That is, ++MyInt is preferred over MyInt++.

This is true at least theoretically because with the postfix operators, the compiler needs to store the initial value temporarily in the event of it needing to be assigned. The effect on performance in these cases is negligible with respect to integers, but in the case of certain classes there might be a point in this argument.

5

Avoid Overflows by Making Wiser Selection of Data Types

Data types such as short, int, long, unsigned short, unsigned int, unsigned long, and the like have a finite capacity for containing numbers. When you exceed the limit imposed by the type chosen in an arithmetic operation, you create an *overflow*.

Take unsigned short for an example. Data type short consumes 16 bits and can hence contain values from 0 through 65535. When you add 1 to 65535 in an unsigned short, the value overflows to 0. It's quite like the odometer of a car that suffers a mechanical overflow when it can support only five digits and the car has done 99,999 kilometers (or miles).

In this case, unsigned short was never the right type for such a counter. The programmer was better off using unsigned int to support numbers higher than 65,535.

In the case of a signed short integer, which has a range of –32768 through 32767, adding 1 to 32767 often results in the signed integer taking the highest negative value—but this is compiler dependent.

Listing 5.3 demonstrates the overflow errors that you can inadvertently introduce via arithmetic operations.

LISTING 5.3   Demonstrating the Ill-Effects of Signed and Unsigned Integer Overflow Errors

```
 0: #include <iostream>
 1: using namespace std;
 2:
 3: int main()
 4: {
 5:    unsigned short UShortValue = 65535;
 6:    cout << "Incrementing unsigned short " << UShortValue << " gives: ";
 7:    cout << ++UShortValue << endl;
 8:
 9:    short SignedShort = 32767;
10:    cout << "Incrementing signed short " << SignedShort<< " gives: ";
11:    cout << ++SignedShort << endl;
12:
13:    return 0;
14:
```

Output ▼

```
Incrementing unsigned short 65535 gives: 0
Incrementing signed short 32767 gives: -32768
```

Analysis ▼

As you see, the output indicates that unintentional overflow situations result in unpredictable and unintuitive behavior for the application. If you were using the integer values in question to allocate memory, then with the unsigned short, you can reach a point where you request zero bytes when your actual need is 65,536 bytes.

Equality Operators (==) and (!=)

Often you need to check for a certain condition being fulfilled or not being fulfilled before you proceed to take an action. Equality operators == (operands are equal) and != (operands are unequal) help you with exactly that.

The result of an equality check is a bool—that is, true or false.

```
int MyNum = 20;
bool CheckEquality = (MyNum == 20); // true
bool CheckInequality = (MyNum != 100); // true

bool CheckEqualityAgain = (MyNum == 200); // false
bool CheckInequalityAgain = (MyNum != 20); // false
```

Relational Operators

In addition to equality checks, you might want to check for inequality of a certain variable against a value. To assist you with that, C++ includes relational operators (see Table 5.1).

TABLE 5.1   Relational Operators

Operator Name	Description
Less than (<)	Evaluates to true if one operand is less than the other (Op1 < Op2), else evaluates to false
Greater than (>)	Evaluates to true if one operand is greater than the other (Op1 > Op2), else evaluates to false
Less than or equal to (<=)	Evaluates to true if one operand is less than or equal to another, else evaluates to false
Greater than or equal to (>=)	Evaluates to true if one operand is greater than or equal to another, else evaluates to false

As Table 5.1 indicates, the result of a comparison operation is always true or false, in other words a bool. The following sample code indicates how the relational operators introduced in Table 5.1 can be put to use:

```
int MyNum = 20; // sample integer value
bool CheckLessThan = (MyNum < 100);  // true
bool CheckGreaterThan = (MyNum > 100); // false
bool CheckLessThanEqualTo = (MyNum <= 20); // true
bool CheckGreaterThanEqualTo = (MyNum >= 20); // true
bool CheckGreaterThanEqualToAgain = (MyNum >= 100); // false
```

Listing 5.4 is a program that demonstrates the effect of using these operators by displaying the result on the screen.

LISTING 5.4   Demonstrating Equality and Relational Operators

```
0: #include <iostream>
1: using namespace std;
2:
3: int main()
```

5

LISTING 5.4 Continued

```
 4: {
 5:     cout << "Enter two integers:" << endl;
 6:     int Num1 = 0, Num2 = 0;
 7:     cin >> Num1;
 8:     cin >> Num2;
 9:
10:     bool Equality = (Num1 == Num2);
11:     cout << "Result of equality test: " << Equality << endl;
12:
13:     bool Inequality = (Num1 != Num2);
14:     cout << "Result of inequality test: " << Inequality << endl;
15:
16:     bool GreaterThan = (Num1 > Num2);
17:     cout << "Result of " << Num1 << " > " << Num2;
18:     cout << " test: " << GreaterThan << endl;
19:
20:     bool LessThan = (Num1 < Num2);
21:     cout << "Result of " << Num1 << " < " << Num2 << " test: " << LessThan <<
     ➥endl;
22:
23:     bool GreaterThanEquals = (Num1 >= Num2);
24:     cout << "Result of " << Num1 << " >= " << Num2;
25:     cout << " test: " << GreaterThanEquals << endl;
26:
27:     bool LessThanEquals = (Num1 <= Num2);
28:     cout << "Result of " << Num1 << " <= " << Num2;
29:     cout << " test: " << LessThanEquals << endl;
30:
31:     return 0;
32: }
```

Output ▼

```
Enter two integers:
365
-24
Result of equality test: 0
Result of inequality test: 1
Result of 365 > -24 test: 1
Result of 365 < -24 test: 0
Result of 365 >= -24 test: 1
Result of 365 <= -24 test: 0
```

Next run:

```
Enter two integers:
101
```

```
101
Result of equality test: 1
Result of inequality test: 0
Result of 101 > 101 test: 0
Result of 101 < 101 test: 0
Result of 101 >= 101 test: 1
Result of 101 <= 101 test: 1
```

Analysis ▼

The program displays the binary result of the various operations. Interesting is to note the output in the event the two supplied integers are the same. The operators ==, >=, and <= produce identical results.

The fact that the output of equality and relational operators is binary makes these perfectly suited to using them in statements that help in decision-making and as loop condition expressions that ensure a loop executes only so long as the condition evaluates to true. You can learn more about conditional execution and loops in Lesson 6.

Logical Operations NOT, AND, OR, and XOR

Logical NOT operation is supported by the operator ! and works on a single operand. Table 5.2 is the truth table for a logical NOT operation, which, as expected, simply inverses the supplied Boolean flag.

TABLE 5.2   Truth Table of Logical NOT Operation

Operand	Result of NOT (Operand)
False	True
True	False

Other operators such as AND, OR, and XOR need two operands. Logical AND operation evaluates to true only when each operand evaluates to true. Table 5.3 demonstrates the functioning of a logical AND operation.

TABLE 5.3   Truth Table of Logical AND Operation

Operand 1	Operand 2	Result of Operand1 AND Operand2
False	False	False
True	False	False
False	True	False
True	True	True

5

Logical AND operation is supported by operator &&.

Logical OR evaluates to `true` when at least one of the operands evaluates to `true`, as demonstrated by Table 5.4.

TABLE 5.4   Truth Table of Logical OR Operation

Operand 1	Operand 2	Result of Operand1 OR Operand2
False	False	False
True	False	True
False	True	True
True	True	True

Logical OR operation is supported by operator ¦¦.

The exclusive OR (abbreviated to XOR) operation is slightly different than the logical OR for it evaluates to `true` when any one operand is `true` but not both, as demonstrated by Table 5.5.

TABLE 5.5   Truth Table of Logical XOR Operation

Operand 1	Operand 2	Result of Operand1 OR Operand2
False	False	False
True	False	True
False	True	True
True	True	False

C++ provides a bitwise XOR in the form of the ^ operator. This operator helps evaluate a result that is generated via an XOR operation on the operand's bits.

Using C++ Logical Operators NOT (!), AND (&&), and OR (¦¦)

Consider these statements:

- "If it is raining AND if there are no buses, I cannot go to work."
- "If there is a deep discount OR if I am awarded a record bonus, I can buy that car."

You need such logical constructs in programming where the result of two operations is used in a logical context in deciding the future flow of your program. C++ provides logical AND and OR operators that you can use in conditional statements, hence conditionally changing the flow of your program.

Listing 5.5 demonstrates the workings of logical AND and logical OR operators.

LISTING 5.5 Analyzing C++ Logical Operators && and ¦¦

```
0: #include <iostream>
1: using namespace std;
2:
3: int main()
4: {
5:    cout << "Enter true(1) or false(0) for two operands:" << endl;
6:    bool Op1 = false, Op2 = false;
7:    cin >> Op1;
8:    cin >> Op2;
9:
10:    cout << Op1 << " AND " << Op2 << " = " << (Op1 && Op2) << endl;
11:    cout << Op1 << " OR " << Op2 << " = " << (Op1 ¦¦ Op2) << endl;
12:
13:    return 0;
14: }
```

Output ▼

```
Enter true(1) or false(0) for two operands:
1
0
1 AND 0 = 0
1 OR 0 - 1
```

Next run:

```
Enter true(1) or false(0) for two operands:
1
1
1 AND 1 = 1
1 OR 1 = 1
```

Analysis ▼

The program actually indicates how the operators supply logical AND and OR functions to you. What the program doesn't do is show you how to use them in making decisions.

Listing 5.6 demonstrates a program that executes different lines of code depending on the values contained in variables using conditional statement processing and logical operators.

5

LISTING 5.6   Using Logical NOT (!) and Logical AND (&&) Operators in `if` Statements for Conditional Processing

```
0: #include <iostream>
1: using namespace std;
2:
3: int main()
4: {
5:    cout << "Use boolean values(0 / 1) to answer the questions" << endl;
6:    cout << "Is it raining? ";
7:    bool Raining = false;
8:    cin >> Raining;
9:
10:    cout << "Do you have buses on the streets? ";
11:    bool Buses = false;
12:    cin >> Buses;
13:
14:    // Conditional statement uses logical AND and NOT
15:    if (Raining && !Buses)
16:      cout << "You cannot go to work" << endl;
17:    else
18:      cout << "You can go to work" << endl;
19:
20:    if (Raining && Buses)
21:      cout << "Take an umbrella" << endl;
22:
23:    if ((!Raining) && Buses)
24:       cout << "Enjoy the sun and have a nice day" << endl;
25:
26:    return 0;
27: }
```

Output ▼

```
Use boolean values(0 / 1) to answer the questions
Is it raining? 1
Do you have buses on the streets? 1
You can go to work
Take an umbrella
```

Next run:

```
Use boolean values(0 / 1) to answer the questions
Is it raining? 1
Do you have buses on the streets? 0
You cannot go to work
```

Last run:

```
Use boolean values(0 / 1) to answer the questions
Is it raining? 0
Do you have buses on the streets? 1
You can go to work
Enjoy the sun and have a nice day
```

Analysis ▼

The program in Listing 5.6 uses conditional statements in the form of the `if` construct that has not been introduced to you. Yet, try to understand the behavior of this construct by correlating it against the output. Line 15 contains the logical expression (`Raining && !Buses`) that can be read as "Raining AND NO buses." This uses the logical AND operator to connect the absence of buses (indicated by the logical NOT on presence of buses) to the presence of rain.

NOTE   If you want to read a little about the `if` construct, you can quickly visit Lesson 6.

Listing 5.7 uses logical NOT (!) and OR (¦¦) operators in a demonstration of conditional processing.

LISTING 5.7   Using Logical NOT and Logical OR Operators to Help You Decide If You Can Buy That Dream Car

```
0: #include <iostream>
1: using namespace std;
2:
3: int main()
4: {
5:    cout << "Answer questions with 0 or 1" << endl;
6:    cout << "Is there a deep discount on your favorite car? ";
7:    bool Discount = false;
8:    cin >> Discount;
9:
10:    cout << "Did you get a fantastic bonus? ";
11:    bool FantasticBonus = false;
12:    cin >> FantasticBonus;
13:
14:    if (Discount ¦¦ FantasticBonus)
15:        cout << "Congratulations, you can buy that car!" << endl;
16:    else
```

5

LISTING 5.7 Continued

```
17:        cout << "Sorry, waiting a while is a good idea" << endl;
18:
19:    return 0;
20: }
```

Output ▼

```
Answer questions with 0 or 1
Is there a deep discount on your favorite car? 0
Did you get a fantastic bonus? 1
Congratulations, you can buy that car!
```

Next run:

```
Answer questions with 0 or 1
Is there a deep discount on your favorite car? 0
Did you get a fantastic bonus? 0
Sorry, waiting a while is a good idea
```

Last run:

```
Answer questions with 0 or 1
Is there a deep discount on your favorite car? 1
Congratulations, you can buy that car!
```

Analysis ▼

Line 14 uses the `if` construct followed by an accompanying `else` in Line 16. The `if` construct executes the following statement in Line 15 when the condition (`Discount ||` `FantasticBonus`) evaluates to `true`. This expression contains the logical OR operator and evaluates to `true` when there is no discount on your favorite car. When the expression evaluates to `false`, the statement following `else` in Line 17 is executed.

Bitwise NOT (~), AND (&), OR (¦), and XOR (^) Operators

The difference between the logical and the bitwise operators is that bitwise operators don't return a boolean result. Instead, they supply a result in which individual bits are governed by executing the operator on the operands' bits. C++ allows you to perform operations such as NOT, OR, AND, and exclusive OR (that is, XOR) operations on a bitwise mode where you can manipulate individual bits by negating them using ~, ORring them using ¦, ANDing them using &, and XORring them using ^. The latter three are performed against a number (typically a bit mask) of your choosing.

Some bitwise operations are useful in those situations where bits contained in an integer—for example, each specify the state of a certain flag. Thus, an integer with 32 bits can be used to carry 32 Boolean flags. Listing 5.8 demonstrates the use of bitwise operators.

LISTING 5.8   Demonstrating the Use of Bitwise Operators to Perform NOT, AND, OR, and XOR on Individual Bits in an Integer

```
0: #include <iostream>
1: #include <bitset>
2: using namespace std;
3:
4: int main()
5: {
6:    cout << "Enter a number (0 - 255): ";
7:    unsigned short InputNum = 0;
8:    cin >> InputNum;
9:
10:    bitset<8> InputBits (InputNum);
11:    cout << InputNum << " in binary is " << InputBits << endl;
12:
13:    bitset<8> BitwiseNOT = (~InputNum);
14:    cout << "Logical NOT ¦" << endl;
15:    cout << "~" << InputBits   << " = " << BitwiseNOT << endl;
16:
17:    cout << "Logical AND, & with 00001111" << endl;
18:    bitset<8> BitwiseAND = (0x0F & InputNum);// 0x0F is hex for 0001111
19:    cout << "0001111 & " << InputBits   << " = " << BitwiseAND << endl;
20:
21:    cout << "Logical OR, ¦ with 00001111" << endl;
22:    bitset<8> BitwiseOR = (0x0F ¦ InputNum);
23:    cout << "00001111 ¦ " << InputBits   << " = " << BitwiseOR << endl;
24:
25:    cout << "Logical XOR, ^ with 00001111" << endl;
26:    bitset<8> BitwiseXOR = (0x0F ^ InputNum);
27:    cout << "00001111 ^ " << InputBits   << " = " << BitwiseXOR << endl;
28:
29:    return 0;
30: }
```

Output ▼

```
Enter a number (0 - 255): 181
181 in binary is 10110101
Logical NOT ¦
~10110101 = 01001010
Logical AND, & with 00001111
0001111 & 10110101 = 00000101
Logical OR, ¦ with 00001111
00001111 ¦ 10110101 = 10111111
```

5

```
Logical XOR, ^ with 00001111
00001111 ^ 10110101 = 10111010
```

Analysis ▼

This program uses bitset—a type you have not seen yet—to make displaying binary data easier. The role of `std::bitset` here is purely to help with displaying and nothing more. In Lines 10, 13, 17, and 22 you actually assign an integer to a bitset object, which is used to display that same integer data in binary mode. The operations are done on integers. For a start, focus on the output, which shows you the original integer 181 fed by the user in binary and then proceeds to demonstrate the effect of the various bitwise operators ~, &, ¦, and ^ on this integer. You see that the bitwise NOT used in Line 14 toggles the individual bits. The program also demonstrates how the operators &, ¦, and ^ work, performing the operations using each bit in the two operands to create the result. Correlate this result with the truth tables introduced earlier, and the workings should become clearer to you.

NOTE

> If you want to learn more about manipulating bit flags in C++, take a look at Lesson 25, "Working with Bit Flags Using STL." It discusses the `std::bitset` in detail.

Bitwise Right Shift (>>) and Left Shift (<<) Operators

Shift operators move the entire bit sequence to the right or to the left, and thus can help with multiplication or division by multiples of two, apart from having other uses in an application.

A sample use of a shift operator used to multiply by two is the following:

```
int DoubledValue = Num << 1; // shift bits one position left to double value
```

A sample use of a shift operator used to halve is the following:

```
int HalvedValue = Num >> 2; // shift bits one position right to halve value
```

Listing 5.9 demonstrates how you can use shift operators to effectively multiply or divide an integer value.

LISTING 5.9   Using Bitwise Right Shift Operator (>>) to Quarter and Half and Left Shift (<<) to Double and Quadruple an Input Integer

```
0: #include <iostream>
1: using namespace std;
2:
```

```
 3: int main()
 4: {
 5:    cout << "Enter a number: ";
 6:    int Input = 0;
 7:    cin >> Input;
 8:
 9:    int Half = Input >> 1;
10:    int Quarter = Input >> 2;
11:    int Double = Input << 1;
12:    int Quadruple = Input << 2;
13:
14:    cout << "Quarter: " << Quarter << endl;
15:    cout << "Half: " << Half << endl;
16:    cout << "Double: " << Double << endl;
17:    cout << "Quadruple: " << Quadruple << endl;
18:
19:    return 0;
20: }
```

Output ▼

```
Enter a number: 16
Quarter: 4
Half: 8
Double: 32
Quadruple: 64
```

Analysis ▼

The input number is 16, which in binary terms is 1000. In Line 9, you move it one bit right to change it to 0100, which is 8, effectively halving it. In Line 10, you move it two bits right changing 1000 to 00100, which is 4. Similarly the effect of the left shift operators in Lines 11 and 12 are exactly the opposite. You move it one bit left to get 10000, which is 32 and two bits left to get 100000, which is 64, effectively doubling and quadrupling the number!

5

NOTE — Bitwise shift operators don't rotate values. Additionally, the result of shifting signed numbers is implementation dependent. On some compilers, most-significant-bit when shifted left is not assigned to the least-significant-bit; rather the latter is zero.

Compound Assignment Operators

Compound assignment operators are assignment operators where the operand to the left is assigned the value resulting from the operation.

Consider the following code:

```
int Num1 = 22;
int Num2 = 5;
Num1 += Num2; // Num1 contains 27 after the operation
```

This is similar to what's expressed in the following line of code:

```
Num1 = Num1 + Num2;
```

Thus, the effect of the += operator is that the sum of the two operands is calculated and then assigned to the operand on the left (which is Num1). Table 5.6 is a quick reference on the many compound assignment operators and explains their working.

TABLE 5.6 Compound Assignment Operators

Operator	Usage	Equivalent
Addition Assignment	Num1 += Num2;	Num1 = Num1 + Num2;
Subtraction Assignment	Num1 -= Num2;	Num1 = Num1 - Num2;
Multiplication Assignment	Num1 *= Num2;	Num1 = Num1 * Num2;
Division Assignment	Num1 /= Num2;	Num1 = Num1 / Num2;
Modulo Assignment	Num1 %= Num2;	Num1 = Num1 % Num2;
Bitwise Left-Shift Assignment	Num1 <<= Num2;	Num1 = Num << Num2;
Bitwise Right-Shift Assignment	Num1 >>= Num2;	Num1 = Num >> Num2;
Bitwise AND Assignment	Num1 &= Num2;	Num1 = Num1 & Num2;
Bitwise OR Assignment	Num1 |= Num2;	Num1 = Num1	Num2;
Bitwise XOR Assignment	Num1 ^= Num2;	Num1 = Num1 ^ Num2;

Listing 5.10 demonstrates the effect of using these operators.

LISTING 5.10 Using Compound Assignment Operators to Add; Subtract; Divide; Perform Modulus; Shift; and Perform Bitwise OR, AND, and XOR

```
0: #include <iostream>
1: using namespace std;
2:
3: int main()
4: {
5:   cout << "Enter a number: ";
6:   int Value = 0;
7:   cin >> Value;
8:
9:   Value += 8;
10:   cout << "After += 8, Value = " << Value << endl;
11:   Value -= 2;
12:   cout << "After -= 2, Value = " << Value << endl;
13:   Value /= 4;
14:   cout << "After /= 4, Value = " << Value << endl;
15:   Value *= 4;
16:   cout << "After *= 4, Value = " << Value << endl;
17:   Value %= 1000;
18:   cout << "After %= 1000, Value = " << Value << endl;
19:
20:   // Note: henceforth assignment happens within cout
21:   cout << "After <<= 1, value = " << (Value <<= 1) << endl;
22:   cout << "After >>= 2, value = " << (Value >>= 2) << endl;
23:
24:   cout << "After |= 0x55, value = " << (Value |= 0x55) << endl;
25:   cout << "After ^= 0x55, value = " << (Value ^= 0x55) << endl;
26:   cout << "After &= 0x0F, value = " << (Value &= 0x0F) << endl;
27:
28:   return 0;
29:}
```

5

Output ▼

```
Enter a number: 440
After += 8, Value = 448
After -= 2, Value = 446
After /= 4, Value = 111
After *= 4, Value = 444
After %= 1000, Value = 444
After <<= 1, value = 888
After >>= 2, value = 222
After |= 0x55, value = 223
After ^= 0x55, value = 138
After &= 0x0F, value = 10
```

Analysis ▼

Note that Value is continually modified throughout the program via the various assignment operators. Each operation is performed using Value, and the result of the operation is assigned back to it. Hence, at Line 9, the user input 440 is added to 8, which results in 448 and is assigned back to Value. In the subsequent operation at Line 11, 2 is subtracted from 448, resulting in 446, which is assigned back to Value, and so on.

Using Operator `sizeof` to Determine the Memory Occupied by a Variable

This operator tells you the amount of memory in bytes consumed by a particular type or a variable. The usage of `sizeof` is the following:

```
sizeof (variable);
```

or

```
sizeof (type);
```

NOTE ·

> sizeof(...) might look like a function call, but it is not a function. sizeof is an operator. Interestingly, this operator cannot be defined by the programmer and hence cannot be overloaded.
>
> You learn more about defining your own operators in Lesson 12, "Operator Types and Operator Overloading."

Listing 5.11 demonstrates the use of `sizeof` in determining memory space occupied by an array. Additionally, you might want to revisit Listing 3.4 to analyze the usage of `sizeof` in determining memory consumed by the most familiar variable types.

LISTING 5.11 Using `sizeof` to Determine the Number of Bytes Occupied by an Array of 100 Integers, and That by Each Element Therein

```
0: #include <iostream>
1: using namespace std;
2:
3: int main()
4: {
5:    cout << "Use sizeof of determine memory occupied by arrays" << endl;
6:    int MyNumbers [100] = {0};
7:
8:    cout << "Bytes occupied by an int: " << sizeof(int) << endl;
```

```
9:      cout << "Bytes occupied by array MyNumbers: " << sizeof(MyNumbers) <<
        ↩endl;
10:     cout << "Bytes occupied by each element: " << sizeof(MyNumbers[0]) <<
        ↩endl;
11:
12:     return 0;
13: }
```

Output ▼

```
Use sizeof of determine memory occupied by arrays
Bytes occupied by an int: 4
Bytes occupied by array MyNumbers: 400
Bytes occupied by each element: 4
```

Analysis ▼

The program demonstrates how sizeof is capable of returning the size of an array of 100 integers in bytes, which is 400 bytes. The program also demonstrates that the size of each element is 4 bytes.

sizeof can be quite useful when you need to dynamically allocate memory for *N* objects, especially of a type created by yourself. You would use the result of the sizeof operation in determining the amount of memory occupied by each object and then dynamically allocate using the operator new.

Dynamic memory allocation is explained in detail in Lesson 8, "Pointers and References Explained."

Operator Precedence

You possibly learned something in school on the order of arithmetic operations called BODMAS (Brackets Orders Division Multiplication Addition Subtraction), indicating the order in which a complex arithmetical expression should be evaluated.

In C++, you use operators and expressions such as the following:

```
int MyNumber = 10 * 30 + 20 - 5 * 5 << 2;
```

The question is, what value would MyNumber contain? This is not left to guesswork of any kind. The order in which the various operators are invoked is very strictly specified by the C++ standard. This order is what is meant by operator precedence. See Table 5.7.

5

TABLE 5.7 The Precedence of Operators

Rank	Name	Operator
1	Scope resolution	`::`

2	Member selection, subscripting, function calls, postfix increment, and decrement	`. ->`
		`()`
		`++ --`

3	`sizeof`, prefix increment and decrement, complement, and, not, unary minus and plus, address-of and dereference, `new, new[], delete, delete[]`, casting, `sizeof()`	`++ --`
		`^ !`
		`- +`
		`& *`
		`()`

4	Member selection for pointer	`.* ->*`
5	Multiply, divide, modulo	`* / %`
6	Add, subtract	`+ -`
7	Shift (shift left, shift right)	`<< >>`
8	Inequality relational	`< <= > >=`
9	Equality, inequality	`== !=`
10	Bitwise AND	`&`
11	Bitwise exclusive OR	`^`
12	Bitwise OR	`¦`
13	Logical AND	`&&`
14	Logical OR	`¦¦`
15	Conditional	`?:`

16	Assignment operators	`= *= /= %=`
		`+= -= <<=`
		`>>=`
		`&= ¦= ^=`

17	Comma	`,`

Have another look at the complicated expression used as the earlier example:

```
int MyNumber = 10 * 30 + 20 - 5 * 5 << 2;
```

In evaluating the result of this expression, you need to use the rules related to operator precedence as shown in Table 5.7 to understand what value the compiler assigns it. As multiply and divide have priority over add and subtract, which in turn have priority over shift, you simplify it to the following:

```
int MyNumber = 300 + 20 - 25 << 2;
```

As add and subtract have priority over shift, this gets simplified to

```
int MyNumber = 295 << 2;
```

Finally, you perform the shift operation. Knowing that one bit left shift doubles, and hence two bits left shift quadruples, you can say that the expression evaluates to 295 * 4, which is 1180.

> **CAUTION**
>
> Use parenthesis to make reading code easy.
>
> The expression used earlier is actually poorly written. It is easy for the compiler to understand, but you should write code that humans can understand, too.
>
> So, the same expression is much better written this way:
>
> ```
> int MyNumber = ((10 * 30) - (5 * 5) + 20) << 2; // leave
> little room for doubt
> ```

DO	DON'T
DO use parentheses to make your code and expressions readable.	**DON'T** program complicated expressions relying on the operator precedence table; your code needs to be human readable, too.
DO use the right variable types and ensure that it will never reach overflow situations.	
DO understand that all l-values (for example, variables) can be r-values, but not all r-values (for example, "Hello World") can be l-values.	**DON'T** confuse ++*Variable* and *Variable*++ thinking they're the same. They're different when used in an assignment.

5

Summary

In this lesson you learned what C++ statements, expressions, and operators are. You learned how to perform basic arithmetic operations such as addition, subtraction, multiplication, and division in C++. You also had an overview on logical operations such as NOT, AND, OR, and xOR. You learned of the C++ logical operators !, &&, and ¦¦ that help you in conditional statements and the bitwise operators such as ~, &, ¦, and ^ that help you manipulate data, one bit at a time.

You learned about operator precedence and how important it is to use parenthesis to write code that can also be understood by fellow programmers. You were given an overview on integer overflow and how important avoiding it actually is.

Q&A

Q Why do some programs use `unsigned int` if `unsigned short` takes less memory and compiles, too?

A `unsigned short` typically has a limit of 65535, and if incremented, overflows to zero. To avoid this behavior, well-programmed applications choose `unsigned int` when it is not certain that the value will stay well below this limit.

Q I need to calculate the double of a number after it's divided by three. So, do you see any problem in my code:

`int result = Number / 3 << 1;?`

A Yes! Why didn't you simply use parenthesis to make this line simpler to read to fellow programmers? Adding a comment or two won't hurt either.

Q My application divides two integer values 5 and 2:

```
int Num1 = 5, Num2 = 2;
int result = Num1 / Num2;
```

On execution, the result contains value 2. Isn't this wrong?

A Not at all. Integers are not meant to contain decimal data. The result of this operation is hence 2 and not 2.5. If 2.5 is the result you expect, change all data types to `float` or `double`. These are meant to handle floating-point (decimal) operations.

Workshop

The Workshop provides quiz questions to help you solidify your understanding of the material covered and exercises to provide you with experience in using what you've learned. Try to answer the quiz and exercise questions before checking the answers in Appendix D, and be certain that you understand the answers before continuing to the next lesson.

Quiz

1. I am writing an application to divide numbers. What's a better suited data type: `int` or `float`?

2. What is the value of 32 / 7?

3. What is the value of 32.0/7?

4. Is `sizeof(...)` a function?

5. I need to compute the double of a number, add 5 to it, and then double it again. Is this correct?

```
int Result = number << 1 + 5 << 1;
```

6. What is the result of XOR operation where the XOR operands both evaluate to true?

Exercises

1. Improve on the code in quiz question 4, using parenthesis to create clarity.

2. What is the value of `result` stored by this expression:

```
int Result = number << 1 + 5 << 1;
```

3. Write a program that asks the user to input two Boolean values and demonstrates the result of various bitwise operators on them.

5

LESSON 6
Controlling Program Flow

Most applications need to perform differently under different situations or with user inputs. To enable your application to react differently, you need to be able to program conditional statements that execute different code segments in different situations.

In this lesson, you find out

- How to make your program behave differently on certain conditions

- How to execute a section of code repeatedly in a loop

- How to better control the flow of execution in a loop

Conditional Execution Using `if … else`

Programs you have seen and composed this far have a serial order of execution—from top down. Every line was executed and no line was ever ignored. But, serial execution of all lines of code in a top-down fashion rarely happens in most applications.

Imagine you want a program that multiplies two numbers if the user presses *m* or adds the numbers if he presses anything else.

As you can see in Figure 6.1, not all code paths are executed in every run. If the user presses *m*, the code that multiplies the two numbers is executed. If he enters anything other than *m*, the code that adds is executed. There is never a situation where both are executed.

FIGURE 6.1
Example of conditional processing required on the basis of user input.

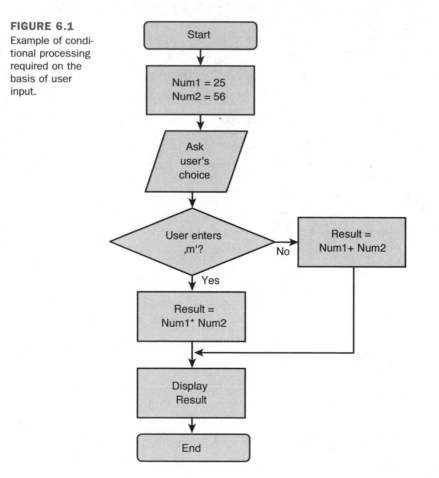

Conditional Programming Using if … else

Conditional execution of code is implemented in C++ using the if … else construct that looks like this:

```
if (conditional expression)
   Do something when expression evaluates true;
else    // Optional
   Do something else when condition evaluates false;
```

So, an if ... else construct that lets a program multiply if the user enters *m* and adds otherwise looks like this:

```
if (UserSelection == 'm')
   Result = Num1 * Num2;  // multiply
else
   Result = Num1 + Num2;  // add
```

NOTE

Note that evaluation of an expression to true in C++ essentially means that the expression does not evaluate to false, false being zero. So, an expression that evaluates to any non-zero number—negative or positive—is essentially considered to be evaluating to true when used in a conditional statement.

Let's analyze this construct in Listing 6.1, which enables the user to decide whether he wishes to either multiply or divide two numbers, hence using conditional processing to generate the desired output.

LISTING 6.1 Multiplying or Adding Two Integers on Basis of User Input

```
0: #include <iostream>
1: using namespace std;
2:
3: int main()
4: {
5:    cout << "Enter two integers: " << endl;
6:    int Num1 = 0, Num2 = 0;
7:    cin >> Num1;
8:    cin >> Num2;
9:
10:    cout << "Enter \'m\' to multiply, anything else to add: ";
11:    char UserSelection = '\0';
12:    cin >> UserSelection;
13:
14:    int Result = 0;
15:    if (UserSelection == 'm')
```

6

LISTING 6.1   Continued

```
16:      Result = Num1 * Num2;
17:   else
18:      Result = Num1 + Num2;
19:
20:   cout << "Result is: " << Result << endl;
21:
22:   return 0;
23: }
```

Output ▼

```
Enter two integers:
25
56
Enter 'm' to multiply, anything else to add: m
Result is: 1400
```

Next run:

```
Enter two integers:
25
56
Enter 'm' to multiply, anything else to add: a
Result is: 81
```

Analysis ▼

Note the use of `if` in Line 15 and `else` in Line 17. What we are instructing the compiler to do is to execute multiplication in Line 15 if the expression (`UserSelection == 'm'`) that follows `if` evaluates to `true` or to execute addition if the expression evaluates to `false`. (`UserSelection == 'm'`) is an expression that evaluates to `true` when the user has entered character *m* (case-sensitive), else it evaluates to `false`. Thus, this simple program models the flowchart in Figure 6.1 and demonstrates how your application can behave differently in different situations.

NOTE

> The `else` part of the `if … else` construct is optional and doesn't need to be used in those situations where there is nothing to be executed in event of failure.

CAUTION

> If in Listing 6.1, Line 15 is
>
> ```
> 15:    if (UserSelection == 'm');
> ```
>
> then the `if` construct is meaningless as it has been terminated in the same line by an empty statement (the semicolon). Be careful and avoid this situation as you won t get a compile error if there is no accompanying `else` to the `if`.
>
> Some good compilers warn you of an "empty control statement" in this situation.

Executing Multiple Statements Conditionally

If you want to execute multiple statements in event of a condition succeeding or failing, you need to enclose them within statement blocks. These are essentially braces {...} enclosing multiple statements to be executed as a block. For example:

```
if (condition)
{
    // condition success block
    Statement 1;
    Statement 2;
}
else
{
    // condition failure block
    Statement 3;
    Statement 4;
}
```

Such blocks are also called compound statements.

Lesson 4, "Managing Arrays and Strings," explained the dangers of using static arrays and crossing its bounds. This problem more often than not manifests itself in character arrays. When writing a string into a character array or copying into it, it is important to check if the array is large enough to hold this character. Listing 6.2 shows you how to perform this very important check to avoid buffer overflows.

6

LISTING 6.2 Check for Capacity Before Copying a String into a char Array

```
0: #include <iostream>
1: #include <string>
2: using namespace std;
3:
```

LISTING 6.2 Continued

```
 4: int main()
 5: {
 6:    char Buffer[20] = {'\0'};
 7:
 8:    cout << "Enter a line of text: " << endl;
 9:    string LineEntered;
10:    getline (cin, LineEntered);
11:
12:    if (LineEntered.length() < 20)
13:    {
14:        strcpy(Buffer, LineEntered.c_str());
15:        cout << "Buffer contains: " << Buffer << endl;
16:    }
17:
18:    return 0;
19: }
```

Output ▼

```
Enter a line of text:
This fits buffer!
Buffer contains: This fits buffer!
```

Analysis ▼

Note how the length of the string is checked against the length of the buffer in Line 12 before copying into it. What is also special about this `if` check is the presence of a statement block in Lines 13 through 16 (also called compound statement) in the event of the check evaluating to `true`.

CAUTION

Note that the `if(condition)` line did NOT have a semicolon after it. This was intentional and ensures that the statement following `if` gets executed in event of success.

The following piece of code

```
if(condition);
    statement;
```

compiles, but you do not experience the desired results because the `if` clause has been terminated by a following semicolon amounting to no conditional processing and resulting in the following statement always being executed.

Nested `if` Statements

Often you have situations where you need to validate against a host of different conditions, many of which are dependent on the evaluation of a previous condition. C++ allows you to nest `if` statements to handle such requirements.

Nested `if` statements are similar to this:

```
if (expression1)
{
   DoSomething1;
   if(expression2)
      DoSomething2;
   else
      DoSomethingElse2;
}
else
    DoSomethingElse1;
```

Consider an application similar to Listing 6.1, in which the user can instruct the application to divide or multiply by pressing a command character *d* or *m*. Now, division should be permitted only when the divisor is non-zero. So, in addition to checking the user input for the intended command, it is also important to check if the divisor is non-zero when the user instructs the program to divide. Listing 6.3 uses a nested `if` construct.

LISTING 6.3   Using Nested `if` Statements in Multiplying or Dividing a Number

```
0: #include <iostream>
1: using namespace std;
2:
3: int main()
4: {
5:    cout << "Enter two numbers: " << endl;
6:    float Num1 = 0, Num2 = 0;
7:    cin >> Num1;
8:    cin >> Num2;
9:
10:    cout << "Enter 'd' to divide, anything else to multiply: ";
11:    char UserSelection = '\0';
12:    cin >> UserSelection;
13:
14:    if (UserSelection == 'd')
15:    {
16:       cout << "You want division!" << endl;
17:       if (Num2 != 0)
18:       {
19:          cout << "No div-by-zero, proceeding to calculate" << endl;
20:          cout << Num1 << " / " << Num2 << " = " << Num1 / Num2 << endl;
```

6

LISTING 6.3   Continued

```
21:     }
22:       else
23:          cout << "Division by zero is not allowed" << endl;
24:   }
25:     else
26:     {
27:        cout << "You want multiplication!" << endl;
28:        cout << Num1 << " x " << Num2 << " = " << Num1 * Num2 << endl;
29:     }
30:
31:     return 0;
32: }
```

Output ▼

```
Enter two numbers:
45
9
Enter 'd' to divide, anything else to multiply: m
You want multiplication!
45 x 9 = 405
```

Next run:

```
Enter two numbers:
22
7
Enter 'd' to divide, anything else to multiply: d
You want division!
No div-by-zero, proceeding to calculate
22 / 7 = 3.14286
```

Last run:

```
Enter two numbers:
365
0
Enter 'd' to divide, anything else to multiply: d
You want division!
Division by zero is not allowed
```

Analysis ▼

The output is the result of running the program three times with three different sets of input, and as you can see, the program has executed different code paths for each of these three runs. This program has quite a few changes over Listing 6.1:

- The numbers are accepted as floating-point variables, to better handle decimals, which are important when dividing numbers.

- The if condition is different than in Listing 6.1. You no longer check if the user has pressed *m*; rather, Line 14 contains an expression (UserSelection == 'd') that evaluates to true when the user enters *d*. If so, you proceed with division.

- Given that this program divides two numbers and the divisor is entered by the user, it is important to check if the divisor is non-zero. This is done using the nested if in Line 17.

Thus, what this program demonstrates is how nested if constructs can be very useful in performing different tasks depending on the evaluation of multiple parameters.

TIP

> The nested tabs that you inserted in the code are optional, but they make a significant contribution to the readability of the nested if constructs.

Note that if... else constructs can also be grouped together. Listing 6.4 is a program that asks the user for the day of the week and then tells what that day is named after using grouped if... else constructs.

LISTING 6.4   Tell What Days of the Week Are Named After

```
0: #include <iostream>
1: using namespace std;
2:
3: int main()
4: {
5:     enum DaysOfWeek
6:     {
7:        Sunday = 0,
8:        Monday,
9:        Tuesday,
10:       Wednesday,
11:       Thursday,
12:       Friday,
13:       Saturday
14:    };
15:
16:    cout << "Find what days of the week are named after!" << endl;
17:    cout << "Enter a number for a day (Sunday = 0): ";
18:
19:    int Day = Sunday;   // Initialize to Sunday
```

6

LISTING 6.4   Continued

```
20:    cin >> Day;
21:
22:    if (Day == Sunday)
23:       cout << "Sunday was named after the Sun" << endl;
24:    else if (Day == Monday)
25:       cout << "Monday was named after the Moon" << endl;
26:    else if (Day == Tuesday)
27:       cout << "Tuesday was named after Mars" << endl;
28:    else if (Day == Wednesday)
29:       cout << "Wednesday was named after Mercury" << endl;
30:    else if (Day == Thursday)
31:       cout << "Thursday was named after Jupiter" << endl;
32:    else if (Day == Friday)
33:       cout << "Friday was named after Venus" << endl;
34:    else if (Day == Saturday)
35:       cout << "Saturday was named after Saturn" << endl;
36:    else
37:       cout << "Wrong input, execute again" << endl;
38:
39:    return 0;
40: }
```

Output ▼

```
Find what days of the week are named after!
Enter a number for a day (Sunday = 0): 5
Friday was named after Venus
```

Next run:

```
Find what days of the week are named after!
Enter a number for a day (Sunday = 0): 9
Wrong input, execute again
```

Analysis ▼

Note the if-else-if construct used in Lines 22 through 37 to check user input and produce the corresponding output. The output in the second run indicates that the program is able to tell the user when he enters a number that is outside of the range 0–6, and hence does not correspond to any day of the week. The advantage of this construct is that it is perfectly suited to validating conditions that are mutually exclusive, that is, Monday can never be a Tuesday and an invalid input cannot be any day of the week. Another interesting thing to note in this program is the use of the enumerated constant called DaysOfWeek declared in Line 5 and used throughout the if statements. You could've simply compared user input against integer values such as 0 for Sunday and so on. However, the use of enumerated constant Sunday makes the code more readable.

Conditional Processing Using `switch-case`

The objective of `switch-case` is to enable you to check a particular expression against a host of possible constants and possibly perform a different action for each of those different values. The new C++ keywords you would often find in such a construct are `switch`, `case`, `default`, and `break`.

The following is the syntax of a switch-case construct:

```
switch(expression)
{
case LabelA:
   DoSomething;
   break;

case LabelB:

   DoSomethingElse;
   break;

// And so on…
default:
   DoStuffWhenExpressionIsNotHandledAbove;
   break;
}
```

What happens is that the resulting code evaluates the `expression` and checks against each of the case labels following it for equality. Each case label needs to be a constant. It then executes the code following that label. When the `expression` does not evaluate to `LabelA`, it checks against `LabelB`. If that check evaluates to `true`, it executes `DoSomethingElse`. This check continues until it encounters a `break`. This is the first time you are seeing `break`. `break` causes execution to exit the code block. `break`s are not compulsory; however, without a `break` the execution simply continues checking against the next labels and so on, which is what you want to avoid in this case. `default` is optional, too, and is the case that is executed when the expression does not equate to any of the labels in the `switch-case` construct.

6

TIP	switch-case constructs are well-suited to being used with enumerated constants. The keyword enum has been introduced to you in Lesson 3, "Using Variables, Declaring Constants."

Listing 6.5 is the `switch-case` equivalent of the program in Listing 6.4 that tells what the days of the week are named after and also uses enumerated constants.

LISTING 6.5   Tell What Days of the Week Are Named After Using switch-case, break, and default

```
0: #include <iostream>
1: using namespace std;
2:
3: int main()
4: {
5:     enum DaysOfWeek
6:     {
7:        Sunday = 0,
8:        Monday,
9:        Tuesday,
10:       Wednesday,
11:       Thursday,
12:       Friday,
13:       Saturday
14:    };
15:
16:    cout << "Find what days of the week are named after!" << endl;
17:    cout << "Enter a number for a day (Sunday = 0): ";
18:
19:    int Day = Sunday;   // Initialize to Sunday
20:    cin >> Day;
21:
22:    switch(Day)
23:    {
24:    case Sunday:
25:       cout << "Sunday was named after the Sun" << endl;
26:       break;
27:
28:    case Monday:
29:       cout << "Monday was named after the Moon" << endl;
30:       break;
31:
32:    case Tuesday:
33:       cout << "Tuesday was named after Mars" << endl;
34:       break;
35:
36:    case Wednesday:
37:       cout << "Wednesday was named after Mercury" << endl;
38:       break;
39:
40:    case Thursday:
41:       cout << "Thursday was named after Jupiter" << endl;
42:       break;
43:
44:    case Friday:
45:       cout << "Friday was named after Venus" << endl;
```

LISTING 6.5   Continued

```
46:        break;
47:
48:    case Saturday:
49:        cout << "Saturday was named after Saturn" << endl;
50:        break;
51:
52:    default:
53:        cout << "Wrong input, execute again" << endl;
54:        break;
55:    }
56:
57:    return 0;
58: }
```

Output ▼

```
Find what days of the week are named after!
Enter a number for a day (Sunday = 0): 5
Friday was named after Venus
```

Next run:

```
Find what days of the week are named after!
Enter a number for a day (Sunday = 0): 9
Wrong input, execute again
```

Analysis ▼

Lines 22–55 contain the switch-case construct that produces different output depending on the integer contained in Day as entered by the user. When the user enters the number 5, the application checks the switch expression Day that evaluates to 5 against the first four labels that are enumerated constants Sunday (value 0) through Thursday (value 4), skipping the code below each of them as none of them are equal to 5. It reaches label Friday where the expression evaluating to 5 equals enumerated constant Friday. Thus, it executes the code under Friday until it reaches break and exits the switch construct. In the second run, when an invalid value is fed, the execution reaches default and runs the code under it, displaying the message asking the user to execute again.

This program using switch-case produces exactly the same output as Listing 6.4 using the if-else-if construct. Yet, the switch-case version looks a little more structured and is possibly well-suited to situations where you want to be doing more that just writing a line to the screen (in which case you would also include code within a case within braces, creating blocks).

6

Conditional Execution Using Operator (?:)

C++ has an interesting and powerful operator called the conditional operator that is similar to a compacted `if-else` construct.

The conditional operator is also called a ternary operator as it takes three operands:

```
(conditional expression evaluated to bool) ? expression1 if true : expression2
if false;
```

Such an operator can be used in compactly evaluating the greater of two given numbers, as seen here:

```
int Max = (Num1 > Num2)? Num1 : Num2; // Max contains greater of Num1 and Num2
```

Listing 6.6 is a demonstration of conditional processing using operator (?:).

LISTING 6.6 Using the Conditional Operator (?:) to Find the Max of Two Numbers

```
0: #include <iostream>
1: using namespace std;
2:
3: int main()
4: {
5:    cout << "Enter two numbers" << endl;
6:    int Num1 = 0, Num2 = 0;
7:    cin >> Num1;
8:    cin >> Num2;
9:
10:    int Max = (Num1 > Num2)? Num1 : Num2;
11:    cout << "The greater of " << Num1 << " and " \
12:       << Num2 << " is: " << Max << endl;
13:
14:    return 0;
15: }
```

Output ▼

```
Enter two numbers
365
-1
The greater of 365 and -1 is: 365
```

Analysis ▼

Line 10 is the code of interest. It contains a very compact statement that makes a decision on which of the two numbers input is larger. This line is another way to code the following using `if-else`:

```
int Max = 0;
if (Num1 > Num2)
   Max = Num1;
else
   Max = Num2;
```

Thus, conditional operators saved a few lines! Saving lines of code, however, should not be a priority. There are programmers who prefer conditional operators and those that don't. It is important to code conditional operators in a way that can be easily understood.

DO	DON'T
DO use constants and enumerates for switch expressions to make code readable.	**DON'T** add two cases with the same label—it won't make sense and won't compile.
DO remember to handle default, unless deemed totally unnecessary.	**DON'T** complicate your case statements by including cases without break and relying on sequence. This can break functionality if you later move the case without paying adequate attention.
DO check if you inadvertently forgot to insert break in each case statement.	**DON'T** use complicated conditions or expressions when programming using conditional operators (:?).

Getting Code to Execute in Loops

This far you have seen how to make your program behave differently when certain variables contain different values—for example, in Listing 6.2 where you multiplied when the user pressed *m*; otherwise, you added. However, what if the user doesn't want the program to just end? What if he wants to perform another add or multiply operation, or maybe five more? This is when you need to repeat the execution of already existing code.

This is when you need to program a loop.

A Rudimentary Loop Using goto

As the name suggests, goto tells the instruction pointer to continue execution from a particular point in code. You can use it to go backward and re-execute certain statements.

The syntax for the goto statement is

```
SomeFunction()
{
```

6

```
JumpToPoint: // Called a label
   CodeThatRepeats;

   goto JumpToPoint;
}
```

You declare a label called JumpToPoint and use goto to repeat execution from this point on, as demonstrated in Listing 6.7. Unless you invoke goto given a condition that can evaluate to false under certain circumstances, or unless the code that repeats contains a return statement executed under certain conditions, the piece of code between the goto command and label will repeat endlessly and keep the program from ending.

LISTING 6.7   Asking the User If He Wants to Repeat Calculations Using goto

```
0: #include <iostream>
1: using namespace std;
2:
3: int main()
4: {
5: JumpToPoint:
6:     int Num1 = 0, Num2 = 0;
7:
8:     cout << "Enter two integers: " << endl;
9:     cin >> Num1;
10:    cin >> Num2;
11:
12:    cout << Num1 << " x " << Num2 << " = " << Num1 * Num2 << endl;
13:    cout << Num1 << " + " << Num2 << " = " << Num1 + Num2 << endl;
14:
15:    cout << "Do you wish to perform another operation (y/n)?" << endl;
16:    char Repeat = 'y';
17:    cin >> Repeat;
18:
19:    if (Repeat == 'y')
20:        goto JumpToPoint;
21:
22:    cout << "Goodbye!" << endl;
23:
24:    return 0;
25: }
```

Output ▼

```
Enter two integers:
56
25
56 x 25 = 1400
56 + 25 = 81
```

```
Do you wish to perform another operation (y/n)?
y
Enter two integers:
95
-47
95 x -47 = -4465
95 + -47 = 48
Do you wish to perform another operation (y/n)?
n
Goodbye!
```

Analysis ▼

Note that the primary difference between Listing 6.7 and Listing 6.1 is that 6.1 needs two runs (two separate executions) to enable the user to enter a new set of numbers and see the result of her addition and multiplication. Listing 6.7 does that in one execution cycle by asking the user if she wishes to perform another operation. The code that actually enables this repetition is in Line 20, where goto is invoked if the user enters *y* for yes. Execution of goto in Line 20 results in the program jumping to the label JumpToPoint declared in Line 5, which effectively restarts the program.

CAUTION

goto is not the recommended form of programming loops because the prolific usage of goto can result in unpredictable flow of code where execution can jump from one line to another in no particular order or sequence, in some cases leaving variables in unpredictable states, too.

A bad case of programming using goto results in what is called *spaghetti code*. You can avoid goto by using while, do... while, and for loops that are explained in the following pages.

The only reason you were taught goto is so that you understand code that uses one.

6

The while Loop

C++ keyword while can help do what goto did in Listing 6.7, but in a refined manner. Its usage syntax is:

```
while(expression)
{
   // Condition evaluates to true
   StatementBlock;
}
```

The statement block is executed so long as the expression evaluates to true. It is hence important to code in a way that there are situations where the expression would also evaluate to false, else the while loop would never end.

Listing 6.8 is an equivalent of Listing 6.7 but uses while instead of goto in allowing the user to repeat a calculation cycle.

LISTING 6.8   Using a while Loop to Help the User Rerun Calculations

```
0: #include <iostream>
1: using namespace std;
2:
3: int main()
4: {
5:    char UserSelection = 'm';   // initial value
6:
7:    while (UserSelection != 'x')
8:    {
9:       cout << "Enter the two integers: " << endl;
10:       int Num1 = 0, Num2 = 0;
11:       cin >> Num1;
12:       cin >> Num2;
13:
14:       cout << Num1 << " x " << Num2 << " = " << Num1 * Num2 << endl;
15:       cout << Num1 << " + " << Num2 << " = " << Num1 + Num2 << endl;
16:
17:       cout << "Press x to exit(x) or any other key to recalculate" << endl;
18:       cin >> UserSelection;
19:    }
20:
21:    cout << "Goodbye!" << endl;
22:
23:    return 0;
24: }
```

Output ▼

```
Enter the two integers:
56
25
56 x 25 = 1400
56 + 25 = 81
Press x to exit(x) or any other key to recalculate
r
Enter the two integers:
365
-5
365 x -5 = -1825
```

```
365 + -5 = 360
Press x to exit(x) or any other key to recalculate
x
Goodbye!
```

Analysis ▼

The `while` loop in Lines 7–19 contains most of the logic in this program. Note how the `while` checks expression (`UserSelection != 'x'`), proceeding only if this expression evaluates to `true`. To enable a first run, you initialized the char variable `UserSelection` to `'m'` in Line 5. This needed to be any value that is not `'x'` (else the condition would fail at the very first loop and the application would exit without letting the user do anything constructive). The first run is very simple, but the user is asked in Line 17 if he wishes to perform another set of calculations. Line 18 containing the user's input is where you modify the expression that `while` evaluates, giving the program a chance to continue or to terminate. When the first loop is done, execution returns to evaluating the expression in the `while` statement at Line 7 and repeats if the user has not pressed *x*. When the user presses *x* at the end of a loop, the next evaluation of the expression at Line 7 results in a `false`, and the execution exits the `while` loop, eventually ending the application after displaying a goodbye statement.

> **NOTE**
> A loop is also called an iteration. Statements involving `while`, `do...while`, and `for` are also called iterative statements.

The do...while loop

There are cases (like the one in Listing 6.8) where you need to ensure that a certain segment of code repeats in a loop and that it executes at least once. This is where the `do...while` loop is useful.

The syntax of the do...while loop is

```
do
{
   StatementBlock; // executed at least once
} while(condition); // ends loop if condition evaluates to false
```

Note how the line containing the `while(expression)` terminates with a semicolon. This is different than the previous `while` loop in which a semicolon would've effectively terminated the loop in the very line, resulting in an empty statement.

Listing 6.9 demonstrates how do...while loops can be implemented in executing statements at least once.

LISTING 6.9   Using do...while to Repeat Execution of a Block of Code

```
0: #include <iostream>
1: using namespace std;
2:
3: int main()
4: {
5:    char UserSelection = 'x';   // initial value
6:    do
7:    {
8:       cout << "Enter the two integers: " << endl;
9:       int Num1 = 0, Num2 = 0;
10:       cin >> Num1;
11:       cin >> Num2;
12:
13:       cout << Num1 << " x " << Num2 << " = " << Num1 * Num2 << endl;
14:       cout << Num1 << " + " << Num2 << " = " << Num1 + Num2 << endl;
15:
16:       cout << "Press x to exit(x) or any other key to recalculate" << endl;
17:       cin >> UserSelection;
18:    } while (UserSelection != 'x');
19:
20:    cout << "Goodbye!" << endl;
21:
22:    return 0;
23: }
```

Output ▼

```
Enter the two integers:
654
-25
654 x -25 = -16350
654 + -25 = 629
Press x to exit(x) or any other key to recalculate
m
Enter the two integers:
909
101
909 x 101 = 91809
909 + 101 = 1010
Press x to exit(x) or any other key to recalculate
x
Goodbye!
```

Analysis ▼

This program is very similar in behavior and output to the previous one. Indeed the only difference is the do keyword at Line 6 and the usage of while later at Line 18. The execution of code happens serially, one line after another until the while is reached at Line 18. This is where while evaluates the expression (UserSelection != 'x'). When the expression evaluates to true (that is, the user doesn't press *x* to exit), execution of the loop repeats. When the expression evaluates to false (that is, the user presses *x*), execution quits the loop and continues with wishing goodbye and ending the application.

The for Loop

The for statement is a more sophisticated loop in that it allows for an initialization statement executed once (typically used to initialize a counter), checking for an exit condition (typically using this counter), and performing an action at the end of every loop (typically incrementing or modifying this counter).

The syntax of the for loop is

```
for (initial expression executed only once;
     exit condition executed at the beginning of every loop;
     loop expression executed at the end of every loop)
{
    DoSomeActivities;
}
```

The for loop is a feature that enables the programmer to define a counter variable with an initial value, check the value against an exit condition at the beginning of every loop, and change the value of the variable at the end of a loop.

Listing 6.10 demonstrates an effective way to access elements in an array using a for loop.

LISTING 6.10   Using for Loops to Enter Elements in a Static Array and Displaying It   6

```
0: #include <iostream>
1: using namespace std;
2:
3: int main()
4: {
5:     const int ARRAY_LENGTH = 5;
6:     int MyInts[ARRAY_LENGTH] = {0};
7:
8:     cout << "Populate array of " << ARRAY_LENGTH << " integers" << endl;
9:
10:     for (int ArrayIndex = 0; ArrayIndex < ARRAY_LENGTH; ++ArrayIndex)
```

LISTING 6.10   Continued

```
11:     {
12:        cout << "Enter an integer for element " << ArrayIndex << ": ";
13:        cin >> MyInts[ArrayIndex];
14:     }
15:
16:     cout << "Displaying contents of the array: " << endl;
17:
18:     for (int ArrayIndex = 0; ArrayIndex < ARRAY_LENGTH; ++ArrayIndex)
19:        cout << "Element " << ArrayIndex << " = " << MyInts[ArrayIndex] <<
endl;
20:
21:     return 0;
22: }
```

Output ▼

```
Populate array of 5 integers
Enter an integer for element 0: 365
Enter an integer for element 1: 31
Enter an integer for element 2: 24
Enter an integer for element 3: -59
Enter an integer for element 4: 65536
Displaying contents of the array:
Element 0 = 365
Element 1 = 31
Element 2 = 24
Element 3 = -59
Element 4 = 65536
```

Analysis ▼

There are two for loops in Listing 6.10—at Lines 10 and 18. The first helps enter elements into an array of integers and the other to display. Both for loops are identical in syntax. Both declare an index variable ArrayIndex to access elements the array. This variable is incremented at the end of every loop; therefore, it helps access the next element in the next run of the loop. The middle expression in the for loop is the exit condition. It checks if ArrayIndex that is incremented at the end of every loop is still within the bounds of the array by comparing it against ARRAY_LENGTH. This way, it is also ensured that the for loop never exceeds the length of the array.

> **NOTE**
>
> A variable such as `ArrayIndex` from Listing 6.10 that helps access elements in a collection such as an array is also called an *iterator*.
>
> The scope of this iterator declared within the `for` construct is limited to the `for` loop. Thus, in the second `for` loop in Listing 6.10, this variable that has been re-declared is effectively a new variable.

However, the usage of the initialization, conditional expression, and the expression to be evaluated at the end of every loop is optional. It is possible to have a `for` loop without some or any of these, as shown in Listing 6.11.

LISTING 6.11 Using a `for` Loop, Omitting Loop Expression, to Repeat Calculations on User Request

```
0: #include <iostream>
1: using namespace std;
2:
3: int main()
4: {
5:     // without loop expression (third expression missing)
6:     for(char UserSelection = 'm'; (UserSelection != x'); )
7:     {
8:         cout << "Enter the two integers: " << endl;
9:         int Num1 = 0, Num2 = 0;
10:        cin >> Num1;
11:        cin >> Num2;
12:
13:        cout << Num1 << " x " << Num2 << " = " << Num1 * Num2 << endl;
14:        cout << Num1 << " + " << Num2 << " = " << Num1 + Num2 << endl;
15:
16:        cout << "Press x to exit or any other key to recalculate" << endl;
17:        cin >> UserSelection;
18:     }
19:
20:     cout << "Goodbye!" << endl;
21:
22:     return 0;
23: }
```

6

Output ▼

```
Enter the two integers:
56
25
56 x 25 = 1400
56 + 25 = 81
Press x to exit or any other key to recalculate
m
Enter the two integers:
789
-36
789 x -36 = -28404
789 + -36 = 753
Press x to exit or any other key to recalculate
x
Goodbye!
```

Analysis ▼

This is identical to Listing 6.8 that used the while loop; the only difference is that this one uses for in Line 8. The interesting thing about this for loop is that it contains only the initialization expression and the conditional expression, ignoring the option to change a variable at the end of each loop.

> **NOTE**
>
> You can initialize multiple variables in a for loop within the first initialization expression that is executed once. A for loop in Listing 6.11 with multiple initializations looks like the following:
>
> ```
> for (int Index = 0, AnotherInt = 5; Index < ARRAY_LENGTH;
> ➥++Index, --AnotherInt)
> ```
>
> Note the new addition called AnotherInt that is initialized to 5.
>
> Interestingly, we also are able to decrement it in the loop expression, once per loop.

Modifying Loop Behavior Using continue and break

There are a few cases— especially in complicated loops handling a lot of parameters with a lot of conditions—where you are not able to program the loop condition efficiently and need to modify program behavior even within the loop. This is where continue and break can help you.

continue lets you resume execution from the top of the loop. It simply skips the code that is within the loop block after it. Thus, the effect of continue in a while, do...while, or for loop is that it results in the loop condition being reevaluated and the loop block being reentered if the condition evaluates to true.

NOTE

In case of a continue within a for loop, the loop expression (the third expression within the for statement typically used to increment the counter) is evaluated before the condition is reevaluated.

break exits the loop's block, effectively ending the loop within which it was invoked.

CAUTION

Usually programmers expect all code in a loop to be executed when the loop conditions are satisfied. continue and break modify this behavior and can result in nonintuitive code.

So, you should use continue and break sparingly and only when you cannot program a loop cannot correctly and efficiently without them.

Listing 6.12 that follows demonstrates using continue to ask the user to reenter the numbers before calculating using them and uses break to exit the loop.

Loops That Don't End, that is, Infinite Loops

Remember that while, do...while, and for loops have a condition expression that results in the loop terminating when the condition evaluates to false. If you program a condition that always evaluates to true, the loop never ends.

An infinite while loop looks like this:

```
while(true)    // while expression fixed to true
{
   DoSomethingRepeatedly;
}
```

An infinite do...while loop would be:

```
do
{
   DoSomethingRepeatedly;
} while(true);    // do…while expression never evaluates to false
```

6

An infinite `for` loop can be programmed the following way:

```
for (;;)   // no condition supplied = unending for
{
   DoSomethingRepeatedly;
}
```

Strange as it may seem, such loops do have a purpose. Imagine an operating system that needs to continually check if you have connected a device such as a USB stick to the USB port. This is an activity that should not stop for so long as the OS is running. Such cases warrant the use of loops that never end. Such loops are also called infinite loops as they execute forever, to eternity.

Controlling Infinite Loops

If you want to end an `infinite loop` (say the OS in the preceding example needs to shut down), you do so by inserting a `break` (typically used within an `if (condition)` block).

The following is an example of using `break` to exit an infinite `while`:

```
while(true)   // while expression fixed to true
{
   DoSomethingRepeatedly;
   if(expression)
      break;  // exit loop when expression evaluates to true
}
```

Using break inside an infinite do..while:

```
do
{
   DoSomethingRepeatedly;
   if(expression)
      break;  // exit loop when expression evaluates to true
} while(true);   // do…while expression never evaluates to false
```

Using break inside an infinite for loop:

```
for (;;)   // no condition supplied = unending for
{
   DoSomethingRepeatedly;
   if(expression)
      break;  // exit loop when expression evaluates to true
}
```

Listing 6.12 shows how to program infinite loops using `continue` and `break` to control the exit criteria.

LISTING 6.12 Using continue to Restart and break to Exit an Infinite for Loop

```
0: #include <iostream>
1: using namespace std;
2:
3: int main()
4: {
5:    for(;;)    // an infinite loop
6:    {
7:       cout << "Enter two integers: " << endl;
8:       int Num1 = 0, Num2 = 0;
9:       cin >> Num1;
10:       cin >> Num2;
11:
12:       cout << "Do you wish to correct the numbers? (y/n): ";
13:       char ChangeNumbers = '\0';
14:       cin >> ChangeNumbers;
15:
16:       if (ChangeNumbers == 'y')
17:          continue;  // restart the loop!
18:
19:       cout << Num1 << " x " << Num2 << " = " << Num1 * Num2 << endl;
20:       cout << Num1 << " + " << Num2 << " = " << Num1 + Num2 << endl;
21:
22:       cout << "Press x to exit or any other key to recalculate" << endl;
23:       char UserSelection = '\0';
24:       cin >> UserSelection;
25:
26:       if (UserSelection == 'x')
27:          break;   // exit the infinite loop
28:    }
29:
30:    cout << "Goodbye!" << endl;
31:
32:    return 0;
33: }
```

Output ▼

```
Enter two integers:
560
25
Do you wish to correct the numbers? (y/n): y
Enter two integers:
56
25
Do you wish to correct the numbers? (y/n): n
56 x 25 = 1400
56 + 25 = 81
Press x to exit or any other key to recalculate
r
Enter two integers:
```

6

```
95
-1
Do you wish to correct the numbers? (y/n): n
95 x -1 = -95
95 + -1 = 94
Press x to exit or any other key to recalculate
x
Goodbye!
```

Analysis ▼

The `for` loop in Line 5 is different from the one in Listing 6.11 in that this is an infinite `for` loop containing no condition expression that is evaluated on every iteration of the loop. In other words, without the execution of a `break` statement, this loop (and hence this application) never exits. Note the output, which is different from the other output you have seen so far in that it allows the user to make a correction to his input integers before the program proceeds to calculate the sum and multiplication. This logic is implemented using a `continue` given the evaluation of a certain condition in Lines 16 and 17. When the user presses *y* on being asked if he wants to correct the numbers, the condition in Line 16 evaluates to `true`, hence executing the following `continue`. When `continue` is encountered, execution jumps to the top of the loop, asking the user again if he wants to enter two integers. Similarly at the end of the loop when the user is asked if he wants to exit, his input is checked against `'x'` in Line 26, and if so, the following `break` is executed, ending the loop.

> **NOTE**
>
> Listing 6.12 uses an empty `for(;;)` statement to create an infinite loop. You can replace that with `while(true)` or a do... `while(true);` to generate the same output using a different loop type.

DO	**DON'T**
DO use do...while when the logic in the loop needs to be executed at least once.	**DON'T** use goto.
	DON'T use continue and break indiscriminately.
DO use while, do...while, or for loops with well-defined condition expressions.	**DON'T** program infinite loops with break unless absolutely necessary.
DO indent code in a statement block contained in a loop to improve readability.	

Programming Nested Loops

Just as you saw nested if statements in the beginning of this lesson, often you do need to nest one loop under another. Imagine two arrays of integers. If you want to find the multiple of each number in Array1 against each in Array2, you use a nested loop to make programming this easy. The first loop iterates Array1, while the second iterates Array2 under the first.

Listing 6.13 demonstrates that you can nest a loop of any type under a loop of any type.

LISTING 6.13   Using Nested Loops to Multiply Each Element in an Array by Each in Another

```
0: #include <iostream>
1: using namespace std;
2:
3: int main()
4: {
5:     const int ARRAY1_LEN = 3;
6:     const int ARRAY2_LEN = 2;
7:
8:     int MyInts1[ARRAY1_LEN] = {35, -3, 0};
9:     int MyInts2[ARRAY2_LEN] = {20, -1};
10:
11:     cout << "Multiplying each int in MyInts1 by each in MyInts2:" << endl;
12:
13:     for(int Array1Index = 0; Array1Index < ARRAY1_LEN; ++Array1Index)
14:         for(int Array2Index = 0; Array2Index < ARRAY2_LEN; ++Array2Index)
15:             cout << MyInts1[Array1Index] << " x " << MyInts2[Array2Index] \
16:             << " = " << MyInts1[Array1Index] * MyInts2[Array2Index] << endl;
17:
18:     return 0;
19: }
```

Output ▼

```
Multiplying each int in MyInts1 by each in MyInts2:
35 x 20 = 700
35 x -1 = -35
-3 x 20 = -60
-3 x -1 = 3
0 x 20 = 0
0 x -1 = 0
```

6

Output ▼

The two nested for loops in question are in Lines 13 and 14. The first for loop iterates the array MyInts1, whereas the second for loop iterates the other array MyInts2. The first for loop executes the second for loop within each iteration. The second for loop iterates over all elements in MyInts2 and in each iteration multiplies that element with the element indexed via Array1Index from the first loop above it. So, for every element in MyInts1, the second loop iterates over all elements in MyInts2, resulting in the first element in MyInts1 at offset 0 being multiplied with all elements in MyInts2. Then the second element in MyInts1 is multiplied with all elements in MyInts2. Finally, the third element in MyInts1 is multiplied with all elements in MyInts2.

> **NOTE**
>
> For convenience and for keeping focus on the loops, the contents of the array in Listing 6.13 are initialized. You should feel free to derive from previous examples, such as Listing 6.10, to get the user to enter numbers into the integer array.

Using Nested Loops to Walk a Multidimensional Array

In Lesson 4, you learned of multidimensional arrays. Indeed in Listing 4.3 you access elements in a two-dimensional array of three rows and three columns. What you did there was to individually access each element in the array, one element per line. There was no automation, and, if the array was to be made larger, you would need to code a lot more, in addition to changing the array's dimensions to access its elements. However, using loops can change all that, as demonstrated by Listing 6.14.

LISTING 6.14   Using Nested Loops to Iterate Elements in a Two-dimensional Array of Integers

```
0: #include <iostream>
1: using namespace std;
2:
3: int main()
4: {
5:    const int MAX_ROWS = 3;
6:    const int MAX_COLS = 4;
7:
8:    // 2D array of integers
9:    int MyInts[MAX_ROWS][MAX_COLS] = { {34, -1, 879, 22},
10:                                       {24, 365, -101, -1},
```

LISTING 6.14 Continued

```
11:                                      {-20, 40, 90, 97} };
12:
13:     // iterate rows, each array of int
14:     for (int Row = 0; Row < MAX_ROWS; ++Row)
15:     {
16:        // iterate integers in each row (columns)
17:        for (int Column = 0; Column < MAX_COLS; ++Column)
18:        {
19:           cout << "Integer[" << Row << "][" << Column \
20:                << "] = " << MyInts[Row][Column] << endl;
21:        }
22:     }
23:
24:     return 0;
25: }
```

Output ▼

```
Integer[0][0] = 34
Integer[0][1] = -1
Integer[0][2] = 879
Integer[0][3] = 22
Integer[1][0] = 24
Integer[1][1] = 365
Integer[1][2] = -101
Integer[1][3] = -1
Integer[2][0] = -20
Integer[2][1] = 40
Integer[2][2] = 90
Integer[2][3] = 97
```

Analysis ▼

Lines 14–22 contain two for loops that you need to access and iterate through a two-dimensional array of integers. A two-dimensional array is in effect an array of an array of integers. Note how the first for loop accesses the rows (each being an array of integers), whereas the second accesses each element in this array—that is, accesses columns therein.

6

NOTE

Listing 6.14 uses braces to enclose the nested for only to improve readability. This nested loop works just fine without the braces, too, as the loop statement is just a single statement to be executed (and not a compound statement that necessitates the use of enclosing braces).

Using Nested Loops to Calculate Fibonacci Numbers

The famed Fibonacci series is a set of numbers starting with 0 and 1, where every following number in the series is the sum of the previous two. So, a Fibonacci series starts with a sequence like this:

0, 1, 1, 2, 3, 5, 8, ... and so on

Listing 6.15 demonstrates how to create a Fibonacci series comprised of as many numbers as you want (limited by the physical capacity of the integer holding the final number).

LISTING 6.15   Using Nested Loops to Calculate a Fibonacci Series

```
0: #include <iostream>
1: using namespace std;
2:
3: int main()
4: {
5:     const int NumsToCal = 5;
6:     cout << "This program will calculate " << NumsToCal \
7:          << " Fibonacci Numbers at a time" << endl;
8:
9:     int Num1 = 0, Num2 = 1;
10:    char WantMore = '\0';
11:    cout << Num1 << " " << Num2 << " ";
12:
13:    do
14:    {
15:       for (int Index = 0; Index < NumsToCal; ++Index)
16:       {
17:          cout << Num1 + Num2 << " ";
18:
19:          int Num2Temp = Num2;
20:          Num2 = Num1 + Num2;
21:          Num1 = Num2Temp;
22:       }
23:
24:       cout << endl << "Do you want more numbers (y/n)? ";
25:       cin >> WantMore;
26:    }while (WantMore == 'y');
27:
28:    cout << "Goodbye!" << endl;
29:
30:    return 0;
31: }
```

Output ▼

```
This program will calculate 5 Fibonacci Numbers at a time
0 1 1 2 3 5 8
Do you want more numbers (y/n)? y
13 21 34 55 89
Do you want more numbers (y/n)? y
144 233 377 610 987
Do you want more numbers (y/n)? y
1597 2584 4181 6765 10946
Do you want more numbers (y/n)? n
Goodbye!
```

Analysis ▼

The outer do...while at Line 13 is basically the query loop that repeats if the user wants to see more numbers. The inner for loop at Line 15 does the job of calculating the next Fibonacci number and displays five numbers at a time. In Line 19 you assign Num2 to a temp value to be able to assign it at Line 21. Note that if you hadn't stored this temp value, you would be assigning the modified value in Line 20 directly to Num1, which is not what you want. The loop repeats with new values in Num1 and Num2 thanks to these three Lines—if the user presses y to repeat.

Summary

This lesson is all about ensuring that you don't just write code that executes only from top to bottom; it shows you how to code conditional statements that create alternative execution paths and make code blocks repeat in a loop. You learned the if...else construct and using switch-case statements to handle different situations in the event of variables containing different values.

In understanding loops, you were taught goto—but you were simultaneously warned against using it due to its ability to create code that cannot be understood. You learned programming loops in C++ using while, do...while, and for constructs. You learned how to make the loops iterate endlessly to create infinite loops and to use continue and break to better control them.

6

Q&A

Q **What happens if I omit a `break` in a `switch-case` statement?**

A The `break` statement enables program execution to exit the `switch` construct. Without it, execution continues evaluating the following `case` statements.

Q **How do I exit an infinite loop?**

A Use `break` to exit the loop. Using `return` exits the function module, too.

Q **My `while` loop looks like `while(Integer)`. Does the `while` loop execute when `Integer` evaluates to -1?**

A Ideally a `while` expression should evaluate to a Boolean value `true` or `false`, else it is interpreted as such: `false` is zero. A condition that does not evaluate to zero is considered to evaluate to `true`. Because -1 is not zero, the `while` condition evaluates to `true` and the loop is executed. If you want the loop to be executed only for positive numbers, write an expression `while(Integer>0)`. This rule is true for all conditional statements and loops.

Q **How do I exit an infinite loop?**

A Use `break` to exit the loop. Using `return` instead of `break` exits the function module, too.

Q **Is there an empty `while` loop equivalent of `for(;;)`?**

A No, `while` always needs an accompanying conditional expression.

Q **I changed a `do…while(exp);` to a `while(exp);` by copying and pasting. Should I anticipate any problems?**

A Yes, big ones! `while(exp);` is already a valid yet empty `while` loop due to the null statement (the semicolon) following the `while`, even if it is followed by a statement block. The statement block in question is executed once, but outside of the loop. You should be careful when copying and pasting code.

Workshop

The Workshop provides quiz questions to help you solidify your understanding of the material covered as well as exercises to provide you with experience in using what you've learned. Try to answer the quiz and exercise questions before checking the answers in Appendix D, and be certain you understand the answers before continuing to the next lesson.

Quiz

1. Why bother to indent code within statements blocks, nested `ifs`, and nested loops when it compiles even without indentation?

2. You can implement a quick fix using `goto`. Why would you still avoid it?

3. Is it possible to write a `for` loop where the counter decrements? How would it look?

4. What is the problem with the following loop?

```
for (int Counter=0; Counter==10; ++Counter)

    cout << Counter << " ";
```

Exercises

1. Write a `for` loop to access elements in an array in the reverse order.

2. Write a nested loop equivalent of Listing 6.13 that adds elements in two arrays, but in reverse order.

3. Write a program that displays Fibonacci numbers similar to Listing 6.15 but asks the user how many numbers she wants to compute.

4. Write a `switch-case` construct that tells if a color is in the rainbow or otherwise. Use enumerated constants.

5. **BUG BUSTERS:** What is wrong with this code?

```
for (int Counter=0; Counter=10; ++Counter)
    cout << Counter << " ";
```

6. **BUG BUSTERS:** What is wrong with this code?

```
int LoopCounter = 0;
while(LoopCounter <5);
{
    cout << LoopCounter << " ";
    LoopCounter++;
}
```

7. **BUG BUSTERS:** What is wrong with this code?

```
cout << "Enter a number between 0 and 4" << endl;
int Input = 0;
cin >> Input;

switch (Input)
```

6

```
{
case 0:
case 1:
case 2:
case 3:
case 4:
   cout << "Valid input" << endl;
default:
   cout << "Invalid input" << endl;
}
```

LESSON 7
Organizing Code with Functions

So far in this book you have seen simple programs where all programming effort is contained in `main()`. This works very well for really small programs and applications. The larger and more complex your program gets, the longer the contents of `main()` become, unless you choose to structure your program using functions.

Functions give you a way to compartmentalize and organize your program's execution logic. They enable you to split the contents of your application into logical blocks that are invoked sequentially.

A function is hence a subprogram that optionally takes parameters and returns a value, and it needs to be invoked to perform its task. In this lesson you learn

- The need for programming functions
- Function prototypes and function definition
- Passing parameters to functions and returning values from them
- Overloading functions
- Recursive functions
- C++11 lambda functions

The Need for Functions

Think of an application that asks the user to enter the radius of a circle and then computes the circumference and area. One way to do this is to have it all inside `main()`. Another way is to break this application into logical blocks: in particular two that compute area and circumference given radius, respectively. See Listing 7.1.

LISTING 7.1 Two Functions That Compute the Area and Circumference of a Circle Given Radius

```cpp
0: #include <iostream>
1: using namespace std;
2:
3: const double Pi = 3.14159;
4:
5: // Function Declarations (Prototypes)
6: double Area(double InputRadius);
7: double Circumference(double InputRadius);
8:
9: int main()
10: {
11:     cout << "Enter radius: ";
12:     double Radius = 0;
13:     cin >> Radius;
14:
15:     // Call function "Area"
16:     cout << "Area is: " << Area(Radius) << endl;
17:
18:     // Call function "Circumference"
19:     cout << "Circumference is: " << Circumference(Radius) << endl;
20:
21:     return 0;
22: }
23:
24: // Function definitions (implementations)
25: double Area(double InputRadius)
26: {
27:     return Pi * InputRadius * InputRadius;
28: }
29:
30: double Circumference(double InputRadius)
31: {
32:     return 2 * Pi * InputRadius;
33: }
```

Output ▼

```
Enter radius: 6.5
Area is: 132.732
Circumference is: 40.8407
```

Analysis ▼

At first look, it looks like the same stuff with a different package. You will appreciate that compartmentalizing the computation of area and circumference into different functions can potentially help reuse as the functions can be invoked repeatedly as and when required. main(), which is also a function, is quite compact and delegates activity to functions such as Area and Circumference that are invoked in Lines 16 and 19, respectively.

The program demonstrates the following artifacts involved in programming using functions:

- Function prototypes are *declared* in Lines 6 and 7, so the compiler knows what the terms Area and Circumference when used in main() mean.
- Functions Area() and Circumference() are *invoked* in main() in Lines 16 and 19.
- Function Area() is *defined* in Lines 25–38, Circumference() in Lines 30–33.

What Is a Function Prototype?

Let's take a look at Listing 7.1 again—Lines 6 and 7 in particular:

```
double Area(double InputRadius);
double Circumference(double InputRadius);
```

Figure 7.1 shows what a function prototype is comprised of.

FIGURE 7.1
Parts of a function prototype.

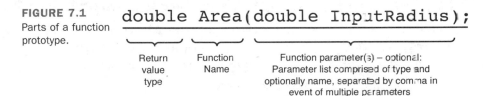

double Area(double InputRadius);

Return value type

Function Name

Function parameter(s) – optional: Parameter list comprised of type and optionally name, separated by comma in event of multiple parameters

7

The function prototype basically tells what a function is called (the name, Area), the list of parameters the function accepts (one parameter, a double called InputRadius) and the return type of the function (a double).

Without the function prototype, on reaching Lines 16 and 19 in main() the compiler wouldn't know what the terms Area and Circumference are. The function prototypes tell the compiler that Area and Circumference are functions; they take one parameter of type double and return a value of type double. The compiler then recognizes these statements as valid and the job of linking the function call to its implementation and ensuring that the program execution actually triggers them is that of the linker.

NOTE

> A function can have multiple parameters separated by commas, but it can have only one return type.
>
> When programming a function that does not need to return any value, specify the return type as void.

What Is a Function Definition?

The actual meat and potatoes—the implementation of a function—is what is called the *definition*. Analyze the definition of function Area:

```
25: double Area(double InputRadius)
26: {
27:    return Pi * InputRadius * InputRadius;
28: }
```

A function definition is always comprised of a statement block. A return statement is necessary unless the function is declared with return type void. In this case, Area needs to return a value because the return type of the function has not been declared as void. The statement block contains statements within open and closed braces ({...}) that are executed when the function is called. Area() uses the input parameter InputRadius that contains the radius as an *argument* sent by the caller to compute the area of the circle.

What Is a Function Call, and What Are Arguments?

Invoking a function is also called making a *function call*. When a function is declared as one with *parameters*, the function call needs to send *arguments* that are values the function requests within its parameter list. Let's analyze a call to Area in Listing 7.1:

```
16:    cout << "Area is: " << Area(Radius) << endl;
```

Here, Area(Radius) is the function call, wherein Radius is the argument sent to the function Area. When invoked, execution jumps to Area that uses the radius sent to compute the area of the circle. When function Area is done, it returns a double. This return value double is then displayed on the screen via the cout statement.

Programming a Function with Multiple Parameters

Assume you were writing a program that computes the area of a cylinder, as shown in Figure 7.2.

FIGURE 7.2
A cylinder.

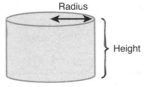

The formula you use would be the following:

```
Area of Cylinder = Area of top circle - Area of bottom circle + Area of Side
                 = Pi * Radius^2 + Pi * Radius ^2 + 2 * Pi * Radius * Height
                 = 2 * Pi * Radius^2 + 2 * Pi * Radius * Height
```

Thus, you need to work with two variables, the radius and the height, in computing the area of the cylinder. In such cases, when writing a function that computes the surface area of the cylinder, you specify at least two parameters in the parameter list, within the function declaration. You do this by separating individual parameters by a comma as shown in Listing 7.2.

LISTING 7.2   Function That Accepts Two Parameters to Compute the Surface Area of a Cylinder

```
0: #include <iostream>
1: using namespace std;
2:
3: const double Pi = 3.14159;
4:
5: // Declaration contains two parameters
6: double SurfaceArea(double Radius, double Height);
7:
8: int main()
9: {
10:    cout << "Enter the radius of the cylinder: ";
11:    double InRadius = 0;
12:    cin >> InRadius;
13:    cout << "Enter the height of the cylinder: ";
14:    double InHeight = 0;
15:    cin >> InHeight;
16:
17:    cout << "Surface Area: " << SurfaceArea(InRadius, InHeight) << endl;
```

7

LISTING 7.2 Continued

```
18:
19:    return 0;
20: }
21:
22: double SurfaceArea(double Radius, double Height)
23: {
24:    double Area = 2 * Pi * Radius * Radius + 2 * Pi * Radius * Height;
25:    return Area;
26: }
```

Output ▼

```
Enter the radius of the cylinder: 3
Enter the height of the cylinder: 6.5
Surface Area: 179.071
```

Analysis ▼

Line 6 contains the declaration of function SurfaceArea with two parameters: Radius and Height, both of type double, separated by a comma. Lines 22–26 show the definition—that is, the implementation of SurfaceArea. As you can see, the input parameters Radius and Height are used to compute the value stored in Area, that is then returned to the caller.

NOTE

Function parameters are like local variables. They are valid within the scope of the function only. So in Listing 7.2, parameters Radius and Height to function SurfaceArea are valid and usable within function SurfaceArea only and not outside it.

Programming Functions with No Parameters or No Return Values

If you delegate the task of saying "Hello World" to a function that does only that and nothing else, you could do it with one that doesn't need any parameters (as it doesn't need to do anything apart from say "Hello"), and possibly one that doesn't return any value (because you don't expect anything from such a function that would be useful elsewhere). Listing 7.3 demonstrates one such function.

LISTING 7.3 A Function with No Parameters and No Return Values

```
0: #include <iostream>
1: using namespace std;
2:
3: void SayHello();
4:
5: int main()
6: {
7:    SayHello();
8:    return 0;
9: }
10:
11: void SayHello()
12: {
13:    cout << "Hello World" << endl;
14: }
```

Output ▼

```
Hello World
```

Analysis ▼

Note that the function prototype in Line 3 declares function SayHello as one with return value of type void—that is, SayHello doesn't return a value. Consequently, in the function definition in Lines 11–14, there is no return statement. Even the function call within main() in Line 7 doesn't assign the function's return value to any variable or use in any expression because the function is one that returns nothing.

Function Parameters with Default Values

In samples thus far, you assumed the value of Pi, fixed it as a constant, and never gave the user an opportunity to change it. However, the user may be interested in a less or more accurate reading. How do you program a function that would assume the value of Pi of your choosing unless another one is supplied?

One way of solving this problem is to supply an additional parameter in function Area() for Pi and supply a value chosen by you as a default one. Such an adaptation of function Area() from Listing 7.1 would look like the following:

```
double Area(double InputRadius, double Pi = 3.14);
```

Note the second parameter Pi and an associated default value of 3.14. This second parameter is now an optional parameter for the caller. So, the calling function can still invoke Area using this syntax:

```
Area(Radius);
```

7

In this case, the second parameter has been ignored, and it defaults to the value of 3.14. However, if the user has supplied a different Pi, then you can specify it in your call to Area, as this:

```
Area(Radius, Pi); // User defined Pi
```

Listing 7.4 demonstrates how you can program functions that contain default values for parameters that can be overridden with a user-supplied value, if available and desired.

LISTING 7.4   Function That Computes the Area of a Circle, Using Pi as a Second Parameter with Default Value 3.14

```
 0: #include <iostream>
 1: using namespace std;
 2:
 3: // Function Declaration (Prototype)
 4: double Area(double InputRadius, double Pi = 3.14);  // Pi with default value
 5:
 6: int main()
 7: {
 8:    cout << "Enter radius: ";
 9:    double Radius = 0;
10:    cin >> Radius;
11:
12:    cout << "Pi is 3.14, do you wish to change this (y / n)? ";
13:    char ChangePi = 'n';
14:    cin >> ChangePi;
15:
16:    double CircleArea = 0;
17:    if (ChangePi == 'y')
18:    {
19:       cout << "Enter new Pi: ";
20:       double NewPi = 3.14;
21:       cin >> NewPi;
22:       CircleArea = Area (Radius, NewPi);
23:    }
24:    else
25:       CircleArea = Area(Radius); // Ignore 2nd param, use default value
26:
27:    // Call function "Area"
28:    cout << "Area is: " << CircleArea << endl;
29:
30:    return 0;
31: }
32:
33: // Function definitions don't specify default values again
34: double Area(double InputRadius, double Pi)
35: {
36:    return Pi * InputRadius * InputRadius;
37: }
```

Output ▼

```
Enter radius: 1
Pi is 3.14, do you wish to change this (y / n)? n
Area is: 3.14
```

Next run:

```
Enter radius: 1
Pi is 3.14, do you wish to change this (y / n)? y
Enter new Pi: 3.1416
Area is: 3.1416
```

Analysis ▼

In the two runs shown in the preceding output, the radius entered by the user was the same—1. In the second run, however, the user opted for the choice to change the precision of Pi, and hence the area computed is slightly different. Note that in both cases, as seen in Line 22 and Line 25, you invoke the same function. Line 25 contains Area invoked without the second parameter Pi, which, in this case, defaults to the value 3.14, supplied as default in the declaration in Line 4.

NOTE

You can have multiple parameters with default values; however, these should all be at the tail end of the parameter list.

Recursion—Functions That Invoke Themselves

In certain cases, you can actually have a function call itself. Such a function is called a *recursive function*. Note that a recursive function should have a very clearly defined exit condition where it returns without invoking itself again.

CAUTION

In the absence of an exit condition or in the event of a bug in the same, your program execution gets stuck at the recursive function that won't stop invoking itself, and this eventually stops when the stack overflows, causing an application crash.

7

Recursive functions can be useful when determining a number in the Fibonacci series as shown in Listing 7.5. This series starts with two numbers, 0 and 1:

```
F(0) = 0
F(1) = 1
```

And the value of a subsequent number in the series is the sum of the previous two numbers. So, the *n*th value (for n > 1) is determined by the (recursive) formula:

```
Fibonacci(n) = Fibonacci(n - 1) + Fibonacci(n - 2)
```

As a result the Fibonacci series expands to

```
F(2) = 1
F(3) = 2
F(4) = 3
F(5) = 5
F(6) = 8, and so on.
```

LISTING 7.5   Using Recursive Functions to Calculate a Number in the Fibonacci Series

```
0: #include <iostream>
1: using namespace std;
2:
3: int GetFibNumber(int FibIndex)
4: {
5:     if (FibIndex < 2)
6:         return FibIndex;
7:     else // recursion if FibIndex >= 2
8:         return GetFibNumber(FibIndex - 1) + GetFibNumber(FibIndex - 2);
9: }
10:
11: int main()
12: {
13:     cout << "Enter 0-based index of desired Fibonacci Number: ";
14:     int Index = 0;
15:     cin >> Index;
16:
17:     cout << "Fibonacci number is: " << GetFibNumber(Index) << endl;
18:     return 0;
19: }
```

Output ▼

```
Enter 0-based index of desired Fibonacci Number: 6
Fibonacci number is: 8
```

Analysis ▼

The function `GetFibNumber` defined in Lines 3–9 is recursive as it invokes itself at Line 8. Note the exit condition programmed in Lines 5 and 6; if the index is less than two, the function is not recursive. Given that the function invokes itself successively with reducing value of `FibIndex`, at a certain point it reaches a level where it enters the exit condition and the recursion stops.

Functions with Multiple Return Statements

You are not restricted to having only one return statement in your function definition. You can return from any point in the function, and multiple times if you want, as shown in Listing 7.6. Depending on the logic and the need of the application, this might or might not be poor programming practice.

LISTING 7.6   Using Multiple Return Statements in One Function

```
0: #include <iostream>
1: using namespace std;
2: const double Pi = 3.14159;
3:
4: void QueryAndCalculate()
5: {
6:    cout << "Enter radius: ";
7:    double Radius = 0;
8:    cin >> Radius;
9:
10:    cout << "Area: " << Pi * Radius * Radius << endl;
11:
12:    cout << "Do you wish to calculate circumference (y/n)? ";
13:    char CalcCircum = 'n';
14:    cin >> CalcCircum;
15:
16:    if (CalcCircum == 'n')
17:        return;
18:
19:    cout << "Circumference: " << 2 * Pi * Radius << endl;
20:    return;
21: }
22:
23: int main()
24: {
25:    QueryAndCalculate ();
26:
27:    return 0;
28: }
```

Output ▼

```
Enter radius: 1
Area: 3.14159
Do you wish to calculate circumference (y/n)? y
Circumference: 6.28319
```

Next run:

```
Enter radius: 1
Area: 3.14159
Do you wish to calculate circumference (y/n)? n
```

7

Analysis ▼

The function `QueryAndCalculate` contains multiple `return` statements: one at Line 17 and the next one at Line 20. This function asks the user if she also wants to calculate circumference. If she presses *n* for no, the program quits by using the `return` statement. For all other values, it continues with calculating the circumference and then returning.

CAUTION

Use multiple returns in a function with caution. It is a lot easier to understand and follow a function that starts at the top and returns at the bottom than one that returns at multiple points in-between.

In Listing 7.6, use of multiple returns could've been avoided simply by changing the `if` condition to testing for `'y'` or yes:

```
if (CalcCircum == 'y')
    cout << "Circumference: " << 2 * Pi * Radius << endl;
```

Using Functions to Work with Different Forms of Data

Functions don't restrict you to passing values one at a time; you can pass an array of values to a function. You can create two functions with the same name and return value but different parameters. You can program a function such that its parameters are not created and destroyed within the function call; instead, you use references that are valid even after the function has exited so as to allow you to manipulate more data or parameters in a function call. In this section you learn about passing arrays to functions, function overloading, and passing arguments by reference to functions.

Overloading Functions

Functions with the same name and return type but with different parameters or set of parameters are said to be overloaded functions. Overloaded functions can be quite useful in applications where a function with a particular name that produces a certain type of output might need to be invoked with different sets of parameters. Say you need to be writing an application that computes the area of a circle and the area of a cylinder. The function that computes the area of a circle needs a parameter—the radius. The other function that computes the area of the cylinder needs the height of the cylinder in addition to the radius of the cylinder. Both functions need to return the data of the same type, containing the area. So, C++ enables you to define two overloaded functions, both called Area, both returning double, but one that takes only the radius as input and another that takes the height and the radius as input parameters as shown in Listing 7 7.

LISTING 7.7 Using an Overloaded Function to Calculate the Area of a Circle or a Cylinder

```cpp
0: #include <iostream>
1: using namespace std;
2:
3: const double Pi = 3.14159;
4:
5: double Area(double Radius);   // for circle
6: double Area(double Radius, double Height); // overloaded for cylinder
7:
8: int main()
9: {
10:     cout << "Enter z for Cylinder, c for Circle: ";
11:     char Choice = 'z';
12:     cin >> Choice;
13:
14:     cout << "Enter radius: ";
15:     double Radius = 0;
16:     cin >> Radius;
17:
18:     if (Choice == 'z')
19:     {
20:         cout << "Enter height: ";
21:         double Height = 0;
22:         cin >> Height;
23:
24:         // Invoke overloaded variant of Area for Cyclinder
25:         cout << "Area of cylinder is: " << Area (Radius, Height) << endl;
26:     }
27:     else
28:         cout << "Area of cylinder is: " << Area (Radius) << endl;
29:
30:     return 0;
31: }
32:
33: // for circle
34: double Area(double Radius)
35: {
36:     return Pi * Radius * Radius;
37: }
38:
39: // overloaded for cylinder
40: double Area(double Radius, double Height)
41: {
```

7

LISTING 7.7   Continued

```
42:    // reuse the area of circle
43:    return 2 * Area (Radius) + 2 * Pi * Radius * Height;
44: }
```

Output ▼

```
Enter z for Cylinder, c for Circle: z
Enter radius: 2
Enter height: 5
Area of cylinder is: 87.9646
```

Next run:

```
Enter z for Cylinder, c for Circle: c
Enter radius: 1
Area of cylinder is: 3.14159
```

Analysis ▼

Lines 5 and 6 declare the prototype for the overloaded forms of Area, one that accepts a single parameter—radius of a circle—and another that accepts two parameters—radius and height of a cylinder. Both functions have the same names, Area; same return types, double; and different sets of parameters —hence they're overloaded. The definitions of the overloaded functions are in Lines 34–44, where the two functions determine the area of a circle given the radius and the area of a cylinder given the radius and height, respectively. Interestingly, as the area of a cylinder is comprised of the area of the two circles it contains (one on top and the other on the bottom) in addition to the area of the sides, the overloaded version for cylinder was able to reuse Area for the circle, as shown in Line 43.

Passing an Array of Values to a Function

A function that displays an integer can be represented like this:

```
void DisplayInteger(int Number);
```

A function that can display an array of integers has a slightly different prototype:

```
void DisplayIntegers(int[] Numbers, int Length);
```

The first parameter tells the function that the data being input is an array, whereas the second parameter supplies the length of the array such that you can use the array without crossing its boundaries. See Listing 7.8.

LISTING 7.8   Function That Takes an Array as a Parameter

```
0: #include <iostream>
1: using namespace std;
2:
3: void DisplayArray(int Numbers[], int Length)
4: {
5:     for (int Index = 0; Index < Length; ++Index)
6:         cout << Numbers[Index] << " ";
7:
8:     cout << endl;
9: }
10:
11: void DisplayArray(char Characters[], int Length)
12: {
13:     for (int Index = 0; Index < Length; ++Index)
14:         cout << Characters[Index] << " ";
15:
16:     cout << endl;
17: }
18:
19: int main()
20: {
21:     int MyNumbers[4] = {24, 58, -1, 245};
22:     DisplayArray(MyNumbers, 4);
23:
24:     char MyStatement[7] = {'H', 'e', 'l', 'l', 'c', '!', '\0' };
25:     DisplayArray(MyStatement, 7);
26:
27:     return 0;
28: }
```

Output ▼

```
24 58 -1 245
H e l l o !
```

Analysis ▼

There are two overloaded functions called DisplayArray here: one that displays the contents of elements in an array of integers and another that displays the contents of an array of characters. In Lines 22 and 25, the two functions are invoked using an array of integers and an array of characters, respectively, as input. Note that in declaring and initializing the array of characters in Line 24, you have intentionally included the null character—as a best practice and a good habit—even though the array is not used as a string in a cout statement or the like (cout << MyStatement;) in this application.

7

Passing Arguments by Reference

Take another look at the function in Listing 7.1 that computed the area of a circle given the radius:

```
24: // Function definitions (implementations)
25: double Area(double InputRadius)
26: {
27:    return Pi * InputRadius * InputRadius;
28: }
```

Here, the parameter `InputRadius` contains a value that is copied in to it when the function is invoked in `main()`:

```
15:    // Call function "Area"
16:    cout << "Area is: " << Area(Radius) << endl;
```

This means that the variable `Radius` in `main` is unaffected by the function call, as `Area()` works on a copy of the value `Radius` contains, held in `InputRadius`. There are cases where you might need a function to work on a variable that modifies a value that is available outside the function, too, say in the calling function. This is when you declare a parameter that takes an argument *by reference*. A form of the function `Area()` that computes and returns the area as a parameter by reference looks like this:

```
// output parameter Result by reference
void Area(double Radius, double& Result)
{
   Result = Pi * Radius * Radius;
}
```

Note how `Area()` in this form takes two parameters. Don't miss the ampersand (&) next to the second parameter `Result`. This sign indicates to the compiler that the second argument should NOT be copied to the function; instead, it is a reference to the variable being passed. The return type has been changed to `void` as the function no longer supplies the area computed as a return value, rather as an output parameter by reference. Returning values by references is demonstrated in Listing 7.9, which computes the area of a circle.

LISTING 7.9   Fetching the Area of a Circle as a Reference Parameter and Not as a Return Value

```
0: #include <iostream>
1: using namespace std;
2:
3: const double Pi = 3.1416;
```

LISTING 7.9 Continued

```
 4:
 5: // output parameter Result by reference
 6: void Area(double Radius, double& Result)
 7: {
 8:    Result = Pi * Radius * Radius;
 9: }
10:
11: int main()
12: {
13:    cout << "Enter radius: ";
14:    double Radius = 0;
15:    cin >> Radius;
16:
17:    double AreaFetched = 0;
18:    Area(Radius, AreaFetched);
19:
20:    cout << "The area is: " << AreaFetched << endl;
21:    return 0;
22: }
```

Output ▼

```
Enter radius: 2
The area is: 12.5664
```

Analysis ▼

Note Lines 17 and 18 where the function Area is invoked with two parameters; the second is one that should contain the result. As Area takes the second parameter by reference, the variable Result used in Line 8 within Area points to the same memory location as the double AreaFetched declared in Line 17 within the caller main(). Thus, the result computed in function Area at Line 8 is available in main and displayed on the screen in Line 20.

NOTE

A function can return only one value using the return statement. So, if your function needs to perform operations that affect many values that are required at the caller, passing arguments by reference is one way to get a function to supply those many modifications back to the calling module.

7

How Function Calls Are Handled by the Microprocessor

Although it is not extremely important to know exactly how a function call is implemented on a microprocessor level, you might find it interesting. Understanding this helps you understand why C++ gives you the option of programming inline functions, which are explained later in this section.

A function call essentially means that the microprocessor jumps to executing the next instruction belonging to the called function at a nonsequential memory location. After it is done with executing the instructions in the function, it returns to where it left off. To implement this logic, the compiler converts your function call into a CALL instruction for the microprocessor specifying the address the next instruction needs to be taken from—this address belongs to your function routine. When compiling the function itself, the compiler converts the return instructions into a RET instruction for the microprocessor.

When the microprocessor encounters CALL, it saves the position of the instruction to be executed after the function call on the stack and jumps to the memory location contained in the CALL instruction.

Understanding the Stack

The stack is a Last-In-First-Out memory structure, quite like a stack of plates where you pick the plate on top, which was the last one to be placed on the stack. Putting data onto the stack is called a *push* operation. Getting data out of the stack is called a *pop* operation. As the stack grows upward, the stack pointer always increments as it grows and points to the top of the stack. See Figure 7.3.

FIGURE 7.3
A visual representation of a stack containing three integers.

INTEGER 3
INTEGER 2
INTEGER 1

Stack Pointer
(always points to the top
where the next element
can be inserted that is,
pushed)

The nature of the stack makes it optimal for handling function calls. When a function is called, all local variables are instantiated on the stack—that is, pushed onto the stack. When the function ends, they're simply popped off it, and the stack pointer returns to where it originally was.

This memory location contains instructions belonging to the function. The microprocessor executes them until it reaches the RET statement (the microprocessor's code for return programmed by you). The RET statement results in the microprocessor popping that address from the stack stored during the CALL instruction. This address contains the location in the calling function where the execution needs to continue from. Thus, the microprocessor is back to the caller and continues where it left off.

Inline Functions

A regular function call is translated into a CALL instruction, which results in stack operations and microprocessor execution shift to the function and so on. This might sound like a lot of stuff happening under the hood, but it happens quite quickly—for most of the cases. However, what if your function is a very simple one like the following?

```
double GetPi()
{
    return 3.14159;
}
```

The overhead of performing an actual function call on this might be quite high for the amount of time spent actually executing GetPi(). This is why C++ compilers enable the programmer to declare such functions as inline. Keyword inline is the programmers' request that these functions be expanded inline where called.

```
inline double GetPi()
{
    return 3.14159;
}
```

Similarly, functions that just double a number and perform such simple operations are good candidates for being inlined, too. Listing 7.10 demonstrates one such case.

LISTING 7.10 Using an Inline Function That Doubles an Integer

```
0: #include <iostream>
1: using namespace std;
2:
3: // define an inline function that doubles
4: inline long DoubleNum (int InputNum)
5: {
6:     return InputNum * 2;
7: }
8:
```

7

LISTING 7.10 Continued

```
 9: int main()
10: {
11:    cout << "Enter an integer: ";
12:    int InputNum = 0;
13:    cin >> InputNum;
14:
15:    // Call inline function
16:    cout << "Double is: " << DoubleNum(InputNum) << endl;
17:
18:    return 0;
19: }
```

Output ▼

```
Enter an integer: 35
Double is: 70
```

Analysis ▼

The keyword in question is `inline` used in Line 4. Compilers typically see this keyword as a request to place the contents of the function `DoubleNum` directly where the function has been invoked—in Line 16—which increases the execution speed of the code.

Classifying functions as inline can also result in a lot of code bloat, especially if the function being inline does a lot of sophisticated processing. Using the `inline` keyword should be kept to a minimum and reserved for only those functions that do very little and need to do it with minimal overhead, as demonstrated earlier.

NOTE

Most modern C++ compilers offer various performance optimization options. Some, such as the Microsoft C++ Compiler, offer you to optimize for size or speed. The former is quite important when developing software for devices and peripherals where memory may be at a premium. When optimizing for size, the compiler might often reject many inline requests as that might bloat code.

When optimizing for speed, the compiler typically sees and utilizes opportunities to inline code where it would make sense and does it for you—sometimes even in those cases where you have not explicitly requested it.

C++11

Lambda Functions

This section is just an introduction to a concept that's not exactly easy for beginners. So, skim through it and try to learn the concept without being disappointed if you don't grasp it all. lambda functions are discussed in depth in Lesson 22, "C++11 Lambda Expressions."

Lambda functions are very useful if you often program using STL algorithms to sort or process data, for example, contained in STL containers such as the std::vector (dynamic array). Typically, a sort requires you to supply a binary predicate that is implemented as an operator in a class, leading to quite a tedious bit of coding. Compilers that are C++11 compliant enable you to program lambda functions and cut quite a bit of flab as shown in Listing 7.11.

LISTING 7.11   Using Lambda Functions to Display Elements in an Array and to Sort Them

```
0: #include <iostream>
1: #include <algorithm>
2: #include <vector>
3: using namespace std;
4:
5: void DisplayNums(vector<int>& DynArray)
6: {
7:    for_each (DynArray.begin(), DynArray.end(), \
8:             [](int Element) {cout << Element << " ";} );// lambda
9:
10:    cout << endl;
11: }
12:
13: int main()
14: {
15:    vector<int> MyNumbers;
16:    MyNumbers.push_back(501);
17:    MyNumbers.push_back(-1);
18:    MyNumbers.push_back(25);
19:    MyNumbers.push_back(-35);
20:
21:    DisplayNums(MyNumbers);
22:
23:    cout << "Sorting them in descending order" << endl;
24:
25:    sort (MyNumbers.begin(), MyNumbers.end(), \
26:          [](int Num1, int Num2) {return (Num2 < Num1); } );
27:
```

7

LISTING 7.11 Continued

```
28:    DisplayNums(MyNumbers);
29:
30:    return 0;
31: }
```

Output ▼

```
501 -1 25 -35
Sorting them in descending order
501 25 -1 -35
```

Analysis ▼

The program contains integers pushed into a dynamic array provided by the C++ Standard Library in the form of a `std::vector`, in Lines 15–19. The function `DisplayNums` uses the STL algorithm to iterate through each element in the array and display its value. In doing so, it uses a lambda function in Line 8 instead of what would've been a long unary function predicate. `std::sort` used in Line 25 also uses a binary predicate (Line 26) in the form of a lambda function that returns `true` if the second number is smaller than the first, effectively sorting the collection in an ascending order.

The syntax of a lambda function is the following:

```
[optional parameters](parameter list){ statements; }
```

Summary

In this lesson, you learned the basics of modular programming. You learned how functions can help you structure your code better and also help you reuse algorithms you write. You learned that functions can take parameters and return values, parameters can have default values that the caller can override, and parameters can also contain arguments passed by reference. You learned how to pass arrays, and you also learned how to program overloaded functions that have the same name and return type but different parameter lists.

Last but not the least, you got a sneak preview into what lambda functions are. Completely new as of C++11, lambda functions have the potential to change how C++ applications will be programmed henceforth, especially when using STL.

Q&A

Q What happens if I program a recursive function that doesn't end?

A Program execution doesn't end. That might not be bad, per se, for there are while(true) and for(;;) loops that do the same; however, a recursive function call consumes more and more stack space, which is finite and runs out, eventually causing an application crash due to a stack overflow.

Q Why not inline every function? It increases execution speed, right?

A That really depends. However, inlining every function results in functions that are used in multiple places to be placed at the point where they're called, and this results in code bloat. That apart, most modern compilers are better judges of what calls can be inlined and do so for the programmer, depending on the compiler's performance settings.

Q Can I supply default parameter values to all parameters in a function?

A Yes, that is definitely possible and recommended when that makes sense.

Q I have two functions, both called Area. One takes a radius and the other takes height. I want one to return float and the other to return double. Will this work?

A Function overloading needs both functions with the same name to also have the same return types. In this case, your compiler shows an error as the name has been used twice in what it expects to be two functions of different names.

Workshop

The Workshop provides quiz questions to help you solidify your understanding of the material covered and exercises to provide you with experience in using what you've learned. Try to answer the quiz and exercise questions before checking the answers in Appendix D, and be certain that you understand the answers before continuing to the next lesson.

Quiz

1. What is the scope of variables declared in a function's prototype?

2. What is the nature of the value passed to this function?

```
int Func(int &SomeNumber);
```

3. I have a function that invokes itself. What is such a function called?

7

4. I have declared two functions, both with the same name and return type but different parameter lists. What are these called?

5. Does the stack pointer point to the top, middle, or bottom of the stack?

Exercises

1. Write overloaded functions that calculate the volume of a sphere and a cylinder. The formulas are the following:

```
Volume of sphere = (4 * Pi * Radius * Radius * Radius) / 3
Volume of a cylinder = Pi * Radius * Radius * Height
```

2. Write a function that accepts an array of double as input.

3. **BUG BUSTERS:** What is wrong with the following code?

```cpp
#include <iostream>
using namespace std;

const double Pi = 3.1416;

void Area(double Radius, double Result)
{
   Result = Pi * Radius * Radius;
}

int main()
{
   cout << "Enter radius: ";
   double Radius = 0;
   cin >> Radius;

   double AreaFetched = 0;
   Area(Radius, AreaFetched);

   cout << "The area is: " << AreaFetched << endl;
   return 0;
}
```

4. **BUG BUSTERS:** What is wrong with the following function declaration?

```cpp
double Area(double Pi = 3.14, double Radius);
```

5. Write a function with return type void that still helps the caller calculate the area and circumference of a circle when supplied the radius.

LESSON 8
Pointers and References Explained

One of the biggest advantages of C++ is that it enables you to write high-level applications that are abstracted from the machine as well as those that work close to the board. Indeed, C++ enables you to tweak the performance of your application on a bytes and bits level. Understanding how pointers and references work is one step toward being able to write programs that are effective in their consumption of system resources.

In this lesson, you find out

- What pointers are

- What the free store is

- How to use operators new and delete to allocate and free memory

- How to write stable applications using pointers and dynamic allocation

- What references are

- Differences between pointers and references

- When to use a pointer and when to use references

What Is a Pointer?

Put simply, a *pointer* is a variable that stores an address in memory. Just the same way as a variable of type int is used to contain an integer value, a pointer variable is one that is used to contain a memory address, as illustrated in Figure 8.1.

FIGURE 8.1
Visualizing a
pointer.

Thus, a pointer is a variable, and like all variables a pointer occupies space in memory (in the case of Figure 8.1, at address 0x101). What's special about pointers is that the value contained in a pointer (in this case, 0x558) is interpreted as a memory address. So, a pointer is a special variable that *points to* a location in memory.

Declaring a Pointer

A pointer being a variable needs to be declared, too. You normally declare a pointer to point to a specific value type (for example, int). This would mean that the address contained in the pointer points to a location in the memory that holds an integer. You can also specify a pointer to a block of memory (also called a void pointer).

A pointer being a variable needs to be declared like all variables do:

```
PointedType * PointerVariableName;
```

As is the case with most variables, unless you initialize a pointer it will contain a random value. You don't want a random memory address to be accessed so you initialize a pointer to NULL. NULL is a value that can be checked against and one that cannot be a memory address:

```
PointedType * PointerVariableName = NULL; // initializing value
```

Thus, declaring a pointer to an integer would be:

```
int *pInteger = NULL; //
```

CAUTION

A pointer, like all data types you have learned, contains a junk value unless it has been initialized. This junk value is particularly dangerous in the case of a pointer because the value of the pointer is expected to contain an address. Uninitialized pointers can result in your program accessing invalid memory locations, resulting in a crash.

Determining the Address of a Variable Using the Reference Operator (&)

Variables are tools the language provides for you to work with data in the memory. This concept was explained in detail in Lesson 3, "Using Variables, Declaring Constants." Pointers are variables, too, but they're a special type that is used exclusively to contain a memory address.

If VarName is a variable, &VarName gives the address in memory where its value is placed.

So, if you have declared an integer, using the syntax that you're quite well acquainted with, such as:

```
int Age = 30;
```

&Age would be the address in memory where the value (30) is placed. Listing 8.1 demonstrates the concept of the memory address of an integer variable that is used to hold the value it contains.

LISTING 8.1   Determining the Addresses of an int and a double

```cpp
0: #include <iostream>
1: using namespace std;
2:
3: int main()
4: {
5:     int Age = 30;
6:     const double Pi = 3.1416;
7:
8:     // Use & to find the address in memory
9:     cout << "Integer Age is at: 0x" << hex << &Age << endl;
10:    cout << "Double Pi is located at: 0x" << hex << &Pi << endl;
11:
12:    return 0;
13: }
```

Output ▼

```
Integer Age is at: 0x0045FE00
Double Pi is located at: 0x0045FDF8
```

Analysis ▼

Note how referencing operator (&) has been used in Lines 9 and 10 to reveal the addresses of variables Age and constant Pi. The text 0x has been appended as a convention that is used when displaying hexadecimal numbers.

NOTE

You know that the amount of memory consumed by a variable is dependent on its type. Listing 3.4 in Lesson 3 uses `sizeof()` to demonstrate that the size of an integer is 4 bytes (on my system, using my compiler). So, using the preceding output that says that integer Age is located at address 0x0045FE08 and using the knowledge that `sizeof(int)` is 4, you know that the four bytes located in the range 0x0045FE00 to 0x0045FE04 belong to the integer Age.

NOTE

The referencing operator (&) is also called the address-of operator.

Using Pointers to Store Addresses

You have learned how to declare pointers and how to determine the address of a variable. You also know that pointers are variables that are used to hold memory addresses. It's time to connect these dots and use pointers to store the addresses obtained using the referencing operator (&).

Assume a variable declaration of the types you already know:

```
// Declaring a variable
Type VariableName = InitialValue;
```

To store the address of this variable in a pointer, you would declare a pointer to the same Type and initialize the pointer to the variable's address using the referencing operator (&):

```
// Declaring a pointer to the same type and initializing to address
Type* Pointer = &Variable;
```

Thus, if you have declared an integer, using the syntax that you're quite well acquainted with, such as

```
int Age = 30;
```

You would declare a pointer to the type `int` to hold the actual address where Age is stored, like this:

```
int* pInteger = &Age; // Pointer to integer Age
```

In Listing 8.2 you see how a pointer can be used to store an address fetched using the referencing operator (&).

LISTING 8.2 Demonstrating the Declaration and Initialization of a Pointer

```
0: #include <iostream>
1: using namespace std;
2:
3: int main()
4: {
5:     int Age = 30;
6:     int* pInteger = &Age;   // pointer to an int, initialized to &Age
7:
8:     // Displaying the value of pointer
9:     cout << "Integer Age is at: 0x" << hex << pIrteger << endl;
10:
11:     return 0;
12: }
```

Output ▼

```
Integer Age is at: 0x0045FE00
```

Analysis ▼

Essentially, the output of this code snippet is the same as the previous one because both the samples are displaying the same thing—the address in memory where Age is stored. The difference here is that the address is first assigned to a pointer at Line 6, and the value of the pointer (now the address) is displayed using cout at Line 9.

NOTE

> Your output might differ in addresses from those you see in these samples. In fact, the address of a variable might change at every run of the application on the very same computer.

Now that you know how to store an address in a pointer variable, it is easy to imagine that the same pointer variable can be reassigned a different memory address and made to point to a different value, as shown in Listing 8.3.

LISTING 8.3 Pointer Reassignment to Another Variable

```
0: #include <iostream>
1: using namespace std;
2:
3: int main()
4: {
5:     int Age = 30;
```

LISTING 8.3 Continued

```
 6:
 7:    int* pInteger = &Age;
 8:    cout << "pInteger points to Age now" << endl;
 9:
10:    // Displaying the value of pointer
11:    cout << "pInteger = 0x" << hex << pInteger << endl;
12:
13:    int DogsAge = 9;
14:    pInteger = &DogsAge;
15:    cout << "pInteger points to DogsAge now" << endl;
16:
17:    cout << "pInteger = 0x" << hex << pInteger << endl;
18:
19:    return 0;
20: }
```

Output ▼

```
pInteger points to Age now
pInteger = 0x002EFB34
pInteger points to DogsAge now
pInteger = 0x002EFB1C
```

Analysis ▼

This program indicates that one pointer to an integer, pInteger, can point to any integer. In Line 7, it has been initialized to &Age, hence containing the address of variable Age. In Line 14 the same pointer is assigned &DogsAge, pointing to another location in the memory that contains DogsAge. Correspondingly, the output indicates that the value of the pointer, that is the address being pointed to, changes as the two integers Age and DogsAge are, of course, stored in different locations in memory, 0x002EFB34 and 0x002EFB1C, respectively.

Access Pointed Data Using the Dereference Operator (*)

You have a pointer to data, containing a valid address. How do you access that location—that is, get or set data at that location? The answer lies in using the de-referencing operator (*). Essentially, if you have a valid pointer pData, use *pData to access the value stored at the address contained in the pointer. Operator (*) is demonstrated by Listing 8.4.

8

LISTING 8.4   Demonstrating the Use of the Dereference Operator (*) to Access
Integer Values

```
0: #include <icstream>
1: using namespace std;
2:
3: int main()
4: {
5:    int Age = 30;
6:    int DogsAge = 9;
7:
8:    cout << "Integer Age = " << Age << endl;
9:    cout << "Integer DogsAge = " << DogsAge << erdl;
10:
11:    int* pInteger = &Age;
12:    cout << "pInteger points to Age" << endl;
13:
14:    // Displaying the value of pointer
15:    cout << "pInteger = 0x" << hex << pInteger << endl;
16:
17:    // Displaying the value at the pointed location
18:    cout << "*pInteger = " << dec << *pInteger << endl;
19:
20:    pInteger = &DogsAge;
21:    cout << "pInteger points to DogsAge now" << erdl;
22:
23:    cout << "pInteger = 0x" << hex << pInteger << endl;
24:    cout << "*pInteger = ' << dec << *pInteger << endl;
25:
26:    return 0;
27: }
```

Output ▼

```
Integer Age = 30
Integer DogsAge = 9
pInteger points to Age
pInteger = 0x0025F788
*pInteger = 30
pInteger points to DogsAge now
pInteger = 0x0025F77C
*pInteger = 9
```

Analysis ▼

In addition to changing the address stored within a pointer as also in the previous sample
in Listing 8.3, this one also uses the dereference operator (*) with the same pointer variable pInteger to print the different values at these two addresses. Note Lines 18 and 24.

In both these lines, the integer pointed to by `pInteger` is accessed using the dereference operator (*). As the address contained in `pInteger` is changed at Line 20, the same pointer after this assignment accesses the variable `DogsAge`, displaying 9.

When the dereference operator (*) is used, the application essentially uses the address stored in the pointer as a starting point to fetch 4 bytes from the memory that belong to an integer (as this is a pointer to integers and `sizeof(int)` is 4). Thus, the validity of the address contained in the pointer is absolutely essential. By initializing the pointer to `&Age` in Line 11, you have ensured that the pointer contains a valid address. When you don't initialize the pointer, it can contain any random value (that existed in the memory location where the pointer variable is located) and dereference of that pointer usually results in an Access Violation—that is, accessing a memory location that your application was not authorized to.

NOTE | The dereferencing operator (*) is also called the indirection operator.

You have used the pointer in the preceding sample to read (get) values from the pointed memory location. Listing 8.5 shows what happens when `*pInteger` is used as an l-value—that is, assigned to instead of just being accessed.

LISTING 8.5   Manipulating Data Using a Pointer and the Dereference Operator (*)

```
0: #include <iostream>
1: using namespace std;
2:
3: int main()
4: {
5:     int DogsAge = 30;
6:     cout << "Initialized DogsAge = " << DogsAge << endl;
7:
8:     int* pAge = &DogsAge;
9:     cout << "pAge points to DogsAge" << endl;
10:
11:    cout << "Enter an age for your dog: ";
12:
13:    // store input at the memory pointed to by pAge
14:    cin >> *pAge;
15:
16:    // Displaying the address where age is stored
17:    cout << "Input stored using pAge at 0x" << hex << pAge << endl;
18:
19:    cout << "Integer DogsAge = " << dec << DogsAge << endl;
```

LISTING 8.5   Continued

```
20:
21:    return 0;
22: }
```

Output ▼

```
Initialized DogsAge = 30
pAge points to DogsAge
Enter an age for your dog: 10
Input stored using pAge at 0x0025FA18
Integer DogsAge = 10
```

Analysis ▼

The key step here is in Line 14 where the integer fed by the user is saved at the location stored in the pointer pAge. Note that even though you store the input number using the pointer pAge, Line 19 displays the variable DogsAge, yet shows that value you stored using the pointer. This is because pAge points to DogsAge, as initialized in Line 8. Any change to that memory location where DogsAge is stored, and where pAge points to, made using one is going to be reflected in the other.

What Is the `sizeof()` of a Pointer?

You have learned that the pointer is just another variable that contains a memory address. Hence, irrespective of the type that is being pointed to, the content of a pointer is an address—a number. The length of an address that is the number of bytes required to store it is a constant for a given system. The sizeof() a pointer is hence dependent on the compiler and the operating system the program has been compiled for and is *not* dependent on the nature of the data being pointed to, as Listing 8.6 demonstrates.

LISTING 8.6   Demonstrating That Pointers to Different Types Have the Same Sizes

```
0: #include <iostream>
1: using namespace std;
2:
3: int main()
4: {
5:     int Age = 30;
6:     double Pi = 3.1416;
7:     char SayYes = 'y';
8:
9:     // initialize pointers to addresses of the variables
10:    int* pInt = &Age;
11:    double* pDouble = &Pi;
```

LISTING 8.6   Continued

```
12:    char* pChar = &SayYes;
13:
14:    cout << "sizeof fundamental types -" << endl;
15:    cout << "sizeof(int) = " << sizeof(int) << endl;
16:    cout << "sizeof(double) = " << sizeof(double) << endl;
17:    cout << "sizeof(char) = " << sizeof(char) << endl;
18:
19:    cout << "sizeof pointers to fundamental types -" << endl;
20:    cout << "sizeof(pInt) = " << sizeof(pInt) << endl;
21:    cout << "sizeof(pDouble) = " << sizeof(pDouble) << endl;
22:    cout << "sizeof(pChar) = " << sizeof(pChar) << endl;
23:
24:    return 0;
25: }
```

Output ▼

```
sizeof fundamental types -
sizeof(int) = 4
sizeof(double) = 8
sizeof(char) = 1
sizeof pointers to fundamental types -
sizeof(pInt) = 4
sizeof(pDouble) = 4
sizeof(pChar) = 4
```

Analysis ▼

The output clearly shows that even though a sizeof(char) is 1 byte and a sizeof(double) is 8 bytes, the sizeof(pointer) is always constant at 4 bytes. This is because the amount of memory required to store an address is the same, irrespective of whether the address points to 1 byte or 8.

NOTE

The output for Listing 8.6 that displays that the sizeof a pointer is 4 bytes might be different than what you see on your system. The output was generated when the code was compiled using a 32-bit compiler. If you use a 64-bit compiler and run the program on a 64-bit system, you might see that the sizeof your pointer variable is 64 bits—that is, 8 bytes.

Dynamic Memory Allocation

When you write a program containing an array declaration such as

```
int Numbers[100]; // a static array of 100 integers
```

your program has two problems:

1. You are actually limiting the capacity of your program as it cannot store more than 100 numbers.

2. You are reducing the performance of the system in cases where only 1 number needs to be stored, yet space has been reserved for 100.

These problems exist because the memory allocation in an array as declared earlier is static and fixed by the compiler.

To program an application that is able to optimally consume memory resources on the basis of the needs of the user, you need to use dynamic memory allocation. This enables you to allocate more when you need more memory and release memory that you have in excess. C++ supplies you two operators, new and delete, to help you better manage the memory consumption of your application. Pointers being variables that are used to contain memory addresses play a critical role in efficient dynamic memory allocation.

Using Operators new and delete to Allocate and Release Memory Dynamically

You use new to allocate new memory blocks. The most frequently used form of new returns a pointer to the requested memory if successful or else throws an exception. When using new, you need to specify the data type for which the memory is being allocated:

```
Type* Pointer = new Type; // request memory for one element
```

You can also specify the number of elements you want to allocate that memory for (when you need to allocate memory for more than one element):

```
Type* Pointer = new Type[NumElements]; // request memory for NumElements
```

Thus, if you need to allocate integers, you use the following syntax:

```
int* pNumber = new int;  // get a pointer to an integer
int* pNumbers = new int[10];  // get a pointer to a block of 10 integers
```

NOTE   Note that new indicates a request for memory. There is no guarantee that a call for allocation always succeeds because this depends on the state of the system and the availability of memory resources.

Every allocation using new needs to be eventually released using an equal and opposite de-allocation via `delete`:

```
Type* Pointer = new Type;
delete Pointer;  // release memory allocated above for one instance of Type
```

This rule also applies when you request memory for multiple elements:

```
Type* Pointer = new Type[NumElements];
delete[] Pointer; // release block allocated above
```

NOTE ___

Note the usage of `delete[]` when you allocate a block using `new[...]` and `delete` when you allocate just an element using `new`.

If you don't release allocated memory after you stop using it, this memory remains reserved and allocated for your application. This in turn reduces the amount of system memory available for other applications to consume and possibly even makes the execution of your application slower. This is called a *leak* and should be avoided at all costs.

Listing 8.7 demonstrates memory dynamic allocation and deallocation.

LISTING 8.7   Accessing Memory Allocated Using new via Operator (*) and Releasing It Using delete

```cpp
0: #include <iostream>
1: using namespace std;
2:
3: int main()
4: {
5:    // Request for memory space for an int
6:    int* pAge = new int;
7:
8:    // Use the allocated memory to store a number
9:    cout << "Enter your dog's age: ";
10:   cin >> *pAge;
11:
12:   // use indirection operator* to access value
13:   cout << "Age " << *pAge << " is stored at 0x" << hex << pAge << endl;
14:
15:   delete pAge; // release memory
16:
17:   return 0;
18: }
```

Output ▼

```
Enter your dog's age: 9
Age 9 is stored at 0x00338120
```

8

Analysis ▼

Line 6 demonstrates the use of operator new to request space for an integer where you plan to store the dog's age as input by the user. Note that new returns a pointer, and that is the reason it is assigned to one. The age entered by the user is stored in this newly allocated memory using cin and the dereference operator (*) in Line 10. Line 13 displays this stored value using the dereference operator (*) again and also displays the memory address where the value is stored. Note that the address contained in pAge in Line 13 still is what was returned by new in Line 6 and hasn't changed since.

CAUTION

> Operator delete cannot be invoked on any address contained in a pointer, rather only those that have been returned by new and only those that have not already been released by a delete.
>
> Thus, the pointers seen in Listing 8.6 contain valid addresses, yet should not be released using delete because the addresses were not returned by a call to new.

Note that when you allocate for a range of elements using new...[...], you would de-allocate using delete[] as demonstrated by Listing 8.8.

LISTING 8.8 Allocating Using new[...] and Releasing It Using delete[]

```cpp
0: #include <iostream>
1: #include <string>
2: using namespace std;
3:
4: int main()
5: {
6:     cout << "Enter your name: ";
7:     string Name;
8:     cin >> Name;
9:
10:     // Add 1 to reserve space for a terminating null
11:     int CharsToAllocate = Name.length() + 1;
12:
13:     // request for memory to hold copy of input
14:     char* CopyOfName = new char [CharsToAllocate];
```

LISTING 8.8 Continued

```
15:
16:     // strcpy copies from a null-terminated string
17:     strcpy(CopyOfName, Name.c_str());
18:
19:     // Display the copied string
20:     cout << "Dynamically allocated buffer contains: " << CopyOfName << endl;
21:
22:     // Done using buffer? Delete
23:     delete[] CopyOfName;
24:
25:     return 0;
26: }
```

Output ▼

```
Enter your name: Siddhartha
Dynamically allocated buffer contains: Siddhartha
```

Analysis ▼

The most important lines in question are the `new` and `delete[]` operators used in Lines 11 and 23, respectively. What makes this sample different is the allocation of a block of memory with space for multiple elements as compared to Listing 8.7 that allocated for only one element. Such allocations for an array of elements need to be matched by de-allocation using `delete[]` to free memory when done. The number of characters to be allocated is calculated in Line 11 as one more than the number of characters entered by the user to accommodate for the terminating NULL character that is important in C-style strings. The need for this terminating NULL is also explained in Lesson 4, "Managing Arrays and Strings." The actual act of copying is done in Line 17 by `strcpy` that uses the `c_str()` function supplied by `std::string Name` as input to copy into the `char` buffer called `CopyOfName`.

NOTE ____ Operators `new` and `delete` allocate memory from the free store. The free store is a memory abstraction in the form of a pool of memory where your application can allocate (that is, reserve) memory to and de-allocate (that is, release) memory from.

to modify, but not others. For example, a function that calculates the area of a circle given radius sent as a pointer should not be allowed to modify the radius. This is where you use const pointers effectively to control what a function is allowed to modify and what it isn't as demonstrated by Listing 8.10.

LISTING 8.10 Use const Keyword in Calculating the Area of a Circle When Radius and Pi Are Supplied as Pointers

```
0: #include <iostream>
1: using namespace std;
2:
3: void CalcArea(const double* const pPi, // const pointer to const data
4:               const double* const pRadius, // i.e. nothing can be changed
5:               double* const pArea) //change pointed value, not address
6: {
7:     // check pointers before using.
8:     if (pPi && pRadius && pArea)
9:         *pArea = (*pPi) * (*pRadius) * (*pRadius);
10: }
11:
12: int main()
13: {
14:     const double Pi = 3.1416;
15:
16:     cout << "Enter radius of circle: ";
17:     double Radius = 0;
18:     cin >> Radius;
19:
20:     double Area = 0;
21:     CalcArea (&Pi, &Radius, &Area);
22:
23:     cout << "Area is = " << Area << endl;
24:
25:     return 0;
26: }
```

Output ▼

```
Enter radius of circle: 10.5
Area is = 346.361
```

Analysis ▼

Lines 3–5 demonstrate the two forms of const where both pRadius and pPi are supplied as "const pointers to const data," so that neither the pointer address nor the data being pointed to can be modified. pArea is evidently the parameter meant to store the output, for the value of the pointer (address) cannot be modified but the data being pointed to can be. Line 7 shows how pointer parameters to a function are checked for validity before using them. You don't want the function to calculate the area if the caller inadvertently sends a NULL pointer as any of the three parameters, for that would result in an application crash.

Similarities Between Arrays and Pointers

Don't you think that the sample in Listing 8.9 where the pointer was incremented using zero-based index to access the next integer in the memory has too many similarities to the manner in which arrays are indexed? When you declare an array of integers

```
int MyNumbers[5];
```

what the compiler does for you is to allocate a fixed amount of memory to hold five integers and give you a pointer to the first element in that array that is identified by the name you assign the array variable. In other words, MyNumbers is a pointer to the first element MyNumber[0]. Listing 8.11 highlights this correlation.

LISTING 8.11   Demonstrate That the Array Variable Is a Pointer to the First Element

```
0: #include <iostream>
1: using namespace std;
2:
3: int main()
4: {
5:     // Static array of 5 integers
6:     int MyNumbers[5];
7:
8:     // array assigned to pointer to int
9:     int* pNumbers = MyNumbers;
10:
11:     // Display address contained in pointer
12:     cout << "pNumbers = 0x" << hex << pNumbers << endl;
13:
14:     // Address of first element of array
15:     cout << "&MyNumbers[0] = 0x" << hex << &MyNumbers[0] << endl;
16:
17:     return 0;
18: }
```

Output ▼

```
pNumbers = 0x004BFE8C
&MyNumbers[0] = 0x004BFE8C
```

Analysis ▼

This simple program demonstrates that an array variable can be assigned to a pointer of the same type as seen in Line 9, essentially confirming that an array is akin to a pointer. Lines 12 and 15 demonstrate that the address stored in the pointer is the same as the address where the first element in the array (at index 0) is placed in memory. This program tells you that an array is a pointer to the first element in it.

Should you need to access the second element via the expression MyNumbers[1], you can also access the same using the pointer pNumbers with syntax *(pNumbers + 1). The third element is accessed in the static array using MyNumbers[2], whereas the third element is accessed in the dynamic array using syntax *(pNumbers - 2).

Because array variables are essentially pointers, it should be possible to use the dereference operator (*) that you have used with pointers to work with arrays. Similarly, it should be possible to use the array operator ([ ]) to work with pointers as demonstrated by Listing 8.12.

LISTING 8.12 Accessing Elements in an Array Using the Dereference Operator (*) and Using the Array Operator ([ ]) with a Pointer

```
0: #include <iostream>
1: using namespace std;
2:
3: int main()
4: {
5:    const int ARRAY_LEN = 5;
6:
7:    // Static array of 5 integers, initialized
8:    int MyNumbers[ARRAY_LEN] = {24, -1, 365, -999, 2011};
9:
10:    // Pointer initialized to first element in array
11:    int* pNumbers = MyNumbers;
12:
13:    cout << "Displaying array using pointer syntax, operator*" << endl;
14:    for (int Index = 0; Index < ARRAY_LEN; ++Index)
15:       cout << "Element " << Index << " = " << *(MyNumbers + Index) << endl;
16:
17:    cout << "Displaying array using pointer with array syntax, operator[]" <<
       endl;
18:    for (int Index = 0; Index < ARRAY_LEN; ++Index)
19:       cout << "Element " << Index << " = " << pNumbers[Index] << endl;
20:
21:    return 0;
22: }
```

Output ▼

```
Displaying array using pointer syntax, operator*
Element 0 = 24
Element 1 = -1
Element 2 = 365
Element 3 = -999
Element 4 = 2011
Displaying array using pointer with array syntax, operator[]
Element 0 = 24
Element 1 = -1
Element 2 = 365
Element 3 = -999
Element 4 = 2011
```

Analysis ▼

The application contains a static array of five integers initialized to five initial values in Line 8. The application displays the contents of this array, using two alternative routes—one using the array variable with the indirection operator (*) in Line 15 and the other using the pointer variable with the array operator ([ ]) in Line 19.

Thus, what this program demonstrates is that both array MyNumbers and pointer pNumbers actually exhibit pointer behavior. In other words, an array declaration is similar to a pointer that will be created to operate within a fixed range of memory. Note that one can assign an array to a pointer as in Line 11, but one cannot assign a pointer to an array because the nature of an array is static and the array hence cannot be a l-value.

CAUTION

> It is important to remember that pointers that are allocated dynamically using operator new still need to be released using operator delete, even if you used syntax similar to that of a static array.
>
> If you forget this, your application leaks memory, and that's bad.

Common Programming Mistakes When Using Pointers

C++ enables you to allocate memory dynamically so that the memory consumption of your application is optimal. Unlike newer languages such as C# and Java that are based on a run-time environment, C++ does not feature an automatic garbage collector that cleans up the memory your program has allocated but can't use. Because pointers can get a bit tricky, a programmer has a host of opportunities to make mistakes.

Memory Leaks

This is probably one of the most frequent problems with C++ applications: The longer they run, the larger the amount of memory they consume and the slower the system gets. This typically happens when the programmer did not ensure that his application releases memory allocated dynamically using new with a matching call to delete after the block of memory is no longer required.

It is up to you—the programmer—to ensure that all allocated memory is also released by your application. Something like this should never be allowed to happen:

```
int* pNumbers = new int [5]; // initial allocation
// use pointer pNumbers
...
// forget to release using delete[] pNumbers;
...
// make another allocation and overwrite the pointer
pNumbers = new int[10]; // leaks the previously allocated memory
```

When Pointers Don't Point to Valid Memory Locations

When you dereference a pointer using operator (*) to access the pointed value, you need to be 100% sure that the pointer contains a valid memory location, else your program will either crash or misbehave. Logical as this may seem, invalid pointers are quite a common reason for application crashes. Pointers can be invalid for a range of reasons, all being attributed to poor memory management. A typical case where a pointer might be invalid is shown in Listing 8.13.

LISTING 8.13   A Demonstration of Bad Programming Using Invalid Pointers

```
0: #include <iostream>
1: using namespace std;
2:
3: int main()
4: {
5:     // uninitialized pointer (bad)
6:     int* pTemperature;
7:
8:     cout << "Is it sunny (y/n)?" << endl;
9:     char UserInput = 'y';
10:    cin >> UserInput;
```

LISTING 8.13   Continued

```
11:
12:    if (UserInput == 'y')
13:    {
14:       pTemperature = new int;
15:       *pTemperature = 30;
16:    }
17:
18:    // pTemperature contains invalid value if user entered 'n'
19:    cout << "Temperature is: " << *pTemperature;
20:
21:    // delete also being invoked for those cases new wasn't done
22:    delete pTemperature;
23:
24:    return 0;
25: }
```

Output ▼

```
Is it sunny (y/n)? y
Temperature is: 30
```

Second run:

```
Is it sunny (y/n)? n
<CRASH!>
```

Analysis ▼

There are many problems in the program, some already commented in the code. Note how memory is allocated and assigned to the pointer in Line 14, which is conditionally executed when the user presses *y* for yes. For all other inputs of the user, this `if` block is not executed, and the pointer `pTemperature` remains invalid. Thus, when the user presses *n* in the second run, the application crashes because `pTemperature` contains an invalid memory address and dereferencing an invalid pointer in Line 19 causes problems.

Similarly, invoking `delete` on this pointer, which has not been allocated for using `new` as seen in Line 22, is equally wrong. Note that if you have a copy of a pointer, you need to be calling `delete` on only one of them (you also need to avoid having copies of a pointer floating around).

A better (safer, more stable) version of the program in Listing 8.13 is one where pointers are initialized, used where their values are valid, and released only once but only when valid.

Dangling Pointers (Also Called Stray or Wild Pointers)

Note that any valid pointer is invalid after it has been released using `delete`. So, if the pointer `pTemperature` were to be used after Line 22, even in those cases where the user did press `y` and the pointer was valid until this point, it gets invalidated after the call to `delete` and should not be used.

To avoid this problem, many programmers assign NULL to a pointer when initializing it or after it has been deleted and check a pointer for validity using it before dereferencing it using operator (`*`).

Pointer Programming Best-Practices

There are some basic rules when it comes to using pointers in your application that will make living with them easier.

DO	DON'T
DO always initialize pointer variables, else they contain junk values. These junk values are interpreted as address locations, but those your application is not authorized to access. If you cannot initialize a pointer to a valid address returned by new or another valid variable, initialize to NULL.	**DON'T** access a block of memory or use a pointer after it has been released using `delete`. **DON'T** invoke delete on a memory address more than once. **DON'T** leak memory by forgetting to invoke delete when done using an allocated block of memory.
DO check pointers for NULL before using them. Checking for NULL will ensure that pointers that have not been assigned valid address in statements following their declaration (where they're initialized to NULL) cannot be used (like they erroneously were in Listing 8.13).	
DO ensure that pointers are programmed in a way that they're used when their validity is ensured, else your program might encounter a crash.	
DO remember to release memory allocated using new by using `delete`, else your application will leak memory and reduce system performance.	

Having learned some programming best practices for using pointers, it's time to correct the extremely faulty code in Listing 8.13 and use the code demonstrated in Listing 8.14.

LISTING 8.14 Safer Pointer Programming, a Correction of Listing 8.13

```
 0: #include <iostream>
 1: using namespace std;
 2:
 3: int main()
 4: {
 5:     cout << "Is it sunny (y/n)? ";
 6:     char UserInput = 'y';
 7:     cin >> UserInput;
 8:
 9:     if (UserInput == 'y')
10:     {
11:         // initialized pointer (good)
12:         int* pTemperature = new int;
13:         *pTemperature = 30;
14:
15:         cout << "Temperature is: " << *pTemperature << endl;
16:
17:         // done using pointer? delete
18:         delete pTemperature;
19:     }
20:
21:     return 0;
22: }
```

Output ▼

```
Is it sunny (y/n)? y
Temperature is: 30
```

Next run:

```
Is it sunny (y/n)? n
```

(Ends without crashing)

Analysis ▼

The main difference is that the pointer is created when needed—that is, when the user presses *y*—and it is initialized on creation as seen in Line 12. The deletion of memory also happens with the same block, thus there are no cases where the pointer is used (in dereference or in call `delete`) when it had not been assigned a valid memory location.

Checking If Allocation Request Using new Succeeded

new succeeds unless asked for an unusually large amount of memory or if the system is in a critical state where it has little to spare. There are applications that need to make requests for large chunks of memory (for example, database applications), and it is generally important to not assume memory allocation to be successful. C++ provides you with two possible methods to ensure that your pointer is valid. The default method uses exceptions wherein unsuccessful allocations result in exception of the form std::bad_alloc to be thrown. This results in the execution of your application being disrupted, and unless you have programmed an exception handler, your application crashes with an error message akin to "unhandled exception."

Lesson 28, "Exception Handling," discusses solving this problem in detail. Listing 8.15 gives you a sneak preview of how exception handling can be used to check for failed allocation requests.

LISTING 8.15   Handle Exceptions, Exit Gracefully When new Fails

```
0: #include <iostream>
1: using namespace std;
2:
3: int main()
4: {
5:    try
6:    {
7:        // Request lots of memory space
8:        int* pAge = new int [336870911];
9:
10:       // Use the allocated memory
11:
12:       delete[] pAge;
13:    }
14:    catch (bad_alloc)
15:    {
16:        cout << "Memory allocation failed. Ending program" << endl;
17:    }
18:    return 0;
19: }
```

Output ▼

```
Memory allocation failed. Ending program
```

Analysis ▼

This program might execute differently on your computer. My environment could not successfully allocate the requested space for 536870911 integers. Had I not programmed an exception handler (the catch block you see in Lines 14–17), the program would have ended quite disgracefully. When using debug mode binaries built using Microsoft Visual Studio, program execution will produce output as shown in Figure 8.2.

FIGURE 8.2
Program Crash
In Absence Of
Exception Handling
in Listing 8.15
(Debug build using
MSVC compiler).

Debug mode binaries have exception handlers inserted by the development environment, and these intervene using the message above. In release mode, the OS (in this case Windows) terminates the application quite unceremoniously as shown by Figure 8.3.

FIGURE 8.3
Program Crash
In Absence Of
Exception Handling
in Listing 8.15
(Release build).

When your application crashes as seen above, it is terminated by the OS and in the absence of an exception handler you have not had the chance to even say "good-bye."

The presence of the exception handler resulted in the application being able to make a decent exit after telling the user that a problem has been encountered, rather than letting the OS display a crash message.

There is a variant of new called new(nothrow) that does not throw an exception, rather results in the operator new returning NULL to the pointer that can be checked for validity before it is used. See Listing 8.16.

LISTING 8.16   Using new(nothrow) That Returns NULL When Allocation Fails

```
0: #include <iostream>
1: using namespace std;
2:
3: int main()
4: {
5:     // Request lots of memory space, use nothrow version
6:     int* pAge = new(nothrow) int [0x1fffffff];
7:
8:     if (pAge) // check pAge != NULL
9:     {
10:        // Use the allocated memory
11:        delete[] pAge;
12:    }
13:    else
14:        cout << "Memory allocation failed. Ending program" << endl;
15:
16:    return 0;
17: }
```

Output ▼

```
Memory allocation failed. Ending program
```

Analysis ▼

The same program using new(nothrow) that returned NULL as the requested memory allocation failed instead of throwing std::bad_alloc as the previous one in Listing 8.15 did. Both forms are good, and the choice is for you to make.

What Is a Reference?

A reference is an alias for a variable. When you declare a reference, you need to initialize it to a variable. Thus, the reference variable is just a different way to access the data stored in the variable being referenced.

You would declare a reference using the reference operator (&) as seen in the following statement:

```
VarType Original = Value;
VarType& ReferenceVariable = Original;
```

To further understand how to declare references and use them, see Listing 8.17.

LISTING 8.17 Demonstrating That References Are Aliases for the Assigned Value

```
0: #include <iostream>
1: using namespace std;
2:
3: int main()
4: {
5:    int Original = 30;
6:    cout << "Original = " << Original << endl;
7:    cout << "Original is at address: " << hex << &Original << endl;
8:
9:    int& Ref = Original;
10:    cout << "Ref is at address: " << hex << &Ref << endl;
11:
12:    int& Ref2 = Ref;
13:    cout << "Ref2 is at address: " << hex << &Ref2 << endl;
14:    cout << "Ref2 gets value, Ref2 = " << dec << Ref2 << endl;
15:
16:    return 0;
17: }
```

Output ▼

```
Original = 30
Original is at address: 0044FB5C
Ref is at address: 0044FB5C
Ref2 is at address: 0044FB5C
Ref2 gets value, Ref2 = 30
```

Analysis ▼

The output demonstrates that references, irrespective of whether they're initialized to the original variable as seen in Line 9 or to a reference as seen in Line 12, address the same location in memory where the original is contained. Thus, references are true aliases— that is, just another name for Original. Displaying the value using Ref2 in Line 14 gets the same value as the Original in Line 6 because Ref2 aliases Original and is contained in the same location in memory.

What Makes References Useful?

References enable you to work with the memory location they are initialized to. This makes references particularly useful when programming functions. As you learned in Lesson 7, "Organizing Code with Functions," a typical function is declared like this:

```
ReturnType DoSomething(Type Parameter);
```

Function DoSomething() is invoked like this:

```
ReturnType Result = DoSomething(argument); // function call
```

The preceding code would result in the argument being copied into Parameter, which is then used by the function DoSomething(). This copying step can be quite an overhead if the argument in question consumes a lot of memory. Similarly, when DoSomething() returns a value, it is copied again into Result. It would be ideal if we could avoid or eliminate the copy steps, enabling the function to work directly on the data in the caller's stack. References enable you to co_ust that.

A version of the function without the copy step looks like this:

```
ReturnType DoSomething(Type& Parameter); // note the reference&
```

This function would be invoked as the following:

```
ReturnType Result = DoSomething(argument);
```

As the argument is being passed by reference, Parameter is not a copy of argument rather an alias of the latter, much like Ref in Listing 8.17. Additionally, a function that accepts a parameter as a reference can optionally return values using reference parameters. See Listing 8.18 to understand how functions can use references instead of return values.

LISTING 8.18 Function That Calculates Square Returned n a Parameter by Reference

```
 0: #include <iostream>
 1: using namespace std;
 2:
 3: void ReturnSquare(int& Number)
 4: {
 5:     Number *= Number;
 6: }
 7:
 8:
 9: int main()
10: {
11:     cout << "Enter a number you wish to square: ";
12:     int Number = 0;
13:     cin >> Number;
14:
15:     ReturnSquare(Number);
16:     cout << "Square is: " << Number << endl;
17:
18:     return 0;
19: }
```

Output ▼

```
Enter a number you wish to square: 5
Square is: 25
```

Analysis ▼

The function that performs the operation of squaring is in Lines 3–6. Note how it accepts the number to be squared as a parameter by reference and returns the result in the same. Had you forgotten to mark the parameter Number as a reference (&), the result would not reach the calling function main() as ReturnSquare() would then perform its operations on a local copy of Number and that would be destroyed when the function exits. Using references, you ensure that ReturnSquare() is operating in the same address space where Number in main() is defined. Thus, the result of the operation is available in main() even after the function ReturnSquare() has exited.

In this sample, the input parameter containing the number sent by the user has been modified. If you need both values, the original and the square, you can have the function accept two parameters: one that contains the input and the other that supplies the square.

Using Keyword const on References

You might need to have references that are not allowed to change the value of the original variable being aliased. Using const when declaring such references is the way to achieve that:

```
int Original = 30;
const int& ConstRef = Original;
ConstRef = 40; // Not allowed: ConstRef can't change value in Original
int& Ref2 = ConstRef; // Not allowed: Ref2 is not const
const int& ConstRef2 = ConstRef; // OK
```

Passing Arguments by Reference to Functions

One of the major advantages of references is that they allow a called function to work on parameters that have not been copied from the calling function, resulting in significant performance improvements. However, as the called function works using parameters directly on the stack of the calling function, it is often important to ensure that the called function cannot change the value of the variable at the caller's end. References that are defined as const help you do just that, as demonstrated by Listing 8.19. A const reference parameter cannot be used as an l-value, so any attempt at assigning to it causes a compilation failure.

LISTING 8.19   Using const Reference to Ensure That the Calling Function Cannot Modify a Value Sent by Reference

```
0: #include <iostream>
1: using namespace std;
2:
3: void CalculateSquare(const int& Number, int& Result) // note "const'
4: {
5:     Result = Number*Number;
6: }
7:
8: int main()
9: {
10:     cout << "Enter a number you wish to square: ";
11:     int Number = 0;
12:     cin >> Number;
13:
14:     int Square = 0;
15:     CalculateSquare(Number, Square);
16:     cout << Number << "^2 = " << Square << endl;
17:
18:     return 0;
19: }
```

Output ▼

```
Enter a number you wish to square: 27
27^2 = 729
```

Analysis ▼

In contrast to the previous program where the variable that sent the number to be squared also held the result, this one uses two variables—one to send the number to be squared and the other to hold the result of the operation. To ensure that the number being sent cannot be modified, it has been marked as a const reference using the const keyword, as shown in Line 3. This automatically makes parameter Number an input parameter—one whose value cannot be modified.

As an experiment, you may modify Line 5 to return the square using the same logic shown in the Listing 8.18:

```
Number *= Number;
```

You are certain to face a compilation error that tells you that a const value cannot be modified. Thus const references are a powerful tool supplied by C++ that indicate a parameter being an input parameter and at the same time ensure that the value being passed by reference cannot be modified by the called function. It might seem trivial at first, but in a multiprogrammer environment where the person writing the first version might be different than the one enhancing it or correcting it, using const references makes an important difference to the quality of programming.

Summary

In this lesson you learned about pointers and references. You learned how pointers can be used to access and manipulate memory and how they're a tool that assists in dynamic memory allocation. You learned operators new and delete that can be used to allocate memory for an element. You learned that their variants new…[] and delete[] help you allocate memory for an array of data. You were introduced to traps in pointer programming and dynamic allocation and found out that releasing dynamically allocated memory is important to avoiding leaks. References are aliases and are a powerful alternative to using pointers when passing arguments to functions in that references are guaranteed to be valid. You learned of "const correctness" when using pointers and references and will hopefully henceforth declare functions with the most restrictive level of const-ness in parameters as possible.

Q&A

Q Why dynamically allocate when you can do with static arrays where you don't need to worry about deallocation?

A Static arrays have a fixed size and will neither scale upward if your application needs more memory nor will they optimize if your application needs less. This is where dynamic memory allocation makes a difference.

Q I have two pointers:

```
int* pNumber = new int;
int* pCopy = pNumber;
```

Am I not better off calling delete using both to ensure that the memory is gone?

A That would be wrong. You are allowed to invoke delete only once on the address returned by new. Also, you would ideally avoid having two pointers pointing to the same address because performing delete on any one would invalidate the other. Your program should also not be written in a way that you have any uncertainty about the validity of pointers used.

8

Q When should I use `new(nothrow)`?

A If you don't want to handle the exception `std::bad_alloc`, you use the nothrow version of operator `new` that returns NULL if the requested allocation fails.

Q I can call a function to calculate area using the following two methods:

```
void CalculateArea (const double* const pRadius, double* const pArea);
void CalculateArea (const double& radius, double& area);
```

Which variant should I prefer?

A The latter, using references as references, is not invalid, whereas pointers can be. Besides, it's simpler, too.

Q I have two pointers:

```
int Number = 30;
const int* pNumber = &Number;
```

I understand that I cannot change the value of `Number` using the pointer `pNumber` due to the const declaration. Can I assign `pNumber` to a non-const pointer and then use it to manipulate the value contained in integer `Number`?

A No, you cannot change the const-correctness of the pointer:

```
int* pAnother = pNumber; // cannot assign pointer to const to a non-const
```

Q Why should I bother passing values to a function by reference?

A You don't need to so long as it doesn't affect you much. However, if your function parameters accept objects that are quite heavy (large in bytes), then passing by value would be quite an expensive operation. Your function call would be a lot more efficient in using references. Remember to use const generously, except where the function needs to store a result in a variable.

Q What is the difference between these two declarations:

```
int MyNumbers[100];
int* MyArrays[100];
```

A `MyNumbers` is an array of integers—that is, `MyNumbers` is a pointer to a memory location that holds 100 integers, pointing to the first at index 0. It is the static alternative of the following:

```
int* MyNumbers = new int [100]; // dynamically allocated array
// use MyNumbers
delete MyNumbers;
```

`MyArrays`, on the other hand, is an array of 100 pointers, each pointer being capable of pointing to an integer or an array of integers.

Workshop

The Workshop provides quiz questions to help you solidify your understanding of the material covered and exercises to provide you with experience in using what you've learned. Try to answer the quiz and exercise questions before checking the answers in Appendix D, and be certain you understand the answers before continuing to the next lesson.

Quiz

1. Why can't you assign a const reference to a non-const reference?

2. Are new and delete functions?

3. What is the nature of value contained in a pointer variable?

4. What operator would you use to access the data pointed by a pointer?

Exercises

1. What is the display when these statements are executed:

```
0: int Number = 3;
1: int* pNum1 = &Number;
2:_*pNum1 = 20;
3: int* pNum2 = pNum1;
4: Number *= 2;
5: cout << *pNum2;
```

2. What are the similarities and differences between these three overloaded functions:

```
int DoSomething(int Num1, int Num2);
int DoSomething(int& Num1, int& Num2);
int DoSomething(int* pNum1, int* pNum2);
```

3. How would you change the declaration of pNum1 in Exercise 1 at Line 1 so as to make the assignment at Line 3 invalid? (*Hint:* It has something to do with ensuring that pNum1 cannot change the data pointed to.)

4. **BUG BUSTERS:** What is wrong with this code?

```
#include <iostream>
using namespace std;
int main()
{
```

```
        int *pNumber = new int;
        pNumber = 9;
        cout << "The value at pNumber: " << *pNumber;
        delete pNumber;
        return 0;
}
```

5. BUG BUSTERS: What is wrong with this code?

```
#include <iostream>
using namespace std;
int main()
{
    int pNumber = new int;
    int* pNumberCopy = pNumber;
    *pNumberCopy = 30;
    cout << *pNumber;
    delete pNumberCopy;
    delete pNumber;
    return 0;
}
```

6. What is the output of the above program when corrected?

LESSON 9
Classes and Objects

So far you have explored the structure of a simple program that starts execution at main() and enables you to declare local and global variables and constants and branch your execution logic into function modules that can take parameters and return values. All this is very similar to a procedural language like C, which has no object-orientation to it. In other words, you need to learn about managing data and connecting methods to it.

In this lesson, you will learn

- What classes are

- How classes help you consolidate data with methods (akin to functions) that work on them

- About constructors, copy constructors, and destructors

- How C++11 helps improve performance via the move constructor

- Object-oriented concepts of encapsulation and abstraction

- What this pointer is about

- What a struct is and how it differs from class

The Concept of Classes and Objects

Imagine you are writing a program that models a human being, like yourself. This human being needs to have an identity: a name, a date of birth, a place of birth, and a gender. The human can perform certain functions, such as talk and introduce him- or herself, among others. Now, the former information is data about the human being, whereas the latter information comprises functions as illustrated by Figure 9.1.

FIGURE 9.1
A broad representation of a human.

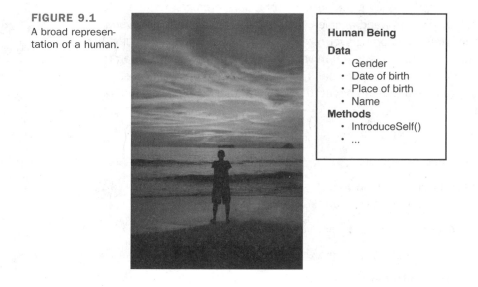

Human Being

Data
- Gender
- Date of birth
- Place of birth
- Name

Methods
- IntroduceSelf()
- ...

To model a human, what you now need is a construct that enables you to group within it the attributes that define a human (data) *and* the activities a human can perform (methods that are similar to functions) using the available attributes. This construct is the *class*.

Declaring a Class

Declaration of a class involves the usage of keyword class followed by the name of the class, followed by a statement block {…} that encloses a set of member attributes and methods within curly braces, finally terminated by a semicolon.

A declaration of a class is akin to the declaration of a function. It tells the compiler about the class and its properties. Declaration of a class alone does not make a difference to the execution of a program, as the class needs to be used just the same way as a function needs to be invoked.

A class that models a human looks like the following (ignore syntactic short-comings for the moment):

```
class Human
{
    // Data attributes:
    string Name;
    string DateOfBirth;
    string PlaceOfBirth;
    string Gender;

    // Methods:
    void Talk(string TextToTalk);
    void IntroduceSelf();
    ...
};
```

Needless to say, IntroduceSelf() uses Talk() and some of the data attributes that are grouped within class Human. Thus, in keyword class, C++ has provided you with a powerful way to create your own data type that allows you to *encapsulate* attributes and functions that work using those. All attributes of a class, in this case Name, DateOfBirth, PlaceOfBirth, and Gender, and all functions declared within it, namely Talk() and IntroduceSelf(), are called members of class Human.

Encapsulation, which is the ability to logically group data and methods that work using it, is a very important property of Object Oriented Programming.

NOTE   *Methods* are essentially functions that are members of a class.

Instantiating an Object of a Class

A class is like a blueprint, and declaring a class alone has no effect on the execution of a program. The real-world avatar of a class at runtime is an object. To use the features of a class, you typically instantiate an object of that class and use that object to access its member methods and attributes.

Instantiating an object of type class Human is similar to creating an instance of another type, say double:

```
double Pi = 3.1415;  // a double declared as a local variable (on stack)
Human Tom;  // An object of class Human declared as a local variable
```

Alternatively, you would dynamically allocate for an instance of class Human as you would an int using new:

```
int* pNumber = new int;  // an integer allocated dynamically on free store
delete pNumber;  // de-allocating the memory
```

```
Human* pAnotherHuman = new Human(); // dynamically allocated Human
delete pAnotherHuman;  // de-allocating memory allocated for a Human
```

Accessing Members Using the Dot Operator .

An example of a human would be Tom, male, born in 1970 in Alabama. Instance Tom is an object of class Human, an avatar of the class that exists in reality, that is at runtime:

```
Human Tom;  // an instance of Human
```

As the class declaration demonstrates, Tom has attributes such as DateOfBirth that can be accessed using the dot operator (.):

```
Tom.DateOfBirth = "1970";
```

This is because attribute DateOfBirth belongs to class Human being a part of its blueprint as seen in the class declaration. This attribute exists in reality—that is, at runtime—only when an object has been instantiated. The dot operator (.) helps you access attributes of an object.

Ditto for methods such as IntroduceSelf():

```
Tom.IntroduceSelf();
```

If you have a pointer pTom to an instance of class Human, you can either use the pointer operator (->) to access members, as explained in the next section, or use the indirection operator (*) to reference the object following the dot operator.

```
Human* pTom = new Human();
(*pTom).IntroduceSelf();
```

Accessing Members Using the Pointer Operator (->)

If an object has been instantiated on the free store using new or if you have a pointer to an object, then you use the pointer operator (->) to access the member attributes and functions:

```
Human* pTom = new Human();
pTom->DateOfBirth = "1970";
pTom->IntroduceSelf();
delete pTom;

// Alternatively when you have a pointer:
Human Tom;
Human* pTom = &Tom; // Assign address using reference operator&
pTom->DateOfBirth = "1970"; // is equivalent to Tom.DateOfBirth = "1970";
pTom->IntroduceSelf(); // is equivalent to Tom.IntroduceSelf();
```

A compile-worthy form of class Human featuring keywords such as private and public is demonstrated by Listing 9.1.

LISTING 9.1   A Compile-worthy Class Human

```
0: #include <iostream>
1: #include <string>
2: using namespace std;
3:
4: class Human
5: {
6: private:
7:     string Name;
8:     int Age;
9:
10: public:
11:     void SetName (string HumansName)
12:     {
13:         Name = HumansName;
14:     }
15:
16:     void SetAge(int HumansAge)
17:     {
18:         Age = HumansAge;
19:     }
20:
21:     void IntroduceSelf()
22:     {
23:         cout << "I am " + Name << " and am ";
24:         cout << Age << " years old" << endl;
25:     }
26: };
27:
28: int main()
29: {
30:     // Constructing an object of class Human with attribute Name as "Adam"
31:     Human FirstMan;
32:     FirstMan.SetName("Adam");
33:     FirstMan.SetAge(30);
34:
35:     // Constructing an object of class Human with attribute Name as "Eve"
36:     Human FirstWoman;
37:     FirstWoman.SetName("Eve");
38:     FirstWoman.SetAge (28);
39:
40:     FirstMan.IntroduceSelf();
41:     FirstWoman.IntroduceSelf();
42: }
```

Output ▼

```
I am Adam and am 30 years old
I am Eve and am 28 years old
```

Analysis ▼

Lines 4–26 demonstrate the construction of a very basic C++ class. These need to be viewed from a very practical point of view, ignoring terms and concepts you don't understand at first sight because they are discussed in detail later in this lesson. Focus on the structure of class Human and how this class has been utilized in main().

This class contains two private variables, one of type string called Name at Line 7 and another of type int called Age at Line 8, and a few public functions (also called methods), SetName(), SetAge(), and IntroduceSelf() at Lines 11, 16, and 21, that use the private variables. Lines 31 and 36 in main() create two objects of class Human, respectively. The lines following this creation of objects set the member variables of the objects FirstMan and FirstWoman using methods SetName() and SetAge() that are called accessor methods. Note how Lines 40 and 41 invoke method IntroduceSelf() on the two objects to create two distinct lines in the output that utilize the member variables you set in the previous lines.

Did you notice keywords private and public in Listing 9.1? It's time you learned features that C++ supplies to help you protect attributes your class should keep hidden from those using it.

Keywords public and private

Each of us has a lot of information. Some of this information is available to people around us—for example, our names. This information can be called public. However, certain attributes are those that you might not want the world to see or know—for example, your income. This information is private and often kept a secret.

C++ enables you to model class attributes and methods as public—implying one with an object of the class can invoke them—or private—implying that only artifacts that belong to the class (or its "friends") can invoke those private members. C++ keywords public and private help you as the designer of a class decide what parts of a class can be invoked from outside it, for instance, from main(), and what cannot.

What advantages does this ability to mark attributes or methods as private present you as the programmer? Consider the declaration of class Human ignoring all but the member attribute Age:

```
class Human
{
private:
    // Private member data:
    int Age;
    string Name;

public:
    int GetAge()
    {
        return Age;
    }

    void SetAge(int InputAge)
    {
        Age = InputAge;
    }

// ...Other members and declarations
};
```

Assume an instance of a Human called Eve:

```
Human Eve;
```

When the user of this instance tries to access Eve's age with

```
cout << Eve.Age; // compile error
```

then this user would get a compile error akin to "Error: Human::Age—cannot access private member declared in class Human." The only permissible way to know the Age would be to ask for it via public method GetAge() supplied by class Human and implemented in a way the programmer of the class thought was an appropriate way to expose the Age:

```
cout << Eve.GetAge(); // OK
```

If the programmer of class Human so desires, he could use GetAge() to show Eve as younger than she is! In other words, this means C++ allows the class to control what attributes it wants to expose and how it wants to expose the same. If there were no GetAge() public member method implemented by class Human, the class would effectively have ensured that the user cannot query Age at all. This feature can be useful in situations that are explained later in this lesson.

Similarly, Human::Age cannot be assigned directly either:

```
Eve.Age = 22; // compile error
```

The only permissible way to set the age is via method SetAge():

```
Eve.SetAge(22); // OK
```

This has many advantages. The current implementation of SetAge() does nothing but directly set the member variable Human::Age. However, you can use SetAge() to verify the Age being set is non-zero and not negative and thus validate external input:

```
class Human
{
private:
   int Age;

public:
   void SetAge(int InputAge)
   {
      if (InputAge > 0)
         Age = InputAge;
   }
};
```

Thus, C++ enables the designer of the class to control how data attributes of the class are accessed and manipulated.

Abstraction of Data via Keyword `private`

While allowing you to design a class as a container that encapsulates data and methods that operate on that data, C++ empowers you to decide what information is unreachable to the outside world (that is, unavailable outside the class) via keyword private. At the same time, you have the possibility to allow controlled access to even information declared private via methods that you have declared as public. Thus your implementation of a class can abstract what you think the world outside it—other classes and functions such as main()—don't need to know.

Going back to the example related to Human::Age being a private member, you know that even in reality many people don't like to reveal their true ages. If class Human was required to tell an age two years younger than the current age, it could do so easily via a public function GetAge() that uses the Human::Age parameter, reduces it by two, and supplies the result as demonstrated by Listing 9.2.

LISTING 9.2   A Model of Class Human Where the True Age Is Abstracted from the User and a Younger Age Is Reported

```
0: #include <iostream>
1: using namespace std;
2:
3: class Human
4: {
```

```
 5: private:
 6:     // Private member data:
 7:     int Age;
 8:
 9: public:
10:     void SetAge(int InputAge)
11:     {
12:         Age = InputAge;
13:     }
14:
15:     // Human lies about his / her Age (if over 30)
16:     int GetAge()
17:     {
18:         if (Age > 30)
19:             return (Age - 2);
20:         else
21:             return Age;
22:     }
23: };
24:
25: int main()
26: {
27:     Human FirstMan;
28:     FirstMan.SetAge(35);
29:
30:     Human FirstWoman;
31:     FirstWoman.SetAge(22);
32:
33:     cout << "Age of FirstMan " << FirstMan.GetAge() << endl;
34:     cout << "Age of FirstWoman " << FirstWoman.GetAge() << endl;
35:
36:     return 0;
37: }
```

Output ▼

```
Age of FirstMan 33
Age of FirstWoman 22
```

Analysis ▼

Note the public method Human::GetAge() at Line 16. As the actual age contained in private integer member Human::Age is not directly accessible, the only resort external users of this class have towards querying an object of class Human for attribute Age is via method GetAge(). Thus, the actual age held in Human::Age is abstracted from the outside world.

Abstraction is a very important concept in object-oriented languages. It empowers programmers to decide what attributes of a class need to remain known only to the class and its members with nobody outside it (with the exception of those declared as its "friends") having access to it.

Constructors

A constructor is a special function (or method) that is invoked when an object is created. Just like functions, constructors can also be overloaded.

Declaring and Implementing a Constructor

A constructor is a special function that has the name of the class and no return value. So, class Human has a constructor that is declared like this:

```
class Human
{
public:
    Human(); // declaration of a constructor
};
```

This constructor can either be implemented inline in the class or can be implemented externally outside the class declaration. An implementation or definition inside the class looks like this:

```
class Human
{
public:
    Human()
    {
        // constructor code here
    }
};
```

A variant enabling you to define the constructor outside the class' declaration looks like this:

```
class Human
{
public:
    Human(); // constructor declaration
};

// constructor definition (implementation)
Human::Human()
{
```

```
    // constructor code here
}
```

9

> **NOTE**
>
> :: is called the scope resolution operator. For example,
> Human::DateOfBirth is referring to variable DateOfBirth declared
> within the scope of class Human. ::DateOfBirth, on the other
> hand, refers to another variable DateOfBirth in a global scope.

When and How to Use Constructors

A constructor is always invoked when an object is created. This makes a constructor a perfect place for you to initialize class member variables such as integers, pointers, and so on to known initial values. Take a look at Listing 9.2 again. Note that if you had forgotten to SetAge(), the integer variable Human::Age would contain an unknown junk value as that variable has not been initialized (try it by commenting out Lines 28 and 31). Listing 9.3 uses constructors to implement a better version of class Human, where variable Age has been initialized.

LISTING 9.3   Using Constructors to Initialize Class Member Variables

```
 0: #include <iostream>
 1: #include <string>
 2: using namespace std;
 3:
 4: class Human
 5: {
 6: private:
 7:     // Private member data:
 8:     string Name;
 9:     int Age;
10:
11: public:
12:     // constructor
13:     Human()
14:     {
15:         Age = 0; // initialized to ensure no junk value
16:         cout << "Constructed an instance of class Human" << endl;
17:     }
18:
19:     void SetName (string HumansName)
20:     {
21:         Name = HumansName;
22:     }
23:
```

LISTING 9.3 Continued

```
24:     void SetAge(int HumansAge)
25:     {
26:        Age = HumansAge;
27:     }
28:
29:     void IntroduceSelf()
30:     {
31:        cout << "I am " + Name << " and am ";
32:        cout << Age << " years old" << endl;
33:     }
34: };
35:
36: int main()
37: {
38:     Human FirstMan;
39:     FirstMan.SetName("Adam");
40:     FirstMan.SetAge(30);
41:
42:     Human FirstWoman;
43:     FirstWoman.SetName("Eve");
44:     FirstWoman.SetAge (28);
45:
46:     FirstMan.IntroduceSelf();
47:     FirstWoman.IntroduceSelf();
48: }
```

Output ▼

```
Constructed an instance of class Human
Constructed an instance of class Human
I am Adam and am 30 years old
I am Eve and am 28 years old
```

Analysis ▼

In the output you see an addition of two very relevant first lines in comparison to Listing 9.1. Now, take a look at main() defined in Lines 36–48. You see that these two lines have been created indirectly via the creation (construction) of two objects FirstMan and FirstWoman in Lines 38 and 42. As these two objects are of type class Human, their creation has automatically resulted in the execution of the constructor of class Human defined in Lines 13–17. This constructor has the cout statement that created this output. Note that the constructor also initializes the integer Age to zero. Should you forget to set the Age of a newly created object, you can rest assured that the constructor ensures that the value is not a random integer (that might look valid) but is instead a zero that indicates a failure in setting the Human::Age class attribute.

A constructor that can be invoked without argument is called the default constructor. Programming a default constructor is optional.

If you don't program any constructor as seen in Listing 9.1, the compiler creates one for you (that constructs member attributes but does not initialize Plain Old Data types such as int to any value).

Overloading Constructors

9

As constructors can be overloaded just like functions, we can create a constructor that requires Human to be created with a name as a parameter, for instance:

```cpp
class Human
{
public:
   Human()
   {
      // default constructor code here
   }

   Human(string HumansName)
   {
      // overloaded constructor code here
   }
};
```

The application of overloaded constructors is demonstrated by Listing 9.4 in creating an object of class Human with a name supplied at the time of construction.

LISTING 9.4 A Class Human with Multiple Constructors

```cpp
0: #include <iostream>
1: #include <string>
2: using namespace std;
3:
4: class Human
5: {
6: private:
7:    // Private member data:
8:    string Name;
9:    int Age;
10:
11: public:
12:    // constructor
13:    Human()
```

LISTING 9.4 Continued

```
14:    {
15:       Age = 0; // initialized to ensure no junk value
16:       cout << "Default constructor creates an instance of Human" << endl;
17:    }
18:
19:    // overloaded constructor that takes Name
20:    Human(string HumansName)
21:    {
22:       Name = HumansName;
23:       Age = 0; // initialized to ensure no junk value
24:       cout << "Overloaded constructor creates " << Name << endl;
25:    }
26:
27:    // overloaded constructor that takes Name and Age
28:    Human(string HumansName, int HumansAge)
29:    {
30:       Name = HumansName;
31:       Age = HumansAge;
32:       cout << "Overloaded constructor creates ";
33:       cout << Name << " of " << Age << " years" << endl;
34:    }
35:
36:    void SetName (string HumansName)
37:    {
38:       Name = HumansName;
39:    }
40:
41:    void SetAge(int HumansAge)
42:    {
43:       Age = HumansAge;
44:    }
45:
46:    void IntroduceSelf()
47:    {
48:       cout << "I am " + Name << " and am ";
49:     cout << Age << " years old" << endl;
50:    }
51: };
52:
53: int main()
54: {
55:    Human FirstMan; // use default constructor
56:    FirstMan.SetName("Adam");
57:    FirstMan.SetAge(30);
58:
59:    Human FirstWoman ("Eve"); // use overloaded constructor
60:    FirstWoman.SetAge (28);
61:
62:    Human FirstChild ("Rose", 1);
```

```
63:
64:    FirstMan.IntroduceSelf();
65:    FirstWoman.IntroduceSelf();
66:    FirstChild.IntroduceSelf();
67: }
```

Output ▼

```
Default constructor creates an instance of Human
Overloaded constructor creates Eve
Overloaded constructor creates Rose of 1 years
I am Adam and am 30 years old
I am Eve and am 28 years old
I am Rose and am 1 years old
```

Analysis ▼

Adam is created using the default constructor; Eve is created using an overloaded constructor that accepts string as parameter that is assigned to Human::Name, whereas Rose is created using a third overloaded constructor that takes a string and an int as a parameter where the int is assigned to Human::Age. This program demonstrates how overloading constructors can be quite useful, helping you initialize variables.

TIP

You can choose to not implement the default constructor to enforce object instantiation with certain minimal parameters.

Class Without a Default Constructor

In Listing 9.5, see how class Human without the default constructor enforces the creator to supply a Name and Age as a prerequisite to creating an object.

LISTING 9.5   A Class with Overloaded Constructor(s) and No Default Constructor

```
0: #include <iostream>
1: #include <string>
2: using namespace std;
3:
4: class Human
5: {
6: private:
7:    // Private member data:
8:    string Name;
```

LISTING 9.5 Continued

```
 9:    int Age;
10:
11: public:
12:
13:    // overloaded constructor (no default constructor)
14:    Human(string HumansName, int HumansAge)
15:    {
16:       Name = HumansName;
17:       Age = HumansAge;
18:       cout << "Overloaded constructor creates " << Name;
19:       cout << " of age " << Age << endl;
20:    }
21:
22:    void IntroduceSelf()
23:    {
24:       cout << "I am " + Name << " and am ";
25:      cout << Age << " years old" << endl;
26:    }
27: };
28:
29: int main()
30: {
31:    // Uncomment next line to try creating using a default constructor
32:    // Human FirstMan;
33:
34:    Human FirstMan("Adam", 30);
35:    Human FirstWoman("Eve", 28);
36:
37:    FirstMan.IntroduceSelf();
38:    FirstWoman.IntroduceSelf();
39: }
```

Output ▼

```
Overloaded constructor creates Adam of age 30
Overloaded constructor creates Eve of age 28
I am Adam and am 30 years old
I am Eve and am 28 years old
```

Analysis ▼

Line 32 in main() begs attention. It is quite similar to the code that creates FirstMan in Listing 9.3, yet if you uncomment it, compilation fails with the message error:

'Human' : no appropriate default constructor available. This is because this version of class Human has only one constructor that takes a string and an int as input parameters, as seen in Line 14. There is no default constructor available, and in the presence of an overloaded constructor, the C++ compiler does not generate a default constructor for you.

Thus, this sample demonstrates the ability to design classes that can enforce creation only when certain parameters have been provided, in this case a Name and an Age for creating an object of type class Human. What this sample in Listing 9.5 also demonstrates is the ability to create an object of class Human with his Name supplied at creation time, and no possibility to change it afterward. This is because the name attribute of the Human is stored in a private variable of type string called Name that cannot be accessed or modified by main() or by any entity that is not a member of class Human. In other words, the user of class Human is forced by the overloaded constructor to specify a name (and age) for every object he creates and is not allowed to change that name—modeling a real-world scenario quite well, don't you think? Your name was given to you by your parents at birth; people are allowed to know it, but nobody (except you) has the authority to change it.

Constructor Parameters with Default Values

Just the same way as functions can have parameters with default values specified, so can constructors. What you see in the following code is a slightly modified version of the constructor from Listing 9.5 at Line 14 where the Age parameter has a default value of 25:

```
class Human
{
private:
   // Private member data:
   string Name;
   int Age;

public:
   // overloaded constructor (no default constructor)
   Human(string HumansName, int HumansAge = 25)
   {
      Name = HumansName;
      Age = HumansAge;
      cout << "Overloaded constructor creates " << Name;
      cout << " of age " << Age << endl;
   }

   // ... other members
};
```

Such a class can be instantiated with the syntax:

```
Human Adam("Adam"); // Adam.Age is assigned a default value 25
Human Eve("Eve, 18); // Eve.Age is assigned 18 as specified
```

<table>
<tr>
<td>NOTE</td>
<td>

Note that a default constructor is one that can be instantiated without arguments, and not necessarily one that doesn't take parameters. So, this constructor with two parameters, both with default values, is a default constructor:

```
class Human
{
private:
    // Private member data:
    string Name;
    int Age;

public:
    // Note default values for the two input parameters
    Human(string HumansName = "Adam", int HumansAge = 25)
    {
        Name = HumansName;
        Age = HumansAge;
        cout << "Overloaded constructor creates " << Name;
        cout << " of age " << Age << endl;
    }
};
```

The reason is that class Human can still be instantiated without arguments:

```
Human Adam; // Human with default Name "Adam", Age 25
```

</td>
</tr>
</table>

Constructors with Initialization Lists

You have seen how constructors are useful to initialize variables. Another way to initialize members is by using initialization lists. An initialization list variant of the constructor in Listing 9.5 that takes two parameters looks like this:

```
class Human
{
private:
    string Name;
    int Age;

public:
    // constructor takes two parameters to initialize members Age and Name
    Human(string InputName, int InputAge)
```

```
      :Name(InputName), Age(InputAge)
  {
     cout << "Constructed a Human called " << Name;
     cout << ", " << Age << " years old" << endl;
  }
// ... other class members
};
```

Thus, the initialization list is characterized by a colon (:) following the parameter declaration contained in parentheses (...), followed by an individual member variable and the
value it is initialized to. This initialization value can be a parameter such as InputName or
can even be a fixed value. Initialization lists can also be useful in invoking base class
constructors with specific arguments and are discussed again in Lesson 10,
"Implementing Inheritance."

You can see class Human that features a default constructor with parameters with
default values and an initialization list in Listing 9.6.

LISTING 9.6   Default Constructor That Accepts Parameters with Default Values to Set
Members Using Initialization Lists

```
 0: #include <iostream>
 1: #include <string>
 2: using namespace std;
 3:
 4: class Human
 5: {
 6: private:
 7:     int Age;
 8:     string Name;
 9:
10: public:
11:     Human(string InputName = "Adam", int InputAge = 25)
12:         :Name(InputName), Age(InputAge)
13:     {
14:         cout << "Constructed a Human called " << Name;
15:         cout << ", " << Age << " years old" << endl;
16:     }
17: };
18:
19: int main()
20: {
21:     Human FirstMan;
22:     Human FirstWoman("Eve", 18);
23:
24:     return 0;
25: }
```

9

Output ▼

```
Constructed a Human called Adam, 25 years old
Constructed a Human called Eve, 18 years old
```

Analysis ▼

The constructor with initialization lists is seen in Lines 11–16, where you can also see that the parameters have been given default values "Adam" for Name and 25 for Age. Hence, when an instance of class Human called FirstMan is created in Line 21, its members are automatically assigned the default values. FirstWoman, on the other hand, has been supplied with an explicit Name and Age as shown in Line 22.

Destructor

Destructors, like constructors, are special functions, too. Unlike constructors, destructors are automatically invoked when an object is destroyed.

Declaring and Implementing a Destructor

The destructor, like the constructor, looks like a function that takes the name of the class, yet has a tilde (~) preceding it. So, class Human can have a destructor that is declared like this:

```
class Human
{
    ~Human(); // declaration of a destructor
};
```

This destructor can either be implemented inline in the class or externally outside the class declaration. An implementation or definition inside the class looks like this:

```
class Human
{
public:
    ~Human()
    {
        // destructor code here
    }
};
```

A variant enabling you to define the destructor outside the class' declaration looks like this:

```
class Human
{
```

```
public:
    ~Human(); // destructor declaration
};

// destructor definition (implementation)
Human::~Human()
{
    // destructor code here
}
```

As you can see, the declaration of the destructor differs from that of the constructor slightly in that this contains a tilde (~). The role of the destructor is, however, diametrically opposite to that of the constructor.

When and How to Use Destructors

Destructors are always invoked when an object of a class goes out of scope or is deleted via delete and is destroyed. This property makes destructors the ideal place to reset variables and release dynamically allocated memory and other resources.

This book has consistently recommended the usage of std::string over a C-style char buffer where you have to manage memory allocation and the likes yourself. std::string and such other utilities are nothing but classes themselves that make the best of constructors and destructors (in addition to operators, that you study in Lesson 12, "Operator Types and Operator Overloading"). Analyze a sample class MyString as shown in Listing 9.7 that allocates memory for a string in the constructor and releases it in the destructor.

LISTING 9.7 A Simple Class That Encapsulates a C-style Buffer to Ensure Deallocation via the Destructor

```
0: #include <iostream>
1: using namespace std;
2:
3: class MyString
4: {
5: private:
6:     char* Buffer;
7:
8: public:
9:     // Constructor
10:     MyString(const char* InitialInput)
11:     {
12:         if(InitialInput != NULL)
13:         {
14:             Buffer = new char [strlen(InitialInput) + 1];
```

9

LISTING 9.7 Continued

```cpp
15:            strcpy(Buffer, InitialInput);
16:         }
17:         else
18:             Buffer = NULL;
19:      }
20:      // Destructor: clears the buffer allocated in constructor
21:      ~MyString()
22:      {
23:         cout << "Invoking destructor, clearing up" << endl;
24:         if (Buffer != NULL)
25:             delete [] Buffer;
26:      }
27:
28:      int GetLength()
29:      {
30:         return strlen(Buffer);
31:      }
32:
33:      const char* GetString()
34:      {
35:          return Buffer;
36:      }
37: }; // end of class MyString
38:
39: int main()
40: {
41:     MyString SayHello("Hello from String Class");
42:     cout << "String buffer in MyString is " << SayHello.GetLength();
43:     cout << " characters long" << endl;
44:
45:     cout << "Buffer contains: ";
46:     cout << "Buffer contains: " << SayHello.GetString() << endl;
47: }
```

Output ▼

```
String buffer in MyString is 23 characters long
Buffer contains: Hello from String Class
Invoking destructor, clearing up
```

Analysis ▼

This class basically encapsulates a C-style string in `MyString::Buffer` and relieves you of the task of allocating memory; it deallocates the same every time you need to use a string. The lines of utmost interest to us are the constructor `MyString()` in Lines 10–19, and the destructor `~MyString()` in Lines 21–26. The constructor enforces construction with an input string via a compulsory input parameter and then copies it to the C-style string Buffer after allocating memory for it in Line 14 where strlen is used to determine the length of the input string and copying into this newly allocated memory in Line 15 using strcpy. In case the user of the class has supplied a NULL as InitialInput, MyString::Buffer is initialized to NULL as well (to keep this pointer from containing a random value that can be dangerous when used to access a memory location). The destructor code does the job of ensuring that the memory allocated in the constructor is automatically returned to the system. It checks if MyString::Buffer is not NULL, and, if so, it performs a delete[] on it that complements the new in the constructor. Note that nowhere in main() has the programmer ever done a new or a delete. This class not only abstracted that implementation from him, but in doing so ensured technical correctness in releasing allocated memory. The destructor ~MyString() is automatically invoked when main returns, and this is demonstrated in the output that executes the cout statements in the destructor.

Classes that handle strings better are one of the many applicable uses of a destructor. Lesson 26, "Understanding Smart Pointers," demonstrates how destructors play a critical role in working with pointers in a smarter way.

9

> **NOTE**
>
> Destructors cannot be overloaded. A class can have only one destructor. If you forget to implement a destructor, the compiler creates and invokes a dummy destructor, that is, an empty one (that does no cleanup of dynamically allocated memory).

Copy Constructor

In Lesson 7, "Organizing Code with Functions," you learned that arguments passed to a function like Area() (shown in Listing 7.1) are copied:

```
double Area(double InputRadius);
```

So, the argument sent as parameter InputRadius is copied when Area() is called. This rule applies to objects or instances of classes as well.

Shallow Copying and Associated Problems

Classes such as MyString, shown in Listing 9.7, contain a pointer member that points to dynamically allocated memory, allocated in the constructor using new and deallocated in the destructor using delete[]. When an object of this class is copied, the pointer member is copied, but not the pointed buffer, resulting in two objects pointing to the same dynamically allocated buffer in memory. This is called a shallow copy and presents a threat to the stability of the program, as Listing 9.8 demonstrates.

LISTING 9.8 The Problem in Passing Objects of a Class Such as `MyString` by Value

```
0: #include <iostream>
1: using namespace std;
2:
3: class MyString
4: {
5: private:
6:     char* Buffer;
7:
8: public:
9:     // Constructor
10:     MyString(const char* InitialInput)
11:     {
12:         if(InitialInput != NULL)
13:         {
14:             Buffer = new char [strlen(InitialInput) + 1];
15:             strcpy(Buffer, InitialInput);
16:         }
17:         else
18:             Buffer = NULL;
19:     }
20:
21:     // Destructor
22:     ~MyString()
23:     {
24:         cout << "Invoking destructor, clearing up" << endl;
25:         if (Buffer != NULL)
26:             delete [] Buffer;
27:     }
28:
29:     int GetLength()
30:     {
31:         return strlen(Buffer);
32:     }
33:
34:     const char* GetString()
35:     {
36:         return Buffer;
37:     }.
38: };
39:
40: void UseMyString(MyString Input)
41: {
42:     cout << "String buffer in MyString is " << Input.GetLength();
43:     cout << " characters long" << endl;
```

```
44:
45:     cout << "Buffer contains: " << Input.GetString() << endl;
46:     return;
47: }
48:
49: int main()
50: {
51:     MyString SayHello("Hello from String Class");
52:
53:     // Pass SayHello as a parameter to the function
54:     UseMyString(SayHello);
55:
56:     return 0;
57: }
```

9

Output ▼

```
String buffer in MyString is 23 characters long
Buffer contains: Hello from String Class
Invoking destructor, clearing up
Invoking destructor, clearing up
<crash as seen in Figure 9.2>
```

FIGURE 9.2
Screenshot of crash caused by executing Listing 9.8 (in MS Visual Studio debug mode).

Microsoft Visual C++ Debug Library

Debug Assertion Failed!

Program: ...tor_CopyMyString\Debug\9.7
NoCopyConstructor_CopyMyString.exe
File: f:\dd\vctools\crt_bld\self_x86\crt\src\dbgdel.cpp
Line: 52

Expression: _BLOCK_TYPE_IS_VALID(pHead->nBlockUse)

For information on how your program can cause an assertion failure, see the Visual C++ documentation on asserts.

(Press Retry to debug the application)

Abort   Retry   Ignore

Analysis ▼

Why does the class that worked just fine in Listing .9.6 cause a crash in Listing 9.7? The only difference between Listing 9.6 and 9.7 is that the job of using the object SayHello of class MyString created in main() has been delegated to function UseMyString(), invoked in Line 54. Delegating work to this function has resulted in object SayHello in main() to be copied into argument Input used in UseMyString(). This is a copy gener-ated by the compiler as the function has been declared to take Input as a parameter by value and not by reference. The compiler performs a binary copy of Plain Old Data such as integers, characters, and raw pointers. So the pointer value contained in SayHello.Buffer has simply been copied to Input—that is, SayHello.Buffer points to the same memory location as Input.Buffer. This is illustrated in Figure 9.3.

FIGURE 9.3
Shallow copy of SayHello into Input when UseMyString() is invoked.

The binary copy did not perform a deep copy of the pointed memory location, and you now have two objects of class MyString pointing to the same location in memory. Thus, when the function UseMyString() returned, variable Input goes out of scope and is destroyed. In doing so, the destructor of class MyString is invoked, and the destructor code in Line 26 in Listing 9.8 releases the memory allocated to Buffer via delete. Note that this call to delete invalidates the memory being pointed to in object SayHello contained in main(). When main() ends, SayHello goes out of scope and is destroyed. This time, however, Line 26 repeats a call to delete on a memory address that is no longer valid (released and invalidated via the destruction of Input). This double delete is what results in a crash. Note that the debug assertion message seen in Figure 9.2 shows Line 52 (Line 51 in the book's zero-based line numbering system) because it's pointing at the object SayHello that was not destructed successfully.

NOTE — The compiler in this case could not automatically ensure a deep copy as it doesn't know for sure the number of bytes pointed to by pointer member MyString::Buffer or the nature of allocation at the time of compilation.

Ensuring Deep Copy Using a Copy Constructor

The copy constructor is a special overloaded constructor that you as the programmer of the class need to supply. The compiler guarantees invocation of the copy constructor every time an object of the class is copied, and this includes passing an object to a function by value.

The declaration syntax of a copy constructor for class MyString is the following:

```
class MyString
{
   MyString(const MyString& CopySource); // copy constructor
};

MyString::MyString(const MyString& CopySource)
{
   // Copy constructor implementation code
}
```

Thus, a copy constructor takes an object of the same class by reference as a parameter. This parameter is an alias of the source object and is the handle you have in writing your custom copy code (where you would ensure a deep copy of all buffers in the source), as Listing 9.9 demonstrates.

LISTING 9.9   Define a Copy Constructor to Ensure Deep Copy of Dynamically Allocated Buffers

```
 0: #include <iostream>
 1: using namespace std;
 2:
 3: class MyString
 4: {
 5: private:
 6:    char* Buffer;
 7:
 8: public:
 9:    // constructor
10:    MyString(const char* InitialInput)
11:    {
12:       cout << "Constructor: creating new MyString" << endl;
13:       if(InitialInput != NULL)
14:       {
15:          Buffer = new char [strlen(InitialInput) + 1];
16:          strcpy(Buffer, InitialInput);
17:
18:          // Display memory address pointed by local buffer
19:          cout << "Buffer points to: 0x" << hex;
20:          cout << (unsigned int*)Buffer << endl;
21:       }
22:       else
23:          Buffer = NULL;
24:    }
25:
26:    // Copy constructor
27:    MyString(const MyString& CopySource)
```

LISTING 9.9   Continued

```
28:    {
29:        cout << "Copy constructor: copying from MyString" << endl;
30:
31:        if(CopySource.Buffer != NULL)
32:        {
33:            // ensure deep copy by first allocating own buffer
34:            Buffer = new char [strlen(CopySource.Buffer) + 1];
35:
36:            // copy from the source into local buffer
37:            strcpy(Buffer, CopySource.Buffer);
38:
39:            // Display memory address pointed by local buffer
40:            cout << "Buffer points to: 0x" << hex;
41:            cout << (unsigned int*)Buffer << endl;
42:        }
43:        else
44:            Buffer = NULL;
45:    }
46:
47:    // Destructor
48:    ~MyString()
49:    {
50:        cout << "Invoking destructor, clearing up" << endl;
51:        if (Buffer != NULL)
52:            delete [] Buffer;
53:    }
54:
55:    int GetLength()
56:    {
57:        return strlen(Buffer);
58:    }
59:
60:    const char* GetString()
61:    {
62:        return Buffer;
63:    }
64: };
65:
66: void UseMyString(MyString Input)
67: {
68:    cout << "String buffer in MyString is " << Input.GetLength();
69:    cout << " characters long" << endl;
70:
71:    cout << "Buffer contains: " << Input.GetString() << endl;
```

```
72:     return;
73: }
74:
75: int main()
76: {
77:     MyString SayHello("Hello from String Class");
78:
79:     // Pass SayHello by value (will be copied)
80:     UseMyString(SayHello);
81:
82:     return 0;
83: }
```

Output ▼

```
Constructor: creating new MyString
Buffer points to: 0x0040DA68
Copy constructor: copying from MyString
Buffer points to: 0x0040DAF8
String buffer in MyString is 17 characters long
Buffer contains: Hello from String Class
Invoking destructor, clearing up
Invoking destructor, clearing up
```

Analysis ▼

Most of the code is similar to Listing 9.8 save for a few lines of cout added to constructor and a new copy constructor in Lines 27–45. To start with, let's focus on main() that (as before) creates an object SayHello in Line 77. Creating SayHello results in the first line of output that comes from the constructor of MyString, at Line 12. For sake of convenience, the constructor also displays the memory address that Buffer points to. main() then passes SayHello by value to function UseMyString() in Line 80, which automatically results in the copy constructor being invoked as shown in the output. The code in the copy constructor is very similar to that in the constructor. The basic idea is the same, check the length of C-style string Buffer contained in the copy source at Line 34, allocate that much memory in one's own instance of Buffer, and then use strcpy to copy from source to destination at Line 37. This is not a shallow copy of pointer values. This is a deep copy where the content being pointed to is copied to a newly allocated buffer that belongs to this object, as illustrated in Figure 9.4.

FIGURE 9.4
Illustration of a
deep copy of
argument
SayHello into
parameter Input
when function
UseMyString()
is invoked.

The output in Listing 9.9 indicates that the memory addresses being pointed to by
Buffer is different in the copy—that is, two objects don't point to the same dynamically
allocated memory address. As a result, when function UseMyString() returns and parameter Input is destroyed, the destructor code does a delete[] on the memory address
that was allocated in the copy constructor and belongs to this object. In doing so, it does
not touch memory that is being pointed to by SayHello in main(). So, both functions
end and their respective objects are destroyed successfully and peacefully without the
application crashing.

NOTE

The copy constructor has ensured deep copy in cases such as
function calls:

```
MyString SayHello("Hello from String Class");
UseMyString(SayHello);
```

However, what if you tried copying via assignment:

```
MyString overwrite("who cares?");
overwrite = SayHello;
```

This would still be a shallow copy due to the default assignment
operator supplied by the compiler as you haven't yet specified any.
To avoid the problem of shallow copies during assignment, you
need to implement the copy assignment operator (=).

The copy assignment operator is discussed in length in Lesson
12. Listing 12.9 is an improved MyString that implements the
same:

```
MyString::operator= (const MyString& CopySource)
{
    //... copy assignment operator code
}
```

CAUTION

> Using const in the copy constructor declaration ensures that the copy constructor does not modify the source object being referred to.
>
> Additionally, the parameter in the copy-constructor is passed by reference as a necessity. If this weren't a reference, the constructor would itself invoke a copy by value, thus causing a shallow copy of the source data—exactly what you set out to avoid.

DO	DON'T
DO always program a copy constructor and copy assignment operator when your class contains raw pointer members (char* and the like). **DO** always program the copy constructor with a const reference source parameter. **DO** use string classes such as std::string and smart pointer classes as members instead of raw pointers as they implement copy constructors and save you the effort.	**DON'T** use raw pointers as class members unless absolutely unavoidable.

NOTE

> The class MyString with a raw pointer member, char* Buffer is used as an example to explain the need for copy constructors.
>
> If you were to program a class that needs to contain string data for storing names and so on, you use std::string instead of char* and might not even need a copy constructor in the absence of raw pointers. This is because the default copy constructor inserted by the compiler would ensure the invocation of all available copy constructors of member objects such as std::string.

C++11

Move Constructors Help Improve Performance

There are cases where your objects are subjected to copy steps automatically, due to the nature of the language and its needs. Consider the following:

```cpp
class MyString
{
```

```
    // pick implementation from Listing 9.9
};
MyString Copy(MyString& Source)
{
    MyString CopyForReturn(Source.GetString());  // create copy
    return CopyForReturn;  // return by value invokes copy constructor
}
int main()
{
    MyString sayHello ("Hello World of C++");
    MyString sayHelloAgain(Copy(sayHello)); // invokes 2x copy constructor

    return 0;
}
```

As the comment indicates, in the instantiation of sayHelloAgain, the copy constructor was invoked twice, thus a deep copy was performed twice because of our call to function Copy(sayHello) that returns a MyString by value. However, this value returned is very temporary and is not available outside this expression. So, the copy constructor invoked in good faith by the C++ compiler actually causes a performance reduction that can become significant if this is a dynamic array of objects of great size.

To avoid this performance bottleneck, program a move constructor in addition to a copy constructor. The syntax of a move constructor is

```
// move constructor
MyString(MyString&& MoveSource)
{
    if(MoveSource.Buffer != NULL)
    {
        Buffer = MoveSource.Buffer; // take ownership i.e.  'move'
        MoveSource.Buffer = NULL;   // set the move source to NULL i.e. free it
    }
}
```

When available, the C++11 compiler automatically opts for a move constructor for "moving" the temporary resource and hence avoiding a deep-copy step. With the move constructor implemented, the comment should be appropriately changed to the following:

```
    MyString sayHelloAgain(Copy(sayHello)); // invokes 1x copy constructor, 1x
move constructor
```

The move constructor is usually implemented with the move assignment operator, which is discussed in greater detail in Lesson 12. Listing 12.11 is a better version of class MyString that implements the move constructor and the move assignment operator.

Different Uses of Constructors and Destructor

You have learned a few important and basic concepts in this lesson, such as the concepts of constructors, destructor, and the abstraction of data and methods via keywords such as `public` and `private`. These concepts enable you to create classes that can control how they're created, copied, destroyed, or expose data.

Let's look at a few interesting patterns that help you solve many important design problems.

Class That Does Not Permit Copying

You are asked to model the constitution of your country. A country has only one president. Your `class President` risks the following:

```
President OurPresident;
DoSomething(OurPresident); // duplicate created in passing by value
President clone;
clone = OurPresident; // duplicate via assignment
```

Clearly, you need to avoid this situation. Beyond modeling a certain constitution, you might be programming an operating system and need to model one local area network, one processor, and so on. You need to avoid situations where resources can be copied. If you don't declare a copy constructor, the C++ compiler inserts a default public copy constructor for you. This ruins your design and threatens your implementation. Yet, the language gives you a solution to this design paradigm.

You would ensure that your class cannot be copied by declaring a private copy constructor. This ensures that the function call `DoSomething(OurPresident)` will cause a compile failure. To avoid assignment, you declare a private assignment operator.

Thus, the solution is the following:

```
class President
{
private:
   President(const President&); // private copy constructor
   President& operator= (const President&); // private copy assignment operator

   // … other attributes
};
```

There is no need for implementation of the private copy constructor or assignment operator. Just declaring them as private is adequate and sufficient toward fulfilling your goal of ensuring non-copyable objects of class President.

Singleton Class That Permits a Single Instance

class President discussed earlier is good, but it has a shortcoming: It cannot help creation of multiple presidents via instantiation of multiple objects:

```
President One, Two, Three;
```

Individually they are non-copyable thanks to the private copy constructors, but what you ideally need is a class President that has one, and only one, real-world manifestation—that is, there is only one object and creation of additional ones is prohibited. Welcome to the concept of singleton that uses private constructors, a private assignment operator, and a static instance member to create this (controversially) powerful pattern.

TIP

When the keyword static is used on a class's data member, it ensures that the member is shared across all instances.

When static is used on a local variable declared within the scope of a function, it ensures that the variable retains its value between function calls.

When static is used on a member function—a method—the method is shared across all instances of the class.

Keyword static is an essential ingredient in creating a singleton class as demonstrated by Listing 9.10.

LISTING 9.10   Singleton class President That Prohibits Copying, Assignment, and Multiple Instance Creation

```
0: #include <iostream>
1: #include <string>
2: using namespace std;
3:
4: class President
5: {
6: private:
7:    // private default constructor (prohibits creation from outside)
8:    President() {};
9:
```

```
10:     //  private copy constructor (prohibits copy creation)
11:     President(const President&);
12:
13:     // private assignment operator (prohibits assignment)
14:     const President& operator=(const President&);
15:
16:     // member data: Presidents name
17:     string Name;
18:
19: public:
20:     // controlled instantiation
21:     static President& GetInstance()
22:     {
23:         // static objects are constructed only once
24:         static President OnlyInstance;
25:
26:         return OnlyInstance;
27:     }
28:
29:     // public methods
30:     string GetName()
31:     {
32:         return Name;
33:     }
34:
35:     void SetName(string InputName)
36:     {
37:         Name = InputName;
38:     }
39: };
40:
41: int main()
42: {
43:     President& OnlyPresident = President::GetInstance();
44:     OnlyPresident.SetName("Abraham Lincoln");
45:
46:     // uncomment lines to see how compile failures prohibit duplicates
47:     // President Second; // cannot access constructor
48:     // President* Third= new President(); // cannot access constructor
49:     // President Fourth = OnlyPresident; // cannot access copy constructor
50:     // OnlyPresident = President::GetInstance(); // cannot access operator=
51:
52:     cout << "The name of the President is: ";
53:     cout << President::GetInstance().GetName() << endl;
54:
55:     return 0;
56: }
```

Output ▼

```
The name of the President is: Abraham Lincoln
```

Analysis ▼

Take a quick look at main() that has a few lines of code and a host of commented lines that show all the combinations in creating new instances or copies of a class President that won't work. Let's analyze them one by one:

```
47:     // President Second; // cannot access constructor
48:     // President* Third= new President(); // cannot access constructor
```

Lines 47 and 48 try object creation on the stack and heap, respectively, using the default constructor, which is unavailable because it's private, as shown in Line 8:

```
49:     // President Fourth = OnlyPresident; // cannot access copy constructor
```

Line 49 is an attempt at creating a copy of an existing object via the copy constructor (assignment at creation time invokes copy constructor), which is unavailable in main() because it is declared private in Line 11:

```
50:     // OnlyPresident = President::GetInstance(); // cannot access operator=
```

Line 50 is an attempt at creating a copy via assignment, which does not work as the assignment operator is declared private in Line 14. So, main() can never create an instance of class President and the only option left is seen in Line 43, where it uses the static function GetInstance() to get an instance of class President. Because GetInstance() is a static member, it is quite like a global function that can be invoked without having an object as a handle. GetInstance(), implemented in Lines 21–27, uses a static variable OnlyInstance to ensure that there is one and only one instance of class President created. To understand that better, imagine that Line 24 is executed only once (static initialization) and hence GetInstance() returns the only one available instance of class President, irrespective of how that instance is used, as shown in Lines 43 and 53 in main().

CAUTION

Use the singleton pattern only where absolutely necessary, keeping future growth of the application and its features in perspective. Note that the very feature that it restricts creation of multiple instances can become an architectural bottleneck when a use case comes up that needs multiple instances of the class.

For example, if our project was growing from modeling a nation to modeling the United Nations that is currently represented by 192 nations with 192 presidents, clearly we have an architectural problem in the making.

Class That Prohibits Instantiation on the Stack

Space on the stack is often limited. If you are writing a database that may contain a gigabyte of data in its internal structures, you might want to ensure that a client of this class cannot instantiate it on its stack; instead it is forced to create instances only on the heap. The key to ensuring this is declaring the destructor private:

```
class MonsterDB
{
private:
   // private destructor
   ~MonsterDB();
   //... collections that reserve a huge amount of data
};
```

Thus, when trying to consume class MonsterDB, one is not allowed to create an instance like this:

```
int main()
{
   MonsterDB myDatabase; // compile error
   // ... more code
   return 0;
}
```

This instance, if successfully constructed, would be on the stack. However, as the compiler knows that myDatabase needs to be destroyed when it goes out of scope, it automatically tries to invoke the destructor at the end of main(), which is not accessible because it is private, resulting in a compile failure.

However, the private destructor does not stop you from instantiating on the heap:

```
int main()
{
   MonsterDB* myDatabase = new MonsterDB(); // no error
   // ... more code
   return 0;
}
```

If you see a memory leak there, you are not mistaken. As the destructor is not accessible from main, you cannot do a delete either. What class MonsterDB needs to support is a static public member function that destroys an instance (as a member, it has access to the destructor). See Listing 9.11.

9

LISTING 9.11   A Database class MonsterDB That Allows Object Creation Only on the Free Store (Using new)

```
 0: #include <iostream>
 1: using namespace std;
 2:
 3: class MonsterDB
 4: {
 5: private:
 6:     ~MonsterDB() {}; // private destructor
 7:
 8: public:
 9:     static void DestroyInstance(MonsterDB* pInstance)
10:     {
11:         // static member can access private destructor
12:         delete pInstance;
13:     }
14:
15:     // ... imagine a few other methods
16: };
17:
18: int main()
19: {
20:     MonsterDB* pMyDatabase = new MonsterDB();
21:
22:     // pMyDatabase -> member methods (....);
23:
24:     // uncomment next line to see compile failure
25:     // delete pMyDatabase; // private destructor cannot be invoked
26:
27:     // use static member to deallocate
28:     MonsterDB::DestroyInstance(pMyDatabase);
29:
30:     return 0;
31: }
```

The code snippet produces no output.

Analysis ▼

The purpose of the code is just to demonstrate how a class that prohibits creation on the stack can be programmed with the help of a private destructor, as shown in Line 6, and a static function DestroyInstance(), as shown in Lines 9–13, used in main() in Line 28.

this **Pointer**

An important concept in C++, this is a reserved keyword applicable within the scope of a class that contains the address of the object. In other words, the value of this is &object. Within a class member method, when you invoke another member method, the compiler sends this pointer as an implicit, invisible parameter in the function call:

```
class Human
{
private:
// … private member declarations
    void Talk (string Statement)
    {
        cout << Statement;
    }

public:

    void IntroduceSelf()
    {
        Talk("Bla bla");
    }
};
```

What you see here is the method IntroduceSelf() using private member Talk() to print a statement on the screen. In reality, the compiler embeds the this pointer in calling Talk, that is invoked as Talk(this, "Bla bla").

From a programming perspective, this does not have too many applications, except those where it is usually optional. For instance, the code to access Age within SetAge(), as shown in Listing 9.1, can have a variant:

```
void SetAge(int HumansAge)
{
    this->Age = HumansAge;    // same as Age = HumansAge
}
```

NOTE

Note that the this pointer is not sent to class methods declared as static as static functions are not connected to an instance of the class. Instead they are shared by all instances.

If you want to use an instance variable in a static function, explicitly declare a parameter that the caller uses to send the this pointer as an argument.

sizeof() a Class

You have learned the fundamentals of defining your own type using keyword class that enables you to encapsulate data attributes and methods that operate on that data. Operator sizeof(), covered in Lesson 3, "Using Variables, Declaring Constants," is used to determine the memory requirement of a specific type, in bytes. This operator is valid for classes, too, and basically reports the sum of bytes consumed by each data attribute contained within the class declaration. Depending on the compiler you use, sizeof() might or might not include padding for certain attributes on word boundaries. Note that member functions and their local variables do not play a role in defining the sizeof() a class. See Listing 9.12.

LISTING 9.12 The Result of Using sizeof on Classes and Their Instances

```
0: #include <iostream>
1: using namespace std;
2:
3: class MyString
4: {
5: private:
6:     char* Buffer;
7:
8: public:
9:     // Constructor
10:    MyString(const char* InitialInput)
11:    {
12:        if(InitialInput != NULL)
13:        {
14:            Buffer = new char [strlen(InitialInput) + 1];
15:            strcpy(Buffer, InitialInput);
16:        }
17:        else
18:            Buffer = NULL;
19:    }
20:
21:    // Copy Constructor
22:    MyString(const MyString& CopySource)
23:    {
24:        if(CopySource.Buffer != NULL)
25:        {
26:            Buffer = new char [strlen(CopySource.Buffer) + 1];
27:            strcpy(Buffer, CopySource.Buffer);
28:        }
29:        else
30:            Buffer = NULL;
31:    }
32:
33:    ~MyString()
34:    {
```

```
35:         if (Buffer != NULL)
36:             delete [] Buffer;
37:     }
38:
39:     int GetLength()
40:     {
41:         return strlen(Buffer);
42:     }
43:
44:     const char* GetString()
45:     {
46:         return Buffer;
47:     }
48: };
49:
50: class Human
51: {
52: private:
53:     int Age;
54:     bool Gender;
55:     MyString Name;
56:
57: public:
58:     Human(const MyString& InputName, int InputAge, bool InputGender)
59:         : Name(InputName), Age (InputAge), Gender(InputGender) {
60:
61:     int GetAge ()
62:     {
63:         return Age;
64:     }
65: };
66:
67: int main()
68: {
69:     MyString FirstMan("Adam");
70:     MyString FirstWoman("Eve");
71:
72:     cout << "sizeof(MyString) = " << sizeof(MyString) << endl;
73:     cout << "sizeof(FirstMan) = " << sizeof(FirstMan) << endl;
74:     cout << "sizeof(FirstWoman) = " << sizeof(FirstWoman) << endl;
75:
76:     Human FirstMaleHuman(FirstMan, 25, true);
77:     Human FirstFemaleHuman(FirstWoman, 18, false);
78:
79:     cout << "sizeof(Human) = " << sizeof(Human) << endl;
80:     cout << "sizeof(FirstMaleHuman) = " << sizeof(FirstMaleHuman) << endl;
81:     cout << "sizeof(FirstFemaleHuman) = " << sizeof(FirstFemaleHuman) <<
endl;
82:
83:     return 0;
84: }
```

Output ▼

```
sizeof(MyString) = 4
sizeof(FirstMan) = 4
sizeof(FirstWoman) = 4
sizeof(Human) = 12
sizeof(FirstMaleHuman) = 12
sizeof(FirstFemaleHuman) = 12
```

Analysis ▼

The sample is admittedly long as it contains class MyString as previously shown in Listing 9.9 (without most of the display text statements) and a variant of class Human that uses type MyString to store Name and has an added parameter bool for Gender.

Let's start with analyzing the output. What you see is that the result of sizeof() on a class is the same as that of an object of the class. Hence, sizeof(MyString) is the same as sizeof(FirstMan) because essentially the number of bytes consumed by such a class are fixed at compile time and are known when the class is designed. Don't be surprised that FirstMan and FirstWoman have the same size in bytes in spite of one containing Adam and the other Eve because these are stored by MyString::Buffer that is a char*, a pointer whose size is fixed at 4 bytes (on my 32-bit system) and is independent of the volume of data being pointed to.

Try calculating the sizeof() a Human manually that is reported as 12. Lines 53, 54, and 55 tell that a Human contains an int, a bool, and a MyString. Referring to Listing 3.4 for a quick refresh on bytes consumed by inbuilt types, you know that an int consumes 4 bytes, a bool 1 byte, and MyString 4 bytes on the system I used for the examples, which do not sum up to 12 as reported by the output. This is because of word padding and other factors that influence the result of sizeof().

How struct Differs from class

struct is a keyword from the days of C, and for all practical purposes it is treated by a C++ compiler very similarly to a class. The exceptions are applicable to the different default access specifiers (public and private) when the programmer has not mentioned any. So, unless specified members in a struct are public by default (private for a class), and unless specified, a struct features public inheritance from a base struct (private for a class). Inheritance is discussed in detail in Lesson 10.

A struct variant of class Human from Listing 9.12 would be the following:

```
struct Human
{
    // constructor, public by default (as no access specified is mentioned)
    Human(const MyString& InputName, int InputAge, bool InputGender)
        : Name(InputName), Age (InputAge), Gender(InputGender) {}

    int GetAge ()
    {
        return Age;
    }

private:
    int Age;
    bool Gender;
    MyString Name;
};
```

As you can see, a struct Human is quite similar to class Human, and instantiation of an object of type struct would be similar to type class as well:

```
Human FirstMan("Adam", 25, true); // is an instance of struct Human
```

Declaring a friend of a class

A class does not permit external access to its data members and methods that are declared private. This rule is waived for those classes and functions that are disclosed as friend classes or functions, using keyword friend as seen in Listing 9.13.

LISTING 9.13   Using the friend Keyword to Allow an External Function DisplayAge() Access to Private Data Members

```
 0: #include <iostream>
 1: #include <string>
 2: using namespace std;
 3:
 4: class Human
 5: {
 6: private:
 7:     string Name;
 8:     int Age;
 9:
10:     friend void DisplayAge(const Human& Person);
11:
12: public:
```

LISTING 9.13   Continued

```
13:     Human(string InputName, int InputAge)
14:     {
15:         Name = InputName;
16:         Age = InputAge;
17:     }
18: };
19:
20: void DisplayAge(const Human& Person)
21: {
22:     cout << Person.Age << endl;
23: }
24:
25: int main()
26: {
27:     Human FirstMan("Adam", 25);
28:     cout << "Accessing private member Age via friend: ";
29:     DisplayAge(FirstMan);
30:
31:     return 0;
32: }
```

Output ▼

```
Accessing private member Age via friend: 25
```

Analysis ▼

Line 10 contains the declaration that indicates to the compiler that function
DisplayAge() in global scope be permitted special access to the private members of
class Human. You can comment Line 10 to see an immediate compile failure at Line 22.

Like functions, external classes can also be designated as a trusted friend, as Listing 9.14
demonstrates.

LISTING 9.14   Using the friend Keyword to Allow an External Class Utility Access to
Private Data Members

```
0: #include <iostream>
1: #include <string>
2: using namespace std;
3:
4: class Human
5: {
6: private:
7:     string Name;
```

```
 8:     int Age;
 9:
10:     friend class Utility;
11:
12: public:
13:     Human(string InputName, int InputAge)
14:     {
15:         Name = InputName;
16:         Age = InputAge;
17:     }
18: };
19:
20: class Utility
21: {
22: public:
23:     static void DisplayAge(const Human& Person)
24:     {
25:         cout << Person.Age << endl;
26:     }
27: };
28:
29: int main()
30: {
31:     Human FirstMan("Adam", 25);
32:     cout << "Accessing private member Age via friend class: ";
33:     Utility::DisplayAge(FirstMan);
34:
35:     return 0;
36: }
```

Output ▼

```
Accessing private member Age via friend class: 25
```

Analysis ▼

Line 10 indicates class Utility to be a friend of class Human. This allows all methods in class Utility access even to the private data members and methods in class Human.

Summary

This lesson taught you one of the most fundamental keywords and concepts in C++, that of a class. You learned how a class encapsulates member data and member functions that operate using the same. You saw how access specifiers such as public and private help you abstract data and functionality that entities external to the class don't need to see.

You learned the concept of copy constructors and how C++11 allows you to optimize on unwanted copy steps with the help of move constructors. You saw some special cases where all these elements come together to help you implement design patterns such as the singleton.

Q&A

Q **What is the difference between the instance of a class and an object of that class?**

A Essentially none. When you instantiate a class, you get an instance that can also be called an object.

Q **What is a better way to access members: using the dot operator (.) or using the pointer operator (->)?**

A If you have a pointer to an object, the pointer operator would be best suited. If you have instantiated an object as a local variable on the stack, then the dot operator is best suited.

Q **Should I always program a copy constructor?**

A If your class' data members are well-programmed smart pointers, string classes, or STL containers such as std::vector, then the default copy constructor inserted by the compiler ensures that their respective copy constructors are invoked. However, if your class has raw pointer members (such as int* for a dynamic array instead of std::vector<int>), you need to supply a correctly programmed copy constructor that ensures a deep copy of an array during function calls where an object of the class is passed by value.

Q **My class has only one constructor that has been defined with a parameter with a default value. Is this still a default constructor?**

A Yes. If an instance of a class can be created without arguments, then the class is said to have a default constructor. A class can have only one default constructor.

Q **Why do some samples in this lesson use functions such as SetAge() to set integer Human::Age? Why not make Age public and assign it as needed?**

A From a technical viewpoint, making Human::Age a public member would work as well. However, from a design point of view, keeping member data private is a good idea. Accessor functions such as GetAge() or SetAge() are a refined and scalable way to access this private data, allowing you to perform error checks for instance before the value of Human::Age is set or reset.

Q Why is the parameter of a copy constructor one that takes the copy source by reference?

A For one, the copy constructor is expected by the compiler to be that way. The reason behind it is that a copy constructor would invoke itself if it accepted the copy source by value, resulting in an endless copy loop.

Workshop

The Workshop provides quiz questions to help you solidify your understanding of the material covered and exercises to provide you with experience in using what you've learned. Try to answer the quiz and exercise questions before checking the answers in Appendix D, and be certain you understand the answers before continuing to the next lesson.

9

Quiz

1. When I create an instance of a class using new, where is the class created?

2. My class has a raw pointer int* that contains a dynamically allocated array of integers. Does sizeof report different sizes depending on the number of integers in the dynamic array?

3. All my class members are private, and my class does not contain any declared friend class or function. Who can access these members?

4. Can one class member method invoke another?

5. What is a constructor good for?

6. What is a destructor good for?

Exercises

1. **BUG BUSTERS:** What is wrong in the following class declaration?

```
Class Human
{
    int Age;
    string Name;

public:
    Human() {}
}
```

2. How would the user of the class in Exercise 1 access member `Human::Age`?

3. Write a better version of the class seen in Exercise 1 that initializes all parameters using an initialization list in the constructor.

4. Write a `class Circle` that computes the area and circumference given a radius that is supplied to the class as a parameter at the time of instantiation. Pi should be contained in a constant private member that cannot be accessed from outside the circle.

LESSON 10
Implementing Inheritance

Object-oriented programming is based on four important aspects: encapsulation, abstraction, inheritance, and polymorphism. Inheritance is a powerful way to reuse attributes and is a stepping stone towards polymorphism.

In this lesson, you find out about

- Inheritance in the context of programming

- The C++ syntax of inheritance

- `public`, `private`, and `protected` inheritance

- Multiple inheritance

- Problems caused by hiding base class methods and slicing

Basics of Inheritance

What Tom Smith inherits from his forefathers is first and foremost his family name that makes him a Smith. In addition, he inherits certain values that his parents have taught him and a skill at sculpting wood that has been the Smith family occupation for many generations. These attributes collectively identify Tom as an offspring of the Smith family tree.

In programming parlance, you are often faced with situations where components being managed have similar attributes, differing minutely in details or in behavior. One way to solve this problem is to make each component a class where each class implements all attributes, even re-implementing the common ones. Another solution is using inheritance to allow classes that are similar to derive from a base class that implements common functionality, overriding this base functionality to implement behavior that makes each class unique. The latter is often the preferred way. Welcome to inheritance in our world of object-oriented programming, as illustrated by Figure 10.1.

FIGURE 10.1
Inheritance
between classes.

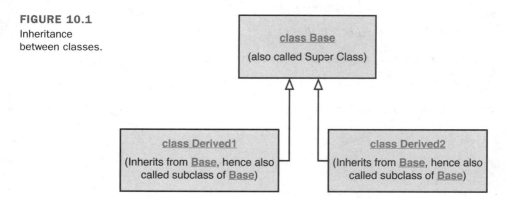

Inheritance and Derivation

Figure 10.1 shows a diagrammatic relationship between a base class and its derived classes. It might not be easy right now to visualize what a base class or a derived class could be; try to understand that a derived class inherits from the base class and in that sense is a base class (just like Tom is a Smith).

NOTE

> The is-a relationship between a derived class and its base is applicable only to public inheritance. This lesson starts with public inheritance to understand the concept of inheritance and the most frequent form of inheritance before moving on to `private` or `protected` inheritance.

To make understanding this concept easy, think of a base class Bird. Classes are derived from Bird are class Crow, class Parrot, or class Kiwi. A class Bird would define the most basic attributes of a bird, such as is feathered, has wings, lays eggs, can fly (for the most part). Derived classes such as Crow, Parrot, or Kiwi inherit these attributes and customize them (for example, a Kiwi would contain no implementation of Fly()). Table 10.1 demonstrates a few more examples of inheritance.

TABLE 10.1 Examples of Public Inheritance Taken from Daily Life

Base Class	Example Derived Classes
Fish	Goldfish, Carp, Tuna (Tuna is a Fish)
Mammal	Human, Elephant, Lion, Platypus (Platypus is a Mammal)
Bird	Crow, Parrot, Ostrich, Kiwi, Platypus (Platypus is a Bird, too!)
Shape	Circle, Polygon (Circle is a Shape)
Polygon	Triangle, Octagon (Octagon is a Polygon, which is a Shape)

What these examples show is that when you put on your object-oriented programming glasses, you see examples of inheritance in many objects around yourself. Fish is a base class for a Tuna because a Tuna, like a Carp, is a Fish and presents all fish-like characteristics such as being cold-blooded. However, Tuna differs from a Carp in the way it looks, swims, and in the fact that it is a saltwater fish. Thus, Tuna and Carp inherit common characteristics from a common base class Fish, yet specialize the base class attributes to distinguish themselves from each other. This is illustrated in Figure 10.2

FIGURE 10.2
Hierarchical relationship between Tuna, Carp, and Fish.

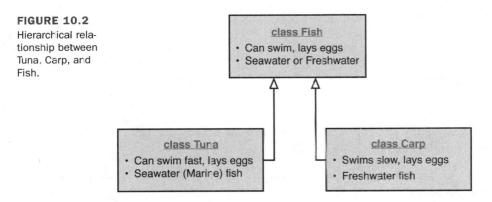

A platypus can swim, yet is a special animal with mammalian characteristics such as feeding its young with milk, avian (bird-like) characteristics as it lays eggs, and reptilian characteristics as it is venomous. Thus, one can imagine a class Platypus inheriting

from two base classes, class Mammal and class Bird, to inherit mammalian and avian features. This form of inheritance is called *multiple inheritance*, which is discussed later in this lesson.

C++ Syntax of Derivation

How would you inherit class Carp from class Fish, or in general a class Derived from class Base? C++ syntax for doing this would be the following:

```
// declaring a super class
class Base
{
    // ... base class members
};
// declaring a sub-class
class Derived: access-specifier Base
{
    // ... derived class members
};
```

The access-specifier can be one of public (most frequently used) for a "derived class is a base class" relationship, private, or protected for a "derived class has a base class" relationship.

An inheritance hierarchical representation for a class Carp that derives from class Fish would be

```
class Fish
{
 // ... Fish's members
};

class Carp:public Fish
{
 // ... Carp's members
};
```

A compile-worthy declaration of a class Carp and class Tuna that derive from class Fish is demonstrated by Listing 10.1.

A Note About Terminology

When reading about inheritance, you will come across terms such as *inherits from* or *derives from*, which essentially mean the same.

Similarly, the base class is also called the *super class*. The class that derives from the base, also known as the *derived class*, can be called the *subclass*.

LISTING 10.1   A Simple Inheritance Hierarchy Demonstrated by the Piscean World

```
 0: #include <iostream>
 1: using namespace std;
 2:
 3: class Fish
 4: {
 5: public:
 6:     bool FreshWaterFish;
 7:
 8:     void Swim()
 9:     {
10:         if (FreshWaterFish)
11:             cout << "Swims in lake" << endl;
12:         else
13:             cout << "Swims in sea" << endl;
14:     }
15: };
16:
17: class Tuna: public Fish
18: {
19: public:
20:     Tuna()
21:     {
22:         FreshWaterFish = false;
23:     }
24: };
25:
26: class Carp: public Fish
27: {
28: public:
29:     Carp()
30:     {
31:         FreshWaterFish = true;
32:     }
33: };
34:
35: int main()
36: {
37:     Carp myLunch;
38:     Tuna myDinner;
39:
40:     cout << "Getting my food to swim" << endl;
41:
42:     cout << "Lunch: ";
43:     myLunch.Swim();
44:
45:     cout << "Dinner: ";
46:     myDinner.Swim();
47:
48:     return 0;
49: }
```

10

Output ▼

```
Getting my food to swim
Lunch: Swims in lake
Dinner: Swims in sea
```

Analysis ▼

Note Lines 37 and 38 in main() that create an object of classes Carp and Tuna, respectively, as myLunch and myDinner. Lines 43 and 46 are where I ask my lunch and dinner to swim by invoking method Swim() that they seem to support. Now, look at the class definitions of Tuna in Lines 17–24 and Carp in Lines 26–33. As you can see, these classes are quite compact, and neither of them seems to define a method Swim() that you have managed to successfully invoke in main(). Evidently, Swim() comes from the class Fish that they inherit from, defined in Lines 3–15. As Fish declares a public method called Swim(), classes Tuna and Carp that inherit from Fish (via public inheritance as shown in Lines 17 and 26) automatically expose the base class' public method Swim(). Note how the constructor of Carp and Tuna initializes base class flag FreshWaterFish, which plays a role in deciding the output displayed by Fish::Swim().

Access Specifier Keyword protected

Listing 10.1 is one where class Fish has a public attribute FreshWaterFish that is set by the derived classes Tuna and Carp so as to customize (also called *specialize*) the behavior of Fish and adapt it to saltwater and freshwater, respectively. However, Listing 10.1 exhibits a serious flaw: If you want, even main() could tamper with this flag that has been marked public and hence open for manipulation from outside class Fish via a simple line such as the following:

```
myDinner.FreshWaterFish = true; // making Tuna a fresh water fish!
```

This obviously needs to be avoided. What you need is a possibility that allows certain attributes in the base class to be accessible only to the derived class but not accessible to the outside world. This means that you want Boolean flag FreshWaterFish in class Fish to be accessible to class Tuna and class Carp that derive from it but not accessible to main() that instantiates classes Tuna or Carp. This is where keyword protected helps you.

> **NOTE**
>
> protected, like public and private, is also an access specifier. When you declare an attribute as protected, you are effectively making the attribute accessible to classes that derive and friends, yet simultaneously making it inaccessible to everyone else outside, including main().

protected is the access specifier you should use if you want a certain attribute in a base class to be accessible to classes that derive from this base, as demonstrated in Listing 10.2.

LISTING 10.2 A Better class Fish Using the protected keyword to Expose Its Member Attribute Only to the Derived Classes

```
0: #include <iostream>
1: using namespace std;
2:
3: class Fish
4: {
5: protected:
6:    bool FreshWaterFish; // accessible only to derived classes
7:
8: public:
9:    void Swim()
10:    {
11:       if (FreshWaterFish)
12:          cout << "Swims in lake" << endl;
13:       else
14:          cout << "Swims in sea" << endl;
15:    }
16: };
17:
18: class Tuna: public Fish
19: {
20: public:
21:    Tuna()
22:    {
23:       FreshWaterFish = false; // set base class protected member
24:    }
25: };
26:
27: class Carp: public Fish
28: {
29: public:
30:    Carp()
31:    {
32:       FreshWaterFish = false;
33:    }
34: };
35:
36: int main()
37: {
38:    Carp myLunch;
39:    Tuna myDinner;
40:
41:    cout << "Getting my food to swim" << endl;
```

10

LISTING 10.2 Continued

```
42:
43:    cout << "Lunch: ";
44:    myLunch.Swim();
45:
46:    cout << "Dinner: ";
47:    myDinner.Swim();
48:
49:    // uncomment line below to see that protected members
50:    // are not accessible from outside the class hierarchy
51:    // myLunch.FreshWaterFish = false;
52:
53:    return 0;
54: }
```

Output ▼

```
Getting my food to swim
Lunch: Swims in lake
Dinner: Swims in sea
```

Analysis ▼

In spite of the fact that the output of Listing 10.2 is the same as Listing 10.1, there are a good number of fundamental changes to class Fish as defined in Lines 3–19. The first and most evident change is that the Boolean member Fish::FreshWaterFish is now a protected attribute, and hence, not accessible via main() as shown in Line 51 (uncomment it to see a compiler error). All the same, this parameter with access specifier protected is accessible from the derived classes Tuna and Carp as shown in Lines 23 and 32, respectively. What this little program effectively demonstrates is the use of keyword protected in ensuring that base class attributes that need to be inherited are protected from being accessed outside the class hierarchy.

This is a very important aspect of object-oriented programming, combining data abstraction and inheritance, in ensuring that derived classes can safely inherit base class attributes that cannot be tampered with by anyone outside this hierarchical system.

Base Class Initialization—Passing Parameters to the Base Class

What if a base class contains an overloaded constructor that enforces arguments at the time of instantiation? How would such a base class be instantiated when the derived class is being constructed? The clue lies in using initialization lists and in invoking the appropriate base class constructor via the constructor of the derived class as shown in the following code:

```
class Base
{
public:
   Base(int SomeNumber) // overloaded constructor
   {
      // Do something with SomeNumber
   }
};
Class Derived: public Base
{
public:
   Derived(): Base(25)  // instantiate class Base with argument 25
   {
      // derived class constructor code
   }
};
```

This mechanism can be quite useful in class Fish wherein, by supplying a Boolean input parameter to the constructor of Fish that initializes Fish::FreshWaterFish, this base class Fish can ensure that every derived class is forced to mention whether the Fish is a freshwater one or a saltwater one as shown in Listing 10.3.

LISTING 10.3   Derived Class Constructor with Initialization Lists

```
0: #include <iostream>
1: using namespace std;
2:
3: class Fish
4: {
5: protected:
6:    bool FreshWaterFish; // accessible only to derived classes
7:
8: public:
9:    // Fish constructor
10:    Fish(bool IsFreshWater) : FreshWaterFish(IsFreshWater){}
11:
12:    void Swim()
13:    {
14:       if (FreshWaterFish)
15:          cout << "Swims in lake" << endl;
16:       else
17:          cout << "Swims in sea" << endl;
18:    }
19: };
```

LISTING 10.3 Continued

```
20:
21: class Tuna: public Fish
22: {
23: public:
24:     Tuna(): Fish(false) {}
25: };
26:
27: class Carp: public Fish
28: {
29: public:
30:     Carp(): Fish(true) {}
31: };
32:
33: int main()
34: {
35:     Carp myLunch;
36:     Tuna myDinner;
37:
38:     cout << "Getting my food to swim" << endl;
39:
40:     cout << "Lunch: ";
41:     myLunch.Swim();
42:
43:     cout << "Dinner: ";
44:     myDinner.Swim();
45:
46:     // uncomment line 48 to see that protected members
47:     // are not accessible from outside the class heirarchy
48:     // myLunch.FreshWaterFish = false;
49:
50:     return 0;
51: }
```

Output ▼

```
Getting my food to swim
Lunch: Swims in lake
Dinner: Swims in sea
```

Analysis ▼

Fish now has a constructor that takes a default parameter initializing Fish::FreshWaterFish. Thus, the only possibility to create an object of Fish is via providing it a parameter that initialized the protected member. This way class Fish ensures that the protected member doesn't contain a random value, especially if a derived class forgets to set it. Derived classes Tuna and Carp are now forced to define a constructor that instantiates the base class instance of Fish with the right parameter (true or false, indicating freshwater or otherwise), as shown in Lines 24 and 30, respectively.

NOTE

In Listing 10.3 you see that boolean member variable Fish::FreshWaterFish was never accessed directly by a derived class in spite of it being a protected member, as this variable was set via the constructor of Fish.

To ensure maximum security, if the derived classes don't need to access a base class attribute, remember to mark the attribute private.

Derived Class Overriding Base Class' Methods

10

If a class Derived implements the same functions with the same return values and signatures as in a class Base it inherits from, it effectively overrides that method in class Base as shown in the following code:

```
class Base
{
public:
   void DoSomething()
   {
      // implementation code… Does something
   }
};
class Derived:public Base
{
public:
   void DoSomething()
   {
      // implementation code… Does something else
   }
};
```

Thus, if method DoSomething() were to be invoked using an instance of Derived, then it would not invoke the functionality in class Base.

If classes Tuna and Carp were to implement their own Swim() method that also exists in the base class as Fish::Swim(), then a call to Swim as shown in main() from the following excerpt of Listing 10.3

```
36:    Tuna myDinner;
// ...other lines
44:    myDinner.Swim();
```

would result in the local implementation of `Tuna::Swim()` being invoked, which essentially overrides the base class' `Fish::Swim()` method. This is demonstrated by Listing 10.4.

LISTING 10.4 Derived Classes `Tuna` and `Carp` Overriding Method `Swim()` in Base Class `Fish`

```
0: #include <iostream>
1: using namespace std;
2:
3: class Fish
4: {
5: private:
6:    bool FreshWaterFish;
7:
8: public:
9:    // Fish constructor
10:    Fish(bool IsFreshWater) : FreshWaterFish(IsFreshWater){}
11:
12:    void Swim()
13:    {
14:       if (FreshWaterFish)
15:          cout << "Swims in lake" << endl;
16:       else
17:          cout << "Swims in sea" << endl;
18:    }
19: };
20:
21: class Tuna: public Fish
22: {
23: public:
24:    Tuna(): Fish(false) {}
25:
26:    void Swim()
27:    {
28:       cout << "Tuna swims real fast" << endl;
29:    }
30: };
31:
32: class Carp: public Fish
33: {
34: public:
35:    Carp(): Fish(true) {}
36:
37:    void Swim()
38:    {
39:       cout << "Carp swims real slow" << endl;
40:    }
41: };
```

```
42:
43: int main()
44: {
45:     Carp myLunch;
46:     Tuna myDinner;
47:
48:     cout << "Getting my food to swim" << endl;
49:
50:     cout << "Lunch: ";
51:     myLunch.Swim();
52:
53:     cout << "Dinner: ";
54:     myDinner.Swim();
55:
56:     return 0;
57: }
```

Output ▼

```
Getting my food to swim
Lunch: Carp swims real slow
Dinner: Tuna swims real fast
```

Analysis ▼

The output demonstrates that myLunch.Swim() in Line 51 invokes Carp::Swim() defined in Lines 37–40. Similarly, myDinner.Swim() from Line 54 invokes Tuna::Swim() defined in Lines 26–29. In other words, the implementation of Fish::Swim() in the base class Fish, as shown in Lines 12–18, is overridden by the identical function Swim() defined by the classes Tuna and Carp that derive from Fish. The only way to invoke Fish::Swim() is either by having the derived class explicitly use it in its member function, or by having main() use the scope resolution operator in explicitly invoking Fish::Swim(), as is shown later in this lesson.

Invoking Overridden Methods of a Base Class

In Listing 10.4, you saw an example of derived class Tuna overriding the Swim() function in Fish by implementing its version of the same. Essentially:

```
Tuna myDinner;
myDinner.Swim(); // will invoke Tuna::Swim()
```

If you want to be invoke Fish::Swim() in Listing 10.4 via main(), you need to use the scope resolution operator (::) in the following syntax:

```
myDinner.Fish::Swim();  // will invoke Fish::Swim() in spite of being a Tuna
```

Listing 10.5 that follows shortly demonstrates invoking a base class member using an instance of the derived class.

Invoking Methods of a Base Class in a Derived Class

Typically, `Fish::Swim()` would contain a generic implementation of swimming applicable to all fishes, tunas and carps included. If your specialized implementations in `Tuna:Swim()` and `Carp::Swim()` need to reuse the base class' generic implementation of `Fish::Swim()`, you use the scope resolution operator (`::`) as shown in the following code:

```
class Carp: public Fish
{
public:
   Carp(): Fish(true) {}

   void Swim()
   {
      cout << "Carp swims real slow" << endl;
      Fish::Swim();  // use scope resolution operator::
   }
};
```

This is demonstrated in Listing 10.5.

LISTING 10.5 Using Scope Resolution Operator (`::`) to Invoke Base Class Methods from Derived Class Methods and `main()`

```
 0: #include <iostream>
 1: using namespace std;
 2:
 3: class Fish
 4: {
 5: private:
 6:    bool FreshWaterFish;
 7:
 8: public:
 9:    // Fish constructor
10:    Fish(bool IsFreshWater) : FreshWaterFish(IsFreshWater){}
11:
12:    void Swim()
13:    {
14:       if (FreshWaterFish)
15:          cout << "Swims in lake" << endl;
16:       else
17:          cout << "Swims in sea" << endl;
18:    }
```

```
19: };
20:
21: class Tuna: public Fish
22: {
23: public:
24:     Tuna(): Fish(false) {}
25:
26:     void Swim()
27:     {
28:         cout << "Tuna swims real fast" << endl;
29:     }
30: };
31:
32: class Carp: public Fish
33: {
34: public:
35:     Carp(): Fish(true) {}
36:
37:     void Swim()
38:     {
39:         cout << "Carp swims real slow" << endl;
40:         Fish::Swim();
41:     }
42: };
43:
44: int main()
45: {
46:     Carp myLunch;
47:     Tuna myDinner;
48:
49:     cout << "Getting my food to swim" << endl;
50:
51:     cout << "Lunch: ";
52:     myLunch.Swim();
53:
54:     cout << "Dinner: ";
55:     myDinner.Fish::Swim();
56:
57:     return 0;
58: }
```

10

Output ▼

```
Getting my food to swim
Lunch: Carp swims real slow
Swims in lake
Dinner: Swims in sea
```

Analysis ▼

`Carp::Swim()` in Lines 37–41 demonstrates calling the base class function `Fish::Swim()` using the scope resolution operator (::). Line 55, on the other hand, shows how you can use the scope resolution operator (::) to invoke base class method `Fish::Swim()` from `main()` given an instance of `Tuna`.

Derived Class Hiding Base Class' Methods

Overriding can take an extreme form where `Tuna::Swim()` can potentially hide all over-loaded versions of `Fish::Swim()` available, even causing compilation failure when the overloaded ones are used (hence, called hidden), as demonstrated by Listing 10.6.

LISTING 10.6   Demonstrating That `Tuna::Swim()` Hides Overloaded Method `Fish::Swim(bool)`

```
0: #include <iostream>
1: using namespace std;
2:
3: class Fish
4: {
5: public:
6:    void Swim()
7:    {
8:       cout << "Fish swims... !" << endl;
9:    }
10:
11:    void Swim(bool FreshWaterFish)
12:    {
13:       if (FreshWaterFish)
14:          cout << "Swims in lake" << endl;
15:       else
16:          cout << "Swims in sea" << endl;
17:    }
18: };
19:
20: class Tuna: public Fish
21: {
22: public:
23:    void Swim()
24:    {
25:       cout << "Tuna swims real fast" << endl;
26:    }
27: };
28:
29: int main()
30: {
31:    Tuna myDinner;
```

```
32:
33:    cout << "Getting my food to swim" << endl;
34:
35:    // myDinner.Swim(false); // compile failure: Fish::Swim(bool) is hidden
by Tuna::Swim()
36:    myDinner.Swim();
37:
38:    return 0;
39: }
```

Output ▼

```
Getting my food to swim
Tuna swims real fast
```

Analysis ▼

This version of class Fish is a bit different than those that you have seen this far. Apart
from being a minimalized version to explain the problem at hand, this version of Fish
contains two overloaded methods for Swim(), one that takes no parameters, as shown in
Lines 6–9, and another that takes a bool parameter, as shown in Lines 11–17. As Tuna
inherits public from Fish as shown in Line 20, one would not be wrong to expect that
both versions of method Fish::Swim() would be available via an instance of class
Tuna. The fact is, however, that Tuna implementing its own Tuna::Swim(), as shown in
Lines 23–26, results in the hiding of Fish::Swim(bool) from the compiler. If you
uncomment Line 35, you see a compilation failure.

So, if you want to invoke the Fish::Swim(bool) function via an instance of Tuna, you
have the following solutions:

- Solution 1: Use the scope resolution operator in main():
  ```
  myDinner.Fish::Swim();
  ```

- Solution 2: Use the using keyword in class Tuna to unhide Swim() in class
  Fish:
  ```
  class Tuna: public Fish
  {
  public:
      using Fish::Swim;    // unhide Swim methods in base class Fish

      void Swim()
      {
          cout << "Tuna swims real fast" << endl;
      }
  };
  ```

- Solution 3: Override all overloaded variants of Swim() in class Tuna (invoke methods of Fish::Swim(...) via Tuna::Fish(...) if you want):

```
class Tuna: public Fish
{
public:
    void Swim(bool FreshWaterFish)
    {
        Fish::Swim(FreshWaterFish);
    }

    void Swim()
    {
        cout << "Tuna swims real fast" << endl;
    }
};
```

Order of Construction

So, when you create an object of class Tuna that derives from class Fish, was the constructor of Tuna invoked before or after the constructor of class Fish? Additionally, within the instantiation of objects in the class hierarchy, what respective order do member attributes such as Fish::FreshWaterFish have? The fact is that base class objects are instantiated before the derived class. So, the Fish part of Tuna is constructed first, so that member attributes—especially the protected and public ones contained in class Fish—are ready for consumption when class Tuna is instantiated. Within the instantiation of class Fish and class Tuna, the member attributes (such as Fish::FreshWaterFish) are instantiated before the constructor Fish::Fish() is invoked, ensuring that member attributes are ready before the constructor works with them. The same applies to Tuna::Tuna().

Order of Destruction

When an instance of Tuna goes out of scope, the sequence of destruction is the opposite to that of construction. Listing 10.7 is a simple example that demonstrates the sequence of construction and destruction.

LISTING 10.7 The Order of Construction and Destruction of the Base Class, Derived Class, and Members Thereof

```
0: #include <iostream>
1: using namespace std;
2:
3: class FishDummyMember
```

```
 4: {
 5: public:
 6:    FishDummyMember()
 7:    {
 8:        cout << "FishDummyMember constructor" << endl;
 9:    }
10:
11:    ~FishDummyMember()
12:    {
13:        cout << "FishDummyMember destructor" << endl;
14:    }
15: };
16:
17: class Fish
18: {
19: protected:
20:    FishDummyMember dummy;
21:
22: public:
23:    // Fish constructor
24:    Fish()
25:    {
26:        cout << "Fish constructor" << endl;
27:    }
28:
29:    ~Fish()
30:    {
31:        cout << "Fish destructor" << endl;
32:    }
33: };
34:
35: class TunaDummyMember
36: {
37: public:
38:    TunaDummyMember()
39:    {
40:        cout << "TunaDummyMember constructor" << endl;
41:    }
42:
43:    ~TunaDummyMember()
44:    {
45:        cout << "TunaDummyMember destructor" << endl;
46:    }
47: };
48:
49:
50: class Tuna: public Fish
51: {
52: private:
53:    TunaDummyMember dummy;
54:
```

10

LISTING 10.7   Continued

```
55: public:
56:    Tuna()
57:    {
58:       cout << "Tuna constructor" << endl;
59:    }
60:    ~Tuna()
61:    {
62:       cout << "Tuna destructor" << endl;
63:    }
64:
65: };
66:
67: int main()
68: {
69:    Tuna myDinner;
70: }
```

Output ▼

```
FishDummyMember constructor
Fish constructor
TunaDummyMember constructor
Tuna constructor
Tuna destructor
TunaDummyMember destructor
Fish destructor
FishDummyMember destructor
```

Analysis ▼

`main()` as shown in Lines 67–70 is spectacularly small for the volume of output it generates. Instantiation of a `Tuna` is enough to generate these lines of output because of the `cout` statements that you have inserted into the constructors and destructors of all objects involved. For the sake of understanding how member variables are instantiated and destroyed, you defined two dummy classes, `FishDummyMember`, and `TunaDummyMember` with `cout` in their constructors and destructors. `class Fish` and `class Tuna` contain a member of each of these dummy classes as shown in Lines 20 and 53. The output indicates that when an object of `class Tuna` is instantiated, instantiation actually starts at the top of the hierarchy. So, the base `class Fish` part of `class Tuna` is instantiated first, and in doing so, the members of the `Fish`—that is, `Fish::dummy`—are instantiated first. This is then followed by the constructor of the `Fish`, which is rightfully executed after the member attributes such as dummy have been constructed. After the base class has been constructed, the instantiation of Tuna continues first with instantiation of member Tuna::dummy, finally followed by the execution of the constructor code in Tuna::Tuna(). The output demonstrates that the sequence of destruction is exactly the opposite.

Private Inheritance

Private inheritance differs from public inheritance (which is what you have seen up to now) in that the keyword private is used in the line where the derived class declares its inheritance from a base class:

```
class Base
{
   // ... base class members and methods

};

class Derived: private Base      // private inheritance
{
   // ... derived class members and methods
};
```

Private inheritance of the base class means that all public members and attributes of the base class are private (that is, inaccessible) to anyone with an instance of the derived class. In other words, even public members and methods of class Base can only be consumed by class Derived, but not by anyone else in possession of an instance of Derived.

This is in sharp contrast to the examples with Tuna and base Fish that you have been following since Listing 10.1. main() in Listing 10.1 could invoke function Fish::Swim() on an instance of Tuna because Fish::Swim() is a public method and because class Tuna derives from class Fish using the public inheritance. Try renaming public to private in Line 17 and see compilation fail.

Thus, for the world outside the inheritance hierarchy, private inheritance essentially does not mean an is-a relationship (imagine a tuna that can't swim!). As private inheritance allows base class attributes and methods to be consumed only by the subclass that derives from it, this relationship is also called a has-a relationship. There are a few examples of private inheritance in some things you see around you in daily life (see Table 10.2).

TABLE 10.2   Examples of Private Inheritance Taken from Daily Life

Base Class	Example Derived Class
Motor	Car (Car has a Motor)
Heart	Mammal (Mammal has a Heart)
Refill	Pen (Pen has a Refill)
Moon	Sky (Sky has a Moon)

Let's visualize private inheritance in a car's relationship to its motor. See Listing 10.8.

LISTING 10.8   A class Car Related to class Motor via private Inheritance

```cpp
0: #include <iostream>
1: using namespace std;
2:
3: class Motor
4: {
5: public:
6:     void SwitchIgnition()
7:     {
8:         cout << "Ignition ON" << endl;
9:     }
10:     void PumpFuel()
11:     {
12:         cout << "Fuel in cylinders" << endl;
13:     }
14:     void FireCylinders()
15:     {
16:         cout << "Vroooom" << endl;
17:     }
18: };
19:
20: class Car:private Motor
21: {
22: public:
23:     void Move()
24:     {
25:         SwitchIgnition();
26:         PumpFuel();
27:         FireCylinders();
28:     }
29: };
30:
31: int main()
32: {
33:     Car myDreamCar;
34:     myDreamCar.Move();
```

```
35:
36:    return 0;
37: }
```

Output ▼

```
Ignition ON
Fuel in cylinders
Vroooom
```

Analysis ▼

class Motor defined in Lines 3–18 is quite simple with three protected member functions that switch ignition, pump fuel, and fire the cylinders. class Car as Line 20 demonstrates inherits from Motor, using keyword private. Thus, public function Car::Move() invokes members from the base class Motor. If you try inserting the following in main():

```
myDreamCar.PumpFuel();
```

it fails compilation with an error similar to error C2247: Motor::PumpFuel not accessible because 'Car' uses 'private' to inherit from 'Motor'.

NOTE

If another class SuperCar had to inherit from Car, then irrespective of the nature of inheritance between SuperCar and Car, SuperCar would not have access to any public member or method of base class Motor. This is because the relationship between Car and Motor is one of private inheritance, meaning that all entities other than Car have private access (that is, no access) even to public members of Base.

In other words, the most restrictive access specifier takes dominance in the compiler's calculation of whether one class should have access to a base class' public or protected members.

10

Protected Inheritance

Protected inheritance differs from public inheritance in that the keyword protected is used in the line where the derived class declares its inheritance from a base class:

```
class Base
{
```

```
    // ... base class members and methods
};

class Derived: protected Base      // protected inheritance
{
    // ... derived class members and methods
};
```

Protected inheritance is similar to private inheritance in the following ways:

- It also signifies a has-a relationship.
- It also lets the derived class access all public and protected members of Base.
- Those outside the inheritance hierarchy with an instance of Derived cannot access public members of Base.

Yet, protected inheritance is a bit different when it comes to the derived class being inherited from:

```
class Derived2: protected Derived
{
    // can access members of Base
};
```

Protected inheritance hierarchy allows the subclass of the subclass (that is, Derived2) access to public members of the Base as shown in Listing 10.9. This would not be possible if the inheritance between Derived and Base were private.

LISTING 10.9   class SuperCar That Derives from class Car That Derives from class Motor Using protected Inheritance

```
0: #include <iostream>
1: using namespace std;
2:
3: class Motor
4: {
5: public:
6:     void SwitchIgnition()
7:     {
8:         cout << "Ignition ON" << endl;
9:     }
10:     void PumpFuel()
11:     {
12:         cout << "Fuel in cylinders" << endl;
13:     }
14:     void FireCylinders()
15:     {
```

```
16:        cout << "Vroooom" << endl;
17:    }
18: };
19:
20: class Car:protected Motor
21: {
22: public:
23:    void Move()
24:    {
25:        SwitchIgnition();
26:        PumpFuel();
27:        FireCylinders();
28:    }
29: };
30:
31: class SuperCar:protected Car
32: {
33: public:
34:    void Move()
35:    {
36:        SwitchIgnition();  // has access to base members
37:        PumpFuel();        // due to "protected" inheritance between Car and
                              Motor
38:        FireCylinders();
39:        FireCylinders();
40:        FireCylinders();
41:    }
42: };
43:
44: int main()
45: {
46:    SuperCar myDreamCar;
47:    myDreamCar.Move();
48:
49:    return 0;
50: }
```

Output ▼

```
Ignition ON
Fuel in cylinders
Vroooom
Vroooom
Vroooom
```

Analysis ▼

class Car inherits using protected from Motor as shown in Line 20. class SuperCar inherits using protected from class Car using protected as shown in Line 31. As you can see, the implementation of SuperCar::Move() uses public methods defined in base class Motor. This access to the ultimate base class Motor via intermediate base class Car is governed by the relationship between Car and Motor. If this were private instead of protected, SuperClass would have no access to the public members of Motor as the compiler would choose the most restrictive of the relevant access specifiers. Note that the nature of relationship between the classes Car and SuperCar plays no role in access to Base. So, even if you change protected in Line 31 to public or to private, the fate of compilation of this program remains unchanged.

> **CAUTION**
>
> Use private or protected inheritance only when you have to.
>
> In most cases where private inheritance is used, such as that of the Car and the Motor, the base class could have as well been a member attribute of the class Car instead of being a super-class. By inheriting from class Motor, you have essentially restricted your Car to having only one motor, for no significant gain over having an instance of class Motor as a private member.
>
> Cars have evolved, and hybrid cars, for instance, have a gas motor in addition to an electric one. Our inheritance hierarchy for class Car would prove to be a bottleneck in being compatible to such developments.

> **NOTE**
>
> Having an instance of Motor as a private member instead of inheriting from it is called *composition* or *aggregation*. Such a class Car looks like this:
>
> ```
> class Car
> {
> private:
>     Motor heartOfCar;
>
> public:
>     void Move()
>     {
>         heartOfCar.SwitchIgnition();
>         heartOfCar.PumpFuel();
>         heartOfCar.FireCylinders();
>     }
> };
> ```
>
> This can be good design as it enables you to easily add more motors as member attributes to an existing Car class without changing its inheritance hierarchy or its design with respect to its clients.

The Problem of Slicing

What happens when a programmer does the following?

```
Derived objectDerived;
Base objectBase = objectDerived;
```

Or, alternatively, what if a programmer does this?

```
void FuncUseBase(Base input);
...
Derived objectDerived;
FuncUseBase(objectDerived);  // objectDerived will be sliced when copied during
  function call
```

In both cases, an object of type Derived is being copied into another of type Base, either explicitly via assignment or by passing as an argument. What happens in these cases is that the compiler copies only the Base part of objectDerived—that is, not the complete object—rather than only that part of it that would fit Base. This is typically not what the programmer expects, and this unwanted reduction of the part of data that makes the Derived a specialization of Base is called *slicing*.

CAUTION	To avoid slicing problems, don't pass parameters by value. Pass them as pointers to the base class or as a (optionally const) reference to the same.

Multiple Inheritance

Earlier in this chapter I mentioned that in some certain cases multiple inheritance might be relevant, such as with the platypus. The platypus is part mammal, part bird, and part reptile. For such cases, C++ allows a class to derive from two or more base classes:

```
class Derived: access-specifier Base1, access-specifier Base2
{
   // class members
};
```

The class diagram for a platypus, as illustrated by Figure 10.3, looks quite different to the previous ones for Tuna and Carp (refer to Figure 10.2).

FIGURE 10.3
Relationship of a
class Platypus,
to classes
Mammal, Reptile
and Bird.

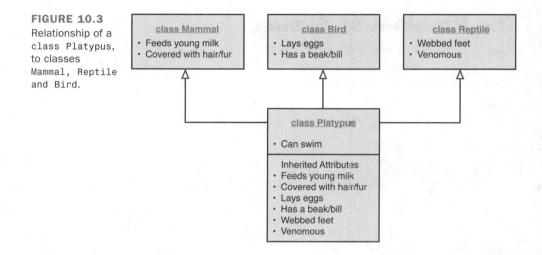

Thus, the C++ representation of class Platypus is the following:

```
class Platypus: public Mammal, public Reptile, public Bird
{
    // ... platypus members
};
```

A manifestation of Platypus that demonstrates multiple inheritance is demonstrated by
Listing 10.10.

LISTING 10.10   Using Multiple Inheritance to Model a Platypus That Is Part Mammal,
Part Bird, and Part Reptile

```
 0: #include <iostream>
 1: using namespace std;
 2:
 3: class Mammal
 4: {
 5: public:
 6:    void FeedBabyMilk()
 7:    {
 8:       cout << "Mammal: Baby says glug!" << endl;
 9:    }
10: };
11:
12: class Reptile
13: {
14: public:
15:    void SpitVenom()
```

```
16:    {
17:        cout << "Reptile: Shoo enemy! Spits venom!" << endl;
18:    }
19: };
20:
21: class Bird
22: {
23: public:
24:    void LayEggs()
25:    {
26:        cout << "Bird: Laid my eggs, am lighter now!" << endl;
27:    }
28: };
29:
30: class Platypus: public Mammal, public Bird, public Reptile
31: {
32: public:
33:    void Swim()
34:    {
35:        cout << "Platypus: Voila, I can swim!" << endl;
36:    }
37: };
38:
39: int main()
40: {
41:    Platypus realFreak;
42:    realFreak.LayEggs();
43:    realFreak.FeedBabyMilk();
44:    realFreak.SpitVenom();
45:    realFreak.Swim();
46:
47:    return 0;
48: }
```

10

Output ▼

```
Bird: Laid my eggs, am lighter now!
Mammal: Baby says glug!
Reptile: Shoo enemy! Spits venom!
Platypus: Voila, I can swim!
```

Analysis ▼

class Platypus features a really compact definition in Lines 30–37. It essentially does nothing more than inherit from the three classes Mammal, Reptile, and Bird. main() in Lines 41–44 is able to invoke these three characteristics of the individual base classes using an object of the derived class Platypus that is aptly named realFreak. In addition to invoking the functions inherited from classes `Mammal`, `Bird`, and `Reptile`, `main()` in Line 45 invokes `Platypus::Swim()`. This program demonstrates the syntax of multiple inheritance and also how a derived class exposes all the public attributes (in this case public member methods) of its many base classes.

NOTE　　Platypus can swim, but it's not a fish. Hence in Listing 10.10, you did not inherit `Platypus` also from `Fish` just for the convenience of using an existing `Fish::Swim()` functior. When making design decisions, don't forget that public inheritance also should signify an is-a relationship and should not be used indiscriminately to fulfill certain goals related to reuse. Those can still be achieved differently.

DO	DON'T
DO create a public inheritance hierarchy to establish an is-a relationship.	**DON'T** create an inheritance hierarchy just to reuse a trivial function.
DO create a `private` or `protected` inheritance hierarchy to establish a has-a relationship.	**DON'T** use private or public inheritance indiscriminately as they can end up being architectural bottlenecks towards the future scalability of your application.
DO remember that public inheritance means that classes deriving from the derived class have access to the public and protected members of the base class.	**DON'T** program derived class functions that unintentionally hide those in the base class by having the same name but a different set of input parameters.
DO remember that private inheritance means that even classes deriving from the derived class have no access to the base class.	
DO remember that protected inheritance means that classes deriving from the derived class have access to the protected and public methods of the base class.	
DO remember that irrespective of the nature of inheritance relationship, `private` members in the base class cannot be accessed by any derived class.	

```
14: public:
15:     // override Fish::Swim
16:     void Swim()
17:     {
18:         cout << "Tuna swims!" << endl;
19:     }
20: };
21:
22: void MakeFishSwim(Fish& InputFish)
23: {
24:     // calling Fish::Swim
25:     InputFish.Swim();
26: }
27:
28: int main()
29: {
30:     Tuna myDinner;
31:
32:     // calling Tuna::Swim
33:     myDinner.Swim();
34:
35:     // sending Tuna as Fish
36:     MakeFishSwim(myDinner);
37:
38:     return 0;
39: }
```

11

Output ▼

```
Tuna swims!
Fish swims!
```

Analysis ▼

class Tuna specializes class Fish via public inheritance as shown in Line 12. It also overrides Fish::Swim(). main() makes a direct call to Tuna::Swim() in Line 33 and passes myDinner (of type Tuna) as a parameter to MakeFishSwim() that interprets it as a reference Fish&, as shown in the declaration at Line 22. In other words, MakeFishSwim(Fish&) doesn't care if the object sent was a Tuna, handles it as a Fish, and invokes Fish::Swim. So, the second line of output indicates that the same object Tuna produced the output of a Fish not indicating any specialization thereof (this could as well be a Carp).

What the user would ideally expect is that an object of type Tuna behaves like a tuna even if the method invoked is Fish::Swim(). In other words, when InputFish.Swim() is invoked in Line 25, he expects it to execute Tuna::Swim(). Such polymorphic behavior where an object of known type `class Fish` can behave as its actual type; namely, derived `class Tuna`, can be implemented by making `Fish::Swim()` a virtual function.

Polymorphic Behavior Implemented Using Virtual Functions

You have access to an object of type `Fish`, via pointer `Fish*` or reference `Fish&`. This object could have been instantiated solely as a `Fish`, or be part of a `Tuna` or `Carp` that inherits from `Fish`. You don't know (and don't care). You invoke method `Swim()` using this pointer or reference, like this:

```
pFish->Swim();
myFish.Swim();
```

What you expect is that the object `Fish` swims as a `Tuna` if it is part of a `Tuna`, as a `Carp` if it is part of a `Carp`, or an anonymous `Fish` if it wasn't instantiated as part of a specialized class such as `Tuna` or `Carp`. You can ensure this by declaring function `Swim()` in the base class `Fish` as a virtual function:

```
class Base
{
    virtual ReturnType FunctionName (Parameter List);
};
class Derived
{
    ReturnType FunctionName (Parameter List);
};
```

Use of keyword `virtual` means that the compiler ensures that any overriding variant of the requested base class method is invoked. Thus, if `Swim()` is declared `virtual`, invoking `myFish.Swim()` (myFish being of type `Fish&`) results in `Tuna::Swim()` being executed as demonstrated by Listing 11.2.

LISTING 11.2 The Effect of Declaring `Fish::Swim()` as a `virtual` Method

```
0: #include <iostream>
1: using namespace std;
2:
3: class Fish
4: {
5: public:
6:    virtual void Swim()
7:       {
```

```
 8:        cout << "Fish swims!" << endl;
 9:    }
10: };
11:
12: class Tuna:public Fish
13: {
14: public:
15:    // override Fish::Swim
16:    void Swim()
17:    {
18:        cout << "Tuna swims!" << endl;
19:    }
20: };
21:
22: class Carp:public Fish
23: {
24: public:
25:    // override Fish::Swim
26:    void Swim()
27:    {
28:        cout << "Carp swims!" << endl;
29:    }
30: };
31:
32: void MakeFishSwim(Fish& InputFish)
33: {
34:    // calling virtual method Swim()
35:    InputFish.Swim();
36: }
37:
38: int main()
39: {
40:    Tuna myDinner;
41:    Carp myLunch;
42:
43:    // sending Tuna as Fish
44:    MakeFishSwim(myDinner);
45:
46:    // sending Carp as Fish
47:    MakeFishSwim(myLunch);
48:
49:    return 0;
50: }
```

11

Output ▼

```
Tuna swims!
Carp swims!
```

Analysis ▼

The implementation of function MakeFishSwim(Fish&) has not changed one bit since Listing 11.1. Yet, the output it produces is dramatically different. For one, Fish::Swim() has not been invoked at all because of the presence of overriding variants Tuna::Swim() and Carp::Swim() that have taken priority over Fish::Swim() because the latter has been declared as a virtual function. This is a very important development. It implies that even without knowing the exact type of Fish being handled, the implementation MakeFishSwim() could result in different implementations of Swim() defined in different derived classes being invoked, given only a base class instance.

This is polymorphism: treating different fishes as a common type Fish, yet ensuring that the right implementation of Swim() supplied by the derived types is executed.

Need for Virtual Destructors

There is a more sinister side to the feature demonstrated by Listing 11.1—unintentionally invoking base class functionality of an instance of type derived, when a specialization is available. What happens when a function calls operator delete using a pointer of type Base* that actually points to an instance of type Derived?

Which destructor would be invoked? See Listing 11.3.

LISTING 11.3   A Function That Invokes Operator delete on Base*

```
0: #include <iostream>
1: using namespace std;
2:
3: class Fish
4: {
5: public:
6:    Fish()
7:    {
8:       cout << "Constructed Fish" << endl;
9:    }
10:    ~Fish()
11:    {
12:       cout << "Destroyed Fish" << endl;
13:    }
14: };
15:
16: class Tuna:public Fish
17: {
18: public:
19:    Tuna()
20:    {
```

```
21:        cout << "Constructed Tuna" << endl;
22:    }
23:    ~Tuna()
24:    {
25:        cout << "Destroyed Tuna" << endl;
26:    }
27: };
28:
29: void DeleteFishMemory(Fish* pFish)
30: {
31:    delete pFish;
32: }
33:
34: int main()
35: {
36:    cout << "Allocating a Tuna on the free store:" << endl;
37:    Tuna* pTuna = new Tuna;
38:    cout << "Deleting the Tuna: " << endl;
39:    DeleteFishMemory(pTuna);
40:
41:    cout << "Instantiating a Tuna on the stack:" << endl;
42:    Tuna myDinner;
43:    cout << "Automatic destruction as it goes out of scope: " << endl;
44:
45:    return 0;
46: }
```

11

Output ▼

```
Allocating a Tuna on the free store:
Constructed Fish
Constructed Tuna
Deleting the Tuna:
Destroyed Fish
Instantiating a Tuna on the stack:
Constructed Fish
Constructed Tuna
Automatic destruction as it goes out of scope:
Destroyed Tuna
Destroyed Fish
```

Analysis ▼

main() creates an instance of Tuna on the free store using new at Line 37 and then releases the allocated memory immediately after using service function DeleteFishMemory() at Line 39. For the sake of comparison, another instance of Tuna is created as a local variable myDinner on the stack at Line 42 and goes out of scope when main() ends. The output is created by the cout statements in the constructors and destructors of classes Fish and Tuna. Note that while Tuna and Fish were both constructed on the free store due to new, the destructor of Tuna was not invoked on delete, rather only that of the Fish. This is in stark contrast to the construction and destruction of local member myDinner where all constructors and destructors are invoked. Lesson 10 demonstrated in Listing 10.7 the correct order of construction and destruction of classes in an inheritance hierarchy, showing that all destructors need to be invoked, including ~Tuna(). Clearly, something is amiss.

This flaw means that code in the destructor of a deriving class that has been instantiated on the free store using new would not be invoked if delete is called using a pointer of type Base*. This can result in resources not being released, memory leaks, and so on and is a problem that is not to be taken lightly.

To avoid this problem, you use virtual destructors as seen in Listing 11.4.

LISTING 11.4 Using virtual Destructors to Ensure That Destructors in Derived Classes Are Invoked When Deleting a Pointer of Type Base*

```
 0: #include <iostream>
 1: using namespace std;
 2:
 3: class Fish
 4: {
 5: public:
 6:    Fish()
 7:    {
 8:       cout << "Constructed Fish" << endl;
 9:    }
10:    virtual ~Fish()   // virtual destructor!
11:    {
12:       cout << "Destroyed Fish" << endl;
13:    }
14: };
15:
16: class Tuna:public Fish
17: {
18: public:
19:    Tuna()
20:    {
21:       cout << "Constructed Tuna" << endl;
22:    }
23:    ~Tuna()
24:    {
25:       cout << "Destroyed Tuna" << endl;
26:    }
27: };
```

In this case, even though objDerived is being interpreted via objBase as an instance of class Base, the VFT pointer in this instance is still pointing to the same table created for class Derived. Thus, Func1() executed via this VFT is certainly Derived::Func1().

This is how Virtual Function Tables help the implementation of (subtype) polymorphism in C++.

The proof of existence of a hidden Virtual Function Table pointer is demonstrated by Listing 11.5, which compares the sizeof two identical classes—one that has virtual functions and another that doesn't.

LISTING 11.5 Demonstrating the Presence of a Hidden VFT Pointer in Comparing Two Classes Identical but for a Function Declared Virtual

```
0: #include <iostream>
1: using namespace std;
2:
3: class SimpleClass
4: {
5:    int a, b;
6:
7: public:
8:    void FuncDoSomething() {}
9: };
10:
11: class Base
12: {
13:    int a, b;
14:
15: public:
16:    virtual void FuncDoSomething() {}
17: };
18:
19: int main()
20: {
21:    cout << "sizeof(SimpleClass) = " << sizeof(SimpleClass) << endl;
22:    cout << "sizeof(Base) = " << sizeof(Base) << endl;
23:
24:    return 0;
25: }
```

Output ▼

```
sizeof(SimpleClass) = 8
sizeof(Base) = 12
```

11

Analysis ▼

This is a sample that has been stripped to the bare minimum. You see two classes, SimpleClass and Base, that are identical in the types and number of members, yet Base has the function FuncDoSomething() declared as virtual (nonvirtual in SimpleClass). The difference in adding this virtual keyword is that the compiler generates a virtual function table for class Base and a reserved place for a pointer to the same in Base as a hidden member. This pointer consumes the 4 extra bytes in my 32-bit system and is the proof of the pudding.

> **NOTE**
>
> C++ also allows you to query a pointer Base* if it is of type Derived* using casting operator dynamic_cast and then perform conditional execution on the basis of the result of the query.
>
> This is called Run Time Type Identificatior (RTTI) and should ideally be avoided even though it is supported by most C++ compilers. This is because needing to know the type of derived class object behind a base class pointer is commonly considered poor programming practice.
>
> RTTI and dynamic_cast are discussed in Lesson 13, "Casting Operators."

Abstract Base Classes and Pure Virtual Functions

A base class that cannot be instantiated is called an *abstract base class*. Such a base class fulfills only one purpose, that of being derived from. C++ allows you to create an abstract base class using pure virtual functions.

A virtual method is said to be *pure* virtual when it has a declaration as shown in the following:

```
class AbstractBase
{
public:
   virtual void DoSomething() = 0;  // pure virtual method
};
```

This declaration essentially tells the compiler that DoSomething() needs to be implemented and by the class that derives from AbstractBase:

```
class Derived: public AbstractBase
{
public:
```

Using virtual **Inheritance to Solve the Diamond Problem**

In Lesson 10 you saw the curious case of a duck-billed platypus that is part mammal, part bird, and part reptile. This is an example where a class Platypus needs to inherits from class Mammal, class Bird, and class Reptile. However, each of these in turn inherit from a more generic class Animal, as illustrated by Figure 11.2.

FIGURE 11.2
The class
diagram of
a platypus
demonstrating
multiple
inheritance.

11

So, what happens when you instantiate a Platypus? How many instances of class Animal are instantiated for one instance of Platypus? Listing 11.7 helps answer this question.

LISTING 11.7 Checking for the Number of Base Class Animal Instances for One
Instance of Platypus

```
0: #include <iostream>
1: using namespace std;
2:
3: class Animal
4: {
5: public:
6:    Animal()
7:    {
8:       cout << "Animal constructor" << endl;
9:    }
10:
11:    // sample method
12:    int Age;
13: };
14:
15: class Mammal:public Animal
16: {
17: };
18:
19: class Bird:public Animal
20: {
21: };
22:
23: class Reptile:public Animal
24: {
25: };
26:
27: class Platypus:public Mammal, public Bird, public Reptile
28: {
29: public:
30:    Platypus()
31:    {
32:       cout << "Platypus constructor" << endl;
33:    }
34: };
35:
36: int main()
37: {
38:    Platypus duckBilledP;
39:
40:    // uncomment next line to see compile failure
41:    // Age is ambiguous as there are three instances of base Animal
42:    // duckBilledP.Age = 25;
43:
44:    return 0;
45: }
```

Output ▼

```
Animal constructor
Animal constructor
Animal constructor
Platypus constructor
```

Analysis ▼

As the output demonstrates, due to multiple inheritance and all three base classes of
Platypus inheriting in turn from class Animal, you have three instances of Animal
created automatically for every instance of a Platypus, as shown in Line 38. This is
quite ridiculous as Platypus is still one animal that has inherited certain attributes from
Mammal, Bird, and Reptile. The problem in the number of instances of base Animal is
not limited to memory consumption alone. Animal has an integer member Animal::Age
(which has been kept public for explanation purposes). When you want to access
Animal::Age via an instance of Platypus, as shown in Line 42, you get a compilation
error simply because the compiler doesn't know if you want to set
Mammal::Animal::Age or Bird::Animal::Age or Reptile::Animal: Age. It can get
even more ridiculous—if you so wanted you could set all three:

```
duckBilledP.Mammal::Animal::Age = 25;
duckBilledP.Bird::Animal::Age = 25;
duckBilledP.Reptile::Animal::Age = 25;
```

11

Clearly, one duck-billed platypus should have only one Age. Yet, you want class
Platypus to be a Mammal, Bird, and Reptile. The solution is in virtual inheritance. If
you expect a derived class to be used as a base class, it possibly is a good idea to define
its relationship to the base using the keyword virtual:

```
class Derived1: public virtual Base
{
   // ... members and functions
};
class Derived2: public virtual Base
{
   // ... members and functions
};
```

A better class Platypus (actually a better class Mammal, class Bird, and class Reptile) is
in Listing 11.8.

LISTING 11.8 Demonstrating How `virtual` Keyword in Inheritance Hierarchy Helps Restrict the Number of Instances of Base Class Animal to One

```
0: #include <iostream>
1: using namespace std;
2:
3: class Animal
4: {
5: public:
6:    Animal()
7:    {
8:       cout << "Animal constructor" << endl;
9:    }
10:
11:    // sample method
12:    int Age;
13: };
14:
15: class Mammal:public virtual Animal
16: {
17: };
18:
19: class Bird:public virtual Animal
20: {
21: };
22:
23: class Reptile:public virtual Animal
24: {
25: };
26:
27: class Platypus:public Mammal, public Bird, public Reptile
28: {
29: public:
30:    Platypus()
31:    {
32:       cout << "Platypus constructor" << endl;
33:    }
34: };
35:
36: int main()
37: {
38:    Platypus duckBilledP;
39:
40:    // no compile error as there is only one Animal::Age
41:    duckBilledP.Age = 25;
42:
43:    return 0;
44: }
```

Output ▼

```
Animal constructor
Platypus constructor
```

Analysis ▼

Do a quick comparison against the output of previous Listing 11.7, and you see that the number of instances of class `Animal` constructed has fallen to one, which is finally reflective of the fact that only one `Platypus` has been constructed as well. This is because of the keyword `virtual` used in the relationship between classes `Mammal`, `Bird`, and `Reptile` ensures that when these classes are grouped together under `Platypus` the common base `Animal` exists only in a single instance. This solves a lot of problems; one among them is Line 41 that now compiles without ambiguity resolution as shown in Listing 11.7.

> **NOTE**
>
> Problems caused in an inheritance hierarchy containing two or more base classes that inherit from a common base, which results in the need for ambiguity resolution in the absence of virtual inheritance, is called the Diamond Problem.
>
> The name "Diamond" is possibly inspired by the shape the class diagram takes (visualize Figure 11.2 with straight and slanted lines relating `Platypus` to `Animal` via `Mammal`, `Bird`, and `Reptile` to see a diamond).

11

> **NOTE**
>
> The `virtual` keyword in C++ often is used in different contexts for different purposes. (My best guess is that someone wanted to save time on inventing an apt keyword.) Here is a summary:
>
> A function declared *virtual* means that an existing overriding function in a derived class is invoked.
>
> An inheritance relationship declared using keyword `virtual` between classes `Derived1` and `Derived2` that inherits from class `Base` means that another class `Derived3` that inherits from `Derived1` and `Derived2` still results in the creation of only one instance of `Base` during instantiation of type `Derived3`.
>
> Thus the same keyword `virtual` is used to implement two different concepts.

Virtual Copy Constructors?

Well, the question mark at the end of the section title is justified. It is technically impossible in C++ to have virtual copy constructors. Yet, such a feature helps you create a collection (for example, a static array) of type `Base*`, each element being a specialization of that type:

```
// Tuna, Carp and Trout are classes that inherit public from base class Fish
Fish* pFishes[3];
Fishes[0] = new Tuna();
Fishes[1] = new Carp();
Fishes[2] = new Trout();
```

Then assigning it into another array of the same type, where the virtual copy constructor ensures a deep copy of the derived class objects as well, ensures that `Tuna`, `Carp`, and `Trout` are copied as `Tuna`, `Carp`, and `Trout` even though the copy constructor is operating on type `Fish*`.

Well, that's a nice dream.

Virtual copy constructors are not possible because the `virtual` keyword in context of base class methods being overridden by implementations available in the derived class are about polymorphic behavior generated at runtime. Constructors, on the other hand, are not polymorphic in nature as they can construct only a fixed type, and hence C++ does not allow usage of the virtual copy constructors.

Having said that, there is a nice workaround in the form of defining your own clone function that allows you to do just that:

```
class Fish
{
public:
   virtual Fish* Clone() const = 0; // pure virtual function
};

class Tuna:public Fish
{
// ... other members
public:
   Tuna * Clone() const  // virtual clone function
   {
      return new Tuna(*this);  // return new Tuna that is a copy of this
   }
};
```

Thus, virtual function `Clone` is a simulated virtual copy constructor that needs to be explicitly invoked, as shown in Listing 11.9.

LISTING 11.9   Tuna and Carp That Support a Clone Function as a Simulated Virtual Copy Constructor

```
0: #include <iostream>
1: using namespace std;
2:
3: class Fish
4: {
5: public:
6:    virtual Fish* Clone() = 0;
7:    virtual void Swim() = 0;
8: };
9:
10: class Tuna: public Fish
11: {
12: public:
13:    Fish* Clone()
14:    {
15:       return new Tuna (*this);
16:    }
17:
18:    void Swim()
19:    {
20:       cout << "Tuna swims fast in the sea" << endl;
21:    }
22: };
23:
24: class Carp: public Fish
25: {
26:    Fish* Clone()
27:    {
28:       return new Carp(*this);
29:    }
30:    void Swim()
31:    {
32:       cout << "Carp swims slow in the lake" << endl;
33:    }
34: };
35:
36: int main()
37: {
38:    const int ARRAY_SIZE = 4;
39:
40:    Fish* myFishes[ARRAY_SIZE] = {NULL};
41:    myFishes[0] = new Tuna();
42:    myFishes[1] = new Carp();
43:    myFishes[2] = new Tuna();
44:    myFishes[3] = new Carp();
45:
46:    Fish* myNewFishes[ARRAY_SIZE];
47:    for (int Index = 0; Index < ARRAY_SIZE; ++Index)
```

11

LISTING 11.9   Continued

```
48:        myNewFishes[Index] = myFishes[Index]->Clone();
49:
50:    // invoke a virtual method to check
51:    for (int Index = 0; Index < ARRAY_SIZE; ++Index)
52:        myNewFishes[Index]->Swim();
53:
54:    // memory cleanup
55:    for (int Index = 0; Index < ARRAY_SIZE; ++Index)
56:    {
57:        delete myFishes[Index];
58:        delete myNewFishes[Index];
59:    }
60:
61:    return 0;
62: }
```

Output ▼

```
Tuna swims fast in the sea
Carp swims slow in the lake
Tuna swims fast in the sea
Carp swims slow in the lake
```

Analysis ▼

Lines 40–44 in main() demonstrate how a static array of pointers to base class Fish* has been declared and individual elements assigned to newly created objects of type Tuna, Carp, Tuna, and Carp, respectively. Note how this array myFishes is able to collect seemingly different types that are all related by a common base type Fish. This is already cool, if you compare it against previous arrays in this book that have mostly been of a simple monotonous type int. If that wasn't cool enough, you were able to copy into a new array of type Fish* called myNewFishes using the virtual function Fish::Clone within a loop, as shown in Line 48. Note that your array is quite small at only four elements. It could've been a lot longer but wouldn't have made much of a difference to the copy logic that would only need to adjust the loop-ending condition parameter. Line 52 is the actual check where you invoke virtual function Fish::Swim() on each stored element in the new array to verify if Clone() copied a Tuna as a Tuna and not just a Fish(). The output demonstrates that it genuinely did copy the Tunas and the Carps just as expected.

DO	DON'T
DO remember to mark virtual those base class functions that need to be overridden by the derived class versions.	**DON'T** forget to supply your base class with a virtual destructor.
DO remember that pure virtual functions make your class an Abstract Base Class, and these functions need to be implemented by a deriving class.	**DON'T** forget that the compiler does not allow you to create a standalone instance of an Abstract Base Class.
DO consider using virtual inheritance.	**DON'T** forget that virtual inheritance is about ensuring that the common base in a diamond hierarchy has only one instance.
	DON'T confuse the function of keyword virtual when used in creating an inheritance hierarchy with the same when used in declaring base class functions.

Summary

In this lesson you learned to tap the power of creating inheritance hierarchies in your C++ code, by using polymorphism. You learned how to declare and program virtual functions—how they ensure that the derived class implementation overrides that in the base class even if an instance of the base class is used to invoke the virtual method. You saw how pure virtual functions were a special type of virtual functions that ensure that the base class alone cannot be instantiated, making it a perfect place to define interfaces that derived classes must fulfill. Finally, you saw the Diamond Problem created by multiple inheritance and how virtual inheritance helps you solve it.

11

Q&A

Q Why use the virtual keyword with a base class function when code compiles without it?

A Without the virtual keyword, you are not able to ensure that someone calling objBase.Function() will be redirected to Derived::Function(). Besides, compilation of code is not a measure of its quality.

Q Why did the compiler create the Virtual Function Table?

A To store function pointers that ensure that the right version of a virtual function is invoked.

Q Should a base class always have a virtual destructor?

A Ideally yes. Only then can you ensure that when someone does a

```
Base* pBase = new Derived();
delete pBase;
```

delete on a pointer of type Base* results in the destructor ~Derived() being invoked only if destructor ~Base() is declared virtual.

Q What is an Abstract Base Class good for when I can't even instantiate it standalone?

A The ABC is not meant to be instantiated as a standalone object; rather it is always meant to be derived from. It contains pure virtual functions that define the minimal blueprint of functions that deriving classes need to implement, thus taking the role of an interface.

Q Given an inheritance hierarchy, do I need to use the keyword virtual on all declarations of a virtual function or just in the base class?

A It is enough to have just one virtual function declaration, and that has to be in the base class.

Q Can I define member functions and have member attributes in an ABC?

A Sure you can. Remember that you still cannot instantiate an ABC as it has at least one pure virtual function that needs to be implemented by a deriving class.

Workshop

The Workshop provides quiz questions to help you solidify your understanding of the material covered and exercises to provide you with experience in using what you've learned. Try to answer the quiz and exercise questions before checking the answers in Appendix D, and be certain you understand the answers before continuing to the next lesson.

Quiz

1. You are modeling shapes—circle and triangle—and want every shape to compulsorily implement functions Area() and Print(). How would you do it?

2. Does a compiler create a Virtual Function Table for all classes?

3. My class Fish has two public methods, one pure virtual function, and some member attributes. Is it still an abstract base class?

Exercises

1. Demonstrate an inheritance hierarchy that implements the question in Quiz 1 for Circle and Triangle.

2. **BUG BUSTERS:** What is the problem in the following code:

```cpp
class Vehicle
{
public:
   Vehicle() {}
   ~Vehicle(){}
};
class Car: public Vehicle
{
public:
   Car() {}
   ~Car() {}
};
```

3. In the (uncorrected) code in Exercise 2, what is the order of execution of constructors and destructors if an instance of car is created and destroyed like this:

```cpp
Vehicle* pMyRacer = new Car;
delete pMyRacer;
```

11

LESSON 12
Operator Types and Operator Overloading

Keyword class enables you to encapsulate not only data and methods, but also operators that make it easy to operate on objects of this class. You can use these operators to perform operations such as assignment or addition on class objects similar to those on integers that you saw in Lesson 5, "Working with Expressions, Statements, and Operators." Just like functions, operators can also be overloaded.

In this lesson, you will learn:

- Using the keyword operator
- Unary and binary operators
- Conversion operators
- C++11 move assignment operator
- Operators that cannot be redefined

What Are Operators in C++?

On a syntactical level, there is very little that differentiates an operator from a function, save for the use of the keyword operator. An operator declaration looks quite like a function declaration:

```
return_type operator operator_symbol (...parameter list...);
```

The operator_symbol in this case could be any of the several operator types that the programmer can define. It could be + (addition) or && (logical AND) and so on. The operands help the compiler distinguish one operator from another. So, why does C++ provide operators when functions are also supported?

Consider a utility class Date that encapsulates the day, month, and year:

```
Date Holiday (25, 12, 2011);  // initialized to 25th Dec 2011
```

Now, if you want this date to point to the next day—26th Dec 2011, in this case—which of the following would be more convenient if not also intuitive?

- Option 1 (using operators):

  ```
  ++ Holiday;
  ```

- Option 2 (using a fictitious Date::Increment()):

  ```
  Holiday.Increment();  // 26th Dec 2011
  ```

Clearly, Option 1 scores over method Increment(). The operator-based mechanism facilitates consumption by supplying ease of use and intuitiveness. Implementing operator (<) in class Date would help you compare two dates like this:

```
if(Date1 < Date2)
{
   // Do something
}
else
{
   // Do something else
}
```

The application of operators is beyond classes such as those that manage dates. Imagine an addition operator (+) that allows easy concatenation of strings in a string utility class such as MyString as shown in Listing 9.9:

```
MyString sayHello ("Hello ");
MyString sayWorld ("world");
MyString sumThem (sayHello + sayWorld);  // uses operator+ (unavailable in
Listing 9.9)
```

<table>
<tr><td>NOTE</td><td>The added effort in implementing relevant operators pays off in the ease with which your class is consumed.</td></tr>
</table>

On a very broad level, operators in C++ can be classified into two types: unary operators and binary operators.

Unary Operators

As the name suggests, operators that function on a single operand are called *unary operators*. The typical definition of a unary operator implemented as a global function or a static member function is

```
return_type operator operator_type (parameter_type)
{
    // ... implementation
}
```

A unary operator that is the member of a class is defined as

```
return_type operator operator_type ()
{
    // ... implementation
}
```

Types of Unary Operators

The unary operators that can be overloaded (or redefined) are shown in Table 12.1.

12

TABLE 12.1   Unary Operators

Operator	Name
++	Increment
—	Decrement
*	Pointer dereference
->	Member selection
!	Logical NOT
&	Address-of
~	One's complement
+	Unary plus
-	Unary negation
Conversion operators	Conversion operators

Programming a Unary Increment/Decrement Operator

A unary prefix increment operator (++) can be programmed using the following syntax within the class declaration: // Unary increment operator (prefix)

```
Date& operator ++ ()
{
    // operator implementation code
    return *this;
}
```

The postfix increment operator (++), on the other hand, has a different return value and an input parameter (that is not always used):

```
Date operator ++ (int)
{
    // Store a copy of the current state of the object, before incrementing day
    Date Copy (*this);

    // operator implementation code (that increments this object)

    // Return the state before increment was performed
    return Copy;
}
```

The prefix and postfix decrement operators have a similar syntax as the increment operators, just that the declaration would contain a − where you see a ++. Listing 12.1 shows a simple class Date that allows incrementing days using operator (++).

LISTING 12.1 A Calendar Class That Handles Day, Month and Year, and Allows Incrementing and Decrementing Days

```
 0: #include <iostream>
 1: using namespace std;
 2:
 3: class Date
 4: {
 5: private:
 6:     int Day;   // Range: 1 - 30 (lets assume all months have 30 days!
 7:     int Month;
 8:     int Year;
 9:
10: public:
```

```
11:    // Constructor that initializes the object to a day, month and year
12:    Date (int InputDay, int InputMonth, int InputYear)
13:        : Day (InputDay), Month (InputMonth), Year (InputYear) {};
14:
15:    // Unary increment operator (prefix)
16:    Date& operator ++ ()
17:    {
18:        ++Day;
19:        return *this;
20:    }
21:
22:    // Unary decrement operator (prefix)
23:    Date& operator — ()
24:    {
25:        —Day;
26:        return *this;
27:    }
28:
29:    void DisplayDate ()
30:    {
31:        cout << Day << " / " << Month << " / " << Year << endl;
32:    }
33: };
34:
35: int main ()
36: {
37:    // Instantiate and initialize a date object to 25 Dec 2011
38:    Date Holiday (25, 12, 2011);
39:
40:    cout << "The date object is initialized to: ";
41:    Holiday.DisplayDate ();
42:
43:    // Applying the prefix increment operator
44:    ++ Holiday;
45:
46:    cout << "Date after prefix-increment is: ";
47:
48:    // Display date after incrementing
49:    Holiday.DisplayDate ();
50:
51:    — Holiday;
52:    — Holiday;
53:
54:    cout << "Date after two prefix-decrements is: ";
55:    Holiday.DisplayDate ();
56:
57:    return 0;
58: }
```

12

Output ▼

```
The date object is initialized to: 25 / 12 / 2011
Date after prefix-increment is: 26 / 12 / 2011
Date after two prefix-decrements is: 24 / 12 / 2011
```

Analysis ▼

The operators of interest are in Lines 16 to 27, and they help in incrementing objects of class Date to add or subtract a day at a time as shown in Lines 44, 51, and 52 in main(). Prefix increment operators are those that first perform the increment operation and return a reference to the same object.

NOTE

> This version of a date class has bare minimum implementation to reduce lines and to explain how prefix operator (++) and operator (−) are to be implemented. In doing so, I have assumed that a month has 30 days and have not implemented rollover functionalities for month and year.

To support postfix increment or decrement, you simply add the following code to class Date:

```
// postfix differs from prefix operator in return-type and parameters
Date operator ++ (int)
{
    // Store a copy of the current state of the object, before incrementing day
    Date Copy (Day, Month, Year);

    ++Day;

    // Return the state before increment was performed
    return Copy;
}
// postfix decrement operator
Date operator − (int)
{
    Date Copy (Day, Month, Year);

    −Day;

    return Copy;
}
```

When your version of class Date supports both prefix and postfix increment and decrement operators, you will be able to use objects of the class using the following syntax:

```
Date Holiday (25, 12, 2011);  // instantiate
++ Holiday;  // using prefix increment operator++
Holiday ++;  // using postfix increment operator++
— Holiday;  // using prefix decrement operator—
Holiday —;  // using postfix decrement operator—
```

NOTE

As the implementation of the postfix operators demonstrates, a copy containing the existing state of the object is created before the increment or decrement operation to be returned thereafter.

In other words, if you had the choice between using ++ object; and object ++; to essentially only increment, you should choose the former to avoid the creation of a temporary copy that is not used.

Programming Conversion Operators

If you use Listing 12.1 and add the following line to main()

```
cout << Holiday;  // error in absence of conversion operator
```

the code would result in the following compile failure: error: binary '<<' : no operator found which takes a right-hand operand of type 'Date' (or there is no acceptable conversion). This error essentially indicates that cout doesn't know how to interpret an instance of Date as class Date does not support the relevant operators.

However, cout can work very well with a const char*:

```
std::cout << "Hello world"; // const char* works!
```

So, getting cout to work with an object of type Date might be as simple as adding an operator that returns a const char* version:

```
operator const char*()
{
    // operator implementation that returns a char*
}
```

Listing 12.2 is a simple implementation of this operator.

12

LISTING 12.2   Implementing Conversion operator const char* for class Date

```
0: #include <iostream>
1: #include <sstream>
2: #include <string>
3: using namespace std;
4:
5: class Date
6: {
7: private:
8:     int Day;   // Range: 1 - 30 (lets assume all months have 30 days!
9:     int Month;
10:     int Year;
11:
12:     string DateInString;
13:
14: public:
15:
16:     // Constructor that initializes the object to a day, month and year
17:     Date (int InputDay, int InputMonth, int InputYear)
18:         : Day (InputDay), Month (InputMonth), Year (InputYear) {};
19:
20:     operator const char*()
21:     {
22:         ostringstream formattedDate;
23:         formattedDate << Day << " / " << Month << " / " << Year;
24:
25:         DateInString = formattedDate.str();
26:         return DateInString.c_str();
27:     }
28: };
29:
30: int main ()
31: {
32:     // Instantiate and initialize a date object to 25 Dec 2011
33:     Date Holiday (25, 12, 2011);
34:
35:     cout << "Holiday is on: " << Holiday << endl;
36:
37:     return 0;
38: }
```

Output ▼

```
Holiday is on: 25 / 12 / 2011
```

Analysis ▼

The benefit of implementing operator const char* as shown in Lines 20 to 27 is visible in Line 35 in main(). Now, an instance of class Date can directly be used in a cout statement, taking advantage of the fact that cout understands const char*. The compiler automatically uses the output of the appropriate (and in this case, the only available) operator in feeding it to cout that displays the date on the screen. In your implementation of operator const char*, you use std::ostringstream to convert the member integers into a std::string object as shown in Lines 23 and 25. You could've directly returned formattedDate.str(), yet you store a copy in private member Date::DateInString in Line 25 because formattedDate being a local variable is destroyed when the operator returns. So, the pointer got via str() would be invalidated on return.

This operator opens up new possibilities towards consuming class Date. You can now even assign a Date directly to a string:

```
string strHoliday (Holiday); // OK! Compiler invokes operator const char*
strHoliday = Date(11, 11, 2011); // also OK!
```

> **NOTE**
>
> Program as many operators as you think your class would be used in. If your application needs an integer representation of a Date then you would program it using:
>
> ```
> operator int()
> {
>     // your conversion code here
> }
> ```
>
> This would allow an instance of Date to be used or transacted as an integer:
>
> ```
> SomeFuncThatTakesInt(Date(25, 12, 2011));
> ```

12

Programming Dereference Operator (*) and Member Selection Operator (->)

The dereference operator (*) and member selection operator (->) are most frequently used in the programming of smart pointer classes. *Smart pointers* are utility classes that wrap regular pointers and make memory management easy by handling memory (or resource) ownership and copy issues. In some cases, they can even help improve the performance of the application. Smart pointers are discussed in detail in Lesson 26, "Understanding Smart Pointers"; this lesson takes a brief look at how overloading operators helps smart pointers work.

Analyze the use of the `std::unique_ptr` in Listing 12.3 and understand how it uses operator (`*`) and operator (`->`) to help you use the smart-pointer class like any normal pointer.

LISTING 12.3 Using Smart Pointer `unique_ptr` to Manage a Dynamically Allocated Instance of class `Date`

```
0: #include <iostream>
1: #include <memory>  // include this to use std::unique_ptr
2: using namespace std;
3:
4: class Date
5: {
6: private:
7:     int Day;
8:     int Month;
9:     int Year;
10:
11:     string DateInString;
12:
13: public:
14:     // Constructor that initializes the object to a day, month and year
15:     Date (int InputDay, int InputMonth, int InputYear)
16:         : Day (InputDay), Month (InputMonth), Year (InputYear) {};
17:
18:     void DisplayDate()
19:     {
20:         cout << Day << " / " << Month << " / " << Year << endl;
21:     }
22: };
23:
24: int main()
25: {
26:     unique_ptr<int> pDynamicAllocInteger(new int);
27:     *pDynamicAllocInteger = 42;
28:
29:     // Use smart pointer type like an int*
30:     cout << "Integer value is: " << *pDynamicAllocInteger << endl;
31:
32:     unique_ptr<Date> pHoliday (new Date(25, 11, 2011));
33:     cout << "The new instance of date contains: ";
34:
35:     // use pHoliday just as you would a Date*
36:     pHoliday->DisplayDate();
37:
38:     // no need to do the following when using unique_ptr:
```

```
39:    // delete pDynamicAllocInteger;
40:    // delete pHoliday;
41:
42:    return 0;
43: }
```

Output ▼

```
Integer value is: 42
The new instance of date contains: 25 / 11 / 2011
```

Analysis ▼

Line 26 is where you declare a smart pointer to type int. This line shows template initialization syntax for smart pointer class unique_ptr. Similarly, Line 32 declares a smart pointer to an instance of class Date. Focus on the pattern, and ignore the details for the moment.

> **NOTE**
> Don't worry if this template syntax looks awkward because templates are introduced later in Lesson 14, "An Introduction to Macros and Templates."

This example not only demonstrates how a smart pointer allows you to use normal pointer syntax as shown in Lines 30 and 36. In Line 30, you are able to display the value of the int using *pDynamicAllocInteger, whereas in Line 36 you use pHoliday->DisplayData() as if these two variables were an int* and Date* respectively. The secret lies in the smart pointer class std::unique_ptr implementing operator (*) and operator (->) respectively. Listing 12.4 is an implementation of a simple and rudimentary smart pointer class.

LISTING 12.4   Implementing operator (*) and Operator (->) in a Simple Smart Pointer Class

```
0: #include <iostream>
1: using namespace std;
2:
3: template <typename T>
4: class smart_pointer
5: {
6: private:
7:    T* m_pRawPointer;
8: public:
9:    smart_pointer (T* pData) : m_pRawPointer (pData) {}    // constructor
```

12

LISTING 12.4 Continued

```
10:       ~smart_pointer () {delete m_pRawPointer ;}          // destructor
11:
12:       T& operator* () const     // dereferencing operator
13:       {
14:           return *(m_pRawPointer);
15:       }
16:
17:       T* operator-> () const    // member selection operator
18:       {
19:           return m_pRawPointer;
20:       }
21:   };
22:
23: class Date
24: {
25: private:
26:     int Day, Month, Year;
27:     string DateInString;
28:
29: public:
30:     // Constructor that initializes the object to a day, month and year
31:     Date (int InputDay, int InputMonth, int InputYear)
32:         : Day (InputDay), Month (InputMonth), Year (InputYear) {};
33:
34:     void DisplayDate()
35:     {
36:         cout << Day << " / " << Month << " / " << Year << endl;
37:     }
38: };
39:
40: int main()
41: {
42:     smart_pointer<int> pDynamicInt(new int (42));
43:     cout << "Dynamically allocated integer value = " << *pDynamicInt;
44:
45:     smart_pointer<Date> pDate(new Date(25, 12, 2011));
46:     cout << "Date is = ";
47:     pDate->DisplayDate();
48:
49:     return 0;
50: }
```

Output ▼

```
Dynamically allocated integer value = 42
Date is = 25 / 12 / 2011
```

Analysis ▼

This is a version of Listing 12.3 that uses your own smart_pointer class defined in Lines 3 to 24. You use template declaration syntax so that your smart pointer can be customized to point to any type, be it an int, as shown in Line 45, or a Date, as shown in Line 48. Our smart pointer class contains a private member of the type it is pointing to, declared in Line 7. Essentially, the smart pointer class aims to automate the management of the resource pointed to by this member, which includes automatically releasing it in the destructor as shown in Line 10. This destructor ensures that even if you did a new, you don't need to do a delete, and not releasing this memory resource manually does not result in a memory leak. Focus on the implementation of operator (*) in Lines 12 to 15 that returns type T& (that is, a reference to the type this template is specialized for). The implementation returns a reference to the instance being pointed to, as shown in Line 14. Similarly, operator (->), as shown in Lines 17 to 20, returns type T* (that is, a pointer of the type this template is specialized for). The implementation of operator (->) in Line 19 returns the member pointer. Collectively, these two operators ensure that class smart_pointer abstracts memory management of a raw pointer and allows usage of regular pointer functionality, thus making it a "smart" pointer.

NOTE

> Smart pointer classes can do a lot more than just parade around as normal pointers, or de-allocate memory when they go out of scope. Find out more about this topic in Lesson 26, "Understanding Smart Pointers."
>
> If the usage of unique_ptr in Listing 12.3 makes you curious, look up its implementation in the header file <memory> as supplied by your compiler or IDE to understand what it does behind the scenes.

12

Binary Operators

Operators that function on two operands are called *binary operators*. The definition of a binary operator implemented as a global function or a static member function is the following:

```
return_type operator_type (parameter1, parameter2);
```

The definition of a binary operator implemented as a class member is

```
return_type operator_type (parameter);
```

The reason the class member version of a binary operator accepts only one parameter is that the second parameter is usually derived from the attributes of the class itself.

Types of Binary Operators

Table 12.2 contains binary operators that can be overloaded or redefined in your C++ application.

TABLE 12.2   Overloadable Binary Operators

Operator	Name
,	Comma
!=	Inequality
%	Modulus
%=	Modulus/assignment
&	Bitwise AND
&&	Logical AND
&=	Bitwise AND/assignment
*	Multiplication
*=	Multiplication/assignment
+	Addition
+=	Addition/assignment
–	Subtraction
–=	Subtraction/assignment
–>*	Pointer-to-member selection
/	Division
/=	Division/assignment
<	Less than
<<	Left shift
<<=	Left shift/assignment
<=	Less than or equal to
=	Assignment, Copy Assignment and Move Assignment
==	Equality
>	Greater than
>=	Greater than or equal to
>>	Right shift
>>=	Right shift/assignment
^	Exclusive OR

Operator	Name
^=	Exclusive OR/assignment
¦	Bitwise inclusive OR
¦=	Bitwise inclusive OR/assignment
¦¦	Logical OR
[]	Subscript operator

Programming Binary Addition (a+b) and Subtraction (a–b) Operators

Similar to the increment/decrement operators, the binary plus and minus, when defined, enable you to add or subtract the value of a supported data type from an object of the class that implements these operators. Take a look at your calendar class Date again. Although you have already implemented the capability to increment Date so that it moves the calendar one day forward, you still do not support the capability to move it, say, five days ahead. To do this, you need to implement binary operator (+), as the code in Listing 12.5 demonstrates.

LISTING 12.5   Calendar Class Featuring the Binary Addition Operator

```
0: #include <iostream>
1: using namespace std;
2:
3: class Date
4: {
5: private:
6:    int Day, Month, Year;
7:
8: public:
9:
10:    // Constructor that initializes the object to a day, month and year
11:    Date (int InputDay, int InputMonth, int InputYear)
12:       : Day (InputDay), Month (InputMonth), Year (InputYear) {};
13:
14:    // Binary addition operator
15:    Date operator + (int DaysToAdd)
16:    {
17:       Date newDate (Day + DaysToAdd, Month, Year);
18:       return newDate;
19:    }
20:
21:    // Binary subtraction operator
22:    Date operator - (int DaysToSub)
23:    {
```

12

LISTING 12.5   Continued

```
24:        return Date(Day - DaysToSub, Month, Year);
25:    }
26:
27:    void DisplayDate ()
28:    {
29:        cout << Day << " / " << Month << " / " << Year << endl;
30:    }
31: };
32:
33: int main()
34: {
35:    // Instantiate and initialize a date object to 25 Dec 2011
36:    Date Holiday (25, 12, 2011);
37:
38:    cout << "Holiday on: ";
39:    Holiday.DisplayDate ();
40:
41:    Date PreviousHoliday (Holiday - 19);
42:    cout << "Previous holiday on: ";
43:    PreviousHoliday.DisplayDate();
44:
45:    Date NextHoliday(Holiday + 6);
46:    cout << "Next holiday on: ";
47:    NextHoliday.DisplayDate ();
48:
49:    return 0;
50: }
```

Output ▼

```
Holiday on: 25 / 12 / 2011
Previous holiday on: 6 / 12 / 2011
Next holiday on: 31 / 12 / 2011
```

Analysis ▼

Lines 14 to 25 contain the implementations of the binary operator (+) and operator (-) that permit the use of simple addition and subtraction syntax as seen in main() in Lines 41 and 45 respectively.

The binary addition operator would also be very useful if you are programming a string class. In Lesson 9, "Classes and Objects," you analyze a simple string wrapper class MyString that encapsulates memory management, copying and the likes for a C-style character string, as shown in Listing 9.9. What this class doesn't support is concatenating two strings using the following syntax:

```
MyString Hello("Hello ");
MyString World(" World");
MyString HelloWorld(Hello + World);  // error: operator+ not defined
```

Needless to say, operator (+) would make using MyString extremely easy and is hence worth the effort:

```
MyString operator+ (const MyString& AddThis)
{
   MyString NewString;

   if (AddThis.Buffer != NULL)
   {
      NewString.Buffer = new char[GetLength() + strlen(AddThis.Buffer) + 1];
      strcpy(NewString.Buffer, Buffer);
      strcat(NewString.Buffer, AddThis.Buffer);
   }

   return NewString;
}
```

Add the preceding code to Listing 9.9 with a private default constructor MyString() with empty implementation to be able to use the addition syntax. You can see a version of class MyString with operator (+) among others in Listing 12.12 later in this lesson.

NOTE

> Operators increase the usability of your class. However, you need to implement operators where they make sense. Note how you implemented addition and subtraction operators for class Date but only addition operator (+) for class MyString. That's because performing subtraction operations on a string is very improbable and such an operator would possibly go waste.

12

Implementing Addition Assignment (+=) and Subtraction Assignment (-=) Operators

The addition assignment operators allow syntax such as "a += b;" that allows the programmer to increment the value of an object a by an amount b. In doing this, the utility of the addition assignment operator is that it can be overloaded to accept different types of parameter b. Listing 12.6 that follows allows you to add an integer value to a CDate object.

LISTING 12.6 Defining Operator (+=) and Operator (-=) to Add or Subtract Days in the Calendar Given an Integer Input

```
0: #include <iostream>
1: using namespace std;
2:
3: class Date
4: {
5: private:
6:     int Day, Month, Year;
7:
8: public:
9:
10:     // Constructor that initializes the object to a day, month and year
11:     Date (int InputDay, int InputMonth, int InputYear)
12:         : Day (InputDay), Month (InputMonth), Year (InputYear) {};
13:
14:     // Binary addition assignment
15:     void operator+= (int DaysToAdd)
16:     {
17:         Day += DaysToAdd;
18:     }
19:
20:     // Binary subtraction assignment
21:     void operator-= (int DaysToSub)
22:     {
23:         Day -= DaysToSub;
24:     }
25:
26:     void DisplayDate ()
27:     {
28:         cout << Day << " / " << Month << " / " << Year << endl;
29:     }
30: };
31:
32: int main()
33: {
34:     // Instantiate and initialize a date object to 25 Dec 2011
35:     Date Holiday (25, 12, 2011);
36:
37:     cout << "Holiday is on: ";
38:     Holiday.DisplayDate ();
39:
40:     cout << "Holiday -= 19 gives: ";
41:     Holiday -= 19;
42:     Holiday.DisplayDate();
43:
44:     cout << "Holiday += 25 gives: ";
45:     Holiday += 25;
46:     Holiday.DisplayDate ();
47:
```

```
48:    return 0;
49: }
```

Output ▼

```
Holiday is on: 25 / 12 / 2011
Holiday -= 19 gives: 6 / 12 / 2011
Holiday += 25 gives: 31 / 12 / 2011
```

Analysis ▼

The addition and subtraction assignment operators of interest are in Lines 14 to 24.
These allow adding and subtracting an integer value for days, as seen in main(), for
instance:

```
41:    Holiday -= 19;
45:    Holiday += 25;
```

Your class Date now allows users to add or remove days from it as if they are dealing
with integers using addition or subtraction assignment operators that take an int as a
parameter. You can even provide overloaded versions of the addition assignment operator
(+=) that takes an instance of a fictitious class CDays :

```
// The addition-assignment operator that add a CDays to an existing Date
void operator += (const CDays& mDaysToAdd)
{
    Day += mDaysToAdd.GetDays ();
}
```

12

NOTE

The multiplication assignment *=, division assignment /=, modulus assignment %=, subtraction assignment -=, left-shift assign-
ment <<=, right-shift assignment >>=, XOR assignment ^=, bitwise
inclusive OR assignment |=, and bitwise AND assignment &= oper-
ators have a similar syntax to the addition assignment operator
shown in Listing 12.6.

Although the ultimate objective of overloading operators is making
the class easy and intuitive to use, there are many situations
where implementing an operator might not make sense. For example, our calendar class Date has absolutely no use for a bitwise
AND assignment &= operator. No user of this class should ever
expect (or even think of) getting useful results from an operation
such as greatDay &= 20;.

Overloading Equality (==) and Inequality (!=) Operators

What do you expect when the user of class Date compares one object to another:

```
if (Date1 == Date2)
{
    // Do something
}
else
{
    // Do something else
}
```

In the absence of an equality operator, the compiler simply performs a binary comparison of the two objects and returns true if they are exactly identical. This might work in some cases (including with the Date class as of now), but it probably does not work to your expectations if the class in question has a non-static string member that contains a string value (char*) such as MyString in Listing 9.9. In such a case, a binary comparison of the member attributes actually compares the string pointers that are not equal (even if the strings pointed to are identical in content) and returns false consistently.

Thus, it is a good practice to define the comparison operators. A generic expression of the equality operator is the following:

```
bool operator== (const ClassType& compareTo)
{
   // comparison code here, return true if equal else false
}
```

The inequality operator can reuse the equality operator:

```
bool operator!= (const ClassType& compareTo)
{
   // comparison code here, return true if inequal else false

}
```

The inequality operator can be the inverse (logical NOT) of the result of the equality operator. Listing 12.7 demonstrates comparison operators defined by our calendar class Date.

LISTING 12.7   Demonstrates Operators == and !=

```
0: #include <iostream>
1: using namespace std;
2:
```

```
 3: class Date
 4: {
 5: private:
 6:     int Day, Month, Year;
 7:
 8: public:
 9:
10:     // Constructor that initializes the object to a day, month and year
11:     Date (int InputDay, int InputMonth, int InputYear)
12:        : Day (InputDay), Month (InputMonth), Year (InputYear) {};
13:
14:     bool operator== (const Date& compareTo)
15:     {
16:        return ((Day == compareTo.Day)
17:             && (Month == compareTo.Month)
18:             && (Year == compareTo.Year));
19:     }
20:
21:     bool operator!= (const Date& compareTo)
22:     {
23:        return !(this->operator==(compareTo));
24:     }
25:
26:     void DisplayDate ()
27:     {
28:        cout << Day << " / " << Month << " / " << Year << endl;
29:     }
30: };
31:
32: int main()
33: {
34:     Date Holiday1 (25, 12, 2011);
35:     Date Holiday2 (31, 12, 2011);
36:
37:     cout << "Holiday 1 is: ";
38:     Holiday1.DisplayDate();
39:     cout << "Holiday 2 is: ";
40:     Holiday2.DisplayDate();
41:
42:     if (Holiday1 == Holiday2)
43:        cout << "Equality operator: The two are on the same day" << endl;
44:     else
45:        cout << "Equality operator: The two are on different days" << endl;
46:
47:     if (Holiday1 != Holiday2)
48:        cout << "Inequality operator: The two are on different days" << endl;
49:     else
50:        cout << "Inequality operator: The two are on the same day" << endl;
51:
52:     return 0;
53: }
```

12

Output ▼

```
Holiday 1 is: 25 / 12 / 2011
Holiday 2 is: 31 / 12 / 2011
Equality operator: The two are on different days
Inequality operator: The two are on different days
```

Analysis ▼

The equality operator (==) is a simple implementation that returns true if the day, month, and year are all equal, as shown in Lines 14 to 19. The inequality operator (!=) simply reuses the equality operator code as seen in line 23. The presence of these operators helps compare two Date objects, Holiday1 and Holiday2, in main() in Lines 42 and 47.

Overloading <, >, <=, and >= Operators

The code in Listing 12.7 made the Date class intelligent enough to be able to tell whether two Date objects are equal or unequal. However, what if the user of the class required to perform a conditional check is akin to this:

```
if (Date1 < Date2) {// do something}
```

or

```
if (Date1 <= Date2) {// do something}
```

or

```
if (Date1 > Date2) {// do something}
```

or

```
if (greatDay >= Date2) {// do something}
```

The user of your calendar class would definitely find it very useful if he could simply compare two dates to know whether one precedes or follows another. The programmer of the class needs to implement this comparison to make using his class as user friendly and intuitive as possible, as demonstrated by the code shown in Listing 12.8.

LISTING 12.8   Demonstrates Implementing <, <=, >, and >= Operators

```
0: #include <iostream>
1: using namespace std;
2:
3: class Date
4: {
5: private:
6:     int Day, Month, Year;
```

```
 7:
 8: public:
 9:
10:     // Constructor that initializes the object to a day, month and year
11:     Date (int InputDay, int InputMonth, int InputYear)
12:        : Day (InputDay), Month (InputMonth), Year (InputYear) {};
13:
14:     bool operator== (const Date& compareTo)
15:     {
16:        return ((Day == compareTo.Day)
17:               && (Month == compareTo.Month)
18:               && (Year == compareTo.Year));
19:     }
20:
21:     bool operator< (const Date& compareTo)
22:     {
23:        if (Year < compareTo.Year)
24:           return true;
25:        else if (Month < compareTo.Month)
26:           return true;
27:        else if (Day < compareTo.Day)
28:           return true;
29:        else
30:           return false;
31:     }
32:
33:     bool operator<= (const Date& compareTo)
34:     {
35:        if (this->operator== (compareTo))
36:           return true;
37:        else
38:           return this->operator< (compareTo);
39:     }
40:
41:     bool operator > (const Date& compareTo)
42:     {
43:        return !(this->operator<= (compareTo));
44:     }
45:
46:     bool operator>= (const Date& compareTo)
47:     {
48:        if(this->operator== (compareTo))
49:           return true;
50:        else
51:           return this->operator> (compareTo);
52:     }
53:
54:     bool operator!= (const Date& compareTo)
55:     {
56:        return !(this->operator==(compareTo));
57:     }
```

12

LISTING 12.8   Continued

```
58:
59:    void DisplayDate ()
60:    {
61:       cout << Day << " / " << Month << " / " << Year << endl;
62:    }
63: };
64:
65: int main()
66: {
67:    Date Holiday1 (25, 12, 2011);
68:    Date Holiday2 (31, 12, 2011);
69:
70:    cout << "Holiday 1 is: ";
71:    Holiday1.DisplayDate();
72:    cout << "Holiday 2 is: ";
73:    Holiday2.DisplayDate();
74:
75:    if (Holiday1 < Holiday2)
76:       cout << "operator<: Holiday1 happens first" << endl;
77:
78:    if (Holiday2 > Holiday1)
79:       cout << "operator>: Holiday2 happens later" << endl;
80:
81:    if (Holiday1 <= Holiday2)
82:       cout << "operator<=: Holiday1 happens on or before Holiday2" << endl;
83:
84:    if (Holiday2 >= Holiday1)
85:       cout << "operator>=: Holiday2 happens on or after Holiday1" << endl;
86:
87:    return 0;
88: }
```

Output ▼

```
Holiday 1 is: 25 / 12 / 2011
Holiday 2 is: 31 / 12 / 2011
operator<: Holiday1 happens first
operator>: Holiday2 happens later
operator<=: Holiday1 happens on or before Holiday2
operator>=: Holiday2 happens on or after Holiday1
```

Analysis ▼

The operators of interest are implemented in Lines 21 to 52 and partially reuse operator (==) that you saw in Listing 12.7. Note how these operators have been implemented: most reuse one or the other.

The usage of the operators inside the main() function between Lines 75 to 84 indicates how the implementation of these operators make using the Date class easy and intuitive.

Overloading Copy Assignment Operator (=)

There are times when you want to assign the contents of an instance of a class to another, like this:

```
Date Holiday(25, 12, 2011);
Date AnotherHoliday(1, 1, 2010);
AnotherHoliday  = Holiday;  // uses copy assignment operator
```

This invokes the default copy assignment operator that the compiler has built in to your class unless you have supplied one. Depending on the nature of your class, the default copy constructor might be inadequate, especially if your class is managing a resource that will not be copied. To ensure deeper copies, as with the copy constructor, you need to specify a copy assignment operator:

```
ClassType& operator= (const ClassType& CopySource)
{
   if(this != &copySource)  // protection against copy into self
   {
      // Assignment operator implementation
   }
   return *this;
}
```

Deep copies are important if your class encapsulates a raw pointer, such as class MyString shown in Listing 9.9. In the absence of an assignment operator, the default copy assignment operator supplied by the compiler simply copies the address contained in char* Buffer from the source to the destination, without performing a deep copy of the memory being pointed to. This is the same scenario as one in the absence of the copy constructor. To ensure deep copy during assignments, define a copy assignment operator as shown in Listing 12.9.

12

LISTING 12.9   A Better class MyString from Listing 9.9 with a Copy Assignment Operator

```
0: #include <iostream>
1: using namespace std;
2:
3: class MyString
4: {
5: private:
6:    char* Buffer;
```

LISTING 12.9   Continued

```
 7:
 8: public:
 9:     // constructor
10:     MyString(const char* InitialInput)
11:     {
12:         if(InitialInput != NULL)
13:         {
14:             Buffer = new char [strlen(InitialInput) + 1];
15:             strcpy(Buffer, InitialInput);
16:         }
17:         else
18:             Buffer = NULL;
19:     }
20:
21:     // insert copy constructor from Listing 9.9
22:     MyString(const MyString& CopySource);
23:
24:     // Copy assignment operator
25:     MyString& operator= (const MyString& CopySource)
26:     {
27:         if ((this != &CopySource) && (CopySource.Buffer != NULL))
28:         {
29:             if (Buffer != NULL)
30:              delete[] Buffer;
31:
32:             // ensure deep copy by first allocating own buffer
33:             Buffer = new char [strlen(CopySource.Buffer) + 1];
34:
35:             // copy from the source into local buffer
36:             strcpy(Buffer, CopySource.Buffer);
37:         }
38:       return *this;
39:     }
40:
41:     // Destructor
42:     ~MyString()
43:     {
44:         if (Buffer != NULL)
45:             delete [] Buffer;
46:     }
47:
48:     int GetLength()
49:     {
50:         return strlen(Buffer);
51:     }
52:
53:     operator const char*()
54:     {
55:         return Buffer;
```

```
56:    }
57: };
58:
59: int main()
60: {
61:     MyString String1("Hello ");
62:     MyString String2(" World");
63:
64:     cout << "Before assignment: " << endl;
65:     cout << String1 << String2 << endl;
66:     String2 = String1;
67:     cout << "After assignment String2 = String1: " << endl;
68:     cout << String1 << String2 << endl;
69:
70:     return 0;
71: }
```

Output ▼

```
Before assignment:
Hello  World
After assignment String2 = String1:
Hello Hello
```

Analysis ▼

I have purposely omitted the copy constructor in this sample to reduce lines of code (but you should be inserting it when programming such a class; refer Listing 9.9 as a reference). The copy assignment operator is implemented in Lines 25 to 39. It is quite similar in function to a copy constructor and performs a starting check to ensure that the same object is not both the copy source and destination. After the checks return true, the copy assignment operator for MyString first deallocates its internal Buffer before reallocating space for the text from the copy source and then uses strcpy() to copy, as shown in Line 36.

12

NOTE

> Another subtle change in Listing 12.9 over Listing 9.9 is that you have replaced function GetString() by operator const char* as shown in Lines 53 to 56. This operator makes it even easier to use class MyString, as shown in Line 68, where one cout statement is used to display two instances of MyString.

CAUTION

When implementing a class that manages a dynamically allocated resource such as a char* C-style string, a dynamic array or the likes, always ensure that you have implemented (or considered implementation of) the copy constructor and the copy assignment operator in addition to the constructor and the destructor.

Unless you clearly evaluate the resource ownership issue when an object of your class is copied, your class is incomplete and even dangerous when used.

TIP

To create a class that cannot be copied, declare the copy constructor and copy assignment operator as private. Declaration (and not even implementation) is sufficient for the compiler to throw error on all attempts at copying this class via passing to a function by value or assigning one instance into another.

Subscript Operator ([ ])

The operator that allow array-style [] access to a class is called *subscript operator*. The typical syntax of a subscript operator is:

```
return_type& operator [] (subscript_type& subscript);
```

So, when creating a class such as MyString that encapsulates a dynamic array class of characters in a char* Buffer, a subscript operator makes it really easy to randomly access individual characters in the buffer:

```
class MyString
{
    // ... other class members
public:
    /*const*/ char& operator [] (int Index) /*const*/
    {
        // return the char at position Index in Buffer
    }
};
```

The sample in Listing 12.10 demonstrates how the subscript operator ([]) helps the user in iterating through the characters contained in an instance of **MyString** using normal array semantics.

LISTING 12.10   Implementing Subscript Operator [ ] in class MyString to Allow
Random Access to Characters Contained in MyString::Buffer

```
0: #include <iostream>
1: #include <string>
2: using namespace std;
3:
4: class MyString
5: {
6: private:
7:     char* Buffer;
8:
9:     // private default constructor
10:     MyString() {}
11:
12: public:
13:     // constructor
14:     MyString(const char* InitialInput)
15:     {
16:         if(InitialInput != NULL)
17:         {
18:             Buffer = new char [strlen(InitialInput) + 1];
19:             strcpy(Buffer, InitialInput);
20:         }
21:         else
22:             Buffer = NULL;
23:     }
24:
25:     // Copy constructor: insert from Listing 9.9 here
26:     MyString(const MyString& CopySource);
27:
28:     // Copy assignment operator: insert from Listing 12.9 here
29:     MyString& operator= (const MyString& CopySource);
30:
31:     const char& operator[] (int Index) const
32:     {
33:         if (Index < GetLength())
34:             return Buffer[Index];
35:     }
36:
37:     // Destructor
38:     ~MyString()
39:     {
40:         if (Buffer != NULL)
41:             delete [] Buffer;
42:     }
43:
44:     int GetLength() const
45:     {
46:         return strlen(Buffer);
47:     }
```

12

LISTING 12.10   Continued

```
48:
49:    operator const char*()
50:    {
51:        return Buffer;
52:    }
53: };
54:
55: int main()
56: {
57:    cout << "Type a statement: ";
58:    string strInput;
59:    getline(cin, strInput);
60:
61:    MyString youSaid(strInput.c_str());
62:
63:    cout << "Using operator[] for displaying your input: " << endl;
64:    for(int Index = 0; Index < youSaid.GetLength(); ++Index)
65:        cout << youSaid[Index] << " ";
66:    cout << endl;
67:
68:    cout << "Enter index 0 - " << youSaid.GetLength() - 1 << ": ";
69:    int InIndex = 0;
70:    cin >> InIndex;
71:    cout << "Input character at zero-based position: " << InIndex;
72:    cout << " is: "<< youSaid[InIndex] << endl;
73:
74:    return 0;
75: }
```

Output ▼

```
Type a statement: Hey subscript operators[] are fabulous
Using operator[] for displaying your input:
H e y    s u b s c r i p t    o p e r a t o r s [ ]    a r e    f a b u l o u s
Enter index 0 - 37: 2
Input character at zero-based position: 2 is: y
```

Analysis ▼

This is just a fun program that takes a sentence you input, constructs a MyString using it, as shown in Line 61, and then uses a for loop to print the string character by character with the help of the subscript operator ([]) using an array-like syntax, as shown in Lines 64 and 65. The operator ([]) itself is defined in Lines 31 to 35 and supplies direct access to the character at the specified position after ensuring that the requested position is not beyond the end of the char* Buffer.

CAUTION

Const-Correctness for Operators

Using keyword const is important even when programming operators. Note how Listing 12.10 has restricted the return value of subscript operator [ ] to const char&. The program works and compiles even without the const keywords, yet the reason you have it there is to avoid this code:

```
MyString sayHello("Hello World");
sayHello[2] = 'k';error: operator[] is const
```

By using const you are protecting internal member MyString::Buffer from direct modifications from the outside via operator [ ]. In addition to classifying the return value as const, you even have restricted the operator function type to const to ensure that this operator cannot modify the class's member attributes.

In general, use the maximum possible const restriction to avoid unintentional data modifications and increase protection of the class's member attributes.

When implementing subscript operators, you can improve on the version shown in Listing 12.10. That one is an implementation of a single subscript operator that works for both reading from and writing to the slots in the dynamic array.

You can, however, implement two subscript operators—one as a const function and the other as a non-const one:

```
char& operator [] (int nIndex);  // use to write / change Buffer at Index
char& operator [] (int nIndex) const; // used only for accessing char at Index
```

The compiler is smart enough to invoke the const function for read operations and the non-const version for operations that write into the MyString object. Thus, you can (if you want to) have separate functionalities in the two subscript functions. For example, one function can log writes into the container while the other can log reads from it. There are other binary operators (enlisted in Table 12.2) that can be redefined or over-loaded but that are not discussed further in this lesson. Their implementation, however, is similar to those that have already been discussed.

Other operators, such as the logical operators and the bitwise operators, need to be pro-grammed if the purpose of the class would be enhanced by having them. Clearly, a calen-dar class such as Date does not necessarily need to implement logical operators, whereas a class that performs string and numeric functions might need them all the time.

Keep the objective of your class and its use in perspective when overloading operators or writing new ones.

Function Operator ( )

The operator ( ) that make objects behave like a function is called a function operator. They find application in the standard template library (STL) and are typically used in STL algorithms. Their usage can include making decisions; such function objects are typically called *unary* or *binary predicate*, depending on the number of operands they work on. Listing 12.11 analyzes a really simple function object so you can first understand what gives them such an intriguing name!

Listing 12.11   A Function Object Created Using Operator ( )

```
1: #include <iostream>
2: #include <string>
3:using namespace std;
4:
5: class CDisplay
6: {
7: public:
8:    void operator () (string Input) const
9:    {
10:       cout << Input << endl;
11:    }
12:};
13:
14:int main ()
15:{
16:    CDisplay mDisplayFuncObject;
17:
18:    // equivalent to mDisplayFuncObject.operator () ("Display this string!");
19:    mDisplayFuncObject ("Display this string!");
20:
21:    return 0;
22: }
```

Output ▼

```
Display this string!
```

Analysis ▼

Lines 8 to 11 implement operator () that is then used inside the function main() at Line 18. Note how the compiler allows the use of object mDisplayFuncObject as a function in Line 18 by implicitly converting what looks like a function call to a call to operator ().

Hence, this operator is also called the function operator () and the object of CDisplay is also called a function object or *functor*. This topic is discussed exhaustively in Lesson 21, "Understanding Function Objects."

C++11

Move Constructor and Move Assignment Operator for High Performance Programming

The move constructor and the move assignment operators are performance optimization features that have become a part of the standard in C++11, ensuring that temporary values (rvalues that don't exist beyond the statement) are not unnecessarily copied. This is particularly useful when handling a class that manages a dynamically allocated resource, such as a dynamic array class or a string class.

The Problem of Unwanted Copy Steps

Take a look at the addition operator as implemented in Listing 12.5. Notice that it actually creates a copy and returns it. The same is true for the subtraction operator. Now, what happens when you create a new instance of MyString using this syntax:

```
MyString Hello("Hello ");
MyString World("World");
MyString CPP(" of C++");
MyString sayHello(Hello + World + CPP);  // operator+, copy constructor
MyString sayHelloAgain ("overwrite this");
sayHelloAgain = Hello + World + CPP;  // operator+, copy constructor, copy
assignment operator=
```

This simple construct is a very intuitive way to concatenate three strings and uses the binary addition operator (+), which is programmed like this:

```
MyString operator+ (const MyString& AddThis)
{
   MyString NewString;

   if (AddThis.Buffer != NULL)
   {
      // copy into NewString
```

12

```
   }
   return NewString;  // return copy by value, invoke copy constructor
}
```

This addition operator (+) that makes it easy to concatenate using intuitive expressions also has the potential to cause performance problems. The creation of sayHello requires the execution of the addition operator twice, each execution of operator (+) results in the creation of a temporary copy as a MyString is returned by value, thus causing the execution of the copy constructor. The copy constructor does a deep copy—to a temporary value that does not exist after the expression. Thus this expression results in temporary copies (rvalues, for the purists) that are not ever required after the statement and hence are a performance bottleneck forced by C++. Well, until recently at least.

This problem has now finally been resolved in C++11 in which the compiler specifically recognizes temporaries and uses move constructors and move assignment operators, if you supply these.

Declaring a Move Constructor and Move Assignment Operator

The syntax of the move constructor is as follows:

```
Class MyClass
{
private:
   Type* PtrResource;

public:
   MyClass(); // default constructor
   MyClass(const MyClass& CopySource); // copy constructor
   MyClass& operator= (const MyClass& CopySource); // copy assignment operator

   MyClass(MyClass&& MoveSource) // Move constructor, note &&
   {
      PtrResource = MoveSource.PtrResource; // take ownership, start move
      MoveSource.PtrResource = NULL;
   }

   MyClass& operator= (MyClass&& MoveSource)//move assignment operator, note &&
   {
      if(this != &MoveSource)
      {
         delete [] PtrResource;  // free own resource
         PtrResource = MoveSource.PtrResource;  // take ownership, start move
         MoveSource.PtrResource = NULL;  // free move source of ownership
      }
   }

};
```

Thus, the declaration of the move constructor and assignment operator are different from the regular copy constructor and copy assignment operator in that the input parameter is of type MyClass&&. Additionally, as the input parameter is the move-source, it cannot be a const parameter as it is modified. Return values remain the same, as these are over-loaded versions of the constructor and the assignment operator respectively.

C++11-compliant compilers ensure that for rvalue temporaries the move constructor is used instead of the copy constructor and the move assignment operator is invoked instead of the copy assignment operator. In your implementation of these two, you ensure that instead of copying, you are simply moving the resource from the source to the destination. Listing 12.12 demonstrates the effectiveness of these two recent additions to C++11 in optimizing class MyString.

LISTING 12.12   class MyString with Move Constructor and Move Assignment Operator in Addition to Copy Constructor and Copy Assignment Operator

```
0: #include <iostream>
1: using namespace std;
2:
3: class MyString
4: {
5: private:
6:     char* Buffer;
7:
8:     // private default constructor
9:     MyString(): Buffer(NULL)
10:    {
11:       cout << "Default constructor called" << endl;
12:    }
13:
14: public:
15:    // Destructor
16:    ~MyString()
17:    {
18:       if (Buffer != NULL)
19:          delete [] Buffer;
20:    }
21:
22:    int GetLength()
23:    {
24:       return strlen(Buffer);
25:    }
26:
27:    operator const char*()
```

LISTING 12.12   Continued

```
28:    {
29:        return Buffer;
30:    }
31:
32:    MyString operator+ (const MyString& AddThis)
33:    {
34:        cout << "operator+ called: " << endl;
35:        MyString NewString;
36:
37:        if (AddThis.Buffer != NULL)
38:        {
39:            NewString.Buffer = new char[GetLength() + strlen(AddThis.Buffer) +
1];
40:            strcpy(NewString.Buffer, Buffer);
41:            strcat(NewString.Buffer, AddThis.Buffer);
42:        }
43:
44:        return NewString;
45:    }
46:
47:    // constructor
48:    MyString(const char* InitialInput)
49:    {
50:        cout << "Constructor called for: " << InitialInput << endl;
51:        if(InitialInput != NULL)
52:        {
53:            Buffer = new char [strlen(InitialInput) + 1];
54:            strcpy(Buffer, InitialInput);
55:        }
56:        else
57:            Buffer = NULL;
58:    }
59:
60:    // Copy constructor
61:    MyString(const MyString& CopySource)
62:    {
63:        cout<<"Copy constructor to copy from: "<<CopySource.Buffer<<endl;
64:        if(CopySource.Buffer != NULL)
65:        {
66:            // ensure deep copy by first allocating own buffer
67:            Buffer = new char [strlen(CopySource.Buffer) + 1];
68:
69:            // copy from the source into local buffer
70:            strcpy(Buffer, CopySource.Buffer);
71:        }
72:        else
73:            Buffer = NULL;
74:    }
```

```
75:
76:      // Copy assignment operator
77:      MyString& operator= (const MyString& CopySource)
78:      {
79:         cout<<"Copy assignment operator to copy from: "<<CopySource.Buffer<< endl;
80:         if ((this != &CopySource) && (CopySource.Buffer != NULL))
81:         {
82:            if (Buffer != NULL)
83:             delete[] Buffer;
84:
85:            // ensure deep copy by first allocating own buffer
86:            Buffer = new char [strlen(CopySource.Buffer) + 1];
87:
88:            // copy from the source into local buffer
89:            strcpy(Buffer, CopySource.Buffer);
90:         }
91:
92:        return *this;
93:      }
94:
95:      // move constructor
96:      MyString(MyString&& MoveSource)
97:      {
98:         cout << "Move constructor to move from: " << MoveSource.Buffer << endl;
99:         if(MoveSource.Buffer != NULL)
00:          {
01:             Buffer = MoveSource.Buffer; // take ownership i.e.  'move'
02:             MoveSource.Buffer = NULL;   // free move source
103:          }
104:       }
105:
106:      // move assignment operator
107:      MyString& operator= (MyString&& MoveSource)
108:      {
109:         cout<<"Move assignment operator to move from: "<<MoveSource.Buffer<<endl;
110:         if((MoveSource.Buffer != NULL) && (this != &MoveSource))
111:         {
112:            delete Buffer; // release own buffer
113:
114:            Buffer = MoveSource.Buffer; // take ownership i.e.  'move'
115:            MoveSource.Buffer = NULL;   // free move source
116:         }
117:
118:         return *this;
119:      }
120: };
121:
122: int main()
123: {
```

12

LISTING 12.12   Continued

```
124:    MyString Hello("Hello ");
125:    MyString World("World");
126:    MyString CPP(" of C++");
127:
128:    MyString sayHelloAgain ("overwrite this");
129:    sayHelloAgain = Hello + World + CPP;
130:
131:    return 0;
132: }
```

Output ▼

Output without the move constructor and move assignment operator (by commenting out Lines 95 to 119):

```
Constructor called for: Hello
Constructor called for: World
Constructor called for:  of C++
Constructor called for: overwrite this
operator+ called:
Default constructor called
```
Copy constructor to copy from: Hello World
```
operator+ called:
Default constructor called
```
Copy constructor to copy from: Hello World of C++
Copy assignment operator to copy from: Hello World of C++

Output with the move constructor and move assignment operator enabled:

```
Constructor called for: Hello
Constructor called for: World
Constructor called for:  of C++
Constructor called for: overwrite this
operator+ called:
Default constructor called
```
Move constructor to move from: Hello World
```
operator+ called:
Default constructor called
```
Move constructor to move from: Hello World of C++
Move assignment operator to move from: Hello World of C++

Analysis ▼

This might be a really long code sample, but most of it has already been demonstrated in previous example and lessons. The most important part of this listing is in Lines 95 to

119 that implement the move constructor and the move assignment operator respectively. Parts of the output that have been influenced by this new addition to C++11 has been marked in bold. Note how the output changes drastically when compared against the same class without these two entities. If you look at the implementation of the move constructor and the move assignment operator again, you see that the move semantic is essentially implemented by taking ownership of the resources from the move source as shown in Lines 101 in the move constructor and 114 in the move assignment operator. This is immediately followed by assigning NULL to the move source pointer as shown in Lines 102 and 115. Thus even when the move source is destroyed, `delete` invoked via the destructor (programmed in Lines 16 to 20) essentially does nothing as the ownership has been moved to the destination object. Note that in the absence of the move constructor, the copy constructor is called that does a deep copy of the pointed string. Thus, the move constructor has saved a good amount of processing time in reducing unwanted memory allocations and copy steps.

Programming the move constructor and the move assignment operator is completely optional. Unlike the copy constructor and the copy assignment operator, the compiler does not add a default implementation for you.

Use this C++11 feature to optimize the functioning of classes that point to dynamically allocated resources that would otherwise be deep copied even in scenarios where they're only required temporarily.

Operators That Cannot Be Overloaded

With all the flexibility that C++ gives you in customizing the behavior of the operators and making your classes easy to use, it still keeps some cards to itself by not allowing you to change or alter the behavior of some operators that are expected to perform consistently. The operators that cannot be redefined are shown in Table 12.3.

TABLE 12.3 Operators That CANNOT Be Overloaded or Redefined

Operator	Name
.	Member selection
.*	Pointer-to-member selection
::	Scope resolution
? :	Conditional ternary operator
sizeof	Gets the size of an object/class type

12

DO	DON'T
DO program as many operators as would help making using your class easy, but not more.	**DON'T** forget that the compiler provides a default copy assignment operator and copy constructor if you don't supply these, and they won't ensure deep copies of any raw pointers contained within the class.
DO always program a copy assignment operator (with a copy constructor and destructor) for a class that contains raw pointer members.	**DON'T** forget that if you don't supply a move assignment operator or move constructor, the compiler does not create these for you, but instead falls back on the regular copy assignment operator and copy constructor.
DO always program a move assignment operator (and move constructor) for classes that manage dynamically allocated resources, such as an array of data, when using a C++11-compliant compiler.	**DON'T** forget that programming operators is optional, yet improves usability of your class.
	DON'T forget that your smart pointer class isn't a pointer until you have programmed operator (*) and operator (->), and it isn't smart enough until you have implemented the destructor and thought out the copy assignment and copy construction cases.

Summary

You learned how programming operators can make a significant difference to the ease with which your class can be consumed. When programming a class that manages a resource, for example a dynamic array or a string, you need to supply a copy constructor and copy assignment operator for a minimum, in addition to a destructor. A utility class that manages a dynamic array can do very well with a move constructor and a move assignment operator that ensures that the contained resource is not deep-copied for temporary objects. Last but not least, you learned that operators such as ., .*, ::, ?:, and sizeof cannot be redefined.

Q&A

Q **My class encapsulates a dynamic array of integers. What functions and operators should I implement for a minimum?**

A When programming such a class, you need to clearly define the behavior in the scenario where an instance is being copied directly into another via assignment or copied indirectly by being passed to a function by value. You typically implement the copy constructor, copy assignment operator, and the destructor. You also implement the move constructor and move assignment operator if you want to tweak the performance of this class in certain cases.

Q **I have an instance `object` of a class. I want to support this syntax: `cout << object;`. What operator do I need to implement?**

A You need to implement a conversion operator that allows your class to be interpreted as a type that `std::cout` can handle upfront. One way is to define operator `char*()` as you also did in Listing 12.2.

Q **I want to create my own smart pointer class. What functions and operators do I need to implement for a minimum?**

A A smart pointer needs to supply the ability of being used as a normal pointer as in `*pSmartPtr` or `pSmartPtr->Func()`. To enable this you implement operator (`*`) and operator (`->`). In addition, for it to be smart, you also take care of automatic resource release/returns by programming the destructor accordingly, and you would clearly define how copy or assignment works by implementing the copy constructor and copy assignment operator or by prohibiting it by declaring these two as `private`.

12

Workshop

The Workshop contains quiz questions to help solidify your understanding of the material covered and exercises to provide you with experience in using what you've learned. Try to answer the quiz and exercise questions before checking the answers in Appendix D, and be certain you understand the answers before going to the next lesson.

Quiz

1. Can my subscript operator [] return const and non-const variants of return types?

```
const Type& operator[](int Index);
Type& operator[](int Index); // is this OK?
```

2. Would you ever declare the copy constructor or copy assignment operator as private?

3. Would it make sense to define a move constructor and move assignment operator for your class Date?

Exercises

1. Program a conversion operator for class Date that converts the date it holds into a unique integer.

2. Program a move constructor and move assignment operator for class DynIntegers that encapsulates a dynamically allocated array in the form of private member int*.

LESSON 13
Casting Operators

Casting is a mechanism by which the programmer can temporarily or permanently change the interpretation of an object by the compiler. Note that this does not imply that the programmer changes the object itself—he simply changes the interpretation thereof. Operators that change the interpretation of an object are called *casting operators*.

In this lesson, you learn

- The need for casting operators

- Why C-style casts are not popular with some C++ programmers

- The four C++ casting operators

- The concepts of upcasting and downcasting

- Why C++ casting operators are not all-time favorites either

The Need for Casting

In a perfectly type-safe and type-strong world comprising well-written C++ applications, there should be no need for casting and for casting operators. However, we live in a real world where modules programmed by a lot of different people and vendors often using different environments have to work together. To make this happen, compilers very often need to be instructed to interpret data in ways that make them compile and the application function correctly.

Let's take a real-world example: Although some C++ compilers might support `bool` as a native type, a lot of libraries are still in use that were programmed years back and in C. These libraries made for C compilers had to rely on the use of an integral type to hold Boolean data. So, a `bool` on these compilers is something akin to:

```
typedef unsigned short BOOL;
```

A function that returns Boolean data would be declared as:

```
BOOL IsX ();
```

Now, if such a library is to be used with a new application programmed in the latest version of the C++ compiler, the programmer has to find a way to make the `bool` data type as understood by his C++ compiler function with the `BOOL` data type as understood by the library. The way to make this happen is by using casts:

```
bool bCPPResult = (bool)IsX ();    // C-Style cast
```

The evolution of C++ saw the emergence of new C++ casting operators and that created a split in the C++ programming community: a group that continued using C-style casts in their C++ applications, and another that religiously converted to casting keywords introduced by C++ compilers. The argument of the former group is that the C++ casts are cumbersome to use, and sometimes differ in functionality to such a small extent that they are of only theoretical value. The latter group, which evidently is comprised of C++ syntax purists, points out at the flaws in the C-style casts to make their case.

Because the real world contains both kinds of code in operation, it would be good to simply read through this lesson, know the advantages and disadvantages of each style, and formulate your own opinion.

Why C-Style Casts Are Not Popular with Some C++ Programmers

Type safety is one of the mantras that C++ programmers swear by when singing praises to the qualities of this programming language. In fact, most C++ compilers won't even let you get away with this:

```
char* pszString = "Hello World!";
int* pBuf = pszString;    // error: cannot convert char* to int*
```

...and quite rightfully so!

Now, C++ compilers still do see the need to be backward compliant to keep old and legacy code building, and therefore automatically allow syntax such as

```
int* pBuf = (int*)pszString; // Cast one problem away, create another
```

However, C-style casts actually force the compiler to interpret the destination as a type that is very conveniently of the programmer's choice—a programmer who, in this case, did not bother thinking that the compiler reported an error in the first place for good reason, and simply muzzled the compiler and forced it to obey. This, of course, does not go well down the throats of C++ programmers who see their type safety being compromised by casts that force anything through.

The C++ Casting Operators

Despite the disadvantages of casting, the concept of casting itself cannot be discarded. In many situations, casts are legitimate requirements to solve important compatibility issues. C++ additionally supplies a new casting operator specific to inheritance-based scenarios that did not exist with C programming.

The four C++ casting operators are

- static_cast
- dynamic_cast
- reinterpret_cast
- const_cast

13

The usage syntax of the casting operators is consistent:

```
destination_type result = cast_type <destination_type> (object_to_be_casted);
```

Using static_cast

static_cast is a mechanism that can be used to convert pointers between related types, and perform explicit type conversions for standard data types that would otherwise happen automatically or implicitly. As far as pointers go, static_cast implements a basic compile-time check to ensure that the pointer is being cast to a related type. This is an improvement over a C-style cast that allows a pointer to one object to be cast to an absolutely unrelated type without any complaint. Using static_cast, a pointer can be upcasted to the base type, or can be down-casted to the derived type, as the following code-sample indicates.

```
Base* pBase = new Derived ();     // construct a Derived object
Derived* pDerived = static_cast<Derived*>(pBase);     // ok!

// CUnrelated is not related to Base via any inheritance heirarchy
CUnrelated* pUnrelated = static_cast<CUnrelated*>(pBase); // Error
//The cast above is not permitted as types are unrelated
```

> **NOTE** Casting a Derived* to a Base* is called upcasting and can be done without any explicit casting operator:
>
> ```
> Derived objDerived;
> Base* pBase = &objDerived;  // ok!
> ```
>
> Casting a Base* to a Derived* is called downcasting and cannot be done without usage of explicit casting operators:
>
> ```
> Derived objDerived;
> Base* pBase = &objDerived; // Upcast -> ok!
> Derived* pDerived = pBase; // Error: Downcast needs explicit cast
> ```

However, note that static_cast verifies only that the pointer types are related. It does *not* perform any runtime checks. So, with static_cast, a programmer could still get away with this bug:

```
Base* pBase = new Base ();
Derived* pDerived = static_cast<Derived*>(pBase); // Still no errors!
```

Here, pDerived actually points to a partial Derived object because the object being pointed to is actually a Base() type. Because static_cast performs only a compile-time check of verifying that the types in question are related and does not perform a runtime check, a call to pDerived->SomeDerivedClassFunction() would get compiled, but probably result in unexpected behavior during runtime.

Apart from helping in upcasting or downcasting, static_cast can, in many cases, help make implicit casts explicit and bring them to the attention of the programmer or reader:

```
double dPi = 3.14159265;
int Num = static_cast<int>(dPi); // Making an otherwise implicit cast, explicit
```

In the preceding code, Num = dPi would have worked as well and to the same effect. However, using a static_cast brings the nature of conversion to the attention of the reader and indicates (to someone who knows static_cast) that the compiler has performed the necessary adjustments based on the information available at compile-time to perform the required type conversion.

Using dynamic_cast and Runtime Type Identification

Dynamic casting, as the name suggests, is the opposite of static casting and actually executes the cast at runtime—that is, at application execution time. The result of a dynamic_cast operation can be checked to see whether the attempt at casting succeeded. The typical usage syntax of the dynamic_cast operator is

```
destination_type* pDest = dynamic_cast <class_type*> (pSource);

if (pDest)     // Check for success of the casting operation before using pointer
   pDest->CallFunc ();
```

For example:

```
Base* pBase = new Derived();

// Perform a downcast
Derived* pDerived = dynamic_cast <Derived*> (pBase);

if (pDerived)     // Check for success of the cast
   pDerived->CallDerivedClassFunction ();
```

As shown in the preceding short example, given a pointer to a base-class object, the programmer can resort to dynamic_cast to verify the type of the destination object being pointed to before proceeding to use the pointer as such. Note that in the code snippet it is apparent that the destination object is a Derived type. So, the sample is of demonstrative value only. Yet, this is not always the case—for example, when a pointer of type Derived* is passed to a function that accepts type Base*. The function can use dynamic_cast given a base-class pointer type to detected type and then perform operations specific to the types detected. Thus dynamic_cast helps determine the type at runtime and use a casted pointer when it is safe to do so. See Listing 13.1 that uses a familiar hierarchy of class Tuna and class Carp related to base class Fish, where the function DetectFishType() dynamically detects if a Fish* is a Tuna* or a Carp*.

13

NOTE Therefore, this mechanism of identifying the type of the object at runtime is called *runtime type identification* or *RTTI*

LISTING 13.1 Using Dynamic Casting to Tell Whether an Fish Object Is a Tuna or a Carp

```
0: #include <iostream>
1: using namespace std;
2:
3: class Fish
4: {
5: public:
6:    virtual void Swim()
7:    {
8:       cout << "Fish swims in water" << endl;
9:    }
10:
11:    // base class should always have virtual destructor
12:    virtual ~Fish() {}
13: };
14:
15: class Tuna: public Fish
16: {
17: public:
18:    void Swim()
19:    {
20:       cout << "Tuna swims real fast in the sea" << endl;
21:    }
22:
23:    void BecomeDinner()
24:    {
25:       cout << "Tuna became dinner in Sushi" << endl;
26:    }
27: };
28:
29: class Carp: public Fish
30: {
31: public:
32:    void Swim()
33:    {
34:       cout << "Carp swims real slow in the lake" << endl;
35:    }
36:
37:    void Talk()
38:    {
39:       cout << "Carp talked crap" << endl;
40:    }
41: };
42:
```

```
43: void DetectFishType(Fish* InputFish)
44: {
45:    Tuna* pIsTuna = dynamic_cast <Tuna*>(InputFish);
46:    if (pIsTuna)
47:    {
48:       cout << "Detected Tuna. Making Tuna dinner: " << endl;
49:       pIsTuna->BecomeDinner();   // calling Tuna::BecomeDinner
50:    }
51:
52:    Carp* pIsCarp = dynamic_cast <Carp*>(InputFish);
53:    if(pIsCarp)
54:    {
55:       cout << "Detected Carp. Making carp talk: " << endl;
56:       pIsCarp->Talk();  // calling Carp::Talk
57:    }
58:
59:    cout << "Verifying type using virtual Fish::Swim " << endl;
60:    InputFish->Swim(); // calling virtual function Swim
61: }
62:
63: int main()
64: {
65:    Carp myLunch;
66:    Tuna myDinner;
67:
68:    DetectFishType(&myDinner);
69:    cout << endl;
70:    DetectFishType(&myLunch);
71:
72:    return 0;
73:}
```

Output ▼

```
Detected Tuna. Making Tuna dinner:
Tuna became dinner in Sushi
Verifying type using virtual Fish::Swim:
Tuna swims real fast in the sea

Detected Carp. Making carp talk:
Carp talked crap
Verifying type using virtual Fish::Swim:
Carp swims real slow in the lake
```

Analysis ▼

This is the hierarchy of Tuna and Carp to the Fish that you were acquainted with in Lesson 10, "Implementing Inheritance." For sake of explanation, not only do the two derived classes implement virtual function Swim(), but they contain a function each that is specific to their types, namely Tuna::BecomeDinner() and Carp::Talk(). What is

13

special in this sample is that given an instance of the base class Fish*, you are able to dynamically detect if that pointer points to a Tuna or a Carp. This dynamic detection or runtime type identification happens in function DetectFishType() defined in Lines 43 to 61. In Line 45, dynamic_cast is used to test the nature of the input base class pointer of type Fish* for type Tuna*. If this Fish* points to a Tuna, the operator returns a valid address, else it returns NULL. Hence, the result of a dynamic_cast always needs to be checked for validity. After the check in Line 46 succeeds, you know that the pointer pIsTuna points to a valid Tuna, and you are able to call function Tuna::BecomeDinner() using it, as shown in Line 49. With the Carp, you use the pointer to invoke function Carp::Talk() as shown in Line 56. Before returning, DetectFishType() does a verification on the type by invoking Fish::Swim(), which being virtual redirects the call to the Swim() method implemented in Tuna or Carp, as applicable.

CAUTION

> The return value of a dynamic_cast operation should always be checked for validity. It is NULL when the cast fails.

Using reinterpret_cast

reinterpret_cast is the closest a C++ casting operator gets to the C-style cast. It really does allow the programmer to cast one object type to another, regardless of whether or not the types are related; that is, it forces a reinterpretation of type using a syntax as seen in the following sample:

```
Base * pBase = new Base ();
CUnrelated * pUnrelated = reinterpret_cast<CUnrelated*>(pBase);
// The code above was not good programming, even when it compiles!
```

This cast actually forces the compiler to accept situations that static_cast would normally not permit. It finds usage in certain low-level applications (such as drivers, for example) where data needs to be converted to a simple type that the API can accept (for example, some APIs work only with BYTE streams; that is, unsigned char*):

```
SomeClass* pObject = new SomeClass ();
// Need to send the object as a byte-stream...
unsigned char* pBytes = reinterpret_cast <unsigned char*>(pObject);
```

The cast used in the preceding code has not changed the binary representation of the source object and has effectively cheated the compiler into allowing the programmer to peek into individual bytes contained by an object of type SomeClass. Because no other C++ casting operator would allow such a conversion, reinterpret_cast explicitly warns the programmer that a potentially unsafe (and nonportable) conversion is occurring.

CAUTION

> As far as possible, you should refrain from using reinterpret_cast in your applications because it allows you to instruct the compiler to treat type X as an unrelated type Y, which does not look like good design or implementation.

Using const_cast

const_cast enables you to turn off the const access modifier to an object. If you are wondering why this cast is necessary at all, you are probably right in doing so. In an ideal situation where programmers write their classes correctly, they remember to use the const keyword frequently and in the right places. The practical world is unfortunately way too different, and code like following is quite prevalent:

```
class SomeClass
{
public:
    // ...
    void DisplayMembers ();    // a display function ought to be const
};
```

So, when you program a function such as

```
void DisplayAllData (const SomeClass& mData)
{
    mData.DisplayMembers ();  // Compile failure
    // reason for failure: call to a non-const member using a const reference
}
```

You are evidently correct in passing the mData object as a const reference. After all, a display function should be read-only and should not be allowed to call non-const member functions—that is, should not be allowed to call a function that can change the state of the object. However, the implementation of DisplayMembers(), which also ought to be const, unfortunately is not. Now, so long as SomeClass belongs to you and the source code is in your control, you can make corrective changes to DisplayMembers(). In many cases, however, it might belong to a third-party library, and making changes to it is not possible. In situations such as these, const_cast is your savior.

The syntax for invoking DisplayMembers() in such a scenario is

```
void DisplayAllData (const SomeClass& mData)
{
    SomeClass& refData = const_cast <SomeClass&>(mData);
    refData.DisplayMembers();    // Allowed!
}
```

13

Note that using `const_cast` to invoke non-const functions should be a last resort. In general, keep in mind that using `const_cast` to modify a const object can result in undefined behavior.

Note also that `const_cast` can be used with pointers:

```
void DisplayAllData (const SomeClass* pData)
{
    // pData->DisplayMembers(); Error: attempt to invoke a non-const function!
    SomeClass* pCastedData = const_cast <SomeClass*>(pData);
    pCastedData->DisplayMembers();    // Allowed!
}
```

Problems with the C++ Casting Operators

Not everyone is happy with all C++ casting operators—not even those who swear by C++. Their reasons range from the syntax being cumbersome and non-intuitive to being redundant.

Let's simply compare this code:

```
double dPi = 3.14159265;

// C++ style cast: static_cast
int Num = static_cast <int>(dPi);     // result: nNum is 3

// C-style cast
int Num2 = (int)dPi;                  // result: Num2 is 3

// leave casting to the compiler
int Num3 = dPi;                       // result: Num3 is 3. No errors!
```

In all the three cases, the programmer achieved the same result. In practical scenarios, the second option is probably the most prevalent, followed by the third. Few people might use the first option. In any case, the compiler is intelligent enough to convert such types correctly. This gives the cast syntax an impression that it makes the code more difficult to read.

Similarly, other uses of `static_cast` are also handled well by C-style casts that are admittedly simpler looking:

```
// using static_cast
Derived* pDerived = static_cast <Derived*>(pBase);
```

```
// But, this works just as well...
Derived* pDerivedSimple = (Derived*)pBase;
```

Thus, the advantage of using static_cast is often overshadowed by the clumsiness of its syntax. Bjarne Stroustrup's own words express the situation accurately: "Maybe, because static_cast is so ugly and so relatively hard to type, you're more likely to think twice before using one? That would be good, because casts really are mostly avoidable in modern C++." (See Bjarne Stroustrup's C++ Style and Technique FAQ at http://www.research.att.com/~bs/bs_faq2.html.)

Looking at other operators, reinterpret_cast is for forcing your way through when static_cast does not work; ditto for const_cast with respect to modifying the const access modifiers. Thus, C++ casting operators other than dynamic_cast are avoidable in modern C++ applications. Only when addressing the needs of legacy applications might other casting operators become relevant. In such cases, preferring C-style casts to C++ casting operators is often a matter of taste. What's important is that you avoid casting as far as possible, and when you do use it, you know what happens behind the scenes.

DO	DON'T
DO remember that casting a Derived* to a Base* is called upcasting and this is safe.	**DON'T** forget to check the pointer for validity after using dynamic_cast.
DO remember that casting a Base* directly to a Derived* is called downcasting, and this can be unsafe unless you use dynamic_cast.	**DON'T** design your application around RTTI using dynamic_cast.
DO remember that the objective of creating an inheritance hierarchy is typically in having virtual functions that when invoked using base class pointers ensure that the available derived class versions are invoked.	

13

Summary

In this lesson, you learned the different C++ casting operators, the arguments for and against using them. You also learned that in general you should avoid the usage of casts.

Q&A

Q Is it okay to modify the contents of a const-object by casting a pointer or reference to it using `const_cast`?

A Most definitely not. The result of such an operation is not defined and is definitely not desired.

Q I need a `Bird*`, but have a `Dog*` at hand. The compiler does not allow me to use the pointer to the `Dog` object as a `Bird*`. However, when I use `reinterpret_cast` to cast the `Dog*` to `Bird*`, the compiler does not complain and it seems I can use this pointer to call `Bird`'s member function, `Fly()`. Is this okay?

A Again, definitely not. `reinterpret_cast` changed only the interpretation of the pointer, and did not change the object being pointed to (that is still a `Dog`). Calling a `Fly()` function on a `Dog` object will not give the results you are looking for, and could possibly cause an application failure.

Q I have a `Derived` object being pointed to by a `pBase` that is a `Base*`. I am sure that `pBase` points to a `Derived` object, so do I really need to use `dynamic_cast`?

A Because you are sure that the object being pointed to is a `Derived` type, you can save on runtime performance by using `static_cast`.

Q C++ provides casting operators, and yet I am advised to not use them as much as possible. Why is that?

A You keep aspirin at home, but you don't make it your staple diet just because it's available, right? Use casts only when you need them.

Workshop

The workshop contains quiz questions to help solidify your understanding of the material covered and exercises to provide you with experience in using what you've learned. Try to answer the quiz and exercise questions before checking the answers in Appendix D, and be certain you understand the answers before going to the next lesson.

Quiz

1. You have a base class object pointer pBase. What cast would you use to determine whether it is a Derived1 type or a Derived2 type?

2. You have a const reference to an object and tried calling a public member function, written by you. The compiler does not allow this because the function in question is not a const member. Would you correct the function or would you use const_cast?

3. reinterpret_cast should be used only when static_cast does not work, and the cast is known to be required and safe. True or false?

4. Is it true that many instances of static_cast-based conversions, especially between simple data types, would be performed automatically by a good C++ compiler?

Exercises

1. **BUG BUSTERS:** What is the problem in the following code?

```
void DoSomething(Base* pBase)
{
    Derived* pDerived = dynamic_cast <Derived*>(pBase);
    pDerived->DerivedClassMethod();
}
```

2. You have pointer pFish* that points to object of class Tuna.

```
Fish* pFish = new Tuna;
Tuna* pTuna = <what cast?>pFish;
```

What cast would you use to get a pointer Tuna* point to this object of type Tuna? Demonstrate using code.

LESSON 14
An Introduction to Macros and Templates

By now, you should have a solid understanding of basic C++ syntax. Programs written in C++ should be understandable and you are poised to learn language features that help you write applications efficiently.

In this lesson, you learn

- An introduction to the preprocessor

- The #define keyword and macros

- An introduction to templates

- How to write templates functions and classes

- The difference between macros and templates

- How C++11 helps program compile time checks using static_assert

The Preprocessor and the Compiler

In Lesson 2, "The Anatomy of a C++ Program," first learned about the preprocessor. The preprocessor, as the name indicates, is what runs before the compiler starts. In other words, the preprocessor actually decides what is compiled on the basis of how you instruct it. Preprocessor directives are characterized by the fact that they all start with a # sign. For example:

```
// tell the preprocessor to insert the contents of header iostream here
#include <iostream>

// define a macro constant
#define ARRAY_LENGTH 25
int MyNumbers[ARRAY_LENGTH]; // array of 25 integers

// define a macro function
#define SQUARE(x) ((x) * (x))
int TwentyFive = SQUARE(5);
```

This lesson focuses on two types of preprocessor directives seen in the code snippet above; one using `#define` to define a constant and another using `#define` define a macro function. Both these directives, irrespective of what role they play, actually tell the preprocessor to replace every instance of the macro (`ARRAY_LENGTH` or `SQUARE`) with the value they define.

> **NOTE**
> Macros are also about text substitution. The preprocessor does nothing intelligent beyond replacing in-place the identifier by another text.

Using `#define` Macros to Define Constants

The syntax of using `#define` to compose a constant quite simple:

```
#define identifier value
```

For example, a constant `ARRAY_LENGTH` that is substituted by 25 would hence be the following:

```
#define ARRAY_LENGTH 25
```

This identifier is now replaced by 25 wherever the preprocessor encounters the text ARRAY_LENGTH:

```
int MyNumbers [ARRAY_LENGTH] = {0};
double Radiuses [ARRAY_LENGTH] = {0.0};
std::string Names [ARRAY_LENGTH];
```

After the preprocessor runs, the three are visible to the compiler as follows:

```
int MyNumbers [25] = {0};   // an array of 25 integers
double Radiuses [25] = {0.0};   // an array of 25 doubles
std::string Names [25];   // an array of 25 std::strings
```

The replacement is applicable to every section of your code, including a for loop such as this one:

```
for(int Index = 0; Index < ARRAY_LENGTH; ++Index)
   MyNumbers[Index] = Index;
```

This for loop is visible to the compiler as

```
for(int Index = 0; Index < 25; ++Index)
   MyNumbers[Index] = Index;
```

To see exactly how such a macro works, review Listing 14.1.

LISTING 14.1 Declaring and Using Macros That Define Constants

```
0: #include <iostream>
1: #include<string>
2: using namespace std;
3:
4: #define ARRAY_LENGTH 25
5: #define PI 3.1416
6: #define MY_DOUBLE double
7: #define FAV_WHISKY "Jack Daniels"
8:
9: int main()
10: {
11:     int MyNumbers [ARRAY_LENGTH] = {0};
12:     cout << "Array's length: " << sizeof(MyNumbers) / sizeof(int) << endl;
13:
14:     cout << "Enter a radius: ";
15:     MY_DOUBLE Radius = 0;
16:     cin >> Radius;
17:     cout << "Area is: " << PI * Radius * Radius << endl;
18:
```

14

LISTING 14.1   Continued

```
19:    string FavoriteWhisky (FAV_WHISKY);
20:    cout << "My favorite drink is: " << FAV_WHISKY << endl;
21:
22:    return 0;
23: }
```

Output ▼

```
Array's length: 25
Enter a radius: 2.1569
Area is: 14.7154
My favorite drink is: Jack Daniels
```

Analysis ▼

ARRAY_LENGTH, PI, MY_DOUBLE, and FAV_WHISKY are the four macro constants defined in Lines 3 to 7 respectively. As you can see, the first is used in defining the length of an array at Line 11, which has been confirmed indirectly by using operator sizeof() in Line 12. MY_DOUBLE is used to declare a variable Radius of type double in Line 15, whereas PI is used to calculate the area of the circle in Line 17. Finally FAV_WHISKY is used to initialize a std::string object in Line 19 and is directly used in the cout statement in Line 20. All these instances show how the preprocessor simply makes a text replacement.

This "dumb" text replacement that seems to have found a ubiquitous application in Listing 14.1 has its drawbacks, too.

TIP

As the preprocessor makes a dumb text substitution, it lets you get away with ransom (but the compiler doesn't always). You could define FAV_WHISKY in line 7 in Listing 14.1 like this:

`#define FAV_WHISKY 42 // "Jack Daniels"`

which would result in a compilation error in Line 19 for the std::string instantiation, but in the absence of it, the compiler would go ahead and print the following:

`My favorite drink is: 42`

This, of course, wouldn't make sense, and most importantly went through undetected. Additionally, you don't have much control on the macro defined constant PI: was it a double or a float? The answer is neither. PI to the preprocessor was just a text substitution element "3.1416". It never was a defined data type.

Constants are better defined using the const keyword with data types instead. So, this is much better:

```
const int ARRAY_LENGTH = 25;
const double PI = 3.1416;
const char* FAV_WHISKY = "Jack Daniels";
typedef double MY_DOUBLE;  // use typedef to alias a type
```

Using Macros for Protection Against Multiple Inclusion

C++ programmers typically declare their classes and functions in .H files called header files. The respective functions are defined in .CPP files that include the header files using the #include <header> preprocessor directive. If one header file—let's call it class1.h—declares a class that has another class declared in class2.h as a member, then class1.h needs to include class2.h. If the design were complicated, and the other class required the former as well, then class2.h would include class1.h, too

For the preprocessor however, two header files that include each other is a problem of recursive nature. To avoid this problem, you can use macros in conjunction with pre-processor directives #ifndef and #endif.

header1.h that includes <header2.h> looks like the following:

```
#ifndef HEADER1_H _//multiple inclusion guard:
#define HEADER1_H_ // preprocessor will read this and following lines once
#include <header2.h>

class Class1
{
    // class members
};
#endif // end of header1.h
```

header2.h looks similar, but with a different macro definition and includes <header1.h>:

```
#ifndef HEADER2_H //multiple inclusion guard
#define HEADER2_H_
#include <header1.h>

class Class2
{
    // class members
};
#endif // end of header2.h
```

14

> **NOTE**
>
> #ifndef can be read as if-not-defined. It is a conditional process-ing command, instructing the preprocessor to continue only if the identifier has not been defined.
>
> #endif marks the end of this conditional processing instruction for the preprocessor.

Thus, when the preprocessor enters header1.h in the first run and encounters #ifndef statement, it notices that the macro HEADER1_H_ has not been defined and proceeds. The first line following #ifndef defines the macro HEADER1_H_ ensuring that a second pre-processor run of this file terminates at the first line containing #ifndef, as that condition now evaluates to false. The same stands true for header2.h. This simple mechanism is arguably one of the most frequently used macro-based functionalities in the world of C++ programming.

Using #define To Write Macro Functions

The ability of the preprocessor to simply replace text elements identified by a macro often results it in being used to write simple functions, for example:

```
#define SQUARE(x) ((x) * (x))
```

This helps determine the square of a number. Similarly, a macro that calculates the area of a circle looks like this:

```
#define PI 3.1416
#define AREA_CIRCLE(r) (PI*(r)*(r))
```

Macro functions are often used for such very simple calculations. They provide the advantage of normal function calls in that these are expanded in-line before compilations and hence can help improve code performance in certain cases. Listing 14.2 demon-strates the use of these macro functions.

LISTING 14.2 Using Macro Functions That Calculate the Square of a Number, Area of a Circle, and Min and Max of Two Numbers

```
0: #include <iostream>
1: #include<string>
2: using namespace std;
3:
4: #define SQUARE(x) ((x) * (x))
5: #define PI 3.1416
```

```
 6: #define AREA_CIRCLE(r) (PI*(r)*(r))
 7: #define MAX(a, b) (((a) > (b)) ? (a) : (b))
 8: #define MIN(a, b) (((a) < (b)) ? (a) : (b))
 9:
10: int main()
11: {
12:    cout << "Enter an integer: ";
13:    int Input1 = 0;
14:    cin >> Input1;
15:
16:    cout << "SQUARE(" << Input1 << ") = " << SQUARE(Input1) << endl;
17:    cout << "Area of a circle with radius " << Input1 << ' is: ";
18:    cout << AREA_CIRCLE(Input1) << endl;
19:
20:    cout << "Enter another integer: ";
21:    int Input2 = 0;
22:    cin >> Input2;
23:
24:    cout << "MIN(" << Input1 << ", " << Input2 << ") = ";
25:    cout << MIN (Input1, Input2) << endl;
26:
27:    cout << "MAX(" << Input1 << ", " << Input2 << ") = ";
28:    cout << MAX (Input1, Input2) << endl;
29:
30:    return 0;
31: }
```

Output ▼

```
Enter an integer: 36
SQUARE(36) = 1296
Area of a circle with radius 36 is: 4071.51
Enter another integer: -101
MIN(36, -101) = -101
MAX(36, -101) = 36
```

Analysis ▼

Lines 4 to 8 contain a few utility macro functions that return the square of a number, area of a circle, and min and max of two numbers. Note how AREA_CIRCLE in Line 6 evaluates the area using a macro constant PI, thus indicating that one macro can reuse another. After all, these are just plain text replacement commands for the preprocessor. Let's analyze Line 25 that uses the macro MIN:

```
cout << MIN (Input1, Input2) << endl;
```

14

This line is essentially fed to the compiler in the following format where the macro is expanded in-place:

```
cout << (((Input1) < (Input2)) ? (Input1) : (Input2)) << endl;
```

Why All the Parentheses?

Take a look at the macro to calculate the circle's area again:

```
#define AREA_CIRCLE(r) (PI*(r)*(r))
```

This calculation has curious syntax in the number of brackets used. In comparison, refer to the function Area() programmed in Listing 7.1 of Lesson 7, "Organizing Code with Functions.".

```
// Function definitions (implementations)
double Area(double InputRadius)
{
   return Pi * InputRadius * InputRadius;  // look, no brackets?
}
```

So, why did you overdo the brackets for the macro while the same formula in a function looks a lot different. The reason lies in the way the macro is evaluated—as a text substitution mechanism supported by the preprocessor.

Consider the macro without most of the brackets:

```
#define AREA_CIRCLE(r) (PI*r*r)
```

What would happen when you invoke this macro using a statement like this:

```
cout << AREA_CIRCLE (4+6);
```

This would be expanded by the compiler into

```
cout << (PI*4+6*4+6);  // not the same as PI*10*10
```

Thus, following the rules of operator precedence where multiplication happens before addition, the compiler actually evaluates the area like this:

```
cout << (PI*4+24+6);    // 42.5664 (which is incorrect)
```

In the absence of parenthesis, plain-text conversion played havoc on our programming logic! Parenthesis help avoid this problem:

```
#define AREA_CIRCLE(r) (PI*(r)*(r))
cout << AREA_CIRCLE (4+6);
```

The expression after substitution is viewed by the compiler as the following:

```
cout << (PI*(4+6)*(4+6));    // PI*10*10, as expected
```

These brackets automatically result in the calculation of an accurate area, making your macro code independent of operator precedence and the effects thereof.

Using Macro assert to Validate Expressions

Although it is good to single step and test every code path immediately after programming, it might be physically impossible. What is possible is to insert checks that validate expressions or variable values.

The assert macro enables you to do just that. To use assert you include <assert.h> and the syntax is as follows:

```
assert (expression that evaluates to true or false);
```

A sample use of assert() that validates the contents of a pointer is:

```
#include <assert.h>
int main()
{
   char* sayHello = new char [25];
   assert(sayHello != NULL); // throws up a message if pointer is NULL

   // other code

   delete [] sayHello;
   return 0;
}
```

assert()ensures that you are notified if the pointer is invalid. For demonstration sake, I initialized sayHello to NULL and on execution in debug mode Visual Studio immediately popped up the screen you see in Figure 14.1.

14

FIGURE 14.1
What happens
when an assert
checking validity of
the pointer fails.

Thus, `assert()`, as implemented in Microsoft Visual Studio, enables you to click the Retry button that brings you back into your application, and the call stack indicates which line failed the assertion test. This makes `assert()` a handy debugging feature; for instance, you can validate input parameters of functions using `assert`. This is highly recommended and helps you improve the quality of your code over the long term.

NOTE

assert() is typically disabled in release modes and provides you with an error message or information only in the debug build of most development environments.

Additionally, some environments have implemented this as a function, not as a macro.

CAUTION

As assert does not make it to the release build, it is important to ensure that checks that are critical to the functioning of your application (for example the return value of a dynamic_cast operation) are still performed using an if-statement. An assert assists you in problem detection; it's not something to replace pointer checks necessary in the code.

Advantages and Disadvantages of Using Macro Functions

Macros enable you to reuse certain utility functions irrespective of the type of variables you are dealing with. Consider the following line from Listing 14.2 again:

```
#define MIN(a, b) (((a) < (b)) ? (a) : (b))
```

You can use this macro function `MIN` on `integers`:

```
cout << MIN(25, 101) << endl;
```

But you can reuse the same on `double`, too:

```
cout << MIN(0.1, 0.2) << endl;
```

Note that if `MIN()` were to be a normal function, you would program two variants of it: `MIN_INT()` that accepted `int` parameters and returned an `int` and `MIN_DOUBLE()` that does the same with type `double` instead. This optimization in reducing lines of code is a slight advantage and entices some programmers into using macros for defining simple utility functions. These macro functions get expanded inline before compilation and hence the performance of a simple macro is superior to that of an ordinary function call doing the same task. This is because the function call requires the creation of a call stack, passing arguments and so on—administrative overload that often takes more CPU time than the calculation of `MIN` itself.

For these advantages, macros present the severe problem of not supporting any form of type safety. If that wasn't enough, debugging a complicated macro is not easy either.

If you need the ability to program generic functions that are type independent, yet type safe, you program a template function instead of a macro function. If you need to boost performance, you call that function `inline`. $I~macro functions;advantages of>

You have already been introduced to programming inline functions using keyword `inline` in Listing 7.10 in Lesson 7, "Organizing Code with Functions".

DO	DON'T
DO program your own macro functions as infrequently as possibly.	**DON'T** forget to envelop every variable in a macro function definition with brackets.
DO use `const` variables where you can instead of macros.	**DON'T** forget to insert multiple inclusion guards using #ifndef, #define, and #endif in your header files.
DO remember that macros are not type safe and the preprocessor performs no type checking.	**DON'T** forget to sprinkle your code with generous number of assert() statements—these don't make it to the release version and are good at improving the quality of your code.

14

It's time to learn generic programming practices using templates!

An Introduction to Templates

Templates are probably one of the most powerful features of the C++ language that often are the least approached, or understood. Before we tackle with this matter, let's first look at the definition of a template as supplied by Webster's Dictionary:

> Pronunciation: \'tem-plét\
>
> Function: noun
>
> Etymology: Probably from French *templet*, diminutive of *temple*, part of a loom, probably from Latin *templum*
>
> Date: 1677
>
> 1: a short piece or block placed horizontally in a wall under a beam to distribute its weight or pressure (as over a door)
>
> 2: (1): a gauge, pattern, or mold (as a thin plate or board) used as a guide to the form of a piece being made (2): a molecule (as of DNA) that serves as a pattern for the generation of another macromolecule (as messenger RNA) b: overlay
>
> 3: something that establishes or serves as a pattern

The last definition probably comes closest to the interpretation of the word *template* as used in the C++ parlance. Templates in C++ enable you to define a behavior that you can apply to objects of varying types. This sounds ominously close to what macros let you do (refer to the simple macro MAX that determined the greater of two numbers), save for the fact that macros are type unsafe and templates are type safe.

Template Declaration Syntax

You begin the declaration of a template using the `template` keyword followed by a type parameter list. The format of this declaration is

```
template <parameter list>
template function / class declaration..
```

The keyword `template` marks the start of a template declaration and is followed by the template parameter list. This parameter list contains the keyword `typename` that defines the template parameter `objectType`, making it a placeholder for the `type` of the object that the template is being instantiated for.

```
template <typename T1, typename T2 = T1>
bool TemplateFunction(const T1& param1, const T2& param2);

// A template class
template <typename T1, typename T2 = T1>
class Template
{
private:
    T1 m_Obj1;
```

```
    T2 m_Obj2;

public:
    T1 GetObj1() {return m_Obj1; }
    // ... other members
};
```

What you see is a template function and a template class, each taking two template parameters T1 and T2, where T2 has been given the default type as that of T1.

The Different Types of Template Declarations

A template declaration can be

- A declaration or definition of a function
- A declaration or definition of a class
- A definition of a member function or a member class of a class template
- A definition of a static data member of a class template
- A definition of a static data member of a class nested within a class template
- A definition of a member template of a class or class template

Template Functions

Imagine a function that would adapt itself to suit parameters of different types. Such a function is possible using template syntax! Let's analyze a sample template declaration that is the equivalent of the previously discussed macro MAX that returns the greater of two supplied parameters:

```
template <typename objectType>
const objectType& GetMax (const objectType& value1, const objectType& value2)
{
    if (value1 > value2)
        return value1;
    else
        return value2;
}
```

Sample usage:

```
int Integer1 = 25;
int Integer2 = 40;
int MaxValue = GetMax <int> (Integer1, Integer2);
double Double1 = 1.1;
double Double2 = 1.001;
double MaxValue = GetMax <double> (Double1, Double2);
```

14

Note the detail `<int>` used in the call to `GetMax`. It effectively defines the template parameter `objectType` as `int`. The preceding code leads to the compiler generating two versions of the template function `GetMax`, which can be visualized as the following:

```
const int& GetMax (const int& value1, const int& value2)
{
    //...
}
const double & GetMax (const double& value1, const double& value2)
{
    // ...
}
```

In reality, however, template functions don't necessarily need an accompanying type specifier. So, the following function call works perfectly well:

```
int MaxValue = GetMax(Integer1, Integer2);
```

Compilers in this case are intelligent enough to understand that the template function is being invoked for the integer type. With template classes, however, you need to explicitly specify type, as shown in Listing 14.3.

LISTING 14.3   A Template Function `GetMax` That Helps Evaluate the Higher of Two Supplied Values

```
 0: #include<iostream>
 1: #include<string>
 2: using namespace std;
 3:
 4: template <typename Type>
 5: const Type& GetMax (const Type& value1, const Type& value2)
 6: {
 7:     if (value1 > value2)
 8:         return value1;
 9:     else
10:         return value2;
11: }
12:
13: template <typename Type>
14: void DisplayComparison(const Type& value1, const Type& value2)
15: {
16:     cout << "GetMax(" << value1 << ", " << value2 << ") = ";
17:     cout << GetMax(value1, value2) << endl;
18: }
19:
20: int main()
21: {
22:     int Int1 = -101, Int2 = 2011;
```

```
23:    DisplayComparison(Int1, Int2);
24:
25:    double d1 = 3.14, d2 = 3.1416;
26:    DisplayComparison(d1, d2);
27:
28:    string Name1("Jack"), Name2("John");
29:    DisplayComparison(Name1, Name2);
30:
31:    return 0;
32: }
```

Output ▼

```
GetMax(-101, 2011) = 2011
GetMax(3.14, 3.1416) = 3.1416
GetMax(Jack, John) = John
```

Analysis ▼

This sample features two template functions: GetMax() in Lines 4 to 11, which is used by DisplayComparison() in Lines 13 to 18. main() demonstrates in Lines 23, 26, and 29 how the same template function has been reused for very different data types: integer, double, and std::string. Not only are these template functions reusable (just like their macro counterparts), but they're easier to program and maintain and are type-safe!

Note that you could've also invoked DisplayComparison with the explicit type:

```
23:    DisplayComparison<int>(Int1, Int2);
```

However, this is unnecessary when calling template functions. You don't need to specify the template parameter type(s) because the compiler is able to infer it automatically. When programming template classes, though, you need to do it.

Templates and Type Safety

Template functions DisplayComparison() and GetMax() shown in Listing 14.3 are type safe. This means that they would not allow a meaningless call like this one:

```
DisplayComparison(Integer, "Some string");
```

This would immediately result in a compile failure.

Template Classes

Lesson 9, "Classes and Objects," taught you that classes are programming units that encapsulate certain attributes and methods that operate on those attributes. Attributes typically are private members, such as int Age in a class Human. Classes are design blueprints, and the real-world representation of a class is an object of the class. So, "Tom"

14

can be thought of as an object of class Human with attribute Age containing value 15, for example. What if you want to store Age in a long long for some humans who are expected to get extraordinarily old, and Age in short for others who are expected to have a low lifespan? This is where template classes could be handy. Template classes are the templatized versions of C++ classes. These are blueprints of blueprints. When using a template class, you are given the option to specify the "type" you are specializing the class for. This enables you to create some humans with template parameter Age as a long long, some with int, and some with Age as an integer of type short.

A simple template class that features a single template parameter T can be written as the following:

```
template <typename T>
class MyFirstTemplateClass
{
public:
    void SetValue  (const T& newValue) { Value = newValue; }
    const T& GetValue() const {return Value;}

private:
    T Value;
};
```

The class MyFirstTemplateClass class has been designed to hold a variable of type T— the type of which is assigned at the time the template is used. So, let's look at a sample usage of this template class:

```
MyFirstTemplateClass <int> HoldInteger;  // Template instantiation
HoldInteger.SetValue(5);
std::cout << "The value stored is: " << HoldInteger.GetValue() << std::endl;
```

You have used this template class to hold and retrieve an object of type int; that is, the Template class is instantiated for a template parameter of type int. Similarly, you can use the same class to deal with character strings in a similar manner:

```
MyFirstTemplateClass <char*> HoldString;
HoldString.SetValue("Sample string");
std::cout << "The value stored is: " << HoldString.GetValue() << std::endl;
```

Thus, the class defines a pattern and gets reused for applying that same pattern it implements on different data types. A customizable Human where you could choose the type of the Age parameter would look like this:

```
template <typename T>
class CustomizableHuman
{
```

```
public:
    void SetAge (const T& newValue) { Age = newValue; }
    const T& GetAge() const {return Age;}

private:
    T Age;    // T is type you choose to customize this template for!
};
```

In using this template, you mention the type in the template instantiation syntax:

```
CustomizableHuman<int> NormalLifeSpan;  // instantiate for type int
  NormalLifeSpan.SetAge(80);
CustomizableHuman<long long> LongLifeSpan;  // instantiate for type long long
  LongLifeSpan.SetAge(3147483647);
CustomizableHuman<short> ShortLifeSpan; // instantiate for type short
  ShortLifeSpan.SetAge(40);
```

Template Instantiation and Specialization

The terminology changes a bit when it comes to templates. The word *instantiation*, when used in the context of classes, normally refers to *objects* as instances of *classes*.

In case of templates, however, *instantiation* is the act *or process of* creating a specific type from a template declaration and one or more template arguments.

So, if you look at a template declaration:

```
template <typename T>
class TemplateClass
{
    T m_member;
};
```

when you use this template, you would write the code as

```
TemplateClass <int> IntTemplate;
```

The specific type created as a result of this instantiation is called a *specialization*.

Declaring Templates with Multiple Parameters

The template parameter list can be expanded to declare multiple parameters separated by a comma. So, if you want to declare a generic class that holds a pair of objects that can be of differing types, you can do so using the construct as shown in the following sample (that displays a template class with two template parameters):

14

```
template <typename T1, typename T2>
class HoldsPair
{
private:
    T1 Value1;
    T2 Value2;
public:
    // Constructor that initializes member variables
    HoldsPair (const T1& value1, const T2& value2)
    {
        Value1 = value1;
        Value2 = value2;
    };
    // ... Other function declarations
};
```

In here, class `HoldsPair` accepts two template parameters named T1 and T2. We can use this class to hold two objects of the same type or of different types as you can see here:

```
// A template instantiation that pairs an int with a double
HoldsPair <int, double> pairIntDouble (6, 1.99);

// A template instantiation that pairs an int with an int
HoldsPair <int, int> pairIntDouble (6, 500);
```

Declaring Templates with Default Parameters

We could modify the previous version of `HoldsPair <...>` to declare int as the default template parameter type.

```
template <typename T1=int, typename T2=int>
class HoldsPair
{
    // ... method declarations
};
```

This is quite similar in construction to functions that define default input parameter values except for the fact that, in this case, we define default *types*.

The second usage of `HoldsPair` can thus be compacted to

```
// A template instantiation that pairs an int with an int (default type)
HoldsPair <> pairIntDouble (6, 500);
```

Sample Template `class<>` `HoldsPair`

It's time to develop further on the template version of `HoldsPair` that been covered so far. Have a look at Listing 14.4.

LISTING 14.4   A Template Class with a Pair of Member Attributes

```
0: // Declaring default paramter types, first int, second float
1: template <typename T1=int, typename T2=double>
2: class HoldsPair
3: {
4: private:
5:     T1 Value1;
6:     T2 Value2;
7: public:
8:     // Constructor that initializes member variables
9:     HoldsPair (const T1& value1, const T2& value2)
10:    {
11:        Value1 = value1;
12:        Value2 = value2;
13:    };
14:
15:    // Accessor functions
16:    const T1 & GetFirstValue () const
17:    {
18:        return Value1;
19:    };
20:
21:    const T2& GetSecondValue () const
22:    {
23:        return Value2;
24:    };
25: };
26:
27: #include <iostream>
28: using namespace std;
29:
30: int main ()
31: {
32:     // Two instantiations of template HoldsPair -
33:     HoldsPair <> mIntFloatPair (300, 10.09);
34:     HoldsPair<short,char*>mShortStringPair(25,"Learn templates,love C++");
35:
36:     // Output values contained in the first object...
37:     cout << "The first object contains -" << endl;
38:     cout << "Value 1: " << mIntFloatPair.GetFirstValue () <<  endl;
39:     cout << "Value 2: " << mIntFloatPair.GetSecondValue () << endl;
```

14

LISTING 14.4 Continued

```
40:
41:    // Output values contained in the second object...
42:    cout << "The second object contains -" << endl;
43:    cout << "Value 1: " << mShortStringPair.GetFirstValue () <<  endl;
44:    cout << "Value 2: " << mShortStringPair.GetSecondValue () << endl;
45:
46:    return 0;
47: }
```

Output ▼

```
The first object contains -
Value 1: 300
Value 2: 10.09
The second object contains -
Value 1: 25
Value 2: Learn templates, love C++
```

Analysis ▼

This simple program illustrates how to declare the template class HoldsPair to hold a pair of values of types that are dependent on the template's parameter list. Line 1 contains a template parameter list that defines two template parameters T1 and T2 with default types as int and double respectively. Accessor functions GetFirstValue () and GetSecondValue() can be used to query the values held by the object. Note how GetFirstValue and GetSecondValue get adapted on the basis of the template instantiation syntax to return the appropriate object types. You have managed to define a pattern in HoldsPair that you can reuse to deliver the same logic for different variable types. Thus, templates increase code reusability.

Template Classes and static Members

We learned how templates are blueprints of classes that are in turn blueprints of objects. How would static member attributes function within a template class? You learned in Lesson 9, "Classes and Objects," that declaring a class member static results in the member being shared across all instances of a class. It's quite similar with a template class, too, save for the fact that a static member is shared across all instances of a template class with the same specialization. So a static member X within a template class T is static within all instances of T specialized for int. Similarly X is static within all instances of T specialized for double, independently of the other specialization for int. In other words, you can visualize it as the compiler creating two versions: X_int for the former and X_double for the latter. Listing 14.5 demonstrates this.

LISTING 14.5   The Effect of Static Variables on Template Class and Instances Thereof

```
0: #include <iostream>
1: using namespace std;
2:
3: template <typename T>
4: class TestStatic
5: {
6: public:
7:     static int StaticValue;
8: };
9:
10: // static member initialization
11: template<typename T> int TestStatic<T>::StaticValue;
12:
13: int main()
14: {
15:     TestStatic<int> Int_Year;
16:     cout << "Setting StaticValue for Int_Year to 2011" << endl;
17:     Int_Year.StaticValue = 2011;
18:     TestStatic<int> Int_2;
19:
20:     TestStatic<double> Double_1;
21:     TestStatic<double> Double_2;
22:     cout << "Setting StaticValue for Double_2 to 1011" << endl;
23:     Double_2.StaticValue = 1011;
24:
25:     cout << "Int_2.StaticValue = " << Int_2.StaticValue << endl;
26:     cout << "Double_1.StaticValue = " << Double_1.StaticValue << endl;
27:
28:     return 0;
29: }
```

Output ▼

```
Setting StaticValue for Int_Year to 2011
Setting StaticValue for Double_2 to 1011
Int_2.StaticValue = 2011
Double_1.StaticValue = 1011
```

Analysis ▼

In Lines 17 and 21, you set member StaticValue for an instantiation of the template for type int and type double respectively. In Lines 25 and 26 in main() you read this value, but using the other instance members Int_2 and Double_1. The output demonstrates that you get two distinct values of StaticValue, 2011, which is set using the other instance specialized for int, and 1011, which is set using the other instance specialized for double.

14

Thus, the compiler ensured that the behavior of the static variable remains intact for the specialization of the class for a type. Each specialization of the template class effectively gets its own static variable.

> **NOTE**
>
> Static member instantiation syntax for a template class is not to be missed in Line 11 in Listing 14.5.
>
> ```
> template<typename T> int TestStatic<T>::StaticValue;
> ```
>
> This follows the pattern:
>
> ```
> template<template parameters> StaticType ClassName<Template
>     Arguments>::StaticVarName;
> ```

C++11

Using `static_assert` to Perform Compile-Time Checks

This is a C++11 feature that enables you to block compilation if certain checks are not fulfilled. Weird as this might sound, it's quite useful with template classes. You might want to ensure that your template class is not instantiated for an integer! `static_assert` is a compile-time assert that can display a custom message on your development environment (or console):

```
static_assert(expression being validated, "Error message when check fails");
```

To ensure that your template class cannot be instantiated for type `int`, you can use `static_assert()` with `sizeof(T)`, comparing it against `sizeof(int)` and displaying an error message if the inequality check fails:

```
static_assert(sizeof(T) != sizeof(int), "No int please!");
```

Such a template class that uses `static_assert` to block compilation for certain instantiation types is seen in Listing 14.6.

LISTING 14.6   A Finicky Template Class That Protests Using `static_assert` When Instantiated for Type `int`

```
0: template <typename T>
1: class EverythingButInt
2: {
3: public:
4:    EverythingButInt()
```

```
 5:    {
 6:        static_assert(sizeof(T) != sizeof(int), "No int please!");
 7:    }
 8: };
 9:
10: int main()
11: {
12:    EverythingButInt<int> test;   // template instantiation with int.
13:    return 0;
14: }
```

Output ▼

There is no output as compile fails, providing you with the note you supplied:

```
error: No int please!
```

Analysis ▼

The protest registered by the compiler is programmed in Line 6. Thus, static_assert is a way C++11 helps you protect your template code against unwanted instantiation.

Using Templates in Practical C++ Programming

The most important and powerful application of templates are in the Standard Template Library (STL). STL is comprised of a collection of template classes and functions containing generic utility classes and algorithms. These STL template classes enable you to implement dynamic arrays, lists, and key-value pair containers, whereas algorithms, such as sort, work on those containers and process the data they contain.

The knowledge of template syntax you gained earlier greatly assists you in using STL containers and functions that are presented in great detail in the following lessons of this book. A better understanding of STL containers and algorithms in turn helps you write efficient C++ applications that use STL's tested and reliable implementation and helps you avoid spending time in boilerplate details.

DO	DON'T
DO use templates for the implementation of generic concepts. **DO** choose templates over macros.	**DON'T** forget to use the principles of const correctness when programming template functions and classes. **DON'T** forget that a static member contained within a template class is static for every type-specialization of the class.

14

Summary

In this lesson, you learned more details about working with the preprocessor. Each time you run the compiler, the preprocessor runs first and translates directives such as `#define`.

The preprocessor does text substitution, although with the use of macros these can be somewhat complex. Macro functions provide complex text substitution based on arguments passed at compile time to the macro. It is important to put parentheses around every argument in the macro to ensure that the correct substitution takes place.

Templates help you write reusable code that supplies the developer with a pattern that can be used for a variety of data types. They also make for a type-safe replacement of macros. With the knowledge of templates gained in this lesson, you are now poised to learn to use the STL!

Q&A

Q Why should I use inclusion guards in my header files?

A Inclusion guards using `#ifndef`, `#define`, and `#endif` protect your header from multiple or recursive inclusion errors, and in some cases they even speed up compilation.

Q When should I favor macro functions over templates if the functionality in question can be implemented in both?

A Ideally, you should always favor templates as the templates allow for generic implementation that is also type safe. Macros don't allow for type-safe implementations and are best avoided.

Q Do I need to specify template arguments when invoking a template function?

A Normally not as the compiler can infer this for you, given the arguments used in the function call.

Q How many instances of static variables exist for a given template class?

A This is entirely dependent on the number of types for which the template class has been instantiated. So, if your class has been instantiated for an `int`, a `string`, and a custom type X, you can expect three instances of your static variable to be available—one per template specialization.

Workshop

The Workshop provides quiz questions to help you solidify your understanding of the material covered and exercises to provide you with experience in using what you've learned. Try to answer the quiz and exercise questions before checking the answers in Appendix D, and be certain you understand the answers.

Quiz

1. What is an inclusion guard?

2. Consider the following macro:

   ```
   #define SPLIT(x) x / 5
   ```

   What is the result if this is called with 20?

3. What is the result if the SPLIT macro in Question 2 is called with 10+10?

4. How would you modify the SPLIT macro to avoid erroneous results?

Exercises

1. Write a macro that multiplies two numbers.

2. Write a template version of the macro in Exercise 1.

3. Implement a template function for swap that exchanges two variables.

4. **BUG BUSTERS**: How would you improve the following macro that computes the quarter of an input value?

   ```
   #define QUARTER(x) (x / 4)
   ```

5. Write a simple template class that holds two arrays of types that are defined via the class's template parameter list. The size of the array is 10, and the template class should have accessor functions that allow for the manipulation of array elements.

14

LESSON 15

An Introduction to the Standard Template Library

Put in simple terms, the standard template library (STL) is a set of template classes and functions that supply the programmer with

- Containers for storing information
- Iterators for accessing the information stored
- Algorithms for manipulating the content of the containers

In this lesson, you get overview on these three pillars of STL.

STL Containers

Containers are STL classes that are used to store data. STL supplies two types of container classes:

- Sequential containers
- Associative containers

In addition to these STL also provides classes called Container Adapters that are variants of the same with reduced functionality which support a specific purpose.

Sequential Containers

As the name suggests, these are containers used to hold data in a sequential fashion, such as arrays and lists. Sequential containers are characterized by a fast insertion time, but are relatively slow in `find` operations.

The STL sequential containers are

- `std::vector`—Operates like a dynamic array and grows at the end. Think of a vector like a shelf of books to which you can add or remove books on one end
- `std::deque`—Similar to `std::vector` except that it allows for new elements to be inserted or removed at the beginning, too
- `std::list`—Operates like a doubly-linked list. Think of this like a chain where an object is a link in the chain. You can add or remove links—that is, objects—at any position
- `std::forward_list`—Similar to a `std::list` except that it is a singly-linked list of elements that allows you to iterate only in one direction

The STL `vector` class is akin to an array and allows for random access of an element; that is, you can directly access or manipulate an element in the `vector` given its position (index) using the subscript operator (`[]`). In addition to this, the STL `vector` is a dynamic array and therefore can resize itself to suit the application's runtime requirements. To keep the property of being able to randomly access an element in the array when given a position, most implementations of the STL `vector` keep all elements in contiguous locations. Therefore, a `vector` that needs to resize itself often can reduce the performance of the application, depending on the type of the object it contains. Lesson 4, "Managing Arrays and Strings," introduced you to the vector briefly in Listing 4.4. This container is discussed extensively in Lesson 17, "STL Dynamic Array Classes."

15

You can think of the STL `list` as STL's implementation of a regular linked list. Although elements in a `list` cannot be randomly accessed, as they can be in the STL `vector`, a `list` can organize elements in noncontiguous sections of memory. Therefore, the `std::list` does not have the performance issues that are applicable to a `vector` when the `vector` needs to reallocate its internal array. STL `list` class is discussed extensively in Lesson 18, "STL `list` and `forward_list`."

Associative Containers

Associative containers are those that store data in a sorted fashion—akin to a dictionary. This results in slower insertion times, but presents significant advantages when it comes to searching.

The associative containers supplied by STL are

- **`std::set`**—Stores unique values sorted on insertion in a container featuring logarithmic complexity.

- **`std::unordered_set`**—Stores unique values sorted on insertion in a container featuring near constant complexity. Available starting C++11.

- **`std::map`**—Stores key-value pairs sorted by their unique keys in a container with logarithmic complexity

- **`std::unordered_map`**—Stores key-value pairs sorted by their unique keys in a container with near constant complexity. Available starting C++11.

- **`std::multiset`**—Akin to a set. Additionally, supports the ability to store multiple items having the same value; that is, the value doesn't need to be unique.

- **`std::unordered_multiset`**—Akin to a unordered_set. Additionally, supports the ability to store multiple items having the same value; that is, the value doesn't need to be unique. Available starting C++11.

- **`std::multimap`**—Akin to a map. Additionally, supports the ability to store key-value pairs where keys don't need to be unique.

- **`std::unordered_multimap`**—Akin to a unordered_map. Additionally, supports the ability to store key-value pairs where keys don't need to be unique. Available starting C++11.

The sort criteria of STL containers can be customized by programming predicate functions.

TIP _____ Some implementations of STL also feature associative containers such as hash_set, hash_multiset, hash_map, and hash_multimap. These are similar to the unordered_* containers, which are supported by the standard. In some scenarios, hash_* and the unordered_* variants can be better at searching for an element as they offer constant time operations (independent of the number of elements in the container). Typically, these containers also supply public methods that are identical to those supplied by their standard counterparts and hence are as easy to use.

Using the standard-compliant variants will result in code that is easier to port across platforms and compilers, and should hence be preferred. It is also possible that the logarithmic reduction in performance of a standard-compliant container might not significantly affect your application.

Choosing the Right Container

Clearly, your application might have requirements that can be satisfied by more than one STL container. There is a selection to be made, and this selection is important because a wrong choice could result in a functional application that under-performs.

Therefore, it is important to evaluate the advantages and disadvantages of the containers before selecting one. See Table 15.1 for more details.

TABLE 15.1 Properties of STL's Container Classes

Container	Advantages	Disadvantages
std::vector (Sequential Container)	Quick (constant time) insertion at the end.	Resizing can result in performance loss.
	Array-like access.	Search time is proportional to the number of elements in the container.
		Insertion only at the end.
std::deque (Sequential Container)	All advantages of the vector. Additionally, offers constant-time insertion at the beginning of the container too.	Disadvantages of the vector with respect to performance and search are applicable to the deque.
		Unlike the vector, the deque by specification does not need to feature the reserve() function that allows the programmer to reserve memory space to be used—a feature that avoids frequent resizing to improve performance.

TABLE 15.1   Continued

Container	Advantages	Disadvantages
std::list (Sequential Container)	Constant time insertion at the front, middle, or end of the list.	Elements cannot be accessed randomly given an index as in an array.
	Removal of elements from a list is a constant-time activity regardless of the position of the element.	Accessing elements can be slower than the vector because elements are not stored in adjacent memory locations.
	Insertion or removal of elements does not invalidate iterators that point to other elements in the list.	Search time is proportional to the number of elements in the container.
std:: forward_list (Sequential Container)	Singly-linked list class that allows iteration only in one direction	Allows insertion only at the front of the list via push_front()
std::set (Associative Container)	Search is not directly proportional to the number of elements in the container, rather to the logarithm thereof and hence is often significantly faster than sequential containers.	Insertion of elements is slower than in sequential counterparts, as elements are sorted at insertion.
std:: unordered_ set (Associative Container)	Search, insertion and removal in this type of container is nearly independent of the number of elements in the container.	As elements are weakly ordered, one cannot rely on their relative position within the container.
std:: multiset (Associative Container)	Should be used when a set needs to contain non-unique values too.	Insertions may be slower than in a sequential container as elements (pairs) are sorted on insertion.
std:: unordered_ multiset (Associative Container)	Should be preferred over an unordered_set when you need to contain non-unique values too.	Elements are weakly ordered, so one cannot rely on their relative position within the container
	Performance is similar to unordered_set, namely constant average time for search, insertion and removal of elements, independent of size of container.	

TABLE 15.1   Continued

Container	Advantages	Disadvantages
std::map (Associative Container)	Key-value pairs container that offers search performance proportional to the logarithm of number of elements in the container and hence often significantly faster than sequential containers.	Elements (pairs) are sorted on insertion, hence insertion will be slower than in a sequential container of pairs.
std:: unordered_ map (Associative Container)	Offers advantage of near constant time search, insertion and removal of elements independent of the size of the container.	Elements are weakly ordered and hence not suited to cases where order is important.
std:: multimap (Associative Container)	To be selected over std::map when requirements necessitate the need of a key-value pairs container that holds elements with non-unique keys.	Insertion or elements will be slower than in a sequential equivalent as elements are sorted on insertion.
std:: unordered_ multimap (Associative Container)	To be selected over multimap when you need a key-value pairs container where keys can be non-unique.	Is a weakly ordered container, so you cannot use it when you need to rely on the relative order of elements.
	Allows constant average time insertion, search and removal of elements, independent of the size of the container	

Container Adapters

Container Adapters are variants of sequential and associative containers that have limited functionality and are intended to fulfill a particular purpose. The main adapter classes are:

- **std::stack**—Stores elements in a LIFO (last-in-first-out) fashion, allowing elements to be inserted (pushed) and removed (popped) at the top.

- **std::queue**—Stores elements in FIFO (first-in-first-out) fashion, allowing the first element to be removed in the order they're inserted.

- **std::priority_queue**—Stores elements in a sorted order, such that the one whose value is evaluated to be the highest is always first in the queue.

These containers are discussed in detail in Lesson 24, "Adaptive Containers: Stack and Queue".

STL Iterators

The simplest example of an iterator is a pointer. Given a pointer to the first element in an array, you can increment it and point to the next element or, in many cases, manipulate the element at that location.

Iterators in STL are template classes that in some ways are a generalization of pointers. These are template classes that give the programmer a handle by which he can work with and manipulate STL containers and perform operations on them. Note that operations could as well be STL algorithms that are template functions. Iterators are the bridge that allows these template functions to work with containers, which are template classes, in a consistent and seamless manner.

Iterators supplied by STL can be broadly classified into the following:

- **Input iterator**—One that can be dereferenced to reference an object. The object can be in a collection, for instance. Input iterators of the purest kinds guarantee read access only.

- **Output iterator**—One that allows the programmer to write to the collection. Output iterators of the strictest types guarantee write access only.

The basic iterator types mentioned in the preceding list are further refined into the following:

- **Forward iterator**—A refinement of the input and output iterators allowing both input and output. Forward iterators may be constant, allowing for read-only access to the object the iterator points to, and otherwise allow for both read and write operations, making it mutable. A forward iterator would typically find use in a singly linked list.

- **Bidirectional iterator**—A refinement of the forward iterator in that it can be decremented to move backward as well. A bidirectional iterator would typically find use in a doubly linked list.

- **Random access iterators**—In general, a refinement over the concept of bidirectional iterators that allow addition and subtraction of offsets or allow one iterator to be subtracted from another to find the relative separation or distance between the two objects in a collection. A random iterator would typically find use in an array.

NOTE

At an implementation level, a *refinement* can be thought of as an *inheritance* or a *specialization*.

STL Algorithms

Finding, sorting, reversing, and the like are standard programming requirements that should not require the programmer to reinvent implementation to support. This is precisely why STL supplies these functions in the form of STL algorithms that work well with containers using iterators to help the programmer with some of the most common requirements.

Some of the most used STL algorithms are

- **std::find**—Helps find a value in a collection
- **std::find_if**—Helps find a value in a collection on the basis of a specific user-defined predicate
- **std::reverse**—Reverses a collection
- **std::remove_if**—Helps remove an item from a collection on the basis of a user-defined predicate
- **std::transform**—Helps apply a user-defined transformation function to elements in a container

These algorithms are template functions in the std namespace and require that the standard header <algorithm> be included.

The Interaction Between Containers and Algorithms Using Iterators

Let's examine how iterators seamlessly connect containers and the STL algorithms using an example. The program shown in Listing 15.1 uses the STL sequential container std::vector, which is akin to a dynamic array, to store some integers and then find one in the collection using the algorithm std::find. Note how iterators form the bridge connecting the two. Don't worry about the complexity of the syntax or functionality. Containers such as std::vector and algorithms such as std::find are discussed in detail in Lesson 17, "STL Dynamic Array Classes" and Lesson 23, "STL Algorithms," respectively. If you find this part complicated, you can skip the section for the moment.

LISTING 15.1   Find an Element and Its Position in a Vector

```
1: #include <iostream>
2: #include <vector>
3: #include <algorithm>
4: using namespace std;
```

```
 5:
 6: int main ()
 7: {
 8:     // A dynamic array of integers
 9:     vector <int> vecIntegerArray;
10:
11:     // Insert sample integers into the array
12:     vecIntegerArray.push_back (50);
13:     vecIntegerArray.push_back (2991);
14:     vecIntegerArray.push_back (23);
15:     vecIntegerArray.push_back (9999);
16:
17:     cout << "The contents of the vector are: " << endl
18:
19:     // Walk the vector and read values using an iterator
20:     vector <int>::iterator iArrayWalker = vecIntegerArray.begin ();
21:
22:     while (iArrayWalker != vecIntegerArray.end ())
23:     {
24:         // Write the value to the screen
25:         cout << *iArrayWalker << endl;
26:
27:         // Increment the iterator to access the next element
28:         ++ iArrayWalker;
29:     }
30:
31:     // Find an element (say 2991) in the array using the 'find' algorithm...
32:     vector <int>::iterator iElement = find (vecIntegerArray.begin ()
33:                             ,vecIntegerArray.end (), 2991);
34:
35:     // Check if value was found
36:     if (iElement != vecIntegerArray.end ())
37:     {
38:         // Value was found... Determine position in the array:
39:         int Position = distance (vecIntegerArray.begin  ), iElement);
40:         cout << "Value "<< *iElement;
41:         cout << " found in the vector at position: " << Position << endl;
42:     }
43:
44:     return 0;
45: }
```

Output ▼

```
The contents of the vector are:
50
2991
23
9999
Value 2991 found in the vector at position: 1
```

Analysis ▼

Listing 15.1 displays the use of iterators in walking through the `vector` and as interfaces that help connect algorithms such as `find` to containers like `vector` that contains the data on which the algorithm is meant to operate. The iterator object `iArrayWalker` is declared in Line 20 and is initialized to the beginning of the container; that is, the `vector` using the return value of the member function `begin()`. Lines 22 to 29 demonstrate how this iterator is used in a loop to locate and display the elements contained in the `vector`, in a manner that is quite similar to how one can display the contents of a static array. The usage of the iterator is quite consistent across all STL containers. They all feature a function `begin()` that points to the first element, and a function `end()` that points to the end of the container `after` the last element. This also explains why the `while` loop in Line 22 stops at the element before `end()` and not with `end()`. Line 32 demonstrates how `find` is used to locate a value in the `vector`. The result of the `find` operation is an iterator as well, and the success of the `find` is tested by comparing the iterator against the end of the container, as seen in Line 36. If an element is found, it can be displayed by dereferencing that iterator (such as how one would dereference a pointer). The algorithm `distance` is applied by computing the offset position of the element found.

If you blindly replace all instances of 'vector' by 'deque' in Listing 15.1, your code would still compile and work perfectly. That's how easy iterators make working with algorithms and containers.

C++11

Using Keyword `auto` to Let Compiler Define Type

Listing 15.1 shows a number of iterator declarations. They look similar to this:

```
20:    vector <int>::iterator iArrayWalker = vecIntegerArray.begin ();
```

This iterator type definition might look quite intimidating. If you are using a C++11-compliant compiler, you can simplify this line to the following:

```
20:    auto iArrayWalker = vecIntegerArray.begin (); // compiler detects type
```

Note that a variable defined as type auto needs initialization (so the compiler can detect type depending on that of the value it is being initialized to).

STL String Classes

STL supplies a template class that has been specially designed for string operations. `std::basic_string<T>` is used popularly in its two template specializations:

- **`std::string`**—A char-based specialization of `std::basic_string` used for the manipulation of simple character strings.
- **`std::wstring`**— A `wchar_t`-based specialization of `std::basic_string` used for the manipulation of wide character strings.

This utility class is extensively discussed in Lesson 16, "The STL String Class," where you see how it makes working with and manipulating strings really simple.

Summary

In this lesson, you learned the concepts on which STL containers, iterators, and algorithms are based. You were introduced to the `basic_string<T>`, which is discussed in detailed in the upcoming lesson. Containers, iterators and algorithms are one of the most important concepts in STL, and a thorough understanding of these will help you efficiently use STL in your application. Lessons 17 through 25 explain the implementation of these concepts and their application in greater detail.

Q&A

Q I need to use an array. I don't know the number of elements it needs to contain. What STL container should I use?

A A `std::vector` or a `std::deque` is perfectly suited to this requirement. Both manage memory and can dynamically scale themselves to an application's increasing requirements.

Q My application has a requirement that involves frequent searches. What kind of container should I choose?

A An associative containers like std::map or std::set or the unordered variants there of are most suited to requirements that involve frequent searches.

Q I need to store key-value pairs for quick lookup. However, the use-case can result in multiple keys that are not unique. What container should I choose?

A An associative container of type `std::multimap` is suited to this requirement. A `multimap` can hold nonunique key-value pairs and can offer a quick lookup that is characteristic of associative containers.

Q **An application needs to be ported across platforms and compilers. There is a requirement for a container that helps in a quick lookup based on a key. Should I use `std::map` or `std::hash_map`?**

A Portability is an important constraint and using standard-compliant containers is necessary. You might also use std::unordered_map if you are using C++11 compliant compilers for all the platforms concerned.

Workshop

The Workshop contains quiz questions to help solidify your understanding of the material covered. Try to answer the quiz questions before checking the answers in Appendix D, and be certain you understand the answers before going to the next lesson.

Quiz

1. What would be your choice of a container that has to contain an array of objects with insertion possible at the top and at the bottom?

2. You need to store elements for quick lookup. What container would you choose?

3. You need to store elements in a `std::set` but still have the storage and lookup criteria altered, based on conditions that are not necessarily the value of the elements. Is this possible?

4. What part of STL helps connect algorithms to containers so that algorithms can work on those elements?

5. Would you choose to use container `hash_set` in an application that needs to be ported to different platforms and built using different C++ compilers?

LESSON 16
The STL String Class

The standard template library (STL) supplies the programmer with a container class that aids in string operations and manipulations. The string class not only dynamically resizes itself to cater to the application's requirement but also supplies useful helper functions or methods that help manipulate the string and work using it. Thus, it helps programmers make use of standard, portable, and tested functionality in their applications and focus time on developing features that are critical to it.

In this lesson, you learn

- Why string manipulation classes are necessary

- How to work with the STL string class

- How STL helps you concatenate, append, find and perform other string operations with ease

- How to use template-based implementation of the STL string

The Need for String Manipulation Classes

In C++, a string is an array of characters. As you saw in Lesson 4, "Managing Arrays and Strings," the simplest character array can be defined as following:

```
char staticName [20];
```

staticName is the declaration of a character array (also called a string) of a fixed (hence static) length of 20 elements. As you see, this buffer can hold a string of limited length and would soon be overrun if you tried to hold a greater number of characters in it. Resizing this statically allocated array is not possible. To overcome this constraint, C++ supplies dynamic allocation of data. Therefore, a more dynamic representation of a string array is

```
char* dynamicName = new char [ArrayLength];
```

dynamicName is a dynamically allocated character array that can be instantiated to the length as stored in the value ArrayLength, determinable at runtime, and hence can be allocated to hold a data of variable length. However, should you want to change the length of the array at runtime, you would first have to deallocate the allocated memory and then reallocate to hold the required data.

Things get complicated if these char* strings are used as member attributes of a class. In situations where an object of this class is assigned to another, in the absence of a correctly programmed copy constructor and assignment operator, the two objects contain copies of a pointer, essentially pointing to the same char buffer. The result is two string pointers in two objects, each holding the same address and hence pointing to the same location in memory. The destruction of the first object results in the pointer in the other object being invalidated, and an impending crash looms on the horizon.

String classes solve these problems for you. The STL string classes std::string that models a character string and std::wstring that models a wide character string helps you in the following ways:

- Reduces the effort of creation and manipulating strings
- Increases the stability of the application being programmed by internally managing memory allocation details
- Supplies copy constructor and assignment operators that automatically ensure that member strings get correctly copied
- Supplies useful utility functions that help in copying, truncating, finding, and erasing to name a few

- Provides operators that help in comparisons
- Focuses efforts on your application's primary requirements rather than on string manipulation details

<table>
<tr><td>NOTE</td><td>Both std::string and std::wstring are actually template specializations of the same class, namely std::basic_string<T> for types char and wchar_t respectively. When you have learned using one, you can use the same methods and operators on the other.</td></tr>
</table>

16

You will soon learn some useful helper functions that STL string classes supply using std::string as an example.

Working with the STL String Class

The most commonly used string functions are:

- Copying
- Concatenating
- Finding characters and substrings
- Truncating
- String reversal and case conversions, which are achieved using algorithms provided by the standard library

To use the STL string class, you must include the header <string>.

Instantiating the STL String and Making Copies

The string class features many overloaded constructors and therefore can be instantiated and initialized in many different ways. For example, you can simply initialize or assign a constant character string literal to a regular STL std::string object:

```
const char* constCStyleString = "Hello String!";
std::string strFromConst (constCStyleString);
```

or

```
std::string strFromConst = constCStyleString;
```

The preceding is quite similar to

```
std::string str2 ("Hello String!");
```

As is apparent, instantiating a `string` object and initializing it to a value did not require supplying the length of the string or the memory allocation details—the constructor of the STL `string` class automatically did this.

Similarly, it is possible to use one `string` object to initialize another:

```
std::string str2Copy (str2);
```

You can also instruct the `string` constructor to accept only the first *n* characters of the supplied input string:

```
// Initialize a string to the first 5 characters of another
std::string strPartialCopy (constCStyleString, 5);
```

You can also initialize a `string` to contain a specific number of instances of a particular character:

```
// Initialize a string object to contain 10 'a's
std::string strRepeatChars (10, 'a');
```

Listing 16.1 analyzes some popularly used `std::string` instantiation and string copy techniques.

LISTING 16.1   STL String Instantiation and Copy Techniques

```
 0: #include <string>
 1: #include <iostream>
 2:
 3: int main ()
 4: {
 5:    using namespace std;
 6:    const char* constCStyleString = "Hello String!";
 7:    cout << "Constant string is: " << constCStyleString << endl;
 8:
 9:    std::string strFromConst (constCStyleString);  // constructor
10:    cout << "strFromConst is: " << strFromConst << endl;
11:
12:     std::string str2 ("Hello String!");
13:    std::string str2Copy (str2);
14:    cout << "str2Copy is: " << str2Copy << endl;
15:
16:    // Initialize a string to the first 5 characters of another
17:    std::string strPartialCopy (constCStyleString, 5);
18:    cout << "strPartialCopy is: " << strPartialCopy << endl;
19:
20:    // Initialize a string object to contain 10 'a's
```

```
21:    std::string strRepeatChars (10, 'a');
22:    cout << "strRepeatChars is: " << strRepeatChars << endl;
23:
24:    return 0;
25: }
```

Output ▼

```
Constant string is: Hello String!
strFromConst is: Hello String!
str2Copy is: Hello String!
strPartialCopy is: Hello
strRepeatChars is: aaaaaaaaaa
```

Analysis ▼

The preceding code sample displays how you can instantiate a STL string object and initialize it to another string, creating a partial copy or initializing your STL string object to a set of recurring characters. constCStyleString is a C-style character string that contains a sample value, initialized in Line 6. Line 9 displays how easy std::string makes it to create a copy using the constructor. Line 12 copies another constant string into a std::string object str2, and Line 13 demonstrates how std::string has another overloaded constructor that allows you to copy a std::string object, to get str2Copy. Line 17 demonstrates how partial copies can be achieved and Line 21 how a std::string can be instantiated and initialized to contain repeating occurrences of the same character. This code sample was just a small demonstration of how std::string and its numerous copy constructors make it easy for a programmer to create strings, copy them, and display them.

NOTE

If you were to use C-style strings to copy another of the same kind, the equivalent of Line 9 in Listing 16.1 would be this:

```
const char* constCStyleString = "Hello World!";

// To create a copy, first allocate memory for one..
char * pszCopy = new char [strlen (constCStyleString) + 1];
strcpy (pszCopy, constCStyleString);  // The copy step

// deallocate memory after using pszCopy
delete [] pszCopy;
```

As you can see, the result is many more lines of code and higher probability of introducing errors, and you need to worry about memory management and deallocations. STL string does all this for you, and more!

Accessing Character Contents of a `std::string`

The character contents of an STL `string` can be accessed via iterators or via an array-like syntax where the offset is supplied, using the subscript operator []. A C-style representation of the `string` can be obtained via member function `c_str ()`. See Listing 16.2.

LISTING 16.2   Two Ways of Accessing Character Clements of an STL `string::Operator[]` and Iterators

```
0: #include <string>
1: #include <iostream>
2:
3: int main ()
4: {
5:    using namespace std;
6:
7:    // The sample string
8:    string strSTLString ("Hello String");
9:
10:     // Access the contents of the string using array syntax
11:    cout<<"Displaying the elements in the string using array-syntax: "<<endl;
12:    for ( size_t nCharCounter = 0
13:        ; nCharCounter < strSTLString.length ()
14:        ; ++ nCharCounter )
15:    {
16:       cout << "Character [" << nCharCounter << "] is: ";
17:       cout << strSTLString [nCharCounter] << endl;
18:    }
19:    cout << endl;
20:
21:    // Access the contents of a string using iterators
22:    cout << "Displaying the contents of the string using iterators: " <<
       endl;
23:    int charOffset = 0;
24:    string::const_iterator iCharacterLocator;
25:    for ( iCharacterLocator = strSTLString.begin ()
26:        ; iCharacterLocator != strSTLString.end ()
27:        ; ++ iCharacterLocator )
28:    {
29:       cout << "Character [" << charOffset ++ << "] is: ";
30:       cout << *iCharacterLocator << endl;
31:    }
32:    cout << endl;
33:
34:    // Access the contents of a string as a C-style string
35:    cout << "The char* representation of the string is: ";
36:    cout << strSTLString.c_str () << endl;
```

```
37:
38:    return 0;
39: }
```

Output ▼

```
Displaying the elements in the string using array-syntax:
Character [0] is: H
Character [1] is: e
Character [2] is: l
Character [3] is: l
Character [4] is: o
Character [5] is:
Character [6] is: S
Character [7] is: t
Character [8] is: r
Character [9] is: i
Character [10] is: n
Character [11] is: g

Displaying the contents of the string using iterators:
Character [0] is: H
Character [1] is: e
Character [2] is: l
Character [3] is: l
Character [4] is: o
Character [5] is:
Character [6] is: S
Character [7] is: t
Character [8] is: r
Character [9] is: i
Character [10] is: n
Character [11] is: g

The char* representation of the string is: Hello String
```

Analysis ▼

The code displays the multiple ways of accessing the contents of a string. Iterators are important in the sense that many of the string's member function return their results in the form of iterators. Lines 12–18 display the characters in the string using array-like semantics via the subscript operator [], implemented by the std::string class. Note that this operator needs you to supply the offset as seen in Line 17. Therefore, it is very important that you do not cross the bounds of the string; that is, you do not read a character at an offset beyond the length of the string. Lines 25–31 also print the content of the string character-by-character, but using iterators.

16

Concatenating One String to Another

String concatenation can be achieved by using either the += operator or the append member function:

```
string strSample1 ("Hello");
string strSample2 (" String!");
strSample1 += strSample2;    // use std::string::operator+=
// alternatively use std::string::append()
strSample1.append (strSample2);  // (overloaded for char* too)
```

Listing 16.3 demonstrates the usage of these two variants.

LISTING 16.3   Concatenate Strings Using Addition Assignment Operator (+=) or Method append()

```
0: #include <string>
1: #include <iostream>
2:
3: int main ()
4: {
5:    using namespace std;
6:
7:    string strSample1 ("Hello");
8:    string strSample2 (" String!");
9:
10:    // Concatenate
11:    strSample1 += strSample2;
12:    cout << strSample1 << endl << endl;
13:
14:    string strSample3 (" Fun is not needing to use pointers!");
15:    strSample1.append (strSample3);
16:    cout << strSample1 << endl << endl;
17:
18:    const char* constCStyleString = " You however still can!";
19:    strSample1.append (constCStyleString);
20:    cout << strSample1 << endl;
21:
22:    return 0;
23: }
```

Output ▼

```
Hello String!

Hello String! Fun is not needing to use pointers!

Hello String! Fun is not needing to use pointers! You however still can!
```

Analysis ▼

Lines 11, 15, and 19 display different methods of concatenating to an STL string. Note the use of the += operator and the capability of the append function, which has many overloads, to accept another string object (as shown in Line 11) and to accept a C-style character string.

Finding a Character or Substring in a String

The STL string supplies a find member function with a few overloaded versions that help find a character or a substring in a given string object.

```
// Find substring "day" in a string strSample, starting at position 0
size_t charPos = strSample.find ("day", 0);

// Check if the substring was found, compare against string::npos
if (charPos != string::npos)
   cout << "First instance of \"day\" was found at position " << charPos;
else
   cout << "Substring not found." << endl;
```

Listing 16.4 demonstrates the utility of std::string::find.

LISTING 16.4 Using string::find() to Locate a Substring or char

```
0: #include <string>
1: #include <iostream>
2:
3: int main ()
4: {
5:     using namespace std;
6:
7:     string strSample ("Good day String! Today is beautiful!");
8:     cout << "The sample string is: " << endl;
9:     cout << strSample << endl << endl;
10:
11:     // Find substring "day" in it...
12:     size_t charPos = strSample.find ("day", 0);
13:
14:     // Check if the substring was found...
15:     if (charPos != string::npos)
16:         cout << "First instance of \"day\" was found at position " << charPos;
17:     else
18:         cout << "Substring not found." << endl;
19:
20:     cout << endl << endl;
21:
22:     cout << "Locating all instances of substring \"day\"" << endl;
```

16

LISTING 16.4   Continued

```
23:    size_t SubstringPos = strSample.find ("day", 0);
24:
25:    while (SubstringPos != string::npos)
26:    {
27:       cout << "\"day\" found at position " << SubstringPos << endl;
28:
29:       // Make find search forward from the next character
30:       size_t nSearchPosition = SubstringPos + 1;
31:
32:       SubstringPos = strSample.find ("day", nSearchPosition);
33:    }
34:
35:    cout << endl;
36:
37:    cout << "Locating all instances of character 'a'" << endl;
38:    const char charToSearch = 'a';
39:    charPos = strSample.find (charToSearch, 0);
40:
41:    while (charPos != string::npos)
42:    {
43:       cout << "'" << charToSearch << "' found";
44:       cout << " at position: " << charPos << endl;
45:
46:       // Make find search forward from the next character
47:       size_t charSearchPos = charPos + 1;
48:
49:       charPos = strSample.find (charToSearch, charSearchPos);
50:    }
51:
52:    return 0;
53: }
```

Output ▼

```
The sample string is:
Good day String! Today is beautiful!

First instance of "day" was found at position 5

Locating all instances of substring "day"
"day" found at position 5
"day" found at position 19

Locating all instances of character 'a'
'a' found at position: 6
'a' found at position: 20
'a' found at position: 28
```

Analysis ▼

Lines 12–18 display the simplest usage of the find function where it ascertains whether a particular substring is found in a string. This is done by comparing the result of the find operation against std::string::npos (that is actually –1) and indicates that the element searched for has not been found. When the find function does not return npos, it returns the offset that indicates the position of the substring or character in the string.

The code thereafter indicates how find can be used in a while loop to locate all instances of a character or a substring in an STL string. The overloaded version of the find function used here accepts two parameters: the substring or character to search for and the search offset that indicates the point from which find should search.

16

NOTE

> The STL string also features functions akin to find(), such as find_first_of(), find_first_not_of(), find_last_of(), and find_last_not_of(), which assist the programmer further in his programming requirements.

Truncating an STL string

The STL string features a function called erase that can erase

- A number of characters when given an offset position and count

```
string strSample ("Hello String! Wake up to a beautiful day!');
strSample.erase (13, 28);  // Hello String!
```

- A character when supplied with an iterator pointing to it

```
strSample.erase (iCharS); // iterator points to a specific character
```

- A number of characters given a range supplied by two iterators that bind the same

```
strSample.erase (strSample.begin (), strSample.end ()); // erase from begin
to end
```

The sample that follows in Listing 16.5 demonstrates different applications of the overloaded versions of string::erase() function.

LISTING 16.5 Using `string::erase` to Truncate a String Starting an Offset Position or Given an Iterator

```
0: #include <string>
1: #include <algorithm>
2: #include <iostream>
3:
4: int main ()
5: {
6:     using namespace std;
7:
8:     string strSample ("Hello String! Wake up to a beautiful day!");
9:     cout << "The original sample string is: " << endl;
10:    cout << strSample << endl << endl;
11:
12:    // Delete characters from the string given position and count
13:    cout << "Truncating the second sentence: " << endl;
14:    strSample.erase (13, 28);
15:    cout << strSample << endl << endl;
16:
17:    // Find a character 'S' in the string using STL find algorithm
18:    string::iterator iCharS = find ( strSample.begin ()
19:                                    , strSample.end (), 'S');
20:
21:    // If character found, 'erase' to deletes a character
22:    cout << "Erasing character 'S' from the sample string:" << endl;
23:    if (iCharS != strSample.end ())
24:        strSample.erase (iCharS);
25:
26:    cout << strSample << endl << endl;
27:
28:    // Erase a range of characters using an overloaded version of erase()
29:    cout << "Erasing a range between begin() and end(): " << endl;
30:    strSample.erase (strSample.begin (), strSample.end ());
31:
32:    // Verify the length after the erase() operation above
33:    if (strSample.length () == 0)
34:        cout << "The string is empty" << endl;
35:
36:    return 0;
37: }
```

Output ▼

```
The original sample string is:
Hello String! Wake up to a beautiful day!

Truncating the second sentence:
Hello String!
```

```
Erasing character 'S' from the sample string:
Hello tring!

Erasing a range between begin() and end():
The string is empty
```

Analysis ▼

The listing indicates the three versions of the erase function. One version erases a set of characters when supplied a staring offset and count, as shown in line 14. Another version erases a specific character given an iterator that points to it, as shown in line 24. The final version erases a range of characters given a couple of iterators that supply the bounds of this range, as shown in line 30. As the bounds of this range are supplied by begin() and end () member functions of the string that effectively include all the contents of the string, calling an erase() on this range clears the string object of its contents. Note that the string class also supplies a clear () function that effectively clears the internal buffer and resets the string object.

C++11

Simplify wordy iterator declarations using auto

C++11 helps simplify wordy iterator declarations as shown in Listing 16.5:

```
18:     string::iterator iCharS = find ( strSample.begin ()
19:                                  , strSample.end (), 'S');
```

To reduce this, use keyword auto as introduced to you in Lesson 3, "Using Variables, Declaring Constants":

```
auto iCharS = find ( strSample.begin ()
                 , strSample.end (), 'S');
```

The compiler automatically deducts type of variable iCharS given return value type information from std::find.

String Reversal

Sometimes it is important to reverse the contents of a string. Say you want to determine whether the string input by the user is a palindrome. One way to do it would be to reverse a copy of the same and then compare the two. STL strings can be reversed easily using the generic algorithm std::reverse algorithm:

```
string strSample ("Hello String! We will reverse you!");
reverse (strSample.begin (), strSample.end ());
```

Listing 16.6 demonstrates the application of algorithm std::reverse to a std::string.

LISTING 16.6   Reversing a STL String Using std::reverse

```
0: #include <string>
1: #include <iostream>
2: #include <algorithm>
3:
4: int main ()
5: {
6:     using namespace std;
7:
8:     string strSample ("Hello String! We will reverse you!");
9:     cout << "The original sample string is: " << endl;
10:    cout << strSample << endl << endl;
11:
12:    reverse (strSample.begin (), strSample.end ());
13:
14:    cout << "After applying the std::reverse algorithm: " << endl;
15:    cout << strSample << endl;
16:
17:    return 0;
18: }
```

Output ▼

```
The original sample string is:
Hello String! We will reverse you!

After applying the std::reverse algorithm:
!uoy esrever lliw eW !gnirtS olleH
```

Analysis ▼

The std::reverse algorithm used in Line 12 works on the bounds of the container that are supplied to it using the two input parameters. In this case, these bounds are the starting and the ending bounds of the string object, reversing the contents of the entire string. It would also be possible to reverse a string in parts by supplying the appropriate bounds as input. Note that the bounds should never exceed end().

String Case Conversion

String case conversion can be effected using the algorithm std::transform, which applies a user-specified function to every element of a collection. In this case, the collection is the string object itself. The sample in Listing 16.7 shows how to switch the case of characters in a string.

LISTING 16.7 Converting an STL String Using `std::transform` to Uppercase

```cpp
0: #include <string>
1: #include <iostream>
2: #include <algorithm>
3:
4: int main ()
5: {
6:    using namespace std;
7:
8:    cout << "Please enter a string for case-convertion:" << endl;
9:    cout << "> ";
10:
11:   string strInput;
12:   getline (cin, strInput);
13:   cout << endl;
14:
15:   transform(strInput.begin(),strInput.end(),strInput.begin(),toupper);
16:   cout << "The string converted to upper case is: " << endl;
17:   cout << strInput << endl << endl;
18:
19:   transform(strInput.begin(),strInput.end(),strInput.begin(),tolower);
20:   cout << "The string converted to lower case is: " << endl;
21:   cout << strInput << endl << endl;
22:
23:   return 0;
24: }
```

Output ▼

```
Please enter a string for case-conversion:
> ConverT thIS StrINg!

The string converted to upper case is:
CONVERT THIS STRING!

The string converted to lower case is:
convert this string!
```

Analysis ▼

Lines 15 and 19 demonstrate how efficiently `std::transform` can be used to change the case of the contents of an STL string.

Template-Based Implementation of an STL String

The `std::string` class, as you have learned, is actually a specialization of the STL template class `std::basic_string <T>`. The template declaration of container class `basic_string` is as follows:

```
template<class _Elem,
    class _Traits,
    class _Ax>
    class basic_string
```

In this template definition, the parameter of utmost importance is the first one: `_Elem`. This is the type collected by the `basic_string` object. The `std::string` is therefore the template specialization of `basic_string` for `_Elem=char`, whereas the `wstring` is the template specialization of `basic_string` for `_Elem=wchar_t`.

In other words, the STL `string` class is defined as

```
typedef basic_string<char, char_traits<char>, allocator<char> >
    string;
```

and the STL `wstring` class is defined as

```
typedef basic_string<wchar_t, char_traits<wchar_t>, allocator<wchar_t> >
    string;
```

So, all string features and functions studied so far are actually those supplied by `basic_string`, and are therefore also applicable to the STL `wstring` class.

TIP

You would use the `std::wstring` when programming an application that needs to better support non-Latin characters such as those in Japanese or Chinese.

Summary

In this lesson, you learned that the STL `string` class is a container supplied by the standard template library that helps the programmer with many string manipulation requirements. The advantage of using this class is apparent in that the need for the programmer to implement memory management, string comparison, and string manipulation functions is taken care of by a container class supplied by the STL framework.

Q&A

Q I need to reverse a string using `std::reverse`. What header has to be included for me to be able to use this function?

A `<algorithm>` is the header that needs to be included for `std::reverse` to be available.

Q What role does `std::transform` play in converting a string to lowercase using the `tolower ()` function?

A `std::transform` invokes `tolower ()` for the characters in the string object that are within the bounds supplied to the transform function.

Q Why do `std::wstring` and `std::string` feature exactly the same behavior and member functions?

A They do so because they are both template specializations of the template class `std::basic_string`.

Q Does the comparison operator `<` of the STL `string` class produce results that are case sensitive or not case sensitive?

A The results are based on a case-sensitive comparison.

Workshop

The Workshop contains quiz questions to help solidify your understanding of the material covered and exercises to provide you with experience in using what you've learned. Try to answer the quiz and exercise questions before checking the answers in Appendix D, and be certain you understand the answers before going to the next lesson.

Quiz

1. What STL template class does the `std::string` specialize?
2. If you were to perform a case-insensitive comparison of two strings, how would you do it?
3. Are the STL string and a C-style string similar?

Exercises

1. Write a program to verify whether the word input by the user is a palindrome. For example: ATOYOTA is a palindrome, as the word does not change when reversed.
2. Write a program that tells the user the number of vowels in a sentence.

16

3. Convert every alternate character of a string into uppercase.

4. Your program should have four string objects that are initialized to "I", "Love", "STL", "String." Append them with a space in between and display the sentence.

LESSON 17
STL Dynamic Array Classes

Unlike static arrays, dynamic arrays supply the programmer with the flexibility of storing data without needing to know the exact volume thereof at the time of programming the application. Naturally, this is a frequently needed requirement, and the Standard Template Library (STL) supplies a ready-to-use solution in the form of the std::vector class.

In this lesson, you learn

- The characteristics of std::vector

- Typical vector operations

- The concept of a vector's size and capacity

- The STL deque class

The Characteristics of `std::vector`

vector is a template class that supplies generic functionality of a dynamic array and features the following characteristics:

- Addition of elements to the end of the array in constant time; that is, the time needed to insert at the end is not dependent on the size of the array. Ditto for removal of an element at the end.

- The time required for the insertion or removal of elements at the middle is directly proportional to the number of elements behind the element being removed.

- The number of elements held is dynamic and the vector class manages the memory usage.

A *vector* being a dynamic array that can be visualized as seen in Figure 17.1.

FIGURE 17.1
The internals of a vector.

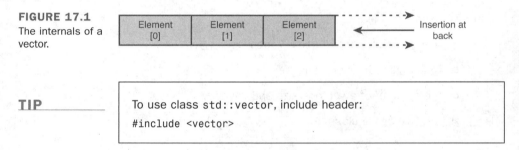

| Element [0] | Element [1] | Element [2] | Insertion at back |

> **TIP**
>
> To use class `std::vector`, include header:
>
> `#include <vector>`

Typical Vector Operations

The behavioral specifications and public members of the `std::vector` class are defined by the C++ standard. Consequently, operations on the vector that you will learn in this lesson are supported by a variety of C++ programming platforms that are standard compliant.

Instantiating a Vector

A vector is a template class that needs to be instantiated in accordance with template instantiation techniques that are covered in Lesson 14, "An introduction to Macros and Templates." The template instantiation of vector needs to specify the type of object that you want to collect in this dynamic array.

```
std::vector<int> vecDynamicIntegerArray;   // vector containing integers
std::vector<float> vecDynamicFloatArray;   // vector containing floats
std::vector<Tuna> vecDynamicTunaArray;     // vector containing Tunas
```

To declare an iterator that points to an element in the list, you would use

```
std::list<int>::const_iterator iElementInSet;
```

If you need an iterator that can be used to modify values or invoke non-const functions, you use iterator instead of const_iterator.

Given that std::vector has a few overloaded constructors, you also have an option of instantiating a vector telling the number of elements it should start with and their initial values, or you can use a part of whole of one vector in instantiating another.

Listing 17.1 demonstrates a few vector instantiations

LISTING 17.1   Different Forms of Instantiating std::vector: Specify Size, Initial Value, and Copying Values from Another

```
0: #include <vector>
1:
2: int main ()
3: {
4:    std::vector <int> vecIntegers;
5:
6:    // Instantiate a vector with 10 elements (it can grow larger)
7:    std::vector <int> vecWithTenElements (10);
8:
9:    // Instantiate a vector with 10 elements, each initialized to 90
10:    std::vector <int> vecWithTenInitializedElements (10, 90);
11:
12:    // Instantiate one vector and initialize it to the contents of another
13:    std::vector <int> vecArrayCopy (vecWithTenInitializedElements);
14:
15:    // Using iterators instantiate vector to 5 elements from another
16:    std::vector <int> vecSomeElementsCopied ( vecWithTenElements.cbegin ()
17:                             , vecWithTenElements.cbegin () + 5 );
18:
19:    return 0;
20: }
```

Analysis ▼

The preceding code features a template specialization of the vector class for type integer; in other words, it instantiates a vector of integers. This vector, named vecIntegers, uses the default constructor that is quite useful when you do not know the minimal size requirements of the container—that is, when you do not know how many integers you want to hold in it. The second and third forms of vector instantiation as seen in Lines 10 and 13 are ones in which the programmer knows that he needs a vector

17

that contains at least 10 elements. Note that this does not limit the ultimate size of the container, rather just sets the initializing size. The fourth form in Lines 16 and 17 is the one in which a vector can be used to instantiate the contents of another—in other words, to create one vector object that is the copy of another, or a part thereof. This is also a construct that works for all STL containers. The last form is the one that uses iterators. vecSomeElementsCopied contains the first five elements from vecWithTenElements.

> **NOTE**
>
> The fourth construct can work only with objects of like types. So, you could instantiate a vecArrayCopy—a vector of integer objects using another vector of integer objects. If one of them were to be a vector of, say, type float, the code would not compile.

> **TIP**
>
> **Are You Facing Errors Compiling** cbegin() **and** cend()**?**
>
> If you are trying to compile this program using a non-C++11-compliant compiler, use begin() and end() instead of cbegin() and cend(), respectively.
>
> cbegin() and cend() are different (and better) in that they return a iterator, but are not supported by older compilers.

Inserting Elements at the End Using push_back()

Having instantiated a vector of integers, the obvious next task is to insert elements (integers) into it. Insertion in a vector happens at the end of the array, and elements are "pushed" into its back using the member method push_back:

```
vector <int> vecIntegers;  // declare a vector of type int

// Insert sample integers into the vector:
vecIntegers.push_back (50);
vecIntegers.push_back (1);
```

Listing 17.2 demonstrates the use of push_back() in the dynamic addition of elements to a std::vector.

LISTING 17.2   Inserting Elements in a Vector Using push_back()

```
0: #include <iostream>
1: #include <vector>
2: using namespace std;
3:
4: int main ()
5: {
6:     vector <int> vecIntegers;
7:
8:     // Insert sample integers into the vector:
9:     vecIntegers.push_back (50);
10:     vecIntegers.push_back (1);
11:     vecIntegers.push_back (987);
12:     vecIntegers.push_back (1001);
13:
14:     cout << "The vector contains ";
15:     cout << vecIntegers.size () << " Elements' << endl;
16:
17:     return 0;
18: }
```

17

Output ▼

```
The vector contains 4 Elements
```

Analysis ▼

push_back(), as seen in Lines 9–12 is the vector class' public member method that inserts objects at the end of the dynamic array. Note the usage of function size(), which returns the number of elements held in the vector.

C++11

Initializer Lists

C++11 features initializer lists via class std::initialize_list<> that, when supported, enables you to instantiate and initialize elements in a vector like you would a static array:

```
vector<int> vecIntegers = {50, 1, 987, 1001};
// alternatively:
vector<int> vecMoreIntegers {50, 1, 987, 1001};
```

This syntax reduces three lines in Listing 17.2. Yet, we haven't used it because at the time of writing this book, initializer lists were not supported by the implementation of std::vector in Microsoft Visual C++ 2010 compiler.

Inserting Elements at a Given Position Using
`insert()`

You use `push_back` to insert elements at the end of a vector. What if you want to insert in the middle? Many other STL containers, including `std::vector`, feature an `insert()` function with many overloads.

In one, you can specify the position at which an element can be inserted into the sequence:

```
// insert an element at the beginning
vecIntegers.insert (vecIntegers.begin (), 25);
```

In another, you can specify the position as well as the number of elements with a value that need to be inserted:

```
// Insert 2 numbers of value 45 at the end
vecIntegers.insert (vecIntegers.end (), 2, 45);
```

You can also insert the contents of one vector into another at a chosen position:

```
// Another vector containing 2 elements of value 30
vector <int> vecAnother (2, 30);

// Insert two elements from another container in position [1]
vecIntegers.insert (vecIntegers.begin () + 1,
                    vecAnother.begin (), vecAnother.end ());
```

You use an iterator, often returned by `begin()` or `end()`, to tell the `insert()` function the position where you want the new elements to be placed.

> **TIP**
>
> Note that this iterator can also be the return value of an STL algorithm, for example the `std::find()` function, which can be used to find an element and then insert another at that position (insertion will shift the element found).

These forms of `vector::insert()` are demonstrated in Listing 17.3.

LISTING 17.3   Using the `vector::insert` Function to Insert Elements at a Set Position

```
0: #include <vector>
1: #include <iostream>
2: using namespace std;
```

```
 3:
 4: void DisplayVector(const vector<int>& vecInput)
 5: {
 6:    for (auto iElement = vecInput.cbegin() // auto and cbegin(): C++11
 7:       ; iElement != vecInput.cerd()  // cend() is new in C++11
 8:       ; ++ iElement )
 9:       cout << *iElement << ' ';
10:
11:    cout << endl;
12: }
13:
14: int main ()
15: {
16:    // Instantiate a vector with 4 elements, each initialized to 90
17:    vector <int> vecIntegers (4, 90);
18:
19:    cout << "The initial contents of the vector: ";
20:    DisplayVector(vecIntegers);
21:
22:    // Insert 25 at the beginning
23:    vecIntegers.insert (vecIntegers.begin (), 25);
24:
25:    // Insert 2 numbers of value 45 at the end
26:    vecIntegers.insert (vecIntegers.end (), 2, 45);
27:
28:    cout << "Vector after inserting elements at beginning and end: ";
29:    DisplayVector(vecIntegers);
30:
31:    // Another vector containing 2 elements of value 30
32:    vector <int> vecAnother (2, 30);
33:
34:    // Insert two elements from another container in position [1]
35:    vecIntegers.insert (vecIntegers.begin () + 1,
36:       vecAnother.begin (), vecAnother.end ());
37:
38:    cout << "Vector after inserting contents from another vector: ";
39:    cout << "in the middle:" << endl;
40:    DisplayVector(vecIntegers);
41:
42:    return 0;
43: }
```

17

Output ▼

```
The initial contents of the vector: 90 90 90 90
Vector after inserting elements at beginning and end: 25 90 90 90 90 45 45
Vector after inserting contents from another vector: in the middle:
25 30 30 90 90 90 90 45 45
```

Analysis ▼

This code effectively demonstrates the power of the `insert` function by enabling you to put values in the middle of the container. `vector` in Line 17 contains four elements, all initialized to 90. Taking this vector as a starting point, we use various overloads of the `vector::insert` member function. In Line 23 you add one element at the beginning. Line 26 uses an overload to add two elements of value 45 at the end. Line 35 demonstrates how elements can be inserted from one vector into the middle (in this example, the second position at offset 1) of another.

Although `vector::insert` is quite a versatile function, `push_back()` should be your preferred way of adding elements to a vector.

Note that `insert()` is an inefficient way to add elements to the `vector` (when adding in a position that is not the end of the sequence) because adding elements in the beginning or the middle makes the `vector` class shift all subsequent elements backward (after making space for the last ones at the end). Thus, depending on the type of the objects contained in the sequence, the cost of this shift operation can be significant in terms of the copy constructor or copy assignment operator invoked. In our little sample, the `vector` contains objects of type `int` that are relatively inexpensive to move around. This might not be the case in many other uses of the `vector` class.

TIP	If your container needs to have very frequent insertions in the middle, you should ideally choose the `std::list`, explained in Lesson 18, "STL `list` and `forward_list`."

CAUTION	**Are You Using an Older C++ Compiler?**
	Function `DisplayVector()` in Listing 17.3 uses the C++11 keyword `auto` to define the type of an iterator in Line 6. In this sample and ahead, to compile using a non-C++11-compliant compiler, you need to replace `auto` by the explicit type, in this case `vector<int>::const_iterator`.

So, `DisplayVector()` for an older compiler would need to be modified to the following:

```
// for older C++ compilers
void DisplayVector(const vector<int>& vecIrput)
{
   for (vector<int>::const_iterator iElenert = vecIrput.begin ()
         ; iElement != vecIrput.end (
         ; ++ iElement )
      cout << *iElement << ' ';

   cout << encl;
}
```

Accessing Elements in a Vector Using Array Semantics

Elements in a vector can be accessed using the following methods: via array semantics using the subscript operator ([ ]), using the member function at( ), or using iterators.

Listing 17.1 showed how an instance of vector can be created that is initialized for 10 elements:

```
std::vector <int> vecArrayWithTenElements (10);
```

You can access and set individual elements using an array-like syntax:

```
vecArrayWithTenElements[3] = 2011; // set 4th element
```

Listing 17.4 demonstrates how elements in a vector can be accessed using the subscript operator ([ ]).

LISTING 17.4   Accessing Elements in a vector Using Array Semantics

```
0: #include <iostream>
1: #include <vector>
2:
3: int main ()
4: {
5:    using namespace std;
6:    vector <int> vecIntegerArray;
7:
8:    // Insert sample integers into the vector
9:    vecIntegerArray.push_back (50);
10:   vecIntegerArray.push_back (1);
```

LISTING 17.4   Continued

```
11:     vecIntegerArray.push_back (987);
12:     vecIntegerArray.push_back (1001);
13:
14:     for (size_t Index = 0; Index < vecIntegerArray.size (); ++Index)
15:     {
16:        cout << "Element[" << Index << "] = " ;
17:        cout << vecIntegerArray[Index] << endl;
18:     }
19:
20:     // changing 3rd integer from 987 to 2011
21:     vecIntegerArray[2] = 2011;
22:     cout << "After replacement: " << endl;
23:     cout << "Element[2] = " << vecIntegerArray[2] << endl;
24:
25:     return 0;
26: }
```

Output ▼

```
Element[0] = 50
Element[1] = 1
Element[2] = 987
Element[3] = 1001
After replacement:
Element[2] = 2011
```

Analysis ▼

At Lines 17, 21, and 23 the vector has been used to access and assign elements the same way you might use a static array using vector's subscript operator ([ ]). This subscript operator accepts an element-index that is zero-based just as in a static array. Note how the for loop has been programmed in Line 15 to ensure that the index doesn't cross the bounds of the vector by comparing it against vector::size().

CAUTION

Accessing elements in a vector using [ ] is fraught with the same dangers as accessing elements in an array; that is, you should not cross the bounds of the container. If you use the subscript operator ([ ]) to access elements in a vector at a position that is beyond its bounds, the result of the operation will be undefined (anything could happen, possibly an access violation).

A safer alternative is to use the at() member function:

```
// gets element at position 2
cout << vecIntegerArray.at (2);
// the vector::at() version of the code above in Listing
   17.4, line 17:
cout << vecIntegerArray.at(Index);
```

at() performs a runtime check against the size of the container and throws an exception if you cross the boundaries (which you shouldn't do anyway).

Subscript operator ([]) is safe when used in a manner that ensures bound integrity, as in the earlier example.

Accessing Elements in a Vector Using Pointer Semantics

17

You can also access elements in a vector using pointer-like semantics by the use of iterators, as shown in Listing 17.5.

LISTING 17.5   Accessing Elements in a Vector Using Pointer Semantics (Iterators)

```
0: #include <iostream>
1: #include <vector>
2:
3: int main ()
4: {
5:    using namespace std;
6:    vector <int> vecIntegers;
7:
8:    // Insert sample integers into the vector:
9:    vecIntegers.push_back (50);
10:    vecIntegers.push_back (1);
11:    vecIntegers.push_back (987);
12:    vecIntegers.push_back (1001);
13:
14:    // Access objects in a vector using iterators:
15:    vector <int>::iterator iElementLocator = vecIntegers.begin ();
16:    // iterator declared using C++11 keyword auto (uncomment next line)
17:    // auto iElementLocator = vecIntegers.begin ();
18:
19:    while (iElementLocator != vecIntegers.end ())
20:    {
21:       size_t Index = distance (vecIntegers.begin (),
```

LISTING 17.5   Continued

```
22:                                iElementLocator);
23:
24:        cout << "Element at position ";
25:        cout << Index << " is: " << *iElementLocator << endl;
26:
27:        // move to the next element
28:        ++ iElementLocator;
29:    }
30:
31:    return 0;
32: }
```

Output ▼

```
Element at position 0 is: 50
Element at position 1 is: 1
Element at position 2 is: 987
Element at position 3 is: 1001
```

Analysis ▼

The iterator in this example behaves more or less like a pointer, and the nature of its usage in the preceding application is quite like pointer arithmetic, as seen in Line 25 where the value stored in the vector is accessed using the dereference operator (*) and Line 29 where the iterator, when incremented using operator (++), points to the next element. Notice how `std::distance()` is used in Line 21 to evaluate the zero-based offset position of the element in the vector (that is, position relative to the beginning), given `begin()` and the iterator pointing to the element.

Removing Elements from a Vector

Just the same way as the `vector` features insertion at the end via the `push_back` method, it also features the removal of an element at the end via the `pop_back` function. Removal of an element from the `vector` using `pop_back` takes constant time—that is, the time required is independent of the number of elements stored in the `vector`. The code that follows in Listing 17.6 demonstrates the use of function `pop_back` to erase elements from the back of the `vector`.

LISTING 17.6   Using pop_back to Erase the Last Element

```
0: #include <iostream>
1: #include <vector>
2: using namespace std;
```

```
 3:
 4: template <typename T>
 5: void DisplayVector(const vector<T>& vecInput)
 6: {
 7:     for (auto iElement = vecInput.cbegin() // auto and cbegin(): C++11
 8:         ; iElement != Input.cend()  // cend() is new in C++11
 9:         ; ++ iElement )
10:       cout << *iElement << ' ';
11:
12:     cout << endl;
13: }
14:
15: int main ()
16: {
17:     vector <int> vecIntegers;
18:
19:     // Insert sample integers into the vector:
20:     vecIntegers.push_back (50);
21:     vecIntegers.push_back (1);
22:     vecIntegers.push_back (987);
23:     vecIntegers.push_back (1001);
24:
25:     cout << "Vector contains " << vecIntegers.size () << " elements: ";
26:     DisplayVector(vecIntegers);
27:
28:     // Erase one element at the end
29:     vecIntegers.pop_back ();
30:
31:     cout << "After a call to pop_back()" << endl;
32:     cout << "Vector contains " << vecIntegers.size () << " elements: ";
33:     DisplayVector(vecIntegers);
34:
35:     return 0;
36: }
```

17

Output ▼

```
Vector contains 4 elements: 50 1 987 1001
After a call to pop_back()
Vector contains 3 elements: 50 1 987
```

Analysis ▼

The output indicates that the pop_back function used at Line 29 has reduced the elements in the vector by erasing the last element inserted into it. Line 32 calls size() again to demonstrate that the number of elements in the vector has reduced by one, as indicated in the output.

NOTE

Function `DisplayVector()` in Lines 4–13 has taken a template form in Listing 17.6 as compared to Listing 17.3 where it accepted only a `vector` for integers. This helps us reuse this template function for a vector of type `float` (instead of `int`):

```
vector <float> vecFloats;
DisplayVector(vecFloats); // works, as this is a generic
    function
```

It now supports a `vector` of any class that supports an operator (*) that returns a value cout would understand.

Understanding the Concepts of Size and Capacity

The *size* of a vector is the number of elements stored in a vector. The *capacity* of a vector is the total number of elements that can potentially be stored in the vector before it reallocates memory to accommodate more elements. Therefore, a vector's size is less than or equal to its capacity.

You can query a vector for the number of elements by calling `size()`:

```
cout << "Size: " << vecIntegers.size ();
```

Or query it for its capacity by calling `capacity()`:

```
cout << "Capacity: " <<  vecIntegers.capacity () << endl;
```

A vector can cause some amount of performance problems when it needs to frequently reallocate the memory of the internal dynamic array. To a great extent, this problem can be addressed by using the member function `reserve (number)`. What `reserve` essentially does is increase the amount of memory allocated for the vector's internal array so as to accommodate that number of elements without needing to reallocate. Depending on the type of the objects stored in the vector, reducing the number of reallocations also reduces the number of times the objects are copied and saves on performance. The code sample in Listing 17.7 demonstrates the difference between `size()` and `capacity()`.

LISTING 17.7 Demonstration of `size()` and `capacity()`

```
0: #include <iostream>
1: #include <vector>
2:
3: int main ()
```

```
 4: {
 5:     using namespace std;
 6:
 7:     // Instantiate a vector object that holds 5 integers of default value
 8:     vector <int> vecIntegers (5);
 9:
10:     cout << "Vector of integers was instantiated with " << endl;
11:     cout << "Size: " << vecIntegers.size ();
12:     cout << ", Capacity: " <<  vecIntegers.capacity () << endl;
13:
14:     // Inserting a 6th element in to the vector
15:     vecIntegers.push_back (666);
16:
17:     cout << "After inserting an additional element... " << endl;
18:     cout << "Size: " << vecIntegers.size ();
19:     cout << ", Capacity: " <<  vecIntegers.capacity () << endl;
20:
21:     // Inserting another element
22:     vecIntegers.push_back (777);
23:
24:     cout << "After inserting yet another element... " << endl;
25:     cout << "Size: " << vecIntegers.size ();
26:     cout << ", Capacity: " <<  vecIntegers.capacity () << endl;
27:
28:     return 0;
29: }
```

17

Output ▼

```
Vector of integers was instantiated with
Size: 5, Capacity: 5
After inserting an additional element...
Size: 6, Capacity: 7
After inserting yet another element...
Size: 7, Capacity: 7
```

Analysis ▼

Line 8 shows the instantiation of a vector of integers containing five integers at default value (0). Lines 11 and 12, which print the size and the capacity of the vector, respectively, display that both are equal at instantiation time. Line 9 inserts a sixth element in the vector. Given that the capacity of the vector was five prior to the insertion, there isn't adequate memory in the internal buffer of the vector to support this new sixth element. In other words, for the vector class to scale itself and store six elements, it needs to reallocate the internal buffer. The implementation of the reallocation logic is smart—in order avoid another reallocation on insertion of another element, it preemptively allocates a capacity greater than the requirements of the immediate scenario.

The output shows that on insertion of a sixth element in a vector that has the capacity for five, the reallocation involved increases the capacity to seven elements. size() always reflects the number of elements in the vector and has a value of six at this stage. The addition of a seventh element in Line 22 results in no increase in capacity—the existing allocated memory meets the demand sufficiently. Both size and capacity display an equal value at this stage, indicating that the vector is used to its full capacity, and insertion of the next element will cause the vector to reallocate its internal buffer, copying existing values before it inserts the new value.

> **NOTE**
>
> The preemptive increase in the capacity of the vector when the internal buffer is reallocated is not regulated by any clause in the standard. This is dependent on the flavor of STL being used.

The STL deque Class

deque (pronunciation rhymes with *deck*) is an STL dynamic array class quite similar in properties to that of the vector except that it allows for the insertion and removal of elements at the front and back of the array. You would instantiate a deque of integers like this:

```
// Define a deque of integers
deque <int> dqIntegers;
```

> **TIP**
>
> To use a std::deque, include header <deque>:
>
> #include<deque>

A deque can be visualized as shown in Figure 17.2.

FIGURE 17.2
Internals of a
deque.

The deque is quite similar to the vector in that it supports element insertions and deletions at the back via the push_back() and pop_back() methods. Just like the vector, the deque also allows you to access it using array semantics via operator ([]). deque is different than the vector in that it also enables you to insert elements at the front using push_front() and remove from the front using pop_front(), as demonstrated by Listing 17.8.

LISTING 17.8 Instantiating an STL deque and Using push_front() and pop_front() Methods to Insert and Delete Elements at the Front

```
0: #include <deque>
1: #include <iostream>
2: #include <algorithm>
3:
4: int main ()
5: {
6:     using namespace std;
7:
8:     // Define a deque of integers
9:     deque <int> dqIntegers;
10:
11:     // Insert integers at the bottom of the array
12:     dqIntegers.push_back (3);
13:     dqIntegers.push_back (4);
14:     dqIntegers.push_back (5);
15:
16:     // Insert integers at the top of the array
17:     dqIntegers.push_front (2);
18:     dqIntegers.push_front (1);
19:     dqIntegers.push_front (0);
20:
21:     cout << "The contents of the deque after inserting elements ";
22:     cout << "at the top and bottom are:" << endl;
23:
24:     // Display contents on the screen
25:     for ( size_t nCount = 0
26:           ; nCount < dqIntegers.size ()
27:           ; ++ nCount )
28:     {
29:         cout << "Element [" << nCount << "] = ";
30:         cout << dqIntegers [nCount] << endl;
31:     }
32:
33:     cout << endl;
34:
35:     // Erase an element at the top
36:     dqIntegers.pop_front ();
37:
38:     // Erase an element at the bottom
39:     dqIntegers.pop_back ();
40:
41:     cout << "The contents of the deque after erasing an element ";
42:     cout << "from the top and bottom are:" << endl;
43:
44:     // Display contents again: this time using iterators
45:     // if on older compilers, remove auto and uncomment next line
46:     // deque <int>::iterator iElementLocator;
47:     for (auto iElementLocator = dqIntegers.begin ()
```

17

LISTING 17.8   Continued

```
48:        ; iElementLocator != dqIntegers.end ()
49:        ; ++ iElementLocator )
50:     {
51:        size_t Offset = distance (dqIntegers.begin (), iElementLocator);
52:        cout << "Element [" << Offset << "] = " << *iElementLocator << endl;
53:     }
54:
55:     return 0;
56: }
```

Output ▼

```
The contents of the deque after inserting elements at the top and bottom are:
Element [0] = 0
Element [1] = 1
Element [2] = 2
Element [3] = 3
Element [4] = 4
Element [5] = 5

The contents of the deque after erasing an element from the top and bottom are:
Element [0] = 1
Element [1] = 2
Element [2] = 3
Element [3] = 4
```

Analysis ▼

Line 10 is where you instantiate a deque of integers. Note how similar this syntax is to the instantiation of a vector of integers. Lines 13–16 display the usage of the deque member function push_back followed by push_front in Lines 18–20. The latter makes the deque unique in comparison to the vector. Ditto for the usage of pop_front, as shown in Line 37. The first mechanism of displaying the contents of deque uses the array-like syntax to access elements, whereas the latter uses iterators. In the case of the latter, as shown in Lines 47–53, the algorithm std::distance is used to evaluate the offset position of the element in the deque in the same manner that you have already seen work with the vector in Listing 17.5.

DO	DON'T
DO use the dynamic arrays vector or deque when you don't know the number of elements you need to store.	**DON'T** forget that the method pop_back() deletes the last element from the collection.
DO remember that a vector can grow only at one end via the method push_back().	**DON'T** forget that the method pop_front() deletes the first element from a deque.
DO remember that a deque can grow on both ends via the methods push_back() and push_front().	**DON'T** access a dynamic array beyond its bounds.

Summary

In this lesson, you learned the basics of using the vector and the deque as dynamic arrays. The concepts of size and capacity were explained, and you saw how the usage of the vector can be optimized to reduce the number of reallocations of its internal buffer, which copies the objects contained and potentially reduces performance. The vector is the simplest of the STL's containers, yet the most used and, arguably, the most efficient one.

17

Q&A

Q Does the vector change the order of the elements stored in it?

A The vector is a sequential container, and elements are stored and accessed in the very order that they are inserted.

Q What function is used to insert items in a vector, and where is the object inserted?

A The member function push_back inserts elements at the end of the vector.

Q What function gets the number of elements stored in a vector?

A The member function size() returns the number of elements stored in a vector. Incidentally, this is true for all STL containers.

Q Does the insertion or removal of elements at the end of the vector take more time if the vector contains more elements?

A No. Insertion and removal of elements at the end of a vector are constant-time activities.

Q What is the advantage of using the `reserve` member function?

A `reserve (...)` allocates space in the internal buffer of the `vector`, and insertion of elements does not need the `vector` to reallocate the buffer and copy existing contents. Depending on the nature of the objects stored in the `vector`, reserving space in a `vector` can result in performance improvements.

Q Are the properties of the `deque` any different than the `vector` when it comes to insertion of elements?

A No, the properties of the `deque` are similar to that of the `vector` when it comes to insertion, which is a constant-time activity for elements added at the end of sequence and a linear-time activity for elements inserted in the middle. However, the `vector` allows insertion at only one end (the bottom), whereas the `deque` allows for insertion at both (the top and the bottom).

Workshop

The Workshop contains quiz questions to help solidify your understanding of the material covered and exercises to provide you with experience in using what you've learned. Try to answer the quiz and exercise questions before checking the answers in Appendix D, and be certain you understand the answers before going to the next lesson.

Quiz

1. Can elements be inserted at the middle or the beginning of a `vector` in constant time?

2. My `vector` returns `size()` as `10` and `capacity()` as `20`. How many more elements can I insert in it without needing the `vector` class to trigger a buffer reallocation?

3. What does the `pop_back` function do?

4. If `vector <int>` is a dynamic array of integers, a `vector <CMammal>` is a dynamic array of what type?

5. Can elements in a `vector` be randomly accessed? If so, how?

6. What iterator type allows random access of elements in a `vector`?

Exercises

1. Write an interactive program that accepts integer input from the user and saves it in the vector. The user should be able to query a value stored in the vector at any time, given an index.

2. Extend the program from Exercise 1 to be able to tell the user whether a value he queries for already exists in the vector.

3. Jack sells jars on eBay. To help him with packaging and shipment, write a program in which he can enter the dimensions of each of these articles, store them in a vector, and have them printed on the screen.

17

LESSON 18
STL list and forward_list

The Standard Template Library (STL) supplies the programmer with a doubly linked list in the form of template class `std::list`. The main advantage of a linked list is in fast and constant time insertion and removal of elements. Starting C++11, you can also use a singly linked list in the form of `std::forward_list` that can be traversed only in one direction.

In this lesson, you learn

- How to instantiate the `list` and `forward_list`
- Using the STL list classes, including insertion and removal
- How to reverse and sort elements

The Characteristics of a `std::list`

A `linked list` is a collection of nodes in which each node, in addition to containing a value or object of interest, also points to the next node; that is, each node links to the next one and previous one as shown in Figure 18.1.

FIGURE 18.1
Visual representation of a doubly linked list.

The STL implementation of the `list` class allows for constant-time insertions in the top, bottom, or middle of the `list`.

TIP	To use class std::list, include header: #include \<list>

Basic `list` Operations

To use STL's `list` class, include header file `<list>`. The template class `list` that exists in the `std` namespace is a generic implementation that needs to be template-instantiated before you can use any of its useful member functions.

Instantiating a `std::list` Object

The template instantiation of `list` needs to specify the type of object that you want to collect in the list. So, the initialization of a list would look like the following:

```
std::list<int> listIntegers;  // list containing integers
std::list<float> listFloats;  // list containing floats
std::list<Tuna> listTunas;  // list containing objects of type Tuna
```

To declare an iterator that points to an element in the list, you would use

```
std::list<int>::const_iterator iElementInSet;
```

If you need an iterator that can be used to modify values or invoke non-`const` functions, you use `iterator` instead of `const_iterator`.

Given that implementations of the `std::list` do provide you with a set of overloaded constructors, you can even create lists that are initialized to contain a number of elements of your choosing, each initialized to a value, as demonstrated by Listing 18.1.

LISTING 18.1 Different Forms of Instantiating std::list, Specifying Number of Elements and Initial Values

```
0: #include <list>
1: #include <vector>
2:
3: int main ()
4: {
5:    using namespace std;
6:
7:    // instantiate an empty list
8:    list <int> listIntegers;
9:
10:   // instantiate a list with 10 integers
11:   list<int> listWith10Integers(10);
12:
13:   // instantiate a list with 4 integers, each initialized to 99
14:   list<int> listWith4IntegerEach99 (10, 99);
15:
16:   // create an exact copy of an existing list
17:   list<int> listCopyAnother(listWith4IntegerEach99);
18:
19:   // a vector with 10 integers, each 2011
20:   vector<int> vecIntegers(10, 2011);
21:
22:   // instantiate a list using values from another container
23:   list<int> listContainsCopyOfAnother(vecIntegers.cbegin(),
24:                                       vecIntegers.cend());
25:
26:   return 0;
27: }
```

Analysis ▼

This program produces no output and demonstrates the application of the various over-loaded constructors in creating a list of integers. In Line 8 you create an empty list, whereas in Line 11 you create a list containing 10 integers. Line 14 is a list, called listWith4IntegersEach99, that contains 4 integers that are each initialized to value 99. Line 17 demonstrates creating a list that is an exact copy of the contents of another. Lines 20–24 are surprising and curious! You instantiate a vector that contains 10 integers, each containing value 2011, and then instantiate a list in Line 23 that contains elements copied from the vector, using const iterators returned by vector::cbegin() and vector::cend() (that are new in C++11). Listing 18.1 is also a demonstration of how iterators help decouple the implementation of one container from another enabling you to use their generic functionality to instantiate a list using values taken from a vector, as shown in Lines 23 and 24.

18

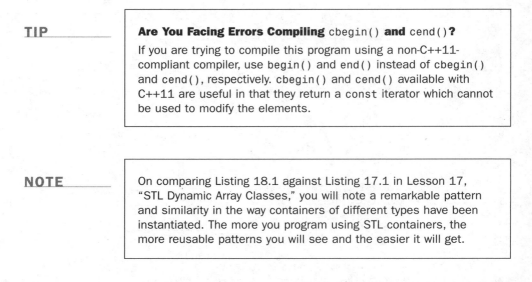

TIP

Are You Facing Errors Compiling cbegin() **and** cend()**?**

If you are trying to compile this program using a non-C++11-compliant compiler, use begin() and end() instead of cbegin() and cend(), respectively. cbegin() and cend() available with C++11 are useful in that they return a const iterator which cannot be used to modify the elements.

NOTE

On comparing Listing 18.1 against Listing 17.1 in Lesson 17, "STL Dynamic Array Classes," you will note a remarkable pattern and similarity in the way containers of different types have been instantiated. The more you program using STL containers, the more reusable patterns you will see and the easier it will get.

Inserting Elements at the Front or Back of the List

Similar to a deque, insertion at the front (or top, depending on your perspective) is effected using the list member method push_front(). Insertion at the end is done using member method push_back(). These two methods take one input parameter, which is the value to be inserted:

```
listIntegers.push_back (-1);
listIntegers.push_front (2001);
```

Listing 18.2 demonstrates the effect of using these two methods on a list of integers.

LISTING 18.2   Inserting Elements in the List Using push_front() and push_back()

```
0: #include <list>
1: #include <iostream>
2: using namespace std;
3:
4: template <typename T>
5: void DisplayContents (const T& Input)
6: {
7:    for (auto iElement = Input.cbegin() // auto and cbegin: C++11
8:        ; iElement != Input.cend()
```

```
 9:            ; ++ iElement )
10:            cout << *iElement << ' ';
11:
12:    cout << endl;
13: }
14:
15: int main ()
16: {
17:    std::list <int> listIntegers;
18:
19:    listIntegers.push_front (10);
20:    listIntegers.push_front (2011);
21:    listIntegers.push_back (-1);
22:    listIntegers.push_back (9999);
23:
24:    DisplayContents(listIntegers);
25:
26:    return 0;
27: }
```

Output ▼

2011 10 -1 9999

Analysis ▼

18

Lines 19–22 demonstrate the usage of push_front() and push_back(). The value being supplied as an argument to push_front() takes the first position in the list, whereas that sent via push_back() takes the last position. The output displays the content of the list via generic template function DisplayContents() demonstrating the order of the inserted elements (and that they aren't stored in order of insertion).

CAUTION

Are You Facing an Error Compiling Keyword auto?

Function DisplayContents() in Lsting 18.2 uses C++11 keyword auto to define the type of an iterator in Line 7. Additionally, it uses cbegin() and cend() that are new in C++11 and return a const_iterator.

In this example and in later examples, to compile using a non-C++11-compliant compiler, you need to replace auto by the explicit type.

So, `DisplayContents()` for an older compiler needs to be modified to the following:

```
template <typename T>
void DisplayContents (const T& Input)
{
   for (T::const_iterator iElement = Input.begin ()
        ; iElement != Input.end ()
        ; ++ iElement )
        cout << *iElement << ' ';

   cout << endl;
}
```

NOTE

`DisplayContents()` in Listing 18.2, Lines 4–13 is a more generic version of the method `DisplayVector()` in Listing 17.6 (note the changed parameter list). Although the latter worked only for the `vector`, generalizing the type of elements stored in one, this version is truly generic even across container types.

You can invoke the version of `DisplayContents()` in Listing 18.2 with a `vector` or a `list` as argument and it will work just fine.

Inserting at the Middle of the List

`std::list` is characterized by its capability to insert elements at the middle of the collection in constant time. This is done using the member function `insert`.

The `list` insert member function is available in three forms:

- **Form 1**

  ```
  iterator insert(iterator pos, const T& x)
  ```

  Here the `insert` function accepts the position of insertion as the first parameter and the value to insert as the second. This function returns an iterator pointing to the recently inserted element in the `list`.

- **Form 2**

  ```
  void insert(iterator pos, size_type n, const T& x)
  ```

  This function accepts the position of insertion as the first parameter, the value to insert as the last parameter, and the number of elements in variable n.

Form 3

```
template <class InputIterator>
void insert(iterator pos, InputIterator f, InputIterator l)
```

This overloaded variant is a template function that accepts, in addition to the position, two input iterators that mark the bounds of the collection to insert into the list. Note that the input type InputIterator is a template-parameterized type and therefore can point to the bounds of any collection—be it an array, a vector, or just another list.

Listing 18.3 demonstrates the use of these overloaded variants of the list::insert function.

LISTING 18.3   The Various Methods of Inserting Elements in a List

```
0: #include <list>
1: #include <iostream>
2: using namespace std;
3:
4: template <typename T>
5: void DisplayContents (const T& Input)
6: {
7:     for (auto iElement = Input.cbegin() // auto and cbegin: C++11
8:         ; iElement != Input.cend()
9:         ; ++ iElement )
10:        cout << *iElement << ' ';
11:
12:     cout << endl;
13: }
14:
15: int main ()
16: {
17:     list <int> listIntegers1;
18:
19:     // Inserting elements at the beginning...
20:     listIntegers1.insert (listIntegers1.begin (), 2);
21:     listIntegers1.insert (listIntegers1.begin (), 1);
22:
23:     // Inserting an element at the end...
24:     listIntegers1.insert (listIntegers1.end (), 3);
25:
26:     cout << "The contents of list 1 after inserting elements:" << endl;
27:     DisplayContents (listIntegers1);
28:
29:     list <int> listIntegers2;
30:
```

18

LISTING 18.3   Continued

```
31:     // Inserting 4 elements of the same value 0...
32:     listIntegers2.insert (listIntegers2.begin (), 4, 0);
33:
34:     cout << "The contents of list 2 after inserting '";
35:     cout << listIntegers2.size () << "' elements of a value:" << endl;
36:     DisplayContents (listIntegers2);
37:
38:     list <int> listIntegers3;
39:
40:     // Inserting elements from another list at the beginning...
41:     listIntegers3.insert (listIntegers3.begin (),
42:                     listIntegers1.begin (), listIntegers1.end ());
43:
44:     cout << "The contents of list 3 after inserting the contents of ";
45:     cout << "list 1 at the beginning:" << endl;
46:     DisplayContents (listIntegers3);
47:
48:     // Inserting elements from another list at the end...
49:     listIntegers3.insert (listIntegers3.end (),
50:                     listIntegers2.begin (), listIntegers2.end ());
51:
52:     cout << "The contents of list 3 after inserting ";
53:     cout << "the contents of list 2 at the beginning:" << endl;
54:     DisplayContents (listIntegers3);
55:
56:     return 0;
57: }
```

Output ▼

```
The contents of list 1 after inserting elements:
1 2 3
The contents of list 2 after inserting '4' elements of a value:
0 0 0 0
The contents of list 3 after inserting the contents of list 1 at the beginning:
1 2 3
The contents of list 3 after inserting the contents of list 2 at the beginning:
1 2 3 0 0 0 0
```

Analysis ▼

begin() and end() are member functions that return iterators pointing to the beginning and the end of the list, respectively. This is generally true for all STL containers, including the std::list. The list insert function accepts an iterator that marks the position before which items are to be inserted. The iterator returned by the end () function, as used in Line 24, points to after the last element in the list. Therefore, that line inserts integer value 3 before the end as the last value. Line 32 indicates the initialization of a list with four elements placed at the beginning—that is, at the front—each with value 0. Lines 41 and 42 demonstrate the usage of the list::insert() function to insert elements from one list at the end of another. Although this example inserts a list of integers into another list, the range inserted could as well have been the limits of a vector, supplied by begin() and end() as also seen in Listing 18.1, or a regular static array.

Erasing Elements from the List

The list member function erase comes in two overloaded forms: one that erases one element given an iterator that points to it and another that accepts a range and therefore erases a range of elements from the list. You can see the list::erase function in action in Listing 18.4, which demonstrates how you erase an element or a range of elements from a list.

LISTING 18.4 Erasing Elements from a List

```
0: #include <list>
1: #include <iostream>
2: using namespace std;
3:
4: template <typename T>
5: void DisplayContents(const T& Input)
6: {
7:     for(auto iElement = Input.cbegin() // auto and cbegin: C++11
8:         ; iElement != Input.cend()
9:         ; ++ iElement )
10:        cout << *iElement << ' ';
11:
12:     cout << endl;
13: }
14:
15: int main()
16: {
17:     std::list <int> listIntegers;
18:
19:     // Insert elements at the beginning and end...
20:     listIntegers.push_back(4);
21:     listIntegers.push_front(3);
22:     listIntegers.push_back(5);
23:
24:     // Store an iterator obtained in using the 'insert' function
25:     auto iValue2 = listIntegers.insert(listIntegers.begin(), 2);
26:
27:     cout << "Initial contents of the list:" << endl;
```

LISTING 18.4   Continued

```
28:    DisplayContents(listIntegers);
29:
30:    listIntegers.erase(listIntegers.begin(), iValue2);
31:    cout << "Contents after erasing a range of elements:" << endl;
32:    DisplayContents(listIntegers);
33:
34:    cout << "After erasing element '"<< *iValue2 << "':" << endl;
35:    listIntegers.erase(iValue2);
36:    DisplayContents(listIntegers);
37:
38:    listIntegers.erase(listIntegers.begin(), listIntegers.end());
39:    cout << "Number of elements after erasing range: ";
40:    cout << listIntegers.size() << endl;
41:
42:    return 0;
43: }
```

Output ▼

```
Initial contents of the list:
2 3 4 5
Contents after erasing a range of elements:
2 3 4 5
After erasing element '2':
3 4 5
Number of elements after erasing range: 0
```

Analysis ▼

Lines 20–25 in `main()` use various methods to insert integers into the `list`. When `insert()` is used to insert a value, it returns an iterator to the newly inserted element. This iterator pointing to an element with value 2 is stored in Line 25 in a variable `iValue2`, to be used later in a call to `erase()` at Line 35 to delete this very element from the list. Lines 30 and 38 demonstrate the usage of `erase()` to delete a range of elements. In the former, you delete a range from `begin()` to the element containing value 2 (but not including that element). Whereas in the latter, you clear a range from `begin()` to `end()`, effectively erasing the entire list.

NOTE

Listing 18.4 demonstrates at Line 40 that the number of elements in a `std::list` can be determined using list method `size()`, very similar to that of a vector. This is a pattern applicable to all STL container classes.

Reversing and Sorting Elements in a List

list has a special property that iterators pointing to the elements in a list remain valid in spite of rearrangement of the elements or insertion of new elements and so on. To keep this important property intact, the list function features sort and reverse as member methods even though the STL supplies these as algorithms that will and do work on the list class. The member versions of these algorithms ensure that iterators pointing to elements in the list are not invalidated when the relative position of the elements is disturbed.

Reversing Elements Using list::reverse()

list features a member function reverse() that takes no parameters and reverses the order of contents in a list for the programmer:

```
listIntegers.reverse();   // reverse order of elements
```

The usage of reverse() is demonstrated in Listing 18.5.

LISTING 18.5   Reversing Elements in a List

```
0: #include <list>
1: #include <iostream>
2: using namespace std;
3:
4: template <typename T>
5: void DisplayContents(const T& Input)
6: {
7:     for(auto iElement = Input.cbegin() // auto and cbegin: C++11
8:        ; iElement != Input.cend()
9:        ; ++ iElement )
10:        cout << *iElement << ' ';
11:
12:     cout << endl;
13: }
14:
15: int main()
16: {
17:     std::list <int> listIntegers;
18:
19:     // Insert elements at the beginning and end
20:     listIntegers.push_front(4);
21:     listIntegers.push_front(3);
22:     listIntegers.push_front(2);
23:     listIntegers.push_front(1);
24:     listIntegers.push_front(0);
25:     listIntegers.push_back(5);
26:
```

18

LISTING 18.5 Continued

```
27:    cout << "Initial contents of the list:" << endl;
28:    DisplayContents(listIntegers);
29:
30:    listIntegers.reverse();
31:
32:    cout << "Contents of the list after using reverse():" << endl;
33:    DisplayContents(listIntegers);
34:
35:    return 0;
36: }
```

Output ▼

```
Initial contents of the list:
0 1 2 3 4 5
Contents of the list after using reverse():
5 4 3 2 1 0
```

Analysis ▼

As shown in Line 30, reverse() simply reverses the order of elements in the list. It is a simple call without parameters that ensures that iterators pointing to elements in the list, if kept by the programmer, remain valid even after the reversal.

Sorting Elements

The list member function sort() is available in a version that takes no parameters:

```
listIntegers.sort();  // sort in ascending order
```

Another version allows you to define your own sort priorities via a binary predicate function as a parameter:

```
bool SortPredicate_Descending (const int& lsh, const int& rsh)
{
   // define criteria for list::sort: return true for desired order
   return (lsh > rsh);
}
// Use predicate to sort a list:
listIntegers.sort (SortPredicate_Descending);
```

These two variants are demonstrated in Listing 18.6.

LISTING 18.6   Sorting a List of Integers in Ascending and Descending Order Using
`list::sort()`

```cpp
0: #include <list>
1: #include <iostream>
2: using namespace std;
3:
4: bool SortPredicate_Descending (const int& lsh, const int& rsh)
5: {
6:    // define criteria for list::sort: return true for desired order
7:    return (lsh > rsh);
8: }
9:
10: template <typename T>
11: void DisplayContents (const T& Input)
12: {
13:    for (auto iElement = Input.cbegin() // auto and cbegin: C++11
14:       ; iElement != Input.cend()
15:       ; ++ iElement )
16:       cout << *iElement << ' ';
17:
18:    cout << endl;
19: }
20:
21: int main ()
22: {
23:    list <int> listIntegers;
24:
25:    // Insert elements at the beginning and end
26:    listIntegers.push_front (444);
27:    listIntegers.push_front (2011);
28:    listIntegers.push_front (-1);
29:    listIntegers.push_front (0);
30:    listIntegers.push_back (-5);
31:
32:    cout << "Initial contents of the list are - " << endl;
33:    DisplayContents (listIntegers);
34:
35:    listIntegers.sort ();
36:
37:    cout << "Order of elements after sort():" << endl;
38:    DisplayContents (listIntegers);
39:
40:    listIntegers.sort (SortPredicate_Descending);
41:    cout << "Order of elements after sort() with a predicate:" << endl;
42:    DisplayContents (listIntegers);
43:
44:    return 0;
45: }
```

18

Output ▼

```
Initial contents of the list are -
0 -1 2011 444 -5
Order of elements after sort():
-5 -1 0 444 2011
Order of elements after sort() with a predicate:
2011 444 0 -1 -5
```

Analysis ▼

This sample displays the sort functionality on a list of integers. The first few lines of code create the list object and insert sample values in it. Line 35 displays the usage of a sort() function without parameters that sorts elements in ascending order by default, comparing integers using operator < (which, in the case of integers, is implemented by the compiler). However, if the programmer wants to override this default behavior, he must supply the sort function with a binary predicate. The function SortPredicate_Descending(), defined in Lines 4–8, is a binary predicate that helps the list's sort function decide whether one element is less than the other. If not, it swaps their positions. In other words, you tell the list what's to be interpreted as less (which, in this case, is the first parameter being greater than the second). This "predicate" is passed as a parameter to the variant of the sort() function as shown in Line 40. The predicate returns true only if the first value is greater than the second. That is, sort that uses the predicate interprets the first value (lsh) to be logically less than the second (rsh) only if the numeric value of the former is greater than that of the latter. On the basis of this interpretation, it swaps position to fulfill the criteria specified by the predicate.

Sorting and Removing Elements from a list That Contains Objects of a class

What if you had a list of a class type, and not a simple built-in type such as int? Say a list of address book entries where each entry is a class that contains name, address, and so on. How would you ensure that this list is sorted on name?

The answer is one of the following:

- Implement operator < within the class-type that the list contains.
- Supply a sort *binary predicate*—a function that takes two values as input and returns a Boolean value indicating whether the first value is smaller than the second.

Most practical applications involving STL containers rarely collect integers; instead, they collect user-defined types such as classes or structs. Listing 18.7 demonstrates one using the example of a contacts list. It seems rather long at first sight but is mostly full of simple code.

LISTING 18.7 A List of Class Objects: Creating a Contacts List

```
0: #include <list>
1: #include <string>
2: #include <iostream>
3: using namespace std;
4:
5: template <typename T>
6: void DisplayContents (const T& Input)
7: {
8:    for(auto iElement = Input.cbegin() // auto, cbegin and cend: c++11
9:       ; iElement != Input.cend()
10:       ; ++ iElement )
11:      cout << *iElement << endl;
12:
13:    cout << endl;
14: }
15:
16: struct ContactItem
17: {
18:    string strContactsName;
19:    string strPhoneNumber;
20:    string strDisplayRepresentation;
21:
22:    // Constructor and destructor
23:    ContactItem (const string& strName, const string & strNumber)
24:    {
25:       strContactsName = strName;
26:       strPhoneNumber = strNumber;
27:       strDisplayRepresentation = (strContactsName + ": " + strPhoneNumber);
28:    }
29:
30:    // used by list::remove() given contact list item
31:    bool operator == (const ContactItem& itemToCompare) const
32:    {
33:       return (itemToCompare.strContactsName == this->strContactsName);
34:    }
35:
36:    // used by list::sort() without parameters
37:    bool operator < (const ContactItem& itemToCompare) const
38:    {
39:       return (this->strContactsName < itemToCompare.strContactsName);
40:    }
41:
```

18

LISTING 18.7   Continued

```
42:    // Used in DisplayContents via cout
43:    operator const char*() const
44:    {
45:       return strDisplayRepresentation.c_str();
46:    }
47: };
48:
49: bool SortOnPhoneNumber (const ContactItem& item1,
50:                            const ContactItem& item2)
51: {
52:    return (item1.strPhoneNumber < item2.strPhoneNumber);
53: }
54:
55: int main ()
56: {
57:    list <ContactItem> Contacts;
58:    Contacts.push_back(ContactItem("Jack Welsch", "+1 7889 879 879"));
59:    Contacts.push_back(ContactItem("Bill Gates", "+1 97 7897 8799 8"));
60:    Contacts.push_back(ContactItem("Angela Merkel", "+49 23456 5466"));
61:    Contacts.push_back(ContactItem("Vladimir Putin", "+7 6645 4564 797"));
62:    Contacts.push_back(ContactItem("Manmohan Singh", "+91 234 4564 789"));
63:    Contacts.push_back(ContactItem("Barack Obama", "+1 745 641 314"));
64:
65:    cout << "List in initial order: " << endl;
66:    DisplayContents(Contacts);
67:
68:    Contacts.sort();
69:    cout << "After sorting in alphabetical order via operator<:" << endl;
70:    DisplayContents(Contacts);
71:
72:    Contacts.sort(SortOnPhoneNumber);
73:    cout << "After sorting in order of phone numbers via predicate:" << endl;
74:    DisplayContents(Contacts);
75:
76:    cout << "After erasing Putin from the list: ";
77:    Contacts.remove(ContactItem("Vladimir Putin", ""));
78:    DisplayContents(Contacts);
79:
80:    return 0;
81: }
```

Output ▼

```
List in initial order:
Jack Welsch: +1 7889 879 879
```

```
Bill Gates: +1 97 7897 8799 8
Angela Merkel: +49 23456 5466
Vladimir Putin: +7 6645 4564 797
Manmohan Singh: +91 234 4564 789
Barack Obama: +1 745 641 314

After sorting in alphabetical order via operator<:
Angela Merkel: +49 23456 5466
Barack Obama: +1 745 641 314
Bill Gates: +1 97 7897 8799 8
Jack Welsch: +1 7889 879 879
Manmohan Singh: +91 234 4564 789
Vladimir Putin: +7 6645 4564 797

After sorting in order of phone numbers via predicate:
Barack Obama: +1 745 641 314
Jack Welsch: +1 7889 879 879
Bill Gates: +1 97 7897 8799 8
Angela Merkel: +49 23456 5466
Vladimir Putin: -7 6645 4564 797
Manmohan Singh: -91 234 4564 789

After erasing Putin from the list:
Barack Obama: +1 745 641 314
Jack Welsch: +1 7889 879 879
Bill Gates: +1 97 7897 8799 8
Angela Merkel: +49 23456 5466
Manmohan Singh: +91 234 4564 789
```

18

Analysis ▼

For a start, focus on main() in Lines 57–81. You have instantiated a list of address book items of type ContactItem in Line 57. In Lines 58–63, you populate this list with some names and (fake) telephone numbers of a few celebrity technologists and politicians and display it in Line 66. Line 68 is when you use list::sort without a predicate function. In the absence of a predicate, this sort function seeks the presence of operator< in ContactItem that has been defined in Lines 37–40. ContactItem::operator< helps list::sort sort its elements in the alphabetical order of the stored names (and not telephone numbers or a random logic). To sort the same list in the order of phone numbers, you use list::sort() supplying a binary predicate function SortOnPhoneNumber() as an argument in Line 72. This function implemented in Lines 49–53 ensures that the input arguments of type ContactItem are compared to each other on the basis of the phone numbers and not the names. Thus, it helps list::sort sort the list of celebrities on the basis of their phone numbers as the output indicates. Finally, Line 77 is where you use `list::remove()` to remove a celebrity contact from the list. You supply an object with the celebrity's name as a parameter. `list::remove()` compares this object to other elements in the list, using `ContactItem::operator=` implemented in Lines 30–34. This operator returns `true` if the names match, helping `list::remove()` decide what the criteria of a match should be.

This example not only demonstrates how STL's template version of the linked `list` can be used to create a `list` of any object type, but also the importance of operators and predicates.

C++11

std::forward_list

Starting with C++11, you have the option of using a `forward_list` instead of a doubly linked list in `std::list`. `std::forward_list` is a singly linked list—that is, it allows iteration in only one direction as shown in Figure 18.2.

FIGURE 18.2
A visual represen-
tation of a singly
linked list.

> **TIP**
>
> To use a `std::forward_list`, you need to include header `<forward_list>`:
>
> `#include<forward_list>`

The usage of the `forward_list` is quite similar to `list`, save for the fact that you can move iterators only in one direction and that you have a `push_front()` function to insert elements but no `push_back()`. Of course, you can always use `insert()` and its overloaded functions to insert an element at a given position.

Listing 18.8 demonstrates some functions of a `forward_list` class.

LISTING 18.8   Basic Insertion and Removal Operations on a forward_list

```
0: #include<forward_list>
1: #include<iostream>
2: using namespace std;
3:
4: template <typename T>
5: void DisplayContents (const T& Input)
6: {
7:    for (auto iElement = Input.cbegin() // auto and cbegin: C++11
8:       ; iElement != Input.cend ()
9:       ; ++ iElement )
10:       cout << *iElement << ' ';
11:
12:    cout << endl;
13: }
14:
15: int main()
16: {
17:    forward_list<int> flistIntegers;
18:    flistIntegers.push_front(0);
19:    flistIntegers.push_front(2);
20:    flistIntegers.push_front(2);
21:    flistIntegers.push_front(4);
22:    flistIntegers.push_front(3);
23:    flistIntegers.push_front(1);
24:
25:    cout << "Contents of forward_list: " << endl;
26:    DisplayContents(flistIntegers);
27:
28:    flistIntegers.remove(2);
29:    flistIntegers.sort();
30:    cout << "Contents after removing 2 and sorting: " << endl;
31:    DisplayContents(flistIntegers);
32:
33:    return 0;
34: }
```

Output ▼

```
Contents of forward_list:
1 3 4 2 2 0
Contents after removing 2 and sorting:
0 1 3 4
```

18

Analysis ▼

As the sample shows, the `forward_list` is quite similar in function to a `list`. As the `forward_list` doesn't support bidirectional iteration, you can use `operator++` on an iterator, but not `operator--`. This sample demonstrates the usage of function `remove(2)` in Line 28 to remove all elements with value 2. Line 29 demonstrates `sort()` using the default sort predicate that uses `std::less<T>`.

The advantage of the `forward_list` is that in being a singly linked list, its memory consumption is slightly lower than that of a `list` (as an element needs to know only the next element but not the previous one).

DO	DON'T
DO choose a `std::list` over `std::vector` where you frequently insert or delete elements, especially in the middle—a vector needs to resize its internal buffer to allow array semantics and causes expensive copy operations, but a list just links or unlinks elements.	**DON'T** use a list when you have infrequent insertions or deletions at the ends and no insertions or deletions in the middle; `vector` or `deque` can be significantly faster in these cases.
DO remember that you can insert in the beginning or end of a list using the `push_front()` or `push_back()` member methods, respectively.	**DON'T** forget to supply a predicate function if you want the list to `sort()` or `remove()` using non-default criteria.
DO remember to program `operator<` and `operator==` in a class that will be collected in a STL container such as `list` to supply the default sort or remove predicate.	
DO remember that you can always determine the number of elements in the `list` using the `list::size()` method, as with any other STL container class.	
DO remember that you can empty a list using `list::clear()` method, as with any other STL container class.	

Summary

This lesson taught you the properties of the list and the different list operations. You now know some of the most useful list functions and can create a list of any object type.

Q&A

Q Why does the list provide member functions such as sort and remove?

A The STL list class is bound to respect the property that iterators pointing to elements in the list should remain valid irrespective of the position of the elements in the list itself. Although STL algorithms work on list too, the list's member functions ensure that the aforementioned property of the list is withheld and iterators pointing to elements in the list before the sort was done continue to point to the same elements even after the sort.

Q You are using a list of type CAnimal, which is a class. What operators should CAnimal define for list member functions to be able to work on it accurately?

A You must provide the default comparison operator == and the default < operator to any class that can be used in STL containers.

Q How would you replace keyword auto by an explicit type declaration in the following line:

```
list<int> listIntegers(10);  // list of 10 integers
auto iFirstElement = listIntegers.begin();
```

A If you are on an older compiler that is not C++11 compatible, you would replace auto by an explicit type declaration:

```
list<int> listIntegers(10);  // list of 10 integers
list<int>::iterator iFirstElement = listIntegers.begin();
```

18

Workshop

The Workshop contains quiz questions to help solidify your understanding of the material covered and exercises to provide you with experience in using what you've learned. Try to answer the quiz and exercise questions before checking the answers in Appendix D, and be certain you understand the answers before going to the next lesson.

Quiz

1. Is there any loss in performance when inserting items in the middle of the STL `list` as compared to the beginning or the end?

2. Two iterators are pointing to two elements in an STL `list` object, and then an element is inserted between them. Are these iterators invalidated by the insert action?

3. How can the contents of a `std::list` be cleared?

4. Is it possible to insert multiple elements in a `list`?

Exercises

1. Write a short program that accepts numbers from the user and inserts them at the top of the `list`.

2. Using a short program, demonstrate that an iterator pointing to an element in a `list` continues to remain valid even after another element has been inserted before it, thus changing the relative position of the former element.

3. Write a program that inserts the contents of a vector into an STL `list` using the `list`'s insert function.

4. Write a program that sorts and reverses a `list` of strings.

LESSON 19
STL Set Classes

The Standard Template Library (STL) supplies the programmer with container classes that help with applications requiring frequent and quick searches. The std::set and std::multiset are used to contain a sorted set of elements and offer you the ability to find elements given a logarithmic complexity. Their unordered counterparts offer constant-time insertion and search capabilities.

This lesson includes

- How STL set and multiset, unordered_set, and unordered_multiset containers can be of use to you

- Insertion, removal, and search of elements

- Advantages and disadvantages in using these containers

An Introduction to STL Set Classes

The set and multiset are containers that facilitate a quick lookup of keys in a container that stores them; that is, the keys are the values stored in the one-dimensional container. The difference between the set and the multiset is that the latter allows for duplicates whereas the former can store only unique values.

Figure 19.1 is only demonstrative and indicates that a set of names contains unique names, whereas a multiset permits duplicates. Being template classes, STL containers are generic and can be used to contain strings the way they contain integers, structures, or class objects.

FIGURE 19.1
Visual representation of a set and a multiset of names.

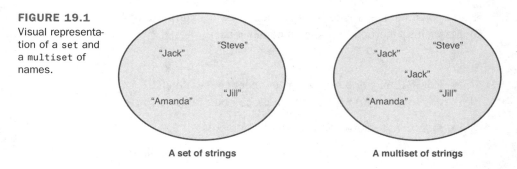

A set of strings   A multiset of strings

To facilitate quick searching, STL implementations of the set and multiset internally look like a binary tree. This means that elements inserted in a set or a multiset are sorted on insertion for quicker lookups. It also means that, unlike in a vector where elements at a position can be replaced by another, an element at a given position in a set cannot be replaced by a new element of a different value. This is true because the set would ideally like to have it placed in a possible different location in accordance with its value relative to those in the internal tree.

TIP

> To use class std::set or std::multiset, include header:
>
> #include <set>

Basic STL set and multiset Operations

STL set and multiset are template classes that need to be instantiated before you can use any of their member functions.

Instantiating a `std::set` Object

Instantiating a set or multiset of a type requires a specialization of the template class
std::set or std::multiset for that type:

```
std::set <int> setIntegers;
std::multiset <int> msetIntegers;
```

To define a set or multiset that contains objects of class Tuna, you would program the
following:

```
std::set <Tuna> setIntegers;
std::multiset <Tuna> msetIntegers;
```

To declare an iterator that points to an element in the set or multiset, you would use
this:

```
std::set<int>::const_iterator iElementInSet;
std::multiset<int>::const_iterator iElementInMultiset;
```

If you need an iterator that can be used to modify values or invoke non-const functions,
you would use iterator instead of const_iterator.

Given that both set and multiset are containers that sort elements on insertion, they use
a default predicate std::less if you don't supply sort criteria. This ensures that your set
contains elements sorted in ascending order.

You create a binary sort predicate by defining a class with operator() that takes two
values of the type contained in the set as input and returns true depending on your criteria. One such sort predicate that sorts in descending order is the following:

```
// used as a template parameter in set / multiset instantiation
template <typename T>
struct SortDescending
{
   bool operator()(const T& lhs, const T& rhs) const
   {
      return (lhs > rhs);
   }
};
```

You then supply this predicate in the set or multiset instantiation as follows:

```
// a set and multiset of integers (using sort predicate)
set <int, SortDescending<int> > setIntegers;
multiset <int, SortDescending<int> > msetIntegers;
```

19

In addition to these variants, you can always create a set or a multiset that copies from another or copies via a supplied range, as demonstrated in Listing 19.1.

LISTING 19.1   Different Instantiation Techniques of set and multiset

```
0: #include <set>
1:
2: // used as a template parameter in set / multiset instantiation
3: template <typename T>
4: struct SortDescending
5: {
6:    bool operator()(const T& lhs, const T& rhs) const
7:    {
8:       return (lhs > rhs);
9:    }
10: };
11:
12: int main ()
13: {
14:    using namespace std;
15:
16:    // a simple set or multiset of integers (using default sort predicate)
17:    set <int> setIntegers1;
18:    multiset <int> msetIntegers1;
19:
20:    // set and multiset instantiated given a user-defined sort predicate
21:    set<int, SortDescending<int> > setIntegers2;
22:    multiset<int, SortDescending<int> > msetIntegers2;
23:
24:    // creating one set from another, or part of another container
25:    set<int> setIntegers3(setIntegers1);
26:    multiset<int> msetIntegers3(setIntegers1.cbegin(), setIntegers1.cend());
27:
28:    return 0;
29: }
```

Analysis ▼

This program produces no output but demonstrates the various instantiation techniques for set and multiset, specialized to contain type int. In Lines 17 and 18, you see the simplest form where the template parameters other than type have been ignored, resulting in the default sort predicate being taken, as implemented in struct (or class) std::less<T>. If you want to override the default sort, you need to specify a predicate like the ones defined in Lines 3–10 and used in main() in Lines 21 and 22. This predicate ensures that the sort is descending (default ascending). Finally, Lines 25 and 26 show instantiation techniques where one set is a copy of another and a multiset instantiates from a range of values taken from a set (but could be a vector or a list or any STL container class that returns iterators that describe bounds via cbegin() and cend()).

Inserting Elements in a set or multiset

Most functions in a set and multiset work in a similar fashion. They accept similar parameters and return similar value types. For instance, inserting elements in both kinds of containers can be done using the member insert, which accepts the value to be inserted:

```
setIntegers.insert (-1);
msetIntegers.insert (setIntegers.begin (), setIntegers.end ());
```

Listing 19.2 demonstrates inserting elements in these containers.

LISTING 19.2   Inserting Elements in an STL set and multiset

```
0: #include <set>
1: #include <iostream>
2: using namespace std;
3:
4: template <typename T>
5: void DisplayContents (const T& Input)
6: {
7:    for(auto iElement = Input.cbegin () // auto, cbegin(): C++11
8:       ; iElement != Input.cend () // cend() is new in C++11
9:       ; ++ iElement )
10:       cout << *iElement << ' ';
11:
12:    cout << endl;
13: }
14:
15: int main ()
16: {
17:    set <int> setIntegers;
```

19

LISTING 19.2 Continued

```
18:    multiset <int> msetIntegers;
19:
20:    setIntegers.insert (60);
21:    setIntegers.insert (-1);
22:    setIntegers.insert (3000);
23:    cout << "Writing the contents of the set to the screen" << endl;
24:    DisplayContents (setIntegers);
25:
26:    msetIntegers.insert (setIntegers.begin (), setIntegers.end ());
27:    msetIntegers.insert (3000);
28:
29:    cout << "Writing the contents of the multiset to the screen" << endl;
30:    DisplayContents (msetIntegers);
31:
32:    cout << "Number of instances of '3000' in the multiset are: '";
33:    cout << msetIntegers.count (3000) << "'" << endl;
34:
35:    return 0;
36: }
```

Output ▼

```
Writing the contents of the set to the screen
-1 60 3000
Writing the contents of the multiset to the screen
-1 60 3000 3000
Number of instances of '3000' in the multiset are: '2'
```

Analysis ▼

Lines 4–13 contain the generic template function DisplayContents(), which you have also seen in Lesson 17, "TL Dynamic Array Classes," and 18, "STL list and forward_list," and writes the contents of an STL container to the console or screen. Lines 17 and 18, as you already know, define a set object and a multiset object. Lines 20–22 insert values into the set using the insert() member function. Line 26 demonstrates how insert()can be used to insert the contents of a set into a multiset, inserting in this case the contents of setIntegers into the multiset msetIntegers. In Line 27 you insert an element with value 3000 that already exists in the multiset. The output demonstrates that the multiset is able to hold multiple values. Lines 25 and 26 demonstrate the utility of the multiset::count() member function, which returns the number of elements in the multiset that hold that particular value.

TIP

> Use multiset::count() to find the number of elements in the multiset that have the same value as that supplied as an argument to this function.

TIP

> **Are You Facing an Error Compiling Keyword auto?**
>
> Function DisplayContents() in Listing 19.2 uses C++11 keyword auto in Line 7 to define the type of an iterator. Additionally, it uses cbegin() and cend() that are new in C++11 and return a const_iterator.
>
> In this sample and ahead, to compile using a non-C++11-compliant compiler, you need to replace auto by the explicit type.
>
> So, DisplayContents() for an older compiler needs to be modified to the following:
>
> ```
> template <typename T>
> void DisplayContents (const T& Input)
> {
>    for (T::const_iterator iElement = Input.begin () //
>   explicit type
>         ; iElement != Input.end ()
>         ; ++ iElement )
>         cout << *iElement << ' ';
>
>    cout << endl;
> }
> ```

19

Finding Elements in an STL set or multiset

Associative containers like set and multiset or map and multimap feature find()—a member function that enables you to find a value given a key:

```
auto iElementFound = setIntegers.find (-);
```

```
// Check if found...
if (iElementFound != setIntegers.end ())
   cout << "Element " << *iElementFound << " found!" << endl;
else
   cout << "Element not found in set!" << endl;
```

The use of `find()` is demonstrated in Listing 19.3. In case of a `multiset` that allows multiple elements with the same value, this function finds the first value that matches the supplied key.

LISTING 19.3   Using the `find` Member Function

```
0: #include <set>
1: #include <iostream>
2: using namespace std;
3:
4: int main ()
5: {
6:    set<int> setIntegers;
7:
8:    // Insert some random values
9:    setIntegers.insert (43);
10:    setIntegers.insert (78);
11:    setIntegers.insert (-1);
12:    setIntegers.insert (124);
13:
14:    // Write contents of the set to the screen
15:    for (auto iElement = setIntegers.cbegin ()
16:        ; iElement != setIntegers.cend ()
17:        ; ++ iElement )
18:       cout << *iElement << endl;
19:
20:    // Try finding an element
21:    auto iElementFound = setIntegers.find (-1);
22:
23:    // Check if found...
24:    if (iElementFound != setIntegers.end ())
25:       cout << "Element " << *iElementFound << " found!" << endl;
26:    else
27:       cout << "Element not found in set!" << endl;
28:
29:    // Try finding another element
30:    auto iAnotherFind = setIntegers.find (12345);
31:
32:    // Check if found...
33:    if (iAnotherFind != setIntegers.end ())
34:       cout << "Element " << *iAnotherFind << " found!" << endl;
35:    else
36:       cout << "Element 12345 not found in set!" << endl;
37:
38:    return 0;
39: }
```

Output ▼

```
-1
43
78
124
Element -1 found!
Element 12345 not found in set!
```

Analysis ▼

Lines 21–27 display the usage of the find() member function. find() returns an iterator that needs to be compared against end(), as shown in Line 24, to verify whether an element was found. If the iterator is valid, you can access the value pointed by it using *iElementFound.

NOTE

> The example in Listing 19.3 works correctly for a multiset, too; that is, if Line 6 s a multiset instead of a set, it does not change the way the application works.

Erasing Elements in an STL set or multiset

Associative containers such as set and multiset or map and multimap feature erase()—a member function that allows you to delete a value given a key:

```
setObject.erase (key);
```

Another form of the erase function allows the deletion of a particular element given an iterator that points to it:

```
setObject.erase (iElement);
```

You can erase a range of elements from a set or a multiset using iterators that supply the bounds:

```
setObject.erase (iLowerBound, iUpperBound);
```

The sample in Listing 19.4 demonstrates the use of erase() in removing elements from the set or multiset.

LISTING 19.4   Using the erase Member Function on a multiset

```
0: #include <set>
1: #include <iostream>
```

19

LISTING 19.4 Continued

```
 2: using namespace std;
 3:
 4: template <typename T>
 5: void DisplayContents (const T& Input)
 6: {
 7:    for(auto iElement = Input.cbegin () // auto, cebgin(): C++11
 8:       ; iElement != Input.cend () // cend() is new in C++11
 9:       ; ++ iElement )
10:       cout << *iElement << ' ';
11:
12:    cout << endl;
13: }
14:
15: typedef multiset <int> MSETINT;
16:
17: int main ()
18: {
19:    MSETINT msetIntegers;
20:
21:    // Insert some random values
22:    msetIntegers.insert (43);
23:    msetIntegers.insert (78);
24:    msetIntegers.insert (78);    // Duplicate
25:    msetIntegers.insert (-1);
26:    msetIntegers.insert (124);
27:
28:    cout << "multiset contains " << msetIntegers.size () << " elements.";
29:    cout << " These are: " << endl;
30:
31:    // Write contents of the multiset to the screen
32:    DisplayContents(msetIntegers);
33:
34:    cout << "Please enter a number to be erased from the set" << endl;
35:    int nNumberToErase = 0;
36:    cin >> nNumberToErase;
37:
38:    cout << "Erasing " << msetIntegers.count (nNumberToErase);
39:    cout << " instances of value " << nNumberToErase << endl;
40:
41:    // Try finding an element
42:    msetIntegers.erase (nNumberToErase);
43:
44:    cout << "multiset contains " << msetIntegers.size () << " elements.";
45:    cout << " These are: " << endl;
46:    DisplayContents(msetIntegers);
47:
48:    return 0;
49: }
```

Output ▼

```
multiset contains 5 elements. These are:
-1 43 78 78 124
Please enter a number to be erased from the set
78
Erasing 2 instances of value 78
multiset contains 3 elements. These are:
-1 43 124
```

Analysis ▼

Note the usage of typedef in Line 15. Line 38 demonstrates the usage of count() to tell the number of elements with a specific value. The actual erase happens in Line 42, which deletes all elements that match the particular number.

Note that erase() is overloaded. You can call erase() on an iterator, say one returned by a find operation to delete one element of the value found, as seen here:

```
MSETINT::iterator iElementFound = msetIntegers.find (nNumberToErase);
if (iElementFound != msetIntegers.end ())
   msetIntegers.erase (iElementFound);
else
   cout << "Element not found!" << endl;
```

Similarly, you can use erase() to remove a range of values from the multiset:

```
MSETINT::iterator iElementFound = msetIntegers.find (nValue);

if (iElementFound != msetIntegers.end ())
   msetIntegers.erase (msetIntegers.begin (), iElementFound);
```

19

The preceding snippet removes all elements from the start to the element of value nValue, not including the latter. Both set and multiset can be emptied of their contents using member function clear().

Now that you have an overview of the basic set and multiset functions, it's time to review a sample that features a practical application made using this container class. The sample in Listing 19.5 is the simplest implementation of a menu-based telephone directory that enables the user to insert names and telephone numbers, find them, erase them, and display them all.

LISTING 19.5 A Telephone Directory Featuring STL set, find, and erase

```
0: #include <set>
1: #include <iostream>
```

LISTING 19.5   Continued

```
 2: #include <string>
 3: using namespace std;
 4:
 5: template <typename T>
 6: void DisplayContents (const T& Input)
 7: {
 8:    for(auto iElement = Input.cbegin () // auto, cebgin(): C++11
 9:        ; iElement != Input.cend () // cend() is new in C++11
10:        ; ++ iElement )
11:        cout << *iElement << endl;
12:
13:    cout << endl;
14: }
15:
16: struct ContactItem
17: {
18:    string strContactsName;
19:    string strPhoneNumber;
20:    string strDisplayRepresentation;
21:
22:    // Constructor and destructor
23:    ContactItem (const string& strName, const string & strNumber)
24:    {
25:       strContactsName = strName;
26:       strPhoneNumber = strNumber;
27:       strDisplayRepresentation = (strContactsName + ": " + strPhoneNumber);
28:    }
29:
30:    // used by set::find()
31:    bool operator == (const ContactItem& itemToCompare) const
32:    {
33:       return (itemToCompare.strContactsName == this->strContactsName);
34:    }
35:
36:    // used as a sort predicate
37:    bool operator < (const ContactItem& itemToCompare) const
38:    {
39:       return (this->strContactsName < itemToCompare.strContactsName);
40:    }
41:
42:    // Used in DisplayContents via cout
43:    operator const char*() const
44:    {
45:       return strDisplayRepresentation.c_str();
46:    }
47: };
48:
49: int main ()
50: {
```

```
51:     set<ContactItem> setContacts;
52:     setContacts.insert(ContactItem("Jack Welsch", "+1 7889 879 879"));
53:     setContacts.insert(ContactItem("Bill Gates", "+1 97 7897 8799 8"));
54:     setContacts.insert(ContactItem("Angela Merkel", '+49 23456 5466"));
55:     setContacts.insert(ContactItem("Vladimir Putin", "+7 6645 4564 737"));
56:     setContacts.insert(ContactItem("Manmohan Singh", "+91 234 4564 739"));
57:     setContacts.insert(ContactItem("Barack Obama", "+1 745 641 314"));
58:     DisplayContents(setContacts);
59:
60:     cout << "Enter a person whose number you wish to delete: ";
61:     string NameInput;
62:     getline(cin, NameInput);
63:
64:     auto iContactFound = setContacts.find(ContactItem(NameInput, ""));
65:     if(iContactFound != setContacts.end())
66:     {
67:         // Erase the contact found in set
68:         setContacts.erase(iContactFound);
69:         cout << "Displaying contents after erasing: " << NameInput << endl;
70:         DisplayContents(setContacts);
71:     }
72:     else
73:         cout << "Contact not found" << endl;
74:
75:     return 0;
76: }
```

Output ▼

```
Angela Merkel: +49 23456 5466
Barack Obama: +1 745 641 314
Bill Gates: +1 97 7897 8799 8
Jack Welsch: +1 7889 879 879
Manmohan Singh: +91 234 4564 789
Vladimir Putin: +7 6645 4564 797

Enter a person whose number you wish to delete: Jack Welsch
Displaying contents after erasing: Jack Welsch
Angela Merkel: +49 23456 5466
Barack Obama: +1 745 641 314
Bill Gates: +1 97 7897 8799 8
Manmohan Singh: +91 234 4564 789
Vladimir Putin: +7 6645 4564 797
```

19

Analysis ▼

This is quite similar to Listing 18.7 that sorted a std::list in alphabetical order, the difference being that in case of the std::set, sort happens on insertion. As the output indicates, you didn't need to invoke any function to ensure that elements in the set are sorted because they're sorted on insertion. You give the user the choice to delete an entry, and Line 64 demonstrates the call to `find()` to locate that entry that is deleted in Line 68 using `erase()`.

> **TIP**
>
> This implementation of the telephone directory is based on the STL `set` and therefore does not allow for multiple entries containing the same value. If you need your implementation of the directory to allow two people with the same name (say, Tom) to be stored, you would choose the STL `multiset`. The preceding code would still work correctly if `setContacts` were to be a `multiset`. To make further use of the `multiset`'s capability to store multiple entries of the same value, you use the `count()` member function to know the number of items that hold a particular value. This is demonstrated in the previous code sample. Similar items are placed adjacently in a `multiset`, and the `find()` function returns an iterator to the first found value. This iterator can be incremented to reach the next found items.

Pros and Cons of Using STL `set` and `multiset`

The STL `set` and `multiset` provide significant advantages in applications that need frequent lookups because their contents are sorted and therefore quicker to locate. However, to provide this advantage, the container needs to sort elements at insertion time. Thus, there is an overhead in inserting elements because elements are sorted—an overhead that might be a worthwhile compromise if you need to use features and functions such as `find()` often.

`find()` makes use of the internal binary tree structure. This sorted binary tree structure results in another implicit disadvantage over sequential containers such as the `vector`. In a `vector`, the element pointed to by an iterator (say, one returned by a `std::find()` operation) can be overwritten by a new value. In case of a `set`, however, elements are sorted by the `set` class according to their respective values, and therefore overwriting an element using an iterator should never be done, even if that were programmatically possible.

C++11

STL Hash Set Implementation `std::unordered_set` and `std::unordered_multiset`

The STL `std::set` and STL `std::multiset` sort elements (that are simultaneously the keys) on the basis of `std::less<T>` or a supplied predicate. Searching in a sorted container is faster than searching in an unsorted container such as a vector, and `std::sort` offers logarithmic complexity. This means that the time spent finding an element in a set is not directly proportional to the number of elements in the set, rather to the LOG thereof. So, on average it takes twice as long to search in a set of 10,000 elements as it would take in a set of 100 (as $100^2 = 10000$, or $\log(10000) = 2 \times \log(100)$).

Yet, this dramatic improvement of performance over an unsorted container (where search is directly proportional to the number of elements) is not enough at times. Programmers and mathematicians alike seek constant-time insertions and sort possibilities, and one of them uses a hash-based implementation, where a hash function is used to determine the sorting index. Elements inserted into a hash set are first evaluated by a hash function that generates a unique index, which is the index of the bucket they're placed in.

The hash set variant provided by STL is container class `std::unordered_set`.

TIP

To use STL containers `std::unordered_set` or `std::unordered_multiset`, include

`#include<unordered_set>`

19

The usage of this class doesn't change too much in comparison to a `std::set`

```
// instantiation:
unordered_set<int> usetInt;

// insertion of an element
usetInt.insert(1000);

// find():
auto iPairThousand = usetInt.find(1000);

if (iPairThousand != usetInt.end())
   cout << *iPairThousand << endl;
```

Yet, one very important feature of an unordered_map is the availability of a hash function that is responsible for deciding the sorting order:

```
unordered_set<int>::hasher HFn = usetInt.hash_function();
```

Listing 19.6 demonstrates the usage of some of the common methods supplied by std::hash_set.

LISTING 19.6   std::unordered_set and the Use of insert(), find(), size(), max_bucket_count(), load_factor(), and max_load_factor()

```
0: #include<unordered_set>
1: #include <iostream>
2: using namespace std;
3:
4: template <typename T>
5: void DisplayContents(const T& Input)
6: {
7:    cout << "Number of elements, size() = " << Input.size() << endl;
8:    cout << "Max bucket count = " << Input.max_bucket_count() << endl;
9:    cout << "Load factor: " << Input.load_factor() << endl;
10:    cout << "Max load factor = " << Input.max_load_factor() << endl;
11:    cout << "Unordered set contains: " << endl;
12:
13:    for(auto iElement = Input.cbegin() // auto, cbegin: c++11
14:       ; iElement != Input.cend()  // cend() is new in C++11
15:       ; ++ iElement )
16:       cout<< *iElement << ' ';
17:
18:    cout<< endl;
19: }
20:
21: int main()
22: {
23:    // instantiate unordered_set of int to string:
24:    unordered_set<int> usetInt;
25:
26:    usetInt.insert(1000);
27:    usetInt.insert(-3);
28:    usetInt.insert(2011);
29:    usetInt.insert(300);
30:    usetInt.insert(-1000);
31:    usetInt.insert(989);
32:    usetInt.insert(-300);
33:    usetInt.insert(111);
34:    DisplayContents(usetInt);
35:    usetInt.insert(999);
36:    DisplayContents(usetInt);
```

```
37:
38:    // find():
39:    cout << "Enter int you want to check for existence in set: ";
40:    int Key = 0;
41:    cin >> Key;
42:    auto iPairThousand = usetInt.find(Key);
43:
44:    if (iPairThousand != usetInt.end())
45:        cout << *iPairThousand << " found in set" << endl;
46:    else
47:        cout << Key << " not available in set" << endl;
48:
49:    return 0;
50: }
```

Output ▼

```
Number of elements, size() = 8
Max bucket count = 8
Load factor: 1
Max load factor = 1
Unordered set contains:
1000 -3 2011 300 -1000 -300 989 111
Number of elements, size() = 9
Max bucket count = 64
Load factor: 0.140625
Max load factor = 1
Unordered set contains:
1000 -3 2011 300 -1000 -300 989 999 111
Enter int you want to check for existence in set: -1000
-1000 found in set
```

Analysis ▼

The sample creates an unordered_set of integers; inserts eight values into it; and then displays contents, including statistics supplied by methods max_bucket_count(), load_factor(), and max_load_factor() as shown in Lines 8–10. The output tells that the bucket count is initially at eight, with eight elements in the container, resulting in a load factor of 1, which is the same as the maximum load factor. When a ninth element is inserted into the unordered_set, it reorganizes itself, creates 64 buckets, and re-creates the hash table and the load factor reduces. The rest of the code in main() demonstrates how the syntax for finding elements in an unordered_set is similar to that in a set. find() returns an iterator that needs to be checked for success of find() as shown in Line 42 before it can be used.

19

NOTE

> As hashes are typically used in a hash table to look up a value given a key, see the section on `std::unordered_map` in Lesson 20, "STL Map Classes."
>
> `std::unordered_map` is an implementation of a hash table that is new in C++11.

DO	DON'T
DO remember that STL `set` and `multiset` containers are optimized for situations that involve frequent search.	**DON'T** forget to program `operator<` and `operator==` for classes that can be collected in containers such as `set` or `multiset`. The former becomes the sort predicate, whereas the latter is used for functions such as `set::find()`.
DO remember that a `std::multiset` allows multiple elements (keys) of the same value whereas `std::set` permits only unique values.	
DO use `multiset::count(value)` to find the number of elements of a particular `value`.	**DON'T** use `std::set` or `std::multiset` in scenarios with frequent insertions and infrequent searches. `std::vector` or `std::list` is usually better suited to such cases.
DO remember that `set::size()` or `multiset::size()` gives you the number of elements in the container.	

Summary

In this lesson, you learned about using the STL `set` and `multiset`, their significant member functions, and their characteristics. You also saw their application in the programming of a simple menu-based telephone directory that also features search and erase functions.

Q&A

Q How would I declare a `set` of integers to be sorted and stored in order of descending magnitude?

A `set <int>` defines a set of integers. This takes the default sort predicate `std::less <T>` to sort items in order of ascending magnitude and can also be expressed as `set <int, less <int> >`. To sort in order of descending magnitude, define the set as `set <int, greater <int> >`.

Q **What would happen if, in a `set` of strings, I inserted the string `"Jack"` twice?**

A A `set` is not meant to be used to insert non-unique values. So, the implementation of the `std::set` class would not allow insertion of the second value.

Q **In the preceding example, if I wanted to have two instances of `"Jack"`, what would I change?**

A By design, a `set` holds only unique values. You would need to change your selection of container to a `multiset`.

Q **What `multiset` member function returns the count of items of a particular value in the container?**

A `count (value)` is the function of interest.

Q **I have found an element in the `set` using the `find` function and have an iterator pointing to it. Would I use this iterator to change the value being pointed to?**

A No. Some STL implementations might allow the user to change the value of an element inside a `set` via an iterator returned by, for example, `find`. However, this is not the correct thing to do. An iterator to an element in the `set` should be used as a const iterator—even when the STL implementation has not enforced it as such.

Workshop

The Workshop contains quiz questions to help solidify your understanding of the material covered and exercises to provide you with experience in using what you've learned. Try to answer the quiz and exercise questions before checking the answers in Appendix D, and be certain you understand the answers before going to the next lesson.

19

Quiz

1. You declare a set of integers as set <int>. What function supplies the sort criteria?

2. Where would you find duplicate elements in a multiset?

3. What set or multiset function supplies the number of elements in the container?

Exercises

1. Extend the telephone directory example in this lesson to find a person's name given a phone number, without changing structure `ContactItem`. (Hint: Define the set with a binary predicate that sorts items in accordance with the number, thus overriding the default sort based on the < operator.)

2. Define a `multiset` to store entered words and their meanings; that is, make a `multiset` work as a dictionary. (Hint: The `multiset` should be one of a structure that contains two strings: the word and its meaning.)

3. Demonstrate via a simple program that a `set` cannot accept duplicate entries whereas a `multiset` can.

LESSON 20
STL Map Classes

The Standard Template Library (STL) supplies the programmer with
container classes that help with applications that require frequent and
quick searches.

This lesson covers

- How STL map and multimap, unordered_map and
  unordered_multimap containers can be of use to you

- Insertion, removal, and search of elements

- Supplying a custom sort predicate

- Basics of how hash tables work

An Introduction to STL Map Classes

The `map` and `multimap` are key-value pair containers that allow for a lookup on the basis of a key as shown in Figure 20.1.

FIGURE 20.1
Visual illustration
of a container for
pairs, each holding
a key and a value.

FIGURE 20.1
Visual illustration of a container for pairs, each holding a key and a value.

The difference between the `map` and the `multimap` is that only the latter allows for duplicates, whereas the former can store only unique keys.

To facilitate quick searching, STL implementations of the `map` and `multimap` internally look like binary trees. This means that elements inserted in a `map` or a `multimap` are sorted on insertion. It also means that, unlike in a vector where elements at a position can be replaced by another, elements in a `map` at a given position cannot be replaced by a new element of a different value. This is because the `map` would ideally like to have it placed in a possible different location in accordance with its value relative to those in the internal tree.

TIP	To use class std::map or std::multimap, include header #include<map>

Basic std::map and std::multimap Operations

STL map and multimap are template classes that need to be instantiated before you can use any of their member functions.

Instantiating a std::map or std::multimap

Instantiating a map or multimap of an integer as key and a string as value requires a specialization of the template class std::map or std::multimap. The template instantiation of the map class needs the programmer to specify the key type, the value type, and optionally a predicate that helps the map class to sort the elements on insertion. Therefore, typical map instantiation syntax looks like this:

```
#include <map>
using namespace std;
...
map <keyType, valueType, Predicate=std::less <keyType> > mapObject;
multimap <keyType, valueType, Predicate=std::less <keyType> > mmapObject;
```

Thus, the third template parameter is optional. When you supply only the key type and the value type, ignoring the third template parameter, std::map and std::multimap default to class std::less<> to define the sort criteria. Thus, a map or multimap that maps an integer to a string looks like this:

```
std::map<int, string> mapIntToString;
std::multimap<int, string> mmapIntToString;
```

Listing 20.1 illustrates instantiation techniques in greater detail.

LISTING 20.1   Instantiating map and multimap Objects That Map an int Key to a string Value

```
0: #include<map>
1: #include<string>
2:
3: template<typename KeyType>
4: struct ReverseSort
5: {
```

20

LISTING 20.1   Continued

```
 6:    bool operator()(const KeyType& key1, const KeyType& key2)
 7:    {
 8:        return (key1 > key2);
 9:    }
10: };
11:
12: int main ()
13: {
14:    using namespace std;
15:
16:    // map and multimap key of type int to value of type string
17:    map<int, string> mapIntToString1;
18:    multimap<int, string> mmapIntToString1;
19:
20:    // map and multimap constructed as a copy of another
21:    map<int, string> mapIntToString2(mapIntToString1);
22:    multimap<int, string> mmapIntToString2(mmapIntToString1);
23:
24:    // map and multimap constructed given a part of another map or multimap
25:    map<int, string> mapIntToString3(mapIntToString1.cbegin(),
26:                                     mapIntToString1.cend());
27:
28:    multimap<int, string> mmapIntToString3(mmapIntToString1.cbegin(),
29:                                           mmapIntToString1.cend());
30:
31:    // map and multimap with a predicate that inverses sort order
32:    map<int, string, ReverseSort<int> > mapIntToString4
33:       (mapIntToString1.cbegin(), mapIntToString1.cend());
34:
35:    multimap<int, string, ReverseSort<int> > mmapIntToString4
36:       (mapIntToString1.cbegin(), mapIntToString1.cend());
37:
38:    return 0;
39: }
```

Analysis ▼

For a start, focus on main() in Lines 12–39. The simplest map and multimap of an integer key to a string value can be seen in Lines 21 and 22. Lines 25–28 demonstrate the creation of a map or a multimap initialized to a range of values from another as input. Lines 31–36 demonstrate how you instantiate a map or multimap with your own custom sort criteria. Note that the default sort (in the previous instantiations) uses std::less<T> that would sort elements in the increasing order. If you want to change this behavior, you supply a predicate that is a class or a struct that implements operator(). Such a predicate struct ReverseSort is in Lines 4–10 and has been used in the instantiation of a map at Line 32 and a multimap at Line 35.

TIP

> **Are You Facing Errors Compiling** cbegin() **and** cend()**?**
>
> If you are trying to compile this program using a non-C++11-compliant compiler, use begin() and end() instead of cbegin() and cend(), respectively. cbegin() and cend() available with C++11 are useful in that they return a const iterator which cannot be used to modify the elements.

Inserting Elements in an STL map or multimap

Most functions in a map and multimap work in a similar fashion. They accept similar parameters and return similar value types. You can insert elements in both kinds of containers by using the insert member function:

```
std::map<int, std::string> mapIntToString1;
// insert pair of key and value using make_pair function
mapIntToString.insert (make_pair (-1, "Minus One"));
```

As these two containers maintain elements in key-value pairs, you can also directly supply a std::pair initialized to the key and value to be inserted:

```
mapIntToString.insert (pair <int, string>(1000, "One Thousand"));
```

Alternatively, you can use an array-like syntax to insert, which does appear quite user friendly and is supported via subscript operator[]:

```
mapIntToString [1000000] = "One Million";
```

You can also instantiate a multimap as a copy of a map:

```
std::multimap<int, std::string> mmapIntToString(mapIntToString.cbegin(),
                                                mapIntToString.cend());
```

Listing 20.2 demonstrates the various instantiation methods.

LISTING 20.2 Inserting Elements in a map and multimap Using Overloads of insert() and Array Semantics via operator[]

```
0: #include <map>
1: #include <iostream>
2: #include<string>
3:
4: using namespace std;
5:
6: // Type-define the map and multimap definition for easy readability
```

20

LISTING 20.2 Continued

```
 7: typedef map <int, string> MAP_INT_STRING;
 8: typedef multimap <int, string> MMAP_INT_STRING;
 9:
10: template <typename T>
11: void DisplayContents (const T& Input)
12: {
13:    for(auto iElement = Input.cbegin() // auto and cbegin(): C++11
14:       ; iElement != Input.cend()  // cend() is new in C++11
15:       ; ++ iElement )
16:       cout << iElement->first << " -> " << iElement->second << endl;
17:
18:    cout << endl;
19: }
20:
21: int main ()
22: {
23:    MAP_INT_STRING mapIntToString;
24:
25:    // Insert key-value pairs into the map using value_type
26:    mapIntToString.insert (MAP_INT_STRING::value_type (3, "Three"));
27:
28:    // Insert a pair using function make_pair
29:    mapIntToString.insert (make_pair (-1, "Minus One"));
30:
31:    // Insert a pair object directly
32:    mapIntToString.insert (pair <int, string>(1000, "One Thousand"));
33:
34:    // Insert using an array-like syntax for inserting key-value pairs
35:    mapIntToString [1000000] = "One Million";
36:
37:    cout << "The map contains " << mapIntToString.size ();
38:    cout << " key-value pairs. They are: " << endl;
39:    DisplayContents(mapIntToString);
40:
41:    // instantiate a multimap that is a copy of a map
42:    MMAP_INT_STRING mmapIntToString(mapIntToString.cbegin(),
43:                           mapIntToString.cend());
44:
45:    // The insert function works the same way for multimap too
46:    // A multimap can store duplicates - insert a duplicate
47:    mmapIntToString.insert (make_pair (1000, "Thousand"));
48:
49:    cout << endl << "The multimap contains " << mmapIntToString.size ();
50:    cout << " key-value pairs. They are: " << endl;
51:    cout << "The elements in the multimap are: " << endl;
52:    DisplayContents(mmapIntToString);
53:
```

LISTING 20.2   Continued

```
54:    // The multimap can also return the number of pairs with the same key
55:    cout << "The number of pairs in the multimap with 1000 as their key: "
56:        << mmapIntToString.count (1000) << endl;
57:
58:    return 0;
59: }
```

Output ▼

```
The map contains 4 key-value pairs. They are:
-1 -> Minus One
3 -> Three
1000 -> One Thousand
1000000 -> One Million


The multimap contains 5 key-value pairs. They are:
The elements in the multimap are:
-1 -> Minus One
3 -> Three
1000 -> One Thousand
1000 -> Thousand
1000000 -> One Million

The number of pairs in the multimap with 1000 as their key: 2
```

Analysis ▼

Note how we typedef the template instantiation of the map and multimap in Lines 7 and 8. You can do this to make your code look a bit simpler (and reduce the template clutter). Lines 10–19 are a form of DisplayContents() adapted for map and multimap in which the iterator is used to access first, which indicates the key, and second, which indicates the value. Lines 26–32 demonstrate the different ways of inserting a key-value pair into a map using overloaded variants of method insert(). Line 35 demonstrates how you can use array-semantics via operator[] to insert elements in a map. Note that these insert mechanisms work as well for a multimap, which is demonstrated in Line 47, where you insert a duplicate into a multimap. Interestingly, the multimap is initialized as a copy of the map, as shown in Lines 42 and 43. The output demonstrates how the two containers have automatically sorted the input key-value pairs in ascending order of keys. The output also demonstrates that the multimap can store two pairs with the same key (in this case 1000). Line 56 demonstrates the usage of multimap::count() to tell the number of elements with a supplied key in the container.

20

TIP

Are You Facing an Error Compiling Keyword auto**?**

Function DisplayContents() in Listing 20.2 uses C++11 keyword auto in Line 13 to define the type of an iterator. In this example and later examples, to compile using a non-C++11-compliant compiler, you need to replace auto by the explicit type.

So, DisplayContents() for an older compiler needs to be modified to:

```
template <typename T>
void DisplayContents (const T& Input)
{
   for (T::const_iterator iElement = Input.begin ()
      ; iElement != Input.end ()
      ; ++ iElement )
      cout << iElement->first << " -> " << iElement->second
<< endl;

   cout << endl;
}
```

Finding Elements in an STL map

Associative containers, such as map and multimap, feature a member function called find that enables you to find a value given a key. The result of a find operation is always an iterator:

```
multimap <int, string>::const_iterator iPairFound = mapIntToString.find(Key);
```

You would first check this iterator for the success of find() and then use it to access the found value:

```
if (iPairFound != mapIntToString.end())
{
   cout << "Key " << iPairFound->first << " points to Value: ";
   cout << iPairFound->second << endl;
}
else
   cout << "Sorry, pair with key " << Key << " not in map" << endl;
```

TIP

If you are using C++11-compliant compilers, the iterator declaration can get simple by the use the auto keyword:

```
auto iPairFound = mapIntToString.find(Key);
```

The compiler determines the type of the iterator automatically by inferring it from the declared return value of map::find().

The example in Listing 20.3 demonstrates the usage of multimap::find.

LISTING 20.3 Using find() Member Function to Locate a Key-Value Pair in a map

```cpp
0: #include <map>
1: #include <iostream>
2: #include <string>
3: using namespace std;
4:
5: template <typename T>
6: void DisplayContents (const T& Input)
7: {
8:    for(auto iElement = Input.cbegin () // auto and cbegin(): C++11
9:       ; iElement != Input.cend()  // cend() is new in C++11
10:      ; ++ iElement )
11:      cout << iElement->first << " -> " << iElement->second << endl;
12:
13:    cout << endl;
14: }
15:
16: int main()
17: {
18:    map<int, string> mapIntToString;
19:
20:    mapIntToString.insert(make_pair(3, "Three"));
21:    mapIntToString.insert(make_pair(45, "Forty Five"));
22:    mapIntToString.insert(make_pair(-1, "Minus One"));
23:    mapIntToString.insert(make_pair(1000, "Thousand"));
24:
25:    cout << "The multimap contains " << mapIntToString.size();
26:    cout << " key-value pairs. They are: " << endl;
27:
28:    // Print the contents of the map to the screen
29:    DisplayContents(mapIntToString);
30:
31:    cout << "Enter the key you wish to find: ";
32:    int Key = 0;
33:    cin >> Key;
34:
35:    auto iPairFound = mapIntToString.find(Key);
36:    if (iPairFound != mapIntToString.end())
37:    {
38:       cout << "Key " << iPairFound->first << ' points to Value: ";
39:       cout << iPairFound->second << endl;
40:    }
41:    else
42:       cout << "Sorry, pair with key " << Key << " not in map" << endl;
43:
44:    return 0;
45: }
```

20

Output ▼

```
The multimap contains 4 key-value pairs. They are:
-1 -> Minus One
3 -> Three
45 -> Forty Five
1000 -> Thousand

Enter the key you wish to find: 45
Key 45 points to Value: Forty Five
```

Next, run (where find() locates no matching value):

```
The multimap contains 4 key-value pairs. They are:
-1 -> Minus One
3 -> Three
45 -> Forty Five
1000 -> Thousand

Enter the key you wish to find: 2011
Sorry, pair with key 2011 not in map
```

Analysis ▼

Lines 20–23 in main() populate a map with sample pairs, each mapping an integer key to a string value. When the user supplies a key to be used in finding in the map, Line 35 uses the find() function to look up the supplied key in the map. map::find() always returns an iterator, and it is always wise to check for the success of the find() operation by comparing this iterator to end(), as shown in Line 36. If the iterator is indeed valid, use member second to access the value, as shown in Line 39. In the second run, you input a key 2011 that is not represented in the map, and an error message is displayed to the user.

CAUTION	Never use the result of a find() operation directly without check-ing the iterator returned for success.

Finding Elements in an STL multimap

If Listing 20.3 were a multimap, opening the possibility that the container contains multiple pairs with the same key, you would need to find the values that correspond to the repeating key. Hence, in the case of a multiset you would use multiset::count() to find the number of values corresponding to a key and increment the iterator to access those consequently placed values.

```
auto iPairFound = mmapIntToString.find(key);

// Check if "find" succeeded
if(iPairFound != mmapIntToString.end())
{
    // Find the number of pairs that have the same supplied key
    size_t nNumPairsInMap = mmapIntToString.count(1000);

    for( size_t nValuesCounter = 0
        ; nValuesCounter < nNumPairsInMap  // stay within bounds
        ; ++ nValuesCounter )
    {
        cout << "Key: " << iPairFound->first;  // key
        cout << ", Value [" << nValuesCounter << "] = ";
        cout << iPairFound->second << endl;    // value

        ++ iPairFound;
    }
}
else
    cout << "Element not found in the multimap";
```

Erasing Elements from an STL map or multimap

The map and multimap feature a member function, erase(), which deletes an element
from the container. The erase() is invoked with the key as the parameter to delete all
pairs with a certain key:

```
mapObject.erase (key);
```

Another form of the erase function allows the deletion of a particular element given an
iterator that points to it:

```
mapObject.erase (iElement);
```

You can erase a range of elements from a map or a multimap using iterators that supply
the bounds:

```
mapObject.erase (iLowerBound, iUpperBound);
```

20

Listing 20.4 illustrates the usage of the erase functions.

LISTING 20.4   Erasing Elements from a multimap

```
0: #include<map>
1: #include<iostream>
2: #include<string>
3: using namespace std;
4:
```

LISTING 20.4   Continued

```
5: template<typename T>
6: void DisplayContents(const T& Input)
7: {
8:    for(auto iElement = Input.cbegin () // auto and cbegin(): C++11
9:       ; iElement != Input.cend()  // cend() is new in C++11
10:       ; ++ iElement )
11:       cout<< iElement->first<< " -> "<< iElement->second<< endl;
12:
13:    cout<< endl;
14: }
15:
16: int main()
17: {
18:    multimap<int, string>  mmapIntToString;
19:
20:    // Insert key-value pairs into the multimap
21:    mmapIntToString.insert(make_pair(3, "Three"));
22:    mmapIntToString.insert(make_pair(45, "Forty Five"));
23:    mmapIntToString.insert(make_pair(-1, "Minus One"));
24:    mmapIntToString.insert(make_pair(1000, "Thousand"));
25:
26:    // Insert duplicates into the multimap
27:    mmapIntToString.insert(make_pair(-1, "Minus One"));
28:    mmapIntToString.insert(make_pair(1000, "Thousand"));
29:
30:    cout<< "The multimap contains "<< mmapIntToString.size();
31:    cout<< " key-value pairs. "<< "They are: "<< endl;
32:    DisplayContents(mmapIntToString);
33:
34:    // Erasing an element with key as -1 from the multimap
35:    auto NumPairsErased = mmapIntToString.erase(-1);
36:    cout<< "Erased " << NumPairsErased << " pairs with -1 as key."<< endl;
37:
38:    // Erase an element given an iterator from the multimap
39:    auto iPairLocator = mmapIntToString.find(45);
40:    if(iPairLocator != mmapIntToString.end())
41:    {
42:       mmapIntToString.erase(iPairLocator);
43:       cout<< "Erased a pair with 45 as key using an iterator"<< endl;
44:    }
45:
46:    // Erase a range from the multimap...
47:    cout<< "Erasing the range of pairs with 1000 as key."<< endl;
48:    mmapIntToString.erase( mmapIntToString.lower_bound(1000)
49:                         , mmapIntToString.upper_bound(1000) );
50:
51:    cout<< "The multimap now contains "<< mmapIntToString.size();
52:    cout<< " key-value pair(s)."<< "They are: "<< endl;
53:    DisplayContents(mmapIntToString);
54:
```

LISTING 20.4   Continued

```
55:    return 0;
56: }
```

Output ▼

```
The multimap contains 6 key-value pairs. They are:
-1 -> Minus One
-1 -> Minus One
3 -> Three
45 -> Forty Five
1000 -> Thousand
1000 -> Thousand

Erased 2 pairs with -1 as key.
Erased a pair with 45 as key using an iterator
Erasing the range of pairs with 1000 as key.
The multimap now contains 1 key-value pair(s).They are:
3 -> Three
```

Analysis ▼

Lines 21–28 insert sample values into the multimap, some of them being duplicates (because a multimap, unlike a map, does support the insertion of duplicate items). After pairs have been inserted into the multimap, the code erases items by using the version of the erase function that accepts a key and erases all items with that key (–1) as shown in Line 35. The return value of map::erase(Key) is the number of elements erased, which is displayed on the screen. In Line 39, you use the iterator returned by find(45) to erase a pair from the map with key 45. Lines 48 and 49 demonstrate how pairs with a key can be deleted given a range specified by lower_bound() and upper_bound().

Supplying a Custom Sort Predicate

20

The map and multimap template definition includes a third parameter that accepts the sort predicate for the map to function correctly. This third parameter, when not supplied (as in the preceding examples), is substituted with the default sort criterion provided by std::less <>, which essentially compares two objects using operator <.

To supply a different sort criterion than what the key-type supports, you would typically program a binary predicate in the form of a class or a struct using operator():

```
template<typename KeyType>
struct Predicate
{
```

```
bool operator()(const KeyType& key1, const KeyType& key2)
{
    // your sort priority logic here
}
};
```

A map that holds a std::string type as the key has a default sort criterion based on the < operator defined by the std::string class, triggered via default sort predicate std::less<T> and therefore is case sensitive. For many applications, such as a telephone directory, it is important to feature an insertion and search operation that is not case sensitive. One way of solving this requirement is to supply the map with a sort predicate that returns either true or false on the basis of a comparison that is not case sensitive:

```
map <keyType, valueType, Predicate> mapObject;
```

Listing 20.5 explains this in detail.

LISTING 20.5 Supplying a Custom Sort Predicate—A Telephone Directory

```
0: #include<map>
1: #include<algorithm>
2: #include<string>
3: #include<iostream>
4: using namespace std;
5:
6: template <typename T>
7: void DisplayContents (const T& Input)
8: {
9:     for(auto iElement = Input.cbegin () // auto and cbegin(): C++11
10:        ; iElement != Input.cend()  // cend() is new in C++11
11:        ; ++ iElement )
12:        cout << iElement->first << " -> " << iElement->second << endl;
13:
14:     cout << endl;
15: }
16:
17: struct PredIgnoreCase
18: {
19:     bool operator()(const string& str1, const string& str2) const
20:     {
21:         string str1NoCase(str1), str2NoCase(str2);
22:         std::transform(str1.begin(), str1.end(), str1NoCase.begin(),
                 tolower);
23:         std::transform(str2.begin(), str2.end(), str2NoCase.begin(),
                 tolower);
24:
25:         return(str1NoCase< str2NoCase);
26:     };
27: };
28:
```

```
29: typedef map<string, string> DIRECTORY_WITHCASE;
30: typedef map<string, string, PredIgnoreCase> DIRECTORY_NOCASE;
31:
32: int main()
33: {
34:     // Case-insensitive directory: case of string-key plays no role
35:     DIRECTORY_NOCASE dirCaseInsensitive;
36:
37:     dirCaseInsensitive.insert(make_pair("John", "2345764"));
38:     dirCaseInsensitive.insert(make_pair("JOHN", "2345764"));
39:     dirCaseInsensitive.insert(make_pair("Sara", "42367236"));
40:     dirCaseInsensitive.insert(make_pair("Jack", "32435348"));
41:
42:     cout << "Displaying contents of the case-insensitive map:"<< endl
43:     DisplayContents(dirCaseInsensitive);
44:
45:     // Case-sensitive map: case of string-key affects insertion & search
46:     DIRECTORY_WITHCASE dirCaseSensitive(dirCaseInsensitive.begin()
47:       , dirCaseInsensitive.end());
48:
49:     cout << "Displaying contents of the case-sensitive map:"<< endl;
50:     DisplayContents(dirCaseSensitive);
51:
52:     // Search for a name in the two maps and display result
53:     cout << "Please enter a name to search: "<< endl<< "> ";
54:     string strNameInput;
55:     cin >> strNameInput;
56:
57:     // find in the map...
58:     auto iPairInNoCaseDir = dirCaseInsensitive.find(strNameInput);
59:     if(iPairInNoCaseDir != dirCaseInsensitive.end())
60:     {
61:         cout << iPairInNoCaseDir->first<< "'s number in the case-insensi-
             tive";
62:         cout << " directory is: "<< iPairInNoCaseDir->second<< endl;
63:     }
64:     else
65:     {
66:         cout << strNameInput<< "'s number not found ";
67:         cout << "in the case-insensitive directory"<< endl;
68:     }
69:
70:     // find in the case-sensitive map...
71:     auto iPairInCaseSensDir = dirCaseSensitive.find(strNameInput);
72:     if(iPairInCaseSensDir != dirCaseSensitive.end())
73:     {
74:         cout<<iPairInCaseSensDir->first<<"'s number in the case-sensitive";
75:         cout << " directory is: "<< iPairInCaseSensDir->second<< endl;
```

20

LISTING 20.5 Continued

```
76:    }
77:    else
78:    {
79:        cout << strNameInput<< "'s number was not found ";
80:        cout << "in the case-sensitive directory"<< endl;
81:    }
82:
83:    return 0;
84:}
```

Output ▼

```
Displaying contents of the case-insensitive map:
Jack -> 32435348
John -> 2345764
Sara -> 42367236

Displaying contents of the case-sensitive map:
Jack -> 32435348
John -> 2345764
Sara -> 42367236

Please enter a name to search:
> sara
Sara's number in the case-insensitive directory is: 42367236
sara's number was not found in the case-sensitive directory
```

Analysis ▼

The code in question contains two directories with equal content, one that has been instantiated with the default sort predicate, using std::less<T> and case-sensitive std::string::operator<, and another that has been instantiated with a predicate struct PredIgnoreCase as shown in Lines 17–27 that compare two strings after reducing them to lowercase. The output indicates that when you search the two maps for 'sara' the map with the case-insensitive instantiation is able to locate Sara in its records whereas the map with default instantiation is unable to find this entry.

NOTE
> In Listing 20.5, struct PredIgnoreCase can also be a class if you add the keyword public for operator(). For a C++ compiler, a struct is akin to a class with members that are public by default and that inherits public by default.

This sample demonstrated how you can use predicates to customize the behavior of a map. It also implies that the key could potentially be of any type, and that the programmer can supply a predicate that defines the behavior of the map for that type. Note that the predicate was a `struct` that implemented `operator()`. It could have also been a `class`. Such objects that double as functions are called Function objects or functors. This topic is addressed in further detail in Lesson 21, "Understanding Function Objects."

NOTE

The `std::map` is well suited for storing key-value pairs where you can look up a value given a key. map does guarantee better performance than an STL `vector` or `list` when it comes to searching. Yet, it does slow down when the number of elements increases. The operational performance of a map is said to be logarithmic in nature—that is, proportional to the LOG of the number of elements placed in the map.

In simple words, a logarithmic complexity means that a container such as `std::map` or `std::set` is twice as slow for 10,000 elements as it is for 100.

An unsorted `vector` presents linear complexity when it comes to search, which means that it is a 100 times slower for 10,000 elements as it is for 100.

So, while logarithmic complexity already looks quite good, one should remember that insertions in a map (or `multimap` or `set` or `multiset`) get slower, too, as these containers sort on insertion. Thus, the search for faster containers continues, and mathematicians and programmers alike seek the holy grail of containers featuring constant-time insertions and searches. The Hash Table is one such container that promises constant-time insertions and near-constant-time searches (in most cases), given a key, independent of the size of the container.

20

C++11

STL's Hash Table–Based Key-Value Container
std::unordered_map

Starting with C++11, the STL supports a hash map in the form of class `std::unordered_map`. To use this template container class include

```
#include<unordered_map>
```

The `unordered_map` promises average constant-time insertion and the removal and lookup of arbitrary elements in the container.

How Hash Tables Work

Although it is not within the scope of this book to discuss this topic in detail (for it has been the subject of one PhD thesis too many), let's just try to grasp the basics of what makes hash tables work.

A hash table can be viewed as a collection of key-value pairs, where given a key, the table can find a value. The difference between the hash table and a simple map is that a hash table stores key-value pairs in buckets, each bucket having an index that defines its relative position in the table (akin to an array). This index is decided by a hash-function that uses the key as input:

```
Index = HashFunction(Key, TableSize);
```

When performing a `find()` given a key, `HashFunction()` is used once again to determine the position of the element and the table returns the value at the position, like an array would return an element stored within it. In cases where `HashFunction()` is not optimally programmed, more than one element would have the same Index, landing in the same bucket—that internally would be a list of elements. In such cases, called *collisions*, a search would be slower and not a constant any more.

Using C++11 Hash Tables: `unordered_map` and `unordered_multimap`

From a usage point of view, these two containers are not too different from `std::map` and `std::multimap`, respectively. They can perform instantiation, insertion, and find and follow similar patterns:

```cpp
// instantiate unordered_map of int to string:
unordered_map<int, string> umapIntToString;

// insert()
umapIntToString.insert(make_pair(1000, "Thousand"));

// find():
auto iPairThousand = umapIntToString.find(1000);
cout << iPairThousand->first << " —> " << iPairThousand->second << endl;

// find value using array semantics:
cout << "umapIntToString[1000] = " << umapIntToString[1000] << endl;
```

Yet, one very important feature of a `unordered_map` is the availability of a hash function that is responsible for deciding the sorting order:

```cpp
unordered_map<int, string>::hasher HFn =
        umapIntToString.hash_function();
```

You can view the priority assigned to a key by invoking the hash function for a key:

```
size_t HashingValue1000 = HFn(1000);
```

As an unordered_map stores key-value pairs in buckets, it does an automatic load balancing when the number of elements in the map reach or tend to reach the number of buckets in the same:

```
cout << "Load factor: " << umapIntToString.load_factor() << endl;
cout << "Max load factor = " << umapIntToString.max_load_factor() << endl;
cout << "Max bucket count = " << umapIntToString.max_bucket_count() << endl;
```

load_factor() is an indicator of the extent to which buckets in the unordered_map have been filled. When load_factor() exceeds max_load_factor() due to an insertion, the map reorganizes itself to increase the number of available buckets and rebuilds the hash table, as demonstrated by Listing 20.6.

TIP

> std::unordered_multimap is similar to unordered_map except that it supports multiple pairs with the same key.
>
> The usage of std::unordered_multimap is quite similar to std::multimap, with certain hash table–specific functions, as shown in Listing 20.6.

LISTING 20.6 Instantiating STL Hash Table Implementation unordered_map, Using insert(), find(), size(), max_bucket_count(), load_factor(), and max_load_factor()

```
0: #include<iostream>
1: #include<string>
2: #include<unordered_map>
3: using namespace std;
4:
5: template <typename T1, typename T2>
6: void DisplayUnorderedMap(unordered_map<T1, T2>& Input)
7: {
8:    cout << "Number of pairs, size(): " << Input.size() << endl;
9:    cout << "Max bucket count = " << Input.max_bucket_count() << endl;
10:   cout << "Load factor: " << Input.load_factor() << endl;
11:   cout << "Max load factor = " << Input.max_load_factor() << endl;
12:   cout << "Unordered Map contains: " << endl;
13:
14:   for(auto iElement = Input.cbegin() // auto, cbegin: c++11
15:      ; iElement != Input.cend()  // cend() is new in C++11
16:      ; ++ iElement )
```

20

LISTING 20.6 Continued

```
17:          cout<< iElement->first<< " -> "<< iElement->second<< endl;
18: }
19:
20: int main()
21: {
22:    unordered_map<int, string> umapIntToString;
23:    umapIntToString.insert(make_pair(1, "One"));
24:    umapIntToString.insert(make_pair(45, "Forty Five"));
25:    umapIntToString.insert(make_pair(1001, "Thousand One"));
26:    umapIntToString.insert(make_pair(-2, "Minus Two"));
27:    umapIntToString.insert(make_pair(-1000, "Minus One Thousand"));
28:    umapIntToString.insert(make_pair(100, "One Hundred"));
29:    umapIntToString.insert(make_pair(12, "Twelve"));
30:    umapIntToString.insert(make_pair(-100, "Minus One Hundred"));
31:
32:    DisplayUnorderedMap<int, string>(umapIntToString);
33:
34:    cout << "Inserting one more element" << endl;
35:    umapIntToString.insert(make_pair(300, "Three Hundred"));
36:    DisplayUnorderedMap<int, string>(umapIntToString);
37:
38:    cout << "Enter key to find for: ";
39:    int Key = 0;
40:    cin >> Key;
41:
42:    auto iElementFound = umapIntToString.find(Key);
43:    if (iElementFound != umapIntToString.end())
44:    {
45:       cout << "Found! Key " << iElementFound->first << " points to value ";
46:       cout << iElementFound->second << endl;
47:    }
48:    else
49:       cout << "Key has no corresponding value in unordered map!" << endl;
50:
51:    return 0;
52: }
```

Output ▼

```
Number of pairs, size(): 8
Max bucket count = 8
Load factor: 1
Max load factor = 1
Unordered Map contains:
-1000 -> Minus One Thousand
```

```
1001 -> Thousand One
1 -> One
-100 -> Minus One Hundred
45 -> Forty Five
-2 -> Minus Two
12 -> Twelve
100 -> One Hundred
Inserting one more element
Number of pairs, size(): 9
Max bucket count = 64
Load factor: 0.140625
Max load factor = 1
Unordered Map contains:
1 -> One
-1000 -> Minus One Thousand
1001 -> Thousand One
-100 -> Minus One Hundred
45 -> Forty Five
-2 -> Minus Two
300 -> Three Hundred
12 -> Twelve
100 -> One Hundred
100 -> One Hundred
Enter key to find for: 300
Found! Key 300 points to value Three Hundred
```

Analysis ▼

Observe the output and note how unordered_map that starts with an initial bucket count of eight, populated with eight pairs, resizes itself when a ninth pair has been inserted. This is when the bucket count is increased to 64. Note the usage of methods max_bucket_count(), load_factor(), and max_load_factor() in Lines 9–11. Apart from these, note that the rest of code really doesn't distinguish heavily compared to a std::map. This includes the usage of find() in Line 42, which returns an iterator as with a std::map that needs to be checked against end() to confirm success of the operation.

20

CAUTION

Don't rely on the order of elements in an unordered_map (hence the name) irrespective of the key. The order of an element relative to other elements in a map depends on many factors, including its key, order of insertion, and number of buckets to name a few.

These containers are optimized for search performance and are not for you to rely on the order of elements when you iterate through them.

<table>
<tr><td>NOTE</td><td>

`std::unordered_map` supplies insertions and searches (in event of no collisions) that are almost constant and independent of the number of elements contained. This, however, doesn't necessarily make the `std::unordered_map` superior to the `std::map` that provides logarithmic complexity in all situations. The constant could be a lot longer, making the former slow in cases where the number of elements contained is not too high.

It is important to base one's decision on the type of container after performing certain benchmark tests that simulate usage in a real scenario.

</td></tr>
</table>

DO	DON'T
DO use a map in those situations where you need a key-value pair where keys are unique.	**DON'T** forget that `multimap::count(Key)` can tell you the number of pairs indexed using `Key` available in the container.
DO use a multimap in those situations where you need a key-value pair where keys can repeat (for example, a telephone directory).	**DON'T** forget to check the result of a `find()` operation by comparing it against the `end()` of a container.
DO remember that both `map` and `multimap`, like other STL containers, feature member method `size()` that tells you the number of pairs they contain.	
DO use an `unordered_map` or `unordered_multimap` when constant-time insertions and searches are absolutely essential (typically when the number of elements is very high).	

Summary

In this lesson, you learned about using the STL `map` and `multimap`, their significant member functions, and their characteristics. You also learned that these containers have a logarithmic complexity and that STL supplies your hash table containers in the form of `unordered_map` and `unordered_multimap`. These feature performance in `insert()` and `find()` operations that is independent of container size. You also learned the importance of being able to customize the sort criterion using a predicate, as demonstrated in the Directory application of Listing 20.5.

Q&A

Q **How would I declare a `map` of integers to be sorted or stored in order of descending magnitude?**

A `map <int>` defines a map of integers. This takes the default sort predicate `std::less <T>` to sort items in order of ascending magnitude and can also be expressed as `map <int, less <int> >`. To sort in order of descending magnitude, define the map as `map <int, greater <int> >`.

Q **What would happen if in a `map` of strings I inserted the string `"Jack"` twice?**

A A map is not meant to be used to insert non-unique values. So, the implementation of the `std::map` class does not allow insertion of the second value.

Q **In the preceding example, what would I change if I wanted to have two instances of `"Jack"`?**

A By design a map holds only unique values. You need to change your selection of container to a `multimap`.

Q **What `multimap` member function returns the count of items of a particular value in the container?**

A `count (value)` is the function of interest.

Q **I have found an element in the `map` using the `find()` function and have an iterator pointing to it. Would I use this iterator to change the value being pointed to?**

A No. Some STL implementations might allow the user to change the value of an element inside a map via an iterator returned by `find()`. This, however, is not the correct thing to do. An iterator to an element in the map should be used as a const iterator—even when your implementation of STL has not enforced it as such.

Q **I am using an older compiler that doesn't support keyword `auto`. How should I declare a variable that holds the return value of a `map::find()`?**

A An iterator is always defined using this syntax:

```
container<Type>::iterator variableName;
```

So the iterator declaration for a map of integers would be the following:

```
std::map<int>::iterator iPairFound = mapIntegers.find(1000);
if (iPairFound != mapIntegers.end())
    ;// Do Something
```

20

Workshop

The Workshop contains quiz questions to help solidify your understanding of the material covered and exercises to provide you with experience in using what you've learned. Try to answer the quiz and exercise questions before checking the answers in Appendix D, and be certain you understand the answers before going to the next lesson.

Quiz

1. You declare a map of integers as map <int>. What function supplies the sort criteria?

2. Where would you find duplicate elements in a multimap?

3. What map or multimap function supplies the number of elements in the container?

4. Where would you find duplicate elements in a map?

Exercises

1. You need to write an application that works as a telephone directory where the names of the people need not be unique. What container would you choose? Write a definition of the container.

2. The following is a map template definition in your dictionary application:

```
map <wordProperty, string, fPredicate> mapWordDefinition;
```

where word is the structure:

```
struct wordProperty
{
    string strWord;
    bool bIsFromLatin;
};
```

Define the binary predicate fPredicate that helps the map sort a key of type wordProperty according to the string attribute it contains.

3. Demonstrate via a simple program that a map cannot accept duplicate entries whereas a multimap can.

LESSON 21
Understanding Function Objects

Function objects or *functors* might sound exotic or intimidating, but they are entities of C++ that you have probably seen, if not also used, without having realized it. In this lesson, you learn

- The concept of function objects
- The usage of function objects as predicates
- How unary and binary predicates are implemented using function objects

The Concept of Function Objects and Predicates

On a conceptual level, function objects are objects that work as functions. On an implementation level, however, function objects are objects of a class that implement `operator()`. Although functions and function-pointers can also be classified as function objects, it is the capability of an object of a class that implements `operator()` to carry `state` (that is, values in member attributes of the class) that makes it useful with Standard Template Library (STL) algorithms.

Function objects as typically used by a C++ programmer working with STL are classifiable into the following types:

- **Unary function**—A function called with one argument; for example, `f(x)`. When a unary function returns a `bool`, it is called a *predicate*.

- **Binary function**—A function called with two arguments; for example, `f(x, y)`. A binary function that returns a `bool` is called a *binary predicate*.

Function objects that return a `boolean` type naturally are used in algorithms that need decision-making. A function object that combines two function objects is called an *adaptive function object*.

Typical Applications of Function Objects

It is possible to explain function objects over pages and pages of theoretical explanations. It is also possible to understand how they look and work via tiny sample applications. Let's take the practical approach and dive straight into the world of C++ programming with function objects or functors!

Unary Functions

Functions that operate on a single parameter are unary functions. A unary function can do something very simple—for example, display an element on the screen. This can be programmed as the following:

```
// A unary function
template <typename elementType>
void FuncDisplayElement (const elementType & element)
{
    cout << element << ' ';
};
```

The function `FuncDisplayElement` accepts one parameter of templatized type `elementType` that it displays using console output statement `std::cout`. The same function can also have another representation in which the implementation of the function is actually contained by the `operator()` of a class or a struct:

```
// Struct that can behave as a unary function
template <typename elementType>
struct DisplayElement
{
    void operator () (const elementType& element) const
    {
        cout << element << ' ';
    }
};
```

TIP
> Note that `DisplayElement` is a struct. If it were a class, `operator()` would need to be given a public access modifier. A struct is akin to a class where members are public by default.

Either of these implementations can be used with the STL algorithm `for_each` to print the contents of a collection to the screen, an element at a time, as shown in Listing 21.1.

LISTING 21.1   Displaying the Contents of a Collection on the Screen Using a Unary Function

```
0: #include <algorithm>
1: #include <iostream>
2: #include <vector>
3: #include <list>
4:
5: using namespace std;
6:
7: // struct that behaves as a unary function
8: template <typename elementType>
9: struct DisplayElement
10: {
11:     void operator () (const elementType& element) const
12:     {
13:         cout << element << ' ';
14:     }
15: };
16:
17: int main ()
18: {
19:     vector <int> vecIntegers;
```

21

LISTING 21.1 Continued

```
20:
21:     for (int nCount = 0; nCount < 10; ++ nCount)
22:         vecIntegers.push_back (nCount);
23:
24:     list <char> listChars;
25:
26:     for (char nChar = 'a'; nChar < 'k'; ++nChar)
27:         listChars.push_back (nChar);
28:
29:     cout << "Displaying the vector of integers: " << endl;
30:
31:     // Display the array of integers
32:     for_each ( vecIntegers.begin ()      // Start of range
33:           , vecIntegers.end ()           // End of range
34:           , DisplayElement <int> () ); // Unary function object
35:
36:     cout << endl << endl;
37:     cout << "Displaying the list of characters: " << endl;
38:
39:     // Display the list of characters
40:     for_each ( listChars.begin ()        // Start of range
41:           , listChars.end ()             // End of range
42:           , DisplayElement <char> () );// Unary function object
43:
44:     return 0;
45: }
```

Output ▼

```
Displaying the vector of integers:
0 1 2 3 4 5 6 7 8 9

Displaying the list of characters:
a b c d e f g h i j
```

Analysis ▼

Lines 8–15 contain the function object DisplayElement, which implements operator(). The usage of this function object is seen with STL algorithm std::for_each in Lines 32–34. for_each accepts three parameters: The first is the starting point of the range, the second is the end of the range, and the third parameter is the function that is called for every element in the specified range. In other words, that code invokes DisplayElement::operator() for every element in the vector vecIntegers. Note that instead of using the struct DisplayElement, you could have also used FuncDisplayElement to the same effect. Lines 40–42 demonstrate the same functionality with a list of characters.

C++11 introduces lambda expressions that are unnamed function objects.

A lambda expression version of struct DisplayElement<T> from Listing 21.1 compacts the entire code, including the definition of the struct and its usage, in three lines within main(), replacing Lines 32–34:

```
// Display the array of integers using lambda expression
for_each ( vecIntegers.begin ()      // Start of range
    , vecIntegers.end ()            // End of range
    , [](int& Element) {cout << element << ' '; } ); //
    Lambda expression
```

Thus, lambdas are a fantastic improvement to C++, and you should not miss learning them in Lesson 22, "C++11 Lambda Expressions." Listing 22.1 demonstrates using lambda functions in a for_each to display the contents of a container, instead of the function object as seen in Listing 21.1.

The real advantage of using a function object implemented in a struct becomes apparent when you are able to use the object of the struct to store information. This is something FuncDisplayElement cannot do the way a struct can because a struct can have member attributes other than the operator(). A slightly modified version that makes use of member attributes is the following:

```
template <typename elementType>
struct DisplayElementKeepCount
{
    int Count;

    DisplayElementKeepCount ()   // constructor
    {
        Count = 0;
    }

    void operator () (const elementType& element)
    {
        ++ Count;
        cout << element << ' ';
    }
};
```

In the preceding snippet, DisplayElementKeepCount is a slight modification over the previous version. operator() is not a const member function anymore as it increments (hence, changes) member Count to keep a count of the number of times it was called to

21

display data. This count is made available via the public member attribute `Count`. The advantage of using such function objects that can also store `state` is shown in Listing 21.2.

LISTING 21.2 Use a Function Object to Hold State

```
0: #include<algorithm>
1: #include<iostream>
2: #include<vector>
3: using namespace std;
4:
5: template<typename elementType>
6: struct DisplayElementKeepCount
7: {
8:     int Count;
9:
10:    // Constructor
11:    DisplayElementKeepCount() : Count(0) {}
12:
13:    // Display the element, hold count!
14:    void operator()(const elementType& element)
15:    {
16:       ++ Count;
17:       cout << element<< ' ';
18:    }
19: };
20:
21: int main()
22: {
23:    vector<int> vecIntegers;
24:    for(int nCount = 0; nCount< 10; ++ nCount)
25:       vecIntegers.push_back(nCount);
26:
27:    cout << "Displaying the vector of integers: "<< endl;
28:
29:    // Display the array of integers
30:    DisplayElementKeepCount<int> Result;
31:    Result = for_each( vecIntegers.begin()   // Start of range
32:                     , vecIntegers.end()     // End of range
33:                     , DisplayElementKeepCount<int>() );// function object
34:
35:    cout << endl<< endl;
36:
37:    // Use the state stores in the return value of for_each!
38:    cout << "'" << Result.Count << "' elements were displayed!"<< endl;
39:
40:    return 0;
41: }
```

Output ▼

```
Displaying the vector of integers:
0 1 2 3 4 5 6 7 8 9

'10' elements were displayed!
```

Analysis ▼

The biggest difference between this sample and the one in Listing 21.1 is the usage of
DisplayElementKeepCount() as the return value of for_each(). operator() implemented in struct DisplayElementKeepCount is invoked by algorithm for_each()
for every element in the container. It displays the element and increments the internal
counter stored in Count. After for_each() is done, you use the object in Line 38 to
display the number of times elements were displayed. Note that a regular function used
in this scenario instead of the function implemented in a struct would not be able to
supply this feature in such a direct way.

Unary Predicate

A unary function that returns a bool is a predicate. Such functions help make decisions
for STL algorithms. Listing 21.3 is a sample predicate that determines whether an input
element is a multiple of an initial value.

LISTING 21.3 A Unary Predicate That Determines Whether a Number Is a Multiple of
Another

```
0: // A structure as a unary predicate
1: template <typename numberType>
2: struct IsMultiple
3: {
4:    numberType Divisor;
5:
6:    IsMultiple (const numberType& divisor)
7:    {
8:       Divisor = divisor;
9:    }
10:
11:    bool operator () (const numberType& element) const
12:    {
13:       // Check if the divisor is a multiple of the divisor
14:       return ((element % Divisor) == 0);
15:    }
16: };
```

21

Analysis ▼

Here the `operator()` returns bool and can work as a unary predicate. The structure has a constructor and is initialized to the value of the divisor. This value stored in the object is then used to determine whether the elements sent for comparison are divisible by it, as you can see in the implementation of `operator()`, using the math operation modulus `%` that returns the remainder of a division operation. The predicate compares that remainder to zero to determine whether the number is a multiple.

In Listing 21.4, we make use of the predicate as seen previously in Listing 21.3 to determine whether numbers in a collection are multiples of a divisor input by the user.

LISTING 21.4   Unary Predicate IsMultiple Used with `std::find_if()` to Find an Element in a `vector` That Is a Multiple of a User-Supplied Divisor

```
0: #include <algorithm>
1: #include <vector>
2: #include <iostream>
3: using namespace std;
4: // Insert struct IsMultiple from Listing 21.3 here
5: int main ()
6: {
7:    vector <int> vecIntegers;
8:    cout << "The vector contains the following sample values: ";
9:
10:    // Insert sample values: 25 - 31
11:    for (int nCount = 25; nCount < 32; ++ nCount)
12:    {
13:       vecIntegers.push_back (nCount);
14:       cout << nCount << ' ';
15:    }
16:    cout << endl << "Enter divisor (> 0): ";
17:    int Divisor = 2;
18:    cin >> Divisor;
19:
20:    // Find the first element that is a multiple of 4 in the collection
21:    auto iElement = find_if ( vecIntegers.begin ()
22:                            , vecIntegers.end ()
23:                            , IsMultiple<int>(Divisor) );
24:
25:    if (iElement != vecIntegers.end ())
26:    {
27:       cout << "First element in vector divisible by " << Divisor;
28:       cout << ": " << *iElement << endl;
29:    }
30:
31:    return 0;
32: }
```

Output ▼

```
The vector contains the following sample values: 25 26 27 28 29 30 31
The first element in the vector that is divisible by 4 is: 28
```

Analysis ▼

The sample starts with a sample container that is a vector of integers. In Lines 11–15, it inserts sample numbers into this container. The usage of the unary predicate is in find_if() as shown in Line 23. In here, the function object IsMultiple() is initialized to a divisor value supplied by the user and stored in variable Divisor. find_if() works by invoking the unary predicate IsMultiple::operator() for every element in the specified range. When the operator() returns true for an element (which happens when that element is divided by 4 and does not produce a remainder), find_if() returns an iterator iElement to that element. The result of the find_if() operation is compared against the end() of the container to verify that an element was found, as shown in Line 25, and the iterator iElement is then used to display the value, as shown in Line 28.

TIP	To see how using lambda expressions compact the program shown in Listing 21.4, take a look at Listing 22.3 in Lesson 22.

Unary predicates find application in a lot of STL algorithms such as std::partition that can partition a range using the predicate, stable_partition that does the same while keeping relative order of the elements partitioned, find functions such as std::find_if(), and functions that help erase elements such as std::remove_if() that erases elements in a range that satisfy the predicate.

Binary Functions

Functions of type f(x, y) are particularly useful when they return a value based on the input supplied. Such binary functions can be used for a host of arithmetic activity that involves two operands, such as addition, multiplication, subtraction, and so on. A sample binary function that returns the multiple of input arguments can be written as the following:

```
template <typename elementType>
class Multiply
{
public:
    elementType operator () (const elementType& elem1,
                             const elementType& elem2)
```

21

```
        {
            return (elem1 * elem2);
        }
};
```

The implementation of interest is again in `operator()` that accepts two arguments and returns their multiple. Such binary functions are used in algorithms such as `std::transform` where you can use it to multiply the contents of two containers. Listing 21.5 demonstrates the usage of such binary functions in `std::transform`.

LISTING 21.5   Using a Binary Function to Multiply Two Ranges

```
 0: #include <vector>
 1: #include <iostream>
 2: #include <algorithm>
 3:
 4: template <typename elementType>
 5: class Multiply
 6: {
 7: public:
 8:     elementType operator () (const elementType& elem1,
 9:         const elementType& elem2)
10:     {
11:         return (elem1 * elem2);
12:     }
13: };
14:
15: int main ()
16: {
17:     using namespace std;
18:
19:     // Create two sample vector of integers with 10 elements each
20:     vector <int> vecMultiplicand, vecMultiplier;
21:
22:     // Insert sample values 0 to 9
23:     for (int nCount1 = 0; nCount1 < 10; ++ nCount1)
24:         vecMultiplicand.push_back (nCount1);
25:
26:     // Insert sample values 100 to 109
27:     for (int nCount2 = 100; nCount2 < 110; ++ nCount2)
28:         vecMultiplier.push_back (nCount2);
29:
30:     // A third container that holds the result of multiplication
31:     vector <int> vecResult;
32:
33:     // Make space for the result of the multiplication
34:     vecResult.resize (10);
35:     transform ( vecMultiplicand.begin (), // range of multiplicands
```

```
36:                   vecMultiplicand.end (), // end of range
37:                   vecMultiplier.begin (),  // multiplier values
38:                   vecResult.begin (), // range that holds result
39:                   Multiply <int> () );    // the function that multiplies
40:
41:     cout << "The contents of the first vector are: " << endl;
42:     for (size_t nIndex1 = 0; nIndex1 < vecMultiplicand.size (); ++ nIndex1)
43:         cout << vecMultiplicand [nIndex1] << ' ';
44:     cout << endl;
45:
46:     cout << "The contents of the second vector are: " << endl;
47:     for (size_t nIndex2 = 0; nIndex2 < vecMultiplier.size (); ++nIndex2)
48:         cout << vecMultiplier [nIndex2] << ' ';
49:     cout << endl << endl;
50:
51:     cout << "The result of the multiplication is: " << endl;
52:     for (size_t nIndex = 0; nIndex < vecResult.size (); ++ nIndex)
53:         cout << vecResult [nIndex] << ' ';
54:
55:     return 0;
56: }
```

Output ▼

```
The contents of the first vector are:
0 1 2 3 4 5 6 7 8 9
The contents of the second vector are:
100 101 102 103 104 105 106 107 108 109

The result of the multiplication held in the third vector is:
0 101 204 309 416 525 636 749 864 981
```

Analysis ▼

Lines 5–13 contain the class Multiply, as shown in the preceeding code snippet. In this sample, you use the algorithm std::transform to multiple the content of two ranges and store in a third. In this case, the ranges in question are held in std::vector as vecMultiplicand, vecMultiplier, and vecResult. In other words, you use std::transform in Lines 35–39 to multiply every element in vecMultiplicand by its corresponding element in vecMultiplier and store the result of the multiplication in vecResult. The multiplication itself is done by the binary function CMultiple::operator () that is invoked for every element in the vectors that make the source and destination ranges. The return value of the operator() is held in vecResult.

21

This sample thus demonstrates the application of binary functions in performing arithmetic operations on elements in STL containers.

Binary Predicate

A function that accepts two arguments and returns a `bool` is a binary predicate. Such functions find application in STL functions such as `std::sort()`. Listing 21.6 demonstrates the usage of a binary predicate that compares two strings after reducing them both to lowercase. Such a predicate can be used in performing a case-insensitive sort on a `vector` of `string`, for instance.

LISTING 21.6   A Binary Predicate for Case-Insensitive String Sort

```
0: #include <algorithm>
1: #include <string>
2: using namespace std;
3:
4: class CompareStringNoCase
5: {
6: public:
7:    bool operator () (const string& str1, const string& str2) const
8:    {
9:       string str1LowerCase;
10:
11:       // Assign space
12:       str1LowerCase.resize (str1.size ());
13:
14:       // Convert every character to the lower case
15:       transform (str1.begin (), str1.end (), str1LowerCase.begin (),
16:                  tolower);
17:
18:       string str2LowerCase;
19:       str2LowerCase.resize (str2.size ());
20:       transform (str2.begin (), str2.end (), str2LowerCase.begin (),
21:                  tolower);
22:
23:       return (str1LowerCase < str2LowerCase);
24:    }
25: };
```

Analysis ▼

The binary predicate implemented in `operator()` first brings the input strings down to lowercase using algorithm `std::transform()` as shown in Lines 15 and 20 before using the string's comparison operator, `operator <`, to return the result of comparison.

You can use this binary-predicate with algorithm std::sort() to sort a dynamic array contained in a vector of string as demonstrated by Listing 21.7.

LISTING 21.7 Using Function Object class CompareStringNoCase to Perform a Case-Insensitive Sort on a vector of string

```
0: // Insert class CompareStringNoCase from Listing 21.6 here
1: #include <vector>
2: #include <iostream>
3:
4: template <typename T>
5: void DisplayContents (const T& Input)
6: {
7:    for(auto iElement = Input.cbegin() // auto, cbegin and cend: c++11
8:       ; iElement != Input.cend ()
9:       ; ++ iElement )
10:       cout << *iElement << endl;
11: }
12:
13: int main ()
14: {
15:    // Define a vector of string to hold names
16:    vector <string> vecNames;
17:
18:    // Insert some sample names in to the vector
19:    vecNames.push_back ("jim");
20:    vecNames.push_back ("Jack");
21:    vecNames.push_back ("Sam");
22:    vecNames.push_back ("Anna");
23:
24:    cout << "The names in vector in order of insertion: " << endl;
25:    DisplayContents(vecNames);
26:
27:    cout << "Names after sorting using default std::less<>: " << endl;
28:    sort(vecNames.begin(), vecNames.end());
29:    DisplayContents(vecNames);
30:
31:    cout << "Names after sorting using predicate that ignores case:" << endl;
32:    sort(vecNames.begin(), vecNames.end(), CompareStringNoCase());
33:    DisplayContents(vecNames);
34:
35:    return 0;
36: }
```

21

Output ▼

```
The names in vector in order of insertion:
jim
Jack
```

```
Sam
Anna
Names after sorting using default std::less<>:
Anna
Jack
Sam
jim
Names after sorting using predicate that ignores case:
Anna
Jack
jim
Sam
```

Analysis ▼

Output displays the contents of the vector in three stages. The first displays contents in order of insertion. The second after a `sort()` at Line 28 reorders using default sort predicate `less<T>`, the output demonstrates that `jim` is not placed after `Jack` because this is a case-sensitive sort via `string::operator<`. The last version uses the sort predicate `class CompareStringNoCase<>` in Line 32 (implemented in Listing 21.6) that ensures that `jim` comes after `Jack` notwithstanding the difference in case.

Binary predicates are required in a variety of STL algorithms. For example, `std::unique()` that erases duplicate neighboring elements, `std::sort()` that sorts, `std::stable_sort()` that sorts while maintaining relative order, and `std::transform()` that can perform an operation on two ranges are some of the STL algorithms that need a binary predicate.

Summary

In this lesson, you gained an insight into the world of functors (or function objects). You learned how function objects are more useful when implemented in a structure or a class than those that are simple functions because the former can also be used to hold state-related information. You got an insight into predicates, which are a special class of function objects, and saw some practical examples that display their utility.

Q&A

Q A predicate is a special category of a function object. What makes it special?

A Predicates always return `boolean`.

Q What kind of a function object should I use in a call to a function such as `remove_if`?

A You should use a unary predicate that would take the value to be processed as the initial state via the constructor.

Q What kind of a function object should I use for a `map`?

A You should use a binary predicate.

Q Is it possible that a simple function with no return value can be used as a predicate?

A Yes. A function with no return values can still do something useful. For example, it can display input data.

Workshop

The Workshop provides quiz questions to help you solidify your understanding of the material covered and exercises to provide you with experience in using what you've learned. Try to answer the quiz and exercise questions before checking the answers in Appendix D.

Quiz

1. What is the term used for a unary function that returns a `bool` result?

2. What would be the utility of a function object that neither modifies data nor returns `bool`? Can you explain using an example?

3. What is the definition of the term *function objects*?

Exercises

1. Write a unary function that can be used with `std::for_each` to display the double of the input parameter.

2. Extend this predicate to indicate the number of times it was used.

3. Write a binary predicate that helps sort in ascending order.

21

LESSON 22
C++11 Lambda Expressions

Lambda expressions are a compact way to define and construct function objects without a name. These expressions are new to C++11. In this lesson, you find out

- How to program a lambda expression

- How to use lambda expressions as predicates

- How to program lambda expressions that can hold and manipulate a state

What Is a Lambda Expression?

A lambda expression can be visualized as a compact version of an unnamed `struct` (or class) with a public `operator()`. In that sense, a lambda expression is a function object like those in Lesson 21, "Understanding Function Objects." Before jumping into analyzing the programming of lambda functions, take a function object from Listing 21.1 (from Lesson 21) as an example:

```
// struct that behaves as a unary function
template <typename elementType>
struct DisplayElement
{
    void operator () (const elementType& element) const
    {
        cout << element << ' ';
    }
};
```

This function object prints an element to the screen and is typically used in algorithms such as `std::for_each`:

```
// Display the array of integers
for_each ( vecIntegers.begin ()      // Start of range
    , vecIntegers.end ()         // End of range
    , DisplayElement <int> () ); // Unary function object
```

A lambda expression compacts the entire code including the definition of the function object in to three lines:

```
// Display the array of integers using lambda expression
for_each ( vecIntegers.begin ()      // Start of range
    , vecIntegers.end ()         // End of range
    , [](int& Element) {cout << element << ' '; } ); // Lambda expression
```

When the compiler sees the lambda expression, in this case

```
[](int Element) {cout << element << ' '; }
```

it automatically expands this expression into a representation that is similar to `struct` `DisplayElement<int>`:

```
struct NoName
{
    void operator () (const int& element) const
    {
        cout << element << ' ';
    }
};
```

How to Define a Lambda Expression

The definition of a lambda expression has to start with square brackets []. These brackets essentially tell the compiler that the lambda expression has started. They are followed by the parameter list, which is the same as the parameter list you would supply your implementation of operator() if you were not using a lambda expression.

Lambda Expression for a Unary Function

The lambda version of a unary operator(Type) that takes one parameter would be the following:

```
[](Type paramName) {  // lambda expression code here;  }
```

Note that you can pass the parameter by reference if you so wish:

```
[](Type& paramName) {  // lambda expression code here;  }
```

Use Listing 22.1 to study the usage of a lambda function in displaying the contents of a Standard Template Library (STL) container using algorithm for_each.

LISTING 22.1   Displaying Elements in a Container via Algorithm for_each() That Is Invoked with a Lambda Expression Instead of a Function Object

```
0: #include <algorithm>
1: #include <iostream>
2: #include <vector>
3: #include <list>
4:
5: using namespace std;
6:
7: int main ()
8: {
9:    vector <int> vecIntegers;
10:
11:    for (int nCount = 0; nCount < 10; ++ nCount)
12:       vecIntegers.push_back (nCount);
13:
14:    list <char> listChars;
15:    for (char nChar = 'a'; nChar < 'k'; ++nChar)
16:       listChars.push_back (nChar);
17:
18:    cout << "Displaying vector of integers using a lambda: " << endl;
19:
20:    // Display the array of integers
21:    for_each ( vecIntegers.begin ()    // Start of range
22:             , vecIntegers.end ()       // End of range
23:             , [](int& element) {cout << element << ' '; } ); // lambda
```

E

LISTING 22.1   Continued

```
24:
25:      cout << endl << endl;
26:      cout << "Displaying list of characters using a lambda: " << endl;
27:
28:      // Display the list of characters
29:      for_each ( listChars.begin ()         // Start of range
30:                 , listChars.end ()          // End of range
31:                 , [](char& element) {cout << element << ' '; } ); // lambda
32:
33:      cout << endl;
34:
35:      return 0;
36: }
```

Output ▼

```
Displaying vector of integers using a lambda:
0 1 2 3 4 5 6 7 8 9

Displaying list of characters using a lambda:
a b c d e f g h i j
```

Analysis ▼

There are two lambda expressions of interest in Lines 23 and 31. They are quite similar, save for the type of the input parameter, as they have been customized to the nature of the elements within the two containers. The first takes one parameter that is an `int`, as it is used to print one element at a time from a `vector` of integers, whereas the second accepts a `char`, as it is used to display elements of type `char` stored in a `std::list`.

NOTE	It is no coincidence that the output produced by Listing 22.1 is the same as that in Listing 21.1. In fact, this program is a lambda version of the one you studied in Listing 21.1 that used function object `DisplayElement<T>`.
	Comparing the two, you realize how lambda functions have the potential to make C++ code simpler and more compact.

Lambda Expression for a Unary Predicate

A predicate helps make decisions. A unary predicate is a unary expression that returns a bool, conveying true or false. Lambda expressions can return values, too. For example, the following is a lambda expression that returns true for even numbers:

```
[](int& Num) {return ((Num % 2) == 0); }
```

The nature of the return value in this case tells the compiler that the lambda expression returns a bool.

You can use a lambda expression that is a unary predicate in algorithms, such as std::find_if(), to find even numbers in a collection. See Listing 22.2 for an example.

LISTING 22.2   Find an Even Number in a Collection Using a Lambda Expression for a Unary Predicate and Algorithm std::find_if()

```
 0: #include<algorithm>
 1: #include<vector>
 2: #include<iostream>
 3: using namespace std;
 4:
 5: int main()
 6: {
 7:    vector<int> vecNums;
 8:    vecNums.push_back(25);
 9:    vecNums.push_back(101);
10:    vecNums.push_back(2011);
11:    vecNums.push_back(-50);
12:
13:    auto iEvenNum = find_if( vecNums.cbegin()
14:                           , vecNums.cend()  // range to find in
15:                           , [](const int& Num){return ((Num % 2) == 0); } );
16:
17:    if (iEvenNum != vecNums.cend())
18:       cout << "Even number in collection is: " << *iEvenNum << endl;
19:
20:    return 0;
21: }
```

Output ▼

```
Even number in collection is: -50
```

E

Analysis ▼

The lambda function that works as a unary predicate is shown in Line 15. Algorithm `find_if()` invokes the unary predicate for every element in the range. When the predicate returns `true`, `find_if()` reports a find by returning an iterator to that element. The predicate in this case is the lambda expression that returns `true` when `find_if()` invokes it with an integer that is even (that is, the result of modulus operation with 2 is zero).

NOTE	Listing 22.2 not only demonstrates a lambda expression as a unary predicate, but also the use of `const` within a lambda expression.
	Remember to use `const` for input parameters, especially when they're a reference.

Lambda Expression with State via Capture Lists [. . .]

In Listing 22.2, you created a unary predicate that returned true if an integer was divisible by 2—that is, the integer is an even number. What if you want a more generic function that returns true when the number is divisible by a divisor of the user's choosing? You need to maintain that "state"—the divisor—in the expression:

```
int Divisor = 2; // initial value
...
auto iElement = find_if ( begin of a range
                        , end of a range
        , [Divisor](int dividend){return (dividend % Divisor) == 0; } );
```

A list of arguments transferred as state variables [. . .] is also called the lambda's capture list.

NOTE	Such a lambda expression is a one-line equivalent of the 16 lines of code seen in Listing 21.3 that defines unary predicate `struct IsMultiple<>`.
	Thus, lambdas improve the programming efficiency in C++11 by leaps and bounds!

Listing 22.3 demonstrates the application of a unary predicate given a state variable in finding a number in the collection that is a multiple of a divisor supplied by the user.

LISTING 22.3   Demonstrating the Use of Lambda Expressions That Hold State to Check If One Number Is Divisible by Another

```
0: #include <algorithm>
1: #include <vector>
2: #include <iostream>
3: using namespace std;
4:
5: int main ()
6: {
7:    vector <int> vecIntegers;
8:    cout << "The vector contains the following sample values: ";
9:
10:   // Insert sample values: 25 - 31
11:   for (int nCount = 25; nCount < 32; ++ nCount)
12:   {
13:      vecIntegers.push_back (nCount);
14:      cout << nCount << ' ';
15:   }
16:   cout << endl << "Enter divisor (> 0): ";
17:   int Divisor = 2;
18:   cin >> Divisor;
19:
20:   // Find the first element that is a multiple of divisor
21:   vector <int>::iterator iElement;
22:   iElement = find_if ( vecIntegers.begin ()
23:                      , vecIntegers.end ()
24:        , [Divisor](int dividend){return (dividend % Divisor) == 0; } );
25:
26:   if (iElement != vecIntegers.end ())
27:   {
28:      cout << "First element in vector divisible by " << Divisor;
29:      cout << ": " << *iElement << endl;
30:   }
31:
32:   return 0;
33: }
```

E

Output ▼

```
The vector contains the following sample values: 25 26 27 28 29 30 31
Enter divisor (> 0): 4
First element in vector divisible by 4: 28
```

Analysis ▼

The lambda expression that contains state and works as a predicate is shown in Line 24. Divisor is a state-variable, comparable to `IsMultiple::Divisor` that you saw in Listing 21.3. Hence, state variables are akin to members in a function object class that you would have composed in days prior to C++11. Thus, you are now able to pass states on to your lambda function and customize its usage on the basis of the same.

NOTE	Listing 22.3 is the lambda expression equivalent of Listing 21.4, without the function object class. A 16-line reduction caused by one C++11 feature!

The Generic Syntax of Lambda Expressions

A lambda expression always starts with square brackets and can be configured to take multiple state variables separated using commas in a capture list [...]:

```
[StateVar1, StateVar2](Type& param) { // lambda code here; }
```

If you want to ensure that these state variables are modified within a lambda, you add keyword `mutable`:

```
[StateVar1, StateVar2](Type& param) mutable { // lambda code here; }
```

Note that here, the variables supplied in the capture list [] are modifiable within the lambda, but changes do not take effect outside it. If you want to ensure that modifications made to the state variables within the lambda are valid outside it, too, then you use references:

```
[&StateVar1, &StateVar2](Type& param) { // lambda code here; }
```

Lambdas can take multiple input parameters, separated by commas:

```
[StateVar1, StateVar2](Type1& var1, Type2& var2) { // lambda code here; }
```

If you want to mention the return type and not leave the disambiguation to the compiler, you use -> as in the following:

```
[State1, State2](Type1 var1, Type2 var2) -> ReturnType
{ return (value or expression ); }
```

Finally, the compound statement {} can hold multiple statements, each separated by a ; as shown here:

```
[State1, State2](Type1 var1, Type2 var2) -> ReturnType
{ Statement 1; Statement 2; return (value or expression); }
```

> **NOTE**
>
> In case your lambda expression spans multiple lines, you are forced to supply an explicit return type.
>
> Listing 22.5 later in this lesson demonstrates a lambda function that specifies a return type and spans multiple lines.

Thus, a lambda function is a compact, fully functional replacement of a function object such as the following:

```
template<typename Type1, typename Type2>
struct IsNowTooLong
{
   // State variables
   Type1 var1;
   Type2 var2;

   // Constructor
   IsNowTooLong(const Type1& in1, Type2& in2): var1(in1), var2(in2) {};

   // the actual purpose
   ReturnType operator()
   {
      Statement 1;
      Statement 2;
      return (value or expression);
   }
};
```

Lambda Expression for a Binary Function

A binary function takes two parameters and optionally returns a value. A lambda expression equivalent of the same would be

```
[...](Type1& param1Name, Type2& param2Name) {  // lambda code here;  }
```

A lambda function that multiplies two equal-sized vectors element by element using std::transform and stores the result in a third vector is shown in Listing 22.4.

LISTING 22.4 Lambda Expression as a Binary Function to Multiply Elements from Two Containers and Store in a Third

```
0: #include <vector>
1: #include <iostream>
2: #include <algorithm>
3:
4: int main ()
5: {
6:    using namespace std;
7:
8:    // Create two sample vector of integers with 10 elements each
9:    vector <int> vecMultiplicand, vecMultiplier;
10:
11:    // Insert sample values 0 to 9
12:    for (int nCount1 = 0; nCount1 < 10; ++ nCount1)
13:       vecMultiplicand.push_back (nCount1);
14:
15:    // Insert sample values 100 to 109
16:    for (int nCount2 = 100; nCount2 < 110; ++ nCount2)
17:       vecMultiplier.push_back (nCount2);
18:
19:    // A third container that holds the result of multiplication
20:    vector <int> vecResult;
21:
22:    // Make space for the result of the multiplication
23:    vecResult.resize (10);
24:
25:    transform ( vecMultiplicand.begin (), // range of multiplicands
26:                vecMultiplicand.end (), // end of range
27:                vecMultiplier.begin (),  // multiplier values
28:                vecResult.begin (), // range that holds result
29:                [](int a, int b) {return a * b; } );  // lambda
30:
31:    cout << "The contents of the first vector are: " << endl;
32:    for (size_t nIndex1 = 0; nIndex1 < vecMultiplicand.size (); ++ nIndex1)
33:       cout << vecMultiplicand [nIndex1] << ' ';
34:    cout << endl;
35:
36:    cout << "The contents of the second vector are: " << endl;
37:    for (size_t nIndex2 = 0; nIndex2 < vecMultiplier.size (); ++nIndex2)
38:       cout << vecMultiplier [nIndex2] << ' ';
39:    cout << endl << endl;
40:
41:    cout << "The result of the multiplication is: " << endl;
42:    for (size_t nIndex = 0; nIndex < vecResult.size (); ++ nIndex)
43:       cout << vecResult [nIndex] << ' ';
44:    cout << endl;
45:
46:    return 0;
47: }
```

Output ▼

```
The contents of the first vector are:
0 1 2 3 4 5 6 7 8 9
The contents of the second vector are:
100 101 102 103 104 105 106 107 108 109

The result of the multiplication is:
0 101 204 309 416 525 636 749 864 981
```

Analysis ▼

The lambda expression in question is shown in Line 29 as a parameter to `std::transform`. This algorithm takes two ranges as input and applies a transformation algorithm that is contained in a binary function. The return value of the binary function is stored in a target container. This binary function is a lambda expression that takes two integers as input and returns the result of the multiplication via the return value. This return value is stored by `std::transform` in `vecResult`. The output demonstrates the contents of the two containers and the result of multiplying them element by element.

> **NOTE**
>
> Listing 22.4 was the demonstration of the lambda equivalent of function object class `Multiply<>` in Listing 21.5.

Lambda Expression for a Binary Predicate

A binary function that returns `true` or `false` to help make a decision is called a binary predicate. These predicates find use in sort algorithms, such as `std::sort()`, that invoke the binary predicate for any two values in a container to know which one should be placed after the other. The generic syntax of a binary predicate is

```
[...](Type1& param1Name, Type2& param2Name) {  // return bool expression; }
```

Listing 22.5 demonstrates a lambda expression used in a sort.

LISTING 22.5   Lambda Expression as a Binary Predicate in `std::sort()` to Enable Case-Insensitive Sort

```
0: #include <algorithm>
1: #include <string>
2: #include <vector>
```

E

LISTING 22.5   Continued

```
 3: #include <iostream>
 4: using namespace std;
 5:
 6: template <typename T>
 7: void DisplayContents (const T& Input)
 8: {
 9:    for(auto iElement = Input.cbegin() // auto, cbegin and cend: c++11
10:       ; iElement != Input.cend ()
11:       ; ++ iElement )
12:       cout << *iElement << endl;
13: }
14:
15: int main ()
16: {
17:    // Define a vector of string to hold names
18:    vector <string> vecNames;
19:
20:    // Insert some sample names in to the vector
21:    vecNames.push_back ("jim");
22:    vecNames.push_back ("Jack");
23:    vecNames.push_back ("Sam");
24:    vecNames.push_back ("Anna");
25:
26:    cout << "The names in vector in order of insertion: " << endl;
27:    DisplayContents(vecNames);
28:
29:    cout << "Names after sorting using default std::less<>: " << endl;
30:    sort(vecNames.begin(), vecNames.end());
31:    DisplayContents(vecNames);
32:
33:    cout << "Names after sorting using predicate that ignores case:" << endl;
34:    sort(vecNames.begin(), vecNames.end(),
35:       [](const string& str1, const string& str2) -> bool  // lambda
36:          {
37:            string str1LowerCase;
38:
39:            // Assign space
40:            str1LowerCase.resize (str1.size ());
41:
42:            // Convert every character to the lower case
43:            transform(str1.begin(), str1.end(),
                         str1LowerCase.begin(),tolower);
44:
45:            string str2LowerCase;
46:            str2LowerCase.resize (str2.size ());
47:            transform (str2.begin (), str2.end (), str2LowerCase.begin (),
```

```
48:                          tolower);
49:
50:              return (str1LowerCase < str2LowerCase);
51:            }  // end of lambda
52:          );  // end of sort
53:      DisplayContents(vecNames);
54:
55:      return 0;
56: }
```

Output ▼

```
The names in vector in order of insertion:
jim
Jack
Sam
Anna
Names after sorting using default std::less<>:
Anna
Jack
Sam
jim
Names after sorting using predicate that ignores case:
Anna
Jack
jim
Sam
```

Analysis ▼

This demonstrates a genuinely large lambda function spanning Lines 35–51— the third parameter of std::sort() starts at Line 34 and ends at Line 52! What this lambda function demonstrates is that a lambda can span multiple statements, the prerequisite being that the return value type is explicitly specified as shown in Line 35 (bool). The output demonstrates the content of the vector as inserted, where jim is before Jack. The content of the vector after a default sort without a supplied lambda or predicate as shown in Line 30 sorts jim after Sam, as this is case sensitive via string::operator<. Finally, a version using a case-insensitive lambda expression is seen in Lines 34–52 that places jim after Jack as the user typically would expect. This sort also uses a lambda expression that spans multiple lines.

E

NOTE

This extraordinarily large lambda in Listing 22.5 is a lambda version of Listing 21.6, class CompareStringNoCase, used in Listing 21.7.

Clearly, this is not an optimal use of a lambda because, in this case, a function object is reusable in multiple std::sort() statements, if required, and also in other algorithms that need a binary predicate.

So, you need to use lambdas when they're short, sweet, and effective.

DO	**DON'T**
DO remember that lambda expressions always start with [] or [state1, state2, ..].	**DON'T** forget that lambda expressions are unnamed representations of a class or a struct with operator().
DO remember that unless specified, state variables supplied within a capture list [] are not modifiable unless you use the keyword mutable.	**DON'T** forget to use const correct parameter types when writing your lambda expressions [](const T& value) { // lambda expression ; }.
	DON'T forget to explicitly mention return type when the lambda expression includes multiple statements within the statement block {}.
	DON'T choose lambda expressions over a function object when the lambda gets extremely long and spans multiple statements, for these are redefined in every use and do not assist code reusability.

Summary

In this lesson, you learned a very important feature in C++11: lambda functions. You saw how lambdas are basically unnamed function objects that can take parameters, have state, return values, and be multiple lined. You learned how to use lambdas instead of function objects in STL algorithms, helping find(), sort(), or transform(). Lambdas make programming in C++ fast and efficient, and you should try to use them as often as possible.

Q&A

Q Should I always prefer a lambda over a function object?

A Lambdas that span multiple lines as shown in Listing 22.5 might not help increase programming efficiency over function objects that are easily reused.

Q How are the state parameters of a lambda transferred, by value or by reference?

A When a lambda is programmed with a capture list as this:

```
[Var1, Var2, ... N](Type& Param1, ... ) { ...expression ;}
```

the state parameters Var1 and Var2 are copied (not supplied as a reference). If you want to have them as reference parameters, you use this syntax:

```
[&Var1, &Var2, ... &N](Type& Param1, ... ) { ...expression ;}
```

In this case, you need to exercise caution as modifications to the state variables supplied within the capture list continue outside the lambda.

Q Can I use the local variables in a function in a lambda?

A You can pass the local variables in a capture list:

```
[Var1, Var2, ... N](Type& Param1, ... ) { ...expression ;}
```

If you want to capture all variables, you use this syntax:

```
[=](Type& Param1, ... ) { ...expression ;}
```

Workshop

The Workshop provides quiz questions to help you solidify your understanding of the material covered and exercises to provide you with experience in using what you've learned. Try to answer the quiz and exercise questions before checking the answers in Appendix D.

Quiz

1. How does a compiler recognize the start of a lambda expression?
2. How would you pass state variables to a lambda function?
3. If you need to supply a return value in a lambda, how would you do it?

E

Exercises

1. Write a lambda binary predicate that would help sort in descending order.

2. Write a lambda function that, when used in `for_each`, adds a user-specified value to that in a container such as vector.

LESSON 23
STL Algorithms

An important part of the Standard Template Library (STL) is a set of
generic functions, supplied by the header <algorithm>, that help
manipulate or work with the contents of a container. In this lesson,
you find out

- How to use STL algorithms to reduce boiler-plate code
- Generic functions to help you count, search, find, and remove in
  addition to other operations in STL containers

What Are STL Algorithms?

Finding, searching, removing, and counting are some generic algorithmic activities that find application in a broad range of programs. STL solves these and many other requirements in the form of generic template functions that work on containers via iterators. To use STL algorithms, the programmer first has to include the header <algorithm>.

NOTE	Although most algorithms work via iterators on containers, not all algorithms necessarily work on containers and hence not all algorithms need iterators. Some, such as swap(), simply accept a pair of values to swap them. Similarly, min() and max() work directly on values, too.

Classification of STL Algorithms

STL algorithms can be broadly classified into two types: non-mutating and mutating algorithms.

Non-Mutating Algorithms

Algorithms that change neither the order nor the contents of a container are called *non-mutating algorithms*. Some of the prominent non-mutating algorithms are shown in Table 23.1.

TABLE 23.1   Quick Reference of Non-Mutating Algorithms

Algorithm	Description
Counting Algorithms	
count	Finds all elements in a range whose values match a supplied value
count_if	Finds all elements in a range whose values satisfy a supplied condition
Search Algorithms	
search	Searches for the first occurrence of a given sequence within a target range either on the basis of element equality (that is, the operator ==) or using a specified binary predicate
search_n	Searches a specified target range for the first occurrence of *n* number of elements of a given value or those that satisfy a given predicate

TABLE 23.1   Continued

Algorithm	Description
find	Searches for the first element in the range that matches the specified value
find_if	Searches for the first element in a range that satisfies the specified condition
find_end	Searches for the last occurrence of a particular subrange in a supplied range
find_first_of	Searches for the first occurrence of any element supplied in one range within a target range; or, in an overloaded version, searches for the first occurrence of an element that satisfies a supplied find criterion
adjacent_find	Searches for two elements in a collection that are either equal or satisfy a supplied condition
Comparison Algorithms	
equal	Compares two elements for equality or uses a specified binary predicate to determine the same
mismatch	Locates the first difference position in two ranges of elements using a specified binary predicate
lexicographical_compare	Compares the elements between two sequences to determine which is the lesser of the two

23

Mutating Algorithms

Mutating algorithms are those that change the contents or the order of the sequence they are operating on. Some of the most useful mutating algorithms supplied by STL are shown in Table 23.2.

TABLE 23.2   A Quick Reference of Mutating Algorithms

Algorithm	Description
Initialization Algorithms	
fill	Assigns the specified value to every element in the specified range.
fill_n	Assigns the specified value to the first n elements in the specified range.
generate	Assigns the return value of a specified function object to each element in the supplied range.
generate_n	Assigns the value generated by a function to a specified count of values in a specified range.

TABLE 23.2   Continued

Algorithm	Description
Modifying Algorithms	
for_each	Performs an operation on every element in a range. When the specified argument modifies the range, for_each becomes a mutating algorithm.
transform	Applies a specified unary function on every element in the specified range.
Copy Algorithms	
copy	Copies one range into another.
copy_backward	Copies one range into another, arranging elements in the destination range in the reverse order.
Removal Algorithms	
remove	Removes an element of a specified value from a specified range.
remove_if	Removes an element that satisfies a specified unary predicate from a specified range.
remove_copy	Copies all elements from a source range to a destination range, except those of a specified value.
remove_copy_if	Copies all elements from a source range to a destination range except those that satisfy a specified unary predicate.
unique	Compares adjacent elements in a range and removes the following duplicates. An overloaded version works using a binary predicate.
unique_copy	Copies all but adjacent duplicate elements from a specified source range to a specified destination range.
Replacement Algorithms	
replace	Replaces every element in a specified range that matches a specified value by a replacement value.
replace_if	Replaces every element in a specified range that matches a specified value by a replacement value.
Sort Algorithms	
sort	Sorts elements in a range using a specified sort criterion, which is a binary predicate that supplies a strict-weak-ordering. sort might change relative positions of equivalent elements.
stable_sort	Stable sort is similar to sort but preserves order, too.
partial_sort	Sorts a specified number of elements in a range.
partial_sort_copy	Copies elements from a specified source range to a destination range that holds them in a sort order.

TABLE 23.2   Continued

Algorithm	Description
Partitioning Algorithms	
partition	Given a specified range, splits elements into two sets within it: those that satisfy a unary predicate come first and the rest after. Might not maintain the relative order of elements in a set.
stable_partition	Partitions an input range into two sets as in partition but maintains relative ordering.
Algorithms That Work on Sorted Containers	
binary_search	Used to determine whether an element exists in a sorted collection.
lower_bound	Returns an iterator pointing to the first position where an element can potentially be inserted in a sorted collection based on its value or on a supplied binary predicate.
upper_bound	Returns an iterator pointing to the last position where an element can potentially be inserted into a sorted collection based on its value or on a supplied binary predicate.

23

Usage of STL Algorithms

The usage of the STL algorithms mentioned in Tables 23.1 and 23.2 is best learned directly by a hands-on coding session. To that end, learn the details of using the algorithms from the code examples that follow and start applying them to your application.

Finding Elements Given a Value or a Condition

Given a container such as a vector, STL algorithms find() and find_if() help you find an element that matches a value or fulfills a condition, respectively. The usage of find() follows this pattern:

```
auto iElementFound = find ( vecIntegers.cbegin () // Start of range
                          , vecIntegers.cend ()   // End of range
                          , NumToFind );          // Element to find

// Check if find succeeded
if ( iElementFound != vecIntegers.cend ())
   cout << "Result: Value found!" << endl;
```

find_if() is similar and requires you to supply a unary predicate (a unary function that returns true or false) as the third parameter.

```
auto iEvenNumber = find_if ( vecIntegers.cbegin () // Start of range
                           , vecIntegers.cend ()   // End of range
                  , [](int element) { return (element % 2) == 0; } );

if (iEvenNumber != vecIntegers.cend ())
   cout << "Result: Value found!" << endl;
```

Thus, both find functions return an iterator, which you need to compare against the end() or cend() of the container to verify the success of the find operation. If this check is successful, you can use this iterator further. Listing 23.1 demonstrates the usage of find() to locate a value in a vector, and find_if() to locate the first even value.

LISTING 23.1 Using find() to Locate an Integer Value in a vector, find_if to Locate the First Even Number Given an Unary Predicate in a Lambda Expression

```
0: #include <iostream>
1: #include <algorithm>
2: #include <vector>
3:
4: int main()
5: {
6:    using namespace std;
7:    vector<int> vecIntegers;
8:
9:    // Inserting sample values -9 to 9
10:    for (int SampleValue = -9; SampleValue < 10; ++ SampleValue)
11:       vecIntegers.push_back (SampleValue);
12:
13:    cout << "Enter number to find in collection: ";
14:    int NumToFind = 0;
15:    cin >> NumToFind;
16:
17:    auto iElementFound = find ( vecIntegers.cbegin () // Start of range
18:                              , vecIntegers.cend ()   // End of range
19:                              , NumToFind );          // Element to find
20:
21:    // Check if find succeeded
22:    if ( iElementFound != vecIntegers.cend ())
23:       cout << "Result: Value " << *iElementFound << " found!" << endl;
24:    else
25:       cout << "Result: No element contains value " << NumToFind << endl;
26:
27:    cout << "Finding the first even number using find_if: " << endl;
28:
29:    auto iEvenNumber = find_if ( vecIntegers.cbegin () // Start of range
30:                               , vecIntegers.cend ()   // End of range
31:                      , [](int element) { return (element % 2) == 0; } );
32:
```

```
33:    if (iEvenNumber != vecIntegers.cend ())
34:    {
35:       cout << "Number '" << *iEvenNumber << "' found at position [';
36:       cout << distance (vecIntegers.cbegin (), iEvenNumber);
37:       cout << "]" << endl;
38:    }
39:
40:    return 0;
41: }
```

Output ▼

```
Enter number to find in collection: 7
Result: Value 7 found!
Finding the first even number using find_if:
Number '-8' found at position [1]
```

Next run:

```
Enter number to find in collection: 2011
Result: No element contains value 2011
Finding the first even number using find_if:
Number '-8' found at position [1]
```

Analysis ▼

main() starts with creating a vector of integers that is initialized to values in the range of
–9 to 9. You use find() in Lines 17–19 to find the number entered by the user. The use
of find_if() to locate the first even number given the range is shown in Lines 29–31.
Line 31 is the unary predicate programmed as a lambda expression. This lambda expression returns true when element is divisible by 2.

CAUTION
Note how Listing 23.1 always checks the iterator returned by
find() or find_if() for validity against cend(). This check
should never be skipped, as it indicates the success of the
find() operation, which should not be taken for granted.

TIP
Listing 17.5 in Lesson 17, "STL Dynamic Array Classes," also
demonstrates the use of std::distance in Line 21 to determine
the offset of the found element from the start of the vector.

Counting Elements Given a Value or a Condition

std::count() and count_if() are algorithms that help in counting elements given a range. std::find()helps you count the number of elements that match a value (tested via equality operator==):

```
size_t nNumZeroes = count (vecIntegers.begin (),vecIntegers.end (),0);
cout << "Number of instances of '0': " << nNumZeroes << endl << endl;
```

std::count_if() helps you count the number of elements that fulfill a unary predicate supplied as a parameter (which can be a function object or a lambda expression):

```
// Unary predicate:
template <typename elementType>
bool IsEven (const elementType& number)
{
    return ((number % 2) == 0); // true, if even
}
...
// Use the count_if algorithm with the unary predicate IsEven:
size_t nNumEvenElements = count_if (vecIntegers.begin (),
                                    vecIntegers.end (), IsEven <int> );
cout << "Number of even elements: " << nNumEvenElements << endl;
```

The code in Listing 23.2 demonstrates the usage of these functions.

LISTING 23.2   Demonstrates the Usage of std::count() to Determine Number of Elements with a Value and count_if() to Determine Number of Elements That Fulfill a Condition

```
 0: #include <algorithm>
 1: #include <vector>
 2: #include <iostream>
 3:
 4: // A unary predicate for the *_if functions
 5: template <typename elementType>
 6: bool IsEven (const elementType& number)
 7: {
 8:     return ((number % 2) == 0); // true, if even
 9: }
10:
11: int main ()
12: {
13:     using namespace std;
14:     vector <int> vecIntegers;
15:
16:     cout << "Populating a vector<int> with values from -9 to 9" << endl;
17:     for (int nNum = -9; nNum < 10; ++ nNum)
```

```
18:          vecIntegers.push_back (nNum);
19:
20:     // Use count to determine the number of '0's in the vector
21:     size_t nNumZeroes = count (vecIntegers.begin (),vecIntegers.end (),0);
22:     cout << "Number of instances of '0': " << nNumZeroes << endl << endl;
23:
24:     // Use the count_if algorithm with the unary predicate IsEven:
25:     size_t nNumEvenElements = count_if (vecIntegers.begin (),
26:                            vecIntegers.end (), IsEven <int> );
27:
28:     cout << "Number of even elements: " << nNumEvenElements << endl;
29:     cout << "Number of odd elements: ";
30:     cout << vecIntegers.size () - nNumEvenElements << endl;
31:
32:     return 0;
33: }
```

23

Output ▼

```
Populating a vector<int> with values from -9 to 9
Number of instances of '0': 1

Number of even elements: 9
Number of odd elements: 10
```

Analysis ▼

Line 21 uses count() to determine the number of instances of 0 in the vector<int>. Similarly, Line 25 uses count_if() to determine the number of even elements in the vector. Note the third parameter, which is a unary predicate IsEven() defined in Lines 6–9. The number of elements in the vector that are odd is calculated by subtracting the return of count_if() with the total number of elements contained in the vector returned by size().

NOTE	Listing 23.2 uses predicate function IsEven() in count_if(), whereas Listing 23.1 used a lambda function doing the work of IsEven() in find_if().
	The lambda version saves lines of code, but you should remember that if the two samples were merged, IsEven() could be used in both find_if() and count_if(), increasing the opportunities for reuse.

Searching for an Element or a Range in a Collection

Listing 23.1 demonstrated how you can find an element in a container. Sometimes, you need to find a range of values or a pattern. In such situations, you should use search() or search_n(). search() can be used to check if one range is contained in another:

```
auto iRange = search ( vecIntegers.begin () // Start of range
                     , vecIntegers.end ()     // End of range to search in
                     , listIntegers.begin ()  // Start of range to search for
                     , listIntegers.end () ); // End of range to search for
```

search_n() can be used to check if *n* instances of a value placed consequently are to be found in a container:

```
auto iPartialRange = search_n ( vecIntegers.begin () // Start range
                              , vecIntegers.end ()    // End range
                              , 3        // Count of item to be searched for
                              , 9 );     // Item to search for
```

Both functions return an iterator to the first instance of the pattern found, and this iterator needs to be checked against end() before it can be used. Listing 23.3 demonstrates the usage of search() and search_n().

LISTING 23.3 Finding a Range in a Collection Using search() and search_n()

```
0: #include <algorithm>
1: #include <vector>
2: #include <list>
3: #include <iostream>
4: using namespace std;
5:
6: template <typename T>
7: void DisplayContents (const T& Input)
8: {
9:    for(auto iElement = Input.cbegin() // auto, cbegin and cend: c++11
10:       ; iElement != Input.cend()
11:       ; ++ iElement )
12:       cout << *iElement << ' ';
13:
14:    cout << endl;
15: }
16:
17: int main ()
18: {
19:    // A sample container - vector of integers - containing -9 to 9
20:    vector <int> vecIntegers;
```

```
21:     for (int nNum = -9; nNum < 10; ++ nNum)
22:         vecIntegers.push_back (nNum);
23:
24:     // Insert some more sample values into the vector
25:     vecIntegers.push_back (9);
26:     vecIntegers.push_back (9);
27:
28:     // Another sample container - a list of integers from -4 to 4
29:     list <int> listIntegers;
30:     for (int nNum = -4; nNum < 5; ++ nNum)
31:         listIntegers.push_back (nNum);
32:
33:     cout << "The contents of the sample vector are: ' << endl;
34:     DisplayContents (vecIntegers);
35:
36:     cout << "The contents of the sample list are: " << endl;
37:     DisplayContents (listIntegers);
38:
39:     cout << "search() for the contents of list in vector:" << endl;
40:     auto iRange = search ( vecIntegers.begin () // Start of range
41:                          , vecIntegers.end () // End range to search in
42:                          , listIntegers.begin () // Start range to search for
43:                          , listIntegers.end () ); // End range to search for
44:
45:     // Check if search found a match
46:     if (iRange != vecIntegers.end ())
47:     {
48:         cout << "Sequence in list found in vector at position: ";
49:         cout << distance (vecIntegers.begin (), iRange) << endl;
50:     }
51:
52:     cout << "Searching {9, 9, 9} in vector using search_n(): " << endl;
53:     auto iPartialRange = search_n ( vecIntegers.begin () // Start range
54:                                   , vecIntegers.end () // End range
55:                                   , 3 // Count of item to be searched for
56:                                   , 9 ); // Item to search for
57:
58:     if (iPartialRange != vecIntegers.end ())
59:     {
60:         cout << "Sequence {9, 9, 9} found in vector at position: ";
61:         cout << distance (vecIntegers.begin (), iPartialRange) << endl;
62:     }
63:
64:     return 0;
65: }
```

23

Output ▼

```
The contents of the sample vector are:
-9 -8 -7 -6 -5 -4 -3 -2 -1 0 1 2 3 4 5 6 7 8 9 9 9
The contents of the sample list are:
-4 -3 -2 -1 0 1 2 3 4
search() for the contents of list in vector:
Sequence in list found in vector at position: 5
Searching {9, 9, 9} in vector using search_n():
```

Analysis ▼

The sample starts with two sample containers, a vector and a list that are initially populated with sample integer values. search() is used to find the presence of the contents of the list in vector, as shown in Line 40. As you want to search in the entire vector for the contents of the entire list, you supply a range as returned by the iterators corresponding to begin() and end() member methods of the two container classes. This actually demonstrates how well iterators connect the algorithms to the containers. The physical characteristics of the containers that supply those iterators are of no significance to algorithms, which search the contents of a list in a vector seamlessly as they only work with iterators. search_n() is used in Line 53 to find the first occurrence of series {9, 9, 9}in the vector.

Initializing Elements in a Container to a Specific Value

fill() and fill_n() are the STL algorithms that help set the contents of a given range to a specified value. fill() is used to overwrite the elements in a range given the bounds of the range and the value to be inserted:

```
vector <int> vecIntegers (3);

// fill all elements in the container with value 9
fill (vecIntegers.begin (), vecIntegers.end (), 9);
```

As the name suggests, fill_n() resets a specified n number of values. It needs a starting position, a count, and the value to fill:

```
fill_n (vecIntegers.begin () + 3, /*count*/ 3, /*fill value*/ -9);
```

Listing 23.4 demonstrates how these algorithms make initializing elements in a vector<int> easy.

LISTING 23.4 Using `fill()` and `fill_n()` to Set Initial Values in a Container

```
0: #include <algorithm>
1: #include <vector>
2: #include <iostream>
3:
4: int main ()
5: {
6:     using namespace std;
7:
8:     // Initialize a sample vector with 3 elements
9:     vector <int> vecIntegers (3);
10:
11:    // fill all elements in the container with value 9
12:    fill (vecIntegers.begin (), vecIntegers.end (), 9);
13:
14:    // Increase the size of the vector to hold 6 elements
15:    vecIntegers.resize (6);
16:
17:    // Fill the three elements starting at offset position 3 with value -9
18:    fill_n (vecIntegers.begin () + 3, 3, -9);
19:
20:    cout << "Contents of the vector are: " << endl;
21:    for (size_t nIndex = 0; nIndex < vecIntegers.size (); ++ nIndex)
22:    {
23:        cout << "Element [" << nIndex << "] = ";
24:        cout << vecIntegers [nIndex] << endl;
25:    }
26:
27:    return 0;
28: }
```

23

Output ▼

```
Contents of the vector are:
Element [0] = 9
Element [1] = 9
Element [2] = 9
Element [3] = -9
Element [4] = -9
Element [5] = -9
```

Analysis ▼

Listing 23.4 uses the `fill()` and `fill_n()` functions to initialize the contents of the container to two separate sets of values, as shown in Lines 12 and 13. Note the usage of the `resize()` function before you filled values into the range, essentially creating elements that were later filled with values. The `fill()` algorithm works on a complete range, whereas `fill_n()` has the potential to work on a partial range.

Using `std::generate()` to Initialize Elements to a Value Generated at Runtime

Just as `fill()` and `fill_n()` functions fill the collection with a specific value, STL algorithms, such as `generate()` and `generate_n()`, are used to initialize collections using values returned by a unary function.

You can use `generate()` to fill a range using the return value of a generator function:

```
generate ( vecIntegers.begin (), vecIntegers.end ()    // range
         , rand );    // generator function to be called
```

`generate_n()` is similar to `generate()` except that you supply the number of elements to be assigned instead of the closing bound of a range:

```
generate_n (listIntegers.begin (), 5, rand);
```

Thus, you can use these two algorithms to initialize the contents of a container to the contents of a file, for example, or simply to random values, as shown in Listing 23.5.

LISTING 23.5   Using `generate()` and `generate_n()` to Initialize Collections to Random Values

```
0: #include <algorithm>
1: #include <vector>
2: #include <list>
3: #include <iostream>
4:
5: int main ()
6: {
7:     using namespace std;
8:
9:     vector <int> vecIntegers (10);
10:     generate ( vecIntegers.begin (), vecIntegers.end ()    // range
11:              , rand );    // generator function to be called
12:
13:     cout << "Elements in the vector of size " << vecIntegers.size ();
14:     cout << " assigned by 'generate' are: " << endl << "{";
15:     for (size_t nCount = 0; nCount < vecIntegers.size (); ++ nCount)
16:         cout << vecIntegers [nCount] << " ";
17:
18:     cout << "}" << endl << endl;
19:
20:     list <int> listIntegers (10);
21:     generate_n (listIntegers.begin (), 5, rand);
22:
23:     cout << "Elements in the list of size: " << listIntegers.size ();
24:     cout << " assigned by 'generate_n' are: " << endl << "{";
```

```
25:      list <int>::const_iterator iElementLocator;
26:      for ( iElementLocator = listIntegers.begin ()
27:         ; iElementLocator != listIntegers.end ()
28:         ; ++ iElementLocator )
29:         cout << *iElementLocator << ' ';
30:
31:      cout << "}" << endl;
32:
33:      return 0;
34: }
```

Output ▼

```
Elements in the vector of size 10 assigned by 'generate' are:
{41 18467 6334 26500 19169 15724 11478 29358 26962 24464 }

Elements in the list of size: 10 assigned by 'generate_n' are:
{5705 28145 23281 16827 9961 0 0 0 0 0 }
```

Analysis ▼

Listing 23.5 uses the generate function to populate all elements in the vector with a random value supplied by the rand function. Note that the generate function accepts a range as an input and consequently calls the specified function object rand for every element in the range. generate_n, in comparison, accepts only the starting position. It then invokes the specified function object, rand, the number of times specified by the count parameter to overwrite the contents of that many elements. The elements in the container that are beyond the specified offset go untouched.

Processing Elements in a Range Using for_each()

The for_each() algorithm applies a specified unary function object to every element in the supplied range. The usage of for_each() is

```
unaryFunctionObjectType mReturn = for_each ( start_of_range
                                           , end_of_range
                                           , unaryFunctionObject );
```

This unary function object can also be a lambda expression that accepts one parameter.

The return value indicates that for_each() returns the function object (also called functor) used to process every element in the supplied range. The implication of this specification is that using a struct or a class as a function object can help in storing state information, which you can later query when for_each() is done. This is demonstrated by Listing 23.6, which uses the function object to display elements in a range and also uses it to count the number of elements displayed.

LISTING 23.6 Displaying the Contents of Sequences Using for_each()

```
 0: #include <algorithm>
 1: #include <iostream>
 2: #include <vector>
 3: #include <string>
 4: using namespace std;
 5:
 6: // Unary function object type invoked by for_each
 7: template <typename elementType>
 8: struct DisplayElementKeepCount
 9: {
10:    int Count;
11:
12:    // Constructor
13:    DisplayElementKeepCount (): Count (0) {}
14:
15:    void operator () (const elementType& element)
16:    {
17:       ++ Count;
18:       cout << element << ' ';
19:    }
20: };
21:
22: int main ()
23: {
24:    vector <int> vecIntegers;
25:    for (int nCount = 0; nCount < 10; ++ nCount)
26:       vecIntegers.push_back (nCount);
27:
28:    cout << "Displaying the vector of integers: " << endl;
29:
30:    // Display the array of integers
31:    DisplayElementKeepCount<int> Functor =
32:       for_each ( vecIntegers.begin ()    // Start of range
33:                , vecIntegers.end ()       // End of range
34:                , DisplayElementKeepCount<int> () );// Functor
34:
35:    cout << endl;
36:
37:    // Use the state stored in the return value of for_each!
38:    cout << "'" << Functor.Count << "' elements were displayed" << endl;
```

```
39:
40:     string Sample ("for_each and strings!");
41:     cout << "String: " << Sample << ", length: ' << Sample.length()) << endl;
42:
43:     cout << "String displayed using lambda:" << endl;
44:     int NumChars = 0;
45:     for_each ( Sample.begin()
46:               , Sample.end ()
47:               , [&NumChars](char c) { cout << c << ' '; ++NumChars; } );
48:
49:     cout << endl;
50:     cout << "'" << NumChars << "' characters were displayed" << erdl;
51:
52:     return 0;
53: }
```

Output ▼

```
Displaying the vector of integers:
0 1 2 3 4 5 6 7 8 9
'10' elements were displayed
String: for_each and strings!, length: 21
String displayed using lambda:
f o r _ e a c h   a n d   s t r i n g s !
'21' characters were displayed
```

Analysis ▼

The code sample demonstrates the utility of for_each() and also of its characteristic to return the function object Result that is programmed to hold information such as the count of the number of times it was invoked. The code features two sample ranges, one contained in a vector of integers, vecIntegers, and the other a std::string object Sample. The sample invokes for_each() on these ranges in Lines 32 and 45, respectively. The first with DisplayElementKeepCount as the unary predicate and the second using a lambda expression. for_each() invokes the operator() for every element in the supplied range, which in turn prints the element on the screen and increments an internal counter. The function object is returned when for_each() is done, and the member Count tells the number of times the object was used. This facility of storing information (or state) in the object that is returned by the algorithm can be quite useful in practical programming situations. for_each() in Line 45 does exactly the same as its previous counterpart in Line 32 for a std::string, using a lambda expression instead of a function object.

Performing Transformations on a Range Using `std::transform()`

`std::for_each()` and `std::transform()` are quite similar in that they both invoke a function object for every element in a source range. However, `std::transform()` has two versions. The first version accepts a unary function and is popularly used to convert a string to upper- or lowercase using functions `toupper()` or `tolower()`:

```
string Sample ("THIS is a TEst string!");
transform ( Sample.begin ()          // start of source range
          , Sample.end ()            // end of source range
          , strLowerCaseCopy.begin ()// start of destination range
          , tolower );               // unary function
```

The second version accepts a binary function allowing `transform()` to process a pair of elements taken from two different ranges:

```
// add elements in two ranges and store in a third
transform ( vecIntegers1.begin ()    // start of source range 1
          , vecIntegers1.end ()      // end of source range 1
          , vecIntegers2.begin ()    // start of source range 2
          , dqResultAddition.begin ()// store result in a deque
          , plus <int> () );         // binary function plus
```

Both versions of the `transform()` always assign the result of the specified transformation function to a supplied destination range, unlike `for_each()`, which works on only a single range. The usage of `std::transform()` is demonstrated in Listing 23.7.

LISTING 23.7   Using `std::transform()` with Unary and Binary Functions

```
 0: #include <algorithm>
 1: #include <string>
 2: #include <vector>
 3: #include <deque>
 4: #include <iostream>
 5: #include <functional>
 6:
 7: int main ()
 8: {
 9:     using namespace std;
10:
11:     string Sample ("THIS is a TEst string!");
12:     cout << "The sample string is: " << Sample << endl;
13:
14:     string strLowerCaseCopy;
15:     strLowerCaseCopy.resize (Sample.size ());
```

```
16:
17:     transform ( Sample.begin ()            // start of source range
18:                , Sample.end ()              // end of source range
19:                , strLowerCaseCopy.begin ()// start of destination range
20:                , tolower );         // unary function
21:
22:     cout << "Result of 'transform' on the string with 'tolower':" << endl;
23:     cout << "\"" << strLowerCaseCopy << "\"" << endl << endl;
24:
25:     // Two sample vectors of integers...
26:     vector <int> vecIntegers1, vecIntegers2;
27:     for (int nNum = 0; nNum < 10; ++ nNum)
28:     {
29:         vecIntegers1.push_back (nNum);
30:         vecIntegers2.push_back (10 - nNum);
31:     }
32:
33:     // A destination range for holding the result of addition
34:     deque <int> dqResultAddition (vecIntegers1.size ());
35:
36:     transform ( vecIntegers1.begin ()      // start of source range 1
37:                , vecIntegers1.end ()        // end of source range 1
38:                , vecIntegers2.begin ()      // start of source range 2
39:                , dqResultAddition.begin ()// start of destination range
40:                , plus <int> () );          // binary function
41:
42:     cout << "Result of 'transform' using binary function 'plus': " << endl;
43:     cout <<endl << "Index    Vector1 + Vector2 = Result (in Deque)" << endl;
44:     for (size_t nIndex = 0; nIndex < vecIntegers1.size (); ++ nIndex)
45:     {
46:         cout << nIndex << "    \t " << vecIntegers1 [nIndex]  << "\t+    ";
47:         cout << vecIntegers2 [nIndex]  << " \t =    ';
48:
49:         cout << dqResultAddition [nIndex] << endl;
50:     }
51:
52:     return 0;
53: }
```

23

Output ▼

```
The sample string is: THIS is a TEst string!
Result of using 'transform' with unary function 'tolower' on the string:
"this is a test string!"

Result of 'transform' using binary function 'plus':
```

```
Index    Vector1 + Vector2 = Result (in Deque)
0        0       + 10      =   10
1        1       + 9       =   10
2        2       + 8       =   10
3        3       + 7       =   10
4        4       + 6       =   10
5        5       + 5       =   10
6        6       + 4       =   10
7        7       + 3       =   10
8        8       + 2       =   10
9        9       + 1       =   10
```

Analysis ▼

The sample demonstrates both versions of `std::transform()`, one that works on a single range using a unary function `tolower()`, as shown in Line 20, and another that works on two ranges and uses a binary function `plus()`, as shown in Line 40. The first changes the case of a string, character-by-character, to lowercase. If you use `toupper()` instead of `tolower()`, you effect a case conversion to uppercase. The other version of `std::transform()`, shown in Lines 36–40, acts on elements taken from two input ranges (two vectors in this case) and uses a binary predicate in the form of the STL function `plus()` (supplied by the header `<functional>`) to add them. `std::transform()` takes one pair at a time, supplies it to the binary function `plus`, and assigns the result to an element in the destination range—one that happens to belong to an `std::deque`. Note that the change in container used to hold the result is purely for demonstration purposes. It only displays how well iterators are used to abstract containers and their implementation from STL algorithms; `transform()`, being an algorithm, deals with ranges and really does not need to know details on the containers that implement these ranges. So, the input ranges happened to be in `vector`, and the output ranges happened to be a `deque`, and it all works fine—so long as the bounds that define the range (supplied as input parameters to `transform`) are valid.

Copy and Remove Operations

STL supplies three prominent copy functions: `copy()`, `copy_if()`, and `copy_backward()`. `copy()` can assign the contents of a source range into a destination range in the forward direction:

```
auto iLastPos = copy ( listIntegers.begin ()  // start source range
                     , listIntegers.end ()     // end source range
                     , vecIntegers.begin () );// start dest range
```

copy_if()copies an element only if a unary predicate supplied by you returns true:

```
// copy odd numbers from list into vector
copy_if ( listIntegers.begin(), listIntegers.end()
       , iLastPos
       , [](int element){return ((element % 2) == 1);} );
```

NOTE

Starting with C++11, copy_if() is an algorithm in the std namespace. If you are using an old or non-C++11-compliant compiler, you might have problems using it.

23

copy_backward() assigns the contents to the destination range in the backward direction:

```
copy_backward ( listIntegers.begin ()
             , listIntegers.end ()
             , vecIntegers.end () );
```

remove(), on the other hand, deletes elements in a container that matches a specified value:

```
// Remove all instances of '0', resize vector using erase()
auto iNewEnd = remove (vecIntegers.begin (), vecIntegers.end (), 0);
vecIntegers.erase (iNewEnd, vecIntegers.end ());
```

remove_if() uses a unary predicate and removes from the container those elements for which the predicate evaluates to true:

```
// Remove all odd numbers from the vector using remove_if
iNewEnd = remove_if (vecIntegers.begin (), vecIntegers.end (),
          [](int element) {return ((element % 2) == 1);} ); //predicate

vecIntegers.erase (iNewEnd , vecIntegers.end ());  // resizing
```

Listing 23.8 demonstrates the usage of the copy and removal functions.

LISTING 23.8   A Sample That Demonstrates copy(), copy_if(), remove(), and remove_if() to Copy a list into a vector and Remove 0s and Even Numbers

```
0: #include <algorithm>
1: #include <vector>
2: #include <list>
3: #include <iostream>
4: using namespace std;
5:
```

LISTING 23.8   Continued

```
 6: template <typename T>
 7: void DisplayContents(const T& Input)
 8: {
 9:    for ( auto iElement = Input.cbegin() // auto, cbegin: c++11
10:         ; iElement != Input.cend()  // cend() is new in C++11
11:         ; ++ iElement)
12:       cout << *iElement << ' ';
13:
14:    cout << "¦ Number of elements: " << Input.size() << endl;
15: }
16: int main ()
17: {
18:    list <int> listIntegers;
19:    for (int nCount = 0; nCount < 10; ++ nCount)
20:       listIntegers.push_back (nCount);
21:
22:    cout << "Source (list) contains:" << endl;
23:    DisplayContents(listIntegers);
24:
25:    // Initialize the vector to hold twice as many elements as the list
26:    vector <int> vecIntegers (listIntegers.size () * 2);
27:
28:    auto iLastPos = copy ( listIntegers.begin ()  // start source range
29:                         , listIntegers.end ()      // end source range
30:                         , vecIntegers.begin () );// start dest range
31:
32:    // copy odd numbers from list into vector
33:    copy_if ( listIntegers.begin(), listIntegers.end()
34:            , iLastPos
35:            , [](int element){return ((element % 2) == 1);});
36:
37:    cout << "Destination (vector) after copy and copy_if:" << endl;
38:    DisplayContents(vecIntegers);
39:
40:    // Remove all instances of '0', resize vector using erase()
41:    auto iNewEnd = remove (vecIntegers.begin (), vecIntegers.end (), 0);
42:    vecIntegers.erase (iNewEnd, vecIntegers.end ());
43:
44:    // Remove all odd numbers from the vector using remove_if
45:    iNewEnd = remove_if (vecIntegers.begin (), vecIntegers.end (),
46:             [](int element) {return ((element % 2) == 1);} ); //predicate
47:
48:    vecIntegers.erase (iNewEnd , vecIntegers.end ());  // resizing
49:
50:    cout << "Destination (vector) after remove, remove_if, erase:" << endl;
51:    DisplayContents(vecIntegers);
52:
53:    return 0;
54: }
```

Output ▼

```
Source (list) contains:
0 1 2 3 4 5 6 7 8 9 ¦ Number of elements: 10
Destination (vector) after copy and copy_if:
0 1 2 3 4 5 6 7 8 9 1 3 5 7 9 0 0 0 0 0 ¦ Number of elements: 20
Destination (vector) after remove, remove_if, erase:
2 4 6 8 ¦ Number of elements: 4
```

Analysis ▼

The usage of copy() is shown in Line 28, where you copy the contents of the list into the vector. copy_if() is used in Line 33, and it copies all but even numbers from the source range listIntegers into the destination range vecIntegers starting at the iterator position iLastPos returned by copy(). remove() is shown in Line 41 and is used to rid the vecIntegers of all instances of 0. remove_if() is used in Line 45 to remove all odd numbers.

23

CAUTION

Listing 23.8 demonstrates that both remove() and remove_if() return an iterator that points to the new end of the container. Yet the container vecIntegers has not been resized yet. Elements have been deleted by the remove algorithms and other elements have been shifted forward, but the size() has remained unaltered, meaning there are values at the end of the vector. To resize the container (and this is important, else it has unwanted values at the end), you need to use the iterator returned by remove() or remove_if() in a subsequent call to erase(), as shown in Lines 42 and 48.

Replacing Values and Replacing Element Given a Condition

replace() and replace_if() are the STL algorithms that can replace elements in a collection that are equivalent to a supplied value or satisfy a given condition, respectively. replace() replaces elements based on the return value of the comparison operator (==):

```
cout << "Using 'std::replace' to replace value 5 by 8" << endl;
replace (vecIntegers.begin (), vecIntegers.end (), 5, 8);
```

replace_if() expects a user-specified unary predicate that returns true for every value that needs to be replaced:

```
cout << "Using 'std::replace_if' to replace even values by -1" << endl;
replace_if (vecIntegers.begin (), vecIntegers.end ()
    , [](int element) {return ((element % 2) == 0); }, -1);
```

The usage of these functions is demonstrated by Listing 23.9.

LISTING 23.9 Using replace() and replace_if() to Replace Values in a Specified Range

```
0: #include <iostream>
1: #include <algorithm>
2: #include <vector>
3: using namespace std;
4:
5: template <typename T>
6: void DisplayContents(const T& Input)
7: {
8:    for ( auto iElement = Input.cbegin() // auto, cbegin: c++11
9:          ; iElement != Input.cend()  // cend() is new in C++11
10:          ; ++ iElement)
11:       cout << *iElement << ' ';
12:
13:    cout << "¦ Number of elements: " << Input.size() << endl;
14: }
15: int main ()
16: {
17:    vector <int> vecIntegers (6);
18:
19:    // fill first 3 elements with value 8, last 3 with 5
20:    fill (vecIntegers.begin (), vecIntegers.begin () + 3, 8);
21:    fill_n (vecIntegers.begin () + 3, 3, 5);
22:
23:    // shuffle the container
24:    random_shuffle (vecIntegers.begin (), vecIntegers.end ());
25:
26:    cout << "The initial contents of the vector are: " << endl;
27:    DisplayContents(vecIntegers);
28:
29:    cout << endl << "Using 'std::replace' to replace value 5 by 8" << endl;
30:    replace (vecIntegers.begin (), vecIntegers.end (), 5, 8);
31:
32:    cout << "Using 'std::replace_if' to replace even values by -1" << endl;
33:    replace_if (vecIntegers.begin (), vecIntegers.end ()
34:        , [](int element) {return ((element % 2) == 0); }, -1);
35:
36:    cout << endl << "Contents of the vector after replacements:" << endl;
```

```
37:     DisplayContents(vecIntegers);
38:
39:     return 0;
40: }
```

Output ▼

```
The initial contents of the vector are:
5 8 5 8 8 5 ¦ Number of elements: 6

Using 'std::replace' to replace value 5 by 8
Using 'std::replace_if' to replace even values by -1

Contents of the vector after replacements:
-1 -1 -1 -1 -1 -1 ¦ Number of elements: 6
```

23

Analysis ▼

The sample fills a vector<int> vecIntegers with sample values and then shuffles it using the STL algorithm std::random_shuffle as shown in Line 24. Line 30 demonstrates the usage of replace() to replace all 5s by 8s. Hence, when replace_if(), in Line 33, replaces all even numbers with –1, the end result is that the collection has six elements, all containing an identical value of –1, as shown in the output.

Sorting and Searching in a Sorted Collection and Erasing Duplicates

Sorting and searching a sorted range (for sake of performance) are requirements that come up in practical applications way too often. Very often you have an array of information that needs to be sorted, say for presentation's sake. You can use STL's sort() algorithm to sort a container:

```
sort (vecIntegers.begin (), vecIntegers.end ()); // ascending order
```

This version of sort() uses std::less<> as a binary predicate that uses operator< implemented by the type in the vector. You can supply your own predicate to change the sort order using an overloaded version:

```
sort (vecIntegers.begin (), vecIntegers.end (),
     [](int lhs, int rsh) {return (lhs > rhs);} ); // descending order
```

Similarly, duplicates need to be deleted before the collection is displayed. To remove adjacently placed repeating values, use algorithm `unique()`:

```
auto iNewEnd = unique (vecIntegers.begin (), vecIntegers.end ());
vecIntegers.erase (iNewEnd, vecIntegers.end ());  // to resize
```

To search fast, STL provides you with `binary_search()` that is effective only on a sorted container:

```
bool bElementFound = binary_search (vecIntegers.begin (), vecIntegers.end (),
2011);

if (bElementFound)
   cout << "Element found in the vector!" << endl;
```

Listing 23.10 demonstrates STL algorithms `std::sort()` that can sort a range, `std::binary_search()` that can search a sorted range, and `std::unique()` that eliminates duplicate neighboring elements (that become neighbors after a `sort()` operation).

LISTING 23.10   Using `sort()`, `binary_search()`, and `unique()`

```
0: #include <algorithm>
1: #include <vector>
2: #include <string>
3: #include <iostream>
4: using namespace std;
5:
6: template <typename T>
7: void DisplayContents(const T& Input)
8: {
9:    for ( auto iElement = Input.cbegin() // auto, cbegin: c++11
10:          ; iElement != Input.cend()  // cend() is new in C++11
11:          ; ++ iElement)
12:       cout << *iElement << endl;
13: }
14: int main ()
15: {
16:    vector<string> vecNames;
17:    vecNames.push_back ("John Doe");
18:    vecNames.push_back ("Jack Nicholson");
19:    vecNames.push_back ("Sean Penn");
20:    vecNames.push_back ("Anna Hoover");
21:
22:    // insert a duplicate into the vector
23:    vecNames.push_back ("Jack Nicholson");
24:
25:    cout << "The initial contents of the vector are:" << endl;
26:    DisplayContents(vecNames);
27:
28:    cout << "The sorted vector contains names in the order:" << endl;
```

```
29:     sort (vecNames.begin (), vecNames.end ());
30:     DisplayContents(vecNames);
31:
32:     cout << "Searching for \"John Doe\" using 'binary_search':" << endl;
33:     bool bElementFound = binary_search (vecNames.begin (), vecNames.end (),
34:                                   "John Doe");
35:
36:     if (bElementFound)
37:        cout << "Result: \"John Doe\" was found in the vector!" << endl;
38:     else
39:        cout << "Element not found " << endl;
40:
41:     // Erase adjacent duplicates
42:     auto iNewEnd = unique (vecNames.begin (), vecNames.end ());
43:     vecNames.erase (iNewEnd, vecNames.end ());
44:
45:     cout << "The contents of the vector after using 'unique':" << endl;
46:     DisplayContents(vecNames);
47:
48:     return 0;
49: }
```

23

Output ▼

```
The initial contents of the vector are:
John Doe
Jack Nicholson
Sean Penn
Anna Hoover
Jack Nicholson
The sorted vector contains names in the order:
Anna Hoover
Jack Nicholson
Jack Nicholson
John Doe
Sean Penn
Searching for "John Doe" using 'binary_search':
Result: "John Doe" was found in the vector!
The contents of the vector after using 'unique':
Anna Hoover
Jack Nicholson
John Doe
Sean Penn
```

Analysis ▼

The preceding code first sorts the sample vector, vecNames in Line 29, before using binary_search() in Line 33 to find John Doe in it. Similarly, std::unique() is used in

Line 42 to delete the second occurrence of an adjacent duplicate. Note that `unique()`, like `remove()`, does not resize the container. It results in values being shifted but not a reduction in the total number of elements. To ensure that you don't have unwanted or unknown values at the tail end of the container, always follow a call to `unique()` with `vector::erase()` using the iterator returned by `unique()`, as demonstrated by Lines 42 and 43.

CAUTION

Algorithms such as `binary_search()` are effective only in sorted containers. Use of this algorithm on an unsorted vector can have undesirable consequences.

NOTE

The usage of `stable_sort()` is the same as that of `sort()`, which you saw earlier. `stable_sort()` ensures that the relative order of the sorted elements is maintained. Maintaining relative order comes at the cost of performance—a factor that needs to be kept in mind, especially if the relative ordering of elements is not essential.

Partitioning a Range

`std::partition()` helps partition an input range into two sections: one that satisfies a unary predicate and another that doesn't:

```
bool IsEven (const int& nNumber)  // unary predicate
{
    return ((nNumber % 2) == 0);
}
...
partition (vecIntegers.begin(), vecIntegers.end(), IsEven);
```

`std::partition()`, however, does not guarantee the relative order of elements within each partition. To maintain relative order, when that is important, you should use `std::stable_partition()`:

```
stable_partition (vecIntegers.begin(), vecIntegers.end(), IsEven);
```

Listing 23.11 demonstrates the usage of these algorithms.

LISTING 23.11 Using partition() and stable_partition() to Partition a Range of Integers into Even and Odd Values

```
0: #include <algorithm>
1: #include <vector>
2: #include <iostream>
3: using namespace std;
4:
5: bool IsEven (const int& nNumber)
6: {
7:    return ((nNumber % 2) == 0);
8: }
9:
10: template <typename T>
11: void DisplayContents(const T& Input)
12: {
13:    for ( auto iElement = Input.cbegin() // auto, cbegin: c++11
14:        ; iElement != Input.cend()  // cend() is new in C++11
15:        ; ++ iElement)
16:       cout << *iElement << ' ';
17:
18:    cout << "| Number of elements: " << Input.size() << endl;
19: }
20: int main ()
21: {
22:    vector <int> vecIntegers;
23:
24:    for (int nNum = 0; rNum < 10; ++ nNum)
25:       vecIntegers.push_back (nNum);
26:
27:    cout << "The initial contents: " << endl;
28:    DisplayContents(vecIntegers);
29:
30:    vector <int> vecCopy (vecIntegers);
31:
32:    cout << "The effect of using partition():" << endl;
33:    partition (vecIntegers.begin (), vecIntegers.end (), IsEven);
34:    DisplayContents(vecIntegers);
35:
36:    cout << "The effect of using stable_partition():" << endl;
37:    stable_partition (vecCopy.begin (), vecCopy.end (), IsEven);
38:    DisplayContents(vecCopy);
39:
40:    return 0;
41: }
```

23

Output ▼

```
The initial contents:
0 1 2 3 4 5 6 7 8 9 ¦ Number of elements: 10
The effect of using partition():
0 8 2 6 4 5 3 7 1 9 ¦ Number of elements: 10
The effect of using stable_partition():
0 2 4 6 8 1 3 5 7 9 ¦ Number of elements: 10
```

Analysis ▼

The code partitions a range of integers, as contained inside vector vecIntegers, into even and odd values. This partitioning is first done using std::partition(), as shown in Line 33, and is done using stable_partition() in Line 37. For the sake of being able to compare, you copy the sample range vecIntegers into vecCopy, the former partitioned using partition(), and the latter using stable_partition(). The effect of using stable_partition rather than partition is apparent in the output. stable_partition() maintains the relative order of elements in each partition. Note that maintaining this order comes at the price of performance that might be small, as in this case, or significant depending on the type of object contained in the range.

NOTE _____ | stable_partition() is slower than partition(), and therefore you should use it only when the relative order of elements in the container is important.

Inserting Elements in a Sorted Collection

It is important that elements inserted in a sorted collection be inserted at the correct positions. STL supplies functions, such as lower_bound() and upper_bound(), to assist in meeting that need:

```
auto iMinInsertPos = lower_bound ( listNames.begin(), listNames.end()
                                   , "Brad Pitt" );
// alternatively:
auto iMaxInsertPos = upper_bound ( listNames.begin(), listNames.end()
                                   , "Brad Pitt" );
```

Hence, lower_bound() and upper_bound()return iterators pointing to the minimal and the maximal positions in a sorted range where an element can be inserted without breaking the order of the sort.

Listing 23.12 demonstrates the usage of lower_bound() in inserting an element at the minimal position in a sorted list of names.

LISTING 23.12 Using `lower_bound()` and `upper_bound(` to Insert in a Sorted Collection

```
0: #include <algorithm>
1: #include <list>
2: #include <string>
3: #include <iostream>
4: using namespace std;
5:
6: template <typename T>
7: void DisplayContents(const T& Input)
8: {
9:    for ( auto iElement = Input.cbegin() // auto, cbegin: c++11
10:        ; iElement != Input.cend()  // cend() is new in C++11
11:        ; ++ iElement)
12:       cout << *iElement << endl;
13: }
14: int main ()
15: {
16:    list<string> listNames;
17:
18:    // Insert sample values
19:    listNames.push_back ("John Doe");
20:    listNames.push_back ("Brad Pitt");
21:    listNames.push_back ("Jack Nicholson");
22:    listNames.push_back ("Sean Penn");
23:    listNames.push_back ("Anna Hoover");
24:
25:    cout << "The sorted contents of the list are: " << endl;
26:    listNames.sort ();
27:    DisplayContents(listNames);
28:
29:    cout << "The lowest index where \"Brad Pitt\" can be inserted is: ";
30:    auto iMinInsertPos = lower_bound ( listNames.begin (), listNames.end ()
31:                                      , "Brad Pitt" );
32:    cout << distance (listNames.begin (), iMinInsertPos) << endl;
33:
34:    cout << "The highest index where \"Brad Pitt\" can be inserted is: ";
35:    auto iMaxInsertPos = upper_bound ( listNames.begin (), listNames.end ()
36:                                      , "Brad Pitt" );
37:    cout << distance (listNames.begin (), iMaxInsertPos) << endl;
38:
39:    cout << endl;
40:
41:    cout << "List after inserting Brad Pitt in sorted order: " << endl;
42:    listNames.insert (iMinInsertPos, "Brad Pitt");
43:
44:    DisplayContents(listNames);
45:    return 0;
46: }
```

23

Output ▼

```
The sorted contents of the list are:
Anna Hoover
Brad Pitt
Jack Nicholson
John Doe
Sean Penn
The lowest index where "Brad Pitt" can be inserted is: 1
The highest index where "Brad Pitt" can be inserted is: 2

List after inserting Brad Pitt in sorted order:
Anna Hoover
Brad Pitt
Brad Pitt
Jack Nicholson
John Doe
Sean Penn
```

Analysis ▼

An element can be inserted into a sorted collection at two potential positions: one is returned by lower_bound() and is the lowest (the closest to the beginning of the collection) and another is the iterator returned by upper_bound() that is the highest (the farthest away from the beginning of the collection). In the case of Listing 23.12, where the string "Brad Pitt" is inserted into the sorted collection already exists in it (inserted in Line 20), the lower and upper bounds are different (else, they would've been identical). The usage of these functions is shown in Lines 30 and 35, respectively. As the output demonstrates, the iterator returned by lower_bound(), when used in inserting the string into the list as shown in Line 42, results in the list keeping its sorted state. Thus, these algorithms help you make an insertion at a point in the collection without breaking the sorted nature of the contents. Using the iterator returned by upper_bound() would have worked fine as well.

DO	DON'T
DO remember to use the container's erase() member method after using algorithms remove(), remove_if(), or unique() to resize the container. **DO** always check the iterator returned by find(), find_if(), search(), or search_n() functions for validity before using it by comparing against the end() of the container. **DO** choose stable_partition() over partition() and stable_sort() over sort() only when the relative ordering of sorted elements is important as the stable_* versions can reduce the performance of the application.	**DON'T** Don't forget sorting a container using sort() before calling unique() to remove repeating adjacent values. sort() will ensure that all elements of a value are aligned adjacent to each other, making unique() effective. **DON'T** forget that binary_search() should be done only on a sorted container.

23

Summary

In this lesson, you learned one of the most important and powerful aspects of STL: algorithms. You gained an insight into the different types of algorithms, and the samples should have given you a clearer understanding of the algorithms application.

Q&A

Q Would I use a mutating algorithm, such as std::transform(), on an associative container, such as std::set?

A Even if it were possible, this should not be done. The contents of an associative container should be treated as constants. This is because associative containers sort their elements on insertion, and the relative positions of the elements play an important role in functions such as find() and also in the efficiency of the container. For this reason, mutating algorithms, such as std::transform(), should not be used on STL sets.

Q I need to set the content of every element of a sequential container to a particular value. Would I use std::transform()for this activity?

A Although std::transform() could be used for this activity, fill() or fill_n() is more suited to the task.

Q Does `copy_backward()` reverse the contents of the elements in the destination container?

A No, it doesn't. The STL algorithm `copy_backward()` reverses the order in which elements are copied but not the order in which elements are stored; that is, it starts with the end of the range and reaches the top. To reverse the contents of a collection, you should use `std::reverse()`.

Q Should I use `std::sort()` on a list?

A `std::sort()` can be used on a list in the same way it can be used on any sequential container. However, the list needs to maintain a special property that an operation on the list does not invalidate existing iterators—a property that `std::sort()` cannot guarantee to upkeep. So, for this reason, STL `list` supplies the `sort()` algorithm in the form of the member function `list::sort()`, which should be used because it guarantees that iterators to elements in the list are not invalidated even if their relative positions in the list have changed.

Q Why is it important to use functions such as `lower_bound()` or `upper_bound()` while inserting into a sorted range?

A These functions supply the first and the last positions, respectively, where an element can be inserted into a sorted collection without disturbing the sort.

Workshop

The Workshop contains quiz questions to help solidify your understanding of the material covered and exercises to provide you with experience in using what you've learned. Try to answer the quiz and exercise questions before checking the answers in Appendix D, and be certain you understand the answers before going to the next lesson

Quiz

1. You need to remove items that meet a specific condition from a list. Would you use `std::remove_if()` or `list::remove_if()`?

2. You have a list of a class type `ContactItem`. How does the `list::sort()` function sort items of this type in the absence of an explicitly specified binary predicate?

3. How often does the `generate()` STL algorithm invoke the `generator()` function?

4. What differentiates `std::transform()` from `std::for_each()`?

Exercises

1. Write a binary predicate that accepts strings as input arguments and returns a value based on case-insensitive comparison.

2. Demonstrate how STL algorithms such as copy use iterators to do their functions without needing to know the nature of the destination collections by copying between two sequences held in two dissimilar containers.

3. You are writing an application that records the characteristics of stars that come up on the horizon in the order in which they rise. In astronomy, the size of the star—as well as information on their relative rise and set sequences—is important. If you're sorting this collection of stars on the basis of their sizes, would you use `std::sort` or `std::stable_sort`?

23

LESSON 24

Adaptive Containers: Stack and Queue

The Standard Template Library (STL) features containers that adapt others to simulate stack and queue behavior. Such containers that internally use another and present a distinct behavior are called *adaptive containers*.

In this lesson, you learn

- The behavioral characteristics of stacks and queues
- Using the STL `stack`
- Using the STL `queue`
- Using the STL `priority_queue`

The Behavioral Characteristics of Stacks and Queues

Stacks and queues are quite like arrays or lists but present a restriction on how elements are inserted, accessed, and removed. Their behavioral characteristics are decided exactly by the placement of elements on insertion or the position of the element that can be erased from the container.

Stacks

Stacks are LIFO (last-in-first-out) systems where elements can be inserted or removed at the top of the container. A stack can be visualized as a stack of plates. The last plate added to the stack is going to be the first one taken off. Plates in the middle and at the bottom cannot be inspected. This method of organizing elements involving "addition and removal at the top" is illustrated by Figure 24.1.

FIGURE 24.1
Operations on a stack.

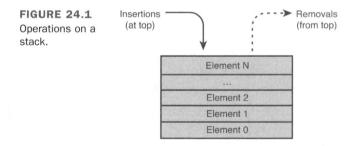

This behavior of a stack of plates is simulated in the generic STL container `std::stack`.

TIP	To use class `std::stack`, include header
	`#include <stack>`

Queues

Queues are FIFO (first-in-first-out) systems where elements can be inserted behind the previous one, and the one inserted first gets removed first. A queue can be visualized as a queue of people waiting for stamps at the post office—those who join the queue earlier, leave earlier. This method of organizing elements involving "addition at the back but removal at the front" is illustrated by Figure 24.2.

FIGURE 24.2
Operations on a
queue.

This behavior of a queue is simulated in the generic STL container `std::queue`.

TIP

To use class `std::queue`, include header

```
#include <queue>
```

Using the STL stack Class

The STL `stack` is a template class that needs the inclusion of header `<stack>`. It is a
generic class that allows insertions and removal of elements at the top and does not permit any access or inspection of elements at the middle. In that sense, the `std::stack` is
quite similar in behavior to a stack of plates.

24

Instantiating the Stack

`std::stack` is defined by some implementations of STL as

```
template <
   class elementType,
   class Container=deque<Type>
> class stack;
```

The parameter `elementType` is the type of object that is collected by the stack. The second template parameter `Container` is the stack's default underlying container implementation class. `std::deque` is the default for the stack's internal data storage and can be
replaced by `std::vector` or the `std::list`. Thus, the instantiation of a stack of integers
will look like

```
std::stack <int> stackInts;
```

If you want to create a stack of objects of any type, for instance `class Tuna`, you would
use the following:

```
std::stack <Tuna> stackTunas;
```

To create a stack that uses a different underlying container, use

```
std::stack <double, vector <double> > stackDoublesInVector;
```

Listing 24.1 demonstrates different instantiation techniques.

LISTING 24.1   Instantiation of an STL Stack

```
0: #include <stack>
1: #include <vector>
2:
3: int main ()
4: {
5:    using namespace std;
6:
7:    // A stack of integers
8:    stack <int> stackInts;
9:
10:    // A stack of doubles
11:    stack <double> stackDoubles;
12:
13:    // A stack of doubles contained in a vector
14:    stack <double, vector <double> > stackDoublesInVector;
15:
16:    // initializing one stack to be a copy of another
17:    stack <int> stackIntsCopy(stackInts);
18:
19:    return 0;
20: }
```

Analysis ▼

The sample produces no output but demonstrates the template instantiation of the STL stack. Lines 8 and 11 instantiate two stack objects to hold elements of type int and double, respectively. Line 14 also instantiates a stack of doubles but specifies a second template parameter—the type of collection class that the stack should use internally, a vector. If this second template parameter is not supplied, the stack automatically defaults to using a std::deque instead. Finally, Line 17 demonstrates that one stack object can be constructed as a copy of another.

Stack Member Functions

The stack, which adapts another container, such as the deque, list, or vector, implements its functionality by restricting the manner in which elements can be inserted or removed to supply a behavior that is expected strictly from a stack-like mechanism. Table 24.1 explains the public member functions of the stack class and demonstrates their usage for a stack of integers.

TABLE 24.1   Member Function of a std::stack

Function	Description
push	Inserts an element at the top of the stack
	stackInts.push (25);
pop	Removes the element at the top of the stack
	stackInts.pop ();
empty	Tests whether the stack is empty; returns bool
	if (stackInts.empty ())
	DoSomething ();
size	Returns the number of elements in the stack
	size_t nNumElements = stackInts.size ();
top	Gets a reference to the topmost element in the stack
	cout << "Element at the top = " << stackInts.top ();

As the table indicates, the public member functions of the stack expose only those methods that allow insertion and removal at positions that are compliant with a stack's behavior. That is, even though the underlying container might be a deque, a vector, or a list, the functionality of that container has not been revealed to enforce the behavioral characteristics of a stack.

Insertion and Removal at Top Using push() and pop()

Insertion of elements is done using member method stack<T>::push():

```
stackInts.push (25); // 25 is atop the stack
```

The stack by definition allows access of elements typically at the top using member top():

```
cout << stackInts.top() << endl;
```

If you want to remove an element at the top, you can use function pop() to help you with the same:

```
stackInts.pop (); // pop: removes topmost element
```

Listing 24.2 demonstrates inserting elements in a stack using push() and removing elements using pop().

LISTING 24.2   Working with a Stack of Integers

```
0: #include <stack>
1: #include <iostream>
2:
```

LISTING 24.2 Continued

```
 3: int main ()
 4: {
 5:    using namespace std;
 6:    stack <int> stackInts;
 7:
 8:    // push: insert values at top of the stack
 9:    cout << "Pushing {25, 10, -1, 5} on stack in that order:" << endl;
10:    stackInts.push (25);
11:    stackInts.push (10);
12:    stackInts.push (-1);
13:    stackInts.push (5);
14:
15:    cout << "Stack contains " << stackInts.size () << " elements" << endl;
16:    while (stackInts.size () != 0)
17:    {
18:       cout << "Popping topmost element: " << stackInts.top() << endl;
19:       stackInts.pop (); // pop: removes topmost element
20:    }
21:
22:    if (stackInts.empty ())  // true: due to previous pop()s
23:       cout << "Popping all elements empties stack!" << endl;
24:
25:    return 0;
26: }
```

Output ▼

```
Pushing {25, 10, -1, 5} on stack in that order:
Stack contains 4 elements
Popping topmost element: 5
Popping topmost element: -1
Popping topmost element: 10
Popping topmost element: 25
Popping all elements empties stack!
```

Analysis ▼

The sample first inserts numbers into a stack of integers, stackInts, using the stack::push() as shown in Lines 9–13. It then proceeds to delete elements using stack::pop(). As stack permits access to only the topmost element, an element at the top can be accessed using member stack::top() as shown in Line 18. Elements can be deleted from the stack one at a time using stack::pop(), as shown in Line 19. The while loop around it ensures that the pop() operation is repeated until the stack is empty. As is visible from the order of the elements that were popped, the element inserted last was popped first, demonstrating the typical LIFO behavior of a `stack`.

Listing 24.2 demonstrates all five member functions of the `stack`. Note that `push_back` and `insert`, which are available with all STL sequential containers, used as underlying containers by the `stack` class, are not available as public member functions of the `stack`. Ditto for iterators that help you peek at elements that are not at the top of the container. All that the `stack` exposes is the element at the top, nothing else.

Using the STL queue Class

The STL queue is a template class that requires the inclusion of the header `<queue>`. It is a generic class that allows insertion only at the end and removal of elements only at the front. A queue does not permit any access or inspection of elements at the middle; however, elements at the beginning and the end can be accessed. In a sense, the `std::queue` is quite similar in behavior to a queue of people at the cashier in a supermarket!

Instantiating the Queue

`std::queue` is defined as

```
template <
   class elementType,
   class Container = deque<Type>
> class queue;
```

Here, `elementType` is the type of elements collected by the queue object. `Container` is the type of collection that the `std::queue` class uses to maintain its data. The `std::list`, `vector`, and `deque` are possible candidates for this template parameter, and the `deque` is the default.

The simplest instantiation of a queue of integers would be the following:

```
std::queue <int> qIntegers;
```

If you want to create a queue containing elements of type `double` inside a `std::list` (instead of a deque, which is default), use the following:

```
std::queue <double, list <double> > qDoublesInList;
```

Just like a stack, a queue can also be instantiated as a copy of another queue:

```
std::queue<int> qCopy(qIntegers);
```

Listing 24.3 demonstrates the various instantiation techniques of `std::queue`.

LISTING 24.3   Instantiating an STL Queue

```
0: #include <queue>
 1: #include <list>
 2:
 3: int main ()
 4: {
 5:    using namespace std;
 6:
 7:    // A queue of integers
 8:    queue <int> qIntegers;
 9:
10:    // A queue of doubles
11:    queue <double> qDoubles;
12:
13:    // A queue of doubles stored internally in a list
14:    queue <double, list <double> > qDoublesInList;
15:
16:    // one queue created as a copy of another
17:    queue<int> qCopy(qIntegers);
18:
19:    return 0;
20: }
```

Analysis ▼

The sample demonstrates how the generic STL class queue can be instantiated to create a queue of integers, as shown in Line 8, or a queue for objects of type double, as shown in Line 11. qDoublesInList, as instantiated in Line 14, is a queue in which you have explicitly specified that the underlying container adapted by the queue to manage its internals be a std::list, as specified by the second template parameter. In the absence of the second template parameter, as in the first two queues, the std::deque is used as the default underlying container for the contents of the queue.

Member Functions of a queue

The std::queue, like std::stack, also bases its implementation on an STL container such as the vector, list, or deque. The queue exposes only those member functions that implement the behavioral characteristics of a queue. Table 24.2 explains the member functions using qIntegers, which Listing 24.3 demonstrates is a queue of integers.

TABLE 24.2   Member Functions of a `std::queue`

Function	Description
push	Inserts an element at the back of the queue; that is, at the last position
	`qIntegers.push (10);`
pop	Removes the element at the front of the queue; that is, at the first position
	`qIntegers.pop ();`
front	Returns a reference to the element at the front of the queue
	`cout << "Element at front: " << qIntegers.front ();`
back	Returns a reference to the element at the back of the queue; that is, the last inserted element
	`cout << "Element at back: " << qIntegers.back ();`
empty	Tests whether the queue is empty; returns a boolean value
	`if (qIntegers.empty ())`
	`cout << "The queue is empty!";`
size	Returns the number of elements in the queue
	`size_t nNumElements = qIntegers.size ();`

STL queue does not feature functions such as `begin()` and `end()`, which are supplied by most STL containers, including the underlying deque, vector, or list, as used by the queue class. This is by intention so that the only permissible operations on the queue are those in compliance with the queue's behavioral characteristics.

Insertion at End and Removal at the Beginning of queue **via** `push()` **and** `pop()`

Insertion of elements in a queue happens at the end and is done using member method `push()`:

```
qIntegers.push (5);   // elements pushed are inserted at the end
```

Removal, on the other hand, happens at the beginning and via `pop()`:

```
qIntegers.pop ();   // removes element at front
```

Unlike the stack, the queue allows elements at both ends—that is, `front` and `back` of the container—to be inspected:

```
cout << "Element at front: " << qIntegers.front() << endl;
cout << "Element at back: " << qIntegers.back () << endl;
```

24

Insertion, removal, and inspection is demonstrated in Listing 24.4.

LISTING 24.4   Inserting, Removing, and Inspecting Elements in a queue of Integers

```
0: #include <queue>
1: #include <iostream>
2:
3: int main ()
4: {
5:    using namespace std;
6:    queue <int> qIntegers;
7:
8:    cout << "Inserting {10, 5, -1, 20} into queue" << endl;
9:    qIntegers.push (10);
10:    qIntegers.push (5);  // elements pushed are inserted at the end
11:    qIntegers.push (-1);
12:    qIntegers.push (20);
13:
14:    cout << "Queue contains " << qIntegers.size () << " elements" << endl;
15:    cout << "Element at front: " << qIntegers.front() << endl;
16:    cout << "Element at back: " << qIntegers.back () << endl;
17:
18:    while (qIntegers.size () != 0)
19:    {
20:       cout << "Deleting element: " << qIntegers.front () << endl;
21:       qIntegers.pop ();  // removes element at front
22:    }
23:
24:    if (qIntegers.empty ())  // true as all elements have been pop()-ed
25:       cout << "The queue is now empty!" << endl;
26:
27:    return 0;
28: }
```

Output ▼

```
Inserting {10, 5, -1, 20} into queue
Queue contains 4 elements
Element at front: 10
Element at back: 20
Deleting element: 10
Deleting element: 5
Deleting element: -1
Deleting element: 20
```

Analysis ▼

Elements were added to qIntegers using push() that inserts them at the end (or back) of the queue in Lines 9–12. Methods front() and back() are used to reference elements at the beginning and the end positions of the queue, as shown in Lines 15 and 16. The `while` loop in Lines 18–22 displays the element at the beginning of the queue, before removing it using a `pop()` operation at Line 21. It continues doing this until the queue is empty. The output demonstrates that elements were erased from the queue in the same order in which they were inserted because elements are inserted at the rear of the queue but deleted from the front.

Using the STL Priority Queue

The STL `priority_queue` is a template class that also requires the inclusion of the header `<queue>`. The `priority_queue` is different from the `queue` in that the element of the highest value (or the value deemed as highest by a binary predicate) is available at the front of the queue and queue operations are restricted to the front.

Instantiating the `priority_queue` Class

`std::priority_queue` class is defined as

```
template <
    class elementType,
    class Container=vector<Type>,
        class Compare=less<typename Container::value_type>
>
class priority_queue
```

Here, `elementType` is the template parameter that conveys the type of elements to be collected in the priority queue. The second template parameter tells the collection class to be internally used by `priority_queue` for holding data, whereas the third parameter allows the programmer to specify a binary predicate that helps the queue determine the element that is at the top. In the absence of a specified binary predicate, the `priority_queue` class uses the default in `std::less`, which compares two objects using `operator<`.

The simplest instantiation of a `priority_queue` of integers would be

```
std::priority_queue <int> pqIntegers;
```

If you want to create a `priority queue` containing elements of type `double` inside a `std::deque`:

```
priority_queue <int, deque <int>, greater <int> > pqIntegers_Inverse;
```

Just like a stack, a queue can also be instantiated as a copy of another queue:

```
std::priority_queue <int>  pqCopy(pqIntegers);
```

The instantiation of a `priority_queue` object is demonstrated by Listing 24.5.

24

LISTING 24.5   Instantiating an STL `priority_queue`

```
0: #include <queue>
1:
2: int main ()
3: {
4:    using namespace std;
5:
6:    // A priority queue of integers sorted using std::less <> (default)
7:    priority_queue <int> pqIntegers;
8:
9:    // A priority queue of doubles
10:    priority_queue <double> pqDoubles;
11:
12:    // A priority queue of integers sorted using std::greater <>
13:    priority_queue <int, deque <int>, greater <int> > pqIntegers_Inverse;
14:
15:    // a priority queue created as a copy of another
16:    priority_queue <int>  pqCopy(pqIntegers);
17:
18:    return 0;
19: }
```

Analysis ▼

Lines 7 and 10 demonstrate the instantiation of two `priority_queues` for objects of type `int` and `double`, respectively. The absence of any other template parameter results in the usage of `std::vector` as the internal container of data, and the default comparison criterion is provided by `std::less`. These queues are therefore so prioritized that the integer of the highest value is available at the `front` of the priority queue. `pqIntegers_Inverse`, however, supplies a `deque` for the second parameter as the internal container and `std::greater` as the predicate. This predicate results in a queue where the smallest number is available at the front.

The effect of using predicate `std::greater<T>` is explained in Listing 24.7 later in this lesson.

Member Functions of `priority_queue`

The member functions `front()` and `back()`, available in the `queue`, are not available in the `priority_queue`. Table 24.3 introduces the member functions of a `priority_queue`.

TABLE 24.3   Member Functions of a std::priority_queue

Function	Description
push	Inserts an element into the priority queue
	`pqIntegers.push (10);`
pop	Removes the element at the top of the queue; that is, the largest element in the queue
	`pqIntegers.pop ();`
top	Returns a reference to the largest element in the queue (which also holds the topmost position)
	`cout << "The largest element in the priority  queue is: " << pqIntegers.top ();`
empty	Tests whether the priority queue is empty; returns a boolean value
	`if (pqIntegers.empty ())`
	`    cout << "The queue is empty!";`
size	Returns the number of elements in the priority queue
	`size_t nNumElements = pqIntegers.size ();`

As the table indicates, queue members can only be accessed using top(), which returns the element of the highest value, evaluated using the user-defined predicate or by std::less in the absence of one.

Insertion at the End and Removal at the Beginning of priority_queue **via** push() **and** pop()

Insertion of elements in a priority_queue is done using member method push():

```
pqIntegers.push (5);  // elements are placed in sorted order
```

Removal, on the other hand, happens at the beginning via pop():

```
pqIntegers.pop ();  // removes element at front
```

The usage of priority_queue members is demonstrated by Listing 24.6.

LISTING 24.6   Working with a priority_queue Using push(), top(), and pop()

```
0: #include <queue>
1: #include <iostream>
2:
3: int main ()
4: {
5:    using namespace std;
6:
```

24

LISTING 24.6 Continued

```
 7:    priority_queue <int> pqIntegers;
 8:    cout << "Inserting {10, 5, -1, 20} into the priority_queue" << endl;
 9:    pqIntegers.push (10);
10:    pqIntegers.push (5);   // placed in sorted order
11:    pqIntegers.push (-1);
12:    pqIntegers.push (20);
13:
14:    cout << "Deleting the " << pqIntegers.size () << " elements" << endl;
15:    while (!pqIntegers.empty ())
16:    {
17:       cout << "Deleting topmost element: " << pqIntegers.top () << endl;
18:       pqIntegers.pop ();
19:    }
20:
21:    return 0;
22: }
```

Output ▼

```
Inserting {10, 5, -1, 20} into the priority_queue
Deleting the 4 elements
Deleting topmost element: 20
Deleting topmost element: 10
Deleting topmost element: 5
Deleting topmost element: -1
```

Analysis ▼

Listing 24.6 inserts sample integers into a priority_queue, as shown in Lines 9–12, and then erases the element on the top/front using pop(), as shown in Line 18. The output indicates that the element of greatest value is available at the top of the queue. Usage of priority_queue::pop() therefore effectively deletes the element that evaluates to having the greatest value among all elements in the container, which is also exposed as the value at the top, via method top() shown in Line 17. Given that you have not supplied a prioritization predicate, the queue has automatically resorted to sorting elements in the descending order (highest value at the top).

The next sample, in Listing 24.7, demonstrates the instantiation of a priority_queue with std::greater <int> as the predicate. This predicate results in the queue evaluating the smallest number as the element with greatest value, which is then available at the front of the priority queue.

LISTING 24.7 Instantiating a Priority Queue That Ho ds the Smallest Value at the Top

```
0: #include <queue>
1: #include <iostream>
2:
3: int main ()
4: {
5:    using namespace std;
6:
7:    // Define a priority_queue object with greater <int> as predicate
8:    priority_queue <int, vector <int>, greater <int> > pqIntegers;
9:
10:   cout << "Inserting {10, 5, -1, 20} into the priority queue" << endl;
11:   pqIntegers.push (10);
12:   pqIntegers.push (5);
13:   pqIntegers.push (-1);
14:   pqIntegers.push (20);
15:
16:   cout << "Deleting " << pqIntegers.size () << " elements" << endl;
17:   while (!pqIntegers.empty ())
18:   {
19:      cout << "Deleting topmost element " << pqIntegers.top () << endl;
20:      pqIntegers.pop ();
21:   }
22:
23:   return 0;
24: }
```

24

Output ▼

```
Inserting {10, 5, -1, 20} into the priority queue
Deleting 4 elements
Deleting topmost element -1
Deleting topmost element 5
Deleting topmost element 10
Deleting topmost element 20
```

Analysis ▼

Most of the code and all the values supplied to the priority_queue in this sample are intentionally the same as those in the previous sample, Listirg 24.6. Yet the output displays how the two queues behave differently. This priority_queue compares the elements in it using the predicate greater <int> as shown in Line 8. As a result of this predicate, the integer with the lowest magnitude is evaluated as greater than others and is therefore placed at the top position. So, function top() used in Line 19 always displays the smallest integer number in the priority_queue, one that is deleted soon after using a pop() operation in Line 20.

Thus, when elements are popped, this `priority_queue` pops the integers in order of increasing magnitude.

Summary

This lesson explained the usage of the three key adaptive containers—the STL `stack`, `queue`, and the `priority_queue`. These adapt sequential containers for their internal storage requirements, yet via their member functions they present the behavioral characteristics that make stacks and queues so unique.

Q&A

Q Can an element in the middle of a stack be modified?

A No, this would be against the behavior of a stack.

Q Can I iterate through all the elements of a queue?

A The queue does not feature iterators, and elements in a queue can be accessed only at its ends.

Q Can STL algorithms work with adaptive containers?

A STL algorithms work using iterators. Because neither the `stack` nor the `queue` class supplies iterators that mark the end of the ranges, the use of STL algorithms with these containers would not be possible.

Workshop

The Workshop contains quiz questions to help solidify your understanding of the material covered and exercises to provide you with experience in using what you've learned. Try to answer the quiz and exercise questions before checking the answers in Appendix D, and be certain you understand the answers before going to the next lesson.

Quiz

1. Can you change the behavior of the `priority_queue` for a certain element, such that the one with the greatest value is popped last?

2. You have a `priority_queue` of `class Coins`. What member operator do you need to define for the `priority_queue` class to present the coin with the greater value at the top position?

3. You have a stack of class `CCoins` and have pushed six objects into it. Can you access or delete the first coin inserted?

Exercises

1. A queue of people (class `CPerson`) are lining up at the post office. `CPerson` contains member attributes that hold age and gender and are defined as

```
class Person
{
    public:
        int Age;
        bool IsFemale;
};
```

   Write a binary predicate for the `priority_queue` that helps service older people and women (in that order) on a priority.

2. Write a program that reverses the user's string input using the `stack` class.

24

LESSON 25
Working with Bit Flags Using STL

Bits can be a very efficient way of storing settings and flags. The Standard Template Library (STL) supplies classes that help organize and manipulate bitwise information. This lesson introduces you to

- The `bitset` class
- The `vector<bool>`

The `bitset` Class

`std::bitset` is the STL class designed for handling information in bits and bit flags. `std::bitset` is not an STL container class because it cannot resize itself. This is a utility class that is optimized for working with a sequence of bits whose length is known at compile time.

Instantiating the `std::bitset`

This template class requires you to supply one template parameter that contains the number of bits the instance of the class has to manage:

`bitset <4> fourBits;  // 4 bits initialized to 0000`

You can also initialize the `bitset` to a bit sequence represented in a `char*` string literal:

`bitset <5> fiveBits ("10101"); // 5 bits 10101`

Copying from one bitset while instantiating another is quite simple:

`bitset <8> eightBitsCopy(eightbits);`

Some instantiation techniques of the `bitset` class are demonstrated by Listing 25.1.

LISTING 25.1   Instantiating a `std::bitset`

```
0: #include <bitset>
1: #include <iostream>
2: #include <string>
3:
4: int main ()
5: {
6:    using namespace std;
7:
8:    // instantiate a bitset object
9:    bitset <4> fourBits;  // 4 bits initialized to 0000
10:    cout << "Initial contents of fourBits: " << fourBits << endl;
11:
12:    bitset <5> fiveBits ("10101"); // 5 bits 10101
13:    cout << "Initial contents of fiveBits: " << fiveBits << endl;
14:
15:    bitset <8> eightbits (255); // 8 bits initialized to long int 255
```

LISTING 25.1   Continued

```
16:    cout << "Initial contents of eightBits: " << eightbits << endl;
17:
18:    // instantiate one bitset as a copy of another
19:    bitset <8> eightBitsCopy(eightbits);
20:
21:    return 0;
22: }
```

Output ▼

```
Initial contents of fourBits: 0000
Initial contents of fiveBits: 10101
Initial contents of eightBits: 11111111
```

Analysis ▼

The sample demonstrates four different ways of constructing a `bitset` object. The default constructor initializes the bit sequence to 0, as shown in Line 9. A C-style string that contains the string representation of the desired bit sequence is used in Line 12. An unsigned `long` that holds the decimal value of the binary sequence is used in Line 15, and the copy constructor is used in Line 19. Note that in each of these instances, you had to supply the number of bits that the `bitset` is supposed to contain as a template parameter. This number is fixed at compile time; it isn't dynamic. You can't insert more bits into a `bitset` than what you specified in your code the way you can insert more elements in a vector than the `size()` planned at compile time.

Using `std::bitset` and Its Members

The `bitset` class supplies member functions that help perform insertions into the `bitset`, set or reset contents, read the bits, or write them into a stream. It also supplies operators that help display the contents of a `bitset` and perform bitwise logical operations among others.

Useful Operators Featured in `std::bitset`

You learned operators in Lesson 12, "Operator Types and Operator Overloading," and you also learned that the most important role played by operators is in increasing the usability of a class. `std::bitset` provides some very useful operators, as shown in Table 25.1, that make using it really easy. The operators are explained using the sample `bitset` you learned in Listing 25.1, `fourBits`.

25

TABLE 25.1   Operators Supported by `std::bitset`

Operator	Description
operator<<	Inserts a text representation of the bit sequence into the output stream
	`cout << fourBits;`
operator>>	Inserts a string into the bitset object
	`"0101" >> fourBits;`
operator&	Performs a bitwise AND operation
	`bitset <4> result (fourBits1 & fourBits2);`
operator¦	Performs a bitwise OR operation
	`bitwise <4> result (fourBits1 ¦ fourBits2);`
operator^	Performs a bitwise XOR operation
	`bitwise <4> result (fourBits1 ^ fourBits2);`
operator~	Performs a bitwise NOT operation
	`bitwise <4> result (~fourBits1);`
operator>>=	Performs a bitwise right shift
	`fourBits >>= (2); // Shift two bits to the right`
operator<<=	Performs a bitwise left shift
	`fourBits <<= (2); // Shift two bits to the left`
operator[N]	Returns a reference to the *n*th bit in the sequence
	`fourBits [2] = 0;  // sets the third bit to 0`
	`bool bNum = fourBits [2]; // reads the third bit`

In addition to these, `std::bitset` also features operators such as `¦=`, `&=`, `^=`, and `~=` that help perform bitwise operations on a `bitset` object.

`std::bitset` **Member Methods**

Bits can hold two states—they are either set (1) or reset (0). To help manipulate the contents of a `bitset`, you can use the member functions as listed in Table 25.2 that can help you work with a `bit`, or with all the `bits` in a `bitset`.

TABLE 25.2   Member Methods of a `std::bitset`

Function	Description
set	Sets all bits in the sequence to 1
	`fourBits.set (); // sequence now contains: '1111'`
set (N, val=1)	Sets the *N*th bit with the value as specified in `val` (default 1)
	`fourBits.set (2, 0); // sets the third bit to 0`

TABLE 25.2   Continued

Function	Description
reset	Resets all bits in the sequence to 0
	fourBits.reset (); // sequence now contains: '0000'
reset (N)	Clears the Nth bit
	fourBits.reset (2); // the third bit is now 0
flip	Toggles all bits in the sequence
	fourBits.flip (); // 0101 changes to 1010
size	Returns the number of bits in the sequence
	size_t NumBits = fourBits.size (); // returns 4
count	Returns the number of bits that are set
	size_t NumBitsSet = fourBits.count ();
	size_t NumBitsReset = fourBits.size () - fourBits.count ();

The usage of these member methods and operators is demonstrated in Listing 25.2.

LISTING 25.2   Performing Logical Operations Using a Bitset

```
0: #include <bitset>
1: #include <string>
2: #include <iostream>
3:
4: int main ()
5: {
6:    using namespace std;
7:    bitset <8> inputBits;
8:    cout << "Enter a 8-bit sequence: ";
9:
10:    cin >> inputBits;  // store user input in bitset
11:
12:    cout << "Number of 1s you supplied: " << inputBits.count () << endl;
13:    cout << "Number of 0s you supplied: ";
14:    cout << inputBits.size () - inputBits.count () << endl;
15:
16:    bitset <8> inputFlipped (inputBits);  // copy
17:    inputFlipped.flip ();  // toggle the bits
18:
19:    cout << "Flipped version is: " << inputFlipped << endl;
20:
21:    cout << "Result of AND, OR and XOR between the two:" << endl;
22:    cout << inputBits << " & " << inputFlipped << " = ";
23:    cout << (inputBits & inputFlipped) << endl;  // bitwise AND
24:
```

LISTING 25.2 Continued

```
25:    cout << inputBits << " ¦ " << inputFlipped << " = ";
26:    cout << (inputBits ¦ inputFlipped) << endl;  // bitwise OR
27:
28:    cout << inputBits << " ^ " << inputFlipped << " = ";
29:    cout << (inputBits ^ inputFlipped) << endl; // bitwise XOR
30:
31:    return 0;
32: }
```

Output ▼

```
Enter a 8-bit sequence: 10110101
Number of 1s you supplied: 5
Number of 0s you supplied: 3
Flipped version is: 01001010
Result of AND, OR and XOR between the two:
10110101 & 01001010 = 00000000
10110101 ¦ 01001010 = 11111111
10110101 ^ 01001010 = 11111111
```

Analysis ▼

This interactive program demonstrates not only how easy performing bitwise operations between two bit-sequences using std::bitset is, but also the utility of its stream operators. Shift operators (>> and <<) implemented by std::bitset made writing a bit sequence to the screen and reading a bit sequence from the user in string format a simple task. inputBits contains a user-supplied sequence that is fed into it in Line 10. count() used in Line 12 tells the number of ones in the sequence, and the number of zeroes is evaluated as the difference between size() that returns the number of bits in the bitset and count(), as shown in Line 14. inputFlipped is at the beginning a copy of inputBits, and then flipped using flip(), as shown in Line 17. It now contains the sequence with individual bits flipped—that is, toggled (0s become 1s and vice versa). The rest of the program demonstrates the result of bitwise AND, OR, and XOR operations between the two bitsets.

NOTE

One disadvantage of STL bitset<> is its inability to resize itself dynamically. You can use the bitset only where the number of bits to be stored in the sequence is known at compile time.

STL supplies the programmer with a class vector<bool> (also called bit_vector in some implementations of STL) that overcomes this shortcoming.

The vector<bool>

The vector<bool> is a partial specialization of the std::vector and is intended for storing boolean data. This class is able to dynamically size itself. Therefore, the programmer does not need to know the number of boolean flags to be stored at compile time.

TIP	To use class std::vector<bool>, include header:
	#include <vector>

Instantiating vector<bool>

Instantiating a vector<bool> is similar to a vector, with some convenient overloads:

```
vector <bool> vecBool1;
```

For instance, you can create a vector with 10 boolean values to start with, each initialized to 1 (that is, true):

```
vector <bool> vecBool2 (10, true);
```

You can also create an object as a copy of another:

```
vector <bool> vecBool2Copy (vecBool2);
```

Some of the instantiation techniques of a vector<bool> are demonstrated by Listing 25.3.

25

LISTING 25.3   The Instantiation of vector<bool>

```
0: #include <vector>
1:
2: int main ()
3: {
4:     using namespace std;
5:
6:     // Instantiate an object using the default constructor
7:     vector <bool> vecBool1;
8:
9:     // Initialize a vector with 10 elements with value true
10:    vector <bool> vecBool2 (10, true);
11:
12:    // Instantiate one object as a copy of another
13:    vector <bool> vecBool2Copy (vecBool2);
14:
15:    return 0;
16: }
```

Analysis ▼

This sample presents some of the ways in which a `vector<bool>` object can be constructed. Line 7 is one that uses the default constructor. Line 10 demonstrates the creation of an object that is initialized to contain 10 `boolean` flags, each holding the value `true`. Line 13 demonstrates how one `vector<bool>` can be constructed as a copy of another.

`vector<bool>` **Functions and Operators**

The `vector<bool>` features the function `flip()` that toggles the state of the Boolean values in the sequence, similar to the function of `bitset<>::flip()`.

Otherwise, this class is quite similar to the `std::vector` in the sense that you can, for example, even push_back flags into the sequence. The example in Listing 25.4 demonstrates the usage of this class in further detail.

LISTING 25.4   Using the `vector<bool>`

```
0: #include <vector>
1: #include <iostream>
2: using namespace std;
3:
4: int main ()
5: {
6:    vector <bool> vecBoolFlags (3);  // instantiated to hold 3 bool flags
7:    vecBoolFlags [0] = true;
8:    vecBoolFlags [1] = true;
9:    vecBoolFlags [2] = false;
10:
11:    vecBoolFlags.push_back (true); // insert a fourth bool at the end
12:
13:    cout << "The contents of the vector are: " << endl;
14:    for (size_t nIndex = 0; nIndex < vecBoolFlags.size (); ++ nIndex)
15:       cout << vecBoolFlags [nIndex] << ' ';
16:
17:    cout << endl;
18:    vecBoolFlags.flip ();
19:
20:    cout << "The contents of the vector are: " << endl;
21:    for (size_t nIndex = 0; nIndex < vecBoolFlags.size (); ++ nIndex)
22:       cout << vecBoolFlags [nIndex] << ' ';
23:
24:    cout << endl;
25:
26:    return 0;
27: }
```

Output ▼

```
The contents of the vector are:
1 1 0 1
The contents of the vector are:
0 0 1 0
```

Analysis ▼

In this sample, the Boolean flags in the vector have been accessed using the operator[], as shown in Lines 7–9, just like you'd access a regular vector. The function flip() used in Line 18 toggles individual bit lags, essentially converting all 0s to 1s and vice versa. Note the usage of push_back() in Line 11. Even though you initialized vecBoolFlags to contain three flags in Line 6, you were able to add more to it dynamically at Line 11. Adding more flags than the number specified at compile time is what you cannot do with a std::bitset.

Summary

In this lesson, you learned about the most effective tool in handling bit sequences and bit flags: the std::bitset class. You also gained knowledge on the vector<bool> class that allows you to store Boolean flags—the number of which does not need to be known at compile time.

Q&A

Q Given a situation where std::bitset and vector<bool> can both be used, which of the two classes would you prefer to hold your binary flags?

A The bitset, as it is most suited to this requirement.

Q I have a std::bitset object called myBitSeq that contains a certain number of stored bits. How would I determine the number of bits that are at value 0 (or false)?

A bitset::count() supplies the number of bits at value 1. This number, when subtracted from bitset::size() (which indicates the total number of bits stored), would give you the number of 0s in the sequence.

Q Can I use iterators to access the individual elements in a vector<bool>?

A Yes. Because the vector<bool> is a partial specialization of the std::vector, iterators are supported.

25

Q **Can I specify the number of elements to be held in a `vector<bool>` at compile time?**

A Yes, by either specifying the number in the overloaded constructor or using `vector<bool>::resize` function at a later instance.

Workshop

The Workshop contains quiz questions to help solidify your understanding of the material covered and exercises to provide you with experience in using what you've learned. Try to answer the quiz and exercise questions before checking the answers in Appendix D, and be certain you understand the answers before going to the next lesson.

Quiz

1. Can the `bitset` expand its internal buffer to hold a variable number of elements?

2. Why is the `bitset` not classified as an STL container class?

3. Would you use the `std::vector` to hold a number of bits that is fixed and known at compile time?

Exercises

1. Write a `bitset` class that contains four bits. Initialize it to a number, display the result, and add it to another bitset object. (The catch: Bitsets don't allow bitsetA = bitsetX + bitsetY.)

2. Demonstrate how you would toggle (that is, switch) the bits in a bitset.

LESSON 26
Understanding Smart Pointers

C++ programmers do not necessarily need to use plain pointer types when managing memory on the heap (or the free store); they can make use of smart pointers.

In this lesson, you learn

- What smart pointers are and why you need them

- How smart pointers are implemented

- Different smart pointer types

- Why you should not use the deprecated `std::auto_ptr`

- The C++11 Standard Library smart pointer `std::unique_ptr`

- Popular smart pointer libraries

What Are Smart Pointers?

Very simply said, a smart pointer in C++ is a class with overloaded operators, which behaves like a conventional pointer. Yet, it supplies additional value by ensuring proper and timely destruction of dynamically allocated data and facilitates a well-defined object lifecycle.

The Problem with Using Conventional (Raw) Pointers

Unlike other modern programming languages, C++ supplies full flexibility to the programmer in memory allocation, deallocation, and management. Unfortunately, this flexibility is a double-edged sword. On one side it makes C++ a powerful language, but on the other it allows the programmer to create memory-related problems, such as memory leaks, when dynamically allocated objects are not correctly released.

For example:

```
CData *pData = mObject.GetData ();
/*
   Questions: Is object pointed by pData dynamically allocated using new?
   Who will perform delete: caller or the called?
   Answer: No idea!
*/
pData->Display ();
```

In the preceding line of code, there is no obvious way to tell whether the memory pointed to by pData

- Was allocated on the heap, and therefore eventually needs to be deallocated

- Is the responsibility of the caller to deallocate

- Will automatically be destroyed by the object's destructor

Although such ambiguities can be partially solved by inserting comments and enforcing coding practices, these mechanisms are much too loose to efficiently avoid all errors caused by abuse of dynamically allocated data and pointers.

How Do Smart Pointers Help?

Given the problems with using conventional pointer and conventional memory management techniques, it should be noted that the C++ programmer is not forced to use them when he needs to manage data on the heap/free store. The programmer can choose a smarter way to allocate and manage dynamic data by adopting the use of smart pointers in his programs:

```
smart_pointer<CData> spData = mObject.GetData ();

// Use a smart pointer like a conventional pointer!
spData->Display ();
(*spData).Display ();

// Don't have to worry about de-allocation
// (the smart pointer's destructor does it for you)
```

Thus, smart pointers behave like conventional pointers (let's call those *raw pointers* now) but supply useful features via their *overloaded operators* and *destructors* to ensure that dynamically allocated data is destroyed in a timely manner.

How Are Smart Pointers Implemented?

This question can for the moment can be simplified to "How did the smart pointer spData function like a conventional pointer?" The answer is this: Smart pointer classes overload derefencing operator (*) and member selection operator (->) to make the programmer use them as conventional pointers. Operator overloading was discussed previously in Lesson 12, "Operator Types and Operator Overloading."

Additionally, to allow you to manage a type of your choice on the heap, almost all good smart pointer classes are template classes that contain a generic implementation of their functionality. Being templates, they are versatile and can be specialized to manage an object of a type of your choice.

Listing 26.1 is a sample implementation of a simple smart pointer class.

26

LISTING 26.1   The Minimal Essential Components of a Smart Pointer Class

```
0: template <typename T>
1: class smart_pointer
2: {
3: private:
4:     T* m_pRawPointer;
5: public:
6:     smart_pointer (T* pData) : m_pRawPointer (pData) {}    // constructor
7:     ~smart_pointer () {delete pData;};                     // destructor
8:
9:     // copy constructor
10:    smart_pointer (const smart_pointer & anotherSP);
11:    // copy assignment operator
12:    smart_pointer& operator= (const smart_pointer& anotherSP);
13:
14:    T& operator* () const       // dereferencing operator
```

LISTING 26.1   Continued

```
15:    {
16:         return *(m_pRawPointer);
17:    }
18:
19:    T* operator-> () const        // member selection operator
20:    {
21:         return m_pRawPointer;
22:    }
23: };
```

Analysis ▼

The preceding smart pointer class displays the implementation of the two operators * and ->, as declared in Lines 14–17 and 19–22, that help this class to function as a "pointer," in the conventional sense. For instance, to use the smart pointer on an object of type class Tuna, you would instantiate it like this:

```
smart_pointer <Tuna> pSmartTuna (new Tuna);
pSmartTuna->Swim();
// Alternatively:
(*pSmartDog).Swim ();
```

This class smart_pointer still doesn't display or implement any functionality that would make this pointer class very smart and make using it an advantage over using a conventional pointer. The constructor, as shown in Line 7, accepts a pointer that is saved as the internal pointer object in the smart pointer class. The destructor frees this pointer, allowing for automatic memory release.

> **NOTE**
>
> The implementation that makes a smart pointer really "smart" is the implementation of the copy constructor, the assignment operator, and the destructor. They determine the behavior of the smart pointer object when it is passed across functions, when it is assigned, or when it goes out of scope (that is, gets destructed). So, before looking at a complete smart pointer implementation, you should understand some smart pointer types.

Types of Smart Pointers

The management of the memory resource (that is, the ownership model implemented) is what sets smart pointer classes apart. Smart pointers decide what they do with the resource when they are copied and assigned to. The simplest implementations often result in performance issues, whereas the fastest ones might not suit all applications. In the end, it is for the programmer to understand how a smart pointer functions before she decides to use it in her application.

Classification of smart pointers is actually a classification of their memory resource management strategies. These are

- Deep copy
- Copy on Write (COW)
- Reference counted
- Reference linked
- Destructive copy

Let's take a brief look into each of these strategies before studying the smart pointer supplied by the C++ standard library—the std::unique_ptr.

Deep Copy

In a smart pointer that implements deep copy, every smart pointer instance holds a complete copy of the object that is being managed. Whenever the smart pointer is copied, the object pointed to is also copied (thus, deep copy). When the smart pointer goes out of scope, it releases the memory it points to (via the destructor).

Although the deep-copy–based smart pointer does not seem to render any value over passing objects by value, its advantage becomes apparent in the treatment of polymorphic objects, as seen in the following, where it can avoid slicing:

```
// Example of Slicing When Passing Polymorphic Objects by Value
// Fish is a base class for Tuna and Carp, Fish::Swim() is virtual
void MakeFishSwim (Fish aFish)    // note parameter type
{
    aFish.Swim(); // virtual function
}

// ... Some function
Carp freshWaterFish;
MakeFishSwim (freshWaterFish);  // Carp will be 'sliced' to Fish
// Slicing: only the Fish part of Carp is sent to MakeFishSwim()

Tuna marineFish;
MakeFishSwim(marineFish); // Slicing again
```

Slicing issues are resolved when the programmer chooses a deep-copy smart pointer, as shown in Listing 26.2.

26

LISTING 26.2   Using a Deep-Copy–Based Smart Pointer to Pass Polymorphic Objects by Their Base Types

```
0: template <typename T>
1: class deepcopy_smart_pointer
2: {
3: private:
4:     T* m_pObject;
5: public:
6:     //... other functions
7:
8:     // copy constructor of the deepcopy pointer
9:     deepcopy_smart_pointer (const deepcopy_smart_pointer& source)
10:    {
11:        // Clone() is virtual: ensures deep copy of Derived class object
12:        m_pObject = source->Clone ();
13:    }
14:
15:    // copy assignment operator
16:     deepcopy_smart_pointer& operator= (const deepcopy_smart_pointer& source)
17:    {
18:      if (m_pObject)
19:         delete m_pObject;
20:
21:      m_pObject = source->Clone ();
22:    }
23:
24: };
```

Analysis ▼

As you can see, `deepcopy_smart_pointer` implements a copy constructor in Lines 9–13 that allows a deep copy of the polymorphic object via a `Clone()` function that the object needs to implement. Similarly, it also implements a copy assignment operator in Lines 16–22. For the sake of simplicity, it is taken for granted in this example that the virtual function implemented by the base class `Fish` is called `Clone`. Typically, smart pointers that implement deep-copy models have this function supplied as either a template parameter or a function object.

Thus, when the smart pointer itself is passed as a pointer to base class type `Fish`:

```
deepcopy_smart_ptr<Carp> freshWaterFish(new Carp);
MakeFishSwim (freshWaterFish);  // Carp will not be 'sliced'
```

The deep-copy implemented in the smart pointer's constructor kicks in to ensure that the object being passed is not sliced, even though syntactically only the base part of it is required by the destination function `MakeFishSwim()`.

The disadvantage of the deep-copy–based mechanism is performance. This might not be a factor for some applications, but for many others it might inhibit the programmer from using a smart pointer for his application. Instead, he might simply pass a base type pointer (conventional pointer, Fish*) to functions such as MakeFishSwim(). Other pointer types try to address this performance issue in various ways.

Copy on Write Mechanism

Copy on Write (*COW* as it is popularly called) attempts to optimize the performance of deep-copy smart pointers by sharing pointers until the first attempt at writing to the object is made. On the first attempt at invoking a non-const function, a COW pointer typically creates a copy of the object on which the non-const function is invoked, whereas other instances of the pointer continue sharing the source object.

COW has its fair share of fans. For those that swear by COW, implementing operators (*) and (->) in their const and non-const versions is key to the functionality of the COW pointer. The latter creates a copy.

The point is that when you chose a pointer implementation that follows the COW philosophy, be sure that you understand the implementation details before you proceed to use such an implementation. Otherwise, you might land in situations where you have a copy too few or a copy too many.

Reference-Counted Smart Pointers

Reference counting in general is a mechanism that keeps a count of the number of users of an object. When the count reduces to zero, the object is released. So, reference counting makes a very good mechanism for sharing objects without having to copy them. If you have ever worked with a Microsoft technology called COM, the concept of reference counting would have definitely crossed your path on at least one occasion.

26

Such smart pointers, when copied, need to have the reference count of the object in question incremented. There are at least two popular ways to keep this count:

- Reference count maintained in the object being pointed to
- Reference count maintained by the pointer class in a shared object

The first variant where the reference count is maintained in the object is called *intrusive reference counting* because the object needs to be modified. The object in this case maintains, increments, and supplies the reference count to any smart pointer class that manages it. Incidentally, this is the approach chosen by COM. The second variant where the reference count is maintained in a shared object is a mechanism where the smart pointer class can keep the reference count on the free store (a dynamically allocated integer, for example) and when copied, the copy constructor increments this value.

Therefore, the reference-counting mechanism makes it pertinent that the programmer works with the smart pointers only when using the object. A smart pointer managing the object and a raw pointer pointing to it is a bad idea because the smart pointer (smartly) releases the object when the count maintained by it goes down to zero, but the raw pointer continues pointing to the part of the memory that no longer belongs to your application. Similarly, reference counting can cause issues peculiar to their situation: Two objects that hold a pointer to each other are never released because their cyclic dependency holds their reference counts at a minimum of 1.

Reference-Linked Smart Pointers

Reference-linked smart pointers are ones that don't proactively count the number of references using the object; rather, they just need to know when the number comes down to zero so that the object can be released.

They are called *reference-linked* because their implementation is based on a double-linked list. When a new smart pointer is created by copying an existing one, it is appended to the list. When a smart pointer goes out of scope or is destroyed, the destructor de-indexes the smart pointer from this list. Reference linking also suffers from the problem caused by cyclic dependency, as applicable to reference-counted pointers.

Destructive Copy

Destructive copy is a mechanism where a smart pointer, when copied, transfers complete ownership of the object being handled to the destination and resets itself:

```
destructive_copy_smartptr <SampleClass> pSmartPtr (new SampleClass ());

SomeFunc (pSmartPtr);    // Ownership transferred to SomeFunc
// Don't use pSmartPtr in the caller any more!
```

Although this mechanism is obviously not intuitive to use, the advantage supplied by `destructive copy` smart pointers is that they ensure that at any point in time, only one active pointer points to an object. So, they make good mechanisms for returning pointers from functions, and are of use in scenarios where you can use their "destructive" properties to your advantage.

The implementation of `destructive copy` pointers deviates from standard, recommended C++ programming techniques, as shown in Listing 26.3.

CAUTION

std::auto_ptr is by far the most popular (or notorious, depending on how you look at it) pointer that follows the principles of destructive copy. Such a smart pointer is useless after it has been passed to a function or copied into another.

std::auto_ptr has been deprecated in C++11. Instead, you should use std::unique_ptr, which cannot be passed by value due to its private copy constructor and copy assignment operator. It can only be passed as a reference argument.

LISTING 26.3   A Sample Destructive Copy Smart Pointer

```
0: template <typename T>
1: class destructivecopy_pointer
2: {
3: private:
4:     T* pObject;
5: public:
6:     destructivecopy_pointer(T* pInput):pObject(pInput) {}
7:     ~destructivecopy_pointer() { delete pObject; }
8:
9:     // copy constructor
10:     destructivecopy_pointer(destructivecopy_pointer& source)
11:     {
12:         // Take ownership on copy
13:         pObject = source.pObject;
14:
15:         // destroy source
16:         source.pObject = 0;
17:     }
18:
19:     // copy assignment operator
20:     destructivecopy_pointer& operator= (destructivecopy_pointer& rhs)
21:     {
22:         if (pObject != source.pObject)
23:         {
24:             delete pObject;
25:             pObject = source.pObject;
26:             source.pObject = 0;
27:         }
28:     }
29: };
30:
31: int main()
32: {
33:     destructivecopy_pointer<int> pNumber (new int);
```

26

LISTING 26.3   Continued

```
34:     destructivecopy_pointer<int> pCopy = pNumber;
35:
36:     // pNumber is now invalid
37:     return 0;
38: }
```

Analysis ▼

Listing 26.3 describes the most important part of the implementation of a destructive-copy–based smart pointer. Lines 10–17 and Lines 20–28 contain the copy constructor and the copy assignment operator, respectively. These functions invalidate the source when making a copy; that is, the copy constructor sets the pointer contained by the source to NULL, after copying it, therefore justifying the name destructive copy. The assignment operator does the same thing. Thus, pNumber is actually invalidated in Line 34 when it is assigned to another pointer. This behavior is counterintuitive to the act of assignment.

CAUTION

The copy constructor and copy assignment operators that are critical to the implementation of destructive copy smart pointers as shown in Listing 26.3 also attract maximum criticism. Unlike most C++ classes, this smart pointer class cannot have the copy constructor and assignment operator accept const references, as it needs to invalidate the source after copying it. This is not only a deviation from traditional copy-constructor and assignment-operator semantics, but also makes using the smart pointer class counter intuitive. Few expect the copy source or the assignment source to be damaged after a copy or assignment step. The fact that such smart pointers destroy the source also makes them unsuitable for use in STL containers, such as the std::vector, or any other dynamic collection class that you might use. These containers need to copy your content internally and end up invalidating the pointers.

So, for more than one reason, there are a lot of programmers who avoid destructive copy smart pointers like the plague.

TIP

The auto_ptr was a destructive-copy–based smart pointer supported by the C++ Standard until now. It has finally been marked as deprecated in C++11, and you should use std::unique_ptr instead.

Similarly, those programming COM applications on Windows platforms should start using the ATL framework's effective smart pointer classes such as CComPtr and CComQIPtr to manage their COM objects, rather than using raw interface pointers.

Summary

In this lesson, you learned how using the right smart pointers can help write code that uses pointers, yet helps reduce allocation and object ownership–related problems. You also learned of the different smart pointer types and that it is important to know the behavior of a smart pointer class before adopting it in your application. You now know that you should not use std::auto_ptr as it invalidates the source during a copy or assignment. You learned about the newest smart pointer class available starting with C++11, the std::unique_ptr.

Q&A

Q I need a vector of pointers. Should I choose auto_ptr as the object type to be held in the vector?

A As a rule, you should never use std::auto_ptr. It is deprecated. A single copy or assignment operation can render the source object unusable.

Q What two operators does a class always need to load to be called a smart pointer class?

A The following: *operator** and *operator ->*. They help use objects of the class with regular pointer semantics.

Q I have an application in which Class1 and Class2 hold member attributes that point to objects of the other's type. Should I use a reference counted pointer in this scenario?

A Probably you wouldn't because of the cyclic dependency that will keep the reference count from going down to zero and will consequently keep objects of the two classes permanently in the heap.

Q How many smart pointers are there in the world?

A. Thousands. No, maybe millions. You should use only smart pointers that have a well-documented functionality and come from a trusted source, such as Boost.

Q A string class also dynamically manages character arrays on the free store. Is a string class therefore a smart pointer, too?

A No, it isn't. These classes typically don't implement both operator* and operator -> and are therefore not classifiable as smart pointers.

26

Workshop

The Workshop contains quiz questions to help solidify your understanding of the material covered and exercises to provide you with experience in using what you've learned. Try to answer the quiz and exercise questions before checking the answers in Appendix D, and be certain you understand the answers before going to the next lesson.

Quiz

1. Where would you look before writing your own smart pointer for your application?

2. Would a smart pointer slow down your application significantly?

3. Where can reference-counted smart pointers hold the reference count data?

4. Should the linked list mechanism used by reference-linked pointers be singly or doubly linked?

Exercises

1. **BUG BUSTER:** Point out the bug in this code:

```
std::auto_ptr<SampleClass> pObject (new SampleClass ());
std::auto_ptr<SampleClass> pAnotherObject (pObject);
pObject->DoSomething ();
pAnotherObject->DoSomething();
```

2. Use the `unique_ptr` class to instantiate a `Carp` that inherits from `Fish`. Pass the object as a `Fish` pointer and comment on slicing, if any.

3. **BUG BUSTER:** Point out the bug in this code:

```
std::unique_ptr<Tuna> myTuna (new Tuna);
unique_ptr<Tuna> copyTuna;
copyTuna = myTuna;
```

LESSON 27
Using Streams for Input and Output

You have actually been using streams all through this book, starting with Lesson 1, "Getting Started," in which you displayed "Hello World" on the screen using std::cout. It's time to give this part of C++ its due attention and learn streams from a practical point of view. In this lesson, you find out

- What streams are and how they are used

- How to write to and read from files using streams

- Useful C++ stream operations

Concept of Streams

You are developing a program that reads from the disk, writes data to the display, reads user input from the keyboard, and saves data on the disk. Wouldn't it be useful if you could treat all read activities and write activities using similar patterns irrespective of what device or location the data is coming from or going to? This is exactly what C++ streams offer you!

C++ streams are a generic implementation of read and write (in other words, input and output) logic that enables you to use certain consistent patterns toward reading or writing data. These patterns are consistent irrespective of whether you are reading data from the disk or the keyboard or whether you are writing to the display or back to the disk. You just need to use the right stream class, and the implementation within the class takes care of device- and OS-specific details.

Let's refer to one relevant line taken from your first C++ program, Listing 1.1 in Lesson 1, again:

```
std::cout << "Hello World!" << std::endl;
```

That's right: `std::cout` is a stream object of `class ostream` for console output. To use `std::cout`, you included header `<iostream>` that supplies this and other functionality such as `std::cin` that allows you to read from a stream.

So, what do I mean when I say that streams allow consistent and device-specific access? If you were to write "Hello World" to a text file, you would use this syntax on a file stream object `fsHW`:

```
fsHW << "Hello World!" << endl;  // "Hello World!" into a file stream
```

As you can see, after you've chosen the right stream class, writing "Hello World" to a file isn't too different in C++ than writing it to the display.

TIP

operator<< used when writing into a stream is called the stream insertion operator. You use it when writing to the display, file, and so on.

operator>> used when writing a stream into a variable is called the stream extraction operator. You use it when reading input from the keyboard, file, and so on.

Going ahead, this lesson studies streams from a practical point of view.

Important C++ Stream Classes and Objects

C++ provides you with a set of standard classes and headers that help you perform some important and frequent I/O operations. Table 27.1 is a list of classes that you use frequently.

TABLE 27.1   Popularly Used C++ Stream Classes in the std Namespace

Class/Object	Purpose
cout	Standard output stream, typically redirected to the console
cin	Standard input stream, typically used to read data into variables
cerr	Standard output stream for errors
fstream	Input and output stream class for file operations; inherits from ofstream and ifstream
ofstream	Output stream class for file operations—that is, used to create files
ifstream	Input stream class for file operations—that is, used to read files
stringstream	Input and output stream class for string operations; inherits from istringstream and ostringstream; typically used to perform conversions from (or to) string and other types

> NOTE
>
> cout, cin, and cerr are global objects of stream classes ostream, istream, and ostream, respectively. Being global objects, they're initialized before main() starts.

When using a stream class, you have the option of specifying manipulators that perform specific actions for you. std::endl is one such manipulator that you have been using thus far to insert a newline character:

```
std::cout  << "This lines ends here" << std::endl;
```

Table 27.2 demonstrates a few other such manipulator functions and flags.

TABLE 27.2   Frequently Used Manipulators in the std Namespace for Working with Streams

Output Manipulators	Purpose
endl	Inserts a newline character
ends	Inserts a null character

27

TABLE 27.2   Continued

Radix Manipulators	Purpose
dec	Instructs stream to interpret input or display output in decimal
hex	Instructs stream to interpret input or display output in hexadecimal
oct	Instructs stream to interpret input or display output in octal

Floating Point Representation Manipulators	Purpose
fixed	Instructs stream to display in fixed point notation
scientific	Instructs stream to display in scientific notation

`<iomanip>` Manipulators	Purpose
setprecision	Set decimal point precision as a parameter
setw	Set field width as a parameter
setfill	Set fill character as a parameter
setbase	Set the radix/base, akin to using dec, hex, or oct as a parameter
setiosflag	Set flags via a mask input parameter of type std::ios_base::fmtflags
resetiosflag	Restore defaults for a particular type specified by that contained in std::ios_base::fmtflags

Using `std::cout` for Writing Formatted Data to Console

`std::cout` used for writing to the standard output stream is possibly the most used stream in this book this far. Yet, it's time to revisit cout and use some of the manipulators in changing the way we are able to align and display data.

Changing Display Number Formats Using `std::cout`

It is possible to ask cout to display an integer in hexadecimal or in octal notations. Listing 27.1 demonstrates using cout to display an input number in various formats.

LISTING 27.1 Displaying an Integer in Decimal, Octal, and Hexadecimal Formats Using cout and <iomanip> Flags

```
0: #include <iostream>
1: #include <iomanip>
2: using namespace std;
3:
4: int main()
5: {
6:     cout << "Enter an integer: ";
7:     int Input = 0;
8:     cin >> Input;
9:
10:    cout << "Integer in octal: " << oct << Input << endl;
11:    cout << "Integer in hexadecimal: " << hex << Input << endl;
12:
13:    cout << "Integer in hex using base notation: ";
14:    cout<<setiosflags(ios_base::hex|ios_base::showbase|ios_base::uppercase);
15:    cout << Input << endl;
16:
17:    cout << "Integer after resetting I/O flags: ";
18:    cout<<resetiosflags(ios_base::hex|ios_base::showbase|ios_base::uppercase);
19:    cout << Input << endl;
20:
21:    return 0;
22: }
```

Output ▼

```
Enter an integer: 253
Integer in octal: 375
Integer in hexadecimal: fd
Integer in hex using base notation: 0XFD
Integer after resetting I/O flags: 253
```

Analysis ▼

The code sample uses the manipulators presented in Table 27.2 to change the way cout displays the same integer object Input, supplied by the user. Note how manipulators oct and hex are used in Lines 10 and 11. In Line 14 you use setiosflags() telling it to display the numbers in hex using uppercase letters, resulting in cout displaying integer input 253 as 0XFD. The effect of resetioflags() used in Line 18 is demonstrated by the

27

integer being displayed by cout using decimal notation again. Another way to change the radix used in displaying integer to decimal would be the following:

```
cout << dec << Input << endl;  // displays in decimal
```

It is also possible to format the manner in which cout displays numbers such as Pi in that you can specify the precision, which in a fixed-point notation specifies the number of places after decimal to be shown, or you can have a number displayed using scientific notation. This and more is demonstrated by Listing 27.2.

LISTING 27.2 Using cout to Display Pi and a Circle's Area Using Fixed-Point and Scientific Notations

```
 0: #include <iostream>
 1: #include <iomanip>
 2: using namespace std;
 3:
 4: int main()
 5: {
 6:     const double Pi = (double)22.0 / 7;
 7:     cout << "Pi = " << Pi << endl;
 8:
 9:     cout << endl << "Setting precision to 7: " << endl;
10:     cout << setprecision(7);
11:     cout << "Pi = " << Pi << endl;
12:     cout << fixed << "Fixed Pi = " << Pi << endl;
13:     cout << scientific << "Scientific Pi = " << Pi << endl;
14:
15:     cout << endl << "Setting precision to 10: " << endl;
16:     cout << setprecision(10);
17:     cout << "Pi = " << Pi << endl;
18:     cout << fixed << "Fixed Pi = " << Pi << endl;
19:     cout << scientific << "Scientific Pi = " << Pi << endl;
20:
21:     cout << endl << "Enter a radius: ";
22:     double Radius = 0.0;
23:     cin >> Radius;
24:     cout << "Area of circle: " << 2*Pi*Radius*Radius << endl;
25:
26:     return 0;
27: }
```

Output ▼

```
Pi = 3.14286

Setting precision to 7:
Pi = 3.142857
```

```
Fixed Pi = 3.1428571
Scientific Pi = 3.1428571e+000

Setting precision to 10:
Pi = 3.1428571429e+000
Fixed Pi = 3.1428571429
Scientific Pi = 3.1428571429e+000

Enter a radius: 9.99
Area of circle: 6.2731491429e+002
```

Analysis ▼

The output demonstrates how increasing the precision to 7 in Line 10 and to 10 in Line 16 changes the display of the value of Pi. Also note how the manipulator scientific results in the calculated area of the circle being displayed as 6.2731491429e+002.

Aligning Text and Setting Field Width Using
std::cout

One can use manipulators such as setw() to set the width of the field in characters. Any insertion made to the stream is right-aligned in this specified width. Similarly, setfill() can be used to determine what character fills the empty area in such a situation, as demonstrated by Listing 27.3.

LISTING 27.3   Set the Width of a Field via setw() and the Fill Characters Using setfill() Manipulators

```
0: #include <iostream>
1: #include <iomanip>
2: using namespace std;
3:
4: int main()
5: {
6:     cout << "Hey - default!" << endl;
7:
8:     cout << setw(35);  // set field width to 25 columns
9:     cout << "Hey - right aligned!" << endl;
10:
11:    cout << setw(35) << setfill('*');
12:    cout << "Hey - right aligned!" << endl;
13:
14:    cout << "Hey - back to default!" << endl;
15:
16:    return 0;
17: }
```

27

Output ▼

```
Hey - default!
              Hey - right aligned!
***************Hey - right aligned!
Hey - back to default!
```

Analysis ▼

The output demonstrates the effect of setw(35) supplied to cout in Line 8 and setfill('*') supplied together with setw(35) in Line 11. You see that the latter results in the free space preceding the text to be displayed to be filled with asterisks, as specified in setfill().

Using std::cin for Input

std::cin is versatile and enables you to read input into the plain old data types, such as the int, double, and char* C-style strings, and you can also read lines or characters from the screen using methods such as getline().

Using std::cin for Input into a Plain Old Data Type

You can feed integers, doubles, and chars directly from the standard input via cin. Listing 27.4 demonstrates the usage of cin in reading simple data types from the user.

LISTING 27.4   Using cin to Read Input into an int, a Floating-Point Number Using Scientific Notation into a double, and Three Letters into a char

```
 0: #include<iostream>
 1: using namespace std;
 2:
 3: int main()
 4: {
 5:    cout << "Enter an integer: ";
 6:    int InputInt = 0;
 7:    cin >> InputInt;
 8:
 9:    cout << "Enter the value of Pi: ";
10:    double Pi = 0.0;
11:    cin >> Pi;
12:
13:    cout << "Enter three characters separated by space: " << endl;
14:    char Char1 = '\0', Char2 = '\0', Char3 = '\0';
15:    cin >> Char1 >> Char2 >> Char3;
16:
```

```
17:    cout << "The recorded variable values are: " << endl;
18:    cout << "InputInt: " << InputInt << endl;
19:    cout << "Pi: " << Pi << endl;
20:    cout << "The three characters: " << Char1 << Char2 << Char3 << endl;
21:
22:    return 0;
23: }
```

Output ▼

```
Enter an integer: 32
Enter the value of Pi: 0.314159265e1
Enter three characters separated by space:
c + +
The recorded variable values are:
InputInt: 32
Pi: 3.14159
The three characters: c++
```

Analysis ▼

The most interesting part about Listing 27.4 is that you entered the value of Pi using exponential notation, and cin filled that data into double Pi. Note how you are able to fill three character variables within a single line as shown in Line 15.

Using std::cin::get for Input into C-Style char Buffer

Just like cin allows you to write directly into an int, you can do the same with a C-style char array, too:

```
cout << "Enter a line: " << endl;
char CStyleStr [10] = {0};  // can contain max 10 chars
cin >> CStyleStr;  // Danger: user may enter more than 10 chars
```

When writing into a C-style string buffer, it is very important that you don't exceed the bounds of the buffer to avoid a crash or a security vulnerability. So, a better way of reading into a C-style char buffer is this:

```
cout << "Enter a line: " << endl;
char CStyleStr[10] = {0};
cin.get(CStyleStr, 9);  // stop inserting at the 9th character
```

This safer way of inserting text into a C-style buffer is demonstrated by Listing 27.5.

27

LISTING 27.5 Inserting into a C-Style Buffer Without Exceeding Its Bounds

```
0: #include<iostream>
1: #include<string>
2: using namespace std;
3:
4: int main()
5: {
6:     cout << "Enter a line: " << endl;
7:     char CStyleStr[10] = {0};
8:     cin.get(CStyleStr, 9);
9:     cout << "CStyleStr: " << CStyleStr << endl;
10:
11:     return 0;
12: }
```

Output ▼

```
Enter a line:
Testing if I can cross the bounds of the buffer
CStyleStr: Testing i
```

Analysis ▼

As the output indicates, you have only taken the first nine characters input by the user into the C-style buffer due to the use of `cin::get` as used in Line 8. This is the safest way to deal with a C-style string.

TIP

> As far as possible, don't use C-style strings and char arrays. Use `std::string` instead of `char*` wherever possible.

Using `std::cin` for Input into a `std::string`

`cin` is quite a versatile tool, and you can even use it to scan a string from the user directly into a `std::string`:

```
std::string Input;
cin >> Input;  // stops insertion at the first space
```

Listing 27.6 demonstrates input using `cin` into a `std::string`.

LISTING 27.6   Inserting Text into a std::string Using cin

```
0: #include<iostream>
1: #include<string>
2: using namespace std;
3:
4: int main()
5: {
6:     cout << "Enter your name: ";
7:     string Name;
8:     cin >> Name;
9:     cout << "Hi " << Name << endl;
10:
11:     return 0;
12: }
```

Output ▼

```
Enter your name: Siddhartha Rao
Hi Siddhartha
```

Analysis ▼

The output did not display my first name alone because the program was designed to. I expected Name populated using cin in Line 8 to contain my full name as input and not just the first name. So what happened? Apparently, cin stops insertion when it encounters the first white space.

To allow the user to enter a complete line, including spaces, you need to use getline():

```
string Name;
getline(cin, Name);
```

This usage of getline() with cin is demonstrated in Listing 27.7.

LISTING 27.7   Reading a Complete Line Input by User Using getline() and cin

```
0: #include<iostream>
1: #include<string>
2: using namespace std;
3:
4: int main()
5: {
6:     cout << "Enter your name: ";
7:     string Name;
8:     getline(cin, Name);
```

27

LISTING 27.7   Continued

```
 9:    cout << "Hi " << Name << endl;
10:
11:    return 0;
12: }
```

Output ▼

```
Enter your name: Siddhartha Rao
Hi Siddhartha Rao
```

Analysis ▼

getline() as shown in Line 8 did the job of ensuring that white space characters are not skipped. The output now contains the complete line fed by the user.

Using `std::fstream` for File Handling

std:fstream is a class that C++ provides for (relatively) platform-independent file access. std::fstream inherits from std::ofstream for writing a file and std::ofstream for reading one.

In other words, std::fstream provides you with both read and write functionality.

TIP	To use class std::fstream or its base classes, include header: #include <fstream>

Opening and Closing a File Using `open()` and `close()`

To use an fstream, ofstream, or ifstream class, you need to open a file using method open():

```
fstream myFile;
myFile.open("HelloFile.txt",ios_base::in¦ios_base::out¦ios_base::trunc);

if (myFile.is_open())
{
   // do reading or writing here

   myFile.close();
}
```

open() takes two arguments: The first is the path and name of the file being opened (if you don't supply a path, it assumes the current directory settings for the application), whereas the second is the mode in which the file is being opened. The modes chosen allow the file to be created even if one exists (ios_base::trunc) and allow you to read and write into the file (in ¦ out).

Note the usage of is_open() to test if open() succeeded.

CAUTION	Remember that closing a file stream is important to save its contents.

There is an alternative way of opening a file stream, which is via the constructor:

```
fstream myFile("HelloFile.txt",ios_base::in¦ios_base::out¦ios_base::trunc);
```

Alternatively, if you want to open a file for writing only, use the following:

```
ofstream myFile("HelloFile.txt", ios_base::out);
```

If you want to open a file for reading, use this:

```
ifstream myFile("HelloFile.txt", ios_base::in);
```

TIP	Irrespective of whether you use the constructor or the member method open(), it is recommended that you check for the successful opening of the file via is_open() before continuing to use the corresponding file stream object.

The various modes in which a file stream can be opened are the following:

- `ios_base::app`—Appends to the end of existing files rather than truncating them
- `ios_base::ate`—Places you at the end of the file, but you can write data anywhere in the file
- `ios_base::trunc`—Causes existing files to be truncated; the default
- `ios_base::binary`—Creates a binary file (default is text)
- `ios_base::in`—Opens file for read operations only
- `ios_base::out`—Opens file for write operations only

27

Creating and Writing a Text File Using `open()` and `operator<<`

After you have opened a file stream, you can write to it using operator <<, as Listing 27.8 demonstrates.

LISTING 27.8 Creating a New Text File and Writing Text into It Using `ofstream`

```
0: #include<fstream>
1: #include<iostream>
2: using namespace std;
3:
4: int main()
5: {
6:    ofstream myFile;
7:    myFile.open("HelloFile.txt", ios_base::out);
8:
9:    if (myFile.is_open())
10:   {
11:      cout << "File open successful" << endl;
12:
13:      myFile << "My first text file!" << endl;
14:      myFile << "Hello file!";
15:
16:      cout << "Finished writing to file, will close now" << endl;
17:      myFile.close();
18:   }
19:
20:    return 0;
21: }
```

Output ▼

```
File open successful
Finished writing to file, will close now
```

Content of file HelloFile.txt:

```
My first text file!
Hello file!
```

Analysis ▼

Line 7 opens the file in mode ios_base::out—that is, exclusively for writing. In Line 9 you test if open() succeeded and then proceed to write to the file stream using the insertion operator << as shown in Lines 13 and 14. Finally, you close at Line 17 and return.

Listing 27.8 demonstrates how you are able to write into a file stream the same way as you would write to the standard output (console) using cout.

This indicates how streams in C++ allow for a similar way of handling different devices, writing text to the display via cout in the same way one would write to a file via ofstream.

Reading a Text File Using open() and operator>>

To read a file, one can use fstream and open it using flag ios_base::in or use ifstream. Listing 27.9 demonstrates reading the file HelloFile.txt created in Listing 27.8.

LISTING 27.9   Reading Text from File HelloFile.txt Created in Listing 27.8

```
0: #include<fstream>
1: #include<iostream>
2: #include<string>
3: using namespace std;
4:
5: int main()
6: {
7:     ifstream myFile;
8:     myFile.open("HelloFile.txt", ios_base::in);
9:
10:     if (myFile.is_open())
11:     {
12:        cout << "File open successful. It contains: ' << endl;
13:        string fileContents;
14:
15:        while (myFile.good())
16:        {
17:           getline (myFile, fileContents);
18:          cout << fileContents << endl;
19:        }
20:
21:        cout << "Finished reading file, will close now" << endl;
22:        myFile.close();
23:     }
24:     else
25:        cout << "open() failed: check if file is in right folder" << endl;
26:
27:     return 0;
28: }
```

27

Output ▼

```
File open successful. It contains:
My first text file!
Hello file!
Finished reading file, will close now
```

NOTE

As Listing 27.9 reads the text file "HelloFile.txt" created using Listing 27.8, you either need to move that file to this project's working directory or merge this code into the previous one.

Analysis ▼

As always, you perform check is_open() to verify if the call to open() in Line 8 succeeded. Note the usage of the extraction operator >> in reading the contents of the file directly into a string that is then displayed on using cout in Line 18. We use getline() in this sample for reading input from a file stream in an exactly identical way as you used it in Listing 27.7 to read input from the user, one complete line at a time.

Writing to and Reading from a Binary File

The actual process of writing to a binary file is not too different from what you have learned thus far. It is important to use ios_base::binary flag as a mask when opening the file. You typically use ofstream::write or ifstream::read as Listing 27.10 demonstrates.

LISTING 27.10   Writing a struct to a Binary File and Reconstructing It from the Same

```
0: #include<fstream>
1: #include<iomanip>
2: #include<string>
3: #include<iostream>
4: using namespace std;
5:
6: struct Human
7: {
8:     Human() {};
9:     Human(const char* inName, int inAge, const char* inDOB) : Age(inAge)
10:    {
11:        strcpy(Name, inName);
12:        strcpy(DOB, inDOB);
13:    }
14:
15:    char Name[30];
```

```
16:    int Age;
17:    char DOB[20];
18: };
19:
20: int main()
21: {
22:    Human Input("Siddhartha Rao", 101, "May 1910");
23:
24:    ofstream fsOut ('MyBinary.bin', ios_base::out | ios_base::binary);
25:
26:    if (fsOut.is_open())
27:    {
28:      cout << "Writing one object of Human to a binary file" << endl;
29:      fsOut.write(reinterpret_cast<const char*>(&Input), sizeof(Input));
30:      fsOut.close();
31:    }
32:
33:    ifstream fsIn ("MyBinary.bin", ios_base::in | ios_base::binary);
34:
35:    if(fsIn.is_open())
36:    {
37:      Human somePerson;
38:      fsIn.read((char*)&somePerson, sizeof(somePerson));
39:
40:      cout << "Reading information from binary file: " << endl;
41:      cout << "Name = " << somePerson.Name << endl;
42:      cout << "Age = ' << somePerson.Age << endl;
43:      cout << "Date of Birth = " << somePerson.DOB << endl;
44:    }
45:
46:    return 0;
47: }
```

Output ▼

```
Writing one object of Human to a binary file
Reading information from binary file:
Name = Siddhartha Rao
Age = 101
Date of Birth = May 1910
```

27

Analysis ▼

In Lines 22–31, you create an instance of struct Human that contains a Name, Age, and DOB and persist it to the disk in a binary file MyBinary.bin using ofstream. This information is then read using another stream object of type ifstream in Lines 33– 44. The output of attributes such as Name and so on is via the information that has been read from the binary file. This sample also demonstrates the usage of ifstream and ofstream for reading and writing a file using ifstream::read and ofstream::write, respectively. Note the usage of reinterpret_cast in Line 29 to essentially force the compiler to interpret the struct as char*. In Line 38, you use the C-style cast version of what is used in Line 29.

NOTE

> If it were not for explanation purposes, I would've rather persisted struct Human with all its attributes in an XML file. XML is a text- and markup-based storage format that allows flexibility and scalability in the manner in which information can be persisted.
>
> If struct Human were to be delivered in this version and after delivery if you were to add new attributes to it (like NumChildren, for instance), you would need to worry about ifstream::read functionality being able to correctly read binary data created using the older versions.

Using std::stringstream for String Conversions

You have a string. It contains a string value 45 in it. How do you convert this string value into an integer with value 45? And vice versa? One of the most useful utilities provided by C++ is class stringstream that enables you to perform a host of conversion activities.

TIP

> To use class std::stringstream, include header:
>
> #include <sstream>

Listing 27.11 demonstrates some simple stringstream operations.

LISTING 27.11   Converting an Integer Value into a String Representation and Vice Versa Using std::stringstream

```
0: #include<fstream>
1: #include<sstream>
2: #include<iostream>
```

```
 3: using namespace std;
 4:
 5: int main()
 6: {
 7:     cout << "Enter an integer: ";
 8:     int Input = 0;
 9:     cin >> Input;
10:
11:     stringstream converterStream;
12:     converterStream << Input;
13:     string strInput;
14:     converterStream >> strInput;
15:
16:     cout << "Integer Input = " << Input << endl;
17:     cout << "String gained from integer, strInput = " << strInput << endl;
18:
19:     stringstream anotherStream;
20:     anotherStream << strInput;
21:     int Copy = 0;
22:     anotherStream >> Copy;
23:
24:     cout << "Integer gained from string, Copy = " << Copy << endl;
25:
26:     return 0;
27: }
```

Output ▼

```
Enter an integer: 45
Integer Input = 45
String gained from integer, strInput = 45
Integer gained from string, Copy = 45
```

Analysis ▼

You ask the user to enter an integer value. You first insert this integer into the stringstream object, as shown in Line 12, using operator<<. Then, you use the extraction operator>> in Line 14 to convert this integer into a string. After that, you use this string as a starting point and get an integer representation Copy of the numeric value held in string strInput.

27

DO	DON'T
DO use `ifstream` when you only intend to read from a file.	**DON'T** forget to close a file stream using method `close()` after you are done using it.
DO use `ofstream` when you only intend to write a file.	**DON'T** forget that extracting from `cin` to a `string` via `cin >> strData`; typically results in the `strData` containing text until the first white space and not the entire line.
DO remember to check if a file stream has opened successfully via `is_open()` before inserting or extracting from the stream.	**DON'T** forget that function `getline(cin, strData)`; fetches you an entire line from the input stream, including white spaces.

Summary

This lesson taught you C++ streams from a practical perspective. You learned that you have been using streams such as I/O streams `cout` and `cin` since the very beginning of the book. You now know how to create simple text files and how to read or write from them. You learned how `stringstream` can help you convert simple types such as integers into strings, and vice versa.

Q&A

Q I see that I can use `fstream` for both writing and reading to a file, so when should I use `ofstream` and `ifstream`?

A If your code or module needs to only be reading from a file, you should instead use `ifstream`. Similarly, if it needs to only write to a file use `ofstream`. In both cases `fstream` would work fine, but for the sake of ensuring data and code integrity, it is better to have a restrictive policy similar to using `const`, which is not compulsory either.

Q When should I use `cin.get()`, and when should I used `cin.getline()`?

A `cin.getline()` ensures that you capture the entire line including white spaces entered by the user. `cin.get()` helps you capture user input one character at a time.

Q When should I use `stringstream`?

A `stringstream` supplies a convenient way of converting integers and other simple types into a string and vice versa, as also demonstrated by Listing 27.11.

Workshop

The Workshop contains quiz questions to help solidify your understanding of the material covered and exercises to provide you with experience in using what you've learned. Try to answer the quiz and exercise questions before checking the answers in Appendix D, and be certain you understand the answers before going to the next lesson.

Quiz

1. You need to only write to a file. What stream would you use?

2. How would you use cin to get a complete line from the input stream?

3. You need to write std::string objects to a file. Would you choose ios_base::binary mode?

4. You opened a stream using open(). Why bother using is_open()?

Exercises

1. **BUG BUSTER:** Find the error in the following code:

```
fstream myFile;
myFile.open("HelloFile.txt", ios_base::out);
myFile << "Hello file!";
myFile.close();
```

2. **BUG BUSTER:** Find the error in the following code:

```
ifstream MyFile("SomeFile.txt");
if(MyFile.is_open())
{
   MyFile << "This is some text" << endl;
   MyFile.close();
}
```

LESSON 28
Exception Handling

The title says it all: dealing with extraordinary situations that disrupt the flow of your program. The lessons thus far have mostly taken an exceedingly positive approach, assuming that memory allocations will succeed files will be found, and so on. Reality is often different.

In this lesson, you learn

- What is an exception
- How to handle exceptions
- How exception handling helps you deliver stable C-+ applications

What Is an Exception?

Your program allocates memory, reads and writes data, saves to a file—the works. All this executes flawlessly on your awesome development environment, and you are even proud of the fact that your application doesn't leak a byte, though it manages a gigabyte! You ship your application and the customer deploys it on his landscape of a thousand workstations. Some of his computers are 10 years old. Some have hard disks that barely spin. It doesn't take much time for the first complaint to reach your inbox. Some complains will be about an "Access Violation," whereas some others will quote an "Unhandled Exception."

There you go—"unhandled" and "exception." Clearly, your application was doing well inside your environment, so why all the fuss?

The fact is that the world out there is very heterogeneous. No two computers, even with the same hardware configuration, are alike. This is because the software running on each computer and the state the machine is in decide the amount of resources that are available at a particular time. It is therefore probable that memory allocation that worked perfectly in your environment fails in another environment.

Such failures are rare, yet they happen. These failures result in "exceptions."

Exceptions disrupt the normal flow of your application. After all, if there is no memory available, there is possibly no way your application can achieve what it set out to do. Yet, your application can handle that exception and display a friendly error message to the user, perform any minimal rescue operation if needed, and exit gracefully.

Handling exceptions helps you avoid those "Access Violation" or "Unhandled Exception" screens or emails. Let's see what tools C++ provides you for dealing with the unexpected.

What Causes Exceptions?

Exceptions can be caused by external factors, such as a system with insufficient resources, or by factors internal to your application, such as a pointer that is used in spite of it containing an invalid value or a divide-by-zero error. Some modules are designed to communicate errors by throwing exceptions to the caller.

NOTE

To protect your code against exceptions, you "handle" exceptions thereby making your code "exception safe."

Implementing Exception Safety via try and catch

try and catch are the most important keywords in C++ as far as implementing exception safety goes. To make statements exception safe, you enclose them within a try block and handle the exceptions that emerge out of the try block in the catch block:

```cpp
vcid SomeFunc()
{
   try
   {
      int* pNumber = new int;
      *pNumber = 999;
      delete pNumber;
   }
   catch(...)  // ... catches all exceptions
   {
      cout << "Exception in SomeFunc(), quitting" << endl
   }
}
```

Using catch(...) to Handle All Exceptions

Remember in Lesson 8, "Pointers and References Explained," that I mentioned that the default form of new returns a valid pointer to a location in memory when it succeeds but throws an exception when it fails. Listing 28.1 demonstrates how you can make memory allocations exception safe using new and handle situations where the computer is not able to allocate the memory you requested.

LISTING 28.1 Using try and catch in Ensuring Exception Safety in Memory Allocations

```cpp
0: #include <iostream>
1: using namespace std;
2:
3: int main()
4: {
5:    cout << "Enter number of integers you wish to reserve: ";
6:    try
7:    {
8:       int Input = 0;
9:       cin >> Input;
10:
11:       // Request memory space and then return it
12:       int* pReservedInts = new int [Input];
13:       delete[] pReservedInts;
14:    }
```

28

LISTING 28.1   Continued

```
15:    catch (...)
16:    {
17:        cout << "Exception encountered. Got to end, sorry!" << endl;
18:    }
19:    return 0;
20: }
```

Output ▼

```
Enter number of integers you wish to reserve: -1
Exception encountered. Got to end, sorry!
```

Analysis ▼

For this example, I used -1 as the number of integers that I wanted to reserve. This input is ridiculous, but users do ridiculous things all the time. In the absence of the exception handler, the program would encounter a very ugly end. But thanks to the exception handler, you see that the output displays a decent message: Got to end, sorry!.

NOTE

If you run the program using Visual Studio, you might also encounter a debug-mode message as illustrated in Figure 28.1.

FIGURE 28.1
Assertion due to Invalid Allocation Size.

Click Ignore to let the exception handler kick in. This is a debug-mode message, but the exception handling helps your program make a clean exit even in release mode.

Listing 28.1 demonstrates the usage of try and catch blocks. catch() takes parameters, just like a function does, and ... means that this catch block accepts all kinds of exceptions. In this case, however, we might want to specifically isolate exceptions of type std::bad_alloc as these are thrown when new fails. Catching a specific type will help you handle that type of problem in particular, for instance, show the user a message telling what exactly went wrong.

Catching Exception of a Type

The exception in Listing 28.1 was thrown from the C++ Standard Library. Such exceptions are of a known type, and catching a particular type is better for you as you can pinpoint the reason for the exception, do better cleanup, or at least show a precise message to the user, as Listing 28.2 does.

LISTING 28.2   Catching Exceptions of Type std::bad_alloc

```
0: #include <iostream>
1: #include<exception>  // include this to catch exception bac_alloc
2: using namespace std;
3:
4: int main()
5: {
6:     cout << "Enter number of integers you wish to reserve: ";
7:     try
8:     {
9:         int Input = 0;
10:        cin >> Input;
11:
12:        // Request memory space and then return it
13:        int* pReservedInts = new int [Input];
14:        delete[] pReservedInts;
15:    }
16:    catch (std::bad_alloc& exp)
17:    {
18:        cout << "Exception encountered: " << exp.what() << endl;
19:        cout << "Got to end, sorry!" << endl;
20:    }
21:    catch(...)
22:    {
23:        cout << "Exception encountered. Got to end, sorry!" << endl;
24:    }
25:    return 0;
26: }
```

28

Output ▼

```
Enter number of integers you wish to reserve: -1
Exception encountered: bad allocation
Got to end, sorry!
```

Analysis ▼

Compare the output of Listing 28.2 to that of Listing 28.1. You see that you are now able to supply a more precise reason for the abrupt ending of the application, namely "bad allocation." This is because you have an additional catch block (yes, two catch blocks), one that traps exceptions of the type catch(bad_alloc&) shown in Lines 16–20, which is thrown by new.

> **TIP**
>
> In general, you can insert as many catch() blocks as you like, one after another, depending on the exceptions you expect and those that would help.
>
> catch(...) as demonstrated in Listing 28.2 catches all those exception types that have not been explicitly caught by other catch statements.

Throwing Exception of a Type Using throw

When you caught std::bad_alloc in Listing 28.2, you actually caught an object of class std::bad_alloc thrown by new. It is possible for you to throw an exception of your own choosing. All you need is the keyword throw:

```
void DoSomething()
{
   if(something_unwanted)
      throw Value;
}
```

Let's study the usage of throw in a custom-defined exception as demonstrated by Listing 28.3 that divides two numbers.

LISTING 28.3 Throwing a Custom Exception at an Attempt to Divide by Zero

```
0: #include<iostream>
1: using namespace std;
2:
3: double Divide(double Dividend, double Divisor)
```

```
 4: {
 5:    if(Divisor == 0)
 6:        throw "Dividing by 0 is a crime";
 7:
 8:    return (Dividend / Divisor);
 9: }
10:
11: int main()
12: {
13:    cout << 'Enter dividend: ";
14:    double Dividend = 0;
15:    cin >> Dividend;
16:    cout << "Enter divisor: ";
17:    double Divisor = 0;
18:    cin >> Divisor;
19:
20:    try
21:    {
22:        cout << "Result of division is: " << Divide(Dividend, Divisor);
23:    }
24:    catch(char* exp)
25:    {
26:        cout << "Exception: " << exp << endl;
27:        cout << "Sorry, can't continue!" << endl;
28:    }
29:
30:    return 0;
31: }
```

Output ▼

```
Enter dividend: 2011
Enter divisor: 0
Exception: Dividing by 0 is a crime
Sorry, can't continue!
```

Analysis ▼

The code not only demonstrates that you are also able to catch exceptions of type char*, as shown in Line 24, but also that you caught an exception thrown in a called function Divide() at Line 6. Also note that you did not include all of main() within try {}; you only include the part of it that you expect to throw. This is generally a good practice, as exception handling can also reduce the execution performance of your code.

28

How Exception Handling Works

In Listing 28.3, you threw an exception of type char* in function Divide() that was caught in the catch(char*) handler in calling function main().

Where an exception is thrown, using throw, the compiler inserts a dynamic lookup for a compatible catch(Type) that can handle this exception. The exception handling logic first checks if the line throwing the exception is within a try block. If so, it seeks the catch(Type) that can handle the exception of this Type. If the throw statement is not within a try block or if there is no compatible catch() for the exception type, the exception handling logic seeks the same in the calling function. So, the exception handling logic climbs the stack, one calling function after another, seeking a suitable catch(Type) that can handle the exception. At each step in the stack unwinding procedure, the variables local to that function are destroyed in reverse sequence of their construction. This is demonstrated by Listing 28.4.

LISTING 28.4   The Destruction Order of Local Objects in Event of an Exception

```
0: #include <iostream>
1: using namespace std;
2:
3: struct StructA
4: {
5:    StructA() {cout << "Constructed a struct A" << endl; }
6:    ~StructA() {cout << "Destroyed a struct A" << endl;  }
7: };
8:
9: struct StructB
10: {
11:    StructB() {cout << "Constructed a struct B" << endl; }
12:    ~StructB() {cout << "Destroyed a struct B" << endl; }
13: };
14:
15: void FuncB()  // throws
16: {
17:       cout << "In Func B" << endl;
18:       StructA objA;
19:       StructB objB;
20:       cout << "About to throw up!" << endl;
21:       throw "Throwing for the heck of it";
22: }
23:
24: void FuncA()
25: {
26:    try
27:    {
```

```
28:          cout << "In Func A" << endl;
29:          StructA objA;
30:          StructB objB;
31:          FuncB();
32:        cout << "FuncA: returning to caller" << endl;
33:      }
34:    catch(const char* exp)
35:      {
36:          cout << "FuncA: Caught exception, it says: " << exp << endl;
37:          cout << "FuncA: Handled it here, will not throw to caller" << endl;
38:          // throw;  // uncomment this line to throw to main()
39:      }
40: }
41:
42: int main()
43: {
44:     cout << "main(): Started execution" << endl;
45:     try
46:     {
47:         FuncA();
48:     }
49:     catch(const char* exp)
50:     {
51:         cout << "Exception: " << exp << endl;
52:     }
53:     cout << "main(): exiting gracefully" << endl;
54:     return 0;
55: }
```

Output ▼

```
main(): Started execution
In Func A
Constructed a struct A
Constructed a struct B
In Func B
Constructed a struct A
Constructed a struct B
About to throw up!
Destroyed a struct B
Destroyed a struct A
Destroyed a struct B
Destroyed a struct A
FuncA: Caught exception, it says: Throwing for the heck of it
FuncA: Handled it here, will not throw to caller
main(): exiting gracefully
```

28

Analysis ▼

In Listing 28.4, `main()` invokes `FuncA()` that invokes `FuncB()`, which throws in Line 21. Both calling functions `FuncA()` and `main()` are exception safe as they both have a `catch(const char*)` block implemented. `FuncB()` that throws the exception has no `catch()` blocks, and hence the catch block within `FuncA()` at Lines 34–39 is the first handler to the thrown exception from `FuncB()`, as `FuncA()` is the caller of `FuncB()`. Note that `FuncA()` decided that this exception is not of a serious nature and did not propagate it to `main()`. Hence, `main()` continues as if no problem happened. If you uncomment Line 38, the exception is thrown to the caller of `FuncB()`—that is, `main()`receives it, too.

The output also indicates the order in which objects are created (the same order as you coded their instantiations) and the order in which they're destroyed as soon as an exception is thrown (in the reverse order of instantiations). This happens not only in `FuncB()` that threw the exception, but also in `FuncA()` that invoked `FuncB()` and handled the thrown exception.

CAUTION

Listing 28.4 demonstrates how destructors of local objects are invoked when an exception is thrown.

Should the destructor of an object invoked due to an exception also throw an exception, it results in an abnormal termination of your application.

Class `std::exception`

In catching `std::bad_alloc` in Listing 28.2, you actually caught an object of class `std::bad_alloc` thrown by `new`. `std::bad_alloc` is a class that inherits from C++ standard class `std::exception`, declared in header `<exception>`.

`std::exception` is the base class for the following important exceptions:

- `bad_alloc`—Thrown when a request for memory using `new` fails
- `bad_cast`—Thrown by `dynamic_cast` when you try to cast a wrong type (a type that has no inheritance relation)
- `ios_base::failure`—Thrown by the functions and methods in the `iostream` library

Class `std::exception` that is the base class supports a very useful and important virtual method `what()` that gives a more descriptive reason on the nature of the problem causing the exception. In Listing 28.2, exp.what() in Line 18 gives the information, "bad alloca-tion," telling you what went wrong. You can make use of std::exception being a base class for many exceptions types and create one catch(const exception&) that can catch all exceptions that have std::exception as base:

```
void SomeFunc()
{
   try
   {
      // code made exception safe
   }
   catch (const std::exception& exp) // catch bad_alloc, bad_cast, etc
   {
      cout << "Exception encountered: " << exp.what() << endl;
   }
}
```

Your Custom Exception Class Derived from std::exception

You can throw an exception of whatever type you want. However, there is a benefit in inheriting from std::exception—all existing exception handlers that catch(const std::exception&) and work for bad_alloc, bad_cast and the like will automatically scale up to catch your new exception class as well because it has the base class in com-mon with them. This is demonstrated in Listing 28.5.

LISTING 28.5   class CustomException That Inherits from std::exception

```
 0: #include <exception>
 1: #include <iostream>
 2: #include <string>
 3: using namespace std;
 4:
 5: class CustomException: public std::exception
 6: {
 7:    string Reason;
 8: public:
 9:    // constructor, needs reason
10:    CustomException(const char* why):Reason(why) {}
11:
12:    // redefining virtual function to return 'Reason'
13:    virtual const char* what() const throw()
14:    {
15:       return Reason.c_str();
16:    }
17: };
```

LISTING 28.5 Continued

```
18:
19: double Divide(double Dividend, double Divisor)
20: {
21:    if(Divisor == 0)
22:       throw CustomException("CustomException: Dividing by 0 is a crime");
23:
24:    return (Dividend / Divisor);
25: }
26:
27: int main()
28: {
29:    cout << "Enter dividend: ";
30:    double Dividend = 0;
31:    cin >> Dividend;
32:    cout << "Enter divisor: ";
33:    double Divisor = 0;
34:    cin >> Divisor;
35:    try
36:    {
37:       cout << "Result of division is: " << Divide(Dividend, Divisor);
38:    }
39:    catch(exception& exp)// catch CustomException, bad_alloc, etc
40:    {
41:       cout << exp.what() << endl;
42:       cout << "Sorry, can't continue!" << endl;
43:    }
44:
45:    return 0;
46: }
```

Output ▼

```
Enter dividend: 2011
Enter divisor: 0
CustomException: Dividing by 0 is a crime
Sorry, can't continue!
```

Analysis ▼

This is the version of Listing 28.3 that threw a simple char* exception on divide by zero. This one, however, instantiates an object of class CustomException defined in Lines 5–17 that inherits from std::exception. Note how our customer exception class implements virtual function what() in Lines 13–16, essentially returning the reason why the exception was thrown. The catch(exception&) logic in main() in Lines 39–43 handles not only class CustomException, but also other exceptions of type bad_alloc that have the same base class exception.

NOTE

Note the declaration of virtual method CustomException::what() in Line 13 in Listing 28.5:

```
virtual const char* what() const throw()
```

It ends with throw(), which means that this function itself is not expected to throw an exception—a very important and relevant restriction on a class that is used as an exception object. If you still insert a throw within this function, you can expect a compiler warning.

If a function ends with throw(int), it means that the function is expected to throw an exception of type int.

DO	DON'T
DO remember to catch exceptions of type std::exception.	**DON'T** throw exceptions from destructors.
DO remember to inherit your custom exception class (if any) from std::exception.	**DON'T** take memory allocations for granted; code that does new should always be exception safe and within a try block with a catch(std::exception&).
DO throw exceptions but with discretion. They're not a substitute for return values such as true or false.	
	DON'T insert any heavy logic or resource allocations inside a catch() block. You don't want to be causing exceptions when you're handling one.

Summary

In this lesson you learned a very important part of practical C++ programming. Making your applications stable beyond your own development environment is important for customer satisfaction and intuitive user experiences, and this is exactly what exceptions help you do. You found out that code that allocates resources or memory can fail and hence needs to be made exception safe. You learned the C++ exception class std::exception and that if you need to be programming a custom exception class, you ideally would be inheriting from this one.

28

Q&A

Q **Why raise exceptions instead of returning an error?**

A Not always do you have the privilege of returning an error. If a call to new fails, you need to handle exceptions thrown by new to prevent your application from crashing. Additionally, if an error is very severe and makes the future functioning of your application impossible, you should consider throwing an exception.

Q **Why should my exception class inherit from `std::exception`?**

A This is, of course, not compulsory, but it helps you reuse all those catch() blocks that already catch exceptions of type std::exception. You can write your own exception class that doesn't inherit from anything else, but then you have to insert new catch(MyNewExceptionType&) statements at all the relevant points.

Q **I have a function that throws an exception. Does it need to be caught at the very same function?**

A Not at all. Just ensure that the exception type thrown is caught at one of the calling functions in the call stack.

Q **Can a constructor throw an exception?**

A Constructors actually have no choice! They don't have return values, and throwing an exception is the best way to demonstrate disagreement.

Q **Can a destructor throw an exception?**

A Technically, yes. However, this is a bad practice as destructors are also called when the stack is unwound due to an exception. So, a destructor invoked due to an exception throwing an exception itself can clearly result in quite an ugly situation for the state of an already unstable application trying to make a clean exit.

Workshop

The Workshop contains quiz questions to help solidify your understanding of the material covered and exercises to provide you with experience in using what you've learned. Try to answer the quiz and exercise questions before checking the answers in Appendix D, and be certain you understand the answers before going to the following lesson.

Quiz

1. What is std::exception?

2. What type of exception is thrown when an allocation using new fails?

3. Is it alright to allocate a million integers in an exception handler (catch block) to back up existing data for instance?

4. How would you catch an exception object of type class MyException that inherits from std::exception?

Exercises

1. **BUG BUSTER:** What is wrong with the following code?

```
class SomeIntelligentStuff
{
   bool StuffGoneBad;
public:
   ~ SomeIntelligentStuff()
   {
      if(StuffGoneBad)
         throw "Big problem in this class, just FYI";
   }
};
```

2. **BUG BUSTER:** What is wrong with the following code?

```
int main()
{
   int* pMillionIntegers = new int [1000000];
   // do something with the million integers

   delete []pMillionIntegers;
}
```

3. **BUG BUSTER:** What is wrong with the following code?

```
int main()
{
   try
   {
      int* pMillionIntegers = new int [1000000];
      // do something with the million integers

      delete []pMillionIntegers;
   }
   catch(exception& exp)
   {
      int* pAnotherMillionIntegers = new int [1000000];
      // take back up of pMillionIntegers and save it to disk
   }
}
```

28

LESSON 29
Going Forward

You have learned the basics of C++ programming. In fact, you have gone beyond theoretical boundaries in understanding how using the Standard Template Library (STL), templates, and the Standard Library can help you write efficient and compact code. It is time to give performance a look and gain a perspective on programming best practices.

In this lesson, you learn

- How today's processors are different
- How your C++ application can best utilize the processor's capabilities
- Threads and multithreading
- Best practices in programming in C++
- Improving your C++ skills beyond this book

What's Different in Today's Processors?

Until recently, computers got faster by using processors that featured faster processing speeds, measured in hertz (Hz), megahertz (Mhz), or gigahertz (GHz). For instance, Intel 8086 (see Figure 29.1) was a 16-bit microprocessor launched in 1978 with a clock speed of about 10MHz.

FIGURE 29.1
The Intel 8086 microprocessor.

Those were the days when processors got significantly faster and so did your C++ application. It was easy to rely on a waiting game to make use of improved hardware performance and improving your software's responsiveness through it. Although today's processors are getting faster, the true innovation is in the number of cores they deploy. At the time of writing this book, Intel was already selling a 64-bit microprocessor with six embedded cores at 3.2GHz, and the trend, as far as the number of cores go, is increasing, as illustrated by Figure 29.2. In fact, even smartphones already feature processors with multiple cores.

FIGURE 29.2
Intel multicore microprocessor.

You can think of a multicore processor as a single chip with multiple processors running in parallel within it. Each processor has its own L1 cache and can work independently of the other.

29

A faster processor increasing the speed of your application is logical. How do multiple cores in a processor help? Each core is evidently capable of running an application in parallel, but this doesn't make your application run any faster. Single-threaded C++ applications of the types you have seen this far are possibly missing the bus as far as using multicore processing capabilities go. The applications run in one thread, and hence on only one core, as shown in Figure 29.3.

FIGURE 29.3
A single-threaded application in a multiple-core processor.

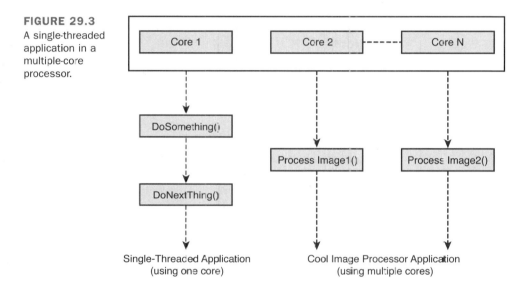

Single-Threaded Application
(using one core)

Cool Image Processor Application
(using multiple cores)

If your application executes all use cases in a serial order, the operating system (OS) will possibly give it only as much time as other applications in the queue and it will occupy only one core on the processor. In other words, your application is running on a multi-core processor in the same way as it would do in those years gone by.

How to Better Use Multiple Cores

The key is in creating applications that are multithreaded. Each thread runs in parallel, allowing the OS to let the threads run on multiple cores. Although it is beyond the scope of this book to discuss threads and multithreading in great detail, I can just touch this topic and give you a head start toward high-performance computing.

What Is a Thread?

Your application code always runs in a thread. A thread is a synchronous execution entity where statements in a thread run one after another. The code inside main() is considered to execute the main thread of the application. In this main thread, you can create new threads that can run in parallel. Such applications that are comprised of one or more threads running in parallel in addition to the main thread are called multithreaded applications.

The OS dictates how threads are to be created, and you can create threads directly by calling those APIs supplied by the OS.

TIP	C++11 specifies thread functions that take care of calling the OS APIs for you, making your multithreaded application a little more portable. If you plan to be writing your application for only one OS, check your OS's APIs on creating multithreaded applications.

NOTE	The actual act of creating a thread is an OS-specific functionality. C++11 tries to supply you with a platform-independent abstraction in the form of `std::thread` in header `<thread>`. At the time of writing this book, most major compilers did not support this functionality very well. Besides, if you are writing for one platform, you are better off just using the OS-specific thread functions. Should you need portable threads in your C++ application, do look up Boost Thread Libraries at www.boost.org.

Why Program Multithreaded Applications?

Multithreading is used in applications that need to do multiple sessions of a certain activity in parallel. Imagine that you are 1 of 10,000 other users trying to make a purchase on Amazon. Amazon's web server can of course not keep 9,999 users waiting at a time. What the web server does is create multiple threads, servicing users at the same time. If the web server is running on a multiple-core processor (which I bet it is), the threads are able to extract the best out of the available cores and provide optimal performance to the user.

Another common example of multithreading is an application that does some work in addition to interacting with the user, for instance via a progress bar. Such applications are often divided into a User Interface Thread that displays and updates the user interface and accepts user input, and the Worker Thread that does the work in the background. A tool that defragments your disk is one such application. After you press the start button, a

Worker Thread is created that starts with the scan and defragmenting activity. At the same time, the User Interface Thread displays progress and also gives you the option to cancel the defragmentation. Note that for the User Interface Thread to show progress, the Worker Thread that does the defragmentation needs to regularly communicate the same. Similarly, for the Worker Thread to stop working when you cancel, the User Interface Thread needs to communicate the same.

NOTE

> Multithreaded applications often need threads to "talk" to each other so that the application can function as a unit (and not a collection of runaway threads that do their stuff irrespective of the other).
>
> Sequence is important, too. You don't want the User Interface Thread to end before the defragmenting Worker Thread has ended. There are situations where one thread needs to wait on another. For instance, a thread that reads from a database should wait until the thread that writes is done.
>
> The act of making threads wait on another is called *thread synchronization*.

How Can Threads Transact Data?

Threads can share variables. Threads have access to globally placed data. Threads can be created with a pointer to a shared object (`struct` or `class`) with data in it, shown in Figure 29.4.

FIGURE 29.4
Worker and User
Interface Threads
sharing data.

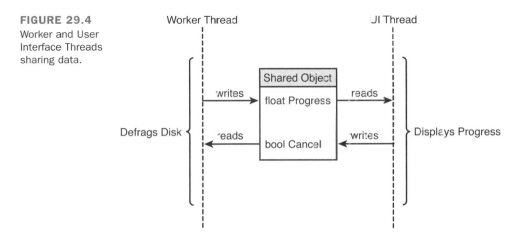

Different threads can communicate by accessing or writing data that is stored in a location in memory that can be accessed by them all and is hence shared. In the example of the defragmenter where the Worker Thread knows the progress and the User Interface Thread needs to be informed of it, the Worker Thread can constantly store the progress in percentage at an integer that the User Interface Thread uses to display the progress.

This is quite a simple case, though—one thread creates information and the other consumes it. What would happen if multiple threads wrote and read from the same location? Some threads might start reading data when some other threads have not finished writing them. The integrity of the data in question would be compromised.

This is why threads need to be synchronized.

Using Mutexes and Semaphores to Synchronize Threads

Threads are OS-level entities, and the objects that you use to synchronize them are supplied by the OS, too. Most operating systems provide you with semaphores and mutexes for performing thread synchronization activity.

Using a mutex, you normally ensure that one thread has access to a piece of code at a time. In other words, a mutex is used to bracket a section of code where a thread has to wait until another thread that is currently executing it is done and releases the mutex. The next thread acquires the mutex, does its job, and releases the same.

Using semaphores, you can control the number of threads that execute a section of code. A semaphore that allows access to only one thread at a time is also called a binary semaphore.

> **NOTE**
> Depending on the OS that you are using, you might have these or more synchronization objects available. Windows, for instance, features critical sections that bracket code that can be executed only one thread at a time.

Problems Caused by Multithreading

Multithreading with its need for good synchronization across threads can also cause a good number of sleepless nights when this synchronization is not effective (read: buggy). Two of the most frequent issues that multithreaded applications face are the following:

- **Race conditions**—Two or more threads trying to write to the same data. Who wins? What is the state of that object?

- **Deadlock**—Two threads waiting on each other to finish resulting in both being in a "wait" state. Your application is hung.

You can avoid race conditions with good synchronization. In general when threads are allowed to write to a shared object, you must take extra care to ensure that

- Only one thread writes at a time.

- No thread is allowed to read that object until the writing thread is done.

You can avoid deadlocks by ensuring that in no situation do two threads wait on each other. You can either have a master thread that synchronizes worker threads or program in a way such that tasks are distributed between threads and result in clear workload distribution. A thread A can wait on B, but B should never need to wait on A.

Programming multithreaded applications is a specialization in itself. Hence, it is beyond the scope of this book to explain this interesting and exciting topic to you in detail. You should either refer to the plenty of online documentation available on the topic or learn multithreading by hands-on programming. Once you master it, you will automatically position your C++ applications optimally as far as using multicore processors being released in the future goes.

Writing Great C++ Code

C++ has not only evolved significantly since the days it was first conceived, but standardization efforts made by major compiler manufacturers and the availability of utilities and functions help you write compact and clean C++ code. It is indeed easy to program readable and reliable C++ applications.

Here is a short list of best practices that help you create good C++ applications:

- Give your variables names that make sense (to others as well as to you). It is worth spending a second more to give variables better names.

- Always initialize variables such as `int`, `float`, and the like.

- Always initialize pointer values to either NULL or a valid address—for instance, that returned by operator `new`.

- When using arrays, never cross the bounds of the array buffer. This is called a buffer overflow and can exploited as a security vulnerability.

- Don't use C-style `char*` string buffers or functions such as `strlen()` and `strcpy()`. `std::string` is safer and provides many useful utility methods including ones that help you find the length, copy, and append.

- Use a static array only when you are certain of the number of elements it will contain. If you are not certain of it, choose a dynamic array such as `std::vector`.

- When declaring and defining functions that take non-POD (plain old data) types as input, consider declaring parameters as reference parameters to avoid the unnecessary copy step when the function is called.

- If your class contains a raw pointer member (or members), give thought to how memory resource ownership needs to be managed in the event of a copy or assignment. That is, consider programming copy constructor and copy assignment operator.

- When writing a utility class that manages a dynamic array or the like, remember to program the move constructor and the move assignment operator for better performance.

- Remember to make your code `const`-correct. A `get()` function should ideally not be able to modify the class' members and hence should be a `const`. Similarly, function parameters should be `const`-references, unless you want to change the values they contain.

- Avoid using raw pointers. Choose the appropriate smart pointers where possible.

- When programming a utility class, take effort in supporting all those operators that will make consuming and using the class easy.

- Given an option, choose a template version over a macro. Templates are type-safe and generic.

- When programming a class that will be collected in a container, such as a vector or a list, or used as a key element in a map, remember to support `operator<` that will help define the default sort criteria.

- If your lambda function gets too large, you should possibly consider making a function object of it—that is, a class with `operator()` as the functor is reusable and a single point of maintenance.

- Never take the success of operator `new` for granted. Code that performs resource allocation should always be made exception safe—bracketed within `try` with corresponding `catch()` blocks.

- Never `throw` from the destructor of a class.

This is not an exhaustive list, but it covers some of the most important points that will help you in writing good and maintainable C++ code.

Learning C++ Doesn't Stop Here!

Congratulations, you have made great progress in learning C++. The best way to continue is to code and code lots more!

C++ is a sophisticated language. The more you program, the higher will be your level of understanding of how stuff works behind the scenes. Development environments such as Visual Studio with intelli-sense features will assist you and feed your curiosity—for instance, by showing you members of a string class you haven't seen yet. It's time to learn by doing!

29

Online Documentation

If you need to learn more about the signatures of STL containers, their methods, their algorithms, and their functional details, visit MSDN (http://msdn.microsoft.com/), which has very good coverage on the Standard Template Library.

TIP

> When reading STL documentation on MSDN, remember to choose the right Visual Studio Version, as C++11 support only started with Visual Studio 2010.

At the time of writing this book, the major C++ compilers did not fully support all C++11 features. For instance, Visual Studio 2010 doesn't support variadic templates. GNU's GCC compiler version 4.6 has an implementation of `std::thread` that is broken. Visiting online documentation of your compiler and seeing what next C++11 feature is planned for support is a good idea in general. The Visual Studio team maintains a blog called "C++11 Core Language Feature Support" that you can visit at http://blogs.msdn.com/b/vcblog/archive/2010/04/06/c-0x-core-language-features-in-vc10-the-table.aspx, and GCC has a support page at http://gcc.gnu.org/projects/cxx0x.html.

NOTE

> Note that at the time of writing this book, these two compilers already supported the major bulk of features recommend by C++11. Rest assured that the code snippets in the book have been tested using them both.

Communities for Guidance and Help

C++ has rich and vibrant online communities. Enroll yourself at sites such as CodeGuru (www.CodeGuru.com) or CodeProject (www.CodeProject.com) to have your technical queries inspected and answered by the community.

When you feel confident, feel free to contribute to these communities. You will find yourself answering challenging questions and learning a lot in the process.

Summary

This concluding lesson is actually an opening page in your quest to learn C++! Having come this far, you have learned the basics and the advanced concepts of the language. In this lesson, you learned the theoretical basics of multithreaded programming. You learned that the only way you can extract the best from multicore processors is to organize your logic in threads and allow parallel processing. You know that there are pitfalls in multithreaded applications and ways to avoid them. Last but not the least, you learned some basic C++ programming best practices. You know that writing good C++ code is not only about using advanced concepts, but also about giving variable names that others understand, handling exceptions to take care of the unexpected, and using utility classes such as smart pointers instead of raw ones. You are now ready to take a leap into the world of professional C++ programming.

Q&A

Q I am quite happy with the performance of my application. Should I still implement multithreaded capabilities?

A Not at all. Not all applications need to be multithreaded. Rather only those that need to perform a task concurrently or that serve many users in parallel.

Q The major compilers still don't support C++11 completely. So, why not use the old style of programming?

A First and foremost, the two major compilers (Microsoft Visual C++ and GNU's GCC) do support most major C++11 features, barring a few. Additionally, C++11 makes programming easy. Keywords such as `auto` save you long and tedious iterator declarations, and lambda functions make your `for_each()` construct compact without the need for a function object. So, the benefits in programming C++11 are already significant.

Workshop

The Workshop contains quiz questions to help solidify your understanding of the material covered. Try to answer the questions before checking the answers in Appendix D.

Quiz

1. My image processing application doesn't respond when it is correcting the contrast. What should I do?

2. My multithreaded application allows for extremely fast access to the database. Yet, sometimes I see that the data fetched is garbled. What am I doing wrong?

APPENDIX A
Working with Numbers: Binary and Hexadecimal

Understanding how the binary and hexadecimal number systems work is not critical to programming better applications in C++, but it helps you to better understand what happens under the hood.

Decimal Numeral System

Numbers that we use on a daily basis are in the range of 0–9. This set of numbers is called the Decimal Numeral System. As the system is comprised of 10 unique digits, it's a system with base of 10.

Hence, as the base is 10, the zero-based position of each digit denotes the power of 10 that the digit is multiplied with. So

```
957 = 9 x 10² + 5 x 10¹ + 7 x 10⁰ = 9 x 100 + 5 x 10 + 7
```

In the number 957, the zero-based position of 7 is 0, that of 5 is 1, and that of 9 is 2. These position indexes become powers of the base 10, as shown in the example. Remember that any number to the power 0 is 1 (so, 10^0 is the same as 1000^0 as both evaluate to 1).

NOTE

> The decimal system is one in which powers of 10 are the most important. Digits in a number are multiplied by 10, 100, 1000, and so on to determine the magnitude of the number.

Binary Numeral System

A system with a base of 2 is called a binary system. As the system allows only two states, it is represented by the numbers 0 and 1. These numbers in C++ typically evaluate to `false` and `true` (`true` being non-zero).

Just as numbers in a decimal system are evaluated to powers of base 10, those in binary are evaluated as powers of their base 2:

```
101 (binary) = 1 x 2² + 0 x 2¹ + 1 x 2⁰ = 4 + 0 + 1 = 5 (decimal)
```

So, the decimal equivalent of binary 101 is 5.

NOTE

> Digits in a binary number are multiplied by powers of 2 such as 4, 8, 16, 32, and so on to determine the magnitude of the number. The power is decided by the zero-based place the digit in question has.

To understand the binary numeral system better, let's examine Table A.1 that enlists the various powers of two.

TABLE A.1 Powers of 2

Power	Value	Binary Representation
0	$2^0 = 1$	1
1	$2^1 = 2$	10
2	$2^2 = 4$	100
3	$2^3 = 8$	1000
4	$2^4 = 16$	10000
5	$2^5 = 32$	100000
6	$2^6 = 64$	1000000
7	$2^7 = 128$	10000000

A

Why Do Computers Use Binary?

Widespread usage of the binary system is relatively new and accelerated by the development of electronics and computers. The evolution of electronics and electronic components resulted in a system that detected states of a component as being ON (under a significant potential difference or voltage) or OFF (no or low potential difference).

These ON and OFF states were very conveniently interpreted as 1 and 0, completely representing the binary number set and making it the method of choice for performing arithmetic calculations. Logical operations, such as NOT, AND, OR and XOR, as covered in Lesson 5, "Working with Expressions, Statements, and Operators" (in Tables 5.2–5.5), were easily supported by the development of electronic gates, resulting in the binary system being whole-heartedly adopted as conditional processing became easy.

What Are Bits and Bytes?

A bit is a basic unit in a computational system that contains a binary state. Thus, a bit is said to be "set" if it contains state 1 or "reset" if it contains state 0. A collection of bits is a byte. The number of bits in a byte is theoretically not fixed and is a hardware-dependent number.

However, most computational systems go with the assumption of 8 bits in a byte, for the simple, convenient reason that 8 is a power of 2. Eight bits in a byte also allows the transmission of up to 2^8 different values, allowing for 255 distinct values. These 255 distinct values are enough for the display or transaction of all characters in the ASCII character set, and more.

How Many Bytes Make a Kilobyte?

1024 bytes (2^{10} bytes) make a kilobyte. Similarly, 1024 kilobytes make a megabyte. 1024 megabytes make a gigabyte. 1024 gigabytes make a terabyte.

Hexadecimal Numeral System

Hexadecimal is a number system with base 16. A digit in the hexadecimal system can be in the range of 0–9 and A–F. So, 10 in decimal is A in hexadecimal, and 15 in decimal is F in hexadecimal:

Decimal	Hexadecimal	Decimal (continued)	Hexadecimal (continued)
0	0	8	8
1	1	9	9
2	2	10	A
3	3	11	B
4	4	12	C
5	5	13	D
6	6	14	E
7	7	15	F

Just as numbers in a decimal system are evaluated to powers of base 10, in binary as powers of their base 2, those in hexadecimal are evaluated to powers of base 16:

```
0x31F = 3 x 16² + 1 x 16¹ + F x 16⁰ = 3 x 256 + 16 + 15 (in decimal) = 799
```

NOTE

It is convention that hexadecimal numbers be represented with a prefix "0x".

Why Do We Need Hexadecimal?

Computers work on binary. The state of each unit of memory in a computer is a 0 or a 1. However, if we as human beings were to interact on computer- or programming-specific information in 0s and 1s, we would need a lot of space to transact small pieces of information. So, instead of writing 1111 in binary, you are a lot more efficient writing F in hexadecimal.

So, a hexadecimal representation can very efficiently represent the state of 4 bits in a digit, using a maximum of two hexadecimal digits to represent the state of a byte.

> A less-used number system is the Octa Numeral System. This is a system with base 8, comprising of numbers from 0 to 7.

Converting to a Different Base

When dealing with numbers, you might see the need to view the same number in a different base—for instance, the value of a binary number in decimal or that of a decimal number in hexadecimal.

A

In the previous examples, you saw how numbers can be converted from binary or hexadecimal into decimal. Take a look at converting binary and hexadecimal numbers into decimal.

The Generic Conversion Process

When converting a number in one system to another, you successively divide with the base, starting with the number being converted. Each remainder fills places in the destination numeral system, starting with the lowest place. The next division uses the quotient of the previous division operation with the base as the divisor.

This continues until the remainder is within the destination numeral system and the quotient is 0.

This process is also called the *breakdown method*.

Converting Decimal to Binary

To convert decimal 33 into binary, you subtract the highest power of 2 possible (32):

Place 1: 33 / 2 = quotient 16, remainder 1
Place 2: 16 / 2 = quotient 8, remainder 0
Place 3: 8 / 2 = quotient 4, remainder 0
Place 4: 4 / 2 = quotient 2, remainder 0
Place 5: 2 / 2 = quotient 1, remainder 0
Place 6: 1 / 2 = quotient 0, remainder 1

Binary equivalent of 33 (reading places): 100001

Similarly, the binary equivalent of 156 is:

Place 1: 156 / 2 = quotient 78, remainder 0

Place 2: 78 / 2 = quotient 39, remainder 0

Place 3: 39 / 2 = quotient 19, remainder 1

Place 4: 19 / 2 = quotient 9, remainder 1

Place 5:   9 / 2 = quotient 4, remainder 1

Place 6:   4 / 2 = quotient 2, remainder 0

Place 7:   2 / 2 = quotient 1, remainder 0

Place 9:   1 / 0 = quotient 0, remainder 1

Binary equivalent of 156: 10011100

Converting Decimal to Hexadecimal

The process is the same as for binary; you divide by base 16 instead of 2.

So, to convert decimal 5211 to hex:

Place 1: 5211 / 16 = quotient 325, remainder B_{16} (11_{10} is B_{16})

Place 2: 325 / 16 = quotient 20, remainder 5

Place 3:   20 / 16 = quotient 1, remainder 4

Place 4:   1 / 16 = quotient 0, remainder 1

$5205_{10} = 145B_{16}$

TIP

To understand better how different number systems work, you can write a simple C++ program similar to Listing 27.1 in Lesson 27, "Using Streams for Input and Output." It uses `std::cout` with manipulators for displaying an integer in hex, decimal, and octal notations.

To display an integer in binary, use `std::bitset` that has been explained in Lesson 25, "Working with Bit Flags Using STL," deriving inspiration from Listing 25.1.

APPENDIX B
C++ Keywords

Keywords are reserved to the compiler for use by the language. You cannot define classes, variables, or functions that have these keywords as their names.

asm	false	signed
auto	final	sizeof
bool	float	static
break	for	static_assert
case	friend	static_cast
catch	goto	struct
char	if	switch
class	inline	template
const	int	this
constexpr	long	throw
const_cast	long long int	true
continue	mutable	try
decltype	namespace	typedef
default	new	typeid
delete	operator	typename
do	override	union
double	private	unsigned
dynamic_cast	protected	using
else	public	virtual
enum	register	void
explicit	reinterpret_cast	volatile
export	return	wchar_t
extern	short	while

In addition, the following keywords are reserved:

and	compl	or_eq
and_eq	not	xor
bitand	not_eq	xor_eq
bitor	or	

APPENDIX C
Operator Precedence

It is a good practice to use parentheses that explicitly compartmentalize your operations. In absence of those parentheses, the compiler resorts to a predefined order of precedence in which the operators are used. This operator precedence, as listed in Table C.1, is what the C++ compiler adheres to in event of ambiguity.

TABLE C.1   The Precedence of Operators

Rank	Name	Operator
1	Scope resolution	`::`
2	Member selection, subscripting, function calls, postfix increment, and decrement	`. ->`
		`()`
		`++ --`
3	`Sizeof`, prefix increment and decrement, complement, and, not, unary minus and plus, address-of and dereference, new, new[], delete, delete[], casting, sizeof()	`++ --` `^ !` `- +` `& *`
		`()`
4	Member selection for pointer	`.* ->*`
5	Multiply, divide, modulo	`* / %`
6	Add, subtract	`+ -`
7	Shift (shift left, shift right)	`<< >>`
8	Inequality relational	`< <= > >=`
9	Equality, inequality	`== !=`
10	Bitwise AND	`&`
11	Bitwise exclusive OR	`^`
12	Bitwise OR	`|`
13	Logical AND	`&&`
14	Logical OR	`||`
15	Conditional	`?:`
16	Assignment operators	`= *= /= %=`
		`+= -= <<=`
		`>>=`
		`&= |= ^=`
17	Comma	`,`

APPENDIX D
Answers

Answers for Lesson 1

Quiz

1. An interpreter is a tool that interprets what you code (or an intermediate byte code) and performs certain actions. A compiler is one that takes your code as an input and generates an object file. In the case of C++, after compiling and linking you have an executable that can run directly by the processor without need for any further interpretation

2. A compiler takes a C++ code file as input and generates an object file in machine language. Often your code has dependencies on libraries and functions in other code files. Creating these links and generating an executable that integrates all dependencies directly and indirectly coded by you is the job of the linker.

3. Code. Compile to create object file. Link to create executable. Execute to test. Debug. Fix errors in code and repeat the steps.

   In many cases, compilation and linking is one step.

4. C++11 supports a portable threading model that enables a programmer to create multithreaded applications using standard C++ threading functions. Thus, it allows a multicore processor to work optimally by simultaneously executing different threads in an application on its multiple cores.

Exercises

1. Display the result of subtracting y from x, multiplying the two, and adding the two.

2. Output should be
   2 48 14

3. A preprocessor command to include `iostream` as seen in Line 1 should start with #.

4. It displays the following:
```
Hello Buggy World
```

Answers for Lesson 2

Quiz

1. Code in C++ is case sensitive. Int is not acceptable to the compiler as an integer type `int`.

2. Yes.
```
/*  if you comment using this C-style syntax
then you can span your comment over multiple lines */
```

Exercises

1. It fails because case-sensitive C++ compilers don't know what `std::Cout` is or why the string following it doesn't start with an opening quote. Additionally, the declaration of `main` should always return an `int`.

2. Here is the corrected version:
```
#include <iostream>
int main()
{
    std::cout << "Is there a bug here?"; // no bug anymore
    return 0;
}
```

3. This program derived from Listing 2.4 demonstrates subtraction and multiplication:
```
##include <iostream>
#using namespace std;
u
// Function declaration
iint DemoConsoleOutput();
{
 int main()
 {
   // Call i.e. invoke the function
   DemoConsoleOutput();

   return 0;
```

```
    }

    // Function definition
    int DemoConsoleOutput()
    {
       cout << "Performing subtraction 10 - 5 = " << 10 - 5 << endl;
       cout << "Performing multiplication 10 * 5 = " << 10 * 5 << endl;

       return 0;
    }
```

Output ▼

```
    Performing subtraction 10 - 5 = 5
    Performing multiplication 10 * 5 = 50
```

Answers for Lesson 3

Quiz

1. A signed integer is one in which the most-significant-bit (MSB) functions as
   the sign-bit and indicates if the value of the integer is positive or negative. An
   unsigned integer in comparison is used to contain only positive integer values.

2. #define is a preprocessor directive that directs the compiler to do a text replacement wherever the defined value is seen. However, it is not type safe and is a
   primitive way of defining constants. Therefore, it is to be avoided.

3. To ensure that it contains a definite, non-random value.

4. 2.

5. The name is nondescriptive and repeats the type. Though this compiles, such code
   becomes difficult for humans to read and maintain and should be avoided. An integer is better declared using a name that reveals its purpose. For example:

```
    int Age = 0;
```

Exercises

1. Many ways of achieving this:

```
    enum YOURCARDS {ACE = 43, JACK, QUEEN, KING};
    // ACE is 43, JACK is 44, QUEEN is 45, KING is 46
    // Alternatively..
    enum YOURCARDS {ACE, JACK, QUEEN = 45, KING};
    // ACE is 0, JACK is 1, QUEEN is 45 and KING is 46
```

D

2. See Listing 3.4 and adapt it (reduce it) to get the answer to this question.

3. Here is a program that asks you to enter radius of a circle and calculates the area and circumference for you:

```cpp
#include <iostream>
using namespace std;

int main()
{
   const double Pi = 3.1416;

   cout << "Enter circle's radius: ";
    double Radius = 0;
   cin >> Radius;

   cout << "Area = " << Pi * Radius * Radius << endl;
   cout << "Circumference = " << 2 * Pi * Radius << endl;

   return 0;
}
```

Output ▼

```
Enter circle's radius: 4
Area = 50.2656
Circumference = 25.1328
```

4. You get a compilation warning (not error) if you store the result of calculating area and circumference in an integer and the output looks like this:

Output ▼

```
Enter circle's radius: 4
Area = 50
Circumference = 25
```

5. auto is a construct where the compiler automatically decides on the type the variable can take depending on the value it is being initialized to. The code in question does not initialize and the statement causes a compilation failure.

Answers for Lesson 4

Quiz

1. 0 and 4 are the zero-based indexes of the first and last elements of an array with five elements.

2. No, as they are proven to be unsafe especially in handling user input, giving the user an opportunity to enter a string longer than the length of the array.

3. One null terminating character.

4. Depending on how you use it. If you use it in a cout statement, for instance, the display logic reads successive characters seeking a terminating null and crosses the bounds of the array, possibly causing your application to crash.

5. That would simply replace the int in the vector's declaration by char.

```
vector<char> DynArrChars (3);
```

Exercises

1. Here you go. The application initializes for ROOKs, but it's enough for you to get an idea:

```
int main()
{
  enum SQUARE
  {
      NOTHING = 0,
      PAWN,
      ROOK,
      KNIGHT,
      BISHOP,
      KING,
      QUEEN
  };

  SQUARE ChessBoard[8][8];

  // Initialize the squares containing rooks
  ChessBoard[0][0] = ChessBcard[0][7] = ROOK;
  ChessBoard[7][0] = ChessBcard[7][7] = ROOK;

  return 0;
}
```

D

2. To set the fifth element of an array, you need to access element MyNumbers[4] as this is a zero-based index.

3. The fourth element of the array is being accessed without ever being initalized or assigned. The resulting output is unpredictable. Always initialize variables and also arrays; otherwise, they contain the last value stored in the memory location they're created in.

Answers for Lesson 5

Quiz

1. Integer types cannot contain decimal values that are possibly relevant for the user who wants to divide two numbers. So, you would use `float`.

2. As the compiler interprets them to be an integer, it is 4.

3. As the numerator is 32.0 and not 32, the compiler interprets this to be a floating-point operation, creating a result in a `float` that is akin to 4.571.

4. No, `sizeof` is an operator, and one that cannot be overloaded.

5. It does not work as intended because the addition operator has priority over shift, resulting in a shift of 1 + 5 = 6 bits instead of just one.

6. The result of XOR is `false` as also indicated by Table 5.5.

Exercises

1. Here is a correct solution:

   ```
   int Result = ((number << 1) + 5) << 1; // unambiguous even to reader
   ```

2. The result contains `number` shifted 7 bits left, as `operator +` takes priority over `operator <<`.

3. Here is a program that stores two Boolean values entered by the user and demonstrates the result of using bitwise operators on them:

   ```
   #include <iostream>
   using namespace std;

   int main()
   {
      cout << "Enter a boolean value true(1) or false(0): ";
      bool Value1 = false;
      cin >> Value1;

      cout << "Enter another boolean value true(1) or false(0): ";
      bool Value2 = false;
      cin >> Value2;

      cout << "Result of bitwise operators on these operands: " << endl;
      cout << "Bitwise AND: " << (Value1 & Value2) << endl;
      cout << "Bitwise OR: " << (Value1 | Value2) << endl;
      cout << "Bitwise XOR: " << (Value1 ^ Value2) << endl;

      return 0;
   }
   ```

Output ▼

```
Enter a boolean value true(1) or false(0): 1
Enter another boolean value true(1) or false(0): 0
Result of bitwise operators on these operands:
Bitwise AND: 0
Bitwise OR: 1
Bitwise XOR: 1
```

Answers for Lesson 6

Quiz

1. You indent not for sake of the compiler, but for the sake of other programmers (humans) who might need to read or understand your code.

2. You avoid it to keep your code from getting unintuitive and expensive to maintain.

3. See the code in the solution to Exercise 1 that uses the decrement operator.

4. As the condition in the for statement is not satisfied, the loop won't execute even once and the cout statement it contains is never executed.

Exercises

1. You need to be aware that array indexes are zero-based and the last element is at index Length − 1:

```cpp
#include <iostream>
using namespace std;

int main()
{
   const int ARRAY_LEN = 5;
   int MyNumbers[ARRAY_LEN]= {-55, 45, 9889, 0, 45};

   for (int nIndex = ARRAY_LEN - 1; nIndex >= 0; —nIndex)
      cout<<"MyNumbers[" << nIndex << "] = '<<MyNumbers[nIndex]<<endl;

   return 0;
}
```

D

Output ▼

```
MyNumbers[4] = 45
MyNumbers[3] = 0
MyNumbers[2] = 9889
```

```
MyNumbers[1] = 45
MyNumbers[0] = -55
```

2. One nested loop equivalent of Listing 6.13 that adds elements in two arrays in the reverse order is demonstrated below:

```cpp
#include <iostream>
using namespace std;

int main()
{
   const int ARRAY1_LEN = 3;
   const int ARRAY2_LEN = 2;

   int MyInts1[ARRAY1_LEN] = {35, -3, 0};
   int MyInts2[ARRAY2_LEN] = {20, -1};

   cout << "Adding each int in MyInts1 by each in MyInts2:" << endl;

   for(int Array1Index=ARRAY1_LEN-1;Array1Index>=0;--Array1Index)
      for(int Array2Index=ARRAY2_LEN-1;Array2Index>=0;--Array2Index)
         cout<<MyInts1[Array1Index]<<" + "<<MyInts2[Array2Index] \
         << " = " << MyInts1[Array1Index] + MyInts2[Array2Index] << endl;

   return 0;
}
```

Output ▼

Adding each int in MyInts1 by each in MyInts2:

```
0 + -1 = -1
0 + 20 = 20
-3 + -1 = -4
-3 + 20 = 17
35 + -1 = 34
35 + 20 = 55
```

3. You need to replace the constant integer with a value fixed at 5 with code that asks the user the following:

```cpp
cout << "How many Fibonacci numbers you wish to calculate: ";
int NumsToCal = 0;
cin >> NumsToCal;
```

4. The switch-case construct using enumerated constants that tells if a color is in the rainbow is as below:

```cpp
#include <iostream>
using namespace std;

int main()
{
   enum COLORS
   {
      VIOLET = 0,
      INDIGO,
      BLUE,
      GREEN,
      YELLOW,
      ORANGE,
      RED,
      CRIMSON,
      BEIGE,
      BROWN,
      PEACH,
      PINK,
      WHITE,
   };

   cout << "Here are the available colors: " << endl;
   cout << "Violet: " << VIOLET << endl;
   cout << "Indigo: " << INDIGO << endl;
   cout << "Blue: " << BLUE << endl;
   cout << "Green: " << GREEN << endl;
   cout << "Yellow: " << YELLOW << endl;
   cout << "Orange: " << ORANGE << endl;
   cout << "RED: " << RED << endl;
   cout << "Crimson: " << CRIMSON << endl;
   cout << "Beige: " << BEIGE << endl;
   cout << "Brown: " << BROWN << endl;
   cout << "Peach: " << PEACH << endl;
   cout << "Pink: " << PINK << endl;
   cout << "White: " << WHITE << endl;

   cout << "Choose one by entering code: ";
   int YourChoice = BLUE; // initial
   cin >> YourChoice;

   switch (YourChoice)
   {
   case VIOLET:
   case INDIGO:
   case BLUE:
   case GREEN:
   case YELLOW:
```

D

```
        case ORANGE:
        case RED:
            cout << "Bingo, your choice is a Rainbow color!" << endl;
            break;

        default:
            cout << "The color you chose is not in the rainbow" << endl;
            break;
    }

    return 0;
}
```

Output ▼

```
Here are the available colors:
Violet: 0
Indigo: 1
Blue: 2
Green: 3
Yellow: 4
Orange: 5
RED: 6
Crimson: 7
Beige: 8
Brown: 9
Peach: 10
Pink: 11
White: 12
Choose one by entering code: 4
Bingo, your choice is a Rainbow color!
```

5. The programmer unintentionally makes an assignment to 10 in the `for` loop condition statement.

6. The `while` statement is followed by a null statement ' ; ' on the same line. Thus, the intended loop following the `while` is never reached and because `LoopCounter` that governs the `while` is never incremented, the `while` does not end and the statements following it are never executed.

7. Missing `break` statement (that is, the default always executes as no case before that breaks execution).

Answers for Lesson 7

Quiz

1. The scope of these variables is the life of the function.

2. SomeNumber is a reference to the variable in the calling function. It does not hold a copy.

3. A recursive function.

4. Overloaded functions.

5. Top! Visualize a stack of plates; the one at the top is available for withdrawal, and that is what the stack pointer points to.

Exercises

1. The function prototypes would look like this:
   ```
   double Area (double Radius); // circle
   double Area (double Radius, double Height); // cylinder
   ```

   The function implementations (definitions) use the respective formulas supplied in the question and return the area to the caller as a return value.

2. Let Listing 7.8 inspire you. The function prototype would be the following:
   ```
   void ProcessArray(double Numbers[], int Length);
   ```

3. The parameter Result ought to be a reference for the function Area to be effective:
   ```
   void Area(double Radius, double &Result)
   ```

4. The default parameter should be listed at the end, or all parameters should have default values specified.

5. The function needs to return its output data by reference to the caller:

   ```
   void Area (double Radius, double &Area, double &Circumference)
   {
      Area = 3.14 * Radius * Radius;
      Circumference = 2 * 3.14 * Radius;
   }
   ```

D

Answers for Lesson 8

Quiz

1. If the compiler let you do that, it would be an easy way to break exactly what const references were meant to protect: the data being referred to that cannot be changed.

2. They're operators.

3. A memory address.

4. operator (*).

Exercises

1. 40.

2. In the first overloaded variant, the arguments are copied to the called function. In the second, they're not copied as they're references to the variables in the caller and the function can change them. The third variant uses pointers, which unlike references can be NULL or invalid, and validity needs to be ensured in such a system.

3. Use the const keyword:
   ```
   1: const int* pNum1 = &Number;
   ```

4. You are assigning an integer to a pointer directly (that is, overwriting the contained memory address by an integer value):
   ```
   *pNumber = 9; // previously: pNumber = 9;
   ```

5. There is a double delete on the same memory address returned by new to pNumber and duplicated in pNumberCopy. Remove one.

6. 30.

Answers for Lesson 9

Quiz

1. On the free store. This is the same as it would be if you allocated for an int using new.

2. sizeof() calculates the size of a class on the basis of the declared data members. As the sizeof(pointer) is constant and independent of the mass of data being pointed to, the sizeof(Class) containing one such pointer member remains constant as well.

3. None except member methods of the same class.

4. Yes, it can.

5. A constructor is typically used to initialize data members and resources.

6. Destructors are typically used for releasing resources and deallocating memory.

Exercises

1. C++ is case sensitive. A class declaration should start with `class`, not `Class`. It should end with a semicolon (;) as shown below:

```
class Human
{
   int Age;
   string Name;

public:
   Human() {}
};
```

2. As `Human::Age` is a private member (remember members of a `class` are `private` by default as opposed to those in a `struct`) and as there is no public accessor function, there is no way that the user of this class can access `Age`.

3. Here is a version of `class Human` with an initialization list in the constructor:

```
class Human
{
   int Age;
   string Name;

public:
   Human(string InputName, int InputAge)
         : Name(InputName), Age(InputAge) {}
};
```

D

4. Note how Pi has not been exposed outside the class as required:

```
#include <iostream>
using namespace std;

class Circle
{
   const double Pi;
   double Radius;

public:
   Circle(double InputRadius) : Radius(InputRadius), Pi(3.1416) {}
```

```
      double GetCircumference()
      {
         return 2*Pi*Radius;
      }

      double GetArea()
      {
         return Pi*Radius*Radius;
      }
};

int main()
{
   cout << "Enter a radius: ";
   double Radius = 0;
   cin >> Radius;

   Circle MyCircle(Radius);

   cout << "Circumference = " << MyCircle.GetCircumference() << endl;
   cout << "Area = " << MyCircle.GetArea() << endl;

   return 0;
}
```

Answers for Lesson 10

Quiz

1. Use access specifier `protected` to ensure that a member of the base class is visible to the derived class, but not to one with an instance of the same.

2. The object of the derived class gets sliced, and only the part of it that corresponds to the base class gets passed by the value. The resulting behavior can be unpredictable.

3. Composition for design flexibility.

4. Use it to unhide base class methods.

5. No, because the first class that specializes `Base`—that is, `class Derived`—has a private inheritance relationship with `Base`. Thus, public members of class `Base` are private to class `SubDerived`, hence are not accessible.

Exercises

1. Construction in order mentioned in the class declaration: `Mammal` - `Bird` - `Reptile` - `Platypus`. Destruction in reverse order. Program is as shown in the following:

```cpp
#include <iostream>
using namespace std;

class Mammal
{
public:
   void FeedBabyMilk()
   {
      cout << "Mammal: Baby says glug!" << endl;
   }

   Mammal()
   {
      cout << "Mammal: Contructor" << endl;
   }
   ~Mammal()
   {
      cout << "Mammal: Destructor" << endl;
   }
};

class Reptile
{
public:
   void SpitVenom()
   {
      cout << "Reptile: Snoo enemy! Spits venom!" << endl;
   }

   Reptile()
   {
      cout << "Reptile: Contructor" << endl;
   }
   ~Reptile()
   {
      cout << "Reptile: Destructor" << endl;
   }
};

class Bird
{
public:
   void LayEggs()
   {
      cout << "Bird: Laid my eggs, am lighter now!" << endl;
   }

   Bird()
   {
      cout << "Bird: Contructor" << endl;
   }
   ~Bird()
   {
```

D

```
        cout << "Bird: Destructor" << endl;
    }
};

class Platypus: public Mammal, public Bird, public Reptile
{
public:
    Platypus()
    {
        cout << "Platypus: Contructor" << endl;
    }
    ~Platypus()
    {
        cout << "Platypus: Destructor" << endl;
    }
};

int main()
{
    Platypus realFreak;
    //realFreak.LayEggs();
    //realFreak.FeedBabyMilk();
    //realFreak.SpitVenom();

    return 0;
}
```

2. Like this:

```
class Shape
{
    // ... Shape members
};

class Polygon: public Shape
{
    // ... Polygon members
}

class Triangle: public Polygon
{
    // ... Triangle members
}
```

3. The inheritance relationship between class `D1` and `Base` should be private to restrict class `D2` from accessing the public members of `Base`.

4. Classes inherit `private` by default. If `Derived` had been a `struct`, that inheritance would've been `public`.

5. `SomeFunc` is taking the parameter of type `Base` by value. This means that a call of this type is subject to slicing, which leads to instability and unpredictable output:

```
Derived objectDerived;
SomeFunc(objectDerived); // will slice
```

Answers for Lesson 11

Quiz

1. Declare an abstract base class Shape with Area() and Print() as pure virtual functions, forcing Circle and Triangle to implement the same. They're forced to comply with your criteria of requiring to support Area() and Print().

2. No. It creates a VFT only for those classes that contain virtual functions, this includes derived classes, too.

3. Yes, as it still cannot be instantiated. As long as a class has at least one pure virtual function, it remains an ABC irrespective of the presence or absence of other fully defined functions or parameters.

Exercises

1. The inheritance hierarchy using an abstract base class Shape for classes Circle and Triangle is as below:

```cpp
#include<iostream>
using namespace std;

class Shape
{
public:
   virtual double Area() = 0;
   virtual void Print() = 0;
};

class Circle
{
   double Radius;
public:
   Circle(double inputRadius) : Radius(inputRadius) {}

   double Area()
   {
      return 3.1415 * Radius * Radius;
   }

   void Print()
   {
      cout << "Circle says hello!" << endl;
   }
```

D

```
};

class Triangle
{
   double Base, Height;
public:
   Triangle(double inputBase, double inputHeight) : Base(inputBase),
Height(inputHeight) {}

   double Area()
   {
      return 0.5 * Base * Height;
   }

   void Print()
   {
      cout << "Triangle says hello!" << endl;
   }
};

int main()
{
   Circle myRing(5);
   Triangle myWarningTriangle(6.6, 2);

   cout << "Area of circle: " << myRing.Area() << endl;
   cout << "Area of triangle: " << myWarningTriangle.Area() << endl;

   myRing.Print();
   myWarningTriangle.Print();

   return 0;
}
```

2. Missing virtual destructor!

3. Without a virtual destructor, the constructor sequence would be `Vehicle()` followed by `Car()`, whereas the nonvirtual destructor would result only in `~Car()` being invoked.

Answers for Lesson 12

Quiz

1. No, C++ does not allow two functions with the same name to have different return values. You can program two implementations of operator `[]` with identical return

types, one defined as a const function and the other not. In this case, C++ compiler picks the non-const version for assignment-related activities and the const version otherwise:

```
Type& operator[](int Index) const;
Type& operator[](int Index);
```

2. Yes, but only if I don't want my class to allow copying or assignment.

3. As there are no dynamically allocated resources contained within class Date that cause unnecessary memory allocation and deallocation cycles within the copy constructor or copy assignment operator, this class is not a good candidate for a move constructor or move assignment operator.

Exercises

1. The conversion operator int() is as below:

```
class Date
{
    int Day, Month, Year;
public:
    operator int()
    {
        return ((Year * 10000) + (Month * 100) + Day);
    }

    // constructor etc
};
```

D

2. The move constructor and move assignment operators are seen below:

```
class DynIntegers
{
private:
    int* pIntegers;

public:
    // move constructor
    DynIntegers(DynIntegers&& MoveSource)
    {
        pIntegers = MoveSource.pIntegers;  // take ownership
        MoveSource.pIntegers = NULL;  // release ownership from source
    }

    // move assignment operator
    DynIntegers& operator= (DynIntegers&& MoveSource)
    {
```

```
        if(this != &MoveSource)
        {
           delete [] pIntegers;  // release own resources
           pIntegers = MoveSource.pIntegers;
           MoveSource.pIntegers = NULL;
        }
        return *this;
     }

     ~DynIntegers() {delete[] pIntegers;}  // destructor

     // implement default constructor, copy constructor, assignment operator
  };
```

Answers for Lesson 13

Quiz

1. dynamic_cast.

2. Correct the function, of course. const_cast and casting operators in general should be a last resort.

3. True.

4. Yes, true.

Exercises

1. The result of a dynamic cast operation should always be checked for validity:

```
void DoSomething(Base* pBase)
{
   Derived* pDerived = dynamic_cast <Derived*>(pBase);

   if(pDerived) // check for validity
      pDerived->DerivedClassMethod();
}
```

2. Use static_cast as you know that the object being pointed to is of type Tuna. Using Listing 13.1 as a base, here is what main() would look like:

```
int main()
{
   Fish* pFish = new Tuna;
   Tuna* pTuna = static_cast<Tuna*>(pFish);
```

```
// Tuna::BecomeDinner will work only using valid Tuna*
pTuna->BecomeDinner();

// virtual destructor in Fish ensures invocation of ~Tuna()
delete pFish;

return 0;
}
```

Answers for Lesson 14

Quiz

1. A preprocessor construct that keeps you from multiplying or recursively including header files.

2. 4.

3. $10 + 10 / 5 = 10 + 2 = 12$.

4. Use brackets:
```
#define SPLIT(x) ((x) / 5)
```

Exercises

1. Here it is:
```
#define MULTIPLY(a,b) ((a)*(b))
```

2. This is the template version of the macro seen in the answer to quiz question 4:
```
template<typename T> T Split(const T& input)
{
    return (input / 5);
}
```

3. The template version of swap would be
```
template <typename T>
void Swap (T& x, T& y)
{
    T temp = x;
    x = y;
    y = temp;
}
```

4. `#define QUARTER(x) ((x)/ 4)`

D

5. The `template` class definition would look like the following:

```
template <typename Array1Type, typename Array2Type>
class TwoArrays
{
private:
        Array1Type Array1 [10];
        Array2Type Array2 [10];
public:
        Array1Type& GetArray1Element(int Index){return Array1[Index];}
        Array2Type& GetArray2Element(int Index){return Array2[Index];}
};
```

Answers for Lesson 15

Quiz

1. A deque. Only a deque allows constant-time insertions at the front and at the back of the container.

2. A `std::set` or a `std::map` if you have key-value pairs. If the elements need to be available in duplicates, too, you would choose `std::multiset` or `std::multimap`.

3. Yes. When you instantiate a `std::set` template, you can optionally supply a second template parameter that is a binary predicate that the `set` class uses as the sort criterion. Program this binary predicate to criteria that are relevant to your requirements. It needs to be strict-weak ordering compliant.

4. Iterators form the bridge between algorithms and containers so that the former (which are generic) can work on the latter without having to know (be customized for) every container type possible.

5. `hash_set` is not a C++ standard-compliant container. So, you should not use it in any application that has portability listed as one of its requirements. You should use the `std::map` in those scenarios.

Answers for Lesson 16

Quiz

1. `std::basic_string <T>`

2. Copy the two strings into two copy objects. Convert each copied string into either lowercase or uppercase. Return the result of comparison of the converted copied strings.

3. No, they are not. C-style strings are actually raw pointers akin to a character array, whereas STL `string` is a class that implements various operators and member functions to make string manipulation and handling as simple as possible.

Exercises

1. The program needs to use `std::reverse`:

```cpp
#include <string>
#include <iostream>
#include <algorithm>

int main ()
{
    using namespace std;

    cout << "Please enter a word for palindrome-check:" << endl;
    string strInput;
    cin >> strInput;

    string strCopy (strInput);
    reverse (strCopy.begin (), strCopy.end ());

    if (strCopy == strInput)
        cout << strInput << " is a palindrome!" << endl;
    else
        cout << strInput << " is not a palindrome." << endl;

    return 0;
}
```

2. Use `std::find`:

```cpp
#include <string>
#include <iostream>

using namespace std;

// Find the number of character 'chToFind' in string "strInput"
int GetNumCharacters (string& strInput, char chToFind)
{
    int nNumCharactersFound = 0;

    size_t nCharOffset = strInput.find (chToFind);
    while (nCharOffset != string::npos)
    {
        ++ nNumCharactersFound;

        nCharOffset = strInput.find (chToFind, nCharOffset + 1);
    }
```

D

```
        return nNumCharactersFound;
    }

    int main ()
    {
        cout << "Please enter a string:" << endl << "> ";
        string strInput;
        getline (cin, strInput);

        int nNumVowels = GetNumCharacters (strInput, 'a');
        nNumVowels += GetNumCharacters (strInput, 'e');
        nNumVowels += GetNumCharacters (strInput, 'i');
        nNumVowels += GetNumCharacters (strInput, 'o');
        nNumVowels += GetNumCharacters (strInput, 'u');

        // DIY: handle capitals too..

        cout << "The number of vowels in that sentence is: " << nNumVowels;

        return 0;
    }
```

3. Use function toupper:

```
    #include <string>
    #include <iostream>
    #include <algorithm>

    int main ()
    {
        using namespace std;

        cout << "Please enter a string for case-conversion:" << endl;
        cout << "> ";

        string strInput;
        getline (cin, strInput);
        cout << endl;

        for ( size_t nCharIndex = 0
            ; nCharIndex < strInput.length ()
            ; nCharIndex += 2)
            strInput [nCharIndex] = toupper (strInput [nCharIndex]);

        cout << "The string converted to upper case is: " << endl;
        cout << strInput << endl << endl;

        return 0;
    }
```

4. This can be simply programmed as

```
#include <string>
#include <iostream>

int main ()
{
    using namespace std;

    const string str1 = "I";
    const string str2 = "Love";
    const string str3 = 'STL";
    const string str4 = 'String.";

    string strResult = str1 + " " + st^2 + " " + str3 + ' " + str4;

    cout << "The sentence reads:" << endl;
    cout << strResult;

    return 0;
}
```

Answers for Lesson 17

Quiz

1. No, they can't. Elements can only be added at the back (that is, the end) of a vector sequence in constant time.

2. 10 more. At the 11th insertion, you trigger a reallocation.

3. Deletes the last element; that is, removes the element at the back.

4. Of type `CMammal`.

5. Via (a) the subscript operator (`[ ]`) (b) Function `at()`.

6. Random-access iterator.

Exercises

1. One solution is

```
#include <vector>
#include <iostream>

using namespace std;

char DisplayOptions ()
```

D

```
    {
        cout << "What would you like to do?" << endl;
        cout << "Select 1: To enter an integer" << endl;
        cout << "Select 2: Query a value given an index" << endl;
        cout << "Select 3: To display the vector" << endl << "> ";
        cout << "Select 4: To quit!" << endl << "> ";

        char ch;
        cin >> ch;

        return ch;
    }

    int main ()
    {
        vector <int> vecData;

        char chUserChoice = '\0';
        while ((chUserChoice = DisplayOptions ()) != '4')
        {
        if (chUserChoice == '1')
            {
                cout << "Please enter an integer to be inserted: ";
                int nDataInput = 0;
                cin >> nDataInput;

                vecData.push_back (nDataInput);
            }
            else if (chUserChoice == '2')
            {
                cout << "Please enter an index between 0 and ";
                cout << (vecData.size () - 1) << ": ";
                int nIndex = 0;
                cin >> nIndex;

                if (nIndex < (vecData.size ()))
                {
                    cout<<"Element ["<<nIndex<<"] = "<<vecData[nIndex];
                    cout << endl;
                }
            }
            else if (chUserChoice == '3')
            {
                cout << "The contents of the vector are: ";
                for (size_t nIndex = 0; nIndex < vecData.size (); ++ nIndex)
                    cout << vecData [nIndex] << ' ';
                cout << endl;
            }
        }
        return 0;
    }
```

2. Use the `std::find` algorithm:

```
vector <int>::iterator iElementFound = std::finc (vecData.begin (),
                                vecData.erd (), nDataInput);
```

3. Derive from the code sample in the solution to Exercise 1 to accept user input and print the contents of a `vector`.

Answers for Lesson 18

Quiz

1. Elements can be inserted in the middle of the list as they can be at either ends. There is no gain or loss in performance due to position.

2. The specialty of the list is that operations such as these don't invalidate existing iterators.

3. `mList.clear ();`

   or

   `mList.erase (mList.begin(), mList.end());`

4. Yes, an overload of the `insert` function enables you to insert a range from a source collection.

Exercises

1. This is like Exercise solution 1 for the `vector` in Lesson 17, "Dynamic Array Classes." The only change is that you would use the list insert function as
   `mList.insert (mList.begin(),nDataInput);`

2. Store iterators to two elements in a list. Insert an element in the middle using the list's insert function. Use the iterators to demonstrate that they are still able to fetch the values they pointed to before the insertion.

3. A possible solution is

```
#include <vector>
#include <list>
#include <iostream>

using namespace std;

int main ()
{
    vector <int> vecData (4);
```

D

```
        vecData [0] = 0;
        vecData [1] = 10;
        vecData [2] = 20;
        vecData [3] = 30;

        list <int> listIntegers;

        // Insert the contents of the vector into the beginning of the list
        listIntegers.insert (listIntegers.begin (),
                            vecData.begin (), vecData.end());

        cout << "The contents of the list are: ";

        list <int>::const_iterator iElement;
        for ( iElement = listIntegers.begin ()
            ; iElement != listIntegers.end ()
            ; ++ iElement)
            cout << *iElement << " ";

        return 0;
};
```

4. A possible solution is

```
#include <list>
#include <string>
#include <iostream>

using namespace std;

int main ()
{
    list <string> listNames;
    listNames.push_back ("Jack");
    listNames.push_back ("John");
    listNames.push_back ("Anna");
    listNames.push_back ("Skate");

    cout << "The contents of the list are: ";

    list <string>::const_iterator iElement;
    for (iElement = listNames.begin(); iElement!=listNames.end();
++iElement)
        cout << *iElement << " ";
    cout << endl;

    cout << "The contents after reversing are: ";
    listNames.reverse ();
    for (iElement = listNames.begin(); iElement!=listNames.end();
++iElement)
```

```
        cout << *iElement << " ";
    cout << endl;

    cout << "The conterts after sorting are: ';
    listNames.sort ();
    for (iElement = listNames.begin(); iElemert!=listVames.end();
++iElement)
        cout << *iElement << " ";
    cout << endl;

    return 0;
}
```

Answers for Lesson 19

Quiz

1. The default sort criterion is specified by std::less<>, which effectively uses operator< to compare two integers and returns true if the first is less than the second.

2. Together, one after another.

3. size(), as is the case with all STL containers.

Exercises

1. The binary predicate can be

```
struct FindContactGivenNumber
{
    bool operator () (const CContactItem& lsh, ccnst CContactItem& rsh)
const
    {
        return (lsh.strPhoneNumber < rsn.strPhoneNumber);
    }
};
```

D

2. The structure and the multiset definition would be

```
#include <set>
#include <iostream>
#include <string>

using namespace std;

struct PAIR_WORD_MEANING
{
```

```
        string strWord;
        string strMeaning;

        PAIR_WORD_MEANING (const string& sWord, const string& sMeaning)
            : strWord (sWord), strMeaning (sMeaning) {}

        bool operator< (const PAIR_WORD_MEANING& pairAnotherWord) const
        {
            return (strWord < pairAnotherWord.strWord);
        }
    };

    int main ()
    {
        multiset <PAIR_WORD_MEANING> msetDictionary;
        PAIR_WORD_MEANING word1 ("C++", "A programming language");
        PAIR_WORD_MEANING word2 ("Programmer", "A geek!");

        msetDictionary.insert (word1);
        msetDictionary.insert (word2);

        return 0;
    }
```

3. One solution is

```
#include <set>
#include <iostream>

using namespace std;

template <typename T>
void DisplayContent (const T& sequence)
{
    T::const_iterator iElement;

    for (iElement = sequence.begin(); iElement!=sequence.end(); ++iElement)
        cout << *iElement << " ";
}

int main ()
{
    multiset <int> msetIntegers;

    msetIntegers.insert (5);
    msetIntegers.insert (5);
    msetIntegers.insert (5);

    set <int> setIntegers;
```

```
    setIntegers.insert (5);
    setIntegers.insert (5);
    setIntegers.insert (5);

    cout << "Displaying the contents of the multiset: ";
    DisplayContent (msetIntegers);
    cout << endl;

    cout << "Displaying the contents of the set: ";
    DisplayContent (setIntegers);
    cout << endl;

    return 0;
}
```

Answers for Lesson 20

Quiz

1. The default sort criterion is specified by `std::less<>`.

2. Next to each other.

3. `size ()`.

4. You would not find duplicate elements in a map!

Exercises

1. An associative container that allows duplicate entries. For example, a `std::multimap`:

   ```
   std::multimap <string, string> multimapPeopleNamesToNumbers;
   ```

2. An associative container that allows duplicate entries.

   ```
   struct fPredicate
   {
       bool operator< (const wordProperty& lsh, const wordProperty& rsh) const
       {
           return (lsh.strWord < rsh. strWord);
       }
   };
   ```

3. Take a hint from the similarly solved exercise 3 in Lesson 19, "STL Set Classes."

D

Answers for Lesson 21

Quiz

1. A unary predicate.

2. It can display data, for example, or simply count elements.

3. Because in C++ all entities that exist during the runtime of an application are objects. In this case, even structures and classes can be made to work as functions, hence the term *function objects*. Note that functions can also be available via function pointers—these are function objects, too.

Exercises

1. A solution is
```
template <typename elementType=int>
struct Double
{
    void operator () (const elementType element) const
    {
        cout << element * 2 << ' ';
    }
};
```

This unary predicate can be used as
```
int main ()
{
    vector <int> vecIntegers;

    for (int nCount = 0; nCount < 10; ++ nCount)
        vecIntegers.push_back (nCount);

    cout << "Displaying the vector of integers: " << endl;

    // Display the array of integers
    for_each ( vecIntegers.begin ()          // Start of range
             , vecIntegers.end ()                    // End of range
             , Double <> () ); // Unary function object

    return 0;
}
```

2. Add a member integer that is incremented every time the operator() is used:
```
template <typename elementType=int>
struct Double
```

```
{
    int m_nUsageCount;

    // Constructor
    Double () : m_nUsageCount (0) {};

    void operator () (const elementType element) const
    {
        ++ m_nUsageCount;
            cout << element * 2 << ' ';
    }
};
```

3. The binary predicate is the following:

```
template <typename elementType>
class CSortAscending
{
public:
    bool operator () (const elementType& num1,
                      const elementType& num2) const
    {
        return (num1 < num2);
    }
};
```

This predicate can be used as

```
int main ()
{
    std::vector <int> vecIntegers;

    // Insert sample numbers: 100, 90... 20, 10
    for (int nSample = 10; nSample > 0; -- nSample)
        vecIntegers.push_back (nSample * 10);

    std::sort ( vecIntegers.begin (), vecIntegers.end (),
                CSortAscending<int> () );

    for ( size_t nElementIndex = 0;
          nElementIndex < vecIntegers.size ();
          ++ nElementIndex )
          cout << vecIntegers [nElementIndex] << ' ';

    return 0;
}
```

D

Answers for Lesson 22

Quiz

1. A lambda always starts with [].
2. Via a capture list [Var1, Var2, …](Type& param) { ...; }
3. Like this:

   [Var1, Var2, ...](Type& param) -> ReturnType { ...; }

Exercises

1. This is how the lambda would look:

```
sort(vecNumbers.begin(), vecNumbers.end(),
    [](int Num1, int Num2) {return (Num1 > Num2); } );
```

2. This is what the lambda would look like:

```
cout << "Number do you wish to add to all elements: ";
int NumInput = 0;
cin >> NumInput;

for_each(vecNumbers.begin(), vecNumbers.end(),
        [=](int& element) {element += NumInput;} );
```

The sample that demonstrates the solutions in Exercise 1 and 2 is

```
#include<iostream>
#include<algorithm>
#include<vector>
using namespace std;

template <typename T>
void DisplayContents (const T& Input)
{
   for(auto iElement = Input.cbegin() // auto, cbegin and cend: c++11
      ; iElement != Input.cend ()
      ; ++ iElement )
      cout << *iElement << ' ';
   cout << endl;
}

int main()
{
   vector<int> vecNumbers;
   vecNumbers.push_back(25);
   vecNumbers.push_back(-5);
   vecNumbers.push_back(122);
```

```
    vecNumbers.push_back(2011);
    vecNumbers.push_back(-10001);
    DisplayContents(vecNumbers);

    sort(vecNumbers.begin(), vecNumbers.end());
    DisplayContents(vecNumbers);

    sort(vecNumbers.begin(), vecNumbers.end(),
       [](int Num1, int Num2) {return (Num1 > Num2); } );
    DisplayContents(vecNumbers);

    cout << "Number do you wish to add to all elements: ";
    int NumInput = 0;
    cin >> NumInput;

    for_each(vecNumbers.begin(), vecNumbers.end(),
       [=](int& element) {element += NumInput;} );

    DisplayContents(vecNumbers);

    return 0;
}
```

Output ▼

```
25 -5 122 2011 -10001
-10001 -5 25 122 2011
2011 122 25 -5 -10001
Number do you wish to add to all elements: 5
2016 127 30 0 -9996
```

D

Answers for Lesson 23

Quiz

1. Use the std::list::remove_if() function because it ensures that existing iterators to elements in the list (that were not removed) still remain valid.

2. list::sort() (or even std::sort()) in the absence of an explicitly supplied predicate resorts to a sort using std::less<>, which employs the operator< to sort objects in a collection.

3. Once per element in the range supplied.

4. for_each() returns the function object, too.

Exercises

1. Here is one solution:

```
struct CaseInsensitiveCompare
{
    bool operator() (const string& str1, const string& str2) const
    {
        string str1Copy (str1), str2Copy (str2);

        transform (str1Copy.begin (),
                   str1Copy.end(), str1Copy.begin (), tolower);
        transform (str2Copy.begin (),
                   str2Copy.end(), str2Copy.begin (), tolower);

        return (str1Copy < str2Copy);
    }
};
```

2. Here is the demonstration. Note how std::copy() works without knowing the nature of the collections. It works using the iterator classes only:

```
#include <vector>
#include <algorithm>
#include <list>
#include <string>
#include <iostream>

using namespace std;

int main ()
{
    list <string> listNames;
    listNames.push_back ("Jack");
    listNames.push_back ("John");
    listNames.push_back ("Anna");
    listNames.push_back ("Skate");

    vector <string> vecNames (4);
    copy (listNames.begin (), listNames.end (), vecNames.begin ());

    vector <string> ::const_iterator iNames;
    for (iNames = vecNames.begin (); iNames != vecNames.end (); ++ iNames)
        cout << *iNames << ' ';

    return 0;
}
```

3. The difference between std::sort() and std::stable_sort() is that the latter, when sorting, ensures the relative positions of the objects. Because the application needs to store data in the sequence it happened, you should choose stable_sort() to keep the relative ordering between the celestial events intact.

Answers for Lesson 24

Quiz

1. Yes, by supplying a predicate.

2. class Coins needs to implement operator<.

3. No, you can only work on the top of the stack. So you can't access the coin at the bottom.

Exercises

1. The binary predicate could be operator<:

```
class Person
{
public:
    int Age;
    bool IsFemale;

    bool operator< (const Person& anotherPerson) const
    {
        bool bRet = false;
        if (Age > anotherPerson.Age)
            bRet = true;
        else if (IsFemale && anotherPerson.IsFemale)
            bRet = true;

        return bRet;
    }
};
```

2. Just insert into the stack. As you pop data, you effectively reverse contents because a stack is a LIFO type of a container.

Answers for Lesson 25

Quiz

1. No. The number of bits a bitset can hold is fixed at compile time.

2. Because it isn't one. It can't scale itself dynamically as other containers do; it doesn't support iterators in the way containers need to.

3. No. std::bitset is best suited for this purpose.

Exercises

1. `std::bitset` featuring instantiation, initialization, display, and addition is demonstrated here:

```cpp
#include <bitset>
#include <iostream>

int main()
{
    // Initialize the bitset to 1001
    std::bitset <4> fourBits (9);

    std::cout << "fourBits: " << fourBits << std::endl;

    // Initialize another bitset to 0010
    std::bitset <4> fourMoreBits (2);

    std::cout << "fourMoreBits: " << fourMoreBits << std::endl;

    std::bitset<4> addResult(fourBits.to_ulong() +
fourMoreBits.to_ulong());
    std::cout << "The result of the addition is: " << addResult;

    return 0;
}
```

2. Call the `flip()` function on any of the bitset objects in the preceding sample:

```cpp
addResult.flip ();
std::cout << "The result of the flip is: " << addResult << std::endl;
```

Answers for Lesson 26

Quiz

1. I would look at www.boost.org. I hope you would, too!
2. No, typically well-programmed (and correctly chosen) smart pointers would not.
3. When intrusive, objects that they own need to hold it; otherwise, they can hold this information in a shared object on the free store.
4. The list needs to be traversed in both directions, so it needs to be doubly linked.

Exercises

1. pObject->DoSomething (); is faulty because the pointer lost ownership of the object during the previous copy step. This will crash (or do something very unpleasant).

2. The code would look like this:

```
#include <memory>
#include <iostream>
using namespace std;

class Fish
{
public:
   Fish() {cout << "Fish: Constructed!" << endl;}
   ~Fish() {cout << "Fish: Destructed!" << endl;}

   void Swim() const {cout << "Fish swims in water" << endl;}
};

class Carp: public Fish
{
};

void MakeFishSwim(const unique_ptr<Fish>& inFish)
{
   inFish->Swim();
}

int main ()
{
   unique_ptr<Fish> myCarp (new Carp); // note this
   MakeFishSwim(myCarp);

   return 0;
}
```

As there is no copy step involved, given that MakeFishSwim() accepts the argument as a reference, there is no question of slicing. Also, note the instantiation syntax of variable myCarp.

3. A unique_ptr does not allow copy or assignment as the copy constructor and copy assignment operator are both private.

D

Answers for Lesson 27

Quiz

1. Use `ofstream` to only write to a file.

2. You would use `cin.getline()`. See Listing 27.7.

3. You wouldn't because `std::string` contains text information and you can stay with the default mode, which is text (no need for binary).

4. To check if `open()` succeeded.

Exercises

1. You opened the file but didn't check for success of `open()` using `is_open()` before using the stream or closing it.

2. You cannot insert into an `ifstream`, which is designed for input, not output, and hence does not support stream insertion `operator<<`.

Answers for Lesson 28

Quiz

1. A class just like any other, but created expressly as a base class for some other exception classes such as `bad_alloc`.

2. `std::bad_alloc`

3. That's a bad idea for it's also possible that the exception was thrown in the first place because of a lack of memory.

4. Using the same `catch(std::exception& exp)` that you can also use for type `bad_alloc`.

Exercises

1. Never throw in a destructor.

2. You forgot to make the code exception safe (missing `try... catch` block).

3. Don't allocate in a catch block! Not a million integers. Assume the data allocated in `try` as lost and continue with damage control.

Answers for Lesson 29

Quiz

1. It seems that your application does all the activity within one thread. So, if the image processing itself (contrast correction) is processor intensive, the UI is unresponsive. You ought to split these two activities into two threads so that the OS switches the two threads, giving processor time to both the UI and the worker that does the correction.

2. Your threads are possibly poorly synchronized. You are writing to and reading from an object at the same time, resulting in inconsistent or garbled data recovery. Insert a binary semaphore and ensure that the table cannot be accessed when it is being modified.

D

APPENDIX E
ASCII Codes

Computers work using bits and bytes, essentially numbers. To represent character data in this numeric system, a standard established by the American Standard Code for Information Interchange (ASCII) is prevalently used. ASCII assigns 7-bit numeric codes to Latin characters A–Z, a–z, numbers 0–9, some special keystrokes (for example, DEL), and special characters (such as backspace).

7 bits allow for 128 combinations of which the first 32 (0–31) are reserved as control characters used to interface with peripherals such as printers.

ASCII Table of Printable Characters

ASCII codes 32–127 are used for printable characters such as 0–9, A–Z, and a–z and a few others such as space. The table below shows the decimal and the hexadecimal values reserved for these symbols.

Symbol	DEC	HEX	Description
	32	20	Space
!	33	21	Exclamation mark
"	34	22	Double quotes (or speech marks)
#	35	23	Number
$	36	24	Dollar
%	37	25	Percent sign
&	38	26	Ampersand
'	39	27	Single quote
(	40	28	Open parenthesis (or open bracket)
)	41	29	Close parenthesis (or close bracket)
*	42	2A	Asterisk
+	43	2B	Plus
,	44	2C	Comma
-	45	2D	Hyphen
.	46	2E	Period, dot or full stop
/	47	2F	Slash or divide
0	48	30	Zero
1	49	31	One
2	50	32	Two
3	51	33	Three
4	52	34	Four
5	53	35	Five
6	54	36	Six
7	55	37	Seven
8	56	38	Eight
9	57	39	Nine
:	58	3A	Colon
;	59	3B	Semicolon
<	60	3C	Less than (or open angled bracket)
=	61	3D	Equals

Symbol	DEC	HEX	Description
>	62	3E	Greater than (or close angled bracket)
?	63	3F	Question mark
@	64	40	At symbol
A	65	41	Uppercase A
B	66	42	Uppercase B
C	67	43	Uppercase C
D	68	44	Uppercase D
E	69	45	Uppercase E
F	70	46	Uppercase F
G	71	47	Uppercase G
H	72	48	Uppercase H
I	73	49	Uppercase I
J	74	4A	Uppercase J
K	75	4B	Uppercase K
L	76	4C	Uppercase L
M	77	4D	Uppercase M
N	78	4E	Uppercase N
O	79	4F	Uppercase O
P	80	50	Uppercase P
Q	81	51	Uppercase Q
R	82	52	Uppercase R
S	83	53	Uppercase S
T	84	54	Uppercase T
U	85	55	Uppercase U
V	86	56	Uppercase V
W	87	57	Uppercase W
X	88	58	Uppercase X
Y	89	59	Uppercase Y
Z	90	5A	Uppercase Z
[	91	5B	Opening bracket
\	92	5C	Backslash
]	93	5D	Closing bracket
^	94	5E	Caret - circumflex
_	95	5F	Underscore
`	96	60	Grave accent

E

Symbol	DEC	HEX	Description
a	97	61	Lowercase a
b	98	62	Lowercase b
c	99	63	Lowercase c
d	100	64	Lowercase d
e	101	65	Lowercase e
f	102	66	Lowercase f
g	103	67	Lowercase g
h	104	68	Lowercase h
i	105	69	Lowercase i
j	106	6A	Lowercase j
k	107	6B	Lowercase k
l	108	6C	Lowercase l
m	109	6D	Lowercase m
n	110	6E	Lowercase n
o	111	6F	Lowercase o
p	112	70	Lowercase p
q	113	71	Lowercase q
r	114	72	Lowercase r
s	115	73	Lowercase s
t	116	74	Lowercase t
u	117	75	Lowercase u
v	118	76	Lowercase v
w	119	77	Lowercase w
x	120	78	Lowercase x
y	121	79	Lowercase y
z	122	7A	Lowercase z
{	123	7B	Opening brace
|	124	7C	Vertical bar
}	125	7D	Closing brace
~	126	7E	Equivalency sign - tilde
	127	7F	Delete

Index

Symbols

A